American Popular Music and Its Business

THE FIRST FOUR HUNDRED YEARS

II
From 1790 to 1909

American Popular Music and Its Business

THE FIRST FOUR HUNDRED YEARS

Volume I. *The Beginning to 1790*
Volume II. *From 1790 to 1909*
Volume III. *From 1900 to 1984*

American Popular Music and Its Business

THE FIRST FOUR HUNDRED YEARS

II
From 1790 to 1909

RUSSELL SANJEK

New York   Oxford
OXFORD UNIVERSITY PRESS
1988

Oxford University Press

Oxford   New York   Toronto
Delhi   Bombay   Calcutta   Madras   Karachi
Petaling Jaya   Singapore   Hong Kong   Tokyo
Nairobi   Dar es Salaam   Cape Town
Melbourne   Auckland

and associated companies in
Berlin   Ibadan

Library of Congress Cataloging-in-Publication Data

Sanjek, Russell.
American popular music and its business.

Bibliography: p.
Includes indexes.
Contents: v. 1. The beginning to 1790—v. 2. From
1790 to 1909—v. 3. From 1900 to 1986.
1. Popular music—United States—History and criticism.
2. Music—United States—History and criticism.   3. Music
trade—United States—History and criticism.   I. Title.
ML200.S26   1988   780'.42'0973   87-18605
ISBN   0-19-504310-3

2 4 6 8 9 7 5 3 1
Printed in the United States of America
on acid-free paper

Contents

PART ONE

1790 to 1860

CHAPTER 1

Music Publishing in the New Republic 1790–1800

Philadelphia, New York, and Boston

On November 18, 1790, Andrew Adgate, a Philadelphia brush-factory operator and mechanic whose love of music had brought about formation of America's earliest and most advanced free school for "spreading the knowledge of vocal music," entered for copyright registration the first musical work printed in the new nation. In accordance with the first copyright law of the United States, passed on May 31, 1790, by the first Congress, "for the encouragement of learning, by securing the copies of maps, charts and books, to the authors and proprietors of such copies," and signed by President George Washington, Adgate paid sixty cents to the Philadelphia District Court clerk, who then entered notice of the work as the tenth title in a new ledger. By this action, Adgate, as a citizen, was assured that his book could not be printed for the next fourteen years without his permission, provided he advertise the fact of registration and deposit a copy of the work within the next two months. Armed with this grant of protection, Adgate sold his new work, the third edition of his *Rudiments of Music, or Philadelphia Harmony,* together with other of his compilations, both at his metal brush- and comb-making establishment and at the Uranian Academy, which he had founded in 1785. This interdenominational institution, dedicated to encouraging participation in church singing, had quickly become one of the new capital city's best-known and important cultural forces.

The first American copyright law was based on England's 1710 Statute of Queen Anne. Like this forerunner, according to copyright expert Barbara Ringer, it was "a narrow stingy law that had to be expanded piecemeal during the century that followed." The British legislation was the result of persistent lobbying by London bookseller publishers and naturally favored their interests, although subsequent revision during the eighteenth century increased authors' rights. The new American republic continually failed to do the same in any truly meaningful way for more than one hundred years.

According to Charles Evans, in *American Bibliography,* some 13,000 books, newspapers, pamphlets, and broadsides were printed during the first decade of American copyright, but only 556 titles were registered, more than half of these in Philadelphia. Only a small number dealt with music in any context. In addition to Adgate's small text, Philadelphia produced, in 1791, the first stamped or punched work—John Aitken's compilation of Catholic *Litanies, Vespers, Hymns, and Anthems*—and also the first piece of sheet music, "The Kentucky Volunteer" (1794). Aitken was his own publisher, but the song was registered in the name of Benjamin Carr, one of the earliest successful full-time music publishers in the United States.

A number of reasons have been advanced for this failure to take advantage of the new law, chiefly that it did not mention music. Virtually all pieces registered were books that contained considerable amounts of text as well as occasional music. Until music was specifically mentioned, in the 1831 revision of the law, many individual pieces of popular music were registered under an engravings, charts, and maps provision.

As was almost every tune book, hymn compilation, and teaching manual published before his, Adgate's work was originally financed by subscription, a merchandising device instituted in Great Britain during the previous century, when authors found that London stationer booksellers were reluctant to finance works of seemingly limited appeal. With support first from the nobility, who paid for and received ostentatious dedications, the list of subscriber purchasers grew in response to solicitations in newspapers and magazines asking for a portion of the special price in advance and the balance on delivery.

Samuel Gerrish, a leading Boston bookseller, involved himself in the "note versus rote" controversy that raged in New England early in the eighteenth century and embarked on a strikingly modern promotion campaign to sell the singing-instruction books he published. He worked with a number of leading Boston clergymen, exponents of reform in psalm singing, who wrote and preached effective messages that encouraged sales by subscription of Gerrish's teaching manuals.

As in Britain during the 1760s, the press carried notices offering engraved secular music to subscribers, whose names and the number of copies each had purchased would be printed in the completed work. This selling scheme was used principally for expensive scores of operas and musical-theater works.

Early in the nineteenth century, the American book trade generally abandoned subscription financing, and the music-printing business soon did the same. By the time of the second war with the British, in 1812, purely religious compilations alone were sold on this basis, and only for the short period of time before organized denominations established their own publishing firms and assumed all costs. Shortly before the Civil War, publishers discovered the money to be made with the popular "religioso" song and so created a profitable industry, whose income often surpassed that of the secular music-printing trade.

Before those developments, however, the publisher owners of presses and music type treated composers and compilers much as did Thomas and Andrews of Boston and Worcester, the first major enterprise to deal with printed music, beginning in the late 1780s. Book authors were obliged to pay production and papers costs, and so, too, were the creators of music. Editions of from 2,000 to 4,000 copies were sold in the publishers' own stores and shipped to dealers around the country. The writers were generally given a portion of the first edition to sell to their pupils, to other singing schoolmasters, or to local grocers, other small merchants, and postmasters. Even under such an evidently unfair arrangement, a successful work could bring its compiler a profit.

Andrew Adgate's temerity in applying for federal protection of his book angered his one-time mentor, Andrew Law, Connecticut minister, compiler, and music-book publisher, who regarded anything competitive as second-rate. Moreover, Adgate had borrowed his title from Law's own successful work, first issued in 1783. It did not matter that Law had himself modeled his effort on that of the Scottish London publisher Robert Bremner. Though he condemned creative larceny in others, Law did not disdain it himself, as his later activities demonstrated. Adgate had assisted the Connecticut clergyman when he first came to Philadelphia in 1783 in search of local dealers to handle his publications. He evidently inspired Law with his dream of cost-free music education for the deserving. The latter quickly borrowed the idea and announced in the New York press in 1786: "Mr. Law, an approved instructor at present teaching private School, has offered to open a general one for the instruction of every person in the art of church music." Though he labored hard to make the project go, Law never enjoyed the success of Adgate and his academy.

Cutting production expenses by printing from engraved music plates, rather than from set music type, Law and his brother William ran off new copies of his book as demand warranted. Law regularly went on teaching and merchandising trips, leaving William in Cheshire, Connecticut, to supervise mail-order sales and to ship plates to his brother for local reprinting. These copies Law sold to young college-graduate music teachers, who bound themselves to him by contract, promising to use only his books in the schools they set up, or to sell them exclusively, on a commission basis, during their travels.

Early in 1790, the Laws sent a number of these employees to work the back country of Virginia, Maryland, and western Pennsylvania, expecting them to establish a Law-influenced singing-school movement. Law was confident that this would lead to annual sales of several hundred copies to each contracted teacher-salesman. However, these young men discovered that Adgate's teaching manuals and hymn, psalm-tune, and anthem collections were not only available but also selling well and effectively cutting Law out of the market. The Philadelphian's accomplishments as the most effective and progressive promoter of music grounded on truly democratic and ecumenical precepts had made him a better-known figure than the cantankerous Law. His stimulating presentations of modern religious music by the Uranian Academy chorus during spectacular "public singings"—concerts open not only to the city's elite but the masses as well—attracted large audiences. The programs had started in 1786, when Adgate offered fifty musicians and a personally trained chorus of 230 voices performing works by William Billings and Handel's crowd-pleasing "Hallelujah Chorus" from *Messiah,* among other pieces. Continued use of

Billings's music was a personal affront indeed to Law, but Adgate's copyright registration proved to be too much. Law set to work on a campaign of complaint, vituperation, and backbiting whose sole purpose was to destroy his former associate as a serious force in American music. It was only Adgate's death in Philadelphia's yellow fever epidemic in 1793 that removed him as a target of Law's wrath.

Law next turned to the "unprovoked robbery" of his own music, from the *Worcester Collection,* the least-expensive, largest, and best-selling work of its kind, which was published by the powerful Thomas and Andrews firm. Equipped with some of the first music type imported from England, Thomas and Andrews issued six profitable editions of the *Collection* before 1797. (Lesser music publishers, including Law and Amos Doolittle, had, before they procured proper fonts, relied on engravings.) Thomas and Andrews lost money on later printings only because Oliver Holden, a composer hired as their editor, received a quarter of each edition in lieu of pay.

The most important publishers and job printers of the time, Thomas and Andrews had issued two dozen tune books prior to 1797, but only three had been deposited for copyright registration. They left that function to their authors and compilers. The firm's monopoly of typographical music printing ended only after other New England businessmen, whose music presses generally specialized in compilations of church music as well as some instruction manuals, began similar production. Soon after the War of 1812 ended, presses capable of producing large volumes were operating west of the Alleghenies, chiefly in Cincinnati. Their availability to frontier preachers, singing teachers, and authors of prose contributed both to general literary and to musical progress there. The business of popular music was not, however, to advance as swiftly, due to the smaller market and the limitations of engraving technology.

It is doubtful that Alexander Reinagle, the immigrant London-trained musician who came to Philadelphia in 1786, would have become the government's favorite musician and the teacher of many of the ruling class's progeny had it not been for the presence there of the talented Scottish metalsmith John Aitken. As the first professional engraver of secular music, Aitken turned out a dozen of the musician's original printed works. These were sold to the master's pupils and to local music lovers and gentleman amateurs who joined with the "greatest musician in the land" in concerts that made Philadelphia the nation's cultural center.

Aitken then withdrew from music engraving until 1807, when John Christopher Moller and Henri Capron opened their music store, publishing business, and music school on North Third Street. Their establishment is generally recognized as the first of its kind in the United States. Composer-pianist Moller and Capron, cellist and sometime operator of a French boarding school, had become important members of the music scene soon after their arrival in America, Moller first in New York City and both in Philadelphia in 1792. Moller owned a set of music punches, with which he produced *Moller & Capron's Monthly Numbers,* eight-page collections mainly of the partners' own compositions, which were sold by subscription, though they appeared only four times.

Following Capron's withdrawal, Moller sold the store and moved back to New York City, where he served as Trinity Church's organist and taught music until his death in 1803.

Most of the earliest sheet-music publishers had arrived prior to 1800. Of German, French, or English extraction, for the most part, the majority came in search of the rich rewards the new nation appeared to offer. They usually were trained professionals of varying degrees of competence—"professors of music" who had been military musicians, choirboys of the Chapel Royal, cathedral organists, theater musicians, or self-proclaimed or authentic intimates of leading European composers. There were also talented amateurs whose skills often overwhelmed those of minor instrumentalists who had failed to gain either fame or fortune on the Continent and now prayed they would find a less discriminating audience. The best of them soon found work in the theater as supporting musicians and singer-actors, from which base they took a leading part in the development of a varied concert life. They supplemented generally small incomes by serving as household musicians or by teaching music to the offspring of the rising middle-class. In this they found small competition from native-born singing teachers, who had little familiarity with European concert music.

Musical instruments could be found during the 1750s in America's first music store—Michael Hillegas's shop in Philadelphia, which this future first treasurer of the United States operated in the same house as his tavern. John Jacob Astor opened the first exclusively musical-instrument and associated supply shop in New York in 1786. Other stores opened in the next four years, and keyboard instruments became commonplace in the parlors of the well-to-do in all sections of the country. The nation's principal keyboard instrument was still, as it long had been England's, the quilled harpsichord. The earliest printed secular music for keyboards—Reinagle's *A Selection of the Most Favorite Scots Tunes* (1787), William Brown's *Three Rondos for the Piano Forte* (1787), and Francis Hopkinson's *Seven Songs for the Harpsichord* (1788), all produced by Aitken— was intended for this older instrument. No craftsmen capable of making a top-notch pianoforte had yet come to America, only a few clever joiners, or woodworkers, who duplicated expensive imports, occasionally with astonishing skill. A member of Philadelphia's Blake family advertised in 1790 "native made pianos . . . braced with screws, not glue as in English pianos, to withstand our dryer climate." A rival boasted of the means taken to prepare wood "to stand the effects of our climate, which imported instruments never do, but are sure to suffer from the saline quality of the seas."

Out of this experimental amateur manufacture came the invention, in 1800, of the upright piano, at the same time it was being created in Vienna. John Isaac Hawkins, a British civil engineer resident in Pennsylvania, used coiled strings for bass notes in an instrument that took up one-fourth the space of a European instrument and remained in tune "five to six times as long." Hawkins gave up piano-making several years later, but not before the mechanical and musical qualities of his invention had impressed Thomas Jefferson.

The presence of newly arrived men who were capable not only of instructing those who wished to play a pianoforte but also of keeping it in tune and good repair helped to build a demand in the major northern cities for both musical supplies and printed music at reasonable cost. Moller and Capron were the earliest to respond to the latter need, and were soon followed by Benjamin Carr, who was deeply rooted in popular-music publishing. A John Carr, as publisher, music seller, and musical-instrument maker of London, had been an associate of John Playford during the reign of Charles II. His son Richard joined young Henry Playford for a brief period in the same business. In 1782, the widow of one Benjamin Carr, musical-instrument maker and publisher, closed her business on The Strand, and it was one of her husband's relatives, Joseph Carr, music dealer in Holborn, who sent his twenty-six-year-old son Benjamin off to America to prepare the way for a family move there. Philadelphia's newest publisher had been taught music by both Samuel Arnold and Charles Wesley, a nephew of Methodism's founder and himself a well-known London church organist. At least one piece of the youth's music had already been published; "Poor Richard" was among the stock at his new Musical Repository, where patrons were offered "an elegant assortment of grand and small Piano Fortes, and all kinds of Musical instruments of the best make, from the first British manufactories." The city was made aware of the enterprise in an advertisement that appeared on New Year's Day 1794: ". . . having settled a correspondence with the principal publishers or suppliers of the newest music—together with several originals in their possession from which they wish to present amateurs with a selection of the most esteemed, they will, for the future, publish *a new song, or piece of music, every Monday,* and by the continuance hope to make their publications a register of fashionable music."

The first in this ambitious, but short-lived, series (there were only four other issues, a piano "lesson" by Reinagle, and three hit songs from the London playhouses) was "The Kentucky Volunteer" by "A Lady of Philadelphia," with music by Raynor Taylor, an old London acquaintance. The plates for this first piece of sheet music to be copyrighted in the United States were probably engraved by Carr himself, since he had practiced the craft in England.

The song's composer was one of the most sophisticated and accomplished musicians to come to the United States in the federal period. In 1792, Taylor sailed to Annapolis, accompanied by a beautiful young singer, a student whose relationship with him had brought about the scandal that speeded his departure from England. He immediately presented "Olios and Burlettas," a one-man show of the type Charles Dibdin was offering to provincial Englishmen with great financial success. Yet local Church of England vestrymen found him to be the "industrious mechanic capable of teaching psalmody and acting as clerk, sexton and organist" of St. Anne's. They did not know exactly how extraordinary an individual they had employed. Taylor was educated at the Chapel Royal. At twelve, while attending Handel's funeral in 1759, he accidentally dropped his hat onto the coffin, with which it was then buried. Later he served as organist at a church near London and also performed appropriate music at Marylebone Gardens during the warm months. His all-sung burletta *Buxom Joan,* based on Congreve's popular *Love for Love,* brought him to the attention of the Sadler's Wells Theatre management, who employed him as staff musician. Taylor also taught many young Englishmen, among them Alexander Reinagle, who preceded him to America by a few years and whose letters prompted him to move to America.

After an argument with his Anglican employers over back pay, Taylor, with his pupil in tow, went to Philadelphia and at once found a position as organist at St. Peter's Church, where he remained until shortly before his death. He was soon at home among old friends, Reinagle, the recently arrived Joseph Carr and his younger son, Thomas, and others, who helped him find work in the theater and afforded a publishing outlet. He was never to realize any great sums from his printed music, however, most of which appeared under the Carr imprint.

Taylor saluted both the occasion and his new home city in January 1794 with a performance of an "Ode to the New Year" and a variety of other pieces, "entirely original." He followed this with regular monthly public concerts of music new to Philadelphia audiences. The city's musicians dipped into his collection of manuscripts and performed a violin concerto, a divertimento, and other pieces; his lovely young protégée sang his songs. Taylor's experience at Sadler's Wells and Covent Garden served to raise the quality of music for ballets and the new professional theater. The production of *Pizarro, or The Spaniards in Peru,* one of the most popular post-Revolution musical plays, for example, was filled with crowds and processions, choruses and dances. It culminated in a scene that invariably brought audiences to their feet, cheering as the fatally wounded hero, on horseback, with a child in his arms, leaped over a chasm to foil the pursuing enemy, all to Taylor's music. American theater technicians were just learning how to employ the innovative techniques of the British and European stage. Transparent and movable scenery was being used for the first time by experimenting "stage machinists," and all scene-shifting and lowering of lights were accompanied by music, written to order by a resident arranger-composer. The highly prolific Taylor excelled in providing music that formed part of the company's regular repertoire.

Until his death, at the age of seventy-eight, Taylor remained in Philadelphia, an active factor in its musical life, both secular and religious.

Lagging sales put a quick end to the Carrs' proposal to issue new music on a regular weekly basis, and because the store could not support all three members of the family, Joseph and Thomas moved to Baltimore, in June 1794, to open a branch store, "entirely in the musical line, having for sale, finger and barrel organs, double and single keyed harpsichords, piano fortes and common guitars." The local population of 15,000 did not provide a sufficiently profitable music trade, so the Carrs were obliged to add a line of beaver hats, blankets, looking glasses, and other variety items to their stock.

Immediately after he arrived, Benjamin Carr had plunged into every musical activity open to him; he appeared as pianist and solo vocalist in concerts, conducted an instrumental group at Philadelphia's version of the Vauxhall Gardens, played organ at the Roman Catholic church where he worshiped, wrote incidental music, made arrangements, and appeared as a singing actor for Reinagle's theatrical company. His publication in 1794 of the music for "Yankee

Doodle,'' in its first printed appearance in the United States, came about because of his demonstrated ability to write popular and instrumental music on order for the theater's orchestra. Carr's New York friend James Hewitt, conductor of the orchestra at the John Street Theatre, had also started to publish music, having just written the score for a new musical play, *Tammany,* financed by the anti-Federalist, pro-Jacobin Tammany Society. On opening night, fighting had broken out in the playhouse over Hewitt's apparent refusal to respond to shouted demands for ''Yankee Doodle.'' The British musician simply did not know the music, or perhaps felt it out of place in such a luxurious setting. Only after the musicians performed as requested did the musical play go on.

When the New York acting company was contracted for a short run in Philadelphia, its manager-owners, Lewis Hallam and John Hodgkinson, determined that the ''Yankee Doodle'' incident would not be repeated, commissioned Carr to write a suitable piece of opening music. The result, his ''Federal Overture,'' a lively potpourri of current popular songs, including ''Yankee Doodle,'' was intended to satisfy all political leanings. It also included the now semiofficial ''President's March,'' written by Philip Phile, a Hessian mercenary who stayed in America after the Revolution and became a professional violinist. It had been published by Carr in mid-1793.

The ''Federal Overture'' was performed by an enlarged group of musicians on September 24, 1794, without incident, though the American theater was becoming known internationally for the rowdy behavior of its audiences. Carr's medley of patriotic and popular songs was repeated several times during the Philadelphia run, and then had similar success back in New York.

Carr had appeared as a minor singing player during the Hallam-Hodgkinson troupe's appearance and apparently enjoyed the experience, for he went to New York with them and made that city his main base of operations for several years. He opened the Musical Magazine Repository in late 1794 and issued printed music under a joint Philadelphia and New York imprint. Also in New York, James Hewitt had already issued some of his own music, and the tavern owner, organist, music dealer George Gilfert soon became one of the city's active music publishers. Neither, however, was the first in New York, for James Harrison, print dealer and owner of a copperplate press, had opened a shop in July 1793 on Maiden Lane. He had middling success, but his stock was large enough to support a circulating music library. He disappeared from the scene early in 1796.

Carr remained an active member of the New York Old American Company throughout his residence there, writing scores for several musical dramas, the best known of which is *The Archers* (1796), the first existing stage musical written by Americans. The book and lyrics were by William Dunlap, ''Father of the American Stage,'' new co-owner of the company. *The Archers* was a musicalization of the William Tell story, written more than thirty years before Rossini made it an opera. Only slightly successful, enjoying a dozen or so performances, *The Archers* was retired from the standard repertory.

Travel between New York and Philadelphia on an overnight stagecoach over generally poor roads proved too tiring, so Carr sold his northern store to Hew-itt. Business in Philadelphia had become brisk for the assortment of pianofortes and other musical wares in his Market Street shop, including an increasing flow of new publications. The city's concert life—the most active in the nation—was further stimulated by the enthusiasm of one of the first of those chief supports of civic culture, an enthusiastic amateur musician and singer. Mrs. Grattan, owner of a linen and muslin emporium, had presented the first of several seasons of Ladies Subscription Concerts in the winter of 1796–97, each concert followed by a formal ball complete with the best musicians. Through-out these programs, Mrs. Grattan offered her own talents for public approval, sometimes in duet with Carr, thus affording the publisher a major showcase for music he was issuing.

Carr's most nationally important popular song publication, a major hit, was advertised for sale on April 27, 1798, two days after it had been introduced in a local theater. It quickly swept the nation, threatening to supplant "Yankee Doodle" in Americans' affections. Its chief partisans were the middle- and upper-class supporters of President John Adams and the Federalist philosophy, which served as inspiration for the words. The young actor and singer Gilbert Fox, in planning attractions to draw an audience to his benefit night, asked his friend Joseph Hopkinson, son of Francis, to write a stirring lyric that might be advertised to attract the President's supporters. The city was full of them for a session of Congress. Fox hoped to bring the audience to its feet with a rousing rendition of new patriotic verse set to "The President's March." None of the theater lyricists had been able to create suitable poetry, but overnight Hopkin-son composed four verses intended to "get up an American spirit which would be independent of, and above the interests, passions, and policy of both bellig-erents." No reference was made to either France or Britain, currently engaged in hostilities, because it was intended to appeal to all Americans in the support of their own nation. The house was sold out when Fox, accompanied by a "full band," sang "Hail Columbia" for the first time and was obliged to give nearly a dozen encores. This "New Federal Song" was printed, without music, in the Philadelphia papers, and then around the country, and it was soon sung and whistled in the streets. Actors in other cities featured it, with similar suc-cess, as Hopkinson reported to George Washington the following month.

Public demand necessitated three printings of "Hail Columbia, Happy Land, the Favorite New Federal Song, Adapted to the President's March." The copy-right law had been in existence for almost ten years, but it appeared to have little effect in protecting popular music. Publishers in Boston, New York, and Philadelphia continued to issue any prospectively attractive new song as their own, and Carr's new patriotic success was equally fair game. For the next century and more, this Phile-Hopkinson song enjoyed a national eminence ri-valed only by "The Star-Spangled Banner," and that, too, was first published by a Carr.

No longer content to be one of the country's most productive music publish-ers, Benjamin Carr suddenly ended his involvement in the business to concen-trate on writing. The local branch of the Carr family's music business was closed, and its good will and customers were turned over to John Chalk, a local book dealer who operated a music store and circulating library. Joseph Carr then announced publication of the *Musical Journal*, "for the pianoforte, selected and arranged by Benjamin Carr of Philadelphia." Weekly collections of songs "worthy of becoming favorites" and of instrumental music were published alternately and sold by subscription or at bookstores. "The weekly expense is trifling," Joseph Carr reminded his customers, "scarce any song in England is now published under one shilling sterling, and in America, a quarter of a dollar for a song of two pages (Note: a fraction of the London price)." Music by Haydn, Corelli, Pleyel, Boccherini, Viotti, and Benjamin Carr first became known to Americans in the instrumental issues, and many songs were introduced in those for pianoforte and voice. When he was not at work on these, Carr devoted himself to teaching, conducting, and overseeing the musical activities of St. Augustine's Roman Catholic Church. In the last capacity, he composed and compiled several collections of ecclesiastical music. He also helped found and organize, with Raynor Taylor and others, the Musical Fund Society of Philadelphia, whose members, the city's finest musicians, regularly gave concerts to raise funds "for the relief and support of decayed musicians and their families, and for the cultivation of skill and the diffusion of taste in music."

A growing market for single-sheet copies of favorite songs brought Benjamin Carr back to music publishing in 1804. George Schetky, Reinagle's nephew and a cellist member of the Musical Fund Society, became his partner in printing and merchandising them, as well as some original music and imported concert pieces. Carr and Schetky formed a distribution chain that originally included the family store in Baltimore, Hewitt in New York, and George Blake, a clarinet teacher. Carr's arrangement of "The Blue Bells of Scotland" contained a publishing innovation that went unmarked at first. His "more elaborated version," employing three staves rather than the usual two, did not come into general use until the 1820s, when it became apparent that piano skills demanded more than just the simplest accompaniment for a popular song.

The Carr-Schetky partnership ended in 1812, but Benjamin assumed the general editing of *Carr's Musical Miscellany in Occasional Numbers*, "a selection of the most fashionable and useful publications," which appeared intermittently between 1812 and 1825. Following his father's death, he ended the series with its eighty-fifth release. Until his death, in 1831, this major figure in the first quarter-century of music publishing in the United States issued both instrumental and vocal secular music, religious works, liturgical music for the Episcopalian and Catholic faiths, and teaching manuals. Philadelphia's entire music fraternity mourned his passing.

Fewer than two hundred miles north of the Quaker City, New York appeared to foreigners to be, like Venice, a place gradually rising from the sea. Its 33,131 residents, counted in the first national census, in 1790, increased by almost 30 percent within a decade. Among them was the violinist George Gilfert, who probably was born in Prague. A few years after his arrival in the mid-1780s he opened the Musical Magazine in John Jacob Astor's former store, selling imported music and a selection of instruments. Despite a thick foreign accent, he fared well financially in the New World, where he also operated a boardinghouse and a tavern at his home in lower Manhattan and served as organist to the New Dutch Church, whose congregation was made up chiefly of people from Central Europe. His service as director of the city's Musical Society from 1789 to 1791 is an indication of the esteem in which musicians held him. Around the time Benjamin Carr first visited New York, in late 1794, Gilfert began to publish music for sale at a store on lower Broadway. Engraving was done by Gilfert and his new partners, Frederick Rausch, a German who had abandoned law for music and then served as a court musician in St. Petersburg. Recently arrived in the city, Rausch was evidently a first-rate pianist, for he was regularly featured as soloist in the city's most important concerts. Before he left in 1796 to go into a short-lived partnership with James Hewitt, the pair issued nearly 100 pieces of printed sheet music. Gilfert himself put out nearly 200 additional titles before the early 1800s, when he concentrated on the sale of imported pianofortes, always an important part of his stock.

On May 11, 1793, James Hewitt, director of the orchestra and house composer at the John Street Theatre, and one of the actresses there, Mary Ann Pownall, advertised the publication, by subscription only, of *A Book of Songs* for pianoforte or harpsichord. The formation of this song-writing team was a logical extension of their musical activities in New York and Philadelphia, the two major cities on a limited theatrical circuit. They were also prominent stars of the instrumental and vocal concerts that were bringing contemporary music to increasing audiences. Although Hewitt's career was to embrace many activities, among them music publishing, in which he was a major figure, he supported himself and a large family for many years as a performing musician. Mrs. Pownall was one of the most important and popular of the British actresses who left England in the early 1790s to take up careers in America.

Despite the evident popularity of the Hewitt-Pownall *Book of Songs,* Hewitt did not engage in further publishing for several years. His time was fully occupied conducting the John Street Theatre orchestra, for which he received fourteen dollars a week, concertizing, playing the organ at Trinity Church, teaching pupils the theory and practice of music, and performing during the off-season summer months at New York Vaux Hall Gardens. He also wrote the now-lost score for *Tammany,* as well as overtures and songs for other productions, some of which was published by his friend Benjamin Carr. Fellow musicians and employers knew him as a capable and conscientious craftsman with an apparently fine musical training.

Hewitt's career as music publisher, which lasted some twenty years and had more financial downs than ups, started in March 1797. Rausch, who had given up his partnership with Gilfert, for reasons unknown, and Hewitt advertised a new monthly, *Ladies Magazine,* which would carry music from "the most celebrated masters never published in America," arranged for piano and flute. No copies exist. They also published some London theater songs, as well as a collection of music to which Hewitt contributed two pieces. The partnership came to an abrupt end when Hewitt took over operation of Benjamin Carr's New York store on William Street, which had continued to serve as an outlet for the publisher's Philadelphia business. Many of the sixty-nine pieces of music Hewitt published during this time bore both his imprint and Carr's Philadelphia and Baltimore imprints.

Hewitt's responsibilities at the John Street Theatre brought him early familiarity with new music from English stage successes being considered for production in America, an advantage that resulted in the first printing of hit songs in the United States. In 1796, he had married Eliza King, sixteen, the daughter of a retired British Army officer, who brought a dowry of money and real estate, including the ground on which the John Street Theatre stood, both of which the musician-publisher eventually managed into bankruptcy.

One of Hewitt's best-known works, *The Battle of Trenton,* appeared for sale at his store and the Carrs' shops in 1797. An unabashed rewrite of Kotzwara's highly successful war-horse *Battle of Prague,* the music was dedicated to George Washington, whose victory in the New Jersey hamlet had been an important event during the Revolution.

Throughout his career as publisher Hewitt understood the commercial viability of popular music from the London playhouses, or American imitations of it, many of which he provided for William Dunlap and the John Street company. Although he retained his British citizenship through the troubled times of 1812 until his death, Hewitt had also learned early that a music publisher could not go wrong with a patriotic song, particularly in the highly charged, chauvinistically emotional state existing in America then.

As the century neared its end, the "European Shakespeare," August von Kotzebue was writing the most successful plays appearing on European and British stages. William Dunlap, keenly aware of what was making money abroad, bought and translated one of his greatest hits, *Pizarro, or The Spaniards in Peru,* for whose New York production Hewitt wrote and arranged all the music. The most financially profitable was the arrangement of a march originally written by Michael Kelly, which Hewitt issued in sheet music and performed with the military bands of New York. Because of the lack of reciprocal international copyright, Hewitt and many others profited from the sale of printed music written by non-Americans.

Hewitt's first son was born on July 12, 1801—John Hill Hewitt, who became a leading American songwriter and literary figure, and was later entitled to be called "Bard of the Confederacy" for his musical services. Other children who had musical careers were Sophia, a pianist; James Lang, who became a leading music publisher; Eliza, a music teacher; Horatio Nelson, later a music dealer; and George Washington, who was a composer and music-publishing executive.

In 1801, the Hewitts moved to Maiden Lane, where Hewitt enjoyed his five most productive years as a publisher and instrument dealer, working in a store located on the street level of this family home. His sense of commercial worth served him well, particularly in the printing of music from plays coinciding with their appearance in an increasing number of new theaters. He made songs by the most popular British songwriter-composers, such as Braham, Mazzinghi, Reeve, Sanderson, Smith, and Stevenson, available for twenty-five cents for each two-page edition. On the back of song collections, he listed the availability of popular music, instruction books, and teaching methods for violin and piano. Having won many friends in social and political circles, thanks in large measure to careless use of his wife's dowry, he did not hesitate to call on these acquaintances for subscriptions to new publications of his music, usually with great success. He won appointment, without pay but with the rank of colonel, as director of all military music in the city of New York. Leading his uniformed musicians on parade, he was an imposing figure in cocked hat, shad-bellied coat, silk sash, gorget, buckskin breeches, boots, spurs, sword, epaulettes, and drum major's baton, the very embodiment of the British military musical director. Throughout his life Hewitt remained "John Bull forever," and so was forced many times to undergo such indignities as he had suffered in the "Yankee Doodle" incident. Named commander of a militia company of artillery in 1805, again without pay, Hewitt used this connection to sell the government the instruments required by his soldier musicians, as well as parts for the marches and other works he wrote for performance by them. Among these were waltzes and grand marches dedicated to powerful and prominent military figures and politicians.

Hewitt began to make regular trips to Boston in connection with concerts and conducting, and in 1808 he was appointed leader there, returning to his family in New York during the summer. Among the friends he made in Boston was James Rowe Parker, member of the Trinity Church choir, and recently elected treasurer of the newly formed Phil-harmonic Society, a group of leading community figures who banded together to play music and offer a regular series of instrumental concerts. Boston had never successfully supported regular occasions of this sort, despite a long record of similar efforts dating back to programs in Peter Pelham's Long Room in 1731. Young Parker was well connected and provided invaluable entree to the city's elite, including Gottlieb Graupner, Boston's most influential musician and music publisher. Hewitt's proposal to Parker in 1810 for joint partnership in a music store did not lead to anything, but it provides a look into trade practices of the time. According to the original at the University of Pennsylvania, Hewitt wrote:

I am willing to put all my plates into the joint-stock, at a fair evaluation, with such music as may be necessary for the use of the Store, to the amount of $2000 but I certainly think that considering I have to make sacrifices of other profits, by giving my personal attention; a consideration ought to be made, either by adding more cash to the concern, or by making some allowance from the Profits; there are many situations in a Music Store which will not only require my attention, but also my *labour,* and it will be very necessary in the commencement, to pay Cash for certain articles. If, goods can be imported, the Sale of the Articles will provide for their payment; therefore the Capital will not be so much wanted—besides one part of the Stock is already provided, in Music, which is a very material consequence, as it takes a long period, time, trouble and expense to collect publications suitable to this Country—respecting the Exchange of Music I perfectly agree with you, not to exchange here—the establishment in New York, will of course be placed in other hands, but it will always be a place [to] import our publications.

The Store ought to be open'd with (if possible) from 8 to 12 pianofortes, besides other instruments. The Capital should be placed in one of the banks, in the name and order of Hewitt for the use of the Concern; as sometimes when speculations offer in Music, where it it useful to have a sum at Command—the profits arising from the Sales, ought to be equally divided, as our care and attention should be mutual to the Interest of the Concern.

Sometime in 1811, Hewitt moved his family to Boston, leaving such good will and customers as he had built up to John Willson, a British singer and music teacher, who became one of New York's music publishers during the War of 1812 by reissuing out-of-print music. Boston's Trinity Church now employed Hewitt as organist, presumably at the regular salary of £200 a year, though his income was being severely stretched by the increasing cost of living due to looming hostilities with England. In spite of the fact that he was British, and hence not entitled to copyright protection, Hewitt registered his major work of this period with Boston's court clerk: the *Harmonia Sacra,* compiled and written for the Trinity choir.

His oldest child, teen-aged Sophia, made her local debut as a pianist and continued to appear with her father, soon gaining the admiration of Boston's music lovers and becoming the most popular artist on her instrument in New England.

War with Great Britain was formally declared in June 1812, and Hewitt, with other English nationals, was moved into the interior in the interest of public safety, but he was soon allowed to go back to Boston. Willson, who had taken over the New York store, was now in Boston and made Hewitt's old plates available for local printing by their former owner.

A musical academy took most of Hewitt's attention, and his interest in publishing waned, but, as the war curtailed access to imported music, he, citing "regular correspondence with all of the most eminent publishers of music in every part of Europe," opened a rental music library of several thousand works, stored at his home. For six dollars a year, or two a quarter, subscribers could borrow from music by the "most eminent Composers, of both the ancient and modern schools." It was evidently not a profitable venture, despite the sideline of "Spanish cigars, in boxes of 250 each."

Until 1816, when he left his wife and youngest children in Boston, supported by Sophia, and took John Hill and James Lang to New York, Hewitt operated out of his home, but scarcely on the scale of his earlier business in Manhattan. Back in New York, after apprenticing his sons to tradesmen, he tried the business once more, with a handful of works. One of these was his setting for Francis Scott Key's poem "The Star-Spangled Banner," which, had it caught on, might have supplanted the unfelicitous melody of the old "To Anacreon in Heaven."

He next wandered about the southeastern states, staying in Charleston, Augusta, and smaller places and earning a living by performing on the violin and conducting local orchestras and theater bands. His music was still available from the original plates, but with newly engraved titles and imprints of the publishers who had acquired them.

He returned to New York in 1824 to work at the new theaters springing up in the Chatham Square area, writing arrangements and directing the playhouse orchestras, but his last years were desperate. The removal of a horrible malignant facial cancer had to be paid for by the children. In his last year, he was taken back to Boston, where his wife of some thirty years cared for him until the end came. The Boston papers recorded on August 3, 1827: "DIED in this city, after a long and painful illness, which he bore with Christian fortitude, James Hewitt, in the 59th year of his age. His friends, acquaintances, and professional brethren are respectfully invited to attend his funeral."

They came in number, from the musical societies of which he was a member, from an organization of loyal Englishmen, and from the Masons, to join the family in laying away a significant figure of the first quarter century of American music publishing. Like his final resting place, most of James Hewitt's music is unknown today.

John and Michael Paff began operating another important New York music-publishing business in 1797. In addition to sheet music, generally published in regular editions of 200 copies, standard for the time, the brothers carried pianos, "every article in the musical line upon reasonable terms," as well as toys, books, prints, and nonmusical merchandise, which many music dealers were obliged to stock. For the next fifteen years, with a catalogue of more than 200 pieces of music, the Paffs were the city's most important publishers, particularly after Gilfert left the field and Hewitt's business faltered. In 1817, the Paff stock of music plates was purchased by William Dubois, who continued to issue their music under his own imprint.

The city of Boston failed to maintain its early lead in music publishing, started with the first printed material dealing with music, the *Bay Psalm Book* (1640) and, during the 1720s, with Samuel Gerrish's intensive promotion campaign to merchandise psalm-singing manuals. Philadelphia quickly took the lead, but Boston continued to be an important force in the development of the nation's music business. In 1783, Ebenezer Battelle opened a music section in his State Street bookstore, offering "a valuable collection of Music Books, consisting of Airs, Songs, Country-Dances, Minuets and Marches—Symphonies, Quartettos, Trios, Oratorios, &c. for the Organ, Harpsichord, Clarinet, French-Horn, Hautboy, Flute, Violin, Violincello, Harp, Piano-Forte, Voice &c." His newspaper advertising called attention to the compilations of New England singing masters, Andrew Law's instruction books and religious music, and, specifically, William Billings's new printing of *The Massachusetts Harmony*. Battelle had first tried his luck in the book trade just before hostilities with Britain started. A Harvard man, he quickly became a major in the Massachusetts militia; when he was appointed colonel of the Boston Regiment in 1785 he gave up his bookshop. His successor was Benjamin Guild, who continued to operate a music and circulating library, adding to his stock lurid imported romantic novels and some printed music books. On his death, the store was purchased by William Pinson Blake, whose principal connection with popular music was the sale of theater music and American editions of the librettos for popular comic operas. Guild's stock of these materials, all reprinted from original European editions, had filled a two-page list.

Blake was the first in Boston to advertise sale, in June 1798, of a new patriotic song that had recently been sung during a dinner honoring President John Adams and was becoming not only a local hit but a favorite around the country among loyal Federalists. "Adams and Liberty" was commissioned by the Massachusetts Charitable Fire Society for its annual dinner. The dinner had given promise of being a very important political occasion, because favorite son John Adams was at the time confronted by the threat of a full-scale war with France. A young local writer, Thomas Paine, the twenty-five-year-old wastrel son of Robert Treat Paine, a signer of the Declaration of Independence, had been engaged to provide a suitable and singable expression of loyalty.

Born in 1773, Paine had been educated at Harvard, where he was hailed for "the vivacity of his wit, the vigor of his imagination, and the variety of his knowledge." Upon graduation, he entered a Boston counting house in deference to his parent's wishes, but when his contributions to magazines and newspapers brought him acclaim, he resigned to embark on a writing career, first editing a biweekly periodical. A prize-winning prologue written in 1793 for the Federal Street Theatre brought him into daily contact with the theater, and his marriage to a "stage person" alienated him from his father.

In 1795, a poem he wrote for the graduation ceremonies at Harvard brought him $1,500, and other large sums followed for poetry and prose. He then became the first young American to devote himself to theatrical criticism. He asked for and received $750 for the song "Adams and Liberty," for which he chose the highly popular melody of "The Anacreontic Song," written specifically for the Anacreontic Society of London by John Stafford Smith, a Chapel Royal graduate who became organist and master of the children. The society, a group of amateur musicians and singers, who admitted some professional musicians to membership to aid in the presentation of annual concerts, first met in 1766. Like similar groups, their activities could be traced back to 1588, when a number of gentlemen gathered in the home of Nicholas Yonge "for the exercise of musick daily," singing from the printed book of madrigals *Musica Transalpina*. The Anacreontic Society, considered one of eighteenth-century London's best clubs, derived its name from the Greek poet Anacreon, who loved both women and wine and wrote of each in verse. Every member was required to sing at each meeting. If he sang out of tune, the penalty was to drink a glass of wine to improve the voice, a bottle of madeira being set out for each three members, and one of sherry for every seven. Words for the "Anacreontic Song," beginning "To Anacreon in Heav'n, where he sat in full glee," were written by Ralph Tomlinson in 1775, when he was society president. They appeared in the first edition of *The Vocal Magazine,* in 1788. This was a songster containing words but no music of "all the English, Scotch and Irish songs, cantatas, glees, catches, airs, ballads, etc., deemed any way worthy of being transmitted to posterity." The society was dissolved in 1794, after the Duchess of Devonshire, Georgiana Spencer Cavendish, whose romantic verse was often set to music during the 1790s, was secreted, with a member's connivance, in a box to spy upon the annual program. Her escapade created such a furor that members resigned.

The Anacreontic tradition was carried on in America when John Hodgkinson formed a Columbian Anacreontic Society of New York around 1795. Neither nobleman nor gentleman, Hodgkinson had run away as a youth from the merchant to whom he had been apprenticed and found work with a traveling acting company by virtue of his native ability as a vocalist and violin player. When he came to America, at the age of twenty-five, and made his local debut, there was considerable surprise at the spectacle of a man who at once was both a first-rate singer and a first-rate actor. Hodgkinson had evidently been present at the exclusive London club at least once, and he attempted to mold the American group into some semblance of its archetype's form. Use there of the "Anacreontic Song" had made it familiar to cultured Americans, many of whom published their own verses to its melody, nine of which had already been printed as sheet music before Paine's ode to John Adams. The success of that song inspired seventy-five more such borrowings prior to 1820, among them "The Star-Spangled Banner" of today.

"Adams and Liberty" was hailed as a triumph on its first performance and then sung at every subsequent Adams political rally. Paine's words summed up the Federalist platform, arguing for the "legitimate powers of the sea . . . the free charter of trade," and warning the French to "beware of collision."

Isaiah Thomas, the leading Boston book and music publisher and job printer, procured a copy of the song prior to the dinner at which it was first sung and advertised printed words on a broadside in May 1798 and its publication as sheet music a few weeks later, sending the first batch of copies to William Blake. Edition after edition came off local printing presses around the country. Paine, flushed with the fame attendant on such national recognition, announced that he would study for the law. Although he attempted several times to write, on commission, similarly successful new lyrics to the "Anacreontic Song," he never duplicated the success of his first one. After an older brother, in line for the family fortune, died in 1801, Paine had his name changed to Robert Treat Paine, that of his father, by an official act of the Massachusetts legislature, citing the collaboration of the original Thomas Paine in the cause of the French Revolution. The American Paine's gesture failed to convince his father of his reformation. His last years were clouded with poverty, illness, and alcohol. He died in the attic of his father's house, hidden there by servants, parent and child never reconciled.

Boston booksellers of this period usually carried music books, sheet music, instruments, and some supplies, but none of them published any music. That was left to Thomas and Andrews, singing-teaching compilers, Billings, Law, and the Norman brothers—engraver John and music and magazine publisher William. Only five music publications of the last have been preserved, including some issues of *The Musical Repository,* a collection of favorite stage songs of 1796, the first sheet music to be printed in Boston. William Norman noted

that the magazine was "for its size and the neatness of its [engraved] work
. . . the cheapest instrumental music ever published in America, it being but
4½ pence per page." Only in the pages of Norman's *Boston Magazine* (1783),
of which William Billings was an early editor, can one find an example of the
"first music type cast in America," according to a note from Isaiah Thomas.
This was made from punches cut by John Norman, who engraved almost all
the religious music published in Boston in the twelve years after 1781, when
Billings's *Psalm Singer's Assistant* appeared, with title page and music done
by John.

Boston's book dealers, like many in New York and Philadelphia, paid for
printings of songsters issued under their imprints and containing lyrics only to
popular songs of all kinds. Among such works were the sixteen-page *History
of a little child found under a haycock* (1794); *Jack Dandy's Delight* (1799),
done for Nathaniel Coverly; and many editions of official Freemason books:
Jachin and Boaz, Freemason's Monitor, and *The Ahiman Rezon,* each of which
contained words to Masonic songs. There were few experienced engravers capable of executing music, so the business of printing and merchandising sheet
music was left to entrepreneurs possessed of both patience and a talent for
improvisation. George Gilfert employed a free-lance artist, who worked on
wood to cut block letters for title pages and composer credits on music printed
by him in the mid-1790s. As the printing business moved away from the large
centers of population, printers in smaller communities used the free time of
printing presses and binding machines to manufacture songsters and jestbooks
containing words only of popular songs and favorite old ballads.

Even as type of all kinds was becoming increasingly available, including
fonts for music publishing imported from Caslon's London foundry, such experiments with type founding as that by the Normans led inevitably to the
creation of another new American industry—type founding. The first was owned
by seventy-five-year-old John Baine, who arrived in Philadelphia sometime in
1787 and immediately offered, for "ready cash or no purchase," products made
in Scottish factories. He had already been famous as a master craftsman for
some forty years, and American printers were familiar with his work. After his
death, in 1790, the business was carried on by his grandson, who provided the
type for the first ten volumes of the first American edition of the *Encyclopaedia
Britannica.* However, it was many years before the Baine factory dealt in music type. Competition first appeared in 1790, when Adam Gerard Mappa, a
thirty-five-year-old Dutch ex-Army officer, took the advice of Thomas Jefferson and moved his type-founding equipment to the United States. Not having
learned the craft through the usual lengthy apprentice-journeyman-master tradition, Mappa was physically and technically incapable of meeting demand for
his products, and, as with the Baine factory, his equipment and stock eventually became the property of Binney & Ronaldson, the first important American
type manufacturers.

A Scotsman trained in the baking trade, James Ronaldson arrived in Philadelphia in 1794 to re-open a biscuit factory, which was destroyed by fire two
years later. He then entered into partnership with a fellow Scotsman, Archibald

Binney, who had arrived in America with $888.80 worth of type-founding equipment. Most Americans preferred imported type but succumbed to the Binney & Ronaldson product when it was offered for three cents a pound less than European letters, and as the nineteenth century dawned, the partners operated the only professional American foundry. It was to them that most publishers turned for type, including Andrew Law when he looked for someone to manufacture the shaped notes he claimed to have invented.

With music type more accessible and affordable, American printers at last began publication of inexpensive collections of popular songs, complete with musical notation. Typical of these, and available in modern reprint, is *The American Musical Miscellany*. Andrew Wright, of Northampton, Massachusetts, and his brother Daniel, issued it in 1798 as the first of a number of similar publications and collections of purely sacred music. There is no indication of the *Miscellany*'s true compiler, but it may have been Timothy Swan, who first learned music during three weeks at a singing school when he was sixteen and then was taught to play the fife by a British soldier. He was much influenced by Billings's work and compiled his first book of sacred music in 1788, *The Federal Harmony,* published by John Norman for schools and singing societies; it went through four editions in four years. Swan was a respected sacred-tune composer, but he also wrote secular music, represented in his 1800 *Songwriter's Assistant,* songs in two parts, half of which were original, and the 1803 *Songwriter's Museum,* in which the influence of Robert Burns is evident. Swan's most ambitious religious work, *The New England Harmony,* printed for the author by the Wrights, failed to sell out its first edition, which at this time was usually between 2,000 and 4,000 copies.

"Humbly dedicated by their friends and humble servants, the Publishers . . . to all true lovers of song in the United States of Columbia," *The American Musical Miscellany* contained 300 pages and was on sale for one dollar in bookstores in Boston and other New England localities. The work contained 111 songs, printed from movable type, the majority with words and melody, but several were set for two, three, and four voices. Only fifty songs indicate an author. English theater writers were in the majority: Charles Dibdin, with twelve songs; James Hook, ten; William Shield, six; Thomas Arne, Samuel Arnold, James Moulds, and William Reeve, two each. Two early songs dealing with the black man are included: Moulds's "I Sold a Guiltless Negro Boy" and Reeve's "The Poor Desponding Negro." In the next two decades, more than 500 such songsters, many with musical notation, came off the American printing press.

Music dealers had also discovered the commercial appeal of another type of music book, one that had its roots in John Playford's *English Dancing Master* of 1650. The French Revolution and subsequent slave uprisings in the West Indies uprooted many dancing teachers, whose livelihood had always depended on the patronage of the wealthy. Opportunity in a new, prosperous nation brought many of them to the major American cities, where they established dancing schools. Many of these displaced men utilized the printing press to prepare lesson books for the convenience of their pupils and for advertising to attract new clients. Mr. Francis, ballet master of the New Theatre in Philadelphia and Baltimore, had printed, for sale at twenty-five cents to subscribers and thirty-seven and a half cents to others, *Mr. Francis's Ballroom Assistant*, "a collection of the most admired cotillions and country dances with their proper figures annexed. Including a variety of marches, minuets, reels, gavottes, hornpipes, etc. The music composed and selected and the whole arranged as lessons for the piano forte by Mr. Reinagle. The work to consist of eight numbers to be published every other week." Pierre Landrin Duport, who migrated to America in 1790 and claimed to have been dancing master to Marie Antoinette's children, settled in Philadelphia and then taught dancing and music in other major cities before making Washington his final home. Duport's dance tunes and figures elevated the standard of excellence in America and were well known to the upper classes. In 1799, William Norman issued the earliest book of music for dancing printed in Boston, a reprint of the London publication *Twenty Four Fashionable Country Dances for the Year 1799.*

The first music publisher in Boston was now facing determined competition from a newcomer, a trained musician and engraver, Peter Albrecht von Hagen. In May 1798, he had opened a Musical Repository in partnership with Benjamin Crehore, an American-born stringed-instrument maker. One of their earliest sheet-music publications was the revised and corrected third edition of "Adams and Liberty," which Thomas and Andrews had first published. The Newbury Street store also contained a "Warranted Piano Forte Warehouse," offering both imported pianos and musical wares as well as some manufactured by Crehore. This early instrument maker worked in a factory in nearby Milton and first met von Hagen at the Federal Street Theatre, where the craftsman's extraordinary skills in woodworking and mechanics were used to construct stage sets and repair musical instruments, and where von Hagen was employed as a conductor, arranger, and composer. Their business association lasted little more than a year, and Crehore returned to making pianos and harpsichords, creating instruments "as correct and elegant as any imported from abroad" for sale in America.

Peter von Hagen had arrived in America just before the Revolution with a new wife, whose skill as a pianist and teacher added to the family's income throughout their life. Once war began, the couple returned to Europe, where von Hagen worked in London and Holland as organist, professor of music, and composer much influenced by Geminiani. A growing family of von Hagens returned to America in 1789, and the father assumed an active role in New York's musical happenings, conducting opera and working as a free-lance musician in concerts and at the theater. Young Peter, at eight, exhibited sufficient skill on the violin to be featured as soloist in subscription concerts sponsored by the growing community of immigrant music masters. There was also a thirteen-year-old daughter who often sang publicly.

The von Hagens moved to Boston in early 1796, after learning of the scarcity of professional musicians in a city where two theaters now functioned. The father, now Van Hagen, found work in both local houses, and also supplied arrangements and new music for productions of comic operas and musical plays;

he became conductor at the Haymarket in January 1797. The family also opened a musical academy and gave lessons there or in the privacy of pupils' homes. Father and son also made regular trips to Boston suburbs as part of their teaching activities. The short-lived partnership with Crehore followed.

The senior Van Hagen was evidently born to be a music publisher, because in the next several years, up to his death in 1803, his firm issued nearly a hundred pieces of music. He added music imported from Holland and Britain to his stock and established working arrangements with music houses in other cities. When Van Hagen died, the family business was left to his oldest son, under whose direction it operated successfully for about a year. Its decline was due not only to new competition, from Gottlieb Graupner, but also to the young man's excessive drinking. Surviving only in the backwaters of Boston's musical life, young Van Hagen died in 1837.

The Van Hagen family's existence was, in great measure, eased through the kindness of Susanna Haswell Rowson, novelist, actress, songwriter, and head of an academy for young females, some of whose popular music had been published by Peter Albrecht.

When the eighteenth century came to an end, only a small number of popular-music publishers had been able to survive the uncertain economic vicissitudes of the business. The Carr family was active only in Baltimore, although Benjamin edited its publications from Philadelphia, where the man who took over Moller and Capron's store, George Willig, and soon his sons, was building the foundation for an enterprise that would last throughout the next century. James Hewitt was at the zenith of his activity in New York, and his sons, eventually to be important figures in popular music, were not yet born. Gottlieb Graupner was chiefly concerned with improving his position in the Boston Theatre orchestra, but was soon to start his own music business.

Philadelphia, the first city in which a full-time regular music publisher worked, had seen the advent and disappearance of thirty-two similar enterprises, with twenty-two printers and nine engravers providing technical services. Twelve New York music-publishing houses had opened, serviced by sixteen printers and eleven engravers. And Boston, the first city in which musical materials were printed and published, was the last in which a music publisher opened a full-time operation.

There were, of course, dozens of newspaper and magazine publishers in whose publications ballads, broadsides, lyrics, and verses appeared, usually intended to be sung to some well-known melody, exactly as had been the practice in Great Britain for almost three centuries.

Oscar Sonneck's ground-breaking *Early Secular Music* (1905) shows clearly that most popular music published in America was English, generally that from the London musical theater, provided by fewer than fifty songwriter-composers, including a small number of Europeans, few of whom were known either to the average Briton or to citizens of the United States. About 450 pieces of secular music were printed in America during the century. Two thirds of these appeared as individual sheet music. Seventy-one patriotic songs, both words and music, were issued, and thirty instrumental pieces of a similar nature.

Irving Lowens's *Bibliography of Songsters* catalogs twenty-six of these collections of words to be sung to familiar tunes published before the Revolution, and an additional 185 by the end. Richard J. Wolfe added, in *Secular Music in America 1801–1825*, almost 200 titles of unrecorded eighteenth-century imprints, and removed from *Early Secular Music* nearly 250 titles that clearly were works published after 1800.

From these beginnings grew the four billion dollars' worth of recorded music and $250 million of printed music sold in 1978.

CHAPTER 2

The Business of Popular Music 1800–1860

Copyright

The first revision of the original American Copyright Act was passed by Congress and signed by President Thomas Jefferson on April 29, 1802. It increased protection for the designers, engravers, and etchers of historical and other prints, raised fines for possession of unauthorized editions of books and engraved prints, and required that every published book henceforth bear the date of its year of copyright. If music publishers had observed the law, the last item would have put an effective end to the traditional custom of printing sheet music without any date, on the time-tested theory, dating back to the elder John Walsh, that only undated music, much like a woman who did not reveal her age, would remain popular. Because music had not been mentioned specifically in the law, it was usually registered as a book or an engraving.

Considerable impetus for passage of the revision had come from the growth of a consumer market for engravings and etchings of paintings, sparked by a rising standard of living and an increasing demand for prints to decorate homes. These dealt in the main with the Revolution and its heroes and allegorical and representational landscapes. In time, public taste made necessary a change of subject material for mass-duplicated art, a demand that the music business was able to satisfy in part with handsome illustrated sheet-music covers.

The plight of John Trumbull, among others, was influential in persuading highly placed politicians of a moral justification for revising the law to increase protection of engraved works of art. American book dealers and art-supply stores had long stocked thousands of imported engravings, to which they had added new works by native artists. A veteran of the Revolution, Trumbull had studied art in Europe and then began painting a series of vast and complex canvases commemorating the great events in America's struggle for independence. He produced reproductions of these works and offered them for sale on a subscription basis. Having invested nearly £2,000 in commissions to European craftsmen for magnificent engraved plates of his first two giant paintings, *Bunker's Hill* and *The Death of Montgomery at Quebec*, Trumbull found the resulting price too high for American purses. When spurious copies began to appear at bargain prices, he looked unsuccessfully to the state for a subsidy, and got copyright revision instead.

Although its American practitioners, from Peter Pelham to Paul Revere, were honored for their work, the quality of native engraving was poor in comparison to that being imported from England and France. Then in 1805, Jacob Perkins, of Massachusetts, developed a new technique for engraving on steel, originally for banknotes, which was almost immediately adopted by the artist engravers. The reduced production costs stemming from this substitution of steel for copper produced art of a harsher quality. Music publishers, nevertheless, found it as irresistible as any succeeding technological development that promised cost reductions.

The 1790 Copyright Act had enabled Noah Webster, the most important lobbyist for its passage, to license exclusively his *Grammatical Institute of the English Language* to seven different booksellers for a period of fourteen years, granting them territorial rights. Each paid a royalty and pledged that prices would remain in line with those of other licensees. The *Grammatical Institute* was divided into three parts—grammar, reader, and speller. The last was known as the *Blue-Backed Speller* and, after the Bible, became America's best-selling book of all time: 5 million copies were sold by 1818, nearly 60 million in the next seventy years, and then approximately a million copies a year for many decades. Webster used the royalty of five cents a copy to finance his *Compendious Dictionary of the English Language*, remembered best simply as "Webster's." It was a declaration of independence from British spelling.

With 1804 fast approaching to put an end to the initial fourteen-year grant of copyright and his licensing agreements with it, Webster went to work again to improve the law. Agitating for permanent copyright, he sought out his congressman, Simeon Baldwin, of Connecticut, and argued that "literary composition is a species of property more peculiarly a man's own than any other, being the production of his mind or inventive faculties. . . . I do not see why an interest in original literary composition should stand on different ground from all other personal property." The original copyright legislation, he added, permitted renewal for an additional fourteen years only if the author was alive; if not, his family or estate lost complete control of the property.

While pretending to live up to the letter of their contracts, the publishers with whom Webster had agreements, chiefly Isaiah Thomas, actually were defrauding him with inaccurate reports of sales and printings, or they leased the type forms to other printers for surreptitious editions. Webster countered by negotiating new agreements with other bookseller distributors and prepared a revised edition of the *Blue-Backed Speller* in order to obtain a new copyright.

Earlier, copyright was indicated on the title page of each work as being so many years from 1776, the year of independence—"Copyrighted April 17 in the twenty-ninth year of the independence of the United States," for instance.

Conforming to the revised act, book publishers began to print the year of issue, in numerals, but music publishers failed to comply fully until around 1820.

The lot of British authors was improved in 1814, when the act of Queen Anne was revised to increase the term of copyright for the writer's life or twenty-eight years from the date of first publication, whichever was longer, legislation that Webster believed was the least America could do for its geniuses.

By 1820, the amount of foreign, and thus not copyrighted, books and music published in the United States rose to its greatest height—70 percent of all literature and a higher share of printed music. No royalties were paid, either to the original publishers or to the authors or composers. The novels of Walter Scott, Maria Edgeworth's stories of British and Irish life, Byron's poetry, and the popular music of Robert Burns, all were "pirated" in this manner.

A few Americans did copyright their works in England, where such protection could be obtained. James Fenimore Cooper and Washington Irving did so and became as popular in the British Isles as they were at home. British law did not require that the author be a citizen, only that the publisher have the writer's permission and that the work not yet have been published elsewhere. Legal precedent for this had been established in 1777, when Johann Christian Bach sued the London house of Longman & Broderip for infringement of his copyright, and the court ruled that the work in question had been issued without his permission, and that, although he was a foreigner, he could publish and register the work in his own name. As a result of this ruling, some American writers took British gold back home, Cooper, for instance, averaging $5,000 annually in English earnings during the 1820s.

Cooper joined Webster in fighting for copyright revision and perpetual protection to a creator of intellectual property, working through a fellow member of New York's artists' and writers' Bread and Cheese Club, the author and editor Gulian C. Verplanck, congressman from Manhattan and chairman of the House committee studying copyright legislation. Webster worked through Daniel Webster, no relation, a congressman, later senator, from Massachusetts. Daniel Webster, a published writer, exerted a powerful influence on national legislation and was looking to the presidency. At Noah's request, he regularly introduced bills that would extend protection to perpetuity, but they failed to move forward. Noah's son-in-law, William W. Ellsworth, of Hartford, was elected to the House of Representatives and joined Verplanck on the Judiciary Committee, a group most vital to change in the law. During the next several years, both men worked toward passage. Noah Webster spent most of his time in Washington, where legislators were pleased to meet the man whose textbooks were educating their children, but they failed to respond to his arguments for perpetual copyright, which had already been granted to inventors, though this was later rescinded in favor of a shorter time.

Music was mentioned for the first time in the revision of 1831. In addition, the estate of a deceased writer could receive extension of copyright for fourteen years. However, the license for international piracy that had been incorporated into the initial act was repeated; the new act covered citizens only. This brought about the tightening of control by the large book publishers of the traffic in reprinting best-selling foreign copyrighted works. They used economic reprisals, and did the same in the music-publishing trade once the market was expanded and profits warranted it. From the early 1820s, a recognized publisher needed only to announce in the trade press that he was issuing an American edition of a new best-selling British novel in order to claim exclusivity in reprinting it. This was respected by his fellow publishers, who received reciprocity. The stakes in this book-pirating business continued to increase as the American educational process produced a growing number of readers, far in excess of those in England. New York, Boston, and Philadelphia publishers sent agents to London to procure unbound advance sheets legitimately from the British publisher in return for economic favors, or to pay the author for a copy of his manuscript. When unable to do either, they bribed printers for copies or, as a last resort, bought the work on its first day of publication. The text was rushed home on the fastest boat, to be set in type and pulled off press in the shortest order. The final printing operation might take as little as thirty-six hours, firmly establishing the American printer-publisher's claim to the so-called full courtesy of the trade. On occasion, typesetters and proofreaders were dispatched to England to wait for the first appearance of a new book and then to set it in type on a returning vessel. Popular music, usually four-to-eight-page affairs easily duplicated by American engravers, was not involved in such a laborious process. The volume of sales and money involved—twenty-five cents or so for the finished product—added up to a much smaller annual gross sales figure than that of the book trade. Only as consumer demand increased and the sales of a popular song began to go into the tens of thousands of copies would the issue of courtesy of the trade enter into the music business.

When a small book publisher infringed on the informal courtesy, the offended larger house might reprint the most valuable copyrighted properties of its infringing competitor and sell them at a drastic reduction, as a lesson in trade etiquette, sometimes driving the pirate out of business as a result. The six-year depression that started in 1837—almost as serious as the one of the 1930s—put a temporary end to courtesy of the trade, but it came back with prosperity and continued as a general practice until the end of the century. After the Civil War, a book-industry trade journal carried the official schedule of all books protected by this system of sanctioned piracy.

Because there was so much profit in the local sale of noncopyrighted books, American authors found it difficult, unless they were a Cooper or Irving, to find publishers willing to risk their money on native talent. Like Webster, America's leading writers found it economically feasible to pay production costs and then have the printer-publisher handle all sales, making his profit from the margin between actual costs and retail discounts. Most bookstores used the same discount and consignment basis for sheet music and music books as it did for printed books. As a result, the music business took the same economic direction as the book trade, changing sales and distribution methods only after the latter did so.

The royalty system for paying book authors, which was to influence dealings with composers and lyric writers, started in the early 1820s, when payment was made to some British writers whose books were being pirated by reprinting in America. It began chiefly to maintain their good will and access to their future writings. These payments were usually a flat fee, with no relation to sales in the beginning, but, with increased competition between publishers, they became based on a percentage payment after production costs were recouped. Music publishers did not do this, as a general practice, until the post–Civil War period, when the growing international business in American music made such reciprocal relations necessary.

Because the Copyright Act of 1831 appeared to indicate that a foreigner might get protection if he resided in the United States, some British writers made an effort to test the new legislation. Captain Frederick Marryat, a professional sailor turned best-selling author of adventure novels dealing with the Royal Navy, came to America in 1838 to observe the young democracy in action. Hearing of his presence, a Philadelphia publisher who had been particularly active in pirating his novels rushed him a check for $2,000 against royalties. Surprised by this unexpected largess, Marryat visited his American ''publisher'' and in gratitude offered the copyright in his newest work. The courts eventually ruled that, despite a year's residence, Marryat would have to file an intention to become a citizen before the copyright was valid. Marryat refused.

Efforts were also made to skirt the law by registering work by an American citizen who supposedly collaborated with a foreign national. These, too, were ruled out of order when the courts found that the exact contribution of each participant must be clearly stated. While this was impossible in novels, it could have been done with popular songs, but the sheet-music publishers were reluctant to compensate songwriters, foreign or not.

A group of well-known British authors, Thomas Moore and William Wordsworth among them, headed by the popular novelist Harriet Martineau, became involved in a more practical venture. On the advice of N. P. Willis, an American newspaperman, author, and sometime songwriter, the London firm of Saunders & Otley dispatched the senior partner's son to New York City to open a publishing office and beat the book pirates at their own game. Young Frederick Saunders used the New York newspapers to agitate for passage of a reciprocal copyright arrangement with England in the mid-1830s, winning the support of prominent American literary figures and politicians, but he lost his fight to best the reprinters. Undaunted, he urged his father to organize British authors in support of those leading American legislators who had displayed an interest in the cause. Miss Martineau persuaded fifty-five of her peers to sign a memorial sent to both houses of Congress, to leading Americans, and to friends of British literature. She then journeyed to the United States to gather material for her new book about Britain's lost colonies and their people. While lobbying for copyright revision, she met Henry Clay in Washington and urged the senator to devote his select committee's attention to the matter. In early 1837, Clay introduced a bill that would provide protection to British and French writers whose works were printed and published within the United States a month after their initial foreign publication. Lobbying by the reprint publishers, as well as the fiscal crisis that triggered the depression of 1837, combined to defeat Clay's proposal. Although he continued to work for revision until 1842, this first serious attempt to bring about international copyright by means of Congressional initiative came to a halt, which continued until after the Civil War.

Charles Dickens made himself a public bore during his first visit to the United States, in 1842, with his endless disputation about the "hornets' nest of copyright" he found in America. Five years earlier, an American reprinter, unexpectedly grateful for his own extraordinary sales of the Englishman's novels, had sent Dickens the sum of $125. Dickens had promptly returned the money, asking only for copies of any American editions. The world-renowned writer was no longer so docile a victim, and determined to get his share of all sales. A journalist found his endless complaints about book pirates the effusions of a "mercenary scoundrel" who abused "the hospitality of the United States."

The act establishing the Smithsonian Institution, passed in 1846, added, to those to whom one copy of every "book, map, chart, musical composition, print, cut, or engraving" was to be delivered for copyright registration, the librarian of that new national storehouse of the arts, as well as the librarian of the Congressional Library. Ten years later, Congress permitted the dispatch of such material through the mail free of charge.

In this same period, a Parisian music publisher opened a New York agency in association with Erich Kerksieg and Charles Breusing, two Europeans who continued in business until 1852, when their store was taken over by a young German, Gustave Schirmer, providing the foundation for a music house that survives to the present day.

Relations between British and American music publishers first began to undergo real changes after the London house of Boosey, instituted a court action, citing rival British publishers who were seeking to violate its copyrights. The son of a parson, Thomas Boosey had opened a bookstore on Old Broad Street, London, around 1792, and in 1816 established a music branch on Oxford Street, putting his twenty-one-year-old son, Thomas, Jr., in charge. That shop became the city's leading source of foreign sheet music, an area in which few dealers were yet specializing. Within eight years, Boosey's boasted a catalogue of 10,000 items, many of them from the operatic stage. Through agreements with the major continental houses, Breitkopf & Härtel and G. Ricordi, and many European composers then in London and employed by the theaters there, Boosey had become the sole British agent for Johann Nepomuk Hummel, Rossini, Vincenzo Bellini, Saverio Mercadante, and Giuseppe Verdi, all composers whose songs were in great demand. When it became quite obvious that music-trade profits exceeded those from books, the firm's name was changed, in 1854, to Boosey & Co., and its resources were expended on promotion of the most important catalogue of contemporary music in England. The firm, in 1930, was amalgamated with Hawkes & Son, music dealers and publishers since 1863, when it became Boosey & Hawkes.

The Boosey zeal for protection of its property, founded on regular deposit of copies with the British Museum within a month of publication and registration at Stationers' Hall, was to set back the possibilities of a reciprocal treaty with the United States. In 1835, Boosey had pressed suit against the music publisher and printer Thomas D'Almaine for unauthorized duplication of an Italian work claimed by Boosey. The court held that such a work could be assigned exclusively to a British publisher, even if its composer had never been in England, changing the thrust of the 1777 decision. Armed with this new precedent, Boosey continued to deal with foreign houses, having little further trouble from British music merchants, and was quick to pounce on any infringement. It was this litigiousness that brought down his empire, as it led to the near destruction of his foreign catalogue.

Shortly after its La Scala premiere in 1831, Vincenzo Bellini's *La Sonnambula* appeared in an English-language production starring the soprano Maria Malibran and became the sensation of London. Bellini's charming arias achieved a popularity equal to that of the popular music of England's best songwriters as the opera was frequently performed, both in its original Italian and in English. In order to meet the requirements of British law, copies of the manuscript score for *La Sonnambula* were dispatched from Milan by Ricordi, the publisher to whom Bellini had sold the copyright, to Boosey in London during the spring of 1831. This was normal practice, prearranged so that British publication would precede the Italian issue, to ensure protection under British regulations.

Almost a generation later, in 1848, the London composer and music seller Charles Jeffrys published 20,000 new copies of one of the opera's arias, which had already sold 50,000 copies for Boosey. Soon after, George Henry Davidson, a music printer, issued five of Bellini's arias, and London music seller Thomas Purday brought out another ten in a separate edition. Boosey's case against Davidson was won the following year, with a decision sent down from the House of Lords that no matter where a foreign author lived, first publication in England clearly established the publisher's right in the work. Within six months, the ruling was reversed, in Boosey's suit against Purday, the court finding that the work of a foreigner written abroad could not require copyright in England. The attention of both the book- and music- publishing trade had been fixed on the Jeffrys case. It was a matter of special interest because any further decision against a music publisher would effectively permit wholesale reprinting of popular American books owned by British houses, thereby putting an end to any effort for reciprocal international copyright. Those British publishers who opposed that possibility formed the Society for Obtaining an Adjustment of the Law of Copyright, headed by Charles Jeffrys's counsel.

Things returned to where they had been pre-Purday when, in 1854, the lords of the law ruled that a foreigner could receive British copyright only if he traveled to the Queen's dominions and remained there long enough to see the actual printed production of his work. Otherwise, sale of copyright to a British subject was outside the law.

Boosey's catalogue of important foreign contemporary music went up in smoke, as though the court had set a match to his building. With it also went the foreign holdings of other major London music houses. Boosey lost Verdi's *La Traviata, Il Trovatore,* and *Rigoletto,* all of Bellini's works, and other commercially successful pieces from which best-selling British sheet-music editions had been extracted. Most foreign music now fell into the public domain, available to all and any.

Although dealing with printed music only, the decision also had a major effect on book publishing. Inexpensively priced reprints of Harriet Beecher Stowe, W. H. Prescott, Melville, Longfellow, and other Americans began to flood the British cheap-book market. This boom was partly depressed when many Americans, including publishers of popular music, discovered that temporary residence in Canada provided the same effect as a stay in England. By going across the northern border, where British copyright law prevailed until 1875, Americans in search of protection throughout the English-speaking world were able to foil London reprinters and music pirates.

Having been stripped of most of its valuable copyrights through the loss of *Boosey* v. *Jeffrys,* the Boosey family joined the reprinters, bringing out cheap editions of the best contemporary foreign music for the pianoforte. Beginning in 1867, however, they retrieved their former good fortune through the new national passion for parlor ballads. Written to order by contract composers and poets, these songs about love, death, God, country, home, and other subjects dear to the hearts of Britons were easy to read, easy to play, easy to sing, and easy to remember, displacing songs much like them from Italian and French operas that had been favorites in the years just before. The new parlor ballads enjoyed so great an international success that Boosey and Chappell & Co., his most formidable rival in merchandising the modern ballad, found it expedient to effect reciprocal arrangements with American music houses.

Although only citizens could obtain copyright, it was possible to work around the law by means of careful coordination with British music merchants, a process made easier by the improvement of international communication. American representatives of London music publishers first deposited a song's title page in Washington, following which the entire work was printed and issued in London. American publication came next, with appropriate deposits at the Library of Congress and the Smithsonian. The last steps in the process took place with the mandatory deposit with the British Museum within one month of publication.

In the early 1850s, a number of British authors were persuaded that only a reciprocal agreement with the Americans would resolve the situation. In 1852, Dickens, Thackeray, Macaulay, and Tennyson, with a doddering Thomas Moore as a sentimental figurehead, joined a group of literary lights and publishers; they raised and sent $5,000 over to their agents in Washington. The money was a first installment in an attempt to facilitate international copyright by the outright bribery of senators and Cabinet members. The group of American lobbyists who had broached the scheme, however, proved to be unable to deliver what they had guaranteed. The plan had been for the Senate to ratify a treaty between the United States and Great Britain agreeing to reciprocal copyright, thus by-passing the House of Representatives, where all attempts at such revision had been defeated. Once the bill was introduced, there was immediate opposition from the New York and Philadelphia book pirates, with the new element of organized labor added. Henry Carey, perennial publisher enemy of such legislation, thundered: "Ideas are common property of all mankind. Facts are everybody's facts. Words are free to all men."

Organized typesetters, stereotypers, printers, and bookbinders spoke out in opposition to what they saw as a political maneuver that would permit importation of cheap British editions and thus put an end to their jobs. Their insistence that a foreign book should receive American copyright only if it was manufactured in the United States was most effective in killing the treaty in committee. It created an element of international copyright that persisted until President Reagan's veto of a bill to end this provision was overridden by Congress in 1982.

George F. Root, teacher, music editor, and successful popular songwriter, learned quickly that the 1856 revision of the copyright law was of little benefit to composers of music, even though it did appear to call for payment for performance of their dramatic works. Dion Boucicault, the Irish-born actor and playwright, was chiefly responsible for passage of the new revision. Soon after his arrival in 1853, this man, who revolutionized the American theater by sending out touring companies while a hit play was still running in New York, learned that, unlike England, the United States did not offer any protection to a dramatist against unauthorized public performance and printing of his scripts. Two leading American playwrights, Robert Montgomery Bird and George Boker, had already been involved in a long fight to get legislation that would protect them. Because managers and star performers usually controlled all rights to plays in their repertoire, including rights to song lyrics interpolated by the writer, the works could not be published by their creators without permission. Consequently, they lost an important source of income. Bird, for example, had received $5,000 from Edwin Forrest for all rights to five original plays that made a fortune for the actor-manager. When Bird wished to publish his collected works, Forrest refused permission, claiming that the plays were his exclusive property by right of purchase. As a result, a disgruntled Bird retired from the theater to become a best-selling novelist, editor, and politician, and used his Washington connections during the 1840s in an unsuccessful effort to have the law changed. In 1853, Boker attempted the same task, and failed as well. Only after Boucicault lobbied for a new bill, to cover performances, did one emerge in 1856; it conferred on the author of a dramatic composition the sole right to copyright, print, publish, and license the performance of his work. The act also provided a minimum fine of $100 for the first and $50 for each subsequent performance given without the consent of the writer. Despite it, for many years only the most successful playwrights were in any position to take advantage of its provisions.

The responsibility of the Department of State to maintain files of all copyrighted works, including a collection of all deposited American music printed since 1819, which was contained in over 200 bound volumes by that time, came to an end in 1859. All matters dealing with copyright were transferred to the Department of the Interior in accordance with an act passed by the 35th Congress.

As the Civil War drew near, the status of American copyright legislation was essentially what it had been shortly after the Constitution was written. Balanced overwhelmingly in favor of the publisher, as under Queen Anne's 1710 Law, it was of little benefit to the creators of words and music, even in the theater, where a performance law obtained. It continued to provide pirates of European literature and music with a license to steal from foreign creators. It remained the narrow and stingy law it had been on passage, and it made abundantly manifest that, as with much legislation, only the most dedicated lobbying by those affected could bring about change.

Changing Technology

During the first twenty-five years of the century some 10,000 musical pieces were published in American commercial compilations or as sheet music, according to Richard J. Wolfe. Most of these were simplified versions for performance by amateurs. The market was too small to support printing of parts of trios or quartets. This also meant that serious, more lengthy compositions remained in manuscript and most have disappeared. As Wolfe has written, the "published repertory should be regarded as the manifestation of the popular or urban taste of the eastern seaboard. This is not to say that Europe's greatest composers were not admired. Nearly 30 of Beethoven's pieces were published in America during his lifetime."

According to Irving Lowens's bibliography, more than 400 songsters—printed songbooks, usually containing words only, although musical notation was sometimes included—were issued from 1801 to 1825. These were printed not only in the major cities, but also by local booksellers and job printers in smaller communities in every one of the states and adjacent territories and possessions. Sung to well-known tunes, these lyrics embraced every type of song, from the patriotic to the "men only" amatory.

A most flourishing business in sacred music had also sprung up. The camp-meeting movement stimulated publication of popular evangelical hymn collections, songs called "Christian" or "gospel" today. The patented shape-note business had found a major market in the South, and a more sophisticated yet evangelical hymnody marked the way for Boston's Lowell Mason, music teacher and compiler, and his disciples. Mason established a market for educational music and built the singing teachers' profession into a major force in public education, which then continued to shape popular culture and taste. The organized Protestant churches understood the yearnings of their communicants for a denominational hymnal that harnessed popular taste for modern and singable melodies to contemporary awareness of the uses of religion in a nation dominated by the middle class, which worshiped at the twin shrines of meeting house and counting house. The Sunday School movement's growth contributed to the establishment of a union catering exclusively to the preparation of literature suitable for children as well as songs that appealed to all generations.

Isaiah Thomas, the major late-eighteenth-century printer, business entrepreneur, and occasional music publisher, whose Worcester, Massachusetts, headquarters employed 150 people in a large complex housing presses, a paper mill, and a bindery, was one of the first to use music type, purchased from British founders. Type continued to be used for printing music books until the 1830s, when the stereotyping process began to replace it. After 1850, electroplating ended the necessity to keep bulky, heavy type standing in case new editions were ordered. The storage of materials to be duplicated was easier for publishers of sheet music, who initially struck off their wares from engraved or punched plates that could easily be housed in the shop or shipped off to a copperplate printer. A publisher's true financial worth was best judged by the number of plates he owned, and they were the most important element in the acquisition of a music house going out of business or in the disposition of an estate left by a music publisher. The eminent house of Ditson & Co., located in a new five-story building on Washington Street, in Boston, stored between 50,000 and 60,000 copperplates in a special fireproof safe in the building's basement just before the Civil War.

As for the printing presses that were essential to the business, there had been no significant improvements. Even in the early nineteenth century, they were rather like those Gutenberg had used 350 years earlier. Technology had not yet devised a press that was lighter, nor taken advantage of modern iron, nor used the lever principle rather than the screw of the 1450 prototype. America's major early contribution to the press's development came from Philadelphia, where foreign technicians were making this publishing center the hub of printing technology. Scottish mechanics Jacob Bay, John Baine, and the partnership of Binney & Ronaldson were engaged in type founding, the last already able to provide American printers with fonts of many kinds, and the equal of the best produced anywhere in the world. The Edinburgh machinist Adam Ramage had built a screw press of his own design in 1795, which quickly replaced older traditional models. His press was superceded in 1813 by Philadelphian George Clymer's Columbian Press, so known because of the giant eagle with a cornucopia in one claw and an olive branch in the other that decorated it. Made of iron and using a series of levers in place of Gutenberg's screw, it was soon in use at the most up-to-date shops, chiefly newspaper offices. Only the British steam-driven cylinder press, first proudly installed by the *Times,* succeeded in replacing Clymer's machine during the 1820s. Richard Hoe's improved machinery permitted printers to turn out 4,000 pages an hour in 1832, doubling British technological capability, and contributed greatly to the growth of large-circulation newspapers and magazines in the United States. Printers who did not need such large production found Clymer's hand press, invented in 1816, most useful for such job orders as music books. Jacob Johnson, a Philadelphia bookseller who had opened his shop shortly after the Revolution, established America's first printing-ink manufacturing company, in 1804, liberating printers from the dirty job of producing their own.

Despite a growing supply of locally made type, which included music symbols and notation, most early American music printers and their immediate successors continued to employ the old and respected punch method, switching to improvements created by Fournier and Breitkopf decades earlier only, with apparent reluctance, after 1820. With pewter plates as the base, usually 13¾ to 11¼ inches long and 7½ to 8½ inches wide, music publishers printed on pages about 13 by 19 inches, or 13 by 9½ when folded.

Owing to the pleasure in possessing sheet music, music publishers' best customers often had their favorites bound together in morocco or calf, in books usually not more than an inch thick. It is these books that have preserved much music of the period. Most of that issued after the 1820s is decorated with examples of the lithographers' art, which range from the crude to strikingly handsome cover illustrations, which have become prized collectors' items.

The discovery of chemical printing, or lithography, by Aloys Senefelder around 1796 came at a time when rising cultural and economic expectations were inspiring newly affluent Americans to search for inexpensive but accurate reproductions of art. By 1830, lithography had come into growing use in both Great Britain and the United States in connection with printed sheet music for the voice and the piano.

A Bohemian Austrian actor and playwright then in his twenties, Senefelder had found the cost of duplicating his scripts by the printing process too expensive and looked around for a simpler and cheaper means. He tried copper and zinc plates but found them almost as costly to use as the methods already available. He later remembered that ''as a child of five or six I had seen a music printery in Frankfurt or Mainz where the notes were etched in black stone. I had played with the broken stones which lay in a heap near our house.'' He began to experiment with native limestone, on which he had been mixing ink for standard engraving, and found that by writing backward and making a sharp impression he produced an accurate reproduction on the polished surface, using an ink made of wax, soap, and lampblack. The result was remarkably similar to a woodblock. Seeking both encouragement and financial backing, Senefelder, after buying some badly printed music, took his work to a Munich court composer-musician, Franz Gleissner, who gave him some music in manuscript to duplicate. Unimpressed by the result, Gleissner revealed an accomplishment that proved to be far more valuable than his music: he was skilled at writing backward. The first joint Senefelder-Gleissner publication, a work for pianoforte, was shown to a local music publisher, who encouraged the project. Further experimentation led to the process known as ''lithography,'' which eventually reduced production costs by seventy-five percent.

Looking for markets outside Munich, Senefelder went to Offenbach, near Frankfurt, where Johan Andre had taken over the music printing and publishing house his father had established in 1774. Having purchased almost all of Mozzart's unpublished manuscripts, as well as the thematic catalogue of every composition he had written, Andre, with almost a monopoly of one of Europe's best-selling concert and operatic composers, needed speedier production methods. Excited by Senefelder's work, he gave him full support and began to retool his shop for the new process.

In Munich, Senefelder found the newest *Wunderkind,* twelve-year-old Karl

Maria von Weber, who had quickly become a nuisance to Andre because of his constant presence in the music shop. Weber had been trained by his musician father to become the next Mozart, and, when his abilities appeared to falter, the unhappy parent turned the boy over to masters in drawing, painting, and engraving. Now young Weber was in Munich to study music once more, and was soon to win the public acclaim as a concert pianist that continued until his death. With the advantage of training in the plastic arts, Weber mastered Senefelder's process well enough to lithograph his second original work, a set of piano variations, making some of his own "improvements" in the method.

Even though the economic benefits of lithography were seen by the young musician, the great music-publishing house of Artaria did not share his vision when Weber offered both his music and his mechanical skills. It appears that Artaria saw the potential and presumably dangerous revolution that lay in use of the new invention, one that would permit a composer to make and print his own music, and merchandise it in quantity himself. The firm did not respond to Weber. Other European music merchants did, however. Breitkopf & Härtel, of Leipzig, G. Ricordi, of Milan, and Schott, of Mainz, bought rights to the process from Senefelder, who established a factory in Vienna in 1803. There he developed the use of metal plates, discarding the stone that broke so easily on printing presses.

Philip Andre, a young relative of the German publishing family who resided in London, assisted Senefelder in patenting the art of "polyautography," as it was known in England. Andre published the first collection using the process in 1803, but British publishers failed to recognize the economic savings inherent in lithography. After Andre's return to Austria, the task of promoting polyautography fell on German-born coachmaker Rudolph Ackerman, who had opened a print and book store combined with an art school on The Strand, where he experimented with lithography and, more important, translated Senefelder's book, *Complete Course of Lithography*.

The first appearance in the United States, in 1818, of Senefelder's book made public the technique that the inventor had worked so hard to keep private. It provided artists and publishers with access to the inexpensive process for multiple reproduction of art, drawn on flat stones with a special grease pencil and then easily colored by hand. The discovery in Kentucky of suitable limestone ended dependence on foreign supplies and gave music publishers an opportunity to follow their European counterparts, principally in England, in using the process for pictorial sheet-music covers. Previously they had used vignettes for their covers, small borderless pictures that George Bickham, Jr., first used during the 1730s in England. The several hundred plates he engraved for two editions of the *Musical Entertainer* were widely imitated for a century in England and then in the United States.

Until the appearance in 1820 of the engraved cover for A. P. Heinrich's 268-page book of printed music, *Dawning of Music in Kentucky*, most examples of the engraver's art used for title pages were rather pedestrian. The first American artist to use lithography in connection with printed music was Henry Stone, of Washington, D.C., whose work decorated the *Miscellany of Music*, a seventy-two-page collection of songs that appeared in 1823. Stone's work was crude, promising none of the artistry of David Claypoole Johnston, the first important American sheet-music illustrator.

Johnston was an unimportant actor in the Philadelphia theater, who probably came into contact with lithographic techniques during travels in northern cities with theatrical troupes, when he watched playhouse designers learning to master the new process. He had learned how to engrave on copper and pewter, and may also have come into possession of the second important English instruction book, *The Art of Drawing on Stone,* by Charles Hullmandell, a British lithographic pioneer, published in 1824. Johnston's artistic abilities were recognized in Boston by John and William Pendleton, owners and operators of the first commercial lithographic shop in America. The Pendletons had set up a press and were teaching apprentices the craft. British-born, the Pendletons had been trained as copperplate engravers, and had found their first work in America installing copper piping for gas fixtures in Charles Willson Peale's Philadelphia Museum. William then moved to Boston, and John to France, where he picked up the fundamentals of lithography, returning with a press and allied supplies to his brother's studio. After the Pendletons' tutelege, Johnston first showed his considerable talent when an old friend, A. P. Heinrich, prepared to publish one of his songs, "The Log House," for sale to his pupils and consignment to Boston music stores. Artist and musician had met in Philadelphia when the lovable Bohemian composer was writing incidental music and songs for local theaters. Johnston now drew the first title page, or sheet-music cover, to be printed by lithography, which showed Heinrich in front of a Kentucky log cabin playing the fiddle, with manuscripts scattered on the ground, while a black man eavesdrops, fiddle in hand.

Another of Johnston's surviving sheet-music covers was also done for a show-business friend, New York theatrical-hotel owner and playwright Micah Hawkins, who asked him to engrave decorative art for his song "Massa Georgee Washington and General Lafayette," written for the popular comic singer James Roberts, who had sung the song to great applause and sufficient encores to warrant its printing. Showing the actor as a black soldier in the American Revolution, the ballad's cover art was the first of a long series of depictions of whites in blackface on sheet music in the United States.

Having mastered the technique and being much in demand, Johnston retired from the theater to specialize in the graphic arts, eventually becoming known as the "American Cruikshank" for the wryly comic caricatured figures that made him famous. His fees were high, so music publishers looked to the less expensive talent being taught by the Pendletons, since the art they had learned not only was cheaper to produce than the engraved kind but also was selling sheet music in greater quantity than sloppily engraved vignettes. These young apprentices became adept in copying the engraved cover art used on the foreign music most dealers specialized in before the 1830s. Consequently, much of the sheet music extant from this time is almost identical to British editions, being altered only to create an American character.

The work of Lowell Mason and his colleagues in educating the young to read and sing music was beginning to bear fruit in other musical idioms, while the piano-playing ability of many young women and some men was growing more sophisticated. Sheet music was a new presence in American homes, gracing the huge family pianos that were often their proudest possession. Piano makers stepped up production in response to demand for the instrument, both as a symbol of social status and as an indication of the rising middle class's wish to hear music of its own choice. Salesrooms featured $300 instruments, alongside racks of the newest printed sheets, which included dance music after society had taken to enjoying each new social dance. Mass-circulation magazines reported new steps and measures, and worked to persuade the American father that dance music had a rightful place alongside the sentimental ballads on which he doted, as well as the genteel "scientific" music he was expected to like.

The Pendletons enjoyed many years of monopoly of lithographic printing, as much because of the abnormal business conditions during Andrew Jackson's first term as president as because of the high cost of imported mechanical equipment and supplies. Good paper for lithographic use was not made in the United States for many years, and the Hoe Printing Press Company made an American lithographic press in the early 1830s.

John Pendleton moved to Philadelphia, where he hired, as his chief draftsman, Rembrandt Peale, the most talented of that artistic family. But a short partnership with a local promoter, Colonel Clephas Childs, ended when Pendleton moved to New York, to open a studio and press there. Childs carried on the business in Philadelphia, hiring another outstanding portraitist, Henry Inman, one of the first American artists to take up lithography as a major medium, to serve as chief artist and master of apprentices. A young French printer, Peter S. Duval, was brought in to head Childs's mechanical operations. He had been trained in leading European lithographic establishments and was the best craftsman in the art that America had yet seen. Duval became part-owner of the business in 1834, when Childs was unable to pay him $750 in back salary.

Duval at once began to publish several magazines with lithographed illustrations. His work came to the attention of government authorities, which provided him with lucrative contracts to make illustrations for reports by various expeditions sent to explore the unknown territories acquired by conquest, purchase, or manifest destiny. Duval's maps, views and landscapes, and drawings of natural and botanic specimens—the major ingredients of these reports—brought lithography to the attention of businessmen, some years after music publishers had become the art's most important users. P. S. Duval's Lithographic Establishment soon operated several dozen presses, with a working force of eighty and more than a hundred colorists. When Duval adapted steam power to his presses, he was accurate in calling the operation the largest in the nation.

James Queen, a local boy who was apprenticed to Duval at the age of fourteen, in 1835, was the firm's outstanding artist for colored music covers. His illustrations for the *U. S. Military Magazine,* created by Duval to exhibit lithography's advantages to a wider market, were often used for sheet music as well. In his later years, Queen was one of the country's leading chromolithographers; many of his famous pieces were issued during the Civil War.

The New York lithographic firm founded in 1828 and operated first by George Endicott and later by his son William remained a leading enterprise until the end of the century. Among its first music-business customers was the house of Firth & Hall, whose cover art featured the earliest racial stereotypes of Jim Crow, the long-tailed Blue, Coal Black Rose, and other characters featured by blackface stage performers. More sophisticated lithographed drawings were used by them on Henry Russell's first hit songs in the late 1830s. Russell brought in the Hutchinson Family, singers whose first songs were published in Boston by Oliver Ditson, who wanted a more aggressive New York outlet. Firth & Hall turned over their first twelve manuscripts to George Endicott, too, for the artwork.

The secret of Endicott's success, as indeed it had to be for all the major cover-illustration houses, was the talent of its artists and the growing facility of its low-paid young apprentices. In order to learn the trade, teen-agers usually signed up for a few dollars a week, until they reached twenty-one and freedom. The Art Students league and other places where an aspiring and talented youngster could find basic training were still in the future, so lithographic establishments served many later important artists as their prime source of training in draftsmanship, the foundation stone of representational art.

Pendleton's Boston establishment was the incubator for a number of major American artists who were to find fame in other fields after they had learned the elements of art there and shown their skills on sheet-music covers. Most Boston publishers used Thayer's, as the Pendleton shop became known after 1840. Among them was the young New Englander Oliver Ditson, who had already shown the sharp business sense that was to make him the music-merchant giant of the century, and Henry Prentiss, a less imposing figure, owner of a jumbled store that carried both the umbrellas he manufactured and sheet music of works usually turned down by all other Boston firms. William Oakes was also a customer, basking in his success as New England distributor for the musician-publisher Charles Edward Horn, whose "Rocked in the Cradle of the Deep" was an important hit song. It was to Oakes that British singer-songwriter Henry Russell went first in Boston. Fitz Hugh Lane and Benjamin Champney, Thayer employees who received between fifteen and eighteen dollars weekly, did Russell's early American song covers for Oakes. When Ditson stole Russell away, Lane and Champney continued to provide cover art for each of Russell's successes of the early 1840s—"The Old Arm Chair," "The Maniac," "The Mad Girl's Song," "The Old Sexton," and many others—which were immediately pirated by London in an atypical reversal of the music trade. Many of Lane's illustrations were copied exactly on the British editions, and some others were only slightly altered. British publishers had not yet learned the commercial appeal of illustrated music, and, being unwilling to spend unnecessary sums, were content to imitate or copy the art.

The son of a pioneer Back Bay family, Lane abandoned the traditional name Nathaniel for a more elegant Fitz Hugh on completing his apprenticeship. He soon became known in Boston as a talented painter of local landscapes as well as the creator of illustrated music covers. He was dismissed from Thayer's following a change of ownership and began to issue collections of his own lithographed work. Later he concentrated on the marine paintings that brought him great success.

After Benjamin Champney, too, was discharged from Thayer's, he went at once to Europe to study with German artists of the Düsseldorf Academy, where he joined a number of young Americans who eventually became first-rate painters. Learning first to draw plaster casts, before moving on to real life, these young men subscribed to the credo that "the public always wants a picture that tells a story." They eventually gained national prominence through chromolithographically reproduced works that sold in the millions. After his return from Europe, Champney became a leading member of the American Academy of Art and well known for his views of New England mountains.

The most talented of Thayer's artists, chief draftsman Robert Cooke was also a skilled musician, with a sensitivity to instrumentalists and theatrical performers beyond that of most contemporary illustrators. Cooke had been an early Pendleton apprentice, but he stayed in the business after he found it difficult to earn a living as a professional painter. His art for the banjo songs written by Joe Sweeney, a leading white virtuoso on that instrument, who is also credited with adding the fifth string to the black man's invention, represented one of the earliest attempts to depict the Southern black as he actually was thought to live and not as depicted by a white man in stage make-up. Henry Prentiss published the Sweeney songs in 1840. The covers he ordered from Thayer's did much to influence the course of minstrel-show art.

The wholesale firing of Thayer's art department added Cooke to the invasion of Europe by out-of-work Boston artists, and he died there a few years later. The man responsible for the purge was John H. Bufford, who had returned to his native city to accept a half-share in his brother-in-law's successful lithographic operation. Originally apprenticed to a bookbinder, Bufford had demonstrated his talent for drawing to William Pendleton in Boston and had been hired as a trainee draftsman. Four years later, he joined the Endicott shop in New York, and then worked for another Pendleton graduate, Nathaniel Currier. When his own shop barely survived the panic of 1837, he disposed of all holdings and went north.

Once all the artists had been dismissed, Bufford assumed control of production, overseeing the work of the teen-age apprentices and trainees recruited by newspaper advertising. Publishers continued to use Thayer's for their covers, and most music art was done by Bufford or under his close supervision. He was one of the first commercial artists to use the new chromolithographic technology, initially experimented with in the United States by a Boston rival, William Sharp, who possibly produced the first piece of popular sheet music illustrated by color lithography—"Blue Beard," issued by William Oakes in the early 1840s.

After 1851, the firm, then known as J. H. Bufford's Lithography, dealt almost exclusively in the production of prints or drawings and well-known paintings, ready for framing. It had great success, and a contemporary wrote: "The landscapes, portraits, architectural designs, already executed by Mr. Bufford, prove him to be a master of the art, and entitle him to the patronage of all who appreciate the beautiful effects of a beautiful art."

Among the apprentices who learned this "beautiful art" and applied it to sheet-music covers in color under Bufford's direction were Joseph Baker and Winslow Homer. Baker eventually became chief artist and produced sheet music in both black and white and color for major New York and Boston music houses. Twenty-year-old Homer chafed for escape from the job he had only recently taken, one paying him five dollars a week when lithographic artists with far less talent were making five times that. He had got the position after seeing a newspaper advertisement asking for "a boy with a taste for drawing. No other wanted." His father's friendship with the studio owner helped. The young man's cartoons and his "inattention" in classes had recently forced his discharge from West Point. His first job of any consequence at Bufford's was to duplicate worn-out stone plates of old music illustrations owned by Ditson, which the publisher intended to use for reissued music. Homer added some personal touches to this work, making many of them valuable collectors' items. One, "The Chair Baby Jumper Song," was printed for distribution only to purchasers of the patented child's furniture, a use of pictorial sheet music that Ditson and others promoted with great success among merchants and manufacturers. Eleven covers for Ditson and one for Harvey Dodsworth, in New York City, are known today as the work of Winslow Homer.

Once he attained his majority and was relieved of the articles of apprenticeship, Homer joined *Harper's Weekly* as a reporter-illustrator, engraving eyewitness pictures on wood as soon after an event as possible. Homer's later reputation as nineteenth-century America's greatest watercolorist and oil painter was considerably enhanced by the chromolithographic industry that mass-produced his work after the Civil War.

Although not the truest talent, the most famous Pendleton alumnus was Nathaniel Currier, whose shrewd perception of popular taste, coupled with a firm awareness of changing technology, created the national business bearing his name that was the leading lithographic firm of its day. It is Currier and Ives prints along with popular songs that give modern Americans a charming insight into that past when sentimental and simple songs and pictures sold in huge quantities. Currier learned the elements of his trade after he was apprenticed to Pendleton in 1826, at the age of thirteen. In five years he had learned enough to be of value to a Philadelphia printer, and later was employed at John Pendleton's New York studio. When John gave up the business, he left Currier on his own, possessed of a single press. Temporary financial aid came to him from a young Englishman, Richard Stodart, a son of the distinguished London piano-making family, who had just sold his interest in a music store and piano warehouse and was looking for a new investment. When business proved poor, Stodart departed, too soon to participate in Currier's first successful lithographic print. The disastrous fire, which destroyed hundreds of New York buildings in mid-December 1835, brought Currier to the attention of buyers, who then remained almost exclusively his for much of the century. His print of an original drawing of *The Ruins of the Merchants Exchange after the Recent Conflagration,* published almost immediately after the event, sold by the thousands. It was the first of Currier's prints to capture the imagination of the curious and the sensation seeker. From this success, Currier learned that fortune lay in giving people what they wanted: pictures of disasters, political figures, celebrities, famous scenic sights, natural wonders, and sentimental and homey subjects. The firm provided the equivalent of what the picture magazine and the television screen offer modern audiences. During the 1830s and 1840s, Currier produced more than eighty music covers for James K. Hewitt, Firth & Hall, and other New York music houses, on all the many subjects used by enterprising music men in order to attract buyers and increase sales.

The business really began to boom in 1852 when Currier hired a member by marriage of his family, James Merritt Ives, as bookkeeper. In 1857, Ives became a full partner, and the new firm of Currier and Ives prospered, issuing more than 7,000 different pictures documenting American life. The prints sold for from twenty cents to four dollars, depending on the subject, and could be ordered from a catalogue or bought at local stores or from traveling peddlers, who bought them wholesale at six dollars per hundred.

Postwar Currier and Ives printed art was made by the chromolithographic process, a modern technique that permitted mass reproduction of oil paintings, watercolors, and other subjects in color. Prior to that, most of the work was done by hand, employees coloring each individual print or tinting it by use of a one-color lithographic stone upon which the drawing, cut on a separate stone, was superimposed. Prints using more than the original black drawing and a single tint required more stones; true chromolithography involved the use of a different stone for each color.

Lithography's father, Aloys Senefelder, had experimented with color early in the century, but its use for sheet music did not take place in England before 1841, five years after a French printer named Engelmann patented the technique. The British pioneer Charles Hullmandell worked with colored prints a few years later and gave the art the English name by which it is known.

Sharp and Bufford, both in Boston, were the first Americans to apply colored lithography to sheet music, and they were followed by Duval in 1843. Customers, particularly women, as well as the living subjects of songs or those to whom songwriters dedicated their pieces, liked the new look of colored sheet music. It cost less to produce than copperplate engraving, but it was more expensive than simple black and white or tinted lithography, so music publishers did what they would always do—passed along the cost to the consumer. The price was raised by a third.

Other production problems arose to plague the music business. Most of the art studios they had been using were still unfamiliar with the new methods, their owners hesitant to purchase the expensive machinery and supplies. Companies formed to meet the demand from other users of reproduced art stepped in, but quality control of sheet-music covers was slow in coming. Only after 1850 did it approach the high level that existed for the rest of the century.

Because stones were good for up to 5,000 impressions, and then could be recycled for other use by grinding away a minute section of the working surface, chromolithographers held onto their work and did not sell it outright, as had been the practice with black-and-white art. This effectively reduced the principal measure of music publishers' assets: the number of plates they owned. Though reasonably suitable American limestone was readily available, workers in chromolithography preferred high-grade materials from the Bavarian fields in which Senefelder had first chanced upon the process. Colored covers became standard only after the music-buying public multiplied in the prosperous period after the Mexican War and the discovery of gold in California, and before the depression of 1857. During this time, more than 50,000 separate items of popular music were issued. The most elegant color sheets were wrapped immediately after printing and placed in colored paper cases, with the titles set in type for the front. They were thus kept clean of the marks of probing fingers, but the prominent type of the titles also caught the customers' attention.

The first music publisher in either England or the United States to become fully aware of the appeal of a title page printed in color was that flambuoyant showman, composer, danceband leader, and writer of polkas, quadrilles, and waltzes, the man who developed the promenade or ''pops'' concert into a national institution in England and influenced the course of popular American concert performances: Louis Antoine Jullien.

Jullien, born in 1812 in a Swiss mountain cottage, was the supreme master of press agentry long before Americans ''invented'' the craft, as the skillful manner in which he manipulated the English-speaking press of the world attests. During his grand tour of the United States in 1853 and 1854, newspapers and magazines were filled with accounts of this conductor who ''with one uprise of his baton had struck universal America with [a] magic wand.'' During that season Jullien recouped a fortune for the syndicate of English gentlemen who had pooled £200,000 to send him and a cadre of the best available European instrumentalists in search of Yankee gold.

Jullien was a master showman, who sat in front of his orchestra of nearly a hundred and a chorus of 85 on an ornate red velvet chair, rising from it to conduct, wearing white kid gloves and using a jeweled baton when his beloved Beethoven's music was played, a lesser rod for others. As an obituary recalled, ''he broke down the barriers and let in the crowds,'' entertaining vast audiences as well as teaching them the excerpted music of Beethoven, Mozart, Handel, Verdi, and Mendelssohn, along with his own dance tunes.

In 1845, at the height of his popularity in England, he opened his own publishing company, in the Royal Musical Conservatory and Musical Library in London. Fans came to admire the great presence and to buy his sheet music, which was decorated with brilliant pictorial covers—piano pieces at four shillings, piano duets for five. To ensure that these were not from the many pirated editions of his successes, Jullien's flowery signature adorned each copy. (Some years earlier, James L. Hewitt, in New York, had published the first Henry Russell hits with the singing songwriter's autograph etched onto the lithographed cover plate for a similar effect.) Jullien's covers were by John Brandard, a young artist who had made his name illustrating pictorial books for women, receiving twenty guineas a plate, or $125, while American artists of exceptional talent were receiving fifteen dollars for a fifty-five-hour week. Brandard also illustrated Jullien's popular annual albums of sheet music, a series of bound copies of his compositions, some of which sold as many as 250,000 copies.

Each year Jullien wrote and published many new quadrilles, those square dances much admired by high society, each based on some popular song or music. His "British Navy Quadrille" was based on Dibdin's and Shield's songs of the sea and the navy, whose melodies had become so ingrained in British music that they were often presumed to be true folk songs. The maestro tickled the ears of his public with highly orchestrated reiterations of familiar music, and Brandard drew elegant cover art for each piece before it appeared in print.

Phineas T. Barnum had already educated Americans to expect an excess of florid exploitation during the months before he sponsored Jenny Lind's concert tour, which grossed three quarters of a million dollars in nine months during the 1850–51 season. However, Jullien taught that master showman and other impresarios some new tricks in the hooplah preceeding his first concert, in 1853. Portraits of the great Jullien and his featured stars were hung in public places all over Manhattan. A monster brass instrument to be featured in his quadrilles was exhibited in a Broadway museum, and stories appeared in print about a drum so large that it took two ships to transport it from Europe, about Jullien's bejeweled baton, his red velvet throne, his kid gloves, his astounding wardrobe, and about other wonders to be seen and heard once he arrived. Castle Garden, remodeled from the circular fortress at the tip of Manhattan constructed during the War of 1812, and now seating 10,000, was rented for an entire month. Vocal and instrumental concerts, drawn from a repertoire of 1,200 numbers, were presented nightly, each evening offering a classical overture, two movements from a symphony, selections from operas, and the concert dance music that had made Jullien famous in England. In the city's cultural climate, dominated by German "puritans" who concentrated on European masters, Jullien provided fresh air by including American music, some of it written by native musicians hired for the national tour, and such current hit songs as Stephen Foster's "Old Folks at Home."

Once he returned home from America, it was all downhill for the great Jullien. A publicly owned company capitalized at $200,000 to operate an immense concert hall seating 10,000 failed. Most of his musical library was destroyed in a fire that gutted Covent Garden. Driven out of England by creditors, he went to France to recoup, only to be arrested for debt, released, and then confined in an asylum after he attempted to kill an adopted daughter. He died there at forty-eight.

Almost immediately after the Frenchman Louis Daguerre took and developed a black-and-white picture, using equipment and a process of his own creation, American artists began to experiment with the technology. Daguerreotypes, or "sun pictures," printed on small metal plates, faithfully reproduced every detail. They were made and collected by American painters to be copied by their students. After 1845, daguerreotypy became a tool of the lithographic trade, offering an inexpensive preserved image that could be easily copied on a stone. It was used for popular music. Pictures of singing families, members of minstrel troups, politicians, and celebrities were copied from daguerreotypes—which accounts for their stiff and frozen qualities on sheet music of this era.

Even as lithography developed into chromolithography, other changes were in the making that would eventually reduce music production costs. The rising price of the highest-grade imported stone outpaced even the inflation factor that brought about the financial disaster of 1857, and thus it encouraged experiments toward a less expensive substitute. Senefelder had used the more easily accessible, lighter, and cheaper zinc, and then, inexplicably, had abandoned that medium in favor of Bavarian stone. Duval used zinc plates in 1849, finding them easy to draw upon, and when scoured with sand capable of absorbing the required water, much as quarried stone did. In addition, a good zinc plate could be used for as many as 8,000 impressions and could be easily stored. One hundred zinc plates took up the same space as a single lithographed stone, and because of their lower cost they could be bought by music publishers, thus adding greatly to their most important asset—their stock of music plates.

In the six decades following Senelder's discovery of the lithographic technique, the number of American printing shops using the process increased from the Pendletons' single Boston office in 1825 to more than sixty major firms around the nation. By 1890, this had grown to 700, which grossed $20 million annually, although their contribution was relatively minor, music publishers had done their part in the technology's growth and helped stimulate American taste for genteel art illustration, reproduced in quantity from a wet stone drawn upon with greased pencils.

CHAPTER 3

Sheet Music Publishing in Pre–Civil War America

America's popular-music business began the century with no more than a few dozen printers equipped with sufficient music type or engravers' tools to engage in the mass duplication of music. Without exception, all were located in the north. About fifty engravers had some connection with the business, among them musicians and composers who, like James Hewitt, Benjamin Carr, Gottlieb Graupner, Thomas Birch, Edward Riley, and a few others, had learned the art of engraving music and possessed the necessary tools and copperplate presses.

By 1825, about 200 men and women had fallen victim to the unpredictable lure of the business of popular music. They included printers, booksellers, engravers; instrument makers, repairers, and dealers; print-shop owners; umbrella manufacturers; music teachers, professional musicians, bandleaders, composers, and songwriters, all of them of English, French, or German extraction. Printers continued to issue broadsides for local or regional consumption, as well as pocket songsters from whose pages those Americans who had not been taught to read music learned the words of the latest new songs or were reminded of old ones. New York, Boston, and Philadelphia continued to dominate such music business as there was in the first quarter of the nineteenth century.

Like booksellers and publishers, whose trade practices shaped the course of music publishing, most of these small operations dealt chiefly in reprinted foreign material, which they could use without any legal obligation to pay for them. As a result, no significant investment was needed to print noncopyright music except production costs, and distributors and retailers could be offered a higher discount than for protected American work. Music with complicated notation or works with more than the two or three pages a popular song demanded necessarily cost more, chiefly because of the effort required to produce them.

As Richard J. Wolfe wrote, in *Early American Music Engraving and Printing:*

> The early printing of music printed from engraved plates was a tedious, repetitious and expensive operation. The publication of a sonata of twenty pages, for example, required that the inking and printing procedure be repeated 1,000 times to produce a mere fifty copies of that work! It is clear why . . . publishers . . . had only a few copies of a given title printed at one time, resorting to reprinting as demand required. The expense and risk involved in engraving and especially in printing large works did not accord with the feeble demand for them. For this reason the more ambitious compositions of many of our early composers—the sonatas of Alexander Reinagle and the larger works of James Hewitt, to mention two examples—never passed beyond their original manuscript form.

The increasing supply of music type and less expensive printing equipment coincided with growing public demand for collections of religious music and for vocal and instrumental music. The new market for evangelistic hymns and songs extended the music business to such remote places as Halifax, North Carolina, Harrisonburg, Virginia, Cincinnati, and Nashville, where publishers of fast-selling camp-meeting hymnals improvised distribution chains that remained in operation for many years. In New England, such works as *The Village Harmony,* an "introduction to the grounds of music," with a collection of appropriate sacred music, demonstrated that there existed a market greater than that enjoyed by any of its predecessors. First published by Henry Ranlet, of Exeter, New Hampshire, in 1795, it sold more than 25,000 copies in six editions issued in the next eleven years, going through seventeen editions by 1825.

Such success made necessary the changes that were beginning to take place in the relationship between American composers and compilers and the businessmen who saw profit in their writings. In 1806, Samuel Holyoke held on to the copyright in his *Instrumental Assistant,* containing "favorite airs" arranged for flute and violin, paid for the paper, and received half of the first edition of 3,000 copies, with printer Ranlet reserving the remainder for sale to the public and to his distributors and retailers. Holyoke sold his portion of the printing to pupils and other music teachers, small-town general stores, postmasters, and others willing to carry the books.

Andrew Law, composer, compiler, his own publisher and distributor, and owner of the patented notation he had "borrowed" from its original creators, had a long and troubled career as a music merchant. Like his friend and occasional salesman on consignment Noah Webster, he found it difficult to collect from dealers who had exclusive territorial rights to his publications. Yet the business in shape-note hymnals grew more significant, particularly in rural areas and throughout the South, where "singing Billy" Walker could boast that 600,000 copies of his *Southern Harmony* were sold between 1835 and 1854.

By then, northern music publishers specializing in "genteel" parlor music as well as educational and sacred materials found their best salesmen and promoters in music teachers, particularly those who followed the educational precepts of Lowell Mason. This Boston bank teller–turned–music educator possessed a creative talent and commercial acumen that brought into being the first significant fortune made from the music-publishing business.

The decades preceding the Civil War also witnessed the first technological advances in printing since Gutenberg created movable type and a printing press. The steam-powered cylindrical press, stereotypy, lithography, and its offspring chromolithography, all made giant contributions to the music trade. Stereotyped plates helped to produce large and inexpensive collections, hymnals, sheet music, and educational materials in response to the demand of a growing and increasingly affluent public. Church-associated music benefited most immediately from this technology, appearing in mass-printed hymnals and sacred collections that added to the wealth of layman entrepreneurs who marketed them with great skill.

Music, in either sheet-music or book form, was guaranteed profits of at least one third of retail price, the remaining amount going for manufacturing costs and trade discounts. In the great financial growth following the Mexican War and the discovery of gold in California, writers of popular hit songs shared in financial returns after all costs were recouped, and were paid on a royalty basis of about 10 percent of retail price, though, unlike composers and authors of the post–World War II period, they had no access to the publishers' financial books.

The most successful music publishers—those in New York, Boston, Philadelphia, and Cincinnati—formed arrangements in most major communities with music stores, which served as co-publishers, sharing expenses in printing editions on whose covers their names appeared with others. A song published in this multiple-imprint fashion by a small syndicate gave a 25 percent discount from retail to all members of the group. They, in turn, had exclusive local sales and distribution monopolies, and were able to act quickly when copyrights were infringed by pirated local editions. Hymnals, collections, and instruction books could be run off from stereotyped plates leased to dealers in large cities, who printed them with their own name and that of the original publisher–copyright owner on the title page.

The music-publishing business, which had become virtually a mirror image of the book trade, shared in the great success of printed books, whose sales increased from $2.5 million in 1820 to just below $20 million at the start of the Civil War. Its chief consumers in that decade were Lowell Mason's progeny: the music teachers of America, who reportedly sold more than three fourths of all printed music, most of it reprinted foreign work, to their pupils after purchasing it from the music trade at a 50 percent discount.

Philadelphia

The first American music house, opened by Moller and Capron in 1793, was only a memory by 1800. The family-operated business owned by the Carrs, started in 1794 by English-born Benjamin Carr, was at this time the branch office, its headquarters in Baltimore, where the father, Joseph Carr, ran it in partnership with his son Thomas. Benjamin devoted his full time to composing, teaching, and public performance, though he did edit music for the family business.

In the early 1800s, a visitor to the City of Brotherly Love wrote about music there that the summit of musical entertainment seldom reached "higher than the accompanying of a song so as to set off a tolerable voice, or aid a weak one, and the attracting of a circle of beaux round a young lady, while she exhibits the nimbleness of her fingers in the execution of a darling waltz; or touches the hearts of fond youths with a plaintive melody accompanied with false notes. . . . Thus music as a science lags in the rear while musical amateurs in myriads twang away in the van." These "amateurs in myriads" could find whatever they needed in the music store operated, in various locations, after 1794 by George Willig, who took over Moller and Capron's business. Before he died in 1851, Willig owned the plates and catalogues of all of Philadelphia's federal period music pioneers.

A music teacher who had engraved music for sale to his pupils in Europe, Willig was in his early thirties when he arrived, in 1793. Among the assets he purchased from Moller and Capron was a set of music punches, which he continued to use for many years, and of which he made and sold duplicates. During his first decade of operation, he specialized in instrumental music for the piano, but he began to broaden his line when other publishers arrived in the city. The *Catalog of Vocal and Instrumental Music* he issued in 1835 contained some 2,400 titles, 1,100 of which he had published prior to 1825, making him the city's second-most-active publisher in that period.

Five years before Willig's death, a directory of Philadelphia's wealthy citizens listed his worth at more than $75,000, a sizable fortune in an era when one could erect a comfortable all-brick house for $2,000.

The Willig business was purchased from his son, George, Jr., in 1856 by two of his former clerks, who were doing business as Lee and Walker. George W. Lee and William W. Walker had been financed by Julius Walker, owner of a local book and music store, and they remained in business until 1875, when Boston music merchant Oliver Ditson acquired both their good will and all their plates. Lee and Walker had been among the first to sell locally published editions of songs from Gilbert and Sullivan, which had been pirated by the time-honored music-publishing device of sending a musical stenographer to the theater to take down the notes and lyrics during a performance.

Eight years after Willig started his business, a flute and clarinet teacher, George E. Blake, who had arrived from England in 1793, enlarged the scope of his flourishing stationer's shop, which carried a large assortment of fashionable music, by beginning to print sheet songs. His 1803 catalogue contained popular London musical-theater music and Vauxhall songs, several musical miscellanies, and some instrumental music, the last engraved by Blake himself. He had learned the craft from the silversmith and engraver John Aitken, whose store occupied the street level, directly below the room in which Blake taught. The year before, John Isaac Hawkins, a young British civil engineer working in Philadelphia, had turned over to Blake all local rights to manufacture and sell the Patent Portable Grand Piano he had developed. It had been built almost simultaneously with a similar instrument in Vienna, where Matthias Muller was now offering it for sale. Both pianos were five feet in length, and each stood on its bottom rather than on four legs for support of the entire frame.

Blake added to his holdings with the purchase of a circulating book library, and in 1805 he married the daughter of a leading local family. By 1815, his business was recognized nationally as having one of the most extensive catalogue of printed music in America, including among its thousand items Blake-engraved editions of Thomas Moore's *Irish Melodies, Sacred Songs,* and *National Melodies* in exact duplication of both decoration and typography, each of the volumes appearing soon after publication in England. Moore's songs were already well known in America, and the Blake editions of his collected works played a definitive role in the contribution this Irish poet-songwriter made to the development of American parlor music. For the next several decades Moore's songs appeared not only in sheet-music form but also in collections and in the pocket songsters that served as the common man's music library.

From his new store, on South 4th Street, Blake issued the first published collection of American military music, *The Martial Music of Camp Dupont* (1816), financed by members of the Philadelphia militia; folios of original American popular songs, many of them ''vanity printings,'' for which the writer paid; and music from local theatrical productions. He was also one of the first American publishers to issue the complete scores of American musicals: the John Bray–J. N. Barker 1810 success *The Indian Princess* and Raynor Taylor's 1814 adaptation of Henry Bishop's London hit *The Ethiop*. His fifteen-volume complete works of Handel for piano, engraved by himself, was one of the most important projects of its time.

The active Blake was a charter member of the Musical Fund Society, the leading piano dealer in the Philadelphia territory for many years, and a member of the Committee on Musical Instruments for the Franklin Institute, which presented, in 1824, the first American exhibition of native-made pianos. Sometime after he completed the Handel work, Blake, nearing sixty, began to cut down on production of printed music, stopping completely in the 1850s.

Among the stock found in his moldering store on his death was all that remained of the music plates John Aitken made after 1806, when he resumed printing music for the first time since the early 1790s. The first to engrave music in the United States, Aitken had created some collections for Alexander Reinagle and other Philadelphia musicians and the earliest volume of Catholic liturgy in English America. He returned to the trade in 1806. Sometime in 1811, he abandoned music publishing to concentrate on work in precious metals. His sometime partners, the Taws family—Scottish piano makers, importers, and manufacturers of the first barrel organ made in America—took over his plates, which came into Blake's possession, with the silversmith's music-engraving tools, sometime after the Taws disappeared from Philadelphia's business directory in 1831.

Allyn Bacon began business in Philadelphia just after the War of 1812 ended. He was among the first American music men to provide an outlet for the work of native songwriters and composers. His *American Musical Miscellany,* brought out in twelve issues between 1818 and 1821, was the first such publication of exclusively American popular songs. His brother George, who joined the business in 1818, did all of the engraving for these and some 300 other works issued under the A. Bacon & Co. imprint. The *Miscellany* introduced Americans to the music of many of their now forgotten fellow countrymen: University of Pennsylvania graduate and surgeon Thomas Van Dyke Weisenthal, who saw service with the U.S. Navy and Marines from 1814 to 1829; Henry W. Young, Philadelphia painter and musical amateur; Jean L'Hulier, teacher of the violin and guitar; Washington musician and bandleader Frederick A. Wagler; the black barber who directed a local military and dance band, James Hemmenway; New York cabinetmaker and music teacher James F. Hance; Charles F. Hupfeld, founder and one of the first leaders of the Musical Fund Society orchestra of Philadelphia; and Irish stage actor and singer Arthur Keene, who sang in the first American production of *Der Freischütz* in 1825 and later retired to Nashville, where he taught piano and guitar and operated a local music store.

The quality of the Bacons' engraved work is to be seen in *The Dawning of Music in Kentucky,* done by George Bacon for A. P. Heinrich, who published it jointly with Allyn Bacon and with one of the many partners with whom he entered into brief relationships, his former salesman Abraham Hart. The largest book of its kind published in America at that time, this 268-page collection of Heinrich's vocal and piano music included some reductions of the composer's orchestral works, many of which were on sale individually, and one piece of engraved pictorial art that has been hailed as "the finest title page published to that time." Shortly after completing this work, Bacon left to open his own business, from which came the first American edition of one of the most successful songs written by an American citizen during the nineteenth century: John Howard Payne's "Home, Sweet Home."

John Howard Payne

Had Henry Bishop offered the "Sicilian Air" to his frequent collaborator Thomas Moore for consideration, John Howard Payne might not be remembered. But he did not, and the melody achieved immortality as "Home, Sweet Home," a smash hit that lasted longer and sold more sheet music than any of its contemporaries except a few penned by the Irish poet Moore. (Moore wrote both the words and the music for "The Minstrel Boy," "The Harp That Once Through Tara's Halls," "Believe Me If All Those Endearing Young Charms," and "'Tis the Last Rose of Summer.") "Home, Sweet Home" was in fact a rejected lyric set to an already published melody, and there was some question as to whether Bishop actually wrote the original.

The first British composer to be awarded a knighthood, Henry Rowley Bishop, a merchant's son, was born in 1786. He began to study music at an early age with an Italian musician, from whose musical influence he broke away to take advantage of an inborn ability to dash off the sort of music on which London theater and opera fans doted. During thirty years in the musical theater, he produced an immense mass of compositions—masques, pageants and dramatic plays, compilations of original and borrowed music, arrangements and incidental music—more than eighty of which were major pieces.

When "Home, Sweet Home" appeared in 1823, Bishop's music was already well known in the United States, particularly the theater songs he wrote for the Haymarket, Covent Garden, and Drury Lane managements. The premiere of his first musical play, *The Circassian Girl,* at Covent Garden in 1809, was followed by a fire that destroyed the theater and, with it, all the parts and the score. Bishop was able to reconstruct the music from memory, a feat that so astounded Covent Garden's owners that they promptly signed him as musical director and chief composer. As one of the founders of London's Philharmonic Society, his intimates included Viotti, Clementi, Philip Anthony Corri (who moved to the United States, where he became a prominent Baltimore musician known as Arthur Clifton), and Vincent Novello, founder of the important London music-publishing house bearing his name.

In 1816, Bishop became director of music at the King's Theatre, in addition to his duties at Covent Garden, but he continued to devote most of his time to the former. James Power, an Irish publisher with a chief office in London, brought Bishop and Moore together in 1819, to work on his new series, *Popular National Airs*. The results of this collaboration, five volumes that appeared between 1820 and 1827, did not include the successful songs that had resulted from Moore's earlier work with James Stevenson and no new hit songs. Whether the fault was Bishop's stern musical exactness or that the flame that had burned so brightly in Moore's earliest Irish songs had been dimmed cannot be known. The Moore-Bishop work is decidedly second-rate.

Covent Garden's 1823 season included the first performance of *Clari, or the Maid of Milan,* a French play purchased from a young American playwright-translator, John Howard Payne. The plot was typical of the time, involving a virtuous peasant lass who is abducted by a dastardly French nobleman when all his other attempts at seduction fail. In the inevitable happy ending, the maiden is restored to her true love and the villain punished, all to singing and dancing. The amiable music written by Bishop for earlier theatrical productions, including adaptations of Walter Scott novels and revisions of Mozart and Rossini operas, had effectively supported the dramatic action, so it was expected that he would provide the same craftsman's work for the new play.

Clari's translator had been a teen-age stage star in America and then in England following the War of 1812, but was now a debt-ridden hack writer whose major ability appeared to be the speed with which he turned out English-language versions of Paris theater successes. Half-Jewish, Payne was born in 1791 on the eastern tip of Long Island; by thirteen he was in Boston, editing a children's magazine in association with Samuel Woodworth, later the author of "The Old Oaken Bucket," which for a time rivaled the success of "Home, Sweet Home." Soon the precocious youth was a dramatic critic, tossing off reviews and judgments with a maturity that amazed or infuriated all who came to know him. His writings appeared in his own magazine of theatrical opinion, *The Thespian Mirror,* for which he wrote most of the copy, with Woodworth, five years his senior, who had come to New York to assist him.

The *Mirror* was a scintillating success, so at the age of fourteen Payne found himself invited to the homes of New York's social elite. He struck up an acquaintance with Washington Irving, the most celebrated American writer of the day and an arbiter of intellectual pursuits in Gotham, who remained a lifelong friend and invaluable source of support in times of trouble. Still in his teens, Payne dashed off his first play, *Julia, or the Wanderer,* which was performed at the Park Theatre in New York in 1806. His friends felt that the boy needed the seasoning of a formal education and raised money to send him to Union College, in central New York State.

When his teacher father declared bankruptcy, Payne took advantage of the situation to start working as an actor on the New York stage, ostensibly to help solve the family's financial problems. Young Master Payne, as he was billed, was an immediate success, playing leading roles in hit productions. His good fortune infuriated the British stars with whom he appeared, and Payne found himself virtually boycotted in New York and working on the road, in Boston, Baltimore, Norfolk, Petersburg, and Washington. In 1809, he played Romeo to Mrs. David Poe's Juliet, soon after she had delivered a son christened Edgar Allan.

In the period of economic blight that enveloped the American theater following the disastrous Richmond, Virginia, theater fire in 1811, and the war with England, Payne looked to foreign fields for success. Friends raised $2,000 and sent him off to Great Britain through the English blockade. He was immediately interned as an enemy alien. Released on the intercession of wealthy British friends, he was signed to appear at the Drury Lane, and became part of the circle that revolved around Thomas Moore.

Until he grew too fat to suit the romantic roles he was usually assigned, Payne played in London theaters and toured the provinces, becoming one of Ireland's favorite stars. During Napoleon's one hundred days of unraveling glory, Payne went to Paris and charmed his way into the Comédie Française's backstage library of playscripts. Out of his plundering of this treasure trove came the second-rate melodramas he sold to Covent Garden and the Drury Lane, many of which provided starring vehicles for great British stars during the next half century. One, *Brutus,* was a mélange of five French tragedies, and another, *Térèse,* kept Payne out of debtor's prison, where he was headed after he botched an appointment as manager of the Sadler's Wells Theatre.

Payne was a workhorse at the royal theaters, hammering out translations or adaptations to order. One of them, *Clari,* was sold outright to Covent Garden for fifty-five pounds. In addition to the script, Payne submitted six song lyrics, among these a set of verses called "Home, Sweet Home," which he had written a few years earlier but discarded. Bishop accepted the verses only after much alteration and set the poetry to the "Sicilian Air" he had included some years before in *Melodies of Various Nations,* a collection of purportedly international folk music. Its original lyric, "To the Home of My Childhood," was written by the poet and playwright Thomas Bayly.

Clari opened May 8, 1823, and was an immediate crowd favorite. "Home, Sweet Home" was sung only once during the play, as a closing chorus, but it became such a hit that London audiences rose en masse at its first notes. So, too, did Americans following the play's New York premiere the following winter.

British editions of the sheet music did not bear Payne's name, nor did the unprecedented seventeen American publications appearing within two years of the song's introduction. Several years later, when a court action was filed in London claiming that Bishop had plagiarized the melody from an original Sicilian song, the composer was forced to admit that when faced with no suitable Sicilian air for Bayly's words he had written a tune himself and passed it off as authentic.

Though Payne never profited from the sales of "Home, Sweet Home," he did make a career out of being its writer. When he returned to America in 1832, he stopped writing for the theater, but his dramas for the British stage continued in great demand. One benefit night in a New York theater brought him some $4,000, at a time when stock companies playing such concoctions of his as *Brutus* earned less than one tenth of that an evening. Near the end of his life Payne mourned to a friend: "How often have I been in the heart of Paris, Berlin, London or some other city and have heard persons singing or hand-organs playing 'Home, Sweet Home' without having a shilling to buy myself the next meal, or a place to put my head. The world has literally sung my song until every heart is familiar with its melody, yet I have been a wanderer from my childhood."

His old friend Washington Irving, who, unfounded rumor had it, was a secret collaborator in Payne's plays, arranged a diplomatic appointment for him. Payne was American counsul in Tunis when he died in 1852.

Payne's words became a symbol of all that nineteenth-century Americans dreamed and expected home to be. His song took the place of "Yankee Doodle" as the most popular one in the United States.

As the quintessence of the nineteenth-century sentimental ballad, "Home, Sweet Home" stands at the head of a torrent of parlor songs, because of its words and in spite of its music, which Maurice Disher, in *Victorian Song,* believes to be "one of the worst tunes" Bishop ever wrote. The tunes of most popular American ballads of the pre–Civil War era usually printed as twenty-five cent sheet music, were no better. But they and their words did reflect a spiritual and social impulse in their buyers, who were searching for basic values while sinking in a sea of mechanical and technological progress that threatened to engulf old-fashioned manners, taste, and morality. Sentiment became prized for itself alone, and songs were written to touch the heart and not to trouble the mind. Not until after the bloody conflict of 1861–65 were the men who had written these songs consigned to oblivion. Even Stephen Foster remained almost forgotten until just before World War II.

Shortly after he printed "Home, Sweet Home", George Bacon moved to New York to open the music store and piano manufactory that became Bacon & Raven in 1841 and was then operated by Bacon's son Francis after George's death in 1856.

The Allyn Bacon plates were purchased after 1834 by Johann A. and A. F. Klemm, descendants of Johann Gottlieb Klemm, who built the first organ for New York's Trinity Church, in 1744. The business stayed under family control until 1881.

The music-publishing business of Augustus Fiot in partnership with Leopold Meignen operated from 1835 until 1839. After that, Fiot continued to print music until 1855, when he sold his interests to John E. Gould, an associate of Oliver Ditson. Meignen devoted all his time to the art of music. A graduate of the Paris Conservatoire and a leading figure in Philadelphia's musical world until his death in 1879, Meignen introduced Beethoven's second and third symphonies to American audiences and wrote a large body of concert music. Among his pupils was William Fry, whose music the colorful Louis Antoine Jullien featured during his 1853–54 American tour. Fry's *Leonora* was the first grand opera by an American to be given a public performance.

Meignen's other illustrious pupil, Septimus Winner, was born in Philadelphia in 1827, the seventh son of a music-loving violin maker. Beginning with an old fiddle his father had repaired, Winner learned to play many different instruments, almost by instinct. He studied with Meignen for a short time in 1853, having already performed with many of the musical organizations in which Philadelphia abounded. After abandoning apprenticeship to a comb maker, Winner began to teach music, giving lessons on violin, guitar, and banjo until 1850. His first publication, "The Village Polka," was written for Lee and Walker, to cash in on the Polish dance, considered genteel by society. His first popular song, "How Sweet Are the Roses," also enjoyed some popularity, but none of his music published by Lee and Walker attained the success of his 1850 "What Is Home Without a Mother?," which almost immediately inspired countless imitations. Winner published this song himself from music plates he had cut in the kitchen, and distributed it from his recently opened music store, in which Joseph Shuster became a partner in 1853.

Winner was the new firm's most prolific songwriter, working under his own name, that of his mother, Alice Hawthorne, and many pseudonyms. Her name appeared on the sheet music of two of Winner's greatest hits, the ones for which he is best remembered—"Whispering Hope" and "Listen to the Mocking Bird." The latter, Winner's "sentimental Ethiopian ballad," came out in 1855 in the midst of the blackface song craze that Stephen Foster and the minstrel stage had created. The melody was by Dick Milburn, a black neighborhood barber who also earned money playing guitar and whistling bird-call imitations along Philadelphia streets. Winner wrote the words after Milburn was hired as a handyman in the music store, where he took to whistling the melody. It was published with Milburn's name on the first edition only, and was then sold for five dollars to Lee and Walker, which issued it under Alice Hawthorne's name. The song made a fortune for its new owners, reportedly selling 20 million copies between 1855 and 1905, three fourths of that in the United States. It was published in a variety of editions, as a quickstep, waltz, fantasia, galop, polka, schottische, march, cotillion, and in many vocal arrangements.

Although he had unwittingly sold a copyright that could have made him a millionaire, Winner remained both cheerful and greatly active throughout a long life. He was music editor for *Peterson's Ladies National Magazine,* the most successful competitor to *Godey's Lady's Book,* and wrote a popular music column for *Graham's Magazine,* another important nineteenth-century periodical.

Winner's series of self-instruction books, employing his famous Eureka Method, taught countless numbers of Americans how to play a musical instrument. More than 200 of these guides to musical self-improvement appeared under the Winner imprint, written for twenty-three different instruments, with more than 2,000 arrangements of original Winner songs.

His most notorious song, "Give Us Back Our Old Commander," was written in 1864 to protest Abraham Lincoln's dismissal of General George B. McClellan. Eighty thousand copies were purchased by McClellan supporters in a few weeks, and, though the President was apparently not bothered by the songwriter's presumptious sentiments, his secretary of war, Edwin Stanton, using existing war powers, had Winner arrested for writing a treasonous song. Lincoln's intercession and pardon won the songwriter's release, though only on condition that he apologize and destroy all the plates and remaining copies of the offending song.

There was no similar national furor over another song Winner wrote in 1864, one of the three that have stayed in the mainstream of popular song to such an extent that they appear to be folk music. It was published as "Der Deutcher's Dog," and its familiar lines—beginning "Oh where! Oh where! ish my liddle dog gone?"—were written by Winner to the German folk song "Im Lauterbach hab'ich mein Strumpf verlorn."

In 1871, long after Joseph Shuster had sold out his interest in the business, around 1856, Winner's son J. Gibson joined the firm, which became known as Sep. Winner & Son. Working with his seemingly tireless father until 1888, young Winner negotiated the sale of all the company's popular-song copyrights and plates, most of them for his father's songs, to the Oliver Ditson interests, where they joined all the Winner hits that had been acquired by the purchase of Lee and Walker some years earlier.

Until his death, in 1902, at seventy-five, Septimus Winner advertised himself as "Music Teacher."

New York

By early 1831, the long and narrow island Dutch sea captains had purchased from its inhabitants for some trinkets had become an inspiration to its songwriters, leading to the publication that year of the earliest known of the large catalogue of paeans to it—"New York, Oh what a charming city!" In the nearly four decades since James Harrison had printed the first popular song offered for sale in New York and Benjamin Carr had sung it at concerts, the music business had gone through many changes. None of the handful of early publishers—Carr, Hewitt, Gilfert, the Paff brothers—was alive. Of the pioneers who had started business there prior to 1800, only John Paff was still active when the United States fought the British Empire from 1812 to 1815.

The Geib brothers, Adam and William, sons of a London piano and organ maker, had arrived in 1798, to engage in the family business at a store in Manhattan and a factory and branch office in nearby Mount Vernon. Their father joined them the following year, after having manufactured 4,910 pianos, 400 "organized" pianos, and "church and chamber organs in proportion" for the English trade, and he now began to make organs for his new country's churches. Difficulty in collecting for an instrument he had installed in a Providence church forced him into bankruptcy, though not until he had put all his assets in his sons's names.

A third brother, young George, made his debut in 1811, playing an original piano concerto. He then advertised his "scientific music school," which featured a new system of fingering. He proved to be the company's best salesman, publicly demonstrating its products and encouraging all of his many pupils to buy it. In 1815, the Geibs added music publishing to the business and printed 400 songs and collections in the next ten years.

The Geibs were known as New York's best piano makers and dealers until the Civil War, and their music-publishing subsidiary, operated by a son-in-law, Daniel Walker, functioned from 1829 until 1843, when it was purchased by Stephen Gordon of Hartford.

A music engraving, printing, selling, and publishing shop operated on The Strand in London by Edward Riley was closed by its thirty-five-year-old owner around 1805. He then took his family, including two sons, to New York. He found work at once, engraving music for local publishers, making instruments, and teaching piano, flute, and voice. In 1811, he opened his own music store on Chatham Street, in which vicinity he stayed until his death in 1829. Riley was one of the city's most active publishers, issuing about 450 pieces, more than any other local music merchant of the period except William Dubois and the Geibs. After his death, his widow, Elizabeth, ran the shop until Edward Riley, Jr., took over. A flute virtuoso and leader of groups of professional musicians, he gave New Yorkers their first organized concert seasons.

He then served the Philharmonic Society in a similar capacity. In its seventh (1851–52) season, he was listed on programs as an "assistant" director. The family business was then being run by Frederick Riley, in conjunction with making and repairing musical instruments. All the Riley plates were purchased by Stephen S. Gordon in 1850.

The music store John Jacob Astor had opened in 1786 passed into the hands of the Paff brothers when the energetic young German from Waldorf determined to give up the music business and seek his fortune in the sale of beaver pelts. In 1817, it fell under the control of William Dubois. Born in the West Indies, Dubois was engaged in shipping merchandise between North America and London when he discovered the growing trade in the sale of pianos and other musical instruments. Without experience in the business, he bought out the Paffs and opened his store at 127 Broadway, where he started to publish sheet music from plates he had acquired. Five years later, Robert Stodart, a grandson of the British piano maker who invented and patented in 1777 the "English grand action" that made British pianos world famous, joined Dubois. Stodart had come to Richmond a few years earlier to sell upright bookcase pianos imported from England, where an uncle made them. Despite their superior qualities, Americans found the instruments priced too high. However, the addition of Stodart's name to the less-expensive instruments Dubois was manufacturing in New York gave the stock of the new firm, Dubois and Stodart, a touch of quality out of keeping with its worth. In 1834, Dubois bought out his British partner, who then went into a partnership with a promising New England artist lithographer, Nathaniel Currier, withdrawing after a short time for other enterprises. In 1836, George Bacon, the Philadelphia engraver, who had been operating a music store and piano dealership in New York, joined Dubois, to operate one of the "big three" music-publishing houses, along with those of the Rileys and the Geibs. This partnership ended in 1839, when Dubois decided to confine himself to piano manufacture. Eventually, Oliver Ditson came into possession of the Dubois music plates.

John Firth, one of the major mid-nineteenth-century American music publishers, has earned a special place in history because of his generally misunderstood dealings with Stephen Foster, who wrote most of Firth and his partners' biggest hit songs. Firth came to the United States as a teen-ager, fought in the War of 1812, and went to work for Edward Riley, making flutes and fifes. In 1815, he went into business on his own. One of his wartime comrades, William Hall, of Tarrytown, New York, also worked for Riley, and the two became good friends. Born in 1796, Hall was apprenticed to an Albany instrument maker and during the war was promoted to the rank of company commander of volunteer militia from upper New York State. In later years, Hall rose to the rank of brigadier general and became known throughout the music trade as "General."

Soon after Firth and Hall each married one of their employer's daughters, they left Riley to open a music store on Pearl Street in New York, adding music publishing in 1827. They began to acquire plates from the estates of music engravers and defunct publishing houses, and soon had built up an imposing catalogue. Their earliest publications included the blackface songs that were promoted by repeated performances on the New York stage by actor George Washington Dixon and his imitators. Firth & Hall was among the first to capitalize on the succeeding public enthusiasm for minstrel music, and brought out songs by Henry Russell and the Hutchinson Family, two of the period's best-known and most popular song-writing theatrical attractions.

In 1832, Firth & Hall moved uptown to Franklin Square, just off Broadway and easily accessible to their growing trade from all sections of lower Manhattan by means of the dozens of licensed omnibuses that went past their doors, carrying passengers for six cents a ride. The house they occupied had been used during the Revolution as Washington's headquarters, and later was the first President's executive mansion, a fact to which the partners constantly referred in their advertising and promotional materials. It was to this building that Henry Russell went in 1837 to sell his first great hit song, "Woodman, Spare That Tree," and with it started a career that influenced the course of American popular songwriting, moving it from an isolated regional form to national exposure that saw its most successful works known to people in every corner of the union.

Henry Russell

Henry Russell was one of the earliest, most successful, and best known of the English songwriters who made the journey to America in order to "put a little money" into their pockets, and his success motivated others to make a similar journey. He was born in Kent at the start of the War of 1812 and first performed as a professional singer when he was eight, on the Drury Lane stage. Following that appearance, King George IV called for the youngster, took him on the royal lap, and kissed the lad, inspiring a "boyish ecstasy" young Russell had never known. At ten, a more significant experience occurred, one that made Russell aware of how to reach an audience: the great actor Edmund Kean, who had himself offset a poor speaking voice with facial expression, said to Russell, "You will never become either a great actor or a great singer unless you learn to speak every word utterly distinctly and clearly."

At the age of thirteen, Russell was sent to Italy, where he apparently studied with Rossini, Bellini, Donizetti, and the young Irish singer and songwriter Michael Balfe. Life there delighted him, and he went back in 1830, after several years in London, to work as a tourist guide, chorus singer, and opera-house musician. Then, learning that a person with his training could readily find employment in Toronto, he sailed to Canada, arriving sometime in 1834. Unsuccessful in his efforts to support himself by giving concerts there, he crossed the border to Rochester, New York, where he was employed as organist and choirmaster in the First Presbyterian Church and formed a "really capital choir." After scoring great success with a local concert, he was hired as a teacher at the recently formed Rochester Academy.

A final but major catalyst in his development came from Henry Clay, as the result of a speech by the politician in Rochester. "It may be a strange sentiment," Russell wrote in his *Autobiography,* "but I don't think I should be talking extravagantly, if I declare the orator was the direct cause of my taking to the composition of descriptive songs. . . . If Henry Clay can make such an impression by the distinct enunciation of every word, should it not be probable for me to make music the vehicle of grand thoughts and noble sentiments to speak to the world through the power of poetry and song?"

Wittingly or not, Russell stumbled on a changing element of the American national character: the doffing of a long-held feeling of inferiority to things foreign, and the growth of national pride. Both were to lead directly to the success of such native entertainment forms as the blackface minstrel, the presentation of embodiments of the Yankee presence in the theater, and the American singing family. "Home, Sweet Home" and "My Country, 'Tis of Thee" had replaced "Yankee Doodle" as favorite American ballads, and attacks on the nation and its culture by English travelers eventually brought about a disenchantment with all things British, among them the English influence on popular music, manifested for long by British singing stars performing the music of British composers and songwriters on the American stage.

Quite shrewdly, Russell perceived in Clay's peculiarly native oratorical style and diction elements he was able to transfer to his own stage personality, and as a result he became successful as a new kind of entertainer who supplied his own new material.

Russell began to set to music Charles Mackay's beautiful poem "Wind of the Winter's Night, Whence Comest Thou?" Mackay later became a friend, although Russell did not yet know him in the mid-1830s. Then only twenty, Mackay was already a recognized journalist poet, whose verses appeared in both British and American newspapers, and he stood on the threshold of a brilliant career. Eventually he became editor of the *Illustrated London News,* a Civil War military correspondent for the London *Times,* author of a history of the Mormons, and, in passing, the father of Minnie Mackay, who, as Marie Corelli, was the author of best-selling purple-tinged late-nineteenth-century novels. Much of Charles Mackay's verse was soon to be set to music, not only by Russell but by many Americans, including Stephen Foster and the Hutchinsons.

Russell worked all through the night on this first original song, trying, he recalled, "to infuse into my music the subtle charm, as it were, of the voice of Henry Clay." When morning came, he had completed the first of seventy popular songs created in the United States, the best known of some 800 he wrote during his lifetime. He was embarked on the creation of a repertory of original music that won world-wide acclaim.

His Italian experience was evident in the music for his "operas in miniature," among them "The Ship on Fire" and "The Maniac," which are descriptive songs combining dramatic narrative with bombastic and virtuosic musical displays whose inspiration was the operatic masters under whom he had studied.

By the autumn of 1836, he was ready to present himself to audiences in New York City, after sharpening his presentations in Rochester and smaller nearby communities. One of his songs had already been issued that summer by Firth & Hall, a ballad, "Some Love to Roam o'er the Dark Sea Foam," words by Mackay; others followed quickly. He was also given the dubious honor of being pirated; Joseph Atwill, of New York, brought out an edition of "The Fine Old English Gentleman," which Russell had already sold to another publisher, with a melody the composer generally assured audiences had been written by Martin Luther.

At first Russell evidently sold his songs to the first local publisher who offered to print them, since, as a British subject, he could not enjoy copyright protection. He was, he said, making his money from performing the songs. As he became more popular, such astute music men as William Hall and Oliver

Ditson bid for the rights to this music, for they were aware that it could be sold for a higher price than songs written by nonperforming writers. Russell wrote: "There was no such thing as a royalty in those days and when a song was sold it was sold outright. My songs brought me an average price of ten shillings each, that is to say, my eight hundred songs have represented about four hundred pounds to me, though they have made the fortune of several publishers."

Russell's first New York appearances were made in conjunction with benefit concerts arranged by Charles Edward Horn and presented by the New York Sacred Music Society, giving Russell an opportunity to display the religious side of his work. The more genteel secular aspect of his musical personality was demonstrated during ballad concerts that attracted the audiences who eventually multiplied into idolizing multitudes.

Russell became acquainted with many leading New York personalities, among them George Pope Morris, editor of the weekly *New York Mirror,* which he had taken over from its founder, Samuel Woodworth. Born in 1802, Morris had come north from Philadelphia as a teen-ager and found a market for his popular verse, which was used to fill spaces between articles and news items in the paper. Under his guidance, the *Mirror* became New York's leading critical and literary periodical. Morris was, like Charles Mackay and John Hill Hewitt, highly regarded as a poet and well known to the musicians who often set his words to their music. Morris's friendship with such songwriters as Russell and Horn, involved him in some of the best-known songs written during the next ten years. Though it was customary to pay only a few dollars to the poet whose words were used for a song, Morris was in a position to receive a greater sum for the use of his verse. He was especially good at rendering the words of blackface songs into highly successful parlor ballads. Horn asked him to rewrite the words of "Long Long Ago," a minstrel song, into the more socially acceptable sentimental ballad "O'er the Lake, Where Droop'd the Willow." In later years, Morris did the same task for P. H. Loder, a British musician who was later conductor of the New York Philharmonic, reworking "Old Dan Tucker" into "The Pastor's Daughter," "De Boatman's Dance" into "Oh! Boatmen Haste!" and "Goin' Over de Mountain" into "Cheerily O'er the Mountain."

None of Morris's sentimental song words, however, had the impact and lasting commercial appeal of those written for Russell's first major hit, which was inspired by a visit the two made to the upstate New York homestead of the poet's forefathers. There a splendid old tree, flourishing in its late summer majesty, was about to be cut down. The gift of a ten-dollar piece to the old man with the ax and the promise of his daughter that the tree should stand as long as she lived saved the giant oak. Russell thought the incident had the making of a good song subject and suggested Morris set it down in verse.

The contemporary who once called Morris "a household poet, whose domestic muse / is soft as silk and sage as Mother Goose" had it right, as the great popular appeal of his simple versifying showed. The new lyric was originally called "The Old Oak Tree," playing upon Russell's often expressed propensity for the word *old,* which he used as often as possible in his songs. Reluctantly, the composer agreed to a title change that may well have made the difference between a typical Russell success and the gigantic international favorite the ballad remained throughout the century. Firth & Hall published it before the end of 1837 as "Woodman, Spare That Tree." In public performance it usually produced an effect that Russell preserved in one of his favorite anecdotes: One evening, as he finished the last verse of the song, and the audience sat spellbound for a moment, as usual, there than "poured out a volume of applause that shook the building to its foundation," he remembered. "A snowy-bearded gentleman, with great anxiety depicted on his venerable features, arose and demanded silence. He asked, with a tremulous voice: 'Mr. Russell, in the name of Heaven, tell me, was the tree spared?' 'It was, sir,' replied the vocalist. 'Thank God! Thank God! I breathe again!' and then he sat down, perfectly overcome by his emotions."

Russell's major success in 1838 was "A Life on the Ocean Wave," which still serves as the official march of the British Royal Marines. The words were by Epes Sargent, a young New England journeyman poet who had won fame while still an adolescent with a series of letters written from Russia, to which he had gone with his father on a business trip. Sargent was part of the literary coterie that made itself at home in the *Mirror*'s offices and was also active in support of Henry Clay's efforts to revise the copyright law. The original text for "A Life on the Ocean Wave" had been by Samuel James Arnold, son of the famous eighteenth-century playhouse composer, but, after Sargent added new verses and rewrote some of the original stanzas, editor Morris wanted a more American lilt to the rhymes before he used the poem in the *Mirror.* Russell chanced to be there when Morris had exclaimed that the words were not suitable. Taking Sargent by the hand, he went to James Hewitt's nearby music store. Seated at a demonstration piano, he dashed off the melody, after a few starts, within ten minutes.

During his five years in the United States, Russell enjoyed almost unparalleled popularity as a public entertainer, never drawing less than fully packed houses. Like Charles Dibdin before him, he appeared only as a soloist, accompanying himself at the piano and giving lengthy spoken introductions to each number. In this, he broke with the American tradition that a program of popular entertainment needed to be made up of performances by several artists.

Although his headquarters remained in New York, Russell spent much time in Baltimore, giving John Hill Hewitt an opportunity to observe him closely, both on stage and off. His baritone voice had a limited register, Hewitt remarked, but the "few good notes he possessed he turned to advantage," writing only songs that, like it, seldom had more than five basic notes in their construction. Russell asked Hewitt to write the words for a new song, "The Old Family Clock." (A wag once sent him verses addressed to "An Old Fine-tooth Comb.") Hewitt wrote a lyric, but Russell changed his mind and, promising good pay, asked for a descriptive song on "The Drunkard," presumably to stir up the temperance people. Hewitt began with "The old lamp burned on the old oaken stool," much to Russell's delight. "He made money on it," Hewitt wrote in 1877, "but I never even got his promise to pay."

"The Old Arm Chair," published in 1840, is a prime example of Russell's skillful manipulation of five notes into a hit song. The words are by Eliza Cook, the daughter of a London brass worker who was hard put to support eleven children and consequently gave them little education. In spite of this, in 1835, at the age of seventeen, Eliza published her first collection of poems that she had been offering anonymously to English newspapers and magazines. When "The Old Arm Chair" was printed, there was a nationwide outcry for the identity of its unknown author, and Eliza Cook became famous. Her name was featured in large print on all editions of Russell's creation.

Finding himself financially secure after eight years in America, chiefly from the profits of personal appearances in the United States, Russell began to think of returning to Britain. Like Dibdin, he had created a new set of miniature but connected musical dramas, detailing life in America. It was such a package he offered Londoners in March 1842 at the famous Hanover Square Rooms, where the London Philharmonic also played its concerts. After twelve months of new triumphs, the sweeter because they were in the land of his birth, Russell went back to America for another grand tour. Stephen Foster heard him in Pittsburgh and was inspired to imitate Russell's songs.

Russell returned home again in 1844, never to return to the land that had given him fame and fortune. New songs written in England continued to pour out but rarely achieved publication in the United States. He was a good friend of Charles Mackay's but chose a young British poet, Leigh Cliffe, to revise the lyrics of his American hits, or to write completely new ones to them, in order to create a body of valid British copyrights. He was not zealous in protecting the rights to his music. When the Hutchinson Family arrived in 1845, he threatened to restrain them legally from singing "The Maniac." When they refused to remove it from their programs, he offered a thousand pounds for exclusive rights to the management of their public appearances in the British Isles. Again the Americans turned him down.

Russell became wholeheartedly interested in Britain's social problems and devoted himself to the improvement of the lot of the poor and oppressed. "Slavery was one of the evils I helped to abolish through the medium of my songs," he later noted with pride. "When I commenced my Anti-slavery Crusade, I did not stop at seeking to relieve the distresses of the unfortunate coloured race. . . . The private lunatic asylums, another sore in our social system, was attacked by my song 'The Maniac', which was written with the object of exposing the horrors of that iniquitous system." He also encouraged poor families to migrate to America. Working with the Canadian government, he was instrumental in assisting thousands of the poor to cross the Atlantic.

His chief propaganda medium was his piano on a stage, from which he offered a production built around his songs, interspersed with appropriate poetry, presented in front of an elaborate diorama. *Far West, or the Emigrant's Progress from the Old World to the New,* with verses by Mackay, featured songs dealing with migration and the beauties of America, culminating in an exhibition of painted pictures of the New World's natural wonders, among them Niagara Falls. *Negro Life in Freedom and Slavery* offered a graphic presentation of the black man's lot, from capture and sale by slave traders in Africa through work in American fields, music and dancing in the slave quarters, to an attempt at escape, with hounds and armed men in pursuit.

The *Negro Melodies* he used included many of the best-known American minstrel songs, many of which he claimed to have written: "One summer afternoon, when I was playing the organ . . . I made a discovery. It was that sacred music played quickly makes the best kind of secular music. It was quite by accident that, playing the 'Old Hundredth' very fast, I produced the air of 'Get out o de way, ole Dan Tucker,' the first of many good minstrel songs that I composed or rather adapted."

This was nonsense, of course, but Russell never hesitated to claim to be a genius. He was never one, but he made a significant contribution to America's popular music, particularly its parlor music, and his influence was great in shaping the manner in which that music would be presented in the years prior to the Civil War.

Although he lived until 1901, his public career came to a sudden end in the early 1860s when he was performing "The Ship on fire," one of his miniature operas, which continued in use as a vaudeville show-stopper on both sides of the Atlantic until the 1920s. Russell suddenly paused, rose from the piano, and uttered a cry. "My nervous system had received a shock," he remembered later. "I cancelled my engagement and abandoned the stage."

Even prior to Henry Russell's appearance on the American scene, John Firth and William Hall had entered the piano-manufacturing business. Sylvanus B. Pond, a forty-year-old New Englander who was trained as an instrument maker and became a partner in 1827 of the Meacham piano factory in Albany, joined Firth & Hall as head of their new factory. Pond was also a compiler and composer of church music and songs for the Sunday school, whose best-known work was his 1841 *United States Psalmody*. He supervised the branch store and instrument manufactory at 239 Broadway, and was named a partner, in Firth, Pond & Hall, instrument makers, which did business there while the music-publishing firm of Firth & Hall continued at the deluxe Franklin Square location.

In 1847, William Hall suddenly withdrew from the partnerships and took over the store on Broadway, continuing to make pianos, sell and repair musical instruments, and publish sheet music, usually of the "scientific" type intended for the parlor-piano trade. His son James F. entered the business at the same time.

Hall's position in New York's political and social worlds, his rank in the state militia, which he commanded with questionable distinction during the infamous 1849 Astor Place riots, and his son's exuberant drive made the handsomely refurbished store at the corner of Broadway and Park Place a rendezvous for the musical community. Music teachers, the most important factor in the Halls' noncopyright foreign sheet-music distribution system, went there to find pieces that would appeal to their pupils. They received a fifty percent discount from retail cost and then sold the pieces for the price indicated on the covers. This growing market, which would account for three fourths of all such sales, eventually forced the Halls and some others specializing in noncopyright music into a price war that brought the richest music houses into alliance against both the smaller firms and music teachers.

Hall's store attracted the newly arrived foreign musicians, mainly through advertising in the music-trade press, which was distributed not only in large American cities but also in England and on the Continent. With space rates at about fifteen cents a line, major music houses found advertising, with the attendant promotion of new songs and piano music in the editorial columns, a most effect sales tool. Hall's boasted in the *New York Musical Review* in 1856 that its music was being sent "from Maine to Oregon, the Sandwich Islands and Australia."

At least twenty periodicals dealing with music had been formed by the early 1850s. The first important one, *The Euterpiad,* was started in 1820 as a promotional house organ for John R. Parker's Franklin Piano Warehouse in Boston, the largest single source of printed sheet music in the northeast after the War of 1812. Few of these publications managed to remain in business for more than a few years until the trade's prosperity and the journals' self-vaunted power over the music-buying public combined to attract industry support. In 1853, it was publicly bruited about that the music business amounted to $27 million annually, of which $12 million came from the pianoforte trade, which music merchants inaccurately claimed exceeded sales of cotton. Such a financial base attracted trade journalism, which depended on trade advertising for its profits.

In the early 1850s, the most important of the new publications were Richard Storr Willis's *Musical World and New York Musical Times,* founded in 1850 after the musician proprietor added *Saroni's Musical Times* and *The Message Bird,* neither more than two years old, to his holdings; *The New York Musical Review and Choral Advocate,* founded in 1850 and published by Lowell Mason's sons; and John Sullivan Dwight's *Journal of Music,* the self-declared most important music periodical of its time, and the sounding board for the Boston music business, chiefly that operated by Oliver Ditson, as well as for all Americans who deplored the direction in which popular music appeared to be drifting.

A small scandal involving the trade press and other critics surfaced after the American tour of diva Henriette Sontag, who had arrived immediately after Jenny Lind's return home in 1852. Madame Sontag's Barnum was Bernard Ullman, an immigrant impresario, "one of that pestilence of musical brokers and *chevaliers d'industrie,''* who, as described in Dwight's *Journal,* "waylay foreign artists, on or before their arrival here, and represent *their* experience, their shrewdness, as indispensible to their success, in guarding them against Yankee craft and imposition, and especially in the sublime art of 'managing the press,' who they represent to be as venal as it is influential and important to be conciliated.''

It was common gossip in the music business, and trade-press editors claimed, that any critic for a New York newspaper collected from $1,000 to $1,500 a year for favorable notices, a rumor that seemed accurate when it was learned that Madame Sontag had presumably engaged in bribing the press. Shortly before her return to Europe, Ullman presented her husband with bills totaling $6,701.32 for advertising her concerts in the cities she had visited.

The *Musical World* headlined in the summer of 1853: THE NEW YORK PRESS BRIBED! / $15,000 EXPENDED BY SONTAG! / WHO HAS THE MONEY???? It was also hinted that the *New York Times* and other local papers had received payment for complimentary reviews of Sontag's performance. Denying such allegations, Ullman wrote to the *Times,* asserting he had given only $300 to the local press, in sums of twenty to twenty-five dollars, at twenty-five cents a line, for publishing extracts from European reviews—a common practice. Naturally, Ullman added, neither the *Times*'s critic nor anyone else connected with that paper had ever asked for or received one penny. However, there had been one attempt, he charged, to blackmail Sontag. A Mr. Dyer of the *Musical World* had proposed that the sum of one dollar each would ensure complimentary notices puffing the singer in the 2,000 country newspapers that Dyer served as correspondent. The offer, Ullman swore before a police justice, was rejected, and the *Musical World* began a vicious campaign of attack on both Sontag and Ullman. Only after the diva left America did Ullman make his peace with the trade press.

Music publishers charged between twenty-five and thirty cents for the four- or five-page copies of printed music by Americans they offered for sale, which was approximately the same as that asked fifty years before. This was no charity, because production costs had decreased, so they were making a greater profit than before. British musicians, however, who had moved to America and taken up permanent residence, thereby qualifying for the copyright protection that would ensure exclusivity to their "superior" offerings, sold their music for as much as a dollar. This inequity resulted from the country's own inferiority complex in matters cultural. Lowell Mason's gospel and that of his fellow teachers and educators, who ascribed the finest quality to European music, principally that from Germany, had done their work successfully.

William Wallace and Louis Moreau Gottschalk

One of the most distinguished visiting European musicians to saunter into Hall's music emporium in the summer of 1850 was William Vincent Wallace, British-born but a permanent resident of New York, whose career and adventures had already been more dramatic than any in the improbable opera librettos for which he wrote highly popular scores. Out of them had already come a number of internationally popular songs, which Hall & Son sold at prices almost double those for work by native songwriters. Born in Ireland in 1812, the son of an army bandmaster, Wallace had played violin in a Dublin theater orchestra in his teens and at eighteen was appointed organist to a local Catholic cathedral. A romantic involvement with one of his Ursuline-convent piano students led to dismissal and sudden marriage. In the midst of these troubles, Wallace saw the satanic violinist Nicolò Paganini, who was on a tour in Ireland, and he determined to devote all his efforts to his instrument, kindling a newborn virtuosity for which he would be acclaimed on three continents.

Overworked to exhaustion by the age of twenty, Wallace, with wife and new son, sailed for Australia to take up sheep farming and pursue a less demanding musical career. After a brilliant debut concert there, he was presented with 100 blooded sheep by Australia's royal governor. In response to a wonderful public reception, Wallace launched an even more strenuous concertizing career, while also operating a music school and store but succeeding in neither. He next tried whaling in New Zealand, and was saved from death at the hands of aborigines by a native princess. On another sailing trip he was one of three survivors of a party of Europeans; the rest were murdered by mutineers.

Heavily in debt, Wallace went to South America and quickly won fame and fortune as an instrumentalist and composer. Back in England, he was introduced to Edward Fitzball, a printer who had made a fortune writing melodramas for the theater and musical librettos for Henry Bishop and Michael Balfe.

Wallace and Fitzball wrote *Maritana* in 1845, the first English grand opera to win acclaim on the European stage. Out of it came some of the best-known popular songs of the 1840s: "Yes, Let me like a Soldier Fall" and "Scenes That Are the Brightest." While at work on a commission from the Paris Opera, Wallace began to lose his sight. His doctor prescribed a sea voyage, so Wallace sailed for Brazil, and during the passage was miraculously cured of his affliction. He returned home, and then, after his investment in a British piano factory was wiped out, he headed for the unknown but green fields of the United States, hoping to mend his purse.

Immediately after settling in New York, Wallace applied for citizenship, invested in another piano factory, married an American concert pianist, despite his now twenty-year-long and still-valid first marriage, and presented himself to Hall and his son. He was promptly signed as an exclusive Hall composer, and plunged into New York's musical life. He participated in programs of the new Philharmonic Society, performed on stage with popular singing stars, conducted revivals of his *Maritana,* and took part in the popular "gift" and "lottery" concerts. Created by merchandisers to dispose of excess stock, these distributions of gifts gave pianos, melodeons, harps, furniture, and various other products to holders of winning tickets.

Wallace's original music for the piano and arrangements of popular songs, the Halls' top-of-the-line items, were usually advertised as being "somewhat more difficult to play than the ordinary commonplace ballad, but [with] a freshness and strength in them that will repay a careful study, and instead of tiring with repetition they become more interesting the oftener they are heard."

Back home in 1855, Wallace found himself in great demand by London publishers, who had marked Hall's success with his music. Yet, in spite of a continuing vast output, he never earned more than £200 annually from his English music before his death in 1860. His poor judgment in business affairs was never more obvious than his assignment of performance rights in his hugely successful last opera, *Lurline,* which he gave to the management of Covent Garden in 1859 for a mere ten shillings. The playhouse made more than £50,000 from the privilege.

Hall & Son's catalogue included an American work that became the most popular and most performed solo piano piece published in America during the nineteenth century, Louis Moreau Gottschalk's "The Last Hope." Early in the next century millions of silent-moving-picture fans wept as its strains accompanied a death scene, and it can still be found in Protestant hymnals as "Mercy," or heard on recordings of sheet music retrieved from old piano benches.

"The Last Hope" was written in the early 1850s for the pleasure of a Cuban lady who promised to expire if young Gottschalk did not assuage her passions. Oliver Ditson bought it from the composer for fifty dollars, and urged him in the future to copy the style of Charles Grobe, who had recently written a best-selling piano piece for the Boston publisher. Shortly after his return from Europe in early 1853, where his music and playing were both favorably received, Gottschalk auditioned for Hall, who told him that if he wanted to make his talent known he should perform in public. Gottschalk responded that this was a luxury he could not afford. "Bah," Hall replied. "I will pay you one hundred dollars for a piano concert at Dodworth's Rooms."

In a few weeks, New York audiences heard the first of a series of concerts given by Gottschalk over the next five years in the small concert hall. He introduced many of his own compositions during these performances, among them "The Banjo," whose inspiration was the instrument that lay at the heart of much of the country's newest popular music. The instrumental pieces Hal acquired from Gottschalk sold in such quantities that his initial investment in the pianist-composer was a bargain. The publisher signed Gottschalk to a contract that gave all United States rights in his works to the New York house, and in order to own all of Gottschalk's music he asked Ditson for the copyright in "The Last Hope." Ditson responded: "It does not sell at all. Pay me the fifty dollars it cost me and it is yours." This mistake by an otherwise infallible publisher was an extremely costly one. Hall issued the piece in 1854 in a "new and only corrected edition, exactly as it is played by the author, simplified with *facilite* passages . . . much easier and more effective than the old edition." "The Last Hope" became Hall's all-time best seller, purchased mostly by the women and young girls who saw Gottschalk in concert both in New York and on the road and doted on the romantic artist and his music.

Gottschalk was only fifteen years old when he composed a piano piece based on "what he saw and heard" in New Orleans' Place Congo, where, for as long as people could remember, black men and woman came to make their own music and dance on Sundays. It was this drawing on local influences, in both the United States and Latin America, that made Gottschalk unique. He became a composer who used his Old World musical training to create little gems for the keyboard based on the American music styles that were growing around him. One of his best-known pieces, "La Bamboula," written around 1844, was first published in Paris by the same firm that issued Verdi's music. It was one of many compositions inspired by the throbbing life of New Orleans, heavily influenced as well by Caribbean elements, and many of his works are a similar blend of seemingly disparate sources.

Gottschalk was born in New Orleans in 1829. His father was an educated Englishman who had learned how to deal successfully with Yankee businessmen, and his mother was a beauteous Creole. That fact led to incorrect speculation that Gottschalk had black blood.

A *Wunderkind,* who took to the piano at three, Gottschalk was performing in Paris by age thirteen for audiences that included Chopin, Berlioz, Offenbach, Victor Hugo, Bizet, and other leaders of the Romantic Movement. His early New Orleans-inspired pieces were written in France while he was recuperating from an illness, and their publication made him famous on the continent.

In late 1852, much like Henry Russell, who wanted to be praised in his own land, Gottschalk sailed to New York, arriving during the first flush of renewed enthusiasm for foreign and exotic artists. Gottschalk was handsome, talented, and certainly as exotic as his music, and P. T. Barnum, who had just achieved a triumph with Jenny Lind, wished to sign him for an American tour. On his father's advice against such "Barnumization," Gottschalk turned down an offer of $20,000 and expenses for a year's exclusive services. It was after the successful series made possible by Hall that Gottschalk did go on tour.

In Europe, Gottschalk had been an eyewitness to monster concerts produced by Jullien and Berlioz, and he had learned from them that showmanship was a key ingredient in achieving public notice. After Americans saw his masterful performances during the next two years, including sixty concerts in New York alone, sales of his music began to boom, and people demanded to see him.

Gottschalk appeared onstage in black evening dress, wearing white kid gloves, which he removed slowly, in the Jullien fashion, finger by finger. Female audiences adored his dreamy, swarthy looks, and his exoticism made him an object of sexual fascination. Women crowded into his concerts, swooning as soon as he sat down and first ran his fingers over the keyboard. Then, as the press noted, "after a few minutes, the fire would kindle him and he would play with all the brilliancy which was so peculiar to him."

In telling Hall of the great number of women who had hysterics and wept when he played "The Last Hope," Gottschalk wrote: "Invariably at every concert a small scribbled note requests me to play [it] . . . 'Would Mr. G. kindly please 36 young girls by playing "The Last Hope" which they all play?' "

When his father died suddenly, Gottschalk found himself responsible for his mother and six brothers and sisters in Paris. He went on a Latin-American tour with the fourteen-year-old "Little Miss Adelina Patti" and remained there after the brilliant child returned home. He had discovered a veritable paradise, peopled, he said, with women "ignorant of evil, sinning with frankness." The next years were also filled with music, "madly squandered, scattered to the winds," as he wandered through the West Indies, absorbing Afro-Cuban music as well as that of island natives. Out of this experience came a somewhat florid musical style that greatly appealed to contemporary Americans. "Ojos Criollos," "La Gallina," "Suis-moi," and the "Caprice Americane-Columbia," with its variations on Foster's "My Old Kentucky Home," resulted, and these and many others were sent off to Hall in New York, who promptly issued them.

The North's fortunes had ebbed almost immediately after the first hostilities of the Civil War, in 1861, when a New York impresario urged Gottschalk to come home for a national tour. Immediately upon his return, in early 1862, he was besieged by those very music publishers who had turned down works he once would have sold for thirty dollars apiece. Ditson offered $1,000 for a single composition; because his Hall contract had expired, Gottschalk accepted the offer, but also signed a new agreement with Hall, as "proof of my gratitude."

Gottschalk left the United States for the last time to concertize in Chile, Uruguay, Argentina, and Brazil. During the summer of 1869, he was stricken with yellow fever, but recovered sufficiently to appear in yet another of the mammoth jubilees with which he won the devotion of Latin Americans. With 800 performers and at least eighty drums of various sizes, the triumphant evening ended with "Grand Fantasy on the Brazilian National Anthem," the last music Gottschalk ever played in public. Within two weeks he was dead.

Hall & Son, of New York, with whom he maintained contact until just a few months before his death, sending them the manuscripts of his newest works, continued to profit from the sale of his piano pieces. Among the several works he had assigned to Ditson, on condition they be sold under the pseudonym "Seven Octaves," was the 1864 "Dying Poet," his second-biggest sheet-music seller. When General William Hall died, in 1875, Hall & Son—the son having lost his taste for the music business—was acquired by Ditson, restoring a profitable body of music to the man who had advised Gottschalk to write more like those commercially inclined Americans of foreign extraction from whom the music-publishing trade was reaping its greatest profits. Gottschalk did not do so, and his music is still heard, unlike that of the others.

After William Hall broke with his old friend and partner John Firth in 1847, the reconstituted company, Firth, Pond & Co., continued to thrive, winning a reputation for integrity, energy, and knowledge of the wants of the public. The firm was well known all over the United States for its extensive catalogue of vocal and instrumental music, and the quality of its pianos and other instruments. Sylvanus Pond had retired from the business in 1850 to devote himself full time to writing and compiling church music. His place was taken by his son William A. Pond, who remained active as a music publisher until his death in 1885.

The total income of the music trades, including instrument manufacture and sales, was estimated to be $24 million in 1855 (total national wealth was $4.5 billion) by a leading music-trade and business paper, *New York Musical Review*. It counted Firth, Pond, Hall & Son, Horace Waters, and the firm of Berry

& Gordon, in which Ditson was a silent partner, as the new giants of New York music publishing. Firth, Pond's sales of sheet music and music books amounted to approximately $70,000 a year. Of this, the greater proportion came from the firm's own catalogue, but it included income made by printing music for others. Some 1,000 plates were engraved annually for about 225 pieces of sheet music, five new works being issued each week. Sales of violins, guitars, strings, and other musical instruments and accessories added $30,000 to gross income. The flutes and guitars were made in a Fluteville, Connecticut, factory, owned jointly with the Halls. The firm was planning a new fireproof piano factory, where, with the aid of the most modern technology and improved machinery, Firth, Pond expected to double sales of the instrument, which already exceeded $4,000 a month. Annual income was: sheet music and music books, $70,000; pianos, $50,000; musical merchandise, $30,000. Firth, Pond employed ninety-two people, forty of whom were in the piano factory, soon to be doubled; twenty in the printing shop, including engravers; fifteen in the water-powered Connecticut factory, seven of whom made and repaired brass instruments, and ten in the stockroom and warehouse.

One asset the *Musical Review* failed to list was the firm's contract for the exclusive services of Stephen Foster, who had already provided a string of hit songs, among them "Old Folks at Home," or " 'Way down upon the Swanee River," one of the most successful songs in any country. It had already sold 150,000 copies and was keeping two of the firm's printing presses busy, at least according to stories released to the trade press.

Stephen Collins Foster

The day of Foster's birth, July 4, 1826, in Pennsylvania, marked the semicentennial anniversary of American independence, and both events were celebrated by an outdoor picnic with thirty-six toasts. The eighth of ten children, young Stephen displayed an early taste for music. When the Fosters bought a pianoforte, the local musician and future music publisher William Cumming Peters was hired to teach the three girls; the two-year-old boy listened with delight.

He was soon able to pick out harmonies on a sister's guitar, and at the age of six picked up a flageolet in a Pittsburgh music store, which he learned to play beautifully. Later he also mastered the piano and could perform with skill on the guitar. He may have heard orchestrated concert music at an early age during summers at the Fosters' vacation home in Economy, Pennsylvania. The family piano teacher and friend wrote original music and made arrangements of contemporary European music for the orchestra maintained at the nearby German communal settlement, whose concerts the Fosters are known to have attended.

Wider horizons and new musical experiences opened for the boy when he was seven and traveled by riverboat with his mother to visit friends in Louisville and Cincinnati. Thomas Dartmouth "Daddy" Rice was rousing the frontier theater circuit with his Jim Crow performances. Stephen knew many of Rice's songs, having seen him perform in Pittsburgh, and he learned more about the region's favorite blackface music as he listened to impromptu entertainment on the boat and in the communities he visited. When the Thespian Company—Foster and neighborhood boys—gave thrice-weekly shows in the summer of 1834, his performances of "Jump Jim Crow," "My Long-Tailed Blue," "Zip Coon," and "Coal Black Rose" were so true to the originals that he was called back again and again. In 1837, when the national depression affected the family finances, Stephen and his mother spent the first of several summers at the home of an eighty-year-old uncle in rural Ohio. In that back country, he came into contact with the same music his older contemporary Daniel Decatur Emmett had been growing up with.

Foster had only a few years of secondary-school education, but he performed for his fellow students the first piece of his social music ever heard outside the family circle, "The Tioga Waltz," written for commencement ceremonies at Athens Academy, a boarding school he attended in 1840. An expected appointment to either West Point or Annapolis never came, and his schooling dwindled into studying arithmetic with a local teacher. His life was, instead, given over to music, studying the works of the masters, especially Mozart, Beethoven, and Weber, or singing one of his own songs or some other favorite.

He spent much time with his older brother Morrison. They heard Henry Russell at a local theater in early 1843, and for the first time the young man witnessed the adulation visited upon a famous parlor-music performer. Inspired by Russell, he wrote a melody for "Open Thy Lattice, Love," by Russell's favorite American writer, George P. Morris, and sometime in 1844 the Fosters sent this sentimental ballad to George Willig in Philadelphia, a music publisher who was not above accepting money to print the work of amateurs ready to pay. Issued in the cheapest possible form on two pages, without a cover, the song incorrectly listed the author as L. C. Foster. It had more of Thomas Moore in it than any of the truly American influences Foster had experienced, and his affection for the Irish songwriter-poet is shown by his later use of the name Milton Moore on a few of his own sentimental ballads.

The influence of blackface music burned within Foster, however, and when he was asked to join a group of teen-agers who gathered together for secret meetings and convivial singing, he wrote the first of the songs he did best, "Lou'siana Belle," followed by "Uncle Ned" who had "no teeth for to eat de corncake, / So he let de corncake be." His sister Ann Eliza claimed after Foster's death that he also composed "O Susanna" during this time. It may have been one of the early Foster songs that began to circulate among Pittsburgh's music-loving young set, and it enjoyed great popularity there, but by the writer's preference, it was never presented in public. For others, Foster wrote genteel ballads. He was also beginning to make contact with professional singers and actor members of minstrel companies that appeared in Pittsburgh.

When he was twenty-one, Foster left home to join his brother Dunning, who had used savings from wages as a riverboat-company clerk to buy a partnership in a Cincinnati commission house. Stephen went to work there as a bookkeeper, in a building that looked out on the dock and loading platform. Soon he found an old friend, W. C. Peters, who was now a music publisher, with a branch office in Louisville operated by family members. Peters took a parlor ballad from Foster, one of those inspired by Russell, "The Good Time Coming," with words by Charles Mackay. No money was involved in this purchase, and Peters brought it out in 1846, copyrighted in his own name.

Meanwhile, Pittsburgh was witnessing a new form of musical entertainment. The owner of Andrews Eagle Ice Cream Saloon had rented the floor over his confection, cake, and frozen delicacies emporium, built a stage, and provided the room with tables and chairs. Admission was a dime, which could be used toward the purchase of refreshments, to be enjoyed during performances by singers and dancers, as well as actors frozen into those living statues that were, in more suggestive poses, attracting New York patrons to exhibitions of "tableaux vivantes."

Nelson Kneass, an itinerant singer, banjo-player, and pianist whose most recent job had been with a touring company that had stranded him, was hired as the Eagle Ice Cream Saloon musical director. As a gimmick to attract new customers, he and Andrews began a series of contests, awarding a bracelet for the best riddle submitted, a ring with a ruby for the best comic song, and a golden chair for the best sentimental song. The most glamorous prize was a genuine silver cup, which was on constant display, to be "presented to the author of the best original Negro song."

Morrison Foster, a regular patron of the Saloon, wrote to Stephen for a manuscript to submit, and got back "Away down souf' whar de corn grows." When the various entries, many of them by anonymous contributors, were sung in competition, audience cheers awarded Foster's plantation ditty the silver cup. The following morning, when Morrison went to the United States District Court in Pittsburgh to deposit the song for copyright, he found Nelson Kneass in line, proposing to register it in his own name.

It had become Stephen Foster's habit to hand out copies of his minstrel songs in Cincinnati in the hope they would be performed publicly by some professional who came into possession of one. A new friend, William Roark, member of the Sable Harmonists, a blackface troupe of which Kneass had been a member, was given a manuscript copy of "O Susanna." By way of the underground communication system then prevalent in the American theater, the song got to Kneass in Pittsburgh. On September 11, 1847, the Eagle Ice Cream Saloon announced an all-singing program, including the performance of "sussana—a new song never before given to the public." It was a rousing hit.

William W. Austin has pointed out that "deprived of its rhythm, smoothed out in sober steady motion, the melody of 'Susanna' resembles a famous hymn by Lowell Mason . . . the 'Missionary Hymn' (From Greenland's icy mountains). . . . The resemblance might be mere coincidence . . . but probably Foster had absorbed Mason's melody from the singing of his mother and sisters; now he fused its firm shape of pitches with the new rhythm and comic words."

Because publishers and professional songwriters knew that the name and picture of E. P. Christy and his minstrels on sheet music and his repeated performances of a new song helped sell sheet music, these New York-based musicians, singers, and dancers had the pick of new blackface songs. Foster therefore included Christy among the performers to whom he sent copies of his new songs, in the hope that their quality would be recognized by the stars of the most important minstrel group in America. "Susanna" was a hit not only in Pittsburgh and Cincinnati. Within a few months, without benefit of printing, it was being spread around the nation by every blackface musical company. Foster was thrilled when Peters sent him two dollar bills for the copy he had sent him, which had the effect, he later said, of "starting me off in my present vocation of song-writer."

In a letter to Christy, now lost, Foster evidently offered to send to him each new "Ethiopian song" for his exclusive use, with five dollars to be paid for every song accepted. Because Foster did not wish to be associated in the public's eye with what he considered a "trashy" kind of music, his name would not appear on the cover, leaving that honor to Christy, but Foster would receive all proper royalties after expenses were paid.

Christy carefully guarded his right to claim the Foster songs as his own, and the first printed edition of "O Susanna" was published in February 1848 by Charles Holt, of New York City, as one of sixteen songs in *Music of the Original CHRISTY MINSTRELS,* which was sold before and after Christy performances. On the strength of material Foster had sent to Firth, Pond, he was asked for any new material. Foster sent a copy of "Nellie Was a Baby" to New York, for hand delivery by a friend there. Not yet aware of the commercial value of black dialect songs, he wrote: "If they will give him $10, $5, or even $1 for it, let him make a donation of the amount to the Orphan Asylum, or any other charitable or praiseworthy institution." When his New York connection failed to contact the proper people at Firth, Pond, Foster dispatched a second copy, with another black dialect song, "My Brudder Gum," asking for only fifty printed copies of each, but a royalty of two cents on all future songs. A few days later he received a reply dated September 12, 1848: his proposition was accepted.

Firth, Pond did not ask for Foster's exclusive services, so before the end of 1848 he entered into a royalty-paying contract with F. D. Benteen, of Baltimore, who immediately brought out printed piano variations on "O Susanna, an Ethiopian melody," following that with a "Susanna Polka" and "Susanna Quickstep." In February 1850, Benteen issued four more Foster songs but neglected to print Christy's name as their author, rousing the impresario to bitter complaint. Foster wrote an explanation and included a few new minstrel songs to assuage Christy. Christy liked them enough to send him five dollars for each.

When royalty payments from both his publishers were slow in coming, Foster had to borrow a hundred dollars, at six percent interest, from his brother William to finance a wedding trip to New York and Baltimore, on which he combined a honeymoon with business, visiting his publishers. He had married Jane McDowell, a Pittsburgh girl, daughter of a prominent physician. After a six week-trip, the Fosters returned to a rented house in a Pittsburgh suburb.

Foster's only child, his daughter, Marian, was born April 18, 1851, and within a few months the new father found that being a parent cost more than his music was bringing in. His letter of June 12, 1851, written to Christy as "one gentleman of the old school" to another, offered a first look at new material at ten dollars for the privilege.

Mail service being speedier in those days, the money was received and another new song sent in about a week. Christy mailed ten dollars for "Massa's in de Cold, Cold Ground," which Foster urged him to have sung in a "pathetic not a comic style." No correspondence survives to explain why the fee went up to fifteen dollars later that summer for "The Old Folks at Home," although Foster explained years later that it was agreed that Christy's name would appear on the sheet music as writer for only a short period, and all royalties would continue to go to the true author. His motivation for anonymity was to keep his name off such popular music, "owing to the prejudice against them by some, which might injure my reputation as the writer of another style of music."

Foster's greatest success began life as " 'Way down upon de Peedee ribber / Far, far away," but became what we know today only when Morrison, after suggesting "Yazoo" in place of "Peedee," took out an atlas, over which the two pored until Stephen found Swanee and wrote the final version. "Old Folks at Home, Ethiopian Melody as sung by Christy's Minstrels, written and composed by E. P. Christy" was published in late 1851 and became an immediate success. Within a year, Firth, Pond & Co. was unable to keep up with demand, although two of its printing presses worked day and night to turn out new copies, advertising that they had already sold 40,000. This was in an era when the trade regarded the sale of 3,000 copies of an instrumental piece and 5,000 of a popular song as a great success, and half of all printed music proved to be a total loss, failing to recoup production costs. On the strength of Firth, Pond's claim, a major trade paper predicted that "Old Folks" would become "one of the most successful songs that has ever appeared in any country."

It was during a trip aboard a riverboat to visit the Mardi Gras in New Orleans in 1852 that Foster learned of the widespread fame of "Old Folks at Home." The jolly party of Pittsburgh's young married couples traveled for six weeks along the Ohio and Mississippi rivers. Although these friends knew about Stephen's song-writing talent, he now met people who did not believe that he, a young white man, like them from backwater America, could have written a song the whole world was singing, of which a famous eastern minstrel performer was publicly known to be author.

Soon after his return home, Foster wrote to Christy, asking for an end to their arrangement. Having seen at first hand the enormous success of his song, he was determined to put his name on the sheet music and "to pursue the Ethiopian business without fear and shame."

Having struck a bargain, the tough-minded minstrel man, who was basking in his public fame as a hit songwriter, refused. Only after renewal of the copyright in his most successful work, in 1879, did Foster's name appear on its cover as author and composer. It was bitter for Foster during 1852 and 1853 to hear that the song "was on everybody's tongue" but "everybody" did not know he wrote it. The Albany *State Register* commented:

Pianos and guitars groan with it, night and day; sentimental young ladies sing it; sentimental young men warble it in midnight serenades; volatile young 'bucks' hum it in the midst of their business and their pleasures; boatmen roar it out stentorially at all times; all the bands play it; amateur flute players agonize over it at every spare moment; the street organs grind it out at every hour; the 'singing stars' carol it on the theatrical boards, and at concerts; the chamber maid sweeps and dusts to the measured cadences of *Old Folks at Home;* the butcher's boy treats you to a strain or two of it as he hands in the steaks for dinner; the milk-man mixes it up strangely with the harsh ding-dong accompaniment of his tireless bell.

The influential John Sullivan Dwight inveighed in his *Journal of Music* against the success of such a piece of "cheap music," much as men like him have done for years at each new popular song of the people.

Even though he could not retrieve "Old Folks at Home" from Christy, Foster continued to deal with the showman on the same basis, selling first-performance rights until Christy retired in 1854, a wealthy man. The Christy Minstrels carried on, and their European tours did much to create a world-wide audience for Foster's music. Among those songs was "My Old Kentucky Home," which appeared as "No. 20 of Foster's Old Plantation Melodies" with the writer's name on the cover, although it was "sung by Christy's Minstrels." In it Foster's approach was genuinely sentimental and aimed at a different market. He explained this new tack to a reporter from the *New York Musical World* in early 1853, who wrote:

We hope he will soon realize enough from his Ethiopian Melodies to enable him to afford to drop them and turn his attention to the production of a higher kind of music. . . . We are glad to learn from Mr. Foster that he intends to devote himself principally hereafter to the production of 'White Men's music'. Firth, Pond & Co. have just published Mr. Foster's last song—My Old Kentucky Home—which he thinks will be more popular than any of his previous productions.

Evidently Foster had written it as "Poor Uncle Ned, Good Night," and it was about the black hero of *Uncle Tom's Cabin,* which sold more than three million copies in hard cover prior to the Civil War. Sensible of his family's antiabolitionist, pro-Democratic political leanings, he borrowed from the book's plot but purged the lyric of all the contemporary black English he had been using with great success in his earlier songs. Foster had effectively turned his back on minstrel songs, despite his great success in a genre in which he was more creative and certainly most commercially successful.

A year later, Firth, Pond advertised that "Old Folks at Home" had sold more than 130,000 copies; "My Old Kentucky Home," 90,000; "Massa's in de Cold, Cold Ground," 74,000; "Old Dog Tray," 48,000. Such figures were most unusual, but not unique. Within a few weeks, Firth, Pond advertised that Francis Brown's "Will You Come to My Mountain Home" had sold 90,000 copies. How much of such advertising was what the present-day music business knows as "hype" cannot be ascertained, but, as Dwight and others complained, these appealing melodies were being hummed and whistled. The printers of songsters, the musically illiterate Americans' sheet music, did pay for permission to print the words, and their writer was making as much as $500 a quarter in sheet-music royalties.

Foster's eternal need for "public recognition" had come to the fore. In return for his exclusive services, Firth, Pond agreed to raise his royalties on all new music to 10 percent of retail price. Doubtlessly, the auspicious beginning of Jullien's Grand American Tour at New York's Castle Garden in August 1853 played some part in that decision. One of the regular features on Jullien's programs was the performance by his European singing star, Anna Zerr, of a refined version of "Old Folks at Home." The resulting public demand for it, as well as Jullien's popular arrangements of songs and operatic arias, may have contributed to the publisher's decision to issue Foster's *The Social Orchestra,* a collection of vocal and dance arrangements of "the most popular operatic and other melodies . . . arranged for flutes, violins and violoncello or piano forte," which sold for one dollar.

Foster had taken up residence in New York prior to the end of 1853, expecting to make a permanent home in that center of entertainment and the music business. The following spring, his wife and daughter joined him in a rented house in Hoboken, New Jersey. *The Social Orchestra* did not come off Firth, Pond's presses until February 1854. The *Musical World* hailed it as a publication destined "to improve the taste of the community for social music." Whatever success it did have among the middle-class households for which it was intended is not reflected in Foster's account books. His normally uncertain financial condition had forced him to sell the manuscript outright to Firth, Pond for $150. The eighty-three pages of engraved notation contained new and polite arrangements of some of Foster's Ethiopian songs, among them "Old Folks at Home," credited to Christy alone, and done in a quadrille as well as in piano and violin variations, and five new instrumental pieces by Foster. There were many arrangements of "tasteful" European music: songs by Franz Abt, a German composer, whose music became popular in America after performances by the growing number of German-American amateur singing societies that dotted the Midwest; songs by Thomas Linley, Samuel Lover, and Vincenzo Bellini, whose charming arias were hit songs in London; Franz Schubert's "Serenade"; pieces by Mozart, Beethoven, Donizetti, Weber; and more contemporary works by Josef Lanner and Johann Strauss.

Foster's songs in his new manner did not achieve the great sales of previous years, despite heavy trade-paper advertising. The most successful, "Willie, We Have Missed You," sold fewer than 3,000 copies in a year, and had earned $497.77 by 1857, when he sold the copyright outright to Firth, Pond. The plantation melodies continued to sell, but in May 1854, Firth, Pond advertised a discount sale on such songs as "Jeanie with the Light Brown Hair," four for a dollar, postage free. Perhaps at Foster's insistence, for he thought it one of his best compositions, Firth, Pond concentrated heavily in their advertising on "Jeanie," calling it "one of the most beautiful of Mr. Foster's melodies. No song writer of the present day can approach Foster in the originality, simplicity and beauty of his melodies, and 'Jeanie' is not an exception." By autumn, the charmer who floated "like a vapor on the soft summer air" was gone from all Firth, Pond advertising, her greatest fame still to come.

The Fosters had been forced to return to live with his parents in western Pennsylvania, but he did negotiate a new contract with Firth, Pond by mail. It was curiously modern in many of its provisions, giving him rights that twentieth-century songwriters fought to gain during the 1930s and after World War II. Foster was freed from his exclusive contract to Firth, Pond; he was to receive a 10 percent royalty on the retail price of all new songs, but a one-and-a-half-cent royalty on all "exclusively instrumental compositions," no matter their price; the publisher was required to send quarterly statements, and pay a penalty if they were late in arriving; copyrights were to be taken out in Firth, Pond's name, and all infringment expenses and legal costs were to be borne by the publisher, any monies resulting to be divided equally; the publisher was to pay all production costs and could grant reprint rights, a source of income the industry had recently discovered, and, if any manuscript was held "for more than a reasonable length of time to publish it," that manuscript would be returned. An additional clause was negotiated several months later, guaranteeing that the publisher would "publish and issue at all times a sufficient number of copies to supply the demand" but could withhold half of Foster's royalties to pay a promissory note granted him.

Foster took over the family home in Pittsburgh following the death of his mother and father in 1855, and in the autumn of that year his brother Dunning also died. These family tragedies conspired to drive Foster to an early but moderate appetite for alcohol, which was abetted by his delight in convivial partying with members of a quasi-political club pledged to the presidential candidacy of James Buchanan.

Foster was not entirely the drunken flawed poet of his last years that some biographers have made of him. Malnutrition, certainly caused by drink, destroyed his health and hastened his death. So, too, did the deteriorating marriage to the "Jeanie" of his songs, his wife, Jane McDowell Foster, who failed to become the doting mother substitute he so much needed, and from whom he was often parted.

The social ballads he was then writing failed to provide sufficient income to continue living in the style of 1854. He wrote one published song, "Gentle Annie," in 1856, but continued to draw consistently on his account with Firth, Pond, soon going into debt. In late January 1857, he took stock of his financial state and tabulated all royalties from Firth, Pond, starting in 1851 with "Old Folks," his best earner, which brought him a total of $1,647.46, and whose future value he computed at $100. Thirty-five songs, a schottische he had rearranged, and *The Social Orchestra,* which he had sold outright, had brought him $9,596.96 in the preceding six years, and he valued their future worth at $2,786.77. His sixteen Benteen publications, including "Camptown Races," with royalties of $101.25, had earned $461.85. Royalties from sheet-music sales had averaged a bit less than $1,500 annually, a small return to the most successful songwriter of the 1850s.

Before moving into a hotel room for ten dollars a week, the Fosters rented out rooms in the family home, and were reduced to living on the $1,500 for which he had sold future royalties on all his songs to Firth, Pond as well as some $200 in past-due royalties paid by Benteen. In almost no time, all the money was gone.

Foster resumed drawing against future earnings in 1858, under a new contract executed in New York with Firth, Pond, who paid for his trip to the city. This fourth agreement cleaned the slate of past debts, tied him up exclusively until August 1860, and endeavored to put a ceiling on all advances. Still, at year's end he was overdrawn by nearly $1,000, and when the contract came to an end, he owed $1,396.64. Jane Foster had, meantime, become a telegrapher for the Pennsylvania Railroad. Foster was told by his publishers to return to the plantation melodies he had abandoned.

"The Glendy Burk," published in May 1860, represents Foster's now old-fashioned vision of the black American. Public taste for such songs had changed, and the minstrel stage was a far cry from the Christy presentations that had propelled Foster's blackface songs to success. Such music publishers as Oliver Ditson had taken to restoring parlor ballads, which had been translated into black English, to their former state. Even Foster's "Old Folks at Home" and his other songs were being sold as purified sheet music. "The Glendy Burk" was Ethiopian only because Foster used the old dialect, though it was a story that could as easily have been sung by an Irish deck hand.

Firth, Pond no longer wanted his services on an exclusive basis, with all its attendant problems. In October 1860, he sold them outright one of his plantation songs in the new manner, "Old Black Joe," which had no dialect. It, too, was inspired by *Uncle Tom's Cabin.* Yet in a curious way its melancholy lyric reflects the despair of Foster himself.

Sometime before "Old Black Joe" 's publication, with Morrison gone from Pittsburgh and William dead, Foster went back to New York with his wife and ten-year-old daughter, in order to be nearer the music houses. The family took up residence in a series of shabby boardinghouses, where they lived until Jane, driven to despair by her husband's self-destructive impulses and frequent absences, took her daughter back home to Pennsylvania, never to see Foster alive again.

Some music publishers were happy to take any new material from him, hoping that lightning would strike again and the fantastic string of hit songs he wrote for Firth, Pond might be repeated. Lee and Walker, of Philadelphia, agreed to take six new songs a year for a $400 advance, and some sentimental executive at Firth, Pond offered him $66.66 monthly for twelve songs annually.

The first Foster song to appear under any imprint other than Firth, Pond's since 1855 was issued in late 1860, published in *Clark's Visitor,* a monthly newspaper for elementary-school pupils. The periodical was printed by Daughaday & Hammond in partnership with Lee and Walker, and five other songs contracted for appeared in subsequent issues of the *Visitor.*

Once President Lincoln's call went out for troops in early 1861, it was clearly evident that the good old days were gone. Almost at once, Firth, Pond was affected by the general recession that immediately hit the music business, and so rejected Foster's new songs. Lee and Walker canceled their agreement with him. From then until his death in January 1864, he wrote 105 new songs, nine of them for Firth, Pond before the firm was dissolved in 1863.

With some assistance from a new friend, John Mahon, who fancied himself a songwriter, Foster was able to sell sixteen songs over the next several years to a minor New York publisher, John J. Daly. But Horace Waters, who had once been a major music man, and was recouping a lost fortune with the publication of successful Sunday songbooks, proved to be even more of a port in a storm, buying forty-seven Foster songs.

Waters's niggardly treatment of the fading songwriter was, in part due to the publisher's dogged dedication to the antislavery cause and the Prohibition Party, of which he was a founding member. The seemingly pro-Southern flavor of Foster's music and his dedication to the bottle evoked Waters's nastiest streak. A woman clerk in his music store recalled how on one occasion a poorly dressed, very dejected man she had never before seen, ill and weak, walked into the shop and was greeted with the clerks' laughter. "His appearance," she said, "was at once so youthful and so aged that it was difficult to determine at a casual glance if he were twenty years old or fifty." He was hardly a figure to elicit the doughty Prohibionist's sympathy.

A friend recalled that Foster was "not one to haggle about the price when selling his songs; and it was not seldom, in consequence, that a publisher would take advantage of his miserable condition, paying him a paltry sum for what other composers would demand and receive fair compensation."

One evening when Foster walked into Waters's store for a few complimentary copies of a song, he was refused and he left with tears rolling down his cheeks. Waters was a hard man, even in the era when the issues of slavery and temperance made unreconstructed zealots out of many Americans. Although his Sunday School songbooks enjoyed great sales, today they are difficult to come by, but it is known that twenty of Foster's children's hymns appeared in Waters's *Choral Harp* and *Athenaeum Collection*. These oblong pocket songsters were compiled for Waters by an amateur hymn-writing clerk, Silas Jones Vail, and were issued in 1863. They include Foster's settings of verse by a new young collaborator, George Cooper, some stanzas by Charles Dickens, others by the popular Baptist hymnist Mary Ann Kidder, and a few by Foster himself. None of these achieved any lasting popularity. Nor did hymns written to Foster melodies, which were used in Sunday School hymnals: setting "Our Shepherd True" to "Swanee River," "Hear the Gentle Voice of Jesus" to "Massa's in de Cold, Cold Ground," "Long from My Heart and All Its Charms" to "Old Black Joe," and "Sorrow Shall Come Again No More" to "Hard Times Come Again No More."

When he was eighty-six years old, in 1926, George Cooper reminisced to a newspaperman about his relationship with Foster, whom he had met in 1861, and "nursed, tidied, fed and looked after" when Jane and young Marian returned to Pittsburgh in 1862. Cooper was a law student who succumbed to that passion of many nineteenth-century attorneys, finding pleasure in writing verse. The pair began to work together, and wrote twenty-three songs before Cooper was called up by the 22nd New York Regiment and served at Gettysburg and in other campaigns. One of the best was "Willie Has Gone to the War," written one cold morning in early 1863, after which they walked the slush-covered streets in search of a buyer, Foster coatless and with holes in his shoes. They came to Wood's Music hall, home of a prominent minstrel company, whose manager was sweeping the sidewalk. A deal was made for the song after Foster sang it, ten dollars in advance and another fifteen after its performance that night.

Weak with fever, which may have denoted tuberculosis, Foster took to bed on the evening of January 9, 1864. Rising to wash, he fainted and fell across the washbasin, which broke and cut a gash in his neck and face. He lay insensible and bleeding until a chambermaid found him, and he was taken to a hospital. Weakened by loss of blood and fever, he died four days later, peacefully and quietly. Morrison rushed to New York in response to Cooper's telegram and claimed the body. Among his effects was a pocket purse that contained thirty-eight cents and a little slip of paper on which was written, perhaps the idea for another song, "Dear hearts and gentle people." He was buried in the hills of western Pennsylvania on January 21, 1864, as the Citizens' Brass Band played "Old Folks at Home."

George Cooper lived long enough to be the last surviving link with Stephen Collins Foster and the music business in which he succeeded and then failed. At the time of his death in 1928, Cooper was existing on a Civil War veteran's pension of thirty dollars a month and a stipend from the American Society of Composers, Authors, and Publishers, which had learned about him through a newspaper account written by a curious reporter. His music, like Foster's, was almost all in the public domain, free for the taking. He had written some of post-Civil War America's most popular songs, among them "Sweet Genevieve," in collaboration with many of that period's most prolific tune writers, Henry Tucker, J. R. Thomas, J. P. Skelly, David Braham, Ira Sankey, Adam Geibel, and Harrison Millard. Cooper had also been active in the New York musical theater in the years between 1866 and 1880, when the stage discovered American popular music and the city became its national nexus.

Almost immediately after Foster's death, New York publishers rushed out new pieces by him, all claiming to be "the last song written" or "composed but a few days previous to his death." Most of them were written on sudden order by hacks. The true last song was "Beautiful Dreamer," with "Jeanie" considered the best of Foster's parlor ballads.

Sales of Foster songs gradually declined, owing partly to the growing popularity of the musical stage, with its spectacles, plays with music, children's operettas, French and German musical comedies and opera buffas, and the Gilbert and Sullivan operettas. These were now the special domain of America's wealthy citizens, who had become the principal market for theater songs arranged for voice and piano.

When an aging John Firth dissolved his partnership with the Pond family in

1863, the firm's assets were divided. Most of the Foster catalogue went to the Ponds, but Firth retained ownership of "Old Folks at Home," "Nellie Bly," "Massa's in the Cold, Cold Ground," and two parlor songs. These became the property of Oliver Ditson in 1867. None of them added perceptibly to his income until the Swedish prima donna Christine Nilsson made the first of her American tours in 1872. According to her press agent, after hearing "Old Folks at Home" she "was so much struck by its plaintive melody and touching words . . . she immediately set herself to learning both" and sang it at each concert. Ditson recognized Nilsson's contribution in promoting the song by issuing a new edition of the piece, with other music the diva was featuring in her programs. No such recognition was given to the Fisk Jubilee Singers, a group of eleven students from the Nashville black college, who included "Old Folks" on all their fund-raising tours, which began in 1871 and eventually took the singers to the nation's major cities and to Europe. A similar black ensemble from Hampton Institute, in Virginia, added "Old Folks at Home" amd "Massa's in de Cold, Cold Ground" to its repertoire of "cabin and plantation songs." These Foster songs became staples in musical programs at other black institutions, whose administrators were seeking to "raise" their charges' musical training by exposing them to white parlor music. Only much later, after black activists crusaded for the removal of their racist words, did "Swanee River," "Massa," and other Ethiopian melodies leave the pages of textbooks.

As time for copyright renewal of Foster's early 1850s hits came near, Ditson executives began a frantic search for Jane Foster. The revised copyright act of July 1870 gave authors or their widows and children exclusive right to extend protection for a second term, of fourteen years. In April 1879, just three months before the date Ditson believed the original copyright of "Old Folks" was to expire, Jane was located in Pittsburgh, now the wife of a merchant. Ditson offered the option of $100 for outright ownership of the song, or a royalty of three cents a copy on sheet music, correctly advising her to take the latter. At a loss in such matters, Jane turned the letter over to Morrison, now a successful Midwestern businessman. His communications with Ditson over the next several decades reveal that Stephen's business ineptitude was not a family trait. Morrison succeeded in obtaining an advance of $100 for "Old Folks at Home" and a three-cents-a-copy royalty after the advance had been earned. He worked out similar deals for other Foster music, with all payments to go to Jane and later Marian. On learning from Ditson that William A. Pond also owned Foster copyrights, similar arrangements were made with that firm.

Between these two publishers, twenty-eight copyrights were renewed and earned a combined total of $4,199.24 for his heirs, according to figures compiled by John Tasker Howard. "Old Folks at Home" alone earned half of that sum, sustaining its stature as Foster's most successful composition. On the other hand, "Jeanie with the Light Brown Hair," his most famous song in the twentieth century, earned only seventy-five cents in sheet-music royalties, in 1892. In all, Foster's songs made a total of $19,290.32 in sheet-music royalties, nearly three fourths of it while he was alive. His professional life lasted a span of fourteen years, the first five of them the most profitable. When he wrote the songs people wanted, he was the best of his time. When he thought he understood public taste and became a composer of parlor ballads rather than plantation melodies, sales of his music steadily declined. He had outlived his prime.

William A. Pond, when he left Firth, went into business with John Mayell, as Wm. A. Pond & Co., to deal in musical merchandise and publishing. The firm eventually ranked among the leading houses in the country. Specializing in songs from the musical theater, where it enjoyed a monopoly, it was later operated by various relatives, one of whom, Nelson Griggs, was active in the affairs of the Music Publishers Association during the 1890s. Once American and British music publishers learned that cooperation in skirting the copyright laws of both nations was good business, Pond & Co. became, for a while, the local representative of Boosey, Chappell, and Novello, the three major British music houses. The business remained in family hands until after World War II, when it became part of Carl Fischer.

Other important pre–Civil War music houses in New York included that owned by William E. Millet, started in 1834 in a brief partnership with Samuel C. Jollie. Millet operated alone in a store on Broadway before his sons William and Francis joined the business. Millett & Sons remained active until 1879. It absorbed Joseph F. Atwill's catalogue in 1849, when that publisher went to California to open Atwill & Co. of San Francisco. Jollie also bought out the Dubois and Warriner piano and music store in 1851, and four years later sold many plates and other assets to Ditson.

William Scharfenberg opened a store on Broadway in 1853 specializing in imported foreign music. He was a German pianist who had studied with Johann Hummel and also played violin under Louis Spohr before coming to America in 1838, at the age of nineteen. He had been preceded by a fellow countryman, Daniel Schlesinger, a pupil of Ignaz Moscheles, who quickly became famous as the best pianist yet heard in America. Shortly after Scharfenberg arrived, he played a two-piano arrangement of the Beethoven *Egmont* Overture with Schlesinger, providing an introduction to the German composer's later works, which had not yet been performed in the United States. Within a few months, Schlesinger died, and Scharfenberg took his place as the top pianist in New York. A memorial concert for the dead musician given a few months later, organized by the Concordia, a fraternal group of German musicians, brought together an orchestra of sixty to give the ''noblest musical performance ever heard in America,'' it was reported, with Scharfenberg as featured artist.

This group of predominantly German-trained musicians formed the nucleus of the New York Philharmonic Society, organized in 1842 under the direction of Uriah Corelli Hill, a Connecticut musician who had studied abroad. Hill's enthusiasm exceeded his musical talent, and his blind devotion to German music was a guiding influence on the Philharmonic's early programming.

Scharfenberg's store became the semiofficial headquarters for the Philharmonic, the place where one could obtain an associate membership in the society for five dollars, entitling one to admission to twelve rehearsals and four concerts annually. By the early 1850s, the store advertised "a more complete assortment of classical and modern European music than any city in Europe, not excepting London, Paris, Vienna or Berlin." For a number of years they employed a teen-ager named Gustave Schirmer as clerk and errand boy. He had come to America in 1840 with his piano-maker father and attended school at night. His familiarity with the German language and the European repertoire brought him to the attention of other music dealers, and he was hired away. In later years, when Schirmer had achieved his ambition and was the most important American publisher of foreign music, he hired his former employer as reader and music editor, in which position Scharfenberg remained until his death in 1895.

New York's second major dealership in imported music, Breusing & Kearsing, opened for business in 1848 in a music store that housed the American piano sales agency for the famous house of Erard Frères of Paris. Formed prior to the French Revolution by a German family, Erard was responsible for many improvements in piano action, eventually producing the instrument preferred by Liszt, Thalberg, and other virtuosos. When the great Sigismund Thalberg came to America in 1856 he brought seven Erards with him, leaving their tuning and shipment around the country to young Schirmer, then manager of the Breusing agency.

Evich Kearsing, who had retired from the partnership before Schirmer was employed, was related to a family of English piano makers who had come to New York in 1802. The Kearsing piano led all others in sales until 1830, when competition began to develop from Firth & Hall, Dubois & Stodart, and other American makers. Soon after the Mexican War, Charles Breusing became hs partner and added a printed music line of imported foreign compositions.

These foreign-owned businesses were proud to be different. Foreign music, Breusing claimed, "exercised a very important and, in the main, healthy influence on the musical tastes of this country. We familiarize Americans with compositions which, aided by the general musical advancement of the people, will lead them to eschew the trashy music now in too common use."

A man who believed in the durability of foreign art music, Gustav Schirmer bought out Breusing in 1861, and in partnership with Bernard Beer, opened Beer & Schirmer. Soon after the Civil War ended, he took over full control as G. Schirmer. His sons were made partners in the business in 1884, and the firm was incorporated after the senior Schirmer's death in 1893. Today, G. Schirmer, which now also specializes in contemporary American concert music, is still a thriving business.

Charles Edward Horn

Typical of Europeans who came to the United States in order to replenish depleted purses in the music business was Charles Edward Horn. With fellow Britons Henry Russell and Charles Dempster, he was eventually responsible in great measure for the success of parlor-ballad music in America before the

Civil War. Parlor ballads became a principal source of income for American music houses, until the nation learned to know and love its own popular music.

The closing of America's theaters following 1837's disastrous financial panic was felt most deeply in New York, the nation's major entertainment center, where all eight playhouses were forced to shut their doors. Among the thousands thrown out of work was Charles Edward Horn, composer, songwriter, and singing actor, who had been considered second only to the great British stage star John Braham. Fortunately, Horn was much in demand as a singing and music teacher, and his recent popular song "Near the Lake Where droop't the Willow" was going through many reprintings to meet demand.

Horn's father was a German-born musician of great natural ability but little formal training, who arrived in London in 1782 and found work in the Longman & Broderip music store before becoming music master to the royal household.

Charles Horn was born in London in 1784 and was taught by his father before he studied voice with the foremost singing master in England, Venanzio Rauzzini, instructor to the brightest stage stars, among them John Braham. Horn began acting in 1809, singing in the royal playhouses and writing musical plays for performance there. For many seasons he was a featured performer, a singing teacher whose pupils included fourteen-year-old Michael Balfe, and a writer of popular songs. His alteration of Robert Herrick's "Cherry Ripe" remained a hit through Queen Victoria's time, as did his "Thro' the Wood" and "I've Been Roaming," all made a success by Madam Vestris, the most popular female ballard singer of the early Victorian era.

Horn arrived in 1827, when New York was in the last throes of its adolescent infatuation with foreign opera and all things Italian. This eventually became so expensive a liaison that it drained the purses of wealthy admirers and made its support dependent upon the lowly masses' uncertain taste. Ever since 1819, when a toothless Italian poet, language teacher, and bookseller named Lorenzo Da Ponte took up permanent residence in the city, high society had been subjected to an unceasing proselytism on behalf of Italian music and letters. Society listened with delight as Da Ponte recounted stories of his friendship with the most glamorous musical, political, and aristocratic figures of Europe. He had written the librettos for Mozart's *Marriage of Figaro, Don Giovanni* and *Così fan Tutte,* and later was a London music publisher.

One of Da Ponte's most zealous converts to the cause of Italian culture was a prosperous Irish wine importer, Dominick Lynch, who was wealthy enough to go to London in 1824 in order to bring back the first Italian opera troupe to visit America. There had yet been no full-scale performance of Italian opera in the United States except for some little-noted programs at the New Orleans Opera House in 1822–23, when Rossini's *Barber of Seville* was offered, just seven years after its premiere in Italy.

Lynch offered a very large sum to Manuel Garcia, once Europe's greatest operatic tenor. The Italian singer turned impresario and contracted to bring to the United States a troupe of singers, among them his seventeen-year-old daughter, at the start of a career that, as Maria Malibran, saw crowds at her feet.

An orchestra of twenty-four musicians, the largest yet to appear in an American theater, rehearsed for one month in order to be approved by Garcia. On November 29, 1825, at the Park Theatre, opposite City Hall, they played for the first long opera ever sung in a foreign language in New York. Box prices were increased to two dollars and pit seats to one dollar for a twice-weekly season that featured Italian opera only.

Once the novelty of these full-length foreign operas wore off, managers returned to English musical plays and comedies, an ideal situation for Horn, whose reputation had been won as a vocalist, producer, and composer of such stage works. He was hailed for the quality of his performances in English-language versions of *Figaro*, Weber's *Abu Hassan, Der Freischütz,* and *Oberon,* and in *The Barber of Seville*. Boston and Philadelphia theaters bid for his services, the latter city giving him half of all box-office receipts.

The New Orleans French Opera began regular visits to New York in 1827, with critical plaudits for the quality of its singers, the skill of its orchestra and corps de ballet, and its "comédies vaudevilles," parodies of opera that developed into opéra comique. The mix was a novelty, attracting audiences despite a general feeling that the American theater was facing hard times. There were a number of reasons. The inroads of sheet music publishing and an increasing availability of parlor pianos had brought about a lessening of interest in the theatre. In addition, the state of New York theaters was deplorable, even the new Chatham, the first theater in the city to be illuminated by gaslight. Pickpockets hovered about the entrances, and rats often ran across the stage.

Despite the dirt and the poor manners of tobacco-spitting audiences, attendance grew when managers discovered the attraction of masquerade balls on the stage. The immense Park, with a seating capacity of 2,500 and a stage sufficient for the most ambitious spectacle, began the masquerades in 1829. Four hundred gentlemen were admitted, each with two ladies, to celebrate the inauguration of Andrew Jackson on March 4. Costumes were available from the theater's wardrobe. These evenings paid better than plays or operas, and they quickly multiplied. The Bowery, the Chatham, the Masonic Hall, Conway's Music Room, all joined in the profitable madness, flooring over their pits to stage height to provide a larger space for dancing and promenades. Lurid stories of improprieties during these fancy-dress parties were splashed over front pages of the local press. It took an act of the state legislature to put the play back into New York's playhouses: a $1,000 fine was imposed on the owners of any establishment who continued to offer boisterous evenings of masked gaiety. It was George Washington Dixon and the blackface song that saved the 1830–31 theatrical season.

Wisely, Horn had returned to London to take up duties as musical director at the Olympia Theatre, recently leased by Lucia Vestris. A stunningly beautiful woman, she had been the darling of London's stage for the past ten years, playing breeches parts and reportedly sharing her bed with a long list of lovers.

The nation's favorite ballad singer, she insisted on sharing all profits from the songs she featured, among them Horn's "Cherry Ripe," and "I've Been Waiting" and Alexander Lee's "Buy a Broom," which went on sale in the United States almost simultaneously with their popularity in England. Vestris ignored the songs of uncooperative writers, or butchered them into ruin, setting a pattern for hit-making stage personalities that followed her.

As the British theater's first woman theatrical manager, Vestris had a formidable ally in James Robinson Planche, an English-born playwright who created her first production, the *Olympia Revels,* starring the luscious actress in the tight-fitting male garments that displayed her considerable attractions. This was the first extravaganza burlesque, which became an important element of the post–Civil War American stage. Classical mythology, Shakespeare, operas, plays, and contemporary fiction were used for burlesque.

After a year in London, Horn returned to New York as director of music at the Park Theatre. He did not attempt to duplicate daring burlesques for American audiences, upon whom Planche's sophisticated punning and literary nuances would be lost. American taste was all for Daddy Rice's caperings, the divine Celine Celeste's naughty French ballet figures, Edwin Forrest's tragedies of American Indian life and Roman slave revolts, and the touring English Kemble family.

The indomitable Da Ponte, in his early eighties, was still fighting for Italian opera, in spite of its inability to pay its way. He persuaded some twenty of New York's wealthiest men to subscribe $6,000 each for boxes in the city's first theater designed for opera, the Italian Opera House, at Church and Leonard Streets, which matched the extravagance and luxury of Europe's finest houses. Unlike them, it did not receive special support from municipal authorities, or guaranteed income above box-office receipts. After three financially disastrous seasons, it closed. People were not ready for the four hours each performance demanded, and the theater was located in a dangerous and unfashionable part of New York.

Yet Horn's productions of English-language Italian opera, with himself in leading roles, brought in money at the Park Theatre, at least until disaster struck and Horn's voice suddenly failed. No longer able to appear on the stage or in concert, Horn announced that he would make the United States his permanent home and open a musical academy with a staff of the finest teachers available to train his new fellow countrymen in the musical arts. The high regard in which Horn was held led to his selection in 1835 to serve with Leopold Meignen, Charles Hupfeld, and others to select the best musical composition written in the United States during the previous year. The competition was in response to an editorial in the leading English periodical, *Blackwood's Magazine,* urging Americans to give up their imitation of European masters and rely on inspiration more closely related to their own experiences and national culture. Horn was particularly singled out as one capable of effecting this change. Despite his presence on the jury, Horn's "Forest Music" won. It was not his only award. The previous year, he had entered a contest sponsored by a New York singing club whose members were looking for new material.

Hewitt and Meignen submitted pieces, but Horn's "Wisdom and Cupid" won him a silver cup and the distinction of being called "the greatest writer of glees in America."

Shortly after he arrived in New York in 1827 Horn's songs had been issued in sheet-music form by American publishers. They were essentially British in character, but *Blackwood's* editorial and his awards awoke in him an awareness of the potential for popular music in the United States. The most successful of his American songs, "Near the Lake Where Droop't the Willow," was a product of this new understanding.

He was on tour in the Southern states in late 1836 when he heard Daddy Rice's

> As I was gwine up Shin Bone Alley
>   Long time ago,
> To buy a bonnet for Miss Sally,
>   Long time ago

sung by a young black with, he wrote later, a "melancholy turn in place of the comic humor I had usually heard thrown into it." Persuaded that a "pathetic and mournful song" might be made of the blackface tune and similar pieces, Horn called on George P. Morris to assist him in redeeming these songs from neglect. The journalist-poet obliged with such success that thousands of copies of "Shin Bone Alley" were sold by James L. Hewitt, who published it in 1837.

Finding himself among the 10,000 New Yorkers thrown out of work by the closing of eight local theaters, and well aware of the profits Hewitt made, Horn opened a publishing company, financed by William J. Davis, a businessman and talented amateur flute player. Their elegant shop at 411 Broadway was also the official sales agency for products of the New York Pianoforte Company, the recently formed cooperative piano manufacturing business, the first ever established in the United States. It was owned by twenty of the finest workmen in the city.

Davis & Horn issued the *National Melodies* series of American folk songs, started with Horn's reworking of "Shin Bone Alley." Five new songs were printed, all using slave melodies, but none achieved the success of the first. Horn promoted his catalogue of imported European music with a series of "Soirees Musicales," which featured the city's outstanding musical talent. With expenses mounting, Davis withdrew, leaving to Horn sole responsibility for a new monthly publication, *Musical Souvenirs,* which sold for a dollar and carried currently popular music. The sagging business was saved by the sudden success of "Rocked in the Cradle of the Deep," which Horn printed soon after its writer, Joseph Philip Knight, introduced it to New York audiences at a solo concert. Horn also served as distributor for the music of many composers who had it printed at their own expense because music houses were reluctant to gamble on copyrighted music.

The economic plight of the American theater was grave. Many of those who could afford the cut-rate entertainment offered to induce them into the playhouses considered the mix of Shakespeare and Jim Crow to be immoral, irreligious, and unfashionable. As the newly arrived John Braham, now a fading sixty-three, was to learn in short order, American gold was hard to get. He could not match the success of the much younger Henry Russell's up-to-date popular songs and new singing style.

Braham was not only a famous tenor, but also a major songwriter. More than 150 of his songs were published in the United States between 1800 and 1825. He was born to a Jewish family named Abraham in 1777. Orphaned while still a young child, he took to the streets to support himself by selling pencils and singing, an experience that brought out an innate sense of the worth of his talent. One day a Jewish stage performer heard him and took him on as an apprentice. He made his debut at Covent Garden at the age of eleven, and won a place with the acting company. When his voice changed, he found a new patron in a wealthy merchant, who paid for piano instruction until the youth was adjudged a true "professor" of the instrument. In 1794, Braham's voice reached maturity, and he was accepted as a pupil by Rauzzini, and soon became a featured performer at the Drury Lane and with the Italian Opera.

Nancy Storace, the original Susannah in Mozart's *Figaro,* became his mistress. They went to Europe, singing in Paris, Florence, and Milan, where Braham won particular plaudits at La Scala. Napoleon's threatening armies forced them back to London, where in 1801, the diminutive, five-foot-three, tenor startled a Covent Garden audience with the voice that would make him a reigning luminary of the musical theater for the next three decades. It had a compass of nineteen notes, with a falsetto extending from D to A in alt, and a volume of sound that was prodigious. He used that instrument to produce tricky crowd-pleasing effects and stunning embellishments.

His first starring vehicle, *The Cabinet,* had a book by Dibdin's younger son, Thomas, and a score mostly by Braham, a practice the singing star insisted on throughout his career. He demanded and received the unprecedented sum of 1,000 guineas for his next production, *The English Fleet in 1343,* again with Dibdin, out of which came two popular hits, equally well known in America, "All's Well" and "The Origin of Gunpowder." He continued to write music for the stage, usually starring in these pieces, and appeared in nearly every major concert, festival, and oratorio presentation in Great Britain, always for tremendous sums.

Although his printed music never contained those flourishes and displays with which he inevitably roused adoring fans to rapture, his songs sold in great quantities to amateurs who hoped to duplicate his vocal triumphs.

During forty years of professional life, Braham made an astounding fortune, but lost most of it in disastrous real estate speculations. By 1840, his voice had lowered, and he had lost the tenor gloss of his better days. Accompanied by a son, he sailed to New York, where Horn was delighted to see his old friend and made every effort to ensure that Braham's public appearances would meet their main objective, fattening the singer's purse. The old-fashioned cadenzas and ornate embellishments that had made Braham a star were unfamiliar to young American audiences at first, but by the time he was ready to go home he had become something of a public rage.

Horn's association with Braham enhanced his position in New York's concert life, as did his activity in the formation of the New York Philharmonic
Society. In 1843, he turned over his publishing business to John F. Nunns, a
New York piano maker and music dealer, and returned to England, where he
became musical director of a playhouse remodeled as an opera theater.

The family were back in America four years later, and Horn immediately
applied for naturalization. Boston's Handel and Haydn Society offered him the
post of its first paid conductor, at $300 a year, hoping that a musician of his
caliber and attainment would bring some semblance of professionalism to its
programs and concerts. In his second year there, his salary increased by $100.
He fell ill of typhoid fever and died on October 21, 1849.

During the two decades in which Charles Edward Horn played an important
part in many aspects of America's musical life, a number of significant changes
were taking place. American secular music was unshackling its British re-
straints, and Horn's popular ballads were losing their appeal to a vitally exuberant development whose ingredients he had dimly perceived in black music.
Then, too, the chief medium for popular music's exploitation, the stage, was
going through major changes. Americans, both the well-to-do and the poor,
were truly equal in the theater, which was therefore required for economic
reasons to be all things to all men. There the lower classes could view entertainment that gave them purposeful self-identification, acted out by players who
served as substitutes for their dreams of accomplishment. Increasing population, a rising standard of living after the Mexican War, and the discovery of
gold in California brought expansion of the nation's economic system, which
gave the stage a new awareness of its special ability to satisfy a broad audience,
rather than the diverse tastes to which it had catered for so long.

The results of these changes were especially vivid in New York, where the
music-publishing business expanded more than in any other American city. For
one, Stephen T. Gordon was contributing to that growth. New Hampshire-
born, he went to Boston while very young and he met and was encouraged in
his musical ambitions by Lowell Mason. He operated a music store in Hartford
for several years before moving to New York in 1850 to work for the local
branch of Philadelphian John E. Gould's operation, which had recently acquired all of the Edward Riley music catalogue. Thomas S. Berry, a New York
piano dealer, joined the firm the following year, and in 1854, with financial
backing from Oliver Ditson, the pair formed Berry & Gordon, in silent partnership with the Boston merchant. The firm became S. T. Gordon the following year and in 1861 took over part of the Russell & Richardson catalogue,
after that Boston firm's dilettante junior partner's death. When the center of
New York's entertainment business moved to the 14th Street area, Gordon and
his son Hamilton moved with it, and in 1890, after Gordon died, his son continued the operation until his death in 1914. The Gordon music interests were
finally absorbed by the Consolidated Music Corporation during the 1960s.

No mid-nineteenth-century musical family was as deeply involved in all fac-
ets of the social dance as the Dodworths, of New York. Harvey and Allen
Dodsworth directed the city's first ''name'' brass band, taught several succeed-

ing generations the latest dance steps, and wrote, arranged, and published music for dancing.

English dancing master Thomas Dodworth had brought eight-year-old Allen and his younger brothers Thomas, Charles, and Harvey, to America in 1825. He became a member of a local Manhattan band, in which Allen played piccolo. All the boys learned to play the brass and wind instruments, and within a decade no local professional musical aggregation was considered complete without the presence of at least one Dodworth.

By the age of fifteen, Allen was a first-rate trombonist, and at twenty-five he was in the first-violin section of the newly formed New York Philharmonic Society orchestra. He was best known, however, for his cornet playing, an instrument for which he created many technical innovations, among them the over-the-shoulder brass horns that directed their sound backward to marching troops. These Dodworth patented horns were made in Austria for sale exclusively at the family's headquarters building at 493 Broadway.

In 1832, the Dodworths formed the first organized brass band in America, which continued regular activity until Harvey's retirement in 1890. It was a national favorite, playing for presidential inaugurations, at civic and fraternal functions, and on significant national occasions. Harvey introduced the saxophone and other reed instruments into the American concert band, invented the open-air band concert, and was the first to play contemporary and classic concert music arranged for band.

In the early 1850s, Allen turned back to the family's original trade, teaching the social dance. He played the violin while directing his own orchestra to provide music for pupils at a series of Dodworth dance academies, which kept moving uptown in Manhattan to keep pace with the best society.

The music to which Dodworth students danced was written and arranged by Allen and published by Harvey from a new building on Astor Place. The firm also brought out a series of pocket-sized manuals, written by Allen, that taught the requirements of basic etiquette and illustrated the steps of new dances allowed by the arbiters of social usage. The Dodworth family instructed upper-class New Yorkers in ballroom dancing until the end of World War I, through numerous dance crazes.

The Nineteenth-Century Social and Stage Dance

In 1885, two years before his retirement to California, Allen Dodworth's *Dancing and Its Relation to Education,* including a complete guide to the cotillion with 250 figures, was published by the prestigious house of Harper. In it the beloved dance master detailed an eyewitness account of the progress of nineteenth-century American dancing. The popular dances of colonial and federal eras had fallen, he believed, to a series of "French invasions."

The Revolution of 1790 had driven many men of high rank from France. They took refuge in large cities and turned their accomplishments into ways of gaining a living. Among the nobility of that time, dancing was considered important as a means of learning proper carriage and manners, so, many of the refugees turned to dance instruction. They were followed by those purposely educated as teachers of social dancing.

The influx of French musicians, noblemen, soldiers, and others to the United States led to many publications of books on dancing and collections of "new cotillions with appropriate figures." Working as hairdressers, fencing masters, music teachers, and in other occupations of service to persons of wealth, these immigrants first used local job printers to prepare their instruction books and music, selling them to pupils. When the early professional music publishers, Blake, Willig, Dubois, and others, recognized the market potential for the French social dance, they took over that function.

There was a third class of French and Europeans, Dodworth wrote, "who, having been educated for the ballet, were removed from the professional dancing master." They became popular among persons who did not "apprehend the difference between ballet and social dancing." Ballet required much exercise to master, producing dances that were "consequently conspicuous at all times for exuberance of motion and manner."

Charles Gilfert, musician, composer, and music publisher, was one of those responsible early for adding on the stage an excess of flesh to that "excess of action" deplored by Dodworth. Gilfert was a successful theater manager in various places, and finally in New York. His credo that a pretty woman will fill the house excited Manhattan in 1826, where he was manager of the Bowery Theatre, the citadel of New York's common folk. He imported, from the opera house in Paris, Mademoiselle Francisque Hutin, whose short flimsy dress created a spectacle new to the Bowery's audience. "When the short petticoats, with lead at the extremities, began to mount and assume a horizontal position . . . the women screamed aloud and the greater part left the theatre," one of the spectators recalled. "The men remained . . . roaring and sobbing with ecstasy."

The partially revealed female figure had been known to both British and American theater audiences for more than a century, starting with the breeches parts played by Charles II's royal playhouse beauties. In 1820, Manhattanites had been particularly thrilled by that "rotundity of form" exhibited by an English actress who played Hamlet in tights. Now the new French ballet style was soon to displace the traditional manner of stage dancing.

Two years after Hutin's appearance, Celine Celeste, who could not speak a word of English, made her debut at the Bowery, dancing a pas de seul that revealed a bit more than her predecessor. On a return trip in the early 1830s, she grossed some $200,000 in three years, dancing and acting, having learned English. Her charming accent added a saucy note to the lyrics of songs written by Henry Bishop for musical versions of European dramas and tragedies.

"Gross and scandalous" display, not only in New York but also around the nation, of high-kicking dances by relatively unencumbered female forms was viewed with alarm by the clergy and the family press. It was reported that actresses danced in "flesh colored pantaloons," that women were often forced to "turn their backs to the stage." A campaign was mounted against these "immodest pranks of half-naked dancers," whose performances were sapping

America's moral fiber. But unblushable women were beginning to imitate the
dancers, and social dancing gradually embraced many vivacious movements of
legs and arms, though contemporary fashion denied any displays of more than
the ankle.

New show-business promotion techniques were being developed during the
1830s, which took advantage of illustrated sheet music being brought out by
such creative houses as Firth & Hall, James L. Hewitt, and Parker & Ditson.
Lithography served first to promote blackface song and its performers, and then
sex appeal, during the triumphant tour of the United States from 1840 to 1843
by the Austrian ballerina Fanny Elssler. She had grown up, during the 1820s,
in the environs of Esterházy Palace, where her father served as copyist to the
aging Haydn. She was recruited by the Royal Austrian Ballet, and in the mid-
1830s had become a favorite in Paris, where she introduced a spirited Polish
peasant dance, the Cracovienne, and made it a favorite with European ballroom
dancers. Americans gaped when she danced it and the Italian tarantella and the
Spanish cachucha during her tour. Elssler mania assumed the proportions of a
national plague wherever she appeared. Shoes, stockings, garters, fans, cigars,
shaving soap, and even bread bore her name, and her plain visage and slender
body, ankles showing, decorated an effusion of sheet music of the dances she
performed, issued to take advantage of the phenomenon.

The "leg-itimate" theater arrived with Elssler. Popular actresses were described as having "the finest leg," "the prettiest foot," "the most magnificent
ankle." Charlotte Cushman, who became one of America's great tragediennes,
was hailed in an 1837 issue of *Godey's Lady's Book* as a paragon of virtue.
But after the Viennese dancer had worked her spell, Miss Cushman appeared
as the leader of some "50 female warriors," providing "a display of ladies'
legs no mortal man could resist the opportunity of seeing."

Elssler was still in America when operators of small theaters, taverns, saloons, hotels, and other drinking houses began to show men and women "in
almost the same state in which Gabriel saw them in the Garden of Eden." The
public was advised that these spectacles, called "leg shows," offered little that
would offend morality, but, instead, would see such educational prospects from
mythology and the Bible as "Venus rising from the sea," "Esther going to the
bath," and the "massacre of Saint Bartholomew." Custodians of public morality, who had succeeded in persuading many to clothe the "limbs" of their
parlor pianofortes with pantaloons made for the purpose, went to work on the
"hyenas of humanity who reveled in the vitals of modesty and worth," and
showed beautiful women who "call themselves models of art and have been
personating all the tableaux of the Holy Scripture from Eve in the Garden down
to Esther in her Persian hot bath." Hounded by these forces, leg shows went
underground, to surface again two decades later in the fashionable musical
theater that appeared after the bloody war against slavery.

Society's young ladies happily embraced Elssler's major contribution to culture, the frenetic new European dances she had introduced. These flowers of
fashion were already afflicted by a craze known as "jiggling," or shaking all
over, that prepared them for the polka. Boston's social authority, Mrs. John

Farrar, observed in *The Young Lady's Friend* in 1838 that "some do it only on entering a room, others do it every time they are introduced to anyone, and whenever they begin to talk to anybody. It must have originated in embarrassment."

Members of America's younger society sent the hornpipe, reel, and allemande the way of the old-fashioned minute, and the lesser classes were quick to imitate their betters. The mazurka, gallopade, and polka became all the rage despite, or perhaps because of the church's warning against "the abomination of permitting a man who was neither your lover nor your husband to encircle you with his arms and slightly press the contour of your waist."

But the new dancing and its rhythms prevailed, and, knowing where the market was, music publishers rushed out hundreds of pieces for dancing in the home to the music of piano or violin, arrangements of popular songs for piano and voice, and instrumental music for the social orchestra.

Many of these new dances had originated among European country people, and thus they repeated the pattern upon which John Playford had been the first to capitalize, two centuries earlier, with his publication of English and Scottish rural dances in *The Country Dancing Master*. The polka craze had started in peasant Bohemia, when a young country girl was observed dancing her own steps to a rhythm she seems to have created, and by the 1840s the rage to copy her had spread throughout Europe and the United States. The mazurka was Polish in origin, and the gallopade a German country round dance. All had in common that they were easily learned and did not require a series of lessons from an expensive dancing teacher. This revolution in social dance had a secondary effect as its rhythms, like those of black Americans who had created an appetite for minstrel songs, began to exert a new influence on songwriters, some of whom borrowed many of the new dances' elements that appealed most to the young, the eternal discoverers and buyers of the "newest thing."

European Music Publishers in New York

The first official representatives of great European publishing houses to appear in America were August and Anthony Andre, sons of Senefelder's partner in the lithographic business, Johann Andre, of Offenbach, the owner of Mozart's entire catalogue. The young men arrived in New York in 1843, at a time when British and Continental music and book publishers had become fully aware of the important inroads being made into their profits because of the failure to achieve international copyright agreement. The Andres' New York store soon offered items from the extensive home-office stock, handsomely lithographed editions of piano and vocal music, with their store's stamp affixed to all foreign printings. In 1841, August, who preferred to be known as Gustav, opened a "depot of foreign music" in Philadelphia and continued to deal in imported music as well as to print locally until his death in 1879, when Ditson assumed ownership. During the 1850s, his distribution chain in the United States included W. C. Peters in Cincinnati, Henry McCaffrey in Baltimore, Fritz in St. Louis, and Gabici in New Orleans.

Realizing that its American agents were not handling the task on a profitable basis, the London firm of Novello & Co. opened its own United States branch, Novello's Sacred Music Store, at 389 Broadway, New York, in 1852. The parent organization had been started in 1811, when Vincent Novello, a thirty-year-old musician, the offspring of an Italian pastry cook and a British domestic, found it impossible to get a publisher for his manuscript *Collection of Sacred Catholic Music.* The compiler, self-taught, had been a choirboy at the Sardinian Embassy in England, and his musical experience also included singing with an Italian opera company as well as teaching and conducting. As a professional Catholic musician, Novello had to rely on manuscripts of the liturgy or expensive imported editions, mainly because of antipathy to the Church of Rome. He had found it necessary to compile a number of Catholic masses and ritual music himself, which he began to print at his own expense and sell from his home.

Novello's first important innovation was to write out organ parts in full, rather than offer the figured bass only. This rendered the music easier to read and perform, and proved to be a major contribution to the choral-singing movement that flourished through the years of Victoria's reign. His publications encompassed a broad range of ritual music, including the Haydn and Mozart masses, many of which thus became available for the first time in printed form. He had interrupted his work on Purcell's sacred music for a trip to Salzburg, where Mozart's sister was still living, in near poverty. Presenting her with a purse of money, he had acquired tacit approval for his Mozart editions, thus by-passing the Andre monopoly.   .

During his absence from England, his nineteen-year-old son, Joseph Alfred, had opened Novello & Co., in a building on Frith Street, in London. As part of a music-loving family, young Novello had become a fine bass singer and chorister. From that experience, he had envisioned the golden future that lay in inexpensive art music printed in Britain.

Vincent Novello completed his Purcell editions, finishing the fifth and final volume in 1832, and thereby provided, for the first time, access to some of the Church of England's most important sacred music. He continued to compile and arrange new editions of other Anglican and Catholic masses, edit music by Beethoven, Hummel, and other works for massed voices, and to write the successful "Infant's Prayer," which sold more than 100,000 copies in his lifetime alone. The ready availability and low price of Novello editions of small choral books and piano scores proved to be a further stimulant to the choir movement that began during the reign of William IV, prompting Queen Adelaide to name the Novello family "Music Sellers to the Court." Stocks at their store also included secular music, much of its publication funded by the sales of religious works and instructional books and textbooks, including a reprint edition of Hawkins's *History of Music,* first published in 1776.

With the establishment of Novello's own printing office and the purchase of extensive supplies of movable music type, the distribution and sales of inexpensive editions increased dramatically, far beyond the family's expectations. Great cases of printed music were shipped from London to the Continent and to American agents. Under the direction of a manager sent from England in the late 1840s, Novello's New York music store cornered the American market in sales of oratorio books and sacred music written by the great masters and used in Catholic and most Protestant churches.

Around the same time the New York branch was opened, Novello's employed young Henry Littleton as a "collector," to pick up newly published music from other London stores. Littleton proved to be an invaluable addition to the business, and when Alfred Novello retired to Italy in 1856, he left Littleton, then thirty-four, in charge of the British business. Through contacts at the royal Sardinian court, Alfred Novello acquired all Italian rights to the Bessemer steel-making process, a business that took up more and more of his time. Littleton was named a partner in the music company in 1861, and purchased the entire business four years later, adding to his holdings Ewer & Co., a London firm that imported music and owned the copyrights to Mendelssohn's later compositions, which were extraordinarily popular in England.

After a visit from Littleton, who was determined to increase his share of the American market, the New York store was enlarged and the owner's son Alfred was placed in charge. Following the new reciprocal copyright arrangement with England in 1891, all sales and distribution of Novello copyrights were handed over to H. Willard Gray, an Englishman who was later in charge of the American office.

Novello's and other British music-publishing houses that had opened American branch operations in the nineteenth century dealt chiefly in concert and sacred music, having lost the exploitation of their popular music to American "pirates" because of the vagaries of copyright legislation. After 1891, the situation changed. International commerce in the music business became equally significant to music publishers in all nations.

Boston

This bastion of rectitude, whose battle cry against secular music was sounded in 1647 by John Cotton, who warned that "to sing man's melody is only a vain show of glory," appeared to take that dictum against an intrusion of the human element into religion as one against any combination of words and music. Boston was the last of federal America's three major cities to house a successful publishing enterprise dealing in popular music.

In 1796, Peter Van Hagen, who had been conducting and playing in New York for several years, arrived in Boston. There he supplemented his salary as a theater conductor by teaching and repairing and tuning harpsichords and pianofortes. Two years later, he opened the city's first Musical Repository. During the next five years, he and his son Peter issued many pieces of secular music, including "Adams and Liberty," one of the new republic's earliest native hit songs. The first challenge to that success came from a young German named Graupner.

Throughout his life in Boston, Johann Christian Gottlieb Graupner was regarded as the city's leading exponent of genteel art music and a prime mover in its association with musical culture, but he also published two thirds of all the popular sheet music printed in the city between 1800 and 1825.

This man, known to Boston's high society as the "Father of American Orchestra Music," was born in 1767 in Hanover, Germany. Like his musician father, he learned to play almost every modern instrument, though with varying degrees of competence. He was regarded, until his death, as America's best player on the double bass and the oboe. After discharge from a regimental band, he had gone to London to work in royal playhouse orchestras and concert rooms. Johann Peter Salomon chose him for the orchestra assembled for Haydn's 1791–92 British tour. As a musician working in almost every form of contemporary music, Graupner became familiar with the cream of new concert and theater music.

He came to America in 1795, first to Charleston, where he worked in the City Theatre orchestra and married one of the company's young actresses, Catherine Hellyer, who was trained at the Drury Lane. When they moved north to Boston, where Catherine had appeared several years before, both were signed by the Federal Street Theatre management, who were looking desperately for professional talent. Graupner moved up from double bass and oboe chair to direct the pit orchestra. In 1801, with François Mallet, who had come to America with Lafayette during the Revolution, he opened the first of several music schools, which subsidized the family when times were difficult. Some months later, Mallet and Graupner announced the opening of a printing office "for the correct and elegant execution of all kinds of Music"; it issued some seventy pieces of music during the next nine months. When Mallet, who preferred teaching, left the partnership, Graupner moved his Musical Academy and Repository of Music to Milk and Franklin Streets. There, using profits from printed music, he set up a new printing press and a stock of movable type to serve alongside the music punches he had been using, and began to sell sheet music and books, imported English-made pianos, and other musical instruments.

Although he became an important musical-wares dealer, Graupner's chief interests during the years he was Boston's most important, and often only, music publisher, were the printing and the merchandising side of his business. Account books exist showing that Graupner instituted lawsuits against delinquent consignees in the South, to whom he shipped, as was his custom for all parts of the country, cartons of his publications. He used both intercoastal shipping and stages, generally offering a 20 percent discount. In the first years of James Hewitt's New York publishing business, Graupner established cordial relations with him, but these suffered when Hewitt's business fell upon hard times and he was in debt to everyone, including Graupner.

Other factors in Graupner's success as a major music publisher were the relationships he developed from his contribution to Boston's increasingly active concert life over a quarter century. One of the best performers on a number of instruments and a conductor of some ability, he was among the founders of the city's Philharmonic Society in 1810. This group of amateurs and professionals met regularly to rehearse Haydn symphonies and other music for their own pleasure, but they soon found a growing interest in their get-togethers among the city's lovers of music. As a man who had actually played under Haydn's direction, Graupner provided a measure of performance authenticity not known to Americans attempting the master's music. Consequently, he became a leading force in the formation of the Handel and Haydn Society, one of the longest-lived musical groups in the nation. A measure of his interest in the orchestra was the fact that he provided printed parts at a wholesale price for mass concerts and sold tickets for these performances at his store.

From 1800 to 1825, Graupner printed 600 of the 900 musical publications issued in Boston, among them folded single-sheet popular music; instruction books for piano, German flute, and clarinet; collections of dance and sacred music; and group songs. He learned how to engrave music of truly professional quality, and served as a job printer for New England composers.

It was family obligation that led partially to the collapse of Graupner's music business, a decline that developed gradually over a decade. Over family objections, his stepdaughter married a Boston bank clerk and amateur flutist, George Cushing, in 1818, and the new bridegroom became a partner in a new and expensively set up G. Graupner & Co. shop. The enterprise lasted for only a few years before looming bankruptcy forced a sale of the entire stock at cut-rate prices, followed by a public auction. The store was shuttered, and Graupner moved back to his first location, to open an operation greatly reduced from the major catalogue he had controlled for so many years.

There is little record of much business activity by Graupner after his wife's death in 1822. He continued to teach, often in the famous private school where Mrs. Susanna Haswell Rowson trained the daughters of Massachusetts' best families. He opened a music school in his own home in 1827, where he also conducted such music business as was left, once advertising the clearance of his stock of music by ''the best European authors'' at wholesale or reduced prices, with customers permitted to try out the music on his own piano before purchase.

It was undoubtedly Graupner's narrow vision of quality in popular music that led to his final fall. Musical tastes were changing as much in Boston as elsewhere. Blackface songs and those from musical plays and operas in English were exerting an influence on the taste of people who bought printed music. It was a change that the man trained in the best music Europe produced would inevitably resist. His friends had died or were in failing health, and even the joy of talented children by his second wife failed to make living what it once had been. None of his family followed Graupner into the music business except a son who was later employed by a neighborhood boy who had made good, Oliver Ditson.

During the years of Graupner's greatest prestige as a leading publisher, some other, smaller, businesses did exist, operated by booksellers, umbrella makers, piano dealers, and instrument makers and repairers. They usually carried the same variety of merchandise for which one went to music dealers everywhere: shoe blacking, stationery, cigars, billiard balls, combs, glassware, drygoods, engravings. Throughout the series of three-year economic depressions that burdened Americans at regular intervals, music dealers were continually obliged to add different lines of merchandise. In Boston, where the publication of religious music was generally controlled by establishment churches, and the sale of popular music was never great until after 1840, music dealers found that diversification of stock was more essential than in most other metropolitan centers.

The saga of how the complexion of the city's music business was changed began when William Pelham, the Virginia-born son of Peter Pelham, who had left Boston years ago for adventure, returned to the family home, in 1796. He took over the Boston Book Store, where, in various locations, flutes, hautboys, violins, strings, music books, and other such stock had been on sale since before the Revolution. In 1804, Pelham turned the business over to a nephew, William Blagrove, who added a stock of playing cards and chessman to a circulating library of music and books.

Blagrove offered his small music section at distress prices in 1810. The following year, he sold the business to Samuel Hale Parker, son of an old New England family, who was a bookbinder. In 1813, Parker added several hundred books of vocal and instrumental music, and some sheet music for the piano, making his circulating library the largest in New England. His competitor in this business was James Hewitt, who advertised borrowing fees of six dollars for annual subscribers, three and a half dollars for six months, and two dollars for three months.

During the following decade, Parker increased the scope of his merchandise, and began to sell pianos and other musical wares, mending glues, concert and theater tickets, new sheet music, and works of fiction. He also printed a few songsters and some sheet music. His most meaningful action, at least for the future, was hiring twelve-year-old Oliver Ditson as a boy of all jobs in 1823 thus starting a significant career.

Other music dealers in this period included the Hayt brothers, Charles and Elna, umbrella makers who added a stock of imported musical instruments and in 1815 joined with Lewis and Alpheus Babcock in the Boston Musical Instrument Manufactory, housed in a new building erected on the site of Benjamin Franklin's 7 Milk Street birthplace. The Babcocks had been taught piano tuning by Peter Van Hagen and piano making by Benjamin Crehore. During the depression of 1819, the Hayts and Babcocks sold out to the umbrella maker John Ashton, who was also a music dealer and served as Gottlieb Graupner's agent in the last years of the German music man's life.

The first important music-trade magazine, devoted to news, criticism, commentary, and information was issued in 1820 by John Rowe Parker, a Boston music publisher who catered to customers looking for the latest "music of the better sort." Immediately after Graupner ended his six months' occupancy of 7 Milk Street, in 1817, Parker opened there the Franklin Music Warehouse, which became America's leading source of music published by such forward-looking men as Klemm, Bacon, and Blake, in Philadelphia, Willig and John Cole, in Baltimore, and a few New Yorkers. The warehouse's stock of music, each piece stamped with its distinctive oval design depicting a bust of Franklin, was focused chiefly on imported and local editions of theater songs. As did most other American dealers, Parker had great difficulty keeping in stock the songs of the day's most famous singing star, John Braham.

Parker was the first American publisher to negotiate with British houses for the use of their music plates, securing the rights from Novello for his successful edition of Handel oratorios, which he issued on a subscription basis for members of the Handel and Haydn Society.

In 1820, Parker brought out his house organ, *The Euterpiad,* "or Musical Intelligencer, devoted to the diffusion of musical information and belles lettres." It appeared weekly at first, then as costs rose every second week, and finally monthly, before its failure in 1825. In four-page editions that sold for three dollars a year, *The Euterpiad* was distributed as far north as Montreal and south to Georgia.

Parker was the first American music dealer to issue a catalogue of his stock as a separate publication. His fifty-five page *Catalog of Music and Musical Instruments* (1820) listed hundreds of works published by American houses, classifying them by category; it is one of the earliest bibliographical treasures dealing with popular music in this country. His growing interest in visual telegraphy hastened Parker's departure from the music business, in the mid-1820s. He took over a marine-telegraph business that employed balls and flags to speed receipt of information brought by incoming ships to within a few minutes, rather than the two days it took a horseman to ride from Martha's Vineyard to Boston. Parker's business was displaced eventually by Samuel Morse's invention of the electrical telegraph. Parker's interest in music continued, and he served as adviser for literary projects dealing with the arts, but he was best known as the author of several books on the semaphoric system of signaling.

Dr. George K. Jackson, a 300-pound musical genius, and his sons Edwin and Charles became the second father-and-sons American music publishers. Jackson was born in Oxford in 1745, studied organ as a boy alongside Samuel Arnold and Raynor Taylor, and became a King's Chapel singer at eighteen. In 1796, he came to America with the oldest of his eleven children and moved through the Middle Atlantic states in search of work as a teacher and organist. After settling in New York, with his family, he directed church choirs and published a few pieces of music in association with John Butler, a British music teacher and instrument maker. When anti-British sentiment flared in New York as war appeared inevitable, Jackson moved to Boston.

In spite of his appointment to the organ loft in the Brattle Street Church and a hugely successful performance of *Messiah* under his direction, Jackson, as a registered alien, was forced into rustication outside Boston until the War of 1812 ended. He then took part in the formation of the Handel and Haydn Society, but was rejected as its musical director. Instead, he became organist for the new handsome St. Paul's Church, at a very high salary. His knowledge of Protestant sacred music was evident at once, and he played elaborate voluntaries that embraced both scientific and classic modulations. His editions of collected church music, which he sold to church members and through local stores, did much to instruct churchgoers in chanting the service. Whenever Dr. Jackson was at St. Paul's organ, Bostonians expected and heard the finest music in their city.

He and his sons opened their Music Warehouse and Variety Store in 1821, selling imported and domestic pianofortes, their father's music, popular songs, and concert music, as well as "ladies' indispensibles of every description, perfumes, soaps, etc." After the father's death in 1822, Charles began to study law, leaving the store to Edwin, who opened a New York branch in 1825. He got out of the business the following year.

With an operation far smaller than that of Isaiah Thomas in Worcester and Boston, Herman Mann, musician, dance-band leader, and printer, operated a bookstore and music press in the small Boston suburb of Dedham from 1798 until 1833, with a subsidiary outlet in Providence. Mann was born in 1771, the brother of Elias Mann, a prominent singing teacher and one of the fifteen founders of the Massachusetts Music Society, predecessor of the Handel and Haydn Society. After teaching school for a time, Herman Mann went to Dedham to open his printing office, publish a newspaper, and engage in job printing. Among his best-known secular publications was Oliver Shaw's *For the Gentlemen*, a collection of instrumental music, written for small four-piece orchestras, the earliest social dance bands. In its pages, many early-nineteenth-century popular musicians found their first source of music. Mann also printed many sacred collections, including Shaw's *Providence Selection of Psalms and Hymns*, one of hundreds of similar locally successful denominational books.

It was out of such a compilation that Shaw's two most popular sacred songs came: "Mary's Tears" and "There's Nothing True but Heaven," which used two of Thomas Moore's "sacred songs." These brought Shaw fame far beyond his native Rhode Island and made him the most popular American songwriter of the 1820s.

Shaw had been blinded in one eye by his penknife in his youth and lost the sight in the other at the age of twenty-one, while on a sea voyage. Two years later, in 1803, he left his Massachusetts home to go to Newport, Rhode Island, to study music with John L. Birkenhead, organist at Trinity Church. The aging Briton was in the last year of his service there, working under a contract that demanded "good behaviour and punctual attendance," imposed on him after he had imbided one tot of New England rum too many and played the wrong music during worship, which led to a public shouting match with the church clerk.

Later Shaw studied with Graupner in Boston, and then began to teach music in nearby Dedham, where one of his pupils was Lowell Mason, and he met Herman Mann, with whom he struck up a lifelong friendship. In 1807, he moved to Providence, opened a music store that was serviced by Graupner, and played organ in the local First Congregational Church. He gave as many as forty classes of music a week in his home, which had a piano in every room and an organ in the center hall. Shaw was also active as a secular musician, conducting concerts at Brown University, where his vocal programs were particular favorites. He published most of his own music, including the setting of

Thomas Moore's verses. "There's Nothing True but Heaven" was especially popular in Boston and was repeated constantly in Handel and Haydn Society concerts, with Shaw himself often soloing. It was often stated that the song made him more than $1,500 in profits.

In 1825, the twenty-two-year-old James Lang Hewitt, the second son of James Hewitt, opened a Boston music store in association with James A. Dickson, a former theater manager and now a publisher. Young James had learned the business in his teens from his father, having accompanied him to New York in 1816, where the Hewitt imprint once again appeared on printed music for a brief period. When his troubled and dying father returned to Boston in the last years of his life, he occupied a room above the Dickson & Hewitt store.

James Lang Hewitt had married a minor New England poet and his business was soon thriving. A catalogue issued in 1827, just after his father's death, embraced an extensive assortment of the latest American and European music, 200 pieces of sheet music, teaching books, and pianos. He also conducted a mail-order business to any part of the United States and the West Indies. Among his best-selling items were two famous American songs: the first sheet-music edition of Lowell Mason's "From Greenland's Icy Mountains" and "The Minstrel's Return'd from the War," by his older brother, John Hill Hewitt.

John Hill Hewitt

Born in 1801 and two years older than his brother James, John Hill Hewitt had been poorly educated, receiving only common-school training in New York and only a brief period more after the Hewitts moved to Boston in 1812. Because his British father had never gained the fortune he wished as a professional musician, he believed that his talented son John, who had a flair for caricature sketching among other abilities, would remain poor if he opted for his father's career. All he wished for the boy was that he become respected, something he considered he had himself never achieved. He therefore apprenticed John to a commercial artist and sign painter.

John's mischievous practical joking quickly ended the apprenticeship, which was followed in rapid order by jobs with a chemist, a commission merchant, a New York jeweler and match maker, and as a clerk for a Manhattan waterfront merchant. Taking destiny into his own hands, John wrote to a family friend, a general in the United States Army, asking for help in securing an appointment to the military academy at West Point. As a member of the class of 1822, he found a kindred spirit in Richard Willis, the bandmaster and teacher of music, who had been born in Dublin, where he learned to play the keyed bugle and was now one of the world's best players on that instrument. Willis had also been employed to travel around Ireland in search of native tunes for one of Thomas Moore's collections; consequently, he had an ear for good popular music, which he imparted to his pupils.

Whatever musical training, other than from his father, John received came entirely from Willis during a stormy academic career. Hewitt took part in a student rebellion in 1820, was confined to quarters for masquerading as an officer, fought duels in spite of the Academy's code, and failed to graduate because of low grades on his mathematics and chemistry examinations. He then joined his father in Augusta, Georgia, where the flawed musician was writing music, leading a six-piece orchestra for the local theater company, and directing concerts. A sudden fire, the constant threat to a theater for much of the century, destroyed almost everything the Hewitts owned, and the father again returned to Boston.

John turned to the only salable talent he had other than his charm and began the teaching career that served to bail him out of similar difficulties for much of his life. He taught piano and flute, learned from Willis, to children of well-to-do families in Georgia and South Carolina. In Augusta, he formed a music and dramatic society and put on original plays with music. In Columbia, South Carolina, he read for the law, and in Greenville became music master for a Baptist Female Academy. Whenever he could, he used his frequently overstated West Point credentials to win a place in the local militia. Working as a part-time journalist, he founded a weekly newspaper and ladies' magazine.

A South Carolina rival for the affections of one of Hewitt's young pupils circulated rumors that the Northerner was no West Point graduate, but a mulatto from the Caribbean. Hewitt's close-cropped curly hair and dark complexion lent credence to this story, resulting in ostracism and a loss of students. With proof to the contrary obtained from friends in the north, Hewitt faced the rumormonger, gun in hand, and collected a written apology restoring his honor. But the scandal was difficult to live down, so he moved on.

James Hewitt's death in 1827 brought his oldest son to Boston for the grand funeral that provided a recognition by his peers the old man would have enjoyed. Among the baggage John took north were the plays he had written for amateur companies, including among them one of his earliest songs, the ballad "The Minstrel's Return'd from the War." As he wrote on the original manuscript, now in the Library of Congress: "I gave him [his brother] a copy to publish—he did it very reluctantly—did not think it worthy of a copyright. It was eagerly taken up by the public, and established my reputation as a ballad composer. It was sung all over the world—and my brother, not securing the right, told me that he missed making at least $10,000."

The song was truly popular all over the world, but it was rarely credited to its author, being usually printed as "Written by J.H.H." Europeans thought so highly of its tragic lyric and martial tune that they believed it was the work of Sir Walter Scott, who was then at his peak and being acclaimed for *Minstrelsy of the Scottish Border,* a collection containing authentic and new folk songs and ballads.

Soon after his father's estate was settled, John moved to Baltimore with his bride, whom he had met and won while at West Point. He remained in Maryland as a journalist-poet for the next twelve years. As always, he taught music and wrote songs, usually published by George Willig, Jr., and sometimes by his brother George, a Philadelphia music publisher for a short period in the late 1830s. Hewitt's reputation as a songwriter was enhanced by the success in 1833 of "The Mountain Bugle" and two years later of "The Knight with the

Raven Black Plume.'' His songs echoed the London playhouse musical style he had learned from his father or the more contemporary songs being written by Henry Bishop, who was now the most successful theater songwriter in the world. There were Italian influences as well: Bellini's pretty arias and Rossini's tunes, favorites of Americans who had adopted the guitar.

People were beginning to learn Hewitt's amiable poetry, which was prominently featured in Baltimore papers and often copied in papers around the country. A collection of this verse appeared in 1834.

As a leading Baltimore journalist, and near Washington, Hewitt came into contact with social and political figures from around the nation and won the friendship of many. He also earned the enmity of Edgar Allan Poe, whose 1829 collection Hewitt criticized derisively. In 1833, relations between the two erupted into a public brawl. Both had submitted entries to a weekly journal whose editors had offered prizes for the best short story and the best poem contributed. Poe's ''Manuscript Found in a Bottle'' won the first, and his poem ''The Coliseum'' was chosen as the best verse. Rather than give two awards to the same person, the editors presented one to Hewitt. The decision did not please Poe, and the pair met in the street and engaged in ''a little unpleasantness.''

Hewitt dipped his feet into the pool of currently popular minstrel songs with *The Crow Quadrilles* in 1838, a ten-page collection of the most popular songs arranged for the piano and illustrated with dance figures. He wrote some original songs for a Baltimore-based minstrel troupe soon after, and for many years provided these entertainers with comic songs that revealed his changing attitude toward slavery and abolition.

In order to clear up some outstanding debts, Hewitt sold his local newspaper interests in 1839 and moved to Washington to lend his pen to the cause of his political idol, the Whig Henry Clay, who was preparing to run for the presidency in the 1844 election. Anticipating a lucrative government post should Clay win, Hewitt became an unofficial member of Clay's political family, writing articles, speeches, and songs. A campaign song he wrote was published, with an engraved portrait of the candidate on the cover.

The pillar for Hewitt's pro-Clay stance was his own paper, *The Capitol,* a Whig periodical he founded in Washington early in the 1840s. As a spokesman for the Whigs, he became close to the family of that party's head, President John Tyler. He taught the Chief Executive's daughter the piano, until he discovered she was taking guitar lessons from a black White House servant. He was persuaded by the President, however, to continue the keyboard instruction on the promise that the offender would be discharged.

When Tyler, a widower, was courting Julia Gardiner, whom he married in the first such ceremony ever held in the White House, Hewitt wrote the music for a ''serenade,'' with which the President wooed his intended.

Clay's defeat in 1844 brought a new and unfriendly party to power. So Hewitt moved to Norfolk, to write for the local paper. In 1848, he accepted an offer from Chesapeake Female College, near Hampton, Virginia, to serve as professor of music. He moved his wife and family there and spent ten reasonably happy years at the school before his wife's death in 1859 and the financial collapse of the school due to fear of war.

With war seemingly inevitable and the probability that much of it would take place in rural Virginia, Hewitt went back to Baltimore. When war started, he went to Richmond to volunteer his services to Jefferson Davis, the Confederacy's president and a fellow West Pointer. Davis offered only the nonmilitary position of volunteer drillmaster. The sixty-year-old songwriter could be seen regularly marching recruits through Richmond streets and leading them through military drill with broomsticks in place of rifles.

In late 1861, Hewitt took over management of the Richmond Theatre, rebuilding a company whose professional members had fled to the north when war broke out. Fire soon destroyed the building, including almost all of the musical plays he had written, over thirty-five years, for amateur and professional actors and students. He moved his actors into an abandoned church to present variety entertainment for Confederate troops. Most of it was anti-Union and anti-Lincoln material and plays of his own heavy with prowar sentiment. *The Vivandiere* (1863) was the first of his works that Hewitt called an "operetta." Deane L. Root, in *American Popular Stage Music, 1860–1880,* calls Hewitt "probably the first significant operetta composer in the United States," whose works "were remarkably varied in their textual and musical imagination." However, Roots points out, because Hewitt wrote only for local production and his work was not published or circulated widely, he had little influence on the operetta form he pioneered in America.

When enemy guns were heard near Richmond in 1864, Hewitt moved his children to Augusta and became manager of a theater there, offering more of his operettas, burlettas, plays with music, and standard theater pieces. He married, for the second time, the eighteen-year-old daughter of a Savannah family that opposed this union of May and December. She bore him four children and walked proudly behind his coffin in 1890.

As the most professional American songwriter to join the Southern cause, Hewitt was much in demand by a music business that started almost overnight, after its Northern suppliers were barred from dealing with it. Among his best-known songs of this time was "Somebody's Darling," a musical setting written on order to verses brought by their writer into the Savannah store of the major Southern music publisher, John C. Schreiner, to whom Hewitt was under exclusive contract as songwriter. The latter wrote a beautiful melody to the original somber lyrics:

> Into the word of the clean, white wash'd halls,
>   Where the dead slept and the dying lay;
> Wounded by bayonets, sabres and balls,
>   Somebody's darling was borne one day

And he insured the song's commercial success by adding an emotional and pleasing refrain that attracted sheet-music buyers:

> Somebody's darling,
> Somebody's pride,

Who'll tell his mother
Where her boy died?

Its popularity was exceeded only by another Hewitt song, "All Quiet Along the Potomac Tonight," written to a poem by a New York housewife who had never seen war, but it captured its essence in five verses and a final four-line refrain. There were a number of other settings, on both sides of the conflict, but none with the impact and appeal of Hewitt's music.

During the last months of the war, Hewitt worked for the Henry C. Blackmar family music business, which had been driven out of New Orleans after Union naval forces captured the city. He operated their Augusta branch store.

Almost all of John Hill Hewitt's 300 songs had been published by the time the war came to an end, and his life thereafter was given over to journalism and playwriting, including children's operettas and other works suitable for schools and singing societies, and historical accounts of his beloved Baltimore. He returned to that city in 1874 after failing as editor of *Southern Music World,* published by the Schreiners.

As was true of so many American songwriters of his time, Hewitt made little financial profit from the success of his music. "The publisher pockets all, gets rich on the brains of the poor fool who is chasing that *ignis fatuus,* reputation," he wrote bitterly.

Like its English counterpart, the early-nineteenth-century American ballad—typified by Hewitt's first hit, "The Minstrel's Return'd from the War"—became a purely sentimental song appealing to genteel audiences, rather than the old narrative poem that told its story in verse-repeating form. A refrain was added to the old pattern, creating a song form intended to move audiences, even though the verse was often bad and the music usually simple. Its roots lay deep in the English-Scots-Irish tradition, with few of the new and peculiarly American elements that influenced the course of contemporary popular entertainment. The most successful parlor ballads were written to move a drawing-room audience to tears or laughter, to stir those basic emotions that lay so close to the surface of middle- and upper-class American psyches.

The American parlor ballad was given its initial commercial impetus by English vocalist-composers who immigrated after 1830 and introduced music in a professional manner that played more skillfully on the emotions and attitudes of audiences than could all the parlor amateurs for whom American publishers had been issuing sheet music. Piano dealers created attractive displays of the latest music to keep buyers returning to their stores, and the market thus created drew new people to the music-publishing business. One of them was Oliver Ditson, who amassed a fortune through his awareness of public taste in popular music.

Oliver Ditson

In 1823, Samuel Parker moved his book and circulating-library business to Washington Street in Boston, along which thoroughfare the city's music-publishing business later extended, and was eventually dominated by the Oliver Ditson Company, at 277 (later 451) Washington Street. A few years later, fifteen-year-old Ditson left his position as Parker's junior salesman and library attendant to learn the printer's trade from Isaac Butts, whose principal account was the *North American Review,* founded in 1815 and already the nation's leading intellectual periodical.

Oliver Ditson was born in 1811, the fifth child of a prosperous shipowner who was bankrupted by the loss of his vessels during the French and Spanish hostilities. The Ditson family had come to New England from Scotland in the seventeenth century, seeking freedom from religious persecution, and Grandfather Samuel Ditson was a veteran of the Revolution. Oliver graduated with honors at the age of twelve from the North End Public School and went out to make his own way in the world.

After several years with Butts, he went to work for one of Boston's leading printers, Alfred Mudge, and was placed in charge of music printing and other work done for Parker, who was becoming a wealthy man from his pirated editions of Walter Scott's Waverley novels. Parker's involvement with the Handel and Haydn Society and his participation in its publication of Lowell Mason's first compilation, *Boston Handel and Haydn Society Collection of Church Music,* made him aware of the possibilities inherent in printed music. In the thirty-five years the hymnal was on sale, the society and the bank-teller compiler each realized more than $30,000.

A great fire in November 1833 destroyed a large portion of Parker's music library, along with two pianos, two printing presses, and a large amount of sheet music, the major part of the assets insured for $13,000. Parker was forced to move, and in 1835 he found himself under the same roof, at 107 Washington Street, as his former employee Oliver Ditson, who had rented a single counter there and was now selling sheet music he published himself.

Though denied the benefits of a full formal education because of his father's bankruptcy, Ditson had sharpened his musical skills by reading, self-education, study with Boston teachers, and through the help of friends. The Graupner family lived across the street from his lodging house, and Ditson renewed friendship with a boyhood chum, Graupner's oldest son, John Henry, who eventually became a Ditson engraver, and Ditson was often able to talk music with the aging publisher. Graupner was now organist at the Bullfinch Street Church and secretary of its singing choir, as well as a music teacher to church classes and a prominent member of a Boston singing society. Ditson had begun to publish music and had a small catalogue of music written and arranged by Charles Zeuner, the Handel and Haydn Society's principal organist. Zeuner's music was being issued by another Boston house, operated by Charles Bradlee, when Ditson won him away to work as his music editor and only staff composer. The music published thereafter was set almost exclusively to the verse of Thomas Moore and Felicia Dorothea Hemans, author of the immortal ''The boy stood on the burning deck.'' Ditson had chosen the latter's poems for Zeuner because of the impact the ''British nightingale'' was making on the sensiblities of New Englanders. He was correct in his appraisal of her sales possibilities, for Mrs. Hemans's verses about death, the graveyard, and women's domestic affairs were set to music that sold in great number for years to come, her eternal lachrymosities touching even young Stephen Foster.

Mrs. Hemans was born in 1793 and died in 1835 of the poor health brought on by her unfaithful Irish soldier husband, who fathered five children in the first six years of marriage and then departed for England. Age fifteen when her first book of verse was published, the young poet inspired such fervid letters from Percy Bysshe Shelley that her mother was forced to call a halt to them. Only Thomas Moore's Irish lyrics were anthologized more frequently in contemporary pocket songsters and music books than those of this "soothing songbird." Even today the titles of her ballads and lays—"If thou hast crush'd a flower," "The hour of death," "The bride's farewell," "He never smiled again," "The child's first grief"—conjure visions of parlor sheet music, decorated with appropriate lithographed illustrations, standing stiffly on pianos and melodeons in countless American homes.

Recognizing Ditson's talent for business, Parker made him a co-partner in 1836, when Oliver was twenty-three, and, as the firm's official historian wrote years later, "he put his whole energy into the business and changed it into a music store." Parker & Ditson sold pianos and printed music, "constantly publishing and receiving from the other publishers in the United States, the fashionable and popular music of the time."

In 1840, Ditson married the daughter of a successful shipowner whose New England ancestors could be traced back to William Bradford, of the first Plymouth colony. Thereafter, he had little difficulty in finding the money to buy out Parker's interest in the business. At twenty-nine, he was the sole owner of an enterprise to which he had come as a boy seventeen years before. His business acumen was perceived also by Boston bankers, and in time he served as trustee, director, and even president of Back Bay financial institutions.

At the start, his staff was a single clerk and, soon, young John C. Haynes, a high-school graduate of fifteen. Haynes opened and closed the shop, dusted, swept, washed windows, made up and stoked the stove, all between 7:00 A.M. and 8:00 P.M.. He also kept the stock in order, ran errands, carried bundles, and collected bills. When Ditson learned that Haynes was considered a more attractive job elsewhere, he gave him a five-dollar gold piece and expressed the hope that he would stay for a long time. The staff was increased slowly to keep pace with the store's growth. Haynes was given an interest in 1852, and made a co-director five years later, when the store's name was changed to Oliver Ditson & Co.

At the time of the Board of Music Trade's formation in 1855, Ditson & Co. was the leading American music house, and, after the purchase of Boston's leading musical-instrument dealership in 1861, it became one of the largest music-supplies store. The five-story building erected in 1857 on Washington Street was the home of a business so prosperous that it was ready to buy any business in trouble and its publications. Twelve of the original founding members of the Board of Music Trade were eventually absorbed in this manner, as were numerous small houses.

Beginning in 1845, with the first American edition of Haydn's *Creation,* Ditson became the leading American publisher of non-copyright European concert music. In 1850, he created a music engraving and printing department, directed by his boyhood friend John Graupner. Out of it came such items as a two-volume engraved edition of all the Beethoven piano sonatas, selling for fifteen dollars; the first American edition of Bach's *Well Tempered Clavier* at ten dollars; Mendelssohn's *Songs Without Words,* the best-selling collection of piano music issued in Victorian England, and his *Four Part Songs* with English words; Kreutzer's *Forty Studies for the Violin;* a series of *Standard Operas;* and *The Complete School of Singing,* by the most famous vocal teacher of the mid-nineteenth century, Manuel Garcia, among whose pupils had been Jenny Lind. More than 200,000 volumes of music of all kinds were housed in the third-floor "Book Room," and the basement contained "cords" of sheet music. The top floor housed the sheet-music printing department. Books were done at another location, in stereotypy on steam-powered presses. Twelve presses ran constantly, tended by twenty workmen, and used some 480 million sheets of paper in 1857.

Acquisition the following year of John Sullivan Dwight's *Journal of Music,* and with it the services of its former owner, still editor, gave Ditson control of America's major music paper. During the following twenty years, it afforded a platform for expressing the company's attitudes toward developments in American music, as well as providing a convenient medium for advertising. Because it was regarded by Europeans as the country's most important voice for its national music, the *Journal* spread Oliver Ditson's reputation around the world. This secured for him the American agency of many foreign publishers.

An investment of $5,000, matched by Lowell Mason, brought Ditson into the growing reed-organ business. The melodeon, a "country cousin" of the piano, spread rapidly through the country's rural regions, and was often the first keyboard instrument available there. In 1854, Ditson introduced a young melodeon mechanic, Emmons Hamlin, to Mason, who in turn introduced him to his son William, just back from study in Paris. The pair formed Mason & Hamlin, to manufacture reed organs. This instrument, inexpensive and easy to maintain and transport, had initially became popular during the 1820s. The hymn collections compiled by Oliver Shaw, Asahel Nettleton, and others, as well as Mason's Handel and Haydn Society volume, touched off a demand for an instrument less costly than the pipe organ, but an effective accompaniment to congregational singing. By 1849, there were forty melodeon makers in the United States, doing an annual business of $650,000, double that of the pipe-organ builders, and comparing favorably with the pianoforte trade. Both rural churches and middle-class households purchased this small chamber organ, which produced tones by forcing air, supplied by the player's pedal pumping, against reed or metal blades. A later development reversed that process, so that the wind was sucked across the blades, leading to a better tonal quality.

Hamlin also improved the tone by adding a number of additional stops, to permit a greater variety of sounds and tone qualities. Selling for $200 to $500, Mason & Hamlin instruments captured a major share of the melodeon market, and within a dozen years sales rose to nearly 4,000 annually, representing a tenth of the country's annual piano-sales business.

In these years prior to the Civil War, Ditson & Co. was reported by a European visitor to have a stock of between 150,000 and 200,000 engraved music plates, capable or producing 20,000 to 30,000 compositions of various sorts. Any musical taste could be satisfied by a Ditson copyright, whether an old ballad from the Scottish or English tradition, songs by little-known composers, songs of cheerful humor and home, elegaic songs, songs of absence, songs from the theater, or songs of the sentimental minstrel stage. An entire gamut of music for the piano was also available, from the complete set of Beethoven's sonatas to currently popular music, priced at fifty cents, and charming little melodies on engraved paper sheets without cover art at twenty-five cents, an additional ten cents for one decorated.

Oliver Ditson's earliest successful native-born songwriters, as well as major promoters of music he published, walked into his Boston store in the summer of 1842 looking for new songs and hoping to persuade the music man to publish their own original material. They were the Hutchinson brothers—John, Asa, and Judson,—all in their twenties and recently arrived in Boston to give public concerts, after a summer of touring smaller New England communities. With their twelve-year-old sister, Abby, completing the ensemble, the Hutchinson Family was creating a new singing style, in which each member merged himself in the whole, forming a perfect quartet, a rarity in those days. None of the men's voices could be distinguished except when heard in a solo. Judson usually took the lead, John the tenor, and Abby the contralto, with Asa the bass and cello accompanist; the other brothers played violin.

They were descendants of an English family that had come to New England in 1634, eventually settling in Milford, New Hampshire, and they were at this time part of a family of sixteen boys and girls. Both parents were musically talented. As John wrote in his memoirs, all through his boyhood he had seen in prophetic visions a company of Hutchinsons, "standing and singing to numerous audiences, heard the plaudits and compliments as they dispersed, and witnessed the gathering-in of piles of money—gold, silver and quantities of paper." In preparation for a career all of them wanted, the boys studied elocution and sang and played their instruments in school entertainments. The Hutchinson boys had bought their first musical instruments in 1833, earning the cost by working on the land. Judson and John joined a local brass band that played for militia companies on the march and for Whig rallies in the 1840 presidential campaign. They remained mostly self-taught, having discovered that many professors of music were more interested in New England rum than in education. This instilled in the boys an aversion to alcohol that shaped their social interests and influenced many of their songs. Such formal musical training as they did get came from a cobbler who conducted evening singing schools. It was, however, enough to make choirmasters and singing teachers out of two other brothers, Joshua and Jesse, and musicians of eleven sons and two daughters.

On Thanksgiving Day of 1839, the Hutchinsons offered their first public concert, in the nearby Baptist meeting house. A sympathetic audience of neighbors received their hymns, glees, and anthems with great enthusiasm. In Lynn, Massachusetts, where Jesse was working as a hardware dealer, five Hutchinsons rented the local hall and gave another successful public recital in late 1841. After it, the brothers were determined, despite their father's objections, to go into the business of giving concerts. Feeling a need for more discipline and culture, John, Asa, and Judson went to Boston to see Lowell Mason, recognized as New England's foremost exponent of ''scientific'' music and education.

A brief interview with Mason produced only the recommendation that they study his newest publication. A meeting with Mason's colleague George Webb resulted in the suggestion that they join the Handel and Haydn Society. Judson and John sat through a rehearsal and left with the feeling that it would not help them much to be part of that group of city people listening to foreign music. Instead, they turned to current popular songs and learned them from sheet music by Henry Russell and the Rainer Family, another singing group. Both had recently been traveling around the northeast, giving concerts to packed houses and collecting that gold, silver, and paper money of which John had dreamed.

The wave of European entertainers that invaded the United States in the late 1830s and early 1840s included a number of singing families. Usually from Middle Europe, these singers entertained audiences with a combination of singing, yodeling, and ''Alpine'' harmony. Four or five in number, they stood on the stage in native dress, with the single woman member placed in the center. The most famous were the Rainers, children of a Swiss cattle farmer. Like the Hutchinsons, they had sung only for people around them until an expected appearance before the Russian and Austrian emperors who, were traveling together through Switzerland, gave them dreams of glory in the outside world.

It was ten years before the family had the opportunity to make those dreams come true. After a single season of appearances in 1827 before the English aristocracy, they took home $27,000 and left behind a vogue for their native dress and music. The composer-pianist Ignaz Moscheles was their patron and also their publisher; he brought out their songs in piano transcriptions, which served as cachets of approval of the singing family and the true Alpine folk songs that were the chief ingredient of their programs.

In 1839, a quartet of distant relatives of the original Rainer Family appeared in New York to give a series of twice-weekly concerts, and they then made successful tours before venturing to Boston. Their first concerts in that city were unsuccessful, but once Lowell Mason urged his fellow townspeople to hear ''the great perfection of their four-voiced songs . . . the excellence of their performances, the peculiarity of their national music,'' packed houses resulted. Parker & Ditson published the Rainers' songs in English translation, and among the customers for this music were the young Hutchinsons.

With the Rainers as a model, and now calling themselves the Aeolian Vocalists, and trading on the popularity of a widely circulated three-dollar songbook, *The Aeolian Lyre,* John, Asa, and Judson began the career that made them international attractions. After Abby joined them at Lynn, dressed in a Swiss costume, the Hutchinsons worked for a few dollars a night or shared in church collections. Each program opened with the Rainers' "Alpine Hunter's Song."

Dozens of other groups took to touring the country with programs of vocal music whose usual content was a repertory of lachrymose narrative songs. Influence by Henry Russell, they stressed a clarity of diction that was in marked contrast to that of the British singing actors who had dominated popular entertainment since the start of the century. No longer would an American audience patiently listen to a stage personality who translated "like a diamond in the sky" into "lake a daymond in the skay."

The greatest of all these new groups was the Hutchinson Family, and its various units made up of other family members and relatives, supplemented by New Englanders chosen only after careful audition. In August 1842, the original Hutchinsons were still the Aeolian Vocalists when an Albany, New York, music-store owner, Luke Newland, changed not only their name but also the content of their performances. He was the first to pay them a fee in advance, one hundred dollars for one night. He then suggested that they concentrate on singing just "selected and original songs and ballads, with humorous ditties, quartets, trios and so forth" and use their instruments only as accompaniment, subordinate to their voices. He also put out their first published song, "The Vulture of the Alps," with the lithographed cover that showed a small child in the carnivore's talons, certain to attract as many buyers as the music itself. The words came from a grammar-school reader, set to original music by Judson. It set the pattern from which the Hutchinsons' songs were always fashioned. "Whenever we found in the paper or had been given anything effective or beautiful in the way of poetry," John wrote, "we would pin it up on a bedpost or side of the house, and start in on a tune, each one making up his own part. Judson usually took [wrote] the air, and so in a sense became the composer of the tune. We have often made our songs and sung them in public without ever having sung a note."

Many songs in their programs were by well-known writers, music of the preceding fifty years that had become standard favorites, or old and new melodies they borrowed, adding their own words. Henry Russell was their special idol. His "The Maniac" usually made the blood of their audiences freeze when sung by John, accompanied by his brothers.

On September 13, 1842, the Hutchinsons gave their first Boston concert, in Melodian Hall. Their uncle Colonel Nathaniel Leavitt, then acting as the group's agent, had advertised in the local papers and dressed the brothers in blue long-tailed coats, close-fitting white trousers, boots, and tall beaver hats, intended to remove the aura of country folk visiting the city for the first time. The concert enjoyed middling success, but it did stimulate word-of-mouth and newspaper praise that resulted in two additional shows, played to full houses. Henry Prentiss bought a few of their songs, and then Oliver Ditson, whose shop they visited, overwhelmed them with attention and discussed publication of their most popular material, including their theme song, "The Old Granite

State,'' which they generally sang at the conclusion of each performance. The words were by Jesse to the tune "Old Church Yard,'' from a hymnbook printed for followers of William Miller, who was then preaching the second coming of Christ and the end of the world before the winter of 1843.

Ditson's enthusiasm increased when the group appeared at a three-day anti-slavery convention held by the major New England abolitionists. The Hutchinsons opened and closed each session with their music, and sometimes entertained during lulls in the activity.

Like many Americans in the rural north, the Hutchinsons had grown up with solitary blacks who had wandered away from the cities to find a peaceful existence in the remote back country. They had known a young black man who had settled in their New Hampshire hometown, married a white woman, and produced four children, all much admired by their neighbors. The Hutchinsons sang emancipation ballads at abolitionist meetings, but their zeal did not extend to singing those songs at paid concerts.

That decision may have been shaped by Ditson, who rejected as too radical their rousing freedom ballad "Get Off the Track,'' which was set to "Old Dan Tucker.'' Like many songs Ditson rejected, it was published by Henry Prentiss, usually the house of last resort for Boston songwriters. Ditson did bring out, in 1843, a number of "safe'' Hutchinson Family songs, in both quartet and solo form with piano accompaniment. Among them were "The Old Granite State'' and some other written by Lyman Heath, a New Hampshire musician who had been one of the family singing group's earliest advocates. His "Snow Storm,'' sung by Abby, was set to words by Seba Smith, a Portland, Maine, journalist-poet. There was more recitation than music in this piece, which began with an arpeggio representing a snowstorm, and then told the tragedy of a young woman struggling through high drifts, a baby in her arms. Tearing the clothes off her body, the mother covered the child and died of exposure. When morning came, a traveler found the two and as he removed the coverings from the child "the babe looked up and sweetly smiled.''

The Hutchinsons went to New York in May 1843, and found a city far more splendid and fickle than Boston in both business matters and art. They met Henry Russell, who suggested that they go to Firth & Hall if they wished to sell their songs. Ditson, he pointed out, had little interest in distributing nationally at discount, much preferring to sell over the counter or by mail. Russell's friend General George Morris, ever on the lookout for musicians who would perform his verse, gave the Hutchinsons some new lyrics. In little more than a week, six were set to music. Learning that Longfellow was at the Astor House, John Hutchinson called on him, to sing his musical setting of the poet's famous "Excelsior.'' Hearing one of his poems sung as a popular song was a new experience for America's favorite poet. Pleased with the performance, he acquiesced in John's suggestion that he write an introduction to the printed music, some lines of prose that appeared on each succeeding edition of the song.

Morris had told William Hall about the family's songwriting talents and, at his urging, Russell took them to the publisher's office, in the main room of the firm's Franklin Square store. John took twelve manuscripts out of his tall beaver hat and presented them for audition. All were accepted, unusual with most publishers. It was agreed that a royalty of between two and three cents would be paid on each copy sold, after expenses, depending on the retail price. The manuscripts were turned over to George Endicott, who did most of Firth & Hall's engraved music covers. He arranged for the brothers and sister to pose for a drawing, which was used on all sheet-music covers of their songs published by Firth & Hall, beginning with "The Old Granite State," even though Ditson, too, had published the piece. Later, demand for a more true-to-life portrait of America's leading family group caused Endicott to prepare a new one, which was used on all street music, advertising lithographs, and in songbooks for the remainder of the Hutchinsons' public career.

For two years, the family made a number of national concert tours, often for a fee of $1,000 a night. The group sailed to the British Isles in the summer of 1845, on the same boat as Frederick Douglass, who was permitted to travel only in steerage, despite their protests to the ship's captain. The poverty they saw everywhere in Britain disturbed these essentially simple New Englanders, who were unused to such extremes of wealth and need. They found that their American popularity mattered little abroad, that they would once again have to sing their way into public favor and overcome prejudice against Yankee talent. Their first audiences in Scotland, Ireland, and England were always the poor; only after leading literary figures commended their performances did the upper classes come to listen. The Hutchinsons ran into Henry Russell in Dublin, where he was repeating his American successes. He offered to manage the quartet, but they refused. He finally prevailed upon them to give several joint appearances. They were placed behind a screen on stage, and sang from there when Russell finished his turn. In the middle of their first chorus, the house nearly came down. Urged by Russell, in response to the clamor, they came out from behind the screen and sang "The Old Granite State," to enthusiastic response. Russell suddenly thought it advisable not to appear again, so the group concluded the concert alone. Before leaving Dublin, they turned down Russell's final offer of £1,000 to make a British tour under his auspices. In retaliation, he threatened to sue them if they continued to sing his songs. The Hutchinsons did well enough without him, admitting when they returned to New Hampshire that they were dollars ahead of what they had when they left.

American audiences generally preferred the Hutchinsons to confine their programs to sentimental and comic music and to leave for those who held similar views the songs of protest over slavery, temperance, the Mexican War, the starving Irish, and countless other causes. Consequently, they played smaller communities in preference to large cities, where audiences occasionally hissed the "radical" pieces. There were times, however, when these "sweet singers" carried even hostile audiences away, as when, in Philadelphia, they appeared before a racially mixed audience, something for which they had long agitated; they were among the first important artists to do so.

The new magic of minstrel bands threatened to end the popularity of all singing families, and the Hutchinsons looked west for new conquests. On one of the subsequent trips Abby met and fell in love with a handsome New Yorker. They were married in 1849, effectively ending her part in the group.

Judson, the moodiest of the family, showed signs of mental disintegration, which eventually ended in his suicide by hanging. He took to throwing silver half dollars at audiences, lecturing them on the sinfulness of eating flesh and wearing clothing made from the skin of animals, and espoused a diet of strict vegetarianism. Jesse, the brother who wrote most of their best songs and served as manager, was so distraught by the death of all his children and then his wife that he left to travel with a rival quartet and died in 1853.

In spite of these family problems, John, with Asa and Judson, filled all engagements, his son occasionally making a fourth partner. Ditson still printed all the sheet music of their new songs on a royalty basis. The family also put together a forty-eight page book of *Words of the Hutchinson Family,* to carry on the road with them. It sold for twenty-five cents, often several hundred copies an evening.

When Harriet Beecher Stowe's best-seller *Uncle Tom's Cabin* appeared in book form in 1852, John wrote to the author for permission to read from the book when he sang antislavery songs at a series of theater appearances. She rejected the proposal, saying that she did not think public sentiment was sufficiently advanced to warrant such a treatment; she regarded the stage as sinful. Other entertainers, less forthright than the Hutchinsons, merely appropriated the property. At least a dozen stage versions of the book were mounted, racking up in excess of 300,000 performances.

There were now a number of official Hutchinson Family presentations, varying from John's solo appearances, when Asa and Judson took time out to rest, to programs by members of three separate groups of relations. "The Tribe of Asa," residing in the town of Hutchinson, Minnesota, named in honor of the family, was made up of Asa, his wife, and their two children, who traveled the western concert circuits. Headquartered in the old family home in New Hampshire, "The Tribe of John" worked before eastern audiences.

Although new generations of Americans were still turning out for any of the groups, the old popularity was waning. The spectacle of a singing family in concert was beginning to pall, not just because of so many similar groups, but because of the audiences' appetite for more variety. With the advent of the Civil War, however, people were once again anxious to hear the Hutchinson Family in person, singing their songs against one of man's injustices. John had worked hard for Lincoln's election, leading crowds of the Illinois lawyer's supporters in songs from a *Republican Songster* he had compiled for the campaign. All the family groups entertained the troops.

John found a stirring marching song in the Massachusetts Second Battalion's defiant parody of a recently published church tune, "Say, Brothers, Will You Meet Us," which was sung by the soldiers to salute their sergeant, John Brown. John Hutchinson began to feature it in concerts for volunteer recruits in New England, and made "John Brown's Body" so popular that within an eight-day period in July 1861 four different versions were copyrighted in Boston; by the end of the war, an additional five dozen had been published from coast to coast.

John took his daughter and son to Washington for the New Year celebrations in 1862, where they entertained soldiers at the YMCA and on January 7 appeared at the White House. The piano there was out of tune, due to lack of use, but after a frantic search for its key and then a missing piano stool, the trio sang, despite the rickety piano accompaniment. When Lincoln called for Henry Russell's "Ship on Fire," John's greatest crowd-pleaser, the family's portable melodeon was brought in from a waiting carriage. A grateful and moved President reportedly gave the Hutchinsons a worn brass thimble his mother had used.

After considerable effort, John was able to obtain a pass permitting his troupe to entertain soldiers within the main lines of the Army of the Potomac. In early 1862, many soldiers did not see the war as one for emancipation of the slaves, and thousands of the New Jersey men they entertained at the first concerts were openly antiabolitionst. After a rousing program of family songs, the group sang their arrangement of Quaker poet John Greenleaf Whittier's "We Will Wait Beneath the Furnace Blast," set by John to Martin Luther's "A Mighty Fortress Is Our God." It was a bold and burning cry for an end to black slavery, and it brought on a near riot, stopped only by the singers when they took up the strains of "The Old Granite State."

George B. McClellan, the commanding general, revoked the pass to the front lines and forbid the Hutchinsons to sing to the troops. The matter reached a Cabinet meeting, where, after all nine of Whittier's verses were read aloud, Lincoln is reported to have said, "I don't see anything very bad about that. If any of the commanders want the Hutchinsons to sing to their soldiers and invite them, they can go."

Seeking relief from the rigors of entertaining the military, and wishing to support the home-front effort, John returned to Old High Rock, a colony of good-sized cottages around the old family home in Milford. Asa came east with his family as well, and the two began a series of outdoor concerts, where a number of new war songs were heard for the first time by a public that paid five cents for admission. These war rallies were the first to hear Walter Kittredge's "Tenting on the Old Camp Ground" and George F. Root's "The Battle Cry of Freedom," both of which remained stirring memories of the bloody conflict for thousands of veterans.

When peace came, John added some Southern states to the family's concert itinerary but met the bitter hostility of people who believed them to be spokesmen for the cause of abolition. They enjoyed far greater success in the Midwest and Pacific states, where they profited from the distribution they had assumed of the sheet music of their songs, purchased wholesale from Ditson at eight cents a copy, as well as from selling the word books, pocket-size collections of song lyrics, printed for them in quantities of 10,000.

The last great and enthusiastic audience for family singers lived away from centers of population, in what has come to be known as "the heartland of America." Whenever the Hutchinsons performed in a large city, they found themselves no longer welcome at large theaters; instead, they appeared in churches and at meetings of temperance groups and rallies of woman-suffrage advocates. The successful Fisk Jubilee Singers' concert tours inspired John and Asa to add to their programs some spirituals the black group was making popular, and they took these expressions of a race in bondage to middle-class Americans who would otherwise never have gotten to know and love them.

In 1893, John Hutchinson was one of the "wonders of America" the promoters of the Chicago World's Fair signed up to entertain the people of the world. Old-timers were pleased to hear a performer who was "a real natural singer." He died fifteen years later, when, after a heart attack, gas escaping from a room heater rendered him unconscious.

He was the last of the singers who, William Lloyd Garrison, a father of abolition, said, made the performance of American ballads "directly and purposely subservient to the freedom, welfare, happiness and moral elevation of the people."

Other Boston Houses

Oliver Ditson was the first music publisher of record to purchase the business of a competitor on the understanding that his rival would refrain from issuing any music for a stipulated period of time. In 1850, Elias Howe, Jr., had become so important a challenge to Ditson that the latter bought him out, on condition that Howe stay out of the business until 1860. A self-taught fiddler, Howe had begun his business with a collection of popular music arranged for the fiddle and printed for him on speculation, the Boston printer agreeing to wait for payment until the book started to sell. Because it contained noncopyright foreign music that other publishers had already put out, dealers were relucant to stock it, for fear of reprisal. Howe, was thus forced to distribute it himself to variety stores, stationers, newspaper dealers, and the general public. Yet the fame of his *Musical Companion* spread beyond New England, and sales made it possible for him to open a shop. He went into partnership with Henry Tolman five years later, in 1845, and the two began to issue a line of self-instruction books for various instruments, each containing several hundred tunes and selling for fifty cents. Performers on the accordion, concertina, melodeon, flute, clarinet, violin, and banjo; singers in search of the latest minstrel songs; and members of small instrumental dance groups, all found Howe's folios outstanding values.

His *Ball-room Hand Book* represented the major mass-produced comprehensive and inexpensive book devoted to the new foreign dance styles that changed that social pastime in the 1840s—the waltz, galop, polka, and other round dances. Many musicians whose social orchestras and quadrille bands provided music for American dancers learned to play their instruments from the pages of Howe's teaching books and collections of music.

The basic dance orchestra of the early 1840s consisted of two violins, one playing the melody and the second serving as rhythmic background and leader, and a cello for the bass line, augmented by flute, clarinet, cornet, harp, piano, and other brass instruments. Howe's teaching books for these various instruments each contained over 150 "favorite marches, quick-steps, waltzes, hornpipes, contra-dances, songs," all accompanied by appropriate figures and instructions the second violin would call out to the dancers.

As America's appetite for public dancing increased, larger halls were needed to accommodate the vogue. The size of dance bands concomitantly increased to ten to sixteen brass instrument, which were usually spelled by a smaller group of winds and strings. The former basic ensemble served only in small rooms, and at home only a piano and / or violin accompanied the dancers. The vast majority of these musicians had been trained by Howe's books.

The Elias Howe Co. reopened in 1860, at the conclusion of the owner's ten-year exile from the business, and at once diversified its wares, opening a drum and accessories manufacturing unit, which won lucrative contracts from the government to supply drums and fifes. Later it added a stringed-instrument division, which became the largest in the nation, selling and repairing violins and other members of the string family. During the war, Howe was offered the newly created post of director of bands for the army, but he refused it.

Until his death, in 1895, Elias Howe, Jr., was a leading publisher of band and popular instrumental music as well as his popular self-instruction books, some of which contained as many as 1,000 tunes.

George Reed, whose music store on Boston's Tremont Row opened in 1839, added publishing in 1850 when he formed G. P. Reed & Co., in partnership with his chief clerk, George D. Russell. That same year a ten-year-old Irish immigrant boy, P. F. Healy, came to work in the shop. He later became one of Oliver Ditson's favorites and was the founder of the Chicago musical-instrument manufacturing and publishing firm of Lyon & Healy.

Because of its publications of music by the major European concert composers, Reed's firm was considered one of Boston's three major houses. When Russell announced that he was leaving to go into business with wealthy Boston concert pianist Nathan Richardson, Reed sold most of his catalogue to them. The younger son of a leading Back Bay family, Richardson had lived in Germany for some years, where he studied with Ignaz Moscheles and with Alexandre Dreyschock, the virtuoso whose diabolic left-hand technique excited the awe of European concertgoers.

Upon returning to America in 1854, Richardson opened a Musical Exchange, financed by his brother, on Washington Street. The surroundings were luxurious, a place where the city's musicians, teachers, and customers for serious music found themselves welcome and where they were given ample opportunity to talk about their art and the newest music.

The thirty-year-old dilettante proprietor had returned to his native land determined to purge the business of popular "trash" and to instill in his fellow Americans an appetite for the high-class music of Europe. He began to publish music written by the young pianists with whom he had studied in Germany, as well as contemporary instrumental and vocal pieces he felt would improve the tastes of the benighted people of the United States. Just as all publishers had been doing for more than fifty years, Richardson never paid any royalties, even to men who had been his teachers or friends in Leipzig.

Modern School for Piano, Richardson's method book, copyrighted in 1853, was little more than a transcript of his lessons with European masters. Soon after it was published, leading musical journals criticized it severely, and persuaded its compiler to revise it, which he did in *New Method for the Piano,* which was not, however, brought out until his death. Published by Ditson, it remained the standard instruction book for many years, enjoying an extraordinary popularity for its pedagogical innovations, in which Richardson had been drilled at the Leipzig Conservatory. Sales rose constantly, reaching more than 500,000 copies of the mid-1880s, for which his widow received some $100,000 in royalties, and it continued to sell 20,000 copies annually for many years.

Despite his high hopes for American taste, Richardson's new publications did not sell well in the 1850s, and on the advice of his businessman brother he determined to recoup his losses by publishing the popular "trash" he despised. A tender of interest was made to George F. Root, the distinguished music educator who masqueraded as G. F. Wurzel (the German word for root) on the title page of his hit song "The Hazel Dell," published by Hall & Son of New York. Root's exclusive three-year contract with that firm was just running out, and he agreed to submit six manuscripts for consideration. When Richardson offered to buy the songs outright, Root countered with the argument that, because a wholesale deal was now at issue, he would sell the whole lot for $600. Hard cash being in short supply, Richardson took the songs on a straight royalty basis. Among them was Root's "Rosalie, the Prairie Flower," which earned its writer more than $3,000 in royalties, indicating a sale of more than 125,000 copies.

Richardson's profits from such ventures into popular music enabled him to concentrate again on foreign art music. When his friend Sigismund Thalberg came to the United States in 1856 for a national tour, Richardson served as official American publisher for him.

Richardon suffered ill health during 1858 and mental delusions as well. He died the following year, and his place in the business was taken by Henry Tolman.

Beginning in February 1860, Russell & Tolman published the *Boston Musical Times,* first as a fortnightly and then as a monthly review of music, art, and literature, generally with original composition inserts and music-trade advertising. The following year, part of the catalogue was sold to S. T. Gordon, of New York, and Russell joined his brother Joseph. Tolman carried on the *Times* alone until 1869, when it was purchased by the composer, music educator, and retailer George W. Stratton.

Joseph Russell had started in the music business with a store and publishing house in partnership with Patrick S. Gilmore, an immigrant cornet virtuoso who came to Boston in 1848. Born in poverty, Gilmore grew up in an Irish garrison town, where band parades were a daily feature. He fell in love with the sound of brass music, took lessons from a local musician, and soon found a place in the town band. At the age of eighteen, he joined the band of an army unit bound for Canada, where he served for a year and then bought his release.

Gilmore made his way to Boston and became manager of the Ordway brothers band-instrument department. With other employees, he formed a minstrel company, featuring himself as cornet soloist, and within weeks Boston was buzzing about the fantastic young musician. He formed a band for the Charlestown militia company, then took over leadership of several more prestigious brass groups. Having heard some of Louis Jullien's concerts, Gilmore recognized the appeal of highly diversified programing, like that of the present-day Boston Pops Orchestra, of which both Jullien and he may correctly be considered parents. He began to write music for the Salem Brass Band, and built up a library for his thirty-two musicians: music from the opera, excerpts from familiar symphonies, quicksteps, quadrilles, polkas, and currently popular stage and minstrel songs. His spreading reputation and musical judgment proved a major asset for Gilmore & Russell. No New England youth who dreamed of wearing the gray, gold-braided uniform of the Gilmore Band ever went anywhere but to the master bandsman for advice on the brass or reed instrument he contemplated purchasing.

When Gilmore's Salem Band marched along Pennsylvania Avenue during James Buchanan's inauguration in 1856, his fame grew nationwide. In 1860, he joined Samuel Greaves, founder and owner of the earliest and most important New England brass-instrument manufactory, to form Gilmore, Greaves & Co. A year later, Gilmore and his entire company of musicians enlisted in a body in the Union Army, and the Irish cornetist moved into the second phase of his career, as the first important American concert bandleader.

G. D. Russell & Co., where Joseph Russell went after Gilmore left him, lasted until 1877, when Ditson took over the plates. Other Boston music merchants sharing the same fate were Henry Prentiss, who began selling musical instruments and umbrellas in 1827, then printed music, and as Prentiss & Clark, was acquired in 1847; umbrella-maker Charles H. Keith, who added music to his general stock in 1835, went into partnership with Alpheus Moore in 1839, and sold plates, stock, and good will in 1846; and J. P. Ordway's Washington Street store, which prospered during Gilmore's employment, and was finally sold in 1856.

The South

It is appropriate that Charleston, South Carolina, where many American musical institutions had their start, was the birthplace of popular-music publishing in that section of the country. In 1803, J. J. Negrin printed there *The Freeman's Vocal Assistant,* "and register of Lodge of Masons of South Carolina," for his fellow members. The 256-page book contained sixteen pages of engraved music for its eighteen songs and two Masonic anthems. As the southernmost dealer for Carr & Schetky, of Philadelphia, E. Morford, of Charleston, was selling popular sheet music in his "fancy store" by 1806. During this period, his name, with those of Blake, Willig, Carr of Baltimore, James Hewitt, and François Mallet, appeared in block letters on the front page of printed songs from the London theater and American music by Benjamin Carr and Reinagle.

In 1813, Charles Gilfert, related to the New York music publisher George Gilfert, moved to Charleston and opened a Music Repository at 40 Broad Street. Born in Bohemia, he had been a pianist, music teacher, and theater musician in New York, but had spent the 1810 season as a member of the Charleston Theatre orchestra. During the next several years he traveled between the two cities. Some of his earliest work was published in New York, including Samuel Woodworth's "Patriotic Diggers," for which he arranged the music, and pieces written for musical plays presented at the Park Theatre. He published sheet and instrumental music in Charleston and sold it at his music store. In 1817, he became manager of the Charleston Theatre, and stayed there until, in 1825, he moved north to Albany.

André Louis Eugene Guilbert, a French refugee musician who had settled in Charleston prior to 1800, began to sell printed editions of his music for harp and piano to pupils and other amateur players in 1817. He had been a respected musician in Europe before the Revolution and became known later far beyond his South Carolina home. Klemm and Willig published his songs and instrumental music, but when the local Seigling store opened in 1819, the French music master's work was included among the 100 pieces published by that Charleston firm during its first five years.

John Seigling's music company, operated by the family until the mid-twentieth century, was the oldest of its kind in America at the time of its closing. It published music by local writers, and then took over Gilfert's plates when the theater demanded all of that musician's time, as well as plates engraved for Philip Muck, whose music business operated from 1813 until 1817. Once the major American music-publishing-and-distribution syndicates evolved in the north, following creation of the Board of Music Trade, the house of Siegling became only a minor regional music printer, although the business continued to be an important merchandising outlet.

Locally printed songsters first appeared in Baltimore in 1794, around the time the Carr family opened a branch store there. The Irish-born bookbinder George Keatinge, who came to America in 1790 with his musician-bookseller brother Henry, issued *The Democratic Songster,* "a collection of the newest and most admired Republican songs, interspersed with many originals," followed by *The Baltimore Songster* and a reprint of the popular *British Jovial Songster,* published in London around 1784. All of these were available at the Keatinge bookstore.

The city's traditional appetite for theatrical entertainment created an early demand for printed songs from the most popular musicals. This was initially met by newspaper and job printers, and by the Keatinge bookstore and circulating library, until the Carr store opened in 1794. Through his Masonic connections, George Keatinge had contact with the city's musical community, and his training as a pianist and flutist got him appointment as leader of the local Maryland militia band. Once music type was available, he printed sheet music, although he was never a serious rival to the Carr family. A young German violinist, Charles Hupfield, served as his music editor, adding his own music instruction book, *Musical Preceptor* (1808), to Keatinge's catalogue. Hupfield had been fourteen when he arrived in Philadelphia from Germany, where he had been trained in music; he moved to Baltimore a few years later to work in the local theater orchestra and was active in concerts and recitals. He left Baltimore for Philadelphia in 1812, and, with Benjamin Carr, Raynor Taylor, George Schetky, and others, founded the Musical Fund Society and was the first leader of its orchestra.

Captain Benjamin Edes III, grandson of the fiery Boston printer and patriot Ben Edes, who had published parodies of the "Liberty Song" in his newspaper just before the Revolution, lost an opportunity to continue the family's involvement in American music history when he closed his Baltimore printing shop and went off with the Maryland militia to fight the British in the late summer of 1814. Immediately after that long night " 'neath the rockets' red glare," during the siege of Fort McHenry on September 13 / 14 1814, Francis Scott Key gave his brother-in-law a copy of the verses his vigil had inspired. A copy was sent to Edes's printing office to be duplicated for distribution. Because the shop was closed, it was taken to another printer, from whom a proof was stolen. This led to dissemination through Baltimore's streets of the printed words that now serve as our national anthem. Shortly after, the lyrics were taken to the city's largest music publisher, the Carr Musical Repository. Key had written the piece with "To Anacreon in Heaven" firmly in mind, for he had already set a number of other poems to the same melody, and Thomas Carr and his father, Joseph, engraved the music, employing tools that were probably brought from England, and edited the words. The first printed sheet music of "The Star-Spangled Banner" went on sale in October 1814.

The handsome and brooding American musician, songwriter, and music publisher Arthur Clifton, who appeared in Baltimore after the War of 1812, was in fact Philip Anthony Corri, the oldest son of the London music publisher Domenico Corri. Corri-Clifton had been a child prodigy and then a leading London musician; he assisted in the formation of the London Philharmonic Society in 1813. When his wife ran off with another man, London gloated over the scandel for months, and he left Europe to settle in Baltimore, remaining there until his death. As Clifton, he married the daughter of a leading Maryland family and resumed his interest in producing concerts and teaching and writing music. He published a substantial amount of music, which was sold through local stores and distributed nationally by George Willig, of Philadelphia. Clifton organized Baltimore's Anacreontic Society, operated a music store, and was the local distributor for a Philadelphia piano maker. When he died in 1832, his wife turned the shop into a dry-goods store. It was not until many years later that people learned Clifton's true identity.

John Cole was one of the two largest Baltimore publishers in the period prior to 1825, during which time he issued 250 of the 1,200 pieces of music printed there. He was in his early teens when his family had moved to the city, looking for religious freedom. His early musical interest was confined to sacred song, in which he was trained by local teachers and by Andrew Law on one of his tours of the United States. Cole's *Episcopalian Harmony* (1800) was the first of more than a dozen original compilations he published in Baltimore. Isaiah Thomas got hold of *Cole's Collection of Psalm Tunes and Anthems* (1803) by flattering its author that "the best judges had pronounced the music too good for the prevailing taste." He sent 100 copies of the completed work in full payment. Cole's *Union Harmony,* printed from the new shape notes, was the first of its kind issued in Maryland.

Cole was also a skilled musician who played several instruments, particularly the clarinet, and directed a marching band that enjoyed great fame in Baltimore during the war with England. When Thomas Carr began to sell off the family music plates in 1821, Cole bought some and started the business that became a major local enterprise. In just four years, he issued more than 200 popular selections, including *Cole's Piano Forte,* which contained music by local musicians, among them Christopher Meineke and Henri-Noel Gilles. His son George joined the business in 1835 and the next year began to dispose of its stock to George Willig, Jr. John Cole continued to write, compile, and print only sacred music until his death in 1855, having gradually sold off all his secular music places to Frederick W. Benteen by 1839.

A dealer in pianos and a protégé of young Willig, Benteen was one of many American publishers who cashed in on the popularity of "O Susanna" in 1848, bringing out an arrangement without any credit to Stephen Foster. The Cincinnati commission-house bookkeeper was initially flattered, but as he became familiar with the workings of music publishers he insisted on a contractual arrangement with Benteen. Some Foster songs and a polka were copyrighted under this agreement. The Benteen business was sold in 1855 to W. C. Miller and J. R. Beecham, who were the major Baltimore music merchants until 1873, when Ditson bought them out.

In 1829, after seven years as his father's representative in Baltimore, George Willig, Jr., opened his own shop. He was the first eastern publisher to bring out Daddy Rice's "Jump Jim Crow" and other blackface songs, and he found a talented professional songwriter as well as a good friend in John Hill Hewitt, who had settled in Baltimore. Willig's store was, Hewitt wrote, "the last resort of many of the musical celebrities of times past and the issues of his press were generally of a classic order, though he secured the copyright of many popular pianoforte compositions and ballads that lived beyond the usual span." Among those that attained great popularity was "The Evergreen Waltz," written by J. T. Stoddard, a pianist and singer associated with Hewitt in formation of a local music academy. The piece outstripped everything in number of editions long after its writer had opted for a business career. Stoddard became sales manager for William C. Knabe, a German piano maker who settled in Baltimore in 1834. His factory opened four years later and in time was known throughout the South as the leading manufacturer of keyboard instruments.

"Since Mr. Willig's early days," Hewitt wrote, "many improvements have been made in the art of stamping and printing sheet music. If anyone would note the difference, let him compare the publications of the beginning of this century with those of the present day. George Willig kept pace with the times, and the publications of his house will compare favorably with any like establishments in the country."

Willig was an early official of the Board of Music Trade, eventually becoming its president, and was highly esteemed by members of that body. In 1866, his firm's name was changed to George Willig & Co., when his sons Joseph and Henry joined him; they took over the old and well-established store after their father died in 1874.

Henry McCaffrey left his position as clerk in Benteen's music store during the late 1840s to open his own business. He quickly became so important a dealer and publisher that he was asked to attend the July 1855 organizational meeting of the Board of Music Trade. McCaffrey stayed in business until 1895, when he turned the stock and good will over to Ditson.

Music dealer John E. Boswell began in business in the mid-1830s, and made pianos after 1851. He, too, was deemed so important a music man that he took part in the first meeting of the Board of Music Trade. Shortly before the Civil War, his catalogue of music plates was purchased by S. T. Gordon, of New York, leaving Boswell to concentrate on piano manufacture.

New Orleans' passion for dancing was one of the earliest orders of business for the first American commissioner in charge of the newly acquired Louisiana Territory. In 1804, William Claiborne took up the problem of civil order at the city's many public balls with his superior, Secretary of State James Madison. The French of New Orleans, it was said, danced all winter "to keep warm and they dance in the summer to keep cool." In time, the upper classes began to attend concerts that were coupled with splendid balls, and owners of real estate increased box-office receipts by adding large ballrooms to new playhouses. All of the city's various racial and ethnic entities took part in the dancing and music making. Even prior to American occupation, the city's black and lower white classes were so devoted to revelry that Spanish authorities had limited the number of dance halls catering to them. The beauty of its women of mixed blood was first exploited by dance-hall owners in 1808, with the creation of "quadroon balls," restricted to white men and free "women of color." In time, the balls were taken up by less affluent citizens, and they later influenced entertainment in the elegant *maisons de plaisir* as well as the shabby crib houses of Storyville, in both of which American jazz was nourished.

The only major American seaport on the Gulf of Mexico, New Orleans was the journey's end for thousands of flatboats that ran with the current and brought cargo and the music of the eastern seaboard from Pittsburgh and the coast. After 1815, speedy keelboats, and by the late 1820s, river steamboats manned by Irish firemen and black deckhands, carried not only the luxuries and necessities of life, but also the latest social ballads and black music to this center of a fast-growing nation.

Early in the century, black and white refugees from the Haitian revolution were among the first professional entertainers in the French language. Within a few years, they had created a sophisticated operatic tradition, with three local companies, one of which toured the northeastern cities, playing more than 250 performances between 1827 and 1833. After a Nashville-based company of actors visited the city in 1817, a prospering English-language theater was installed, extending touring companies through the Deep South and the frontier in the next twenty years.

This stage activity and the continuing requirements of music for social dancing did not tax the capabilities of Crescent City musicians. Many of them had sharpened their skills by providing music for militia companies formed by various ethnic groups, which reached an estimated 3,000 members by 1840. Residents became accustomed to regular competition between musicians marching in funeral parades, patriotic parades, political parades, and social processions, all accompanied by exceptional brass bands, and daily filling downtown streets almost without cease. Traveling instrumentalists were presented regularly in the lucrative New Orleans theaters, inspiring the city's young musicians to imitation.

Professional composers made an early appearance in the city, but whether there were publishers to merchandise their compositions is not yet known. In 1805, local musicians presented the first of 147 musical programs, extending to 1830, during which original music by local composers was offered. Harry A. Kmen has unearthed records of more than a hundred performances or original music by twenty-three resident musicians in that period.

The violinist and orchestra conductor Louis Desfarges learned early how to thwart American river boatmen in their cries for "Yankee Doodle," which he had inadvertently omitted from a Fourth of July celebration overture. Having been deafened at the Battle of New Orleans in 1815, he was able to ignore the shouting, but, to guard against any further such incident, the theater manager commissioned suitable arrangements of favorite American popular music. During many seasons in the theater, Desfarges wrote music for full orchestra and solo instrumentalists, and for Masonic holidays and parades dedicated to French and American military heroes.

Only one of New Orleans' composers and songwriters in the pre-1825 period attracted the attention of the new American publishing business—Philip Laroque, probably the city's best musician. In 1815, George Willig, Sr., put out Laroque's sixteen-page sonata honoring the *Battle of the Memorable 8th of January,* written for a celebratory concert performed in New Orleans a few weeks after the victory. As a composer in the operatic tradition, Laroque had provided the New Orleans Opera with at least three original works before 1810.

The name of George Pfeiffer began to appear on printed music covers in 1823, when he became the New Orleans distributor for George Blake, part of a chain that included music stores in New York, Boston, Baltimore, Washington, Richmond, Charleston, and Savannah. Until others are authenticated, Emile Johns must be recognized as the first New Orleans music publisher. The city directory carried his name first in 1822, as a teacher of the pianoforte, and newspaper accounts reported his appearances as soloist at benefit concerts for local musicians. After a visit to Paris, Johns became the New Orleans distributor for the Pleyel piano, and it is highly probably that Louis Moreau Gottschalk learned to play on a pianoforte purchased from Johns. In 1837, E. Johns & Co. was listed as a bookseller, printer, importer, and publisher of music, some of which was written by Johns himself. In 1842, a commission merchant, W. T. Mayo, took over the Johns business and was in turn bought out in 1854, by Philip Werlein. Then forty-two, Werlein had come to the United States in 1831, had then studied music and become a teacher. He opened a music store in Vicksburg, Mississippi, in 1842, and moved to New Orleans in 1850 to work at Ashbrand's Music Store, buying a partnership three years later. His purchase of the Johns-Mayo catalogue and stock in 1854 made P. F. Werlein the major music publisher in the South. Werlein was the only music man from that section of the nation to be admitted to the Board of Music Trade prior to the Civil War. He had representatives in Mobile, Natchez, and Memphis, and was the first Southern publisher to issue "Dixie," after he pirated it from its Yankee owners in 1860, and thus incurred a reprimand and a fine from the music board.

Werlein's chief competitor in the South was Armand Edward Blackmar, a Vermonter born in 1826, who moved as a child to Cleveland, where he was graduated from Western Reserve College at the age of nineteen. He went south to teach music and train brass bands and orchestras in Huntsville, Alabama, and then was hired as a professor of music in 1852 by Centenary College in Jackson, Mississippi. Four years later, he opened a local music store and later another in Vicksburg. His younger brother, Henry Clay Blackmar, came down from Ohio to clerk in the shop and became Armand's sole partner in 1859. The Blackmar brothers opened a store on Camp Street, New Orleans, in 1860, publishing music and selling pianos, musical instruments, and other wares. During the war, Blackmar shifted his headquarters to Augusta, Georgia, here John Hill Hewitt worked for him until the publisher was jailed owing to marital difficulties, and Hewitt, the "Bard of the Stars and Bars," bought the business. Following the war, the Blackmars reopened their New Orleans store, and Armand Blackmar remained the major music dealer in the mid-Southern territory for the rest of the century.

Frontier and Western Music Publishers

Financed by an exclusive contract for all official printing in the recently acquired Louisiana Territory north of New Orleans, the Irish refugee printer James Charless opened St. Louis's first printing office in 1808 and printed the area's first newspaper and official book of law there. His facilities were used in 1821 for the territory's first book of ballad lyrics, a collection, *Missouri Lays and Other Western Ditties* by Angus Humphraville, published by John A. Paxton, who had moved west from Philadelphia. Eighteen years later, in 1839, the former Boston umbrella maker Nathaniel Phillips advertised "the first Piece of Music published WEST of the Mississippi," on sale in his variety store and men's furnishings shop on Market Street—"The St. Louis Grand March" by G. H. Draper, which occupied a place of honor among the sheet music Phillips carried. In 1842, when the first lithographic press was installed in the city,

Phillips had already established mail-order relations with Oliver Ditson, but he continued to issue music by residents of St. Louis and the Mississippi valley. Among the several dozen titles he published before 1852 were several by Nelson Kneass, the minstrel singer in charge of entertainment at the Eagle Ice Cream Saloon in Pittsburgh. J. W. Postlewaite's "St. Louis Quick Step" (1849) was reissued many times by local publishers in the following years. A freeborn mulatto, Postlewaite was a coffee-house and music-store owner as well as a musician and singer, and leader of dance and marching bands. According to Dr. Samuel Floyd, of the Institute of Black Music Studies, Postlewaite was a significant influence on Scott Joplin, who lived within several blocks of the St. Louis music store when he arrived in that city at the age of fifteen. Fifteen Postlewaite compositions, published by various St. Louis firms, have been located by Dr. Floyd in the files of the Missouri Historical Society, and a number of others are listed in the Board of Music Trade's 1870 *Complete Catalog*.

The German music teacher Charles Balmer, who is believed to have taught Postlewaite, published his own "St. Louis Fireman's Parade March" in 1847. However, Nathaniel Phillips had no serious competition before 1847, when James and J. R. Phillips, no relations, printed an edition, copyrighted in their name, of Stephen Foster's "Lou'siana Belle." In an attempt to make his music more widely known, Foster had sent around handwritten copies of his new songs to professional entertainers, and Kneass introduced the snappy tune in St. Louis, where the Phillips brothers first heard and then issued it. Their firm continued in business for several years, until Balmer and Henry Weber bought it. These two German musicians had opened a music store in 1848 and began to print music shortly after, later taking over the Nathaniel Phillips catalogue. At the initial formation of the Board of Music Trade, Balmer & Weber was qualified for membership, printing more than 1,200 pieces of sheet music before 1860. In 1907, the firm, which had since become a major Midwestern piano dealership and music outlet, was purchased by Leo Feist, of New York.

There were other St. Louis publishers in business during the middle of the century. They usually operated as dealers associated with national firms, but none of them was of particular significance except John Green, who was a member of the Board of Music Trade in 1873, his name appearing on its roster for only that year.

In 1840, the Mexican-born, Paris-trained concert violinist Joseph Tosso published his own "General Harrison's Grand March" in Cincinnati in order to salute Ohio's native son, who was campaigning for the presidency. The splendidly lithographed sheet music bore the imprint of Tosso & Douglas, a music store and instrument dealership, and possibly Cincinnati's first music publisher. Tosso's death in 1887 in Kentucky was marked in the European press, the notice including this sentence: "His musical warhorse was 'The Arkansas Traveler' which is popularly, though erroneously, considered to be his composition."

Until 1860, when Chicago became the chief cultural center of the Midwest, after the expanding railroad system made it the hub of inland transportation, Cincinnati, the largest city west of the Alleghenies, was the capital of the frontier publishing and job-printing business. Two paper mills were in operation by 1811 and nine printing offices had opened by 1826, turning out 185,000 books, all printed from type founded locally. The first steam-powered presses followed soon after, and thus made the city a logical center for the area's music trade.

In 1832, Uriah and Joseph James, two printers who had moved from New Jersey, issued their first publication, *The [A]Eolian Songster,* a collection of popular song lyrics, which was also being printed throughout the United States by many other local job houses. A short-lived piano factory was doing business in Cincinnati in 1822, with a staff of three men and a boy, making instruments that sold for from $200 to $400. In the early 1830s, a British couple named Nixon ran the Queen City of the West's first musical seminary, offering piano lessons to young ladies only. The local piano factory had closed, but pianos could be shipped from the east by way of the Erie Canal.

The *Guide to Instruction on the Pianoforte* published by Mr. Nixon in 1834 was not the first locally printed teaching manual. Early in the 1830s, Timothy B. Mason had been impressed by his brother Lowell's success with publications of sacred music and the large financial returns they enjoyed, and so had brought the Mason method of music training to Cincinnati, where he began to preach the gospel of new *do-re-mi* solmization, rather than the popular patent shape notation. Mason fumed when he was told that the congregation of Cincinnati's Second Presbyterian Church, with which he was affiliated, still sang in the old William Billings style, four-note *fa-so-la,* using books printed with shape notes. In 1834, he compiled a 240-page instruction and song book, *The Ohio Sacred Harp,* and took his manuscript to the local printing house of Truman & Smith. Rugged fundamentalists, the publishers insisted on using shape-notation type for Mason's book, believing that it would be more acceptable to the majority.

In time, Mason put an end to the old singing-school methods of music instruction for Cincinnati's young and introduced his brother's system in the city's elementary schools. In 1849, he formed the music business of Mason & Colborn, with W. F. Colburn, a Lowell Mason disciple and leading public-school music educator. The firm specialized in materials and printed music for the music-convention movement.

One of America's major pre–Civil War publishers appeared in Cincinnati for the first time in 1845. He was William Cumming Peters, who opened W. C. Peters & Co., with his son as assistant. Most of Peters's earliest publications were his own music, but in 1846 he copyrighted a new setting for Charles Mackay's poem "There's a Good Time Coming," the second published piece written by Stephen Foster, whom he had known since the songwriter's childhood. The following year he also published Foster's first song, "Open Thy Lattice, Love," under an arrangement with George Willig, of Philadelphia, who had printed it after being paid to do so by Foster's family.

Peters had been born in Devonshire, England, in 1805 and had gone to Canada as a teen-ager with his family. His father was employed there as bandmaster for a group in which William played the clarinet. When the family moved to western Pennsylvania a few years later, William settled in Pittsburgh sometime between 1824 and 1827, and earned a living by teaching flute, piano, and violin. He also entered into partnership with two local piano dealers in one of Pittsburgh's earliest music stores, where the Foster family bought its musical instruments, including the flute and guitar to which Stephen was devoted. During these years, Peters also spent considerable time in Louisville as a performing musician.

His musical activities brought him to the attention of the communal religious settlements of Moravian refugee disciples of George Rapp, established in Pennsylvania and Indiana. He became active at the Rappite communities at Economy, near Pittsburgh, and Harmony. The Harmony group employed him to teach music and to arrange and compose for their small instrumental groups, writing overtures, marches, fanfares, and making arrangements of music by leading European composers. At Economy between 1829 and 1831 the community orchestra gave regular concerts of Peters's music and arrangements, attracting audiences from the surrounding region. During this time, when Thomas "Daddy" Rice was starting the blackface career that made him famous, he walked into the Peters music store in Pittsburgh and had the owner write down the music and words for his "Jump Jim Crow," which Peters then issued in printed form.

In 1830, Peters moved to Louisville, where he opened a music store eight years later, and then one in Cincinnati in 1839. The Kentucky store was the locale for discussions leading to the establishment of a colony in Dallas, Texas, of twenty Americans and Britons, among them members of the Peters family. The group took advantage of an offer by the Republic of Texas granting land to responsible settlers. The Peters Colony, as it became known, prospered when the Dallas area in which it settled became economically important and real estate values soared.

Peters's move to Cincinnati in 1845 marked the true start of a music business and publishing empire. His son Henry took over the Louisville store and remained in business there until 1877. Another branch continued in Pittsburgh, from which Peters issued his musical magazine *The Olio*. With the Cincinnati store as a base of operations, he, with his sons William and Alfred, scored an initial success because of the presence there of Stephen Foster. Foster did not yet have any notion of making a living as a songwriter, but he gloried in the actual publication of any of his efforts by Peters, who considered himself the youth's friend and adviser. After printing two of Foster's earliest songs, Peters neglected to bring out immediately two very professional ones, "Uncle Ned" and "O Susanna." E. P. Christy, leader of the most famous minstrel company of the time, got his hands on a copy of the latter and began to feature it, leading to its publication, without writer credit, by at least nine eastern houses. At the end of 1848, Peters issued the "official" edition, giving Foster two ten-dollar bills, the first hard cash he had ever earned from his music.

During the next year, "O Susanna" became a marching song for the westward trek of Americans to the goldfields of California, and then made its way around the world. A dozen more editions appeared, generally without any mention of Foster. Peters eventually worked out an arrangement to release the writer to a New York firm.

Whether or not, as some historians insist, Peters made $10,000 out of his Foster copyrights, which enabled him to expand his business, he had become the major Midwestern music publisher within two years. A promotional book, *Cincinnati in 1851,* detailed his assets: a catalogue of 1,600 pieces, sixty of which had been published in the last six months of 1850; and a stock of engraved zinc and copper plates valued at more than $30,000. He had paid out $3,000 for "copyrights," presumably royalties. He employed thirty people and had sold more than 3,000 pianos since 1845.

W. C. Peters was present at the formation of the Board of Music Trade in 1855 and became part of the national music syndicate that followed. When a fire destroyed his business, including all of his engraved music plates, on March 22, 1866, it was reported that Peters had sustained a loss in excess of $1.75 million. Within a month he was dead of a heart attack, at sixty-one.

In 1834, the Brainard family moved from New Hampshire to Cleveland, where father Nathan opened a music store, and his four sons—Silas, age twenty, and the younger Henry, George Washington, and Joseph—learned the trade by hard work, and the value of a dollar by poor times. Cleveland was then a small frontier town of less than 4,000 population, many of whom got to know Silas from his skill on the flute. Sometime in 1837, Nathan Brainard went into partnership with Briton Henry J. Mould, the first of many unions between members of the two families. Silas married Emily Mould in 1840, when their parents had begun to manufacture candles and confectionary and sold a line of imported pickles, fruits, and preserves.

Silas Brainard printed his first sheet music in 1845, and the following year his brother Henry, now married to Laura Mould, moved to Chicago to open the city's first Music Salon and Fancy Goods and Confectionary, in association with Brooks Mould, a brother-in-law. A few years later, Henry returned to Cleveland, where he worked for his father until his death two years later.

When W. C. Peters moved the last of his Louisville holdings to Cincinnati, George Washington Brainard, twenty, and his seventeen-year-old brother Joseph opened a music store in the Kentucky community, which was already well supplied with music dealers, chief of whom were Henry Peters and David P. Faulds. The latter first entered the music business during the early 1840s and opened his own store ten years later. A founder of the Board of Music Trade, Faulds was regarded as the territory's most important publisher and instrument dealer until well into the 1890s, when his assets were sold to Ditson.

Piano makers Timothy and Thomas Cragg joined Henry Peters in 1851, to form Peters, Cragg & Co. Thomas Cragg went to work for Faulds in 1855 but rejoined his brother in 1859, after Louis Tripp, of Louisville, bought out Peters, and Tripp & Cragg was formed. In the late 1850s, the company was admitted to membership in the Board of Music Trade, an indication of its importance in the business.

After the depression of 1857 disrupted American business, Joseph Brainard went back to the family home in Cleveland, where the Brainards were, with W. C. Peters, the leading publishers in the Midwest, both of them in the Board of Music Trade, after having weathered the country's financial disaster. Silas's sons, Charles and Henry, became partners in the firm, and the name was changed to S. Brainard's Sons.

Chicago's first but short-lived daily newspaper, the *American,* was just a year old in 1836 when it carried advertising by Osbourn & Strail, dealers in dry goods, groceries, and crockery, offering residents of the small prairie village at the head of Lake Michigan various musical instruments, printed songs for voice, piano, and guitar, and "a wide variety of the latest Marches, Waltzes, arranged for the piano." Live entertainment had been presented three years before in a tavern owned by Chicago's official ferryman, Marc Beaubien, a French-Canadian fiddler whose music for dancing attracted to the establishment the most convivial of the 600 local inhabitants. Beaubien's brother, Jean Baptiste, arrived shortly after, bringing his piano by lake schooner. In addition to Osbourn & Strail Musical Supplies, a local art dealer offered pianos imported from the east, and a "man of colour," Wilson Perry, advertised that he "was ready at all times to furnish music at assemblies, balls and parties on as reasonable a basis as can be furnished in this place." The first music school, Miss Myther's, was a few years old, and a vocal quartet had been organized at St. James' Church, where Chicago's first pipe organ was installed. When the Old Settlers' Harmonic Society produced its second annual concert in 1836, the local population had nearly quadrupled.

In 1837, Beaubien's tavern dining room was transformed into Chicago's first theater, for such attractions as Joseph Jefferson, with the true star of that family acting company, his nine-year-old boy, Joseph III, four years after an appearance in Washington, D.C., with Daddy Rice in which the child had appeared as a Jim Crow in miniature. In order to accommodate increased audiences, a new theater was improvised on the second floor of a Dearborn Street tenement, and the silver coins thrown onstage to young Jefferson exceeded any he had picked up elsewhere.

The popular blackface show made its first appearance in 1840, when P. T. Barnum arrived with his singing-dancing star Master Jack Diamond. Chicago's musical life was in full swing, new citizens arriving almost daily now that the Indians had been routed. The Brainard & Mould music and confectionary store opened in 1848, the first such in Chicago. The Sacred Musical Society, Mozart Society and Choral Union were all thriving in a new building erected exclusively as a public theater to house them. The audience that came to see the first concert performed by a European pianist was so large that the courthouse was opened for the occasion. The Hutchinson Family came, as did some of their innumerable imitators, as well as such disparate attractions as Kunkel's Nightingales, Gray's Ethiopian Warblers, Signor Blitz's Trained Canaries, and the reigning dramatic stars Edwin Booth and Edwin Forrest. The city's first operatic presentation, a performance of Bellini's *La Sonnambula,* ended almost before it began when fire sent the audience rushing out into the streets and destroyed Chicago's first opera house. The opening of the Illinois-Michigan Canal connecting Chicago with the Mississippi provided almost daily transportation to eastern America, and construction was begun on the steel rails that eventually linked the city and the Midwest to both coasts. In short, the Windy City was preparing to become the major center for all types of music that it continued to be until after World War II, when television's coaxial cables relegated it to a second-class power.

After Henry Brainard went back to Cleveland, Brooks Mould sold his candy-making and bakery business in 1849 to concentrate on music and issued Chicago's first piece of copyrighted music in 1853, the "Garden City Polka," written by the conductor of the local second Philharmonic Society. Music printed locally from music type was first available that year, when Joseph Cockroft produced the first of a series of promotional magazines for Chicago bookseller William Danehower, whose *Literary Budget* carried reviews and advertisements of new books, short stories, piano pieces, and songs "to help set the literary fashions of the community." Cockroft made plaster impressions of music type for the magazine and used these to form metal stereotype molds from which the musical selections were printed. Although he advertised his Chicago Electro-Stereotype Foundry and General Printing Establishment, specializing in "letter press printing and music work, job, Music & Book Stereotyping of every description," Mould's sheet music, like that of most other local publishers, was printed for many years by eastern houses.

The Apollo Music Store carried music from leading Boston and New York firms, and Eli A. Benson dealt at wholesale and retail in all kinds of musical merchandise, as well as sheet music. Benson's name disappeared from the local directory in 1854, perhaps because he moved to Tennessee when Charles D. Benson operated a music store and printed music for sale at his shop on Union Street, Nashville, in 1858. His name also appeared as the local distributor and secondary publisher of the "Prize Banner Polka," copyrighted in the federal district of Western Tennessee in 1861. That same music was sold by Eli A. Benson in Chicago between 1864 and 1866. Three years later, an Eli A. Benson was again in Tennessee, at 317 Main Street, Memphis.

The name B. K. Mould on covers of eastern sheet-music publications during the early 1850s marked him as a link in the national distribution chain. Robert G. Greene joined him in 1854 to form a new "wholesale and retail business in all kinds of musical merchandise." A number of the illustrious Greene family of Rhode Island, Greene was secretary of the Chicago Philharmonic Society, in which Mould had been active since the formation, in 1850, of the city's first concert orchestra, twenty-two German musicians under Carl Dyhrenfurth. Following a disastrous first season, the conductor worked with Mould to salvage the project by means of a number of concerts and public balls.

Mould & Greene occupied a three-story building on Lake Street, where the retail business was conducted on the first floor. The second served as a display room and warehouse for melodeons, and on the third a pianoforte showroom was decorated with engraved portraits of leading musicians and composers.

After having observed the music trade in action on a trip east in 1855, Greene declared that he, too, would print sheet music but use only local craftsmen. He initiated Chicago's first music magazine, the *Western Journal of Music,* an eighty-page biweekly that contained printed music as well as articles of criticism and on other matters pertaining to music. Greene also invested $10,000 in Chicago's first musical-instrument manufactory, a melodeon plant employing twenty workmen that produced 300 instruments in 1855, with sales of $25,000.

When Greene died, in 1857, not yet thirty, Mould had already quit the firm to open his own music store, and he stayed in business for several years, until he turned to the practice of accountancy. Before he left music, he did some business with a newcomer to Chicago who eventually became the Midwest's major piano and organ maker. When the nation plunged into financial ruin in 1857, William Wallace Kimball, a New Englander who had gone west in the early 1850s, closed an Iowa real estate and insurance business and moved to Chicago, which, like the rest of the country, was in the midst of a deep depression. A chance encounter with a Yankee piano salesman, who had four eastern-made square instruments to sell, led to a swap for some land Kimball owned in Iowa. Looking about for space to house his new wares, Kimball found Mould happy to lease room in his storehouse. There, Kimball started a piano rental business and, the following year opened a music store, out of which he sold and rented pianos until he began to manufacture his own, which in time made Chicago the country's second major center of musical-instrument making.

Chicago's first nationally prominent song surfaced in 1857, when the Higgins brothers, Adoniram Judson and Hiram Murray, published "Lorena," words by the Reverend H. D. L. Webster, music by Joseph P. Webster, who were not related. The Higginses had come from upper New York State. In the early 1850s, when Hiram was thirty, the brothers and two sisters traveled through Kentucky as a singing family group. Hiram had worked in that state for the past ten years as an itinerant singing master. His younger brother Adoniram had also taught music in Kentucky and in Ohio and had become known as one of the best. The brothers traveled to New York in 1854 to study with Lowell Mason and George Root, and then went to Chicago, where they opened their own business, publishing music written chiefly by members of the family.

J. P. Webster came to their store in the summer of 1856 and began to use the premises as a business office and mailing address—not uncommon in this time when publishers depended to a great extent on the custom of music teachers and did everything possible to maintain their friendship. Webster was self-taught on the violin and flute and had then studied with Mason and George Webb in Boston before going to New York. He found regular employment as a church soloist until an attack of bronchitis stopped that career. Moving around the Midwest, he ran into the Reverend H. D. L. Webster, who showed him the words for two songs, "Lorena" and "Willie's Gone." After setting them to music, he played both on his Stradivarius for the Higgines, who bought and immediately printed them. "Willie's Gone" was another in the spate of similarly named ballads appearing all over America—"Little Willie," "Poor Willie's Gone," "Poor Willie's All Alone," "Willie Lee"—all equally macabre and dealing with the death of their protagonist. Out of all the "Willie" songs, including some by Foster, the Webster-and-Webster concoction became the most famous.

Soon after his first appearance in Chicago, J. P. Webster was hired by the Higginses to edit their new monthly magazine and promotional paper *The Flower Queen*, named after the popular "little opera for young ladies" written by George Root and Fanny Crosby. Ten thousand copies of the first issue were distributed, all presumably to potential customers.

"Lorena" had become a national success by the late summer of 1857, and its popularity continued throughout the Civil War. Confederate music publishers issued their own editions of the melancholy words and music, which became inextricably bound to the Southern cause. The Reverend Webster had written the lyrics in memory of a long-lost love who had refused his offer of marriage.

Many popular songs flowed from J. P. Webster's violin during and after the Civil War, among them his second great success, in 1867, "In the Sweet By and By," written with a frequent collaborator, Sanford Fillmore Bennett. Throughout the war, Webster was under exclusive contract to the Higginses, but he also recruited and trained soldiers for service in the Union Army, from which his poor eyesight kept him.

When the hostilities ended, he returned to his family in Elkhart, Wisconsin, and opened a billiard parlor, attracting many young men who already knew and sang his songs. Bennett ran a nearby pharmacy, into which Webster went one day and was handed the lyrics for a new song. After he had picked out a melody on his Stradivarius, Webster returned to the pharmacy and, with some customers joining in, sang "In the Sweet By and By." It had intensive promotion by his new publisher, Lyon & Healy, as both a hymn and a popular song, which helped to establish its unusual fame.

After his death, in 1875, after years of serious depression, induced by the loss of his favorite violin in the 1871 Chicago fire, funeral mourners sang "In the Sweet By and By" and three bars of the melody were chiseled into Joseph Philbrick Webster's headstone.

Webster had resigned the editorship of *The Flower Queen* after only a few issues, to pursue a full-time songwriting career, and Chauncey Marvin Cady was hired to replace him. Cady had started in the business as a songwriter and was first published by Hall & Son, of New York. For a time, he worked as an associate editor of the *New York Musical Review*. The son of an upper New York State Congregationalist family, he had studied at Oberlin College for a year, was graduated from the University of Michigan, and then attended Union Theological Seminary, in New York. He first met his future publishing associate, George Root, at the seminary, where the educator was on the faculty and collaborating with the blind poet Fanny Crosby on *The Flower Queen*. Cady's temperance song "Cold Clear Water" had just been printed by Hall, and, as a reward for a prize-winning essay on music in America he was employed by the *New York Musical Review*.

In the summer of 1854, Cady, in the Midwest to take part in local music conventions, decided to try the music business in Chicago. Every publisher was on the lookout for visiting music educators—the trade's best customers—and the presence in the city of a New York editor, composer, and teacher was an event. The Higgins brothers offered him free use of their store and then the editorship of their magazine. His first move was to change its name to *Musical Review and Flower Queen*. Under his guidance, it became so important a voice among Midwestern music buyers and teachers that Oliver Ditson bought it in 1858. At that point, Cady resigned to devote his time to purely musical matters.

The growth of the Higgins brothers' business had necessitated a move into a remodeled four-story building on Lake Street, but in the midst of their success they severed their relationship, in early 1859. H. M. Higgins carried on in the Lake Street store with a stock he proclaimed to be "the largest and most complete in the Northwest," and a catalogue of his own sheet music, "now the finest of any publisher in the United States to which I am constantly adding from the best composers in the Eastern and Western states." For a short time his brother A. J. sold music and occasionally wrote some popular material, but he soon devoted himself exclusively to the practice of medicine.

As Chicago's oldest continuous music publisher, Hiram Higgins prospered, many of his most successful songs coming from Webster's Stradivarius. He was rivaled during the 1860s only by Root & Cady, formed in 1859 by Chauncey Cady and Ebenezer Root, with wartime hit songs by George F. Root and Henry Clay Work, which dominated contemporary popular music. In 1867, Higgins sold off the song business to J. L. Peters, of New York and St. Louis, but continued the musical-instrument trade and published the *Musical Review*. These interests were finally turned over to the Demotte Brothers, who in turn sold them to Peters. When friends became increasingly concerned over Higgins's interest in the occult, he moved to San Diego, where he was reported to be experimenting with seedless lemons at the time of his death in 1879.

The business of popular music moved ever westward, expanding with the local economy and the standard of living, following the printing press and the stage. Detroit, however, founded as early as 1701, did not have any semblance of a music business until 1844. That year, Adam Couse, a dancing teacher from Pittsburgh, where he evidently knew Stephen Foster's family, opened a music store. Ten years later, he carried a stock of 12,000 pieces of music, among it a small catalogue of copyrighted material written by local people and music for dancing. In 1850, Stephen Foster dedicated his ballad "The Voice of Days Gone By" to Couse. It was published by Firth, Pond, as was a single piece of Couse's instrumental music. In 1854, his clerks Dwight Amsden and Henry Hawley, the latter leader of a local orchestra, took over the store, and Couse dealt exclusively in pianos.

In that year, Detroit's most important mid-nineteenth-century music store was opened by two German musicians, Charles F. Stein and and William Buckheister. Until the war, when Stein went back to Germany, their Boston Music Store also printed a number of songs and instrumental pieces. Songwriter and publisher J. J. Whittemore opened a Detroit music store in 1857, and achieved considerable fame, not only for his songs written during the Civil War, but also for his flamboyant advertising of them.

The earliest significant music publishing in San Francisco began in 1851, when Joseph F. Atwill moved there from New York. He remained active in the trade until after the war. In 1852, he published the first known locally engraved and printed sheet music, "The California Pioneers," whose cover, depicting two buckskin-garbed settlers, has become a highly prized collector's item. Atwill also printed California editions of his earlier copyrights, many of the "Negro Melodies" he had put out in New York during the heyday of blackface music printing.

Mathias Gray's San Francisco publishing and music store, established in 1859, became sufficiently important as a western distributor and publisher for it to be absorbed by Ditson in 1889.

The Board of Music Trade

On January 1, 1855, Hall & Son, of New York threw a bombshell into the printed-music business with the announcement that the firm was cutting in half the price of all noncopyrighted foreign sheet music and books, but was maintaining the price of its copyrighted American works. Music publishers had long taken advantage of the American copyright law and pirated unprotected European works of all sorts. Sheet music of works for the piano by Mendelssohn, Schubert, Beethoven, Chopin, Liszt, Thalberg, and others, sold for higher prices than similar American music, as did pieces by Englishmen living in America. This discrepancy was based on the generally accepted music-business theory that these compositions were inherently superior to native works. For that reason, as well as the ready free accessibility provided by a chauvinistic federal law, the proportion of foreign to American published music had been as high as ten to one for a time and had changed little through ensuing decades.

The Copyright Bureau, housed in the Department of State, where printed music was required to be deposited in order to receive protection, maintained a collection of every work received. It filled 120 thick bound volumes by 1854— sixty of songs and sixty of instrumental music. Each of these held an average of 250 pages, some 30,000 in all, representing most of the music deposited for copyright since 1819. The British sack of Washington and the fires set during that attack in 1814 had destroyed most previously deposited music, and little care was taken of registrations while government offices were being rebuilt. None of the foreign music that was published in America was ever offered for copyright, and many publishers did not pay the necessary fees to register popular music, even though most of them printed a notice of copyright.

On the basis of the Copyright Bureau's collection, as well as bibliographical deduction, D. W. Krummel has made the following estimates of production, supplementing the 10,000 publications, copyrighted and not, collated by Richard Wolfe:

1826–30	600 titles a year
1831–35	900 "

1836–40	1,200	"
1841–45	1,600	"
1846–50	3,000	"
1851–54	5,000	"

These number some 57,000 up to the time Hall & Son made its announcement. Copyrighted music could be printed only by the owner or his assigns, whereas noncopyrighted foreign music, most in demand, was generally issued by many publishers. As a result, a backlog of unsold foreign music filled the shelves of music dealers around the country. The major publishers were not affected to any great extent, owing to the over-the-counter and mail-order business they did with music teachers and educators who bought three quarters of all such music for resale to their pupils. The teachers did enforce a 50 percent discount on all sales, which cut into profits substantially.

The *Washington Globe* of November 11, 1854, which carried an account of the government's copyrighted music collection, commented that the 120 volumes afford "material for interesting reflections of a national character, as touching this department of industry and the fine arts, and the genius in musical composition and artistical and mechanical execution thereof evinced."

The increase in the number of songs entered for copyright during the early 1850s was due in no small part to the sudden growth in sales of popular sheet music. Foster's "Old Folks at Home" and George Root's Wurzel songs, for example sold several hundred thousand copies. Consequently, it was more necessary for a publisher to protect his property against piracy by federal copyright. This is evident by the increased number of songs registered.

The *New York Times,* closely connected with the world's largest book-publishing firm, Harper, which had become an active supporter of mutual international copyright protection, supported Hall & Son's price reduction. "The great revolution in the music trade," an editorial said, ". . . is destined to have a very important bearing on the musical taste in America. We have wondered that so high prices should be charged for music where nothing is paid for a copyright, and the expense was only for engraving, printing and paper."

Yet the economics of the music trade had changed dramatically in the years since James Harrison opened for business on Maiden Lane in 1793. There had been not only increased competition and a rising cost of living, but also major advances in printing and distribution technology, in promotion and merchandising. All costs had gone up, but a song could still be bought for between twenty-five and fifty cents, depending on the number of pages and the lithographed illustration. The basic cost for a printed page of music was about two and a half cents, if done by outside printers, less if a publisher owned his own press. A title page cost from five dollars up, depending on its complexity and the use of colors. The songwriters who sold best demanded royalties of about 10 percent—two to three cents a copy after initial expenses were recouped. As the business took on an interstate nature, extending to the West Coast, the cost of distribution rose. In addition, the half-price discount music teachers enjoyed reduced profits further, as did the cost of advertising in the music press, a factor unknown in the days when several inches of type in the local press served and customers were attracted by the display of new material in store windows.

The music business gladly cooperated with printed reviews in the trade papers in which they advertised, expecting and receiving this important promotion. The *New York Musical Review,* for example, regularly reviewed new publications submitted by advertisers in a column, "New Music Reviews." Management policy was stated over the judgments:

> Our friends are hereby informed that all music sent us is more carefully and conscientiously examined, and such only as is considered worthy of recommendation is mentioned. Dealers can therefore use our NEW MUSIC REVIEWS as a guide in selecting their stock of Sheet-music; and we think that purchasers who rely with confidence upon our recommendations, and are governed thereby in their purchases, will be saved much trouble and disappointment.

In the next several years, the major publishers effected an end to the power of the music periodicals, which were read not only by the trade but by the music-buying public as well, either by buying them out, as did Oliver Ditson when he took over Dwight's *Journal,* or by printing their own for sale to the public.

The growth of the postal service, which carried the musical press to subscribers and advertisers, had extended the lines of distribution of printed music to dealers and music teachers all around the country. During the fifteen years immediately preceding the Civil War, westward expansion forced an increase from a total of 144,000 miles of steamboat, coach, and railroad routes in 1845 to nearly 250,000 miles in 1860. The seventy-five post offices serving Americans in 1789 had grown to about 14,000 in 1845 and 28,500 in 1860. Only because the government effectively subsidized this service could Ditson offer to fill any music order at one cent per ounce under 3,000 miles and double that beyond.

Ditson mailed packages to sheet and music-book buyers and to dealers as far away as the Pacific coast; they arrived in less than a month. All California mail went by ship to Panama, then by the Panama Railroad to the Pacific and by ship to San Francisco and other coast ports.

Only Horace Waters and Schuberth & Co., both of New York, joined Hall in reducing the price of noncopyrighted foreign music. They were seeking to attain several objectives by this action. Any piece of foreign music for which a sizable market developed was quickly duplicated by other musicians, its new publishers finding it cheaper to reengrave than to purchase it from the original publisher, and then, in the ensuing competition, offering it at trade discounts of as much as 40 percent in addition to the usual 50 percent trade discount. Consequently, the major publishers were losing customers to the cut-rate houses, all of whom were beyond control.

There had been an earlier effort to regulate the business by the formation of a Board of Music Trade, to which Hall alluded in an open letter to the New York press. The board intended to establish its own controls over publication price and sale of noncopyrighted and all printed music. The members wanted no interference by Hall, considered a New York maverick. Consequently, they were obliged to ostracize him and bound themselves, under heavy penalty, not to sell any music to him or supply anyone who dealt with him or retailers who were also offering half-price reductions. The fact that Hall was willing to print the reduced price on his sheet music, using established currency rather than the fractioned shillings, still in use, that confused many buyers, added further annoyance.

Echoing the board's disapproval, John Sullivan Dwight clouded the issue by writing that Hall had reduced the price only of foreign music, which the publisher quickly denied. The *Journal*'s editor took the high road on behalf on "good" music, maintaining that it should be made accessible as cheaply as possible. If publishers and dealers can get only half price for it, "will they not soon cease reprinting such, and confine their operations to the more paying task of issuing only copyright pieces? "But, he continued, what kind of music does that mean? It would be "the most superficial, trashy stuff that is in vogue: the negro melodies, the namby-pamby sentimental ballads, the flashy fantasias, polkas, waltzes, marches, etc., of native Americans, or tenth-rate resident German manufacture. What absurdity to pay five cents per page for Wallace, Strakosch, Hutchinsons, or Woodbury, and only two-and-one-half for the Sonatas of Beethoven!''

Despite the board's boycott, within a month Hall & Son boasted to a New York music paper that business was booming and sales of price-cut copyright music "ranged from $200 to $500 a day.'' As the Stationers' Company had done with its rebels in Queen Elizabeth's time, and the music business would do in the future, they made peace with the man who threatened their profits, and William Hall was taken into their councils in May 1855.

Hall thereafter had the privilege of announcing to the New York press the board's decisions: all noncopyrighted music would now be sold at a 20 percent reduction from the old prices; all music being offered at reduced prices in the future would not carry that information, instead being marked with an asterisk; and the decimal monetary system would be used industry-wide.

The last point was another result of Hall's rebellion. He had earlier suggested that the music industry adopt a coinage system based on the Spanish milled dollar first proposed in 1785 by Jefferson and enacted by Congress a few years later. The failure of the new system to achieve national usage brought about a growing state of chaos in American currency. An Illinois banknote could not be used in New England. In going to Boston from New York, or vice versa, one had to change money into that of the new location. A banknote of either city would be closely scrutinized in the other and then accepted only at a discount. In many cities there were no such things as dimes and nickels. New England's smallest silver coins were nine pence (twelve and a half cents) and four pence half penny (six and a quarter cents). In New York these coins were called "shilling" and "six pence." The price of sheet music varied in different states, creating many accounting problems for the music business.

New York's gaslighted luxury hotel the Astor House, where such radical departures from standard practice as individual room keys and free soap were found, was the scene of a sumptuous banquet following the meeting of the music merchants in July 1855. General Hall was chosen chairman of the dinner as a symbol of the unity of twenty-seven representatives of major publishers, who constituted themselves as the Board of Trade of the Music Publishers of the United States.

Publishers who wished to join the board were required to own a stock of more than 1,000 engraved music plates, to subscribe to never-revealed articles of agreement, and to be unanimously approved by members. The initiation fee was twenty-five dollars. The trust-busters of the current century would have had a field day with this combination, created to restrain trade, fix prices, lock out competition, and engage in other practices agreed upon behind closed doors.

The *New York Musical Review* reported after the initial meeting that most prices would now be indicated in decimals, clearing up the interstate currency differences; that songs selling for less than twenty-five cents would bear no price, so that the retailer could fix his own; and that all members would mark prices with a figure inside a star. Most important, no member would reprint a noncopyrighted or foreign piece that had already been issued by another member. This left the now price-fixed catalogue of "good" European music to major publishers, ending the cutthroat competition in reprinting such works.

At the second annual meeting, held in Boston, Oliver Ditson was elected president, succeeding George Root. Leaks to the press, which had been barred from the meetings, reported "a very satisfactory state of affairs growing out of last year's organization. The uniform plan of conducting business is universally approved . . . there is a peculiarity in the business of sheet music which makes some general regulations to govern it absolutely necessary. . . . All seemed satisfied."

Most affected by the "general regulations" to govern the business were those music teachers, many of them isolated from the large cities, who were accustomed to rely on profits from discounted music they sold to pupils. The traditional 50 percent discount was no longer available in dealing with the important publishers. The formalized "courtesy of the trade," alloting foreign-music copyrights to a handful of houses, cut deeply into the teachers' income. Competing editions were a thing of the past. Music publishers now argued that it was no longer the music teacher who chose the piano pieces they wished their pupils to learn, but, rather, the young ladies who used their services.

A group of teachers, predominantly German, headed by Paul Schmidt, of Lexington, Kentucky, planned the formation in late 1857 of the National Association of Music Teachers to fight the board's regulations. A multipointed program was announced, calling for a new code of ethics, a national price scale for music lessons, creation of a pension fund for "superannuated teachers" and their widows and orphans, creation of musical festivals and concerts, and "personal agreements and more harmonious action amongst members."

More to the point was a proposal to establish a general publishing house that would reprint noncopyrighted music, to be sold at dramatically reduced wholesale prices, and publish new music by members who would withhold their compositions from board members. A committee of publication would supervise the selection of new music as well as the works that would be reprinted. The association would also engage in preparation of official instruction books.

There can be little doubt that such an organization, supported by all music teachers, with its own publishing company and a national resolve to use only its own publications, would have been a major threat to publishers. However, even as Schmidt and his colleages announced their plans, the effects of the country's most serious economic depression thus far were beginning to be felt across the land, and this grass-roots group died aborning.

Music teachers were faced with far more immediate threats to their livelihoods than the trade's refusal to grant them a discount on sheet music and teaching books. Their purpose at last became a partial reality in 1876, with formation of the Music Teachers National Association.

Most Board of Music Trade members weathered the dire economic state far better than the teachers. In 1858, Oliver Ditson purchased the *Journal of Music,* retaining its founder, John Dwight, as editor and chief advocate for the Ditson interests, which usually coincided with those of the board. Ditson's Boston headquarters moved to a new building, where twelve music presses were kept at work pouring out sheet music as well as custom printing, with which he expected to remove any vestige of the teachers' association publishing plans. As an example, by paying approximately fifty dollars, a music teacher could receive one hundred copies of an eight-page instrumental work of his own composition or, indeed, any music, sell each for one dollar to his pupils, and realize a profit of 100 percent. To amateur songwriters who intended to engage in the vanity printing that had been a trade practice since the early 1800s, Ditson pointed out that so much new music was being offered for sale that success was limited unless the work was "particularly striking or original in its character." Only one out of ten new songs paid back its initial costs, and only one in fifty had any measure of success.

One of the matters dealt with at the board's June 1859 meeting, held in Baltimore, involved the Southern dealer P. F. Werlein, who had applied for affiliation but neglected to send in his proof of eligibility on time. W. C. Peters was elected president, and some new members were in attendance, among them a Canadian, A. S. Nordheimer. His presence may be explained as a result of the loss of Thomas Boosey's suit in England, which eventually made it possible for an American to obtain British copyright by publication in Canada. As that nation's most important piano dealer and manufacturer and Canada's oldest and leading music man, Nordheimer played an important role as collaborator with Americans who wished to secure international protection.

The board's constituency had changed little from that of the first meeting, and Dwight reported that the entente cordiale between members remained unimpaired, that all enjoyed sumptuous meals, "the feast of reason and the flow of soul." A highlight was the concert by Charles Grobe, an eminent and profitable composer of fantasias, variations on the day's best-selling popular songs and instrumental pieces. A native of Germany, Grobe was in the United States prior to 1840 and then taught for many years at the Wilmington, Delaware, Wesleyan Female Seminary, where he composed hugely successful piano variations crafted for the average competent female parlor pianist. Shortly before the meeting, Grobe's Opus 1000 had been brought out. He was a music publisher's delight.

Hall's son, "Prince" James, was elected president at the 1860 meeting, held in New York, where Werlein was admitted to membership, which lasted less than a year, owing to the war; he was the only Southern publisher ever admitted to the board. The group's meetings had taken on the atmosphere of a trade market, it was reported, the business transacted between sessions amounting to $2,000 to $3,000 from the leasing and sale of copyrights, plates, and other special deals.

The Other Music-Publishing Business

The nationwide industry of contemporary counterparts of those early English broadside-ballad printers who were barred from admission to the Stationers' Company and denied possession of a royal patent, and made their income from publishing the darling songs of the common people, was never represented on the Board of Music Trade. However, because a national market for printed words of popular songs did flourish, the members of the board saw another source of income in reprint rights to their song words. Customers were that majority of people who did not own, and could not afford to buy, the musical instruments that adorned the parlors of the genteel middle and upper classes.

This vast market learned the melodies of the day's hit songs by hearing them sung in saloons and cheap theaters, whistled on the streets, or ground out by hand organs. Occasionally, printers of the words used engraved illustrations and sold their wares wholesale to dealers and retail to bookstores, stationery shops, and street peddlers. The cheapest collections of words sold for a penny retail, and were usually manufactured in New York, Boston, or Philadelphia, the nation's printing centers. The people who bought them formed the major market for popular music, but they did not make any real contribution to the music trade's income. Usually printers did not pay for the right to reprint song words, but in time some did get permission.

A similar craze for printed song words existed in Queen Victoria's Britain, but there the taste was more for the traditional news ballad, particularly gory ditties inspired by bloody murders and crimes of passion. A ballad appearing immediately after the execution of a mass murderer sold two and a half million copies in a single year.

Because it was older and more formalized, the British street-ballad trade was more businesslike than the American, to the point of providing sales figures, statistics against which to measure the American trade. Ballads on quarter sheets cost one shilling a gross wholesale, and sold for a British penny each. Half sheets were two shillings, and whole, or broadsheets, three shillings fourpence on the day of publication. Once initial demand was satisfied, the prices were reduced to five shillings sixpence for a ream of forty dozen copies.

There are no comparable figures for American song sheets, slip ballads, and broadsides of the Civil War period, but the trade had grown since the late

1840s, and during the war millions of copies were printed. Unlike the British, Americans preferred to have the words to old songs and new popular music introduced to them by the most celebrated vocalists or sidewalk musicians. Printers advertised that their stocks contained all the "new and popular senti-mental, comic, Ethiopian, national and naval songs." These seemed to be everywhere in large cities, not only in stores but also "upon fences and rails, wherever you go, you'll see the penny ballads sticking up in a row," as Ste-phen Foster wrote in his "Song of All Songs" (1863). The five verses told a story made up of song titles, linked by verbs, and concluded with a call for victory "from Maine to Oregon!"

The pocket-songster trade became a truly national business in the 1850s. Started when Benjamin Franklin printed a ninety-four-page compilation, *The Constitution of the Free-Masons,* in 1734, containing five songs, American presses had regularly turned out inexpensive collections of "wit, wisdom, and song words," bound into about two-by-three-inch paperbacks. During the War of 1812 dozens of songsters of this size and slightly larger were printed in Philadelphia, New York, Boston, Baltimore, and in smaller communities. Wa-gon trains, canal boats, steam riverboats, and railroads carried the cheap books west as the country grew. Clarke & Appleton, Printers, of San Francisco, is-sued a forty-page descriptive catalogue in 1861 of "song books, dream, astrol-ogy & cookery books, novels, Toy Books, &c." The firm also carried a line of cloth-bound books, each containing "over 1,000 songs," words only, at prices ranging from a dollar to two fifty.

The New York mass printer Leavitt & Allen was typical of the eastern com-panies that distributed songbooks nationally. An important change in the me-chanical reproduction of type, the steam-driven "Lightning Press," had made mass distribution of the inexpensive songbooks possible. Devised by Richard Hoe in 1846, this rotary or cylinder press had a revolving printing surface onto which curved type forms were locked. One revolution printed multiple sheets, surpassing the output of the best old flatbed presses by 400 percent an hour. By 1860, almost all sheet music and songbooks were printed by the stereotype process, ideally suited to the cylinder press.

Using the new machinery, Leavitt & Allen, the Beadle brothers, and many others catered to the new market for songbooks and "dime novels." The latter, inexpensive paperbacks, received the name from the Beadles' first novels, which did indeed sell for ten cents, though after the war and through their heyday in the 1880s the cheap books could be purchased for five cents.

The Beadle brothers—master stereotyper Erastus, printer James, and book-binder Irwin—joined in business after a series of disastrous individual publish-ing and real estate ventures. Irwin sold off a failing New York magazine in 1859, and used his capital to print by the stereotype process the first *Beadle's Dime Song Book,* whose profits funded additional successful paperbacks, *The Dime Recipe Book, Dime Dialogues, the Dime Cook Book,* and others in the Dime series. On June 7, 1860, the brothers' new joint venture issued the first of a profitable series of "books for the million . . . a dollar book for a dime! 128 pages complete!" The first Beadle novel, *Waleska, the Indian Wife of a*

White Hunter, reportedly sold half a million copies, far in excess of the Dime line's usual sales of 50,000 to 100,000. The enthusiasm of Northern soldiers as well as their Confederate opponents, who found Beadle books among the belongings of military prisoners, created a mass market for pocket-fitting novels and other Dime collections, including lyrics to popular songs. Unlike most trade-book publishers, the cheap-book printers flourished during the war, the "most singing" conflict in which the nation ever engaged.

The mail-order firm of Dick & Fitzgerald, of New York, was a business giant equal to the Beadles'; it had been in the ten-cent paperback trade since 1851. William Brisbane Dick and Lawrence F. Fitzgerald had come to New York from Philadelphia in 1844 as young apprentices to a bookselling firm housed under P. T. Barnum's American Museum, on Broadway. Seven years later, they bought the business from their employer and began a partnership located on Ann Street, in the center of the cheap-book trade. They were among the first to print copyrighted lyrics with proper credit to the owners. For example, in *George Christy's Essence of Old Kentucky* a notice appears at the head of the words to "No One to Love": "Published by permission of Messrs. LEE AND WALKER, Philadelphia, owners of the copyright, and publishers of the music, with pianoforte accompaniments." By 1870, this type of acknowledgment of permission to use, for which a few dollars were paid, was commonplace.

Neither Dick & Fitzgerald, nor the Beadles, nor any of the cheap-book publishers of song words was ever considered worthy of admission to the Board of Music Trade. The fact is, however, that these huckstering book manufacturers provided the great masses of untrained poor and lower-middle-class musical Americans with more awareness of the popular music of their time than all the music-merchant members of the board.

CHAPTER 4

American Musical
Theater 1800–1860

In Search of a National Popular Music

"Democracy is too new a comer upon the earth to have been able yet to organize its pleasures and amusements," a visiting young French economist wrote in 1833. "In Europe our pleasures are essentially exclusive, they are aristocratic like Europe itself. In that matter, then, as in politics, the American democracy has yet to create anything fresh."

The British clergyman-satirist Sydney Smith had been even less kind in his 1820 attack on American culture and those who shaped it:

> During the thirty or forty years of their independence they have done nothing for the Sciences, for the Arts, for Literature, or even for the statesman-like studies of Politics or Political Economy. . . . In the four quarters of the globe, who reads an American book? or goes to an American play? or looks at an American picture or statue? . . . Finally, under which of the tyrannical governments of Europe is every sixth man a Slave, whom his fellow creatures may buy and sell and torture? When these questions are fairly and favourably answered, their laudatory epithets may be allowed."

America did indeed look to Europe for its culture when the Reverend Smith spoke. Although the colonies were more than two centuries old, no significant musical work of cultural worth created by an American had yet been duly recognized, either abroad or at home. Both the man hailed in 1780 as "a rival to Handel," William Billings, and his peculiarly American popular religious songs had been virtually eradicated within four decades from the church hymnody they had enriched. Ninety percent of the 10,000 printed sheets of popular music produced before 1825 were the work of foreigners. That astounding international success "Home, Sweet Home," words by John Howard Payne, did not bear his name on the sheet music. The first internationally popular ballad written by an American-born songwriter and issued by an American-born publisher, John Hill Hewitt's "The Minstrel's Return'd from the War," was believed by Europeans to have come from the pen of Sir Walter Scott.

Royall Tyler's *The Contrast,* the first American comedy, was never staged in England, nor were the plays of American William Dunlap, even his *André,* a sympathetic portrait of that ill-fated amateur secret agent. The British continued to see Americans as "Jonathan Yank," descended from the Yankee Doodle who, unbelievably, had won a revolution but had no connection to the British Puritan and Cavalier colonists who had sailed for the New World. Practically all patrician Americans shared that haughty assumption.

Several factors led to the financial bankruptcy of William Dunlap's New York theater in 1805. His high-flown original tragedies and tedious translations of that "European Shakespeare," Kotzebue, who dulled the international stage, brought in ticket buyers only when augmented by music Dunlap considered "foolish"—countless variations on "Yankee Doodle" and other popular tunes of the day. Although clearly the leading creative force in the American theater, Dunlap, too, relied on low comedians, who took from life around them and caricatured the "average" American. Dunlap did not perceive that Americans came to the theater for a romantic view of themselves in familiar situations. A similar misjudgment by Boston and Philadelphia theater managers, coupled with the serious effects of early-nineteenth-century economic depressions, kept the national stage in constant crisis.

The regular advent of the dreaded yellow jack and malaria, making their way from the West Indies, made most people reluctant to gather in large numbers. Winters were dreadful, with temperatures often far below zero, and torrid summers encouraged the spread of pestilence in crowded, garbage-laden streets. A mass burial of the sixty-one patrons who had died in the Richmond Theatre conflagration in 1811 shocked the nation, and added another fear that kept audiences away. Moreover, clergymen and lay intellectuals alike viewed the dubious character of city audiences as sufficient reason for reform.

The major theaters along a circuit connecting Boston, New York, Philadelphia, Annapolis, Baltimore, and Washington slowly began to fill the gaps between depressions and outbreaks of disease. The London stage, to which American producers looked for new acting blood, new plays, and new musical materials, had found itself catering to the offspring of the Industrial Revolution, who, as soon as they had discovered such entertainment, insisted on grand action spectacles appealing to the senses rather than the intellect. Immense new playhouses seating thousands were built in the largest cities. The required broad acting style, out of place in America's smaller theaters, necessitated similar large new edifices in America in which to present equally grandiose productions involving pageantry and spectacle.

Popular music provided the major ingredient of every such presentation, alongside comic operas and farces. It also made up the chief repertory of performers who appeared between the acts or the variety entertainment that served to distract restive audiences during long evenings, which often lasted from past six until midnight.

David Grimsted wrote, in *Melodrama Unveiled:* "In the nineteenth century music was generally used to underline the emotional feelings at high points during a performance. Many plays were printed with musical cues telling where and what kind of music should be inserted and their climactic tableaux commonly gained effectiveness from the music or songs that accompanied them.''

As had been true in England, where, once royal charters precluded all but two licensed houses from offering all-spoken drama, early-nineteenth-century American audiences had a full evening. At the start of the bill was the full-length drama and at its end a short comic opera or farce, which, with its popular music, served to provide an economic base for the pre-1825 music business. Between the two was an omnium gatherum of songs, dancing, and vajriety entertainment, accompanied increasingly by a theater orchestra, made up of immigrant musicians trained in Europe, who brought their music with them.

American audiences' demand for new things to see and hear, most vociferously expressed by the galleries, compelled managers to make a place on their programs for animal acts, acrobatic performers, horse riders, clowns, eccentric dancers, and vocalists. As the century progressed, the dramatic theater shared its stage with ever more exotic variety acts and opening melodramas. The latter included the plays of Shakespeare in new happy-ending adaptations, though often played to the popular music written for them during the eighteenth century; works by Sheridan, Goldsmith, Ottway, and others; William Dunlap's translations of European hits; and Covent Garden and Drury Lane pantomimed adaptations of old fairy tales. Music was a major component of this theater. Every acting company, whether housed permanently in a major city or a touring group, had its own orchestra of about fifteen musicians, singers, dancers, and instrumental soloists.

There was a certain merit to the continued elitist complaint, added to by the clergy, about the character of the American audience throughout the first half of the century. As children of a revolution and ardent devourers of the fruit of that triumph, audiences brought along their political articles of faith. Demanding the strains of ''Yankee Doodle'' and shouting their desires and judgments, they tyrannized actors and musicians, until a bloody New York riot in 1850 butchered twenty-two of them, signaling the splintering of national entertainment into a number of separate forms. In the years preceding this event, however, the voice of the people, in a mixture of idolatry and violence, was responsible for the distinctly national social components of the American stage and insured their survival.

The repertoire continued mainly to be British plays performed and sung by British actors. Anti-English sentiment waxed beyond past proportions as, before and during the War of 1812, the Royal Navy continued to search American merchant shipping and thus to make audiences ever more hostile to foreign actors. The shrewdest managers catered to nationalistic sentiment. Advertising directed at the rising tide of confidence that began to expand with each American victory drew houses full of patriots who thrilled to war songs and war plays. It was in this hothouse atmosphere that the ''Star-Spangled Banner'' was first heard.

Yankee Doodle on the Stage

The years-long contention between the United States and the Barbary pirates over freedom of the seas first gave playwrights and songwriters, beginning with Susannah Rowson, in *Slaves in Algeria* (1794), the inspiration that attracted Americans looking to see themselves as extraordinary and triumphant. Before his career as mayor of Philadelphia and controller of the Treasury, James Nelson Barker wrote for the country's most important company, the New Chestnut Street actors. His usual collaborator was an English actor and musician, John Bray, who had succeeded Alexander Reinagle as musical director and house composer. In *Tears and Smiles* (1807), Barker and Bray made an effort to restore recognized American types on the order of Royall Tyler's stage Yankee. The broadly comic role they created for the popular British actor Joseph Jefferson kept audiences returning. When the play was presented in London two years later, it cemented a British perception of Yankees as low-comedy country bumpkins.

Although it was neither performed nor printed prior to 1815, David Humphreys's *The Yanky in England* proved also to be extremely influential in forging the stage Yankee Doodle. Upon graduation from Yale, Humphreys had served as aide-de-camp to General Washington during the Revolution. He was sent to Paris in 1784 as Franklin's confidential secretary and proved to possess outstanding qualities that made him an effective espionage agent as well. In 1794, John Adams appointed him ambassador to Spain, when it appeared that France was going to export its bloody revolution to its neighbor, but the narrow anti-populist leanings Humphreys expressed forced his recall by Jefferson in 1801. He returned with the small flock of Merino sheep that started New England's wool industry, out of which he became an extremely wealthy man.

Humphreys was a prolific versifier and a leading member of the Hartford Wits—mostly Yale men whose conservative Calvinist notions, reaching back to the Mathers, and staunchly capitalistic view of the common man stirred up New England's antagonism to Jeffersonian democracy. Before his diplomatic and mercantile career, Humphreys had written for the theater, and he continued to work in that idiom while abroad. His *Yanky in England,* the first play to put such an American in a British locale, was pulled out of Humphreys's yellowing and unpublished manuscripts in 1815 for performance by an amateur group of Humphreysville, Connecticut, actors and was printed in conjunction with that production. Although the play never received a professional performance, it made its way to England, where the playscript and the accompanying ten-page glossary of "perculiar idiom and pronunciation" served as the basis for an operatic farce, *Jonathan Doubikins or Jonathan in England.* It was written expressly for the comic actor Charles Matthews, whose "entertainments of satiric impressions and imitations" had made him a British theater idol.

In spite of his rarely concealed distaste for lower-class Americans, Humphreys painted a portrait of Yankee Doodle that mixed admiration with disdain, and Matthews's success in the part created the stereotype from which most characterizations of Americans were drawn. Not only in Britain but later in

America, playwrights and performers continued to view Yankee Doodle as, one wrote, "credulous, from inexperience and want of knowledge of the world; believing himself to be perfectly acquainted with whatever he partially knows; tenacious of prejudices; docile, when rightly managed; when otherwise treated, independent to obstinacy; easily betrayed into ridiculous mistakes; incapable of being overawed by external circumstances."

Other than Joseph Hutton's 1815 *Fashionable Follies,* first performed in Philadelphia and quickly forgotten, no major play about Americans by an American appeared for most of the following decade. Native dramatists appeared to have found little inspiration in the country around them. A typical theater work of the period was Barker and Bray's *The Indian Princess,* written in 1808, and available on a modern recording. A three-act "operatic melodrama," it was based on the Captain John Smith–Pocahontas legend. George Blake published the songs and incidental music in a forty-two-page original-score edition that appeared immediately after its first performance. The music has been characterized by H. Wiley Hitchcock as "vaguely early-Beethoven," although Bray's experiment with syncopation provides a glimpse into the future.

The Indian Princess's first American performance was canceled to make way for presentations saluting an American military victory. By the time of war with Britain, theaters in New York, Philadelphia, and Boston were regularly exhibiting masterly illuminated transparencies that celebrated recent victories or events of similar significance. These presentations, with appropriate music and songs, were a sort of stage version of television's newscasts, bringing the scene of action to the spectators.

Yankee Chronology was a ballad initially sung at such an occasion in 1812, the celebration of the birthday of independence. It was written by William Dunlap, but soon became so long from the addition of new verses that the dramatist made it into a one-act playlet with singing dialogue. It chronologically detailed American history from colonization and showed each subsequent feat on land and sea. It continued to serve as a theater staple for years.

The patriotic songs used in the Philadelphia theater to stir up national pride were collected by a local printer and bookseller, William McCulloch, in the *American Patriotic Song Book,* a compilation of "political, descriptive and humorous songs of national character and productions of American poets only." This first pocket songster to be inspired by the music of a national war contained more than two dozen lyrics, music printed from type, and nine war songs for which appropriate music was indicated. Among these was the ever-present "To Anacreon in Heaven."

Dozens of verses set to the tune had been published and countless hundreds of parodies set to its music printed in the United States, among them "Adams and Liberty" in 1798, one of the nation's first native hit songs. Every would-be songwriter produced at least one set of lyrics to that English drinking song. These included the young Baltimore lawyer Francis Scott Key, who wrote the longest-lived, "The Star-Spangled Banner."

The September 20, 1814, issue of the *Baltimore Patriot* had carried an account of the British bombardment of the city's defenses at Fort McHenry six weeks earlier, when Key wrote his words. The verses were then circulated through the city in a typical broadside, with no credit to Key, and *Patriot* gave a version of the writing of this "beautiful and animated effusion which is destined to outlast the occasion and outlive the impulse which produced it."

Key, a young attorney who was also a volunteer Light Artillery officer and had President Madison's permission to seek the release of a friend captured by the British, was the unnamed gentleman whose song the paper praised so fulsomely. Baltimore's other paper, the *American,* took up the story and suggested that Key's verses be sung to the "Anacreontic Song," as the author had intended. Key was familiar with the tune; he had already used it to honor Stephen Decatur for his actions against the Barbary pirates in 1805, a set of verses in which the phrase "star-spangled banner" was first used.

It is believed that the volunteer soldier Ferdinand Durang, of the famous acting family, first sang the words and proper music in a tavern next to Baltimore's Holiday Square Theatre, standing on a chair to do so, and was joined in the refrain by merrymakers assembled to celebrate the British defeat. The public premiere took place October 19 when the actor, Mr. Hardinge, sang it during the presentation of an illuminated transparency of a "grand scene representing the two fleets"—probably stock scenery. Out of this developed an ambitious piece of stage business, *The Bombardment of Baltimore,* "a new military, patriotic naval entertainment," with Key's song performed throughout the northern theater circuit.

Writers of the patriotic songs offered on playhouse stages to celebrate American victories were seldom pure amateurs like Key, but were, instead, professional scriveners earning a living by hackwork, as had their British Grub Street and pothouse poet predecessors, men out of whose ranks came the earliest popular songwriters. One of them was Samuel Woodworth, whose name has been forgotten for more than a century and his best-known work, "The Old Oaken Bucket," for almost as long. Poet, lyricist, playwright, and journalist, Woodworth had been born in 1784 in Scituate, Massachusetts, son of a Revolutionary War Soldier and the descendant of a 1640 freeman of the town. The family was poor, and Samuel's schooling meager. At sixteen, he apprenticed himself, as a printer, to Boston bookseller and publisher Benjamin Russell, owner of the strongly pro-Federalist *Columbian Centinel.* Russell had learned to set type in Isaiah Thomas's Boston shop, and was recognized as a newspaperman who aimed for excellence in news writing. Under his tutelage, young Woodworth developed his writing skills and contributed verse to the *Centinel* and other local papers. During 1805–06 he edited *The Fly,* a magazine for young people, with John Howard Payne. After he completed his contract with Russell, he established several papers in Connecticut and Maryland, and then took up residence in New York City, where he married in 1810.

Woodworth supplemented his small income by writing both verse and prose for magazines and newspapers. A devout Swedenborgian, he founded a magazine devoted to the teachings of that engineer–religious philosopher. During the War of 1812, he edited *War,* a weekly news magazine that reported only on the progress of the struggle. In August 1814, when the British were reported within sight of Washington, New York's mayor, DeWitt Clinton, to prepare for the worst, organized the Committee of Defense, which was authorized to draft civilians to work on fortifications around the city. To support that effort, Woodworth wrote "Patriotic Diggers," set to a popular song. The Park Theatre's musical director, Charles Gilfert, arranged for its publication.

Woodworth's 1816 novel *The Champion of Freedom*, a mix of prose and poetic narrative about the recent war, won critical praise but few sales. Some local songwriters did set a few of its most appealing verses to music, but with little success. He then founded a women's magazine, devoted to beauty and hair styling, which was sprinkled with poetry and essays written by him under the pen name Selim. Later in his career, he formed the weekly literary magazine *New York Mirror*, which he edited for a while before turning it over to his friend George Pope Morris, the five-foot-two essayist, critic, and later leading lyricist.

Ready to essay any medium producing money, Woodworth offered several evenings of "Literary and Musical Entertainments" in New York recital halls and theaters. Recognizing his facility, producers began to commission him to write special material to order: funeral orations, odes, epilogues, and dramatic character pieces. He entered and generally won competitions sponsored by theaters that offered either a free season pass or a gold medal worth fifty dollars for the best poetic address, with which performances were usually begun.

The first of his seven plays, *Deed of Gift*, was produced in 1822. It contained several songs set to currently popular melodies. His second play, dealing with Lafayette during the French Revolution and a plot to rescue him from prison, was written to take advantage of the great furor over the Frenchman's visit to America in 1825.

It was his third play, *The Forest Rose*, that proved to be Woodworth's most successful comic opera. In it he created the first fully fleshed and realistic American Yankee to appear on the stage: the young farmer-merchant Jonathan Ploughboy. This served as the starring role for a number of leading men, including the greatest of all in the part, George Handel Hill. Music for the overture and the play's thirteen songs was written and arranged by a New York church organist, John Davies.

Fewer than one hundred people were in the Chatham Garden Theatre when *The Forest Rose* opened in early 1826. George Morris's spirited editorial defense of his friend's stage piece in the pages of the *Mirror*, as well as the masterful ability of the actor playing Jonathan, then won audiences and growing fame for this play.

All of the lyrics of Woodworth's songs in his seven stage plays appeared in collected editions of his writings, as were those for the two hit songs that appeared first as newspaper verse and then were set to music: "The Hunters of Kentucky" and "The Old Oaken Bucket."

The extraordinary victory won by American forces under Andrew Jackson outside New Orleans in 1815, weeks after the war had ended officially, inspired the first of these songs. Five months before the battle, a British proclamation, intended to discourage continued backwoods support of American policy and force a national split, had been addressed to "Inhabitants of Kentucky." Frontier Americans found this propaganda to be nonsense and responded quickly to Jackson's call for riflemen. Some 2,000 Kentuckians arrived in the port city four days before battle was joined on January 8. Nearly, 15,000 British Army regulars and Royal Marines, the best-trained troops in the world, men who had defeated Napoleon at Waterloo, went into action against them and met defeat. Woodworth's eight verses, set to the tune of "Miss Bailey's Ghost," were heard with music for the first time between scenes in a New York theater. They were sung by Arthur Keane, a teacher, singing actor, and music seller, who spent the last years of his life in Nashville. A clipping of Woodworth's verses, with the melody indicated, which appeared in the national press, eventually made its way west to the Kentucky-Tennessee frontier. There they were introduced to a particularly receptive theater audience, which related to the song's braggadocio and its identification with the war's hero, Jackson, who was making his mark in national politics as the voice of the frontier. Acting companies that played the western circuit featured the song regularly, and it became the marching song of Jackson's supporters.

In 1824, when the war hero made an unsuccessful run for the presidency against John Quincy Adams, the song was heard throughout the states wherever Jackson appeared. In New York's Chatham Garden Theatre, the roost of local Jacksonians, an actor named Petrie came onstage between acts dressed like a Kentucky rifleman and sang Woodworth's ballad, accompanied by the house orchestra, one of whom, William Blondell, had made a new arrangement of the tune. Alerted to the performance and an ensuing clamor for a printed version of the song, Thomas Birch, a painter who dabbled in music engraving, issued Blondell's version in a twenty-five-cent four-page edition, with a lithographed vignette of Petrie in costume, both with his rifle's butt on the ground and firing the long rifle. After Jackson was elected president in 1828, "The Hunters of Kentucky" became the quasi-official President's March.

"The Old Oaken Bucket" first appeared in print as part of Woodworth's 1826 collection *Melodies, Duets, Trios, Songs and Ballads,* which contained no printed music but did specify suggested music for many of the verses. For this song, the writer had chosen the Scottish folk tune used by the highland weaver Robert Tannahill in 1817 for "Jessie the Flower o'Dunblane," a song that remained popular long after the Civil War.

Countless editions of Woodworth's song were published in the following years, and, as the cultural historian Ray B. Brown clearly proved, "The Old Oaken Bucket" was the most reprinted popular lyric appearing in songsters and songbooks during the nineteenth century. The verses got a second lease on life in the 1870s, when they were published to be sung to "Araby's Daughter," a melody written in 1826 by George Kiallmark, a London theater musician, for words by Thomas Moore. Though Woodworth's verses do not once mention alcohol or refer to any spirituous liquors, the song became a favorite of temperance advocates.

Woodworth made little profit from either of the songs by which he is best remembered. He continued to write for the theater, and received his income chiefly from the proceeds of the dramatist's customary benefit nights. This small amount barely kept Woodworth and his family out of complete poverty. In 1837, he suffered an apoplectic stroke and remained paralyzed until his death, in 1842.

Early Growth of the Frontier Theater

By 1825, New York City had wrested domination of the American stage away from Philadelphia and become the hub of all popular entertainment, as well as of the music business that depended on it for almost all promotion of printed sheet music. When the Erie Canal was built, it provided an all-water route from New York to New Orleans and offered actors, singers, dancers, and musicians access, by a crowded and uncomfortable means, to the show business opening up around Pittsburgh, in the new states of Kentucky and Tennessee, and along the Ohio and Mississippi rivers.

Late in the eighteenth century, itinerant entertainers had first traveled along the Cumberland Road to Lexington, in Kentucky, to offer music, dancing, magic shows, acrobatic displays, and other diversions to second-generation pioneers, most of whom had never seen such sights before. An amateur actor in blackface played Mungo and sang Charles Dibdin's hit music from *The Padlock* in a program that included *Douglas,* a British tragedy, and the comic opera *Love-a-la-Mode,* with "Aileen Aroon," a song that had long been a favorite in both England and the colonies. An amateur company was formed in Cincinnati sometime in 1801, and other groups offered occasional nights of comic opera, farce, comedy, and tragedy, interspersed with hornpipe dancing, popular songs, and instrumental music, much the same fare the English-speaking theater had presented since the days of Henry Purcell and John Gay.

After traveling from Albany to Kentucky, Samuel Drake's company of performers arrived in Frankfort, the state capital, in December 1815, ready to entertain those gathered there for the legislature's annual meeting. Drake and his actors had come by stagecoach, horse, wagon, and flat-bottomed boat, encountering wolves and rushing rivers, and had been on the road since early May with their costumes, scenery, and stage equipment. They had paid their way with the proceeds from performances in whatever theater, courthouse, large room, or barn could be used for the purpose. Drake, an actor who doubled as a fiddle player, was born in England, where he studied for the church until he saw his first play, at Covent Garden, and deserted the cloth for grease paint. In 1810, he was working in Boston's Federal Street Theatre, and the next year, with wife and children, he moved to Albany. The offer to reestablish a suspended three-city circuit in Kentucky tempted him west. There he and his Company of Comedians founded a theatrical empire that dominated the southern United States for years.

In 1817, one of Drake's players, twenty-year-old Noah Miller Ludlow, who had joined the company as an advance man and bit player, accepted the proposal of some fellow actors to form a Commonwealth of Players, typical of the cooperative ventures that extended the theater from the eastern seaboard to remote wilderness reaches. Ludlow was cool to the plan until he met a young widow from Tennessee, on her way home. He then agreed to join the troupe on a visit to the sections of Tennessee and the South where no theatrical company had ever appeared. The group purchased a horse and wagon, and, after a hazardous trip, got to the growing settlement on the Cumberland River, Nashville, the home of the widow he admired, in the early autumn of 1817. They played a three-week season, creating an improvised theater in an old salt house, and Ludlow wooed and won the Tennessee belle, who then joined the Commonwealth of Players.

Hearing from travelers that New Orleans, part of the United States since 1803, had never seen an English-speaking production, the actors agreed to try their luck in that thriving seaport, through whose harbor passed an immense traffic in slaves, cotton, sugar, tobacco, and other inland produce. Ludlow was named captain-manager of a keelboat purchased for $200 and dubbed *Noah's Ark*.

This first American showboat passed down the Cumberland, to the Ohio and the Mississippi. The troupe play to any group that would pay, performing on a sandbar or in a smoke-filled grogshop or tavern. In December 1817, they landed at Natchez-under-the-Hill and packed a 500-seat theater at a dollar a head. They then climbed up the hill to Memphis and presented David Garrick's ballad-farce version of Shakespeare's *Taming of the Shrew*. *Noah's Ark* was sold to pay for passage on a cotton transport bound for New Orleans, which the actors reached at the beginning of 1818. They opened in a local theater, with a program that included Michael Kelly's comic opera *The Honeymoon,* several of whose songs were already well known by way of printed sheet music, and continued on a four-times-weekly schedule until April. Ludlow's actors cleared $15,000, and with his third of the receipts tucked into a saddlebag, the actor-manager made his way on horseback north through hostile Choctaw and Cherokee territory to his new wife and home, arriving in July 1818.

Working from a base in Nashville, and later in Huntsville, Alabama, the Ludlows played seasons in New Orleans and St. Louis, touring whenever possible through the hinterland to bring theater to rural audiences. Until the Civil War, Ludlow managed playhouses throughout the South, and with Drake, Sol Smith, and a few other producers, developed the Mississippi and Deep South theater circuits.

In his early years, Ludlow became famous for singing "The Hunters of Kentucky," generally to the real thing. He had introduced the song after learning the words from a *New York Mirror* clipping. Dressed in a buckskin hunting shirt and leggings, with rifle in hand, he brought crowds of river boatmen and frontiersmen to their feet as he recounted the glories of Andrew Jackson and the men who fought the British in the Battle of New Orleans.

The first important American stage character rooted in black contemporary culture, Jim Crow, as played by Thomas Dartmouth "Daddy" Rice, emerged out of the frontier theater. Many of the audiences that cheered Rice's performances in blackface along the Kentucky and Ohio show-business trail were backwoodsmen, typified by Jackson's mobocracy. These "half-horse and half-alligator" characters, as someone called them, became legendary around the world, particularly after they evolved into the twentieth-century's white-hatted cowboy. With Jonathan Ploughboy, the typification of Yankee Doodle, and Jim Crow or Sambo, the black man, three idealizations of the American character were ready to shape the course of American popular entertainment and popular music. Of them, the black American was to make the heaviest contribution to the popular music of the next century.

The Black American Discovered

There is something mysterious, deep-rooted, and still unexplained in the white Anglo-Saxon psyche that obliges many people to sing and dance and speak in, and pay money to hear and see, what is perceived to be "black" style and character. This tradition goes back in theater history to the masque Ben Jonson wrote for James I's Danish queen, who wished to appear in lavish white costume and black make-up, and has moved through the ballad theater and the nineteenth-century stage to the present, with Mick Jagger moving hundreds of thousands to near-ecstasy singing "like a black."

One of the first foreigners to appropriate American types for his own uses was Charles Matthews, a British actor who made his first tour of America in 1822–23. The son of a stationer, he was born in 1776 and revealed early an incomparable genius for mimicry. He became a professional actor at the age of eighteen, serving a poorly paid apprenticeship before he triumphed as a low comedian in 1808 at the Little Theatre in the Haymarket. He had the magical ability to transform himself into many characters, male and female, using many dialects with unerring accuracy. His chief vehicle was the one-man show *Matthews at Home,* which attracted the poor, the aristocracy, and leading figures alike. Using songs and stories, as Dibdin had, he added ventriloquism, quick costume changes, and a fantastic sense of impersonation to create a connected story line that involved "monopolylogues" between the various individuals he brought to life on the stage.

He went to America not only to gain gold but also to collect new material based on close examination of the genus Americanus, and the audiences who came to see "the greatest comedian on the London stage" were never disappointed. After touring the eastern seaboard, he returned home with most of the proceeds from big fees and benefit performances for each of which he got more than $1,000. His initial view of America and its people, as detailed in letters to his wife, was one of disappointment and shock. "If this must be the effect of a republican form of government," he wrote, "give me a monarch, even if he be a despot." He scorned American food, loathed the means of transportation, hated the weather, and mourned the lack of British sophistication. He did, however, collect a storehouse of character types, all culled from conversations with obliging Americans of all social and economic levels and all races.

Out of his investigations came several perceptions, which made up the major part of his stage presentation. They had an immediate, and lasting, effect on the American actors and playwrights who saw his performances.

During a stroll around New York, Matthews chanced upon the African Grove Theater, located in 1822 near Broadway and Mercer Street. There, a number of free blacks were attempting to create a world of show business rooted in the white man's culture that would entertain fellow Afro-Americans who wished to become part of the American way of life. The company, victim of contempt in the local press, suffered the abuse of poor whites who came to jeer and remained to disrupt. The police arrested its actors in the interest of preserving peace.

There were a number of accomplished performers in the African Grove Theater company, and in other times and social climates they might have become darlings of white audiences, as Paul Robeson and Sammy Davis, Jr., did in the twentieth century. A singer and dancer named James Hewlett, a West Indian mulatto, was one. He had worked as a dresser for leading British actors touring in New York and had developed considerable talent as an impressionist, with a repertoire based on their stage performances. Hewlett also appeared during summers in Saratoga, New York, where he entertained with songs and excerpts from Shakespeare.

The African Grove Theater's most talented performer was Ira Aldridge, born in 1807 and educated in the white-supported Manumission Society's African Free School, established even before free education was supplied to the city's white children. A building on Mulberry Street near Grand housed the school, in which 500 black boys were taught the basic elements and trained as merchant sailors. Although his father intended Ira to be a clergyman, the youth often frequented the Park Theatre's topmost gallery, the home of pickpockets, trulls, and blacks. When he discovered the African Grove Theater and saw James Hewlett sing, dance, and play in Shakespearean works, Ira felt that his true destiny had at last been revealed, and after 1820 he was a member of the company.

Charles Matthews claimed to have seen Aldridge play Hamlet one evening in 1822 and drew on that experience for material he used in his *Trip to America,* in which he toured until his death. He viewed the experience as a lesson in ''nigger'' comedy, particularly after unruly white interlopers responded to the melancholy Dane's soliloquy by screaming after the lines ''Or to take arms against a sea of troubles, / And by opposing end them?'' The actor had no chance to speak the next words: ''To die: to sleep,'' as the cries rose from the whites for ''Opposum Up a Gum Tree,'' which Matthews was assured was ''a national air, a sort of 'God Save the King' of the Negroes.'' The incident as played onstage by Matthews became one of the most requested parts of his *Trip to America,* and did much to make the song a favorite in Britain. The sheet music published by a London music house credited the words and music of this ''South Carolinian Negro Air, as sung by Mr. Matthews'' as the ''only correct copy of this Original Negro Melody.''

A quarter of a century later, after Aldridge had played with great success in British, European, and Russian theaters, in both ''white'' and ''black'' roles, the then famous black star gave his own account of that evening. He denied that the "whole of the ludicrous scene so well and humorously described by Mr. Matthews" had ever occurred. But Aldridge did sing the song, as well as many other pieces of "black minstrelsy," accompanying himself on the guitar, during his early career in England prior to his tours of the Continent. British managers insisted that the "African Roscius," as Aldridge was billed, interpolate "Opposum Up a Gum Tree" in productions of *The Padlock.* Aldridge's playing of the black servant Mungo was hailed as "equal to anything we have ever witnessed, [displaying] humor and histrionic art in setting forth the salient points of that very facetious specimen of sable servants."

In the late 1830s and early 1840s, Aldridge lifted Matthews's interpretation of his own New York theater performance for the "Entertainments" he offered in England, and combined it with scenes from the great plays, pleas to end slavery in America, and the songs that white blackface minstrels were introducing to British audiences: "Jump Jim Crow," "Lubly Rose," "Miss Lucy Long," and other pieces. It was an era when the British were in the throes of their first infatuation with the minstrel show, and a London critic wrote of Aldridge's performance: "No mock 'Ethiopian Serenader' could come near this 'veritable nigger', whose good nature, humour and wit are so commodiously ridiculed."

Once Aldridge made his first tour of Europe, in 1852, he had no more need for minstrel songs, for he had gained the respect of audiences that included the crowned heads of the world for his portrayals of Othello, Lear, Macbeth, Richard III, and the Merchant of Venice. His tour of Russia in 1858 restored Shakespeare's works to the standard repertory there. When Aldridge died in 1864, while on a tour of Poland, he was considered one of the greatest actors of the time, and his memory as such a star is preserved by portrait in Leningrad.

During his second tour of America, in 1834, Matthews made a point of listening to blacks of all classes—household servants, stagecoach drivers, and ministers in evangelical churches—and he took notes of their speech patterns and dialects, the songs they sang at work. He transcribed this material and shaped it into his own special presentations. "I shall be rich in black fun," he wrote to his wife. "I have studied their broken English carefully. It is pronounced the real thing, even by the Yankees."

While arriving at his perceptions of Americans, Matthews had enjoyed a short friendship with John Wesley Jarvis, an American humorist and storyteller whose contribution the British actor acknowledged only by making Jarvis one of his stage characters. Jarvis was an early-nineteenth-century eccentric, part genius, part wastrel, the English-born grandnephew of Methodism's Wesley brothers. He made his fame as one of the best American artists during the War of 1812, when he painted full-scale portraits of the hero generals and commodores, which were hung in New York's City Hall. Upon learning that the jokes and witty lampoons he shared with his barber were being repeated around the nation, Jarvis evolved his personal style of storytelling, one that almost equaled his skill as an artist. He was one of the first American painters to make a special study of anatomy, generally preferring to examine the live female body

and in the process fathering a brood of illegitimate offspring, to the consterna-
tion of less free-spirited literary and social acquaintances.

Jarvis executed commissions in many cities, all the while playing practical
jokes and collecting anecdotes, dialects, local mannerisms, which he assembled
into seemingly impromptu performances for friends after dinner was ended and
the cigars and port came out. As a frequent guest of James Fenimore Cooper,
William Dunlap, and other prominent New Yorkers, Matthews had ample opportunity to see Jarvis, the "best story teller that ever lived," in action. Many
of that amateur comedian's best narratives turned up in *A Trip to America,*
including one dealing with a French admirer of Andrew Jackson, in which
Matthews burlesqued "The Hunters of Kentucky."

A second important contribution to Matthews's sometimes accurate view of
the new nation came from David Humphreys's five-act comedy *The Yanky in
England* and, especially, the *Glossary of Yankee Words,* which Matthews found
in the United States and passed on to his co-writer of the operatic farce *Jonathan in England,* the actor's first successful American role. "Yankee Doodle"
was featured in it, as was Matthews's blackface rendition of "Opposum Up a
Gum Tree."

Though the musical depicted cultured and wealthy Americans as being much
like their British counterparts, the playwright, Richard Brinsley Peake, drew
the lower classes at their worst—as ignorant, mean, slave-beating, bragging,
and uncouth—qualities perceived by many Englishmen. More sensitive Britons
were troubled by the piece and the images it presented, though both earned the
applause of English audiences for many years.

The three-and-a-half-hour *A Trip to America,* which Matthews offered on
March 25, 1824, presented in speech and song a view of the lost colonies and
their people as seen through the eyes of this shrewd, if superficial, observer of
the human condition. Matthews had learned the Yankee, black, Scottish, Irish,
Dutch, and French accents of America north of the Mason-Dixon line. Seated
in an armchair, with only a reading lamp for stage decoration, to preserve the
"at home" atmosphere, he told and sang of his trip. A dozen recognizable
types—French émigrés, black Shakespearean actors, New England Jonathan
Ploughboys, a fiddle-playing black stagecoach driver, a Negro waiter, an Irish
social climber, a Jacksonian Kentucky shoemaker who was colonel of militia—
peopled the stage, each in the correct costume. As he advertised, he offered a
more "correct picture of the habits, manners, and characteristics of the Americans than ever was presented to Englishmen, exaggerated, occasionally for
effect, but never so caricatured as to leave any doubt of the truth of the portrait." the most popular of his creations was the black actor; the most cruelly
accurate, his Yankees.

The pre–Civil War theater's view of the common American man, white or
black, and the songs he sang was fixed once a twenty-six-year-old American
actor appeared at Covent Garden as a guest star in 1827. Not a true Yankee,
Henry Hackett had been taken from his native Holland to the United States at
the age of three. He read for the law, but could find work only as a grocery
wholesaler's clerk. At the age of nineteen, he married a young actress and

moved with her to Utica, New York, to engage in trade, supplying groceries and wines and liquors to the surrounding territory, and amassing $18,000 within five years, then reckoned a small fortune. His daily contact in that remote area with New England Yankees and French Canadian runners-of-the-woods gave Hackett an insight into their characters fare more intimate than that of Jarvis or Matthews. He first put it to good use when business reverses brought him to near-bankruptcy, and so forced his return to New York City, where he found work in the theater.

Hackett had appeared in amateur theatricals in Utica and was known to friends there as a crackerjack storyteller, but his debut in *Love in a Village* proved to be a minor disaster. The following week he saved himself by appearing in a piece of old fluff that permitted him to imitate leading stage personalities, including Charles Matthews. Hackett triumphed with a story about "Uncle Ben and the Squirrel Hunt," the rambling account of a Yankee's reluctance to part with the shilling promised his nephew for retrieval of a treed rodent. Jarvis had once told the story to Matthews, and Hackett wrote later than he, too, had recounted the tale to the British actor.

Advertising himself as a "Leading American Comic Actor," Hackett went to London in 1827 and was signed by Covent Garden for a single appearance. He intended to present a program that had always pleased American audiences, an assemblage of material based on his life in upper New York State, heavily peppered with Jarvis by way of Matthews, some popular American songs, and cameos of Yankees, Dutchmen, immigrant French, Southern colonels, and backwoods Kentuckians. The house applauded at the start, when he appeared in standard Yankee clothing—black hat, blue coat, blue-striped pantaloons, and floral vest, with his hair in a pigtail—but he was soon hissed offstage, for the crowd saw him as a thief of the stories and songs for which Matthews was famous. Even the true-to-life mimicries of British actors now working in America, in which Hackett excelled, failed to win any more engagements.

Five years passed before Hackett appeared again in London. In the interim he had won American affections with his Falstaff; the Dutch Rip Van Winkle; Yankee Solomon Swap, "the most natural and exaggerated Yankee ever seen on stage"; Melodious Migrate, a New England singing master who preferred the music of a Negro band to "Eye-talian opery"; and Colonel Nimrod Wildfire, half-horse and half-alligator Kentucky congressman, clearly modeled after Davy Crockett and Andrew Jackson's riflemen. Wildfire was created for Hackett by James Kirke Paulding, a literary crony of Washington Irving, Cooper, Dunlap, and other New York intellectuals. The influence of Jarvis also is clearly evident in *The Lion of the West,* Paulding's prize-winning entry in a competition Hackett sponsored in order to obtain exclusive publication and copyright in the vehicles created for him.

Such caricatures of regional Americans, presented as audiences wished to see them and played by Hackett and his contemporaries, as well as by blackface actors pretending to be transplanted Africans, and the stage Irishmen, Germans, French, and other European immigrants, provided the bulk of popular entertainment. Around it the major element of popular theater music and its business was forming.

The American Stage Black and His Music

Beginning with John Gay's suppressed comic opera *Polly* (1729), the British public theater had offered from time to time musical plays in which black characters played important roles, usually as servants. None was as successful as the Isaac Bickerstaffe–Charles Dibdin comic creation Mungo, guardian of *The Padlock* (1768), a stage work that remained in both the English and the American repertory for a century.

The new form of popular song coming to life in the United States after 1820 derived indirectly from the blacks, slave and free, who were becoming more evident everywhere in America. White authors and composers had come to see these blacks, as one late-eighteenth-century traveler saw them, as "the greatest humorists in the nation." The word *humorist* was not used in its presently preferred definition, as "an entertainer specializing in humor," but, rather, as "peculiar or eccentric, indulging in odd or whimsical ways." There were, of course, Americans who saw the black man at first hand, having grown up with him and his music, and now wrote such songs themselves. One of them was the author of the first black-dialect song known to have been published in the United States, "Back Side of Albany Stands Lake Champlain."

It was sung first to an Albany theater audience in February 1815, and then on the professional stage in New York City by Hopkins Robinson, an actor better known to his fans as Mr. Robertson. The first occasion was Robinson's benefit evening, and, as he did later, the actor appeared in a sailor's costume and blackface to sing the set of four verses, to the Irish tune "Boyne Water." Soon after its first performance, "Back Side of Albany" was printed in Albany in a 180-page songster, *The Columbian Harmonist,* and it appeared in countless similar collections until just before the Civil War. The author was Michael "Micah" Hawkins, then a thirty-eight-year-old grocer and hotelkeeper who had learned the fiddle from a black man and was also proficient on the piano and flute. His first teacher was a family slave, the black fiddler Toney Clapp, after whose death and burial in the Hawkinses' slave burying ground, Micah wrote: "His artless music was a language universal and its effect, most irresistable . . . though of a race despis'd." Vera Brodsky Lawrence's indefatigable research first limned the details of Hawkins's contributions to the American theater and its music in 1978.

During an apprenticeship to a New Jersey coachmaker, Hawkins laboriously compiled a handwritten *Book of Notes for the German Flute,* a personal tune-book of some 200 melodies, among which was "Boyne Water," used for his first known printed work. This manuscript eventually came into the possession of a nephew and music pupil, the brilliant nineteenth-century painter William Sidney Mount.

Hawkins forsook the coach-making trade to become a grocer and in 1810 moved his prospering business to Catherine Street in lower Manhattan, near the ferry landing from Brooklyn. He added to his holdings the Catherine Street Ferry House, a hotel and tavern, where patrons were served not only food and potables, but also music, played by the owner on his fiddle or a piano beneath the bar. "Persons just landed from vessels in the East River [were] completely overpowered by the exquisitely touching style in which Hawkins played some air likely to arouse their feelings," a contemporary wrote, "[and] often requested their host to cease playing upon the ground that so long as he played they could not leave."

Only a handful of the songs Hawkins wrote have survived. One was written during the exuberant outpouring of affection and music welcoming General Lafayette on his triumphal tour of America. "Massa Georgee Washington and General Lafayette" is a piece of what was later called "special material," written for a patron actor from the nearby Chatham Gardens Theatre district. In the song, Hawkins anticipated not only the minstrel theater, but also such twentieth-century blackface comedians as Amos and Andy, in the patter between the sung verses. The song was introduced on October 24, 1825, by an actor in burned ham-fat make-up, dressed in the uniform of a Continental trooper, with cocked hat and sword. Shortly after, Edward Riley, whose music store was on Chatham Street, brought it out in an eight-page edition, including song and patter.

A few weeks later, Hawkins's play with music *The Saw-mill* opened at the Chatham Garden Theatre. A tiring James Hewitt, buffeted by the fates and alienated from his family, wrote arrangements of Hawkins's music for the theater orchestra and probably conducted the performance. The following summer, Micah Hawkins was dead, and soon forgotten except for the four songs that had appeared in print, all that remained from a creative career spanning more than twenty years. As his nephew Mount wrote, "His good wife, a member of the Presbyterian Church, felt that she would be serving the Lord by giving her servant his plays and writings in manuscript to heat the tea kettle with."

Charles Matthews's successful first American tour, with his caricatures and songs, led to growing use of dialect comedy and music on the stage. Young Edwin Forrest, destined to be one of the century's greatest native-born stage stars, was learning his craft as a member of Sol Smith's frontier touring theater company. In the early 1820s, when cast as a slave, Forrest carefully studied black people's "odd and eccentric ways" in order to achieve a believable performance. In blackface and appropriate costume, he walked through Cincinnati streets to provoke a public reaction. An elderly and patently near-sighted black woman mistook him for a relative, so true, Forrest bragged, was his appearance. The actor persuaded her to join him onstage that evening, and the pair sang and danced for an enthusiastic audience.

Like Matthews and Forrest, American actors began to pay close attention to the blacks around them, probably eliciting in response the sort of performance that whites expected to see: "odd" persons acting in "peculiar ways." The most talented of these white actors achieved sufficient acclaim by the late 1820s to be remembered by the people who worked with them in traveling shows, circuses, and on big-city stages. George Nichols, a clown working the Mississippi River circuit was, according to Colonel T. Allston Brown, in *Fun in Black or Sketches of Minstrel Life,* "an original. He would compose the verses of his comic songs within ten minutes of his appearances before an audience. . . . Nichols first sang 'Jim Crow' as clown, and afterwards as a Negro. He first conceived the idea from a French darkie, a banjo player known from New Orleans to Cincinnati as 'Picayune Butler.' "

According to the colonel some half century later, Nichols was the writer of "Zip Coon," whose authorship was also claimed by the New York stage performer Bob Farrell and was first performed by him in New York in 1834. As Brown points out, the melody is Irish in origin, "taken from a rough jig called 'Natchez under the hill.' " Brown also avers that Nichols wrote "Clar de Kitchin," a combination of humorous references to black life as lived by Aesop -like animals, which he performed after having heard a rude version sung by black Mississippi riverboat stokers. Most of these popular songs were, Brown adds, "taken after hearing the darkies of the south singing after the labor of the day was over on the plantation." Virtually all early blackface melodies were European in origin, first heard from whites and then altered by blacks. "Sich a gittin" was a morris-dance melody; "Gumbo Chaff" used the old British tune "Bow Wow Wow," the refrain of an old song known as the "Barking Barber"; a Scottish melody served for "Long Tail Blue"; and the song that precipitated an international vogue for black minstrelsy, "Jump Jim Crow," was a London royal playhouse melody based on an Irish folk tune.

George Washington Dixon, the first popular blackface singing actor to give performances of what became known as "plantation melodies," first appeared on stage in Albany in 1827, singing a mixture of comic black English and frontier humor, and then made his New York debut the following year at the Chatham. "Coal Black Rose," the song for which he was best known, was published in songsters and as sheet music, with appropriate credit to him on the cover. In order to keep others from singing the song, Dixon claimed to have registered it for copyright, but, in the general carefree atmosphere prevailing for songwriters in that period, the ruse failed, and many others took up his material. In spite of them, Dixon ruled in Manhattan as the favorite of the lower classes, until a native son, Thomas Dartmouth Rice, returned from triumphs along the Ohio River circuit with a new song and a new kind of stage dance.

Rice was born to poor Irish parents in New York in 1808 and apprenticed to a wood-carver while still a boy. He began to work at the Park Theatre as an extra, and developed those "stage eccentricities" or "scene stealing" that brought him applause from the gallery but complaints from the principals he upstaged, and, eventually, dismissal. Rice headed for the West and found work with Sol Smith as property man, lamplighter and stage carpenter; he also doubled in small comic roles. In 1828, he volunteered to sing between the acts of a now-lost play written by Smith, *The Rifle,* in which Rice was cast as a Kentucky fieldhand. He had been watching an old black slave, Jim, who belonged to the local white Crow family, working in the stable at the rear of the Cincinnati theater. Jim was deformed, his right shoulder contorted and his left leg stiff and crooked at the knee. His limping walk was a source of amusement to the actors, but it provided a spark of inspiration to Rice. Jim also was in the habit of crooning a rhythmic tune, to which he sang verses of his own making. At the end of each quatrain, he turned completely around, pivoting on one heel, and sang:

> Ebery time I wheel 'bout I jump Jim Crow,
> Wheel 'bout, turn 'bout,
> Do jes' so,
> An' ebery time I wheel 'bout
> I jump Jim Crow.

Blackface comedy and singing had already become popular, but Rice discerned something new in Jim's singing and dancing. After borrowing clothing from a hotel porter for his first appearance in *The Rifle,* Rice blackened his face, put on a black curly wool wig, and went onstage to perform Jim's song and imitate his grotesque but comic dancing.

"Daddy" Rice's name began to creep slowly up the posters advertising Smith's company as they moved along the Ohio River, and the new comedy star now added comic topical allusions to the song he had appropriated. In Pittsburgh, he was visited backstage by young Stephen Foster, who tried to sell him some songs, and he realized that he, too, should put his words and music down on paper. W. C. Peters did that for the musically illiterate young actor and brought out the printed sheet music of "Jim Crow," Many other publishers did the same, usually with a lithographed picture of Rice in costume, sometimes giving him credit as writer. To keep his material fresh, Rice found it necessary to provide new comic lines, which he may have written himself or he may have used some written by professionals.

Rice made his triumphant return to New York at the Bowery Theatre in November 1832 after a week during which the city was saturated with posters promising his appearance. He had added new songs to his repertory, usually the old favorites but with far more sophisticated comical material than had been common. He sang "Long Tail Blue" in a long-tailed dress coat and red-and-white trousers, and he ripped off five- and ten-dollar gold pieces serving as coat and vest buttons to throw to the audience.

The songs that Rice and his imitators were making popular provided the popular-music business with new material, for which public demand was met with lithographed four-page editions, generally illustrated with vulgar depictions of men and women in blackface and eccentric clothing, drawn to satisfy the stereotyped vision of blacks as heavy-lipped, foolishly happy, lazy, shuffling, dancing, and generally gaudily clad.

After a decade during which the blackface song had made its way into everyone's consciousness, J. K. Kinnard asked, in an October 1845 issue of *Knickerbocker Magazine,* "Who are our national poets?" and answered that they were indeed blacks, the country's "truly original American poets."

Thomas Dartmouth "Daddy" Rice, the first to make an international reputation through the songs of American blacks, enjoyed a fame not unlike that of

Elvis Presley in the late 1950s. However, Rice's best-known song, "Jim Crow," never suffered the vigorous denunciation in the press and from the pulpit and Congress that Presley's "Hound Dog" endured. When Rice made his first appearance in Washington, it was before an enthusiastic audience of national leaders. He presented his youngest imitator, four-year-old Joseph Jefferson, dressed as a miniature Jim Crow, carrying him onstage in a sack.

To accommodate his fame, Rice expanded his presentation, appearing in short playlets, supported by singing and dancing male and female actors. These skits were next enlarged to become "Ethiopian Operas," to which new stage business and spoken dialogue were added regularly. Following the British tradition of burlesquing successful stage works, Rice created *O Hush* and *Bone Squash Diavolo,* his best-known works, the latter a travesty of the then popular comic opera *Fra Diavolo* by Daniel Auber to a libretto by Augustin Scribe. In all his works, Rice, and those who followed him, used two kinds of stage blacks, what he called "nigga gemmen and common niggas." They represented the middle-class, social striving, urban Afro-American and the lowest-class black workmen.

Hans Nathan has written, in *Dan Emmett and Negro Minstrelsy,* that Rice's best-known plays are

> examples of a form which descended from English ballad operas and thus contained spoken dialogue and a great deal of music to verses, crudely rhymed. The vocal numbers were always Negro minstrel songs or songs popular on the minstrel stage, performed as solos or divided among several actors and sung in duets, trios and other ensemble numbers. As a rule, this type of play concluded with a refrain that was usually sung by everyone present on the stage. At times no more than a single tune served to enliven an entire scene. Between the stanzas and sometimes at their conclusion, a dance such as a "breakdown" or a "reel" would be interjected. Instrumental music was not neglected; it introduced a scene, accompanied a dance, or else announced and underlined a sudden and exciting event, such as the appearance of the devil. Climaxes in these plays always crystallized into an action which even the least sophisticated could understand.

With a swarm of imitators on the New York stage, Rice took Jim Crow and his first two Ethiopian operas to England, where he starred in *Bone Squash Diavolo* at London's Surrey Theatre, playing to packed houses for three months, starting in July 1836. This first taste of American blackface entertainment gave middle- and lower-class Britons an appetite that persisted without surfeit until after World War II, when the long-running radio program "The Black and White Show," a BBC burnt-cork minstrel production, came to an end.

The management of the more fashionable Adelphi Theatre hired Rice away from the Surrey. He starred there first in a new burletta, *A Flight to America,* a variation on Matthews's one-man shows, but with a large cast playing the many parts. Rice also appeared as the "King of the Blacks," mounted on a white horse, in the "Grade Procession of Niggers on July 4th."

Whenever possible, the Adelphi featured Rice in afterpieces and in its famous Christmas pantomime. Rice cemented himself in British affections when he married a London girl. Later, he went to Ireland, where he made nearly

$2,000 for a single night's work, which prompted managers to ask Ira Aldridge to add Jim Crow to his repertoire.

The Rices made trips regularly between America and England, on each of which it was observed that his popularity was slowly diminishing in both nations. Rice's monopoly as "the best representative of the American negro we have ever seen," as the *Knickerbocker* reported, was nearing its end. There were talented youngsters everywhere stealing his routines and adding their own new material. While he was being lionized in England and on the Continent, a new breed of "negro specialists" had developed, men who had been bitten by the virus while working for equestrian circuses.

The American Circus—Incubator of the Minstrel Show

The founding father of theatrical burnt-cork minstrelsy, Hopkins Robertson (or Robinson), singer of "Back Side of Albany" in 1815, was a singing circus clown before he made his American stage debut in 1801. Appearing in Boston, New York, and Philadelphia he gave bird imitations, danced a hornpipe blindfolded, threw forward and backward somersets, and, as a *pièce de résistance,* leaped through a hoop of fire held fourteen feet above the stage. Occasionally, he offered his "antipodean whirligig," rotating on his head, without using his hands, and with fireworks attached to his body, at a rate of 60 to 100 times a minute.

William Dunlap, for the benefit of whose bankrupt theater Robertson often performed the "human firecracker" turn, pointed to the actor's spectacular accomplishment as an example of the hard times on which popular entertainment had fallen. "To support the treasury," he moaned, "the stage was degraded by the exhibitions of a man who could whirl around on his head with crackers and fireworks attached."

Before Robertson went on the stage, he had been a tailor in the Park Theatre's costume department, but left that to become a supporting player in a number of Dunlap's productions. When the British equestrian John Ricketts was drowned at sea, and his principal competitor, the French circus impresario Lailson, fled to Haiti to avoid bankruptcy, the American theatrical-equestrian circus came to a temporary end. In the fall of 1802, Robertson took up some of the slack temporarily, playing the clown in displays of horse-riding in a New York theater and appearing as a singing actor in the stage presentations that concluded each performance. Only when winter came and the legitimate theater opened did Robertson abandon the circus, while his associates went on the road in warmer climes.

Open-air equestrian circuses become commonplace in northeastern cities during the summer, offering music, songs, hornpipe dancing, and scenes from popular stage plays and pantomimes, as well as displays of horsemanship. Sometime before 1810, these shows went indoors in the major cities, where the stage presentations became more elaborate, and in time the animals were used exclusively in gaudy melodramas.

Owners of trained American animals and African lions, camels, and other imported beasts had been touring the colonies for much of the preceding century, but the principal animal attraction of the modern circus, the elephant, did not appear until 1797. That year, Captain Jacob Crowninshield brought the first elephant to the country and exhibited it on tour. In the winter of 1812, he first allowed it to appear indoors, renting the pachyderm to New York's Park Theatre to appear in revivals of *Blue Beard* and *The Forty Thieves*.

New York's dramatic and equestrian circus finally found an indoor home in a number of wooden buildings around lower Broadway, many of which were built for the purpose at considerable expense. British performers who had learned the business from Philip Astley and his Royal Circus came to join the American companies, as did actors from the musical theater, variety artists, and ballet dancers, all of whom took part in shows whose pattern had been established by Astley and Dibdin. A three-city circuit developed—New York, Philadelphia, Boston—in permanent circus buildings, each trying to be more lavish than the others. Every summer, circus companies combined the best of circus with ambitious musical theater productions and appearances by outstanding musicians, dancers, comedians, and variety artists.

The legitimate theater's quest for novelty, with which to fill the new buildings that grew ever bigger, eventually absorbed the circus theater. Equestrian displays became an important part of variety entertainment. Out of this, ''horsetrionic drama'' evolved, *Mazeppa* and others, grandiose action melodramas that starred a series of lissome actresses who made strong men blush and chaste women faint at the sight of their seemingly unclad bodies draped across the broad back of a crazed stallion galloping on a concealed treadmill in mad flight from pursuing villains.

The American circus as it was known in the twentieth century was started in 1816 by Nathan Howes, who purchased the second elephant imported into the United States from her owner, Hackaliah Bailey, of Somers, New York. With ''old Bet'' as the star, Howes' Menagerie took to the roads of New England, traveling by night to keep the elephant away from curiosity seekers. When he returned home far richer, his neighbors followed his example. Within ten years, syndicates of New York Staters controlled both the animal circus and the business of importing creatures from abroad.

By the mid-1820s, thirty circus companies were touring, reaching as far north as Detroit in 1830. These were small affairs at first, consisting of a few wagons, four trained horses, and some half-dozen performers, mostly tumblers and vaulters, with the essential trick rider and a singing clown, who often wore blackface. Except for a fiddle or two, there was no band. The wagons carried some six-foot poles, around which, in a circle, a canvas was hung to contain the paying trade. The stage was a few boards raised just above the ground, on which acrobatic performances and Irish and Scottish jig dancing took place. The site was open to both sun and rain before a covering suspended from a high center pole was introduced. There were no seats. On occasion, wagons were drawn in for those at the rear to perch on. A crowd of 250 paying customers, at twenty-five cents a head, was considered big. An ''advance man'' traveled ahead of the circus to placard every strategically located post with advertising, secure a license from local authorities for, usually, five dollars, and hire the best site. The circus's approach was heralded by a bugler on horseback, and a clown made his way to the village green to announce the time of the performance as well as the great attractions available to all who paid. By 1828, there is an account of a circus with forty horses, eight wagons, thirty-five performers, and a tent seventy-five feet in diameter that accommodated 800 persons. Aaron Turner, a neighbor of Howes, was the first to put his circus under canvas, and within a few years most troupes were performing under "the big top."

The most talented clowns left the circus, where the pay was low, to try the "big time" in large cities. Among them was George Washington Dixon, who had served his apprenticeship in a New York State company, and then won fame on the New York stage as a blackface singer and actor. When the changing character of the minstrel theater and the number of talented performers it attracted made it difficult for him to compete, he became a soldier of fortune in Latin America and later the publisher of a scandalmongering and blackmailing gossip sheet. He died in a Louisiana hospital at the beginning of the Civil War.

George Nichols, who was one of several claiming authorship of "Zip Coon," left the Southern circus where he had learned his craft to go north. With him, he brought the song "Clar de Kitchin." He had first heard the melody sung by riverboat firemen and added his own words. Uneducated, Nichols had a gift for almost instant improvisation, which he put to good use in regularly adding new verses to the best of the Ethiopian songs. Many of the minstrel stage stars—"Zip Coon" Farrell, Frank Whitaker, Ben Cotton, Horatio Eversell, Barney Burns, Billy Whitlock, and Dan Rice, among others—first succumbed to the lure of traveling shows, for which they worked as equestrian clowns and blackface singers, appearing in costume as deckhands or plantation slaves, and singing songs and telling stories in a black English dialect picked up from Southern blacks. Late in the century, Cotton remembered that he "used to sit with them in front of their cabins and we would start the banjo twanging, and their voices would ring out in the quiet night air in their weird melodies. They did not quite understand me. I was the first white man they saw who sang as they did; but we were brothers for the time being and were perfectly happy."

The dance steps men like Cotton learned from the plantation blacks also influenced the work of both the blackface circus clown and minstrel singers, and the nature of the music they sang. Clowns usually worked on the raised wooden boards inside the circus ring, which amplified the toe-tapping that accompanied their songs. To this they added British heel-and-toe jig-step dancing, which the American Negro had also picked up by watching white dancers.

In her classic *American Humor,* Constance Rourke noted the coincidences inherent in the rise of the blackface white stage performer and the changing place of the black man in the American fabric:

Little Jim Crow appeared at almost the precise minute when *The Liberator* [an abolitionist journal] and minstrelsy spread over the land and grew in popularity as the struggle for emancipation gained in power through the '40s and '50s. The

Negro minstrel joined with the Yankee and the backwoodsman to make a comic trio, appearing in the same era as the Jacksonian democracy. . . . The Negro minstrel was grounded in reality, even though the impersonators were white, even though the figure was a myth. . . . But each of the trio remained distinct. None left a deeper print than the Negro in minstrelsy, even though his shadowy figure was the slowest to emerge, and though the minstrel never assumed the many distinct parts taken by the Yankee and the backwoodsman.

Americans of all ages and all social classes found irresistible the Ethiopian songs and dance steps played for them by an ever-increasing troop of actors in blackface. Daily, the demand increased from song-word and sheet-music publishers as well as stage performers for new Negro music. Singer and playwright Edward Harper modified the traditional Virginia reel into a new black dance, done to the song "Jim Along Josey," and a new national craze followed, almost equaling that for "Jim Crow."

Dan "Ole Bull" Myers, a country fiddler, collaborated with the successful journalist-poet Silas S. Steele to write "Dandy Jim of Caroline," which was featured by one of the first blackface dancers, Barney Williams. Born Bernard O'Flaherty in Cork, Williams was just under twenty when he won fame on the American stage in the late 1830s, combining Gaelic stepdancing with the leg- and foot-work of plantation dancers in the Camptown hornpipes and "Virginny" breakdowns that audiences demanded. Williams's inability to shed his brogue for an acceptable black dialect forced him off the minstrel stage, but he made a comeback in the 1850s as the 'celebrated Irish Comic Boy."

In this period of transition from the solo blackface performer to the minstrel show, the traditional American banjo underwent a change that is usually attributed to Joe Sweeney, considered the best banjoist of the day. By adding a fifth "thumb" string and stretching the guts over a cigar box, Sweeney provided an Africanlike syncopation that had long been lacking in the white man's music.

The quality of white Negro specialty dancing improved dramatically, sparked by the ambition of many dancers to match the skills of the free black dancer Master Juba. Born William Henry Lane, in Rhode Island in 1825, he apparently became the ward of New York's entire burnt-cork community, who recognized his great talent. Growing up in the cross-acculturation of the infamous Five Points neighborhood, an Irish-Negro slum area, Juba took the best from both and created an incomparable kind of dancing. His black teacher was a jig and reel dancer who toured the city's saloons and dance halls, working for food and tips. The Irish steps he learned from his desperately poor white neighbors. Surpassing all his teachers, he began to haunt shabby drinking houses and brothels, dancing for a meal of eels and ale or an occasional coin tossed to him by a white performer looking for something new to offer on the stage. He was still a teen-ager when Charles Dickens saw him dance in a dive by candlelight. As he wrote in his *American Notes* (1842), the youth showed incomparable agility in "single shuffle, double shuffle, cut and cross-cut; snapping his fingers, rolling his eyes, turning in his knees, presenting the backs of his legs up in front, spinning about on his toes and heels like nothing but the man's fingers on the tamourine; dancing with two left legs, two right legs, two wooden legs, two wire legs, two spring legs—all sorts of legs and no legs— what is this to him?" Many dancers, white and black, borrowed from Master Juba, but none surpassed him, especially in a series of competitions staged by showman P. T. Barnum. These culminated in 1844 in a great public contest, the last such occasion, when the grand prize went to "the wonder of the world, Juba, acknowledged to be the Greatest Dancer in the World."

Juba Lane went to England in 1848 as a member of the otherwise all-white Pell's Ethiopian Serenaders and was taken to the hearts of Britons at once. A member of a private party at which he entertained in late 1848 wrote of him: "The manner in which he beats time with his feet, and the extraordinary command he possesses over them, can only be believed by those who have been present at his exhibition. Scarcely less singular is the rapidity with which he sings one of his favorite songs."

From the perspective of a century, Marian Winters in *Chronicles of the American Dance,* saw Master Juba as "the most influential single performer of nineteenth-century American dance. . . . Juba was actually an initiator and determinant of the form itself. The repertoire of any current tap dancer contains elements which were established theatrically by him. That is the cornerstone of his memorial."

Master Juba Lane died in England in 1852, never having returned to the United States.

The Arrival of the Minstrel Show

Though no audience witnessed the impromptu concert that took place in a lower Manhattan lodging house off Chatham Square on a night in the winter of 1843, it was an occasion of tremendous significance in the course of American popular music.

"Negro specialists," white men and, occasionally, women and teen-age boys, had been working with black song, dance, and comedy in major theaters and in traveling shows and circuses crisscrossing rural America. "Heelologists," circus clowns and equestrians, banjo and dance teams, Ethiopian operas, experts in "Negro peculiarities," comic extravaganzas (short skits involving a cast of blackface comedians), burnt-cork impressionists who offered "correct imitations of a locomotive in operation or the screech of a steamboat whistle in the night"—these were the principal fare Americans were paying to see.

The 1842–43 theatrical season was one of the worst in man's memory. Admission prices were pared to offset the effects of a continuing business depression. Actors' salaries were cut. Employment opportunities on the stage decreased steadily. Yet on that night in 1843, four men met to rehearse, against the possibility they might be called in to work. They gathered in the room rented by Dan Emmett in Mrs. Brooke's lodging house at 37 Catherine Street in New York City. With William Whitlock on violin, Frank Brower on the bone castenets, Richard Pelham on tambourine, and Emmett on banjo, with all singing solo and in various combinations, a new sound was created. The Virginia Minstrels were born.

After an audition in a hotel billiard room nearby, the group was signed to appear at the Bowery Theatre, to play for the circus owned by "Uncle" Nate Howes, who had launched that business in 1816. The Minstrels, singing, dancing, and performing some comedy sketches, were advertised as being "entirely exempt from the vulgarities and other objectionable features which have hitherto characterized negro extravaganzas." Daddy Rice's type of blackface show business was coming to the end of its road, at least in America.

The creator of the burnt-cork minstrel or "Ethiopian" business that swept the white world after 1843, Daniel Emmett Decatur, had been born to Irish-American parents in Mount Vernon, Ohio, in 1815. Educated in a one-room schoolhouse that was open only in the winter and then taught the printer's trade, Emmett was nearly eighteen when he left his blacksmith father's house to work for an Ohio newspaper as a journeyman printer. Still underage, he joined the United States Army in 1834, but was soon sent home. Working during the winter months as a typesetter, in warm weather he traveled with circuses, playing fiddle and banjo, on both of which he was proficient, and capering in blackface as a clown. His first song was written for an equestrian comedy rider, but, after its favorable reception, he decided to use his material himself. Frank Brewer, a celebrated dancer and singer, joined the circus and formed an act with Emmett. During one of their performances, Brewer introduced the art of "bone playing," using a set of dried horse bones cut to a length of twelve inches to make a rhythm instrument he had seen used by Southern blacks. Later one of the Virginia Minstrels, Francis Marion Brewer had begun working as an entertainer when he was fifteen, and became one of the best blackface vocalists. Emmett and Brewer worked in Midwestern and Southern circuses until 1842, when they arrived in the nation's entertainment capital, New York, in search of work.

William Whitlock, a New Yorker and a printer, had also worked for a Southern circus, where he learned from Joe Sweeney how to play the banjo. Within a year he was so highly regarded an instrumentalist that P. T. Barnum sent him on the road with one of his blackface boy dancers. During the tour, Whitlock, too, became a specialist in black "peculiarities, dances, and extravagancies." Also a native New Yorker, Richard Pelham was a singer and dancer who regularly appeared on the Gotham stage.

Immediately after their debut, the Virginia Minstrels received offers of other work and began to extend their repertory with new sketches: "A Negro Lecture on Locomotives," "A Definition of the Bankruptcy Laws," and "Dan Tucker on Horseback," all played in black make-up to the music of banjo, violin, bones, and tambourine. Emmett's song "Old Dan Tucker" became an overnight hit, its fame spreading after New York publisher Joseph Atwill brought it out in sheet music.

When Howes rejected their offer to work for him at ten dollars a week per man, the Minstrels got a personal manager, who was charged with procuring bookings and top prices. They next went to Boston, where, sitting on the stage in a semicircle in the traditional shabby dress of the stage plantation darky, their virtuosic playing, exaggerated postures, and vulgar comedy won the hearts of people Lowell Mason was trying to save from the horrors of popular music.

Most Boston publishers quickly turned down Emmett's songs, because of their lack of refinement, but the former umbrella maker Charles H. Keith bought all that were available and issued them exactly "as performed by the Virginia Minstrels."

After further record-breaking engagements in New York and Boston, the Minstrels sailed for England in April 1843. Blackface entertainment was certainly not new to the British. In 1839, a group of English blackface entertainers, James Buckley and his three sons, had made their way to the United States, where, as the Congo Melodists, they had won some fame, chiefly by burlesquing Italian operas. Daddy Rice had returned to London the previous winter to appear at the Adelphi as Julius Caesar Washington Hickery Dock in a new farce set in Saratoga Springs, with a cast of predominantly white Americans, all attempting to win the favor and fortune of Miss Zip Coon, a young black heiress.

The banjoist Joe Sweeney was already playing in London and Scotland when the Minstrels arrived. Although they had been hired by Liverpool, Manchester, and other theater managers, the four Americans failed to stir up any great enthusiasm until a London magician hired them at £100 a week. Their "true copy" of slave life in America was hailed by the *Times* and reviewed favorably by Michael Balfe, a young singer and teacher. In spite of those recommendations, and because of their employer's legerdemain with box-office receipts, they had yet to earn enough to pay their board. So the group broke up, the men working singly for various theaters, visiting American circuses, or as supporting players to other entertainers. By the end of 1844, all but Pelham had sailed home. Sadler's Wells employed Pelham for a two-month run as the "Genuine Yankee Nigger of the U.S.," and he remained in England—and married an English actress—until the 1870s.

The Virginia Minstrels left not only Pelham behind, but also the roots of an extremely popular kind of entertainment, which has continued to delight the British through changing media—recordings, motion pictures, radio, and television. The literature of British minstrel songs has grown from Dan Emmett's *Celebrated Negro Melodies,* published in 1844 by the Soho piano maker and music printer Thomas D'Almaine.

On their return home, the three remaining Minstrels learned that a number of similar companies had been organized and had received such favorable reception that a command performance by a blackface minstrel company was scheduled for President John Tyler's wedding. This latest thing in popular musical show business was also beginning to spread from coast to coast. By the end of the decade, the *New York Tribune*'s best feature writer, Bayard Taylor, reported from California, of the popular songs springing from the minstrel show: "They are in fact, the national airs of America. Their quaint, mock-sentimental cadences, so well suited to the broad absurdity of the words—their reckless gaiety and irreverent familiarity with serious subjects—and their spirit of antagonism and perseverence—are true expressions of the more popular sides of the national character.''

Edition after edition of these songs was issued, but they usually called attention to the performer rather than the creator of the music, though he was often the same person. Songwriters usually got little more for their efforts than a line on the sheet-music cover and some free copies for friends or to offer to professional performers in the hope they would use the song. They gave up royalties for the exposure and paid no attention to copyright, which was invariably taken out by the publisher.

In the face of this proliferation of minstrel songs and groups, Dan Emmett found it impossible to win the acclaim he hoped for. During the summer he traveled with circuses and in the winter played in burlesque comedy skits, mostly in New York. Many of the banjo tunes he played were his own, or melodies whose origins were lost to memory and therefore claimed as his own. The words were original and were soon used, at greater profit, by new minstrel stars.

Chief among these was E. P. Christy, who had capitalized on the Virginia Minstrels' success during their trip to Europe, labeling his company of entertainers ''The Original Band of Virginia Minstrels.'' Ned Christy was born sometime before the War of 1812, in Philadelphia. In 1827, he was foreman of a rope-making factory in New Orleans, where black workers introduced him to their music. He learned more on Sunday afternoons in Congo Square, where black men and women gathered by the hundreds to enjoy a weekly Southern variation of Pinkster Day (Whitsuntide). Dancing jigs, breakdowns, and fandangos to the music of banjos, fifes, fiddles, bones, and other instruments, the black people of New Orleans sang many tunes that eventually were found in white popular music.

After traveling as a shoe salesman, Christy became one of George Washington Dixon's many imitators. He worked as a banjo-playing blackface comic singer. As was true with many white entertainers, Christy's source of exposure to ''down-home'' black English was a slave, in his case hymn-singing ''One-legged'' Harrison. In Buffalo, Christy formed a company of singers and dancers that became favorites in the bars frequented by sailors and deckhands who worked in canal and lake shipping. A British actor who chanced upon the Christy group during this time observed that the ''staple of E. P. Christy's entertainment was fun—genuine negro fun.''

When word of the unparalleled success of the Virginia Minstrels reached Buffalo, Christy immediately preempted the name. Though he later dropped it, he never stopped advertising his group as ''the oldest established company in existence. The model troupe of the world. The first to harmonize Negro melodies, and originators of the present popular style of Ethiopian entertainments.''

In 1846, believing his time had come, Christy booked a number of appearances in small New York theaters, which were successful. He then took on a hall in the Mechanics' Building, on Broadway near Grand Street. There he made the minstrel show palatable family entertainment, charging twenty-five cents for adults and half that for children. The hall was packed almost every evening for 2,792 performances, and Christy made a profit of half the $317,000 grossed. The fame of Christy's Minstrels spread across America, for a trip to Mechanics' Hall was mandatory for all visitors to the country's biggest city.

Unlike the early days of rock 'n' roll—whose music has much in common with that of the minstrel show in intention if not rhythmic patterns—when a storm of fearful protest greeted performances by white men of music that had been the special property of black people for decades, white audiences of the 1840s did not feel especially threatened by minstrel shows. They came back again and again to hear the comedy and "peculiar" music. Many of them had never seen a black man and often thought the blackface entertainers were real Afro-Americans. To make clear this was not the fact, some music publishers used lithographs on sheet-music covers showing leading minstrel groups in both stage costume and the street clothing of bourgeois Americans that many of them in fact were. Some companies dealt with this by presenting the first portion of each show in whiteface. When Americans, moved by Harriet Beecher Stowe's *Uncle Tom's Cabin* and abolitionist propaganda, were becoming aware of the destructive realities of traffic in black flesh, the minstrel show's caricaturization of blacks as lazy, simple-minded, eternally happy people showed them as no special threat, social or economic.

There were, however, those who yearned for the music of the "good old days," and looked back at the time when Daddy Rice sang "Jim Crow." Things had moved fast, and they could no longer find a copy of the sheet music for Rice's hit song. Instead, they complained that people who never saw an alligator or smelled magnolia blossoms wrote "African" songs filled with incorrect or far-fetched lyrics.

Whether they were aware of it or not, Ned Christy and the Bryants, who followed him, provided a more sophisticated and professional quality to the minstrel show in making it acceptable for family viewing. In its more formalized state it was being slowly changed from a collection of solo turns and specialty acts to a three-part offering whose form remained fixed past the end of the century. Not until the consciousness-raising of the 1960s were the last fund-raising amateur blackface minstrel shows abandoned by white social and fraternal groups. And only a decade or so before did Eddie Cantor, Al Jolson, and other twentieth-century veterans give up burnt-cork make-up and woolly wigs.

As the most famous minstrel company, Christy's men had the pick of new songs, not only the plantation melodies, but also the sentimental ditties of the day. The songs were those Americans sang around their pianos or melodeons, on which Charles Grobe and other Europeans wrote innumerable variations for two and four hands, permitting smitten lovers to touch flesh with impunity while crossing hands over the keyboard in following the carefully calculated fingering instructions.

Stephen Foster was not alone in turning over many of his rights in new songs to such men as Christy. He knew that continued performances led to success and sheet-music sales. Only because Foster was genuinely talented as well as prolific did Christy allow him to sell his music to Firth, Pond and receive royalties from all sales. Lesser songwriters had to be satisfied with a small outright amount of cash for their music, the big money going to the minstrel star on the sheet-music cover.

By the 1850s, New York City had become the pinnacle of American show business, the place where every actor, singer, and minstrel man hoped to find fame. It was there that innovations that continued to change the pattern of the minstrel show took form, created by Christy, the Bryants, and a half-dozen other resident companies. Boston and Philadelphia, too, were the strongholds of some permanent local troupes, though none as famous as those in New York. Lesser companies roved the country's back roads and waterways, occasionally masquerading as nationally known groups.

The man who had started this new form of musical theater, Dan Emmett, became, in 1854, musical director for Lea's Female Opera Troupe, which combined black minstrelsy with the popular female tableaus. He also conducted the minstrel band, which accompanied the young ladies in their body shows. In 1855, Emmett moved to Chicago and opened a small theater on Randolph Street, where he presented Burlesque Ethiopian Varieties, but he sold his lease within a year to go on the road with yet another minstrel company.

Unlike most public entertainment, the large minstrel companies took the financial crisis in stride. Eleven resident troupes were highly successful, and on the road hundreds of lesser groups regularly provided entertainment to a public desperate for something to laugh at. Christy's Minstrels had been taken over by one of the original members, George Christy, after Ned retired in 1854, sufficiently wealthy to spend his days in luxurious but solitary brooding that eventually brought on madness. The troupe found serious competition in Bryant's Minstrels, owned by three young brothers who were hailed as "a combination of comical talent never before witnessed." Daniel Webster O'Brien Bryant, the leader, was a brilliant banjoist and bones manipulator whose black-English dialect won the approval of Edwin Forrest. As a hotel baggage porter, he had learned the blackface craft while perched high in theater balconies. His brothers, Jerry and Neil, were equally gifted. Bryant's Minstrels brought a new element to the theater, combining "old and original" ways with more sophisticated and slick offerings of the "comicalities and eccentricities of negro life." In addition, "prominent public matters" were also dealt with on their stage when the Bryants lampooned white American social and political life. Each performance ended, after a depiction of life on a Southern plantation, with virtuosic singing and dancing by all the members of the company, who engaged in a carefully organized competition with one another done to a "walk-around" musical composition.

In late 1858, Dan Bryant located Emmett and offered him a job as orchestra musician, stage performer, and composer of new songs and jig tunes. Bryant's Minstrels had been active for more than a year, appearing in the same Mechanic's Hall where Christy had made his fortune, when Emmett joined them in the late fall of 1858. He stayed with the Minstrels until after the Civil War, his major responsibility becoming the creation of music for the walk-around finale. The ghost of Master Juba and a thousand plantation dancers hovered over the stage where white specialty dancers worked to music that Emmett often borrowed.

A chord from the orchestra brought the entire company to its feet from the great semicircle in which they stood, patting time to the music. The same lively breakdown tune in 2 / 4 time was used as each minstrel man stepped downstage to "walk around" in a circle for sixteen bars while the others clapped hands in rhythm. As in the traditional African challenge dances, each man strove to win the laurels of applause. Dan Bryant made an internationally famous specialty out of his "Essence of Old Virginia," a distillation of many plantation dances in which he appeared to move without moving his feet. At this midpoint in the development of dancing from Rice's African shuffle and jump to the twentieth century's soft-shoe stepping, Bryant's Essence was the best-known step created by white minstrelsy out of authentic Afro-American dances married to Anglo-Saxon clogs and jigs. Doing the walking jawbone, sugar-cane reel, Congo cocoanut dance, double trouble, smokehouse reel, corn-shuck jig, country breakdown, or one of a hundred other colorfully named steps, each dancer attempted to outdo his peers, and before the final curtain fell all mixed in together.

Emmett's thirty-two-bar walk-around composition was usually original, although he often borrowed the music. The words and music for "Turkey in the Straw," which he wrote for the Bryants in 1859, were presumably new, but an instrumental passage from George Dixon's printed "Zip Coon" was a part of the final arrangement Emmett penned.

The words were almost all his in "Mr. Dan Emmett's new and original Plantation Song and Dance DIXIE'S LAND," created for the April 4, 1859, performance at Mechanics' Hall. However, such phrases as "I wish I was" had appeared in "Clar de Kitchin," and "away down souf whar I was born" was in the Picayune Butler song published in 1840. The origin of the word *Dixie* has been attributed to a number of sources, among them the Citizens' Bank of New Orleans, whose ten-dollar-notes bore the French word *dix,* or ten, on the reverse side and were known as "dixeys"; a kindhearted Long Island farmer-slaveowner named Dixey, whose "Dixey's Land" farm was a veritable heaven on earth for blacks; and Jeremiah Dixon of the surveying team of Mason and Dixon, whose 1767 line between Pennsylvania and Maryland purportedly separated free and slave states before the Civil War. The 1850 minstrel play *United States Mail or Dixie in Difficulties* was the first to use the word on stage, in describing a black postboy character.

At its first performance, Emmett's song was used next to the closing, where it remained for many months. Only mounting public clamor moved the Bryants to put it into the important finale position in the autumn of 1860. The cheap-book publisher Dick & Fitzgerald first included the words, alone, in a twenty-five cent pocket songster, *Bryant's Essence of Old Virginny,* printed in September 1859, but they were also being circulated in a broadsheet.

New Orleans publisher Philip Werlein issued an unauthorized first edition in 1860 as "I Wish I Was in Dixie," with no credit to Emmett. The second Werlein edition, a few months later, bore the name of young minstrel Bobby

Newcombe as writer, with no mention of Emmett. When Werlein learned the true identity of "Dixie's" author, he offered Emmett five dollars for all rights, but was refused. Emmett finally sold the song in June 1860, more than a year after it was written, to Firth, Pond for $300; all of his rights, including copyright renewal, were in the contract. Brought out immediately as sheet music, with Emmett's name on it, the song went through a number of editions.

When Werlein went to New York for the 1860 meeting of the Board of Music Trade, to which he had recently been elected, he heard himself denounced by Henry W. Pond for having published "I Wish I Was in Dixie's Land" in violation of the association's constitution, which mandated full rights to the owner of the original copyright. There was considerable debate as to who had brought the song out first, and after a secret vote Werlein was directed to share rights in the song with Firth, Pond. After Lincoln's election to the presidency, the New Orleans music man turned his back on the understanding.

Just before the war began, a New Orleans production of John Brougham's burlesque *Po-Co-Hon-Tas, or the Gentle Savage* included an interpolation of "Dixie" into the score. Forty young women dressed in clinging military uniforms stopped the show nightly while marching to its strains. Werlein brought out a new edition, again without mention of Emmett. After secession sundered the union, "Dixie" became the new Confederacy's marching song, though both Northern and Southern military units marched to it. It was performed at Jefferson Davis's inauguration as the South's first president. A Yankee partisan through and through, Emmett mumbled, "If I had known to what use they were going to put my song, I'll be damned if I'd have written it."

Once the conflict was over and Robert E. Lee had surrendered, a crowd gathered outside the White House in Washington, waiting for Lincoln to speak a few words. When he had done so, he asked the band to play "Dixie": "I had heard that our adversaries over the way attempted to appropriate it. I insisted yesterday that we had fairly captured it. I presented the question to the Attorney-General, and he gave his opinion that it is our lawful prize. I ask the band to give us a good turn on it."

Dan Emmett left the Bryants in 1866, moving to Chicago to join a new minstrel company. However, his voice was soon gone, so he was forced to play the fiddle in a lakeside tavern. When the fire of 1871 destroyed most of his possessions, he became manager of a Canal Street saloon for an owner who hoped to attract trade by advertising the minstrel star's regular presence. When the place closed, Emmett wrote to a friend: "I find myself all alone in the world, humbly trying in my old age to eke out a living as a musician."

Once the *Clipper,* the leading show-business paper, to which Emmett regularly submitted dialect and comedy material and lyrics, learned he was no longer able to support himself and a new wife, members of the profession rallied to him. Eventually, the Actors' Fund of America put him on a dole of five dollars a week until his death. In 1888, Emmett returned to his birthplace, Mount Vernon, Ohio, where he bought a cottage and some land, on which he raised chickens. Occasionally, a tourist, astonished to find the writer of "Dixie" still alive, bought an autographed copy of the music from its author.

Daniel Decatur Emmett was eighty-eight when he died in 1904, and they buried him in the dress suit he had worn on a final tour in 1895 with the minstrel star Al Fields. His younger neighbors had never seen him in such splendor. They knew him only as a raggedy old man who raised chickens and bored them with old jokes and songs.

At the time of his death, all the great figures of pre–Civil War minstrelsy were long dead. Daddy Rice had died in 1860. E. P. Christy had jumped from a window in 1862. The man who wanted to be the best Ethiopian songwriter, and succeeded, Stephen Foster, was dead, a penniless drunk. The three Bryants were gone, having seen the old business become a slick variety show that relied on sex for much of its appeal. The music publishers who had profited from the rage for plantation songs were long dead, too, and their catalogues reposed in the vaults of the Oliver Ditson Company in Boston.

CHAPTER 5

The Music of God's Americans 1800–1860

The continuing struggle for political separation of church and state that found its first tentative victory in the Constitution's text had Thomas Jefferson for its chief strategist when the new century dawned. That commonsensical genius saw Christianity as becoming perverted into "an engine for enslaving mankind, and aggrandizing their oppressors in church and state." The growing popularity among the people of Jefferson's articles of intellectual and political faith that swept him into the presidency in 1800 was but one of the factors aiding the growth of belief in a rational God at one pole and a surge of freethinking at the other. While upper-class Federalists indulged themselves in the pursuit of profits and pleasures, and their children began to dally with Rousseau's and Voltaire's rational infidelities, many of their fellow citizens were being seduced into deism by Tom Paine's *Age of Reason*. The aging torch of the Revolution was in France, extending the boundaries of his concern for the rights of man by serving in bloody combat against the excesses of Bourbon aristocracy. Sometime between polemics and politics, Paine found opportunity to write the tract urging that one's mind was one's own, and all religious institutions were "no other than human inventions, set up to terrify and enslave mankind, and monopolize power and profit."

Paine's new piece almost immediately attracted wide attention, as had his writings during the dark and uncertain days at Valley Forge, when he was similarly idolized by the poor and reviled by the wealthy. Taverns, college rooms, stagecoaches, newspapers, and magazines were filled with argument. Wandering chapmen carried *The Age of Reason* in the same pack with Webster's *Blue-Backed Speller* and the latest pocket songster. Americans who had lost faith in the nation's semiofficial denominations found its pages entrancing. The Federalist establishment church, the United States branch of Anglican Episcopalianism, was regarded by many as the continuing power base of the Hanoverian monarchy which had spawned the fight for independence. New England's smug merchant Congregationalists were preoccupied with maintaining

179

their hold on the national government and profiting from the region's state-granted economic monopolies. Most of the 800,000 Yankees who had left their New England homes between 1790 and 1829 to go west had lost all interest in both of these religious institutions and looked for a more rigid faith, something closer to the old Calvinist severity.

The populist doctrines of the two leading minorities, Wesleyan Methodism and the South's Baptist Church of Christ, proved to be far more accommodating to the needs of those who were extending the frontier past the Alleghenies. Throughout the century, until the mail-order catalogue and the automobile brought in the outside world, both faiths served a growing majority of Protestant pioneers well, providing not only a house of worship but also a social hall. It was out of their rituals and observances that the phenomenon of nineteenth-century revivalism grew, giving birth in turn to a major viable popular-religious-music publishing industry. Throughout the nation, men began to engage in printing innumerable editions of collected gospel music, those sacred songs that served the multitudes as meaningfully as did the outpourings of commercial music publishers catering to a growing market for music written for the parlor and the piano.

Worship Under the Open Skies

Outdoor Christian worship was as old as the faith itself, witnessed by chronicles of Jesus speaking to the multitudes under the open sky. English Protestants watched the Wesley brothers take their Methodist flocks into the fields as early as 1739, when the doors of Anglican houses of worship were barred to them. George Whitefield spoke to his thousands both indoors and out in the course of his visits preceding the American Revolution. The for-men-only outdoor camp meetings conducted by the unlettered Baptist preacher John Waller in Virginia during that fight for freedom of thought and worship were yet another step along the path to the revival meeting. "Raised up" by God's voice, Waller inspired others to meet under the open sky in services that in time became outpourings of whites and blacks joined to sing, dance, shout, and weep. The quarterly conferences of Southern Baptists were often forced out of doors for lack of space to accommodate all who wished to join in the love feasts.

Among the 221,000 Americans living in Kentucky in the late 1790s were the denizens of "Rogues Harbour," on the Green River in Logan County. These thieves, murderers, and runaway white and black slaves lived in a state of tentative peace with the border Scots-Irish settlers who had been moving into the region since the days of their great expulsions from England. An inelegant, ugly minister named James McGready used a masterful evangelical preaching fervor that won over murderous outlaws to his brand of Calvinist Presbyterianism, which urged a "new birth" to escape the vengeance of an angry Jehovah. McGready's fame spread quickly throughout the surrounding territory, attracting converts as well as the scorn of conservative Presbyterians, who found his exhortations a serious challenge to accepted practice. By June 1800, McGready's adherents, both old and new, had grown so numerous that the Red River Church, was unable to contain his flock. The time had come for a "religious service of several days' length, held outdoors, for a group that was obliged to take shelter on the spot because of the distance from home"— a certifiable definition of the ensuing phenomenon. This moment was the birth of the true evangelical camp meeting of the Great Revival, or Second Awakening of American Protestantism.

The "divine flame" of religious excitement stirred up by McGready and other Southern ministers, who came to observe and then left to imitate, burst into full light in the last week of July 1800, at the nearby Gaspar River Church. An area around the small meeting house was cleared and a platform and seats were built. From Saturday evening until Tuesday morning, Presbyterian, Methodist, and Baptist clergy and several hundred worshipers, some of them from points more than 100 miles away, forgot sleep and sustenance as the light of the sun and the glare of nightime torch and bonfire illuminated the work of awakening and converted souls, which went on without pause. Within the year, revival meetings had found their pattern.

Starting on August 6, a week-long "sacramental occasion" took place at Cane Ridge, not far from Kentucky's largest city, Lexington. Assembled there were 25,000 men, women, and children, both saints and sinners, for, as skeptics noted, "more souls were made than saved" in the darkness of the forest's remote glens. Physical manifestations of converts' emotional responses were witnessed: falling as though dead, jerking, dancing, running, barking, and hysterical laughter. Of the singing, one clergyman wrote: "[It was] . . . unaccountable. . . . The subject in a very happy state of mind would sing most melodiously, not from the mouth or nose, but entirely in the breast, the sounds issuing from thence. Such music silenced everything, and attracted the attention of all. It was heavenly! None could ever be tired of hearing it."

The character of these heavenly religious songs took its untrammeled shape only after Presbyterian officialdom ended all connection with the movement, claiming it was being "used to contend for an educated ministry, for pews, for instrumental music, for a congregational or stated salaried ministry." By 1805, organized Presbyterians had left the movement in the hands of theological revolutionaries and "illiterate" Methodist preachers.

In one of his last acts, John Wesley had sent Francis Asbury to America, just before the Revolution. Faced with the wilderness's vast distances, Asbury transplanted the British system of a traveling Methodist ministry by creating circuit-riding preachers who went from settlement to hamlet on horseback to seek out co-religionists or win new ones. Even after being named bishop, Asbury rode more than 275,000 miles during the four decades of his American ministry. Like him, many circuit riders were accompanied by assistants, some of them black, who took an active part in the work. All Methodist clergymen also served as agents for the oldest American religious-publishing enterprise, the Methodist Book Concern, formed in Philadelphia five years after Asbury established the Methodist Episcopal Church of America during the 1784 Christmas conference in Baltimore. Each rider's saddlebag carried samples of the Concern's catalogue, Bibles, hymn books, and other church literature, which could be ordered from a new building in New York. The earliest *Pocket Hymn Book* for American Methodists was reprinted from the English model before 1791. It contained only the words of hymns, no musical notation, and thus required the old method of lining-out. The books were often cut up, the pages being passed around so the the illiterate could learn the words and assist in the singing.

Order had been brought early to the camp meeting, a pattern of worship observed before 1803 in the northeast, Ohio, western Georgia, and the Carolinas moving into the mid-South and then the far north, where some Canadians held outdoor meetings. When the Louisiana Purchase opened up a new frontier, the revival meeting moved with the wagons and pack animals that took pioneers into the vast rich lands Napoleon had thrown away for a mere 80 million francs. In spite of Bishop Asbury's adoption of the old interdiction that only an approved hymnal could serve Methodists, the general scarcity of such books led to the printing of many unauthorized words-only pocket hymnals. The earliest were issued in the South, where musical type was scarce: Stith Mead's *Hymns and Spiritual Songs,* Richmond, and David S. Mintz's *Spiritual Song Book,* Halifax, North Carolina, both in 1805. Others issued prior to 1830 included Solomon Watt's *Impartial Selections of Hymns and Spiritual Songs,* Philadelphia, 1809; John C. Totten's *A Collection of the Most Admired Hymns and Spiritual Songs, with choruses affixed as usually sung at camp-meetings,* New York, 1809; Thomas S. Hinde's *The Pilgrim Songster,* Cincinnati, 1810; Peggy Dow's *Collection of Camp-meeting Hymns,* Philadelphia, 1816; John J. Harrod's *Social and Camp Meeting Sings for the Pious,* Baltimore, 1817; *The American Camp Meeting Hymn Book,* 1818, compiled by Enoch Mudge, minister and member of the Massachusetts legislature, "the first native-born converted American Methodist"; J. Clarke's *The Camp-Meeting Chorister,* Philadelphia, and Orange Scott's *New and Improved Camp-Meeting Hymn Book,* Brookfield, Massachusetts, both 1829.

Because these were used chiefly by illiterates, compilers and publishers, as had the British earlier, looked for catchy popular tunes. Much of the music was therefore purely secular, with roots in British theater and "folk" music, some of it dating back to the earliest ballad broadsides issued in Queen Elizabeth's time. Hinde, a British immigrant who settled in Newport, Kentucky, went across the river to Cincinnati in 1810 to have a printer there prepare his *Pilgrim Chorister.* The small book went through many editions. It was essentially a collection of original hymns by Caleb Jarvis Taylor and John A. Granade. The latter was a hard-drinking Carolina doctor who became known as "the Wild Man of the West" after he found God during a camp meeting and turned minister himself. A long period of melancholia preceded each of Granade's three following conversions before he finally became a "shining and burning light as a public advocate for the cause of Christ." During three years of traveling in the Carolinas and Tennessee, he wrote many of the best-loved songs of his time, earning him the title "Western Poet."

Twenty-five years later, the father of modern revivalism, Charles Grandison Finney, remembered the Granade hymns he had heard during his youth in central New York State: "His poetry was . . . was bold, towering, often tinctured with the awfully sublime, yet flowing with ease and naturalness and sometimes extremely tender and pathetic. . . . Some vestiges of [his songs], occasionally found in compilations, are so mangled and distorted that the author, if living, would hardly recognize them."

Mead's *Hymns and Spiritual Songs* included a response to Paine's *Age of Reason:*

> The World, the devil, and Tom Paine,
> Have done their best, but all in vain,
> They can't prevail, the reason is
> The Lord defends the Methodist.

Peggy Dow, compiler of an 1816 collection of camp-meeting hymns, was married to "Crazy" Lorenzo Dow, of Connecticut, an eccentric free-lance evangelist who took the open-air message of salvation to almost all of the United States and to England. There, he learned that English Wesleyanism, much like its American counterpart, frowned on such unofficial innovations, finding them "highly improper." Before his death in 1834, Dow preached, as he described in his *History of Cosmopolite,* to "Presbyterians, Methodists, Quakers, Baptists, Church of England, and Independents . . . Gentlemen and Lady, black and white, the aged and the youth, rich and poor, without exception." This reference to the presence of blacks at camp meetings is but one of many, from which it may be reasonably deduced that the white man's religious frontier revival songs entered the black consciousness early. Until the custom was ended, frontier democracy practiced in mixed worship made both races aware of their separate musical pasts.

Another of the earliest camp-meeting hymnals was the "New and Improved" collection compiled by Orange Scott, a militant abolitionist Methodist preacher. It was printed for him in 1829 by E. & G. Merriam. Brothers Ebenezer and Daniel Merriam started their business in 1797, using one of Franklin's old presses. Ebenezer operated the Brookfield, Massachusetts, printing house; Daniel, a Worcester bookshop that served as their principal outlet. Both were experienced job printers, who first brought out a local newspaper and also issued several editions of a pocket songster, *The Echo.* Like many others, the Merriams cashed in on the popularity of Webster's *Blue-Backed Speller,* and desisted from this piracy only after Webster warned them. Four of Daniel's sons were also apprenticed to printers, one of them, George, being assigned to set the Scott hymnal. After attaining master-printer state, George opened the G. & C. Merriam business in Springfield, with a younger brother, Charles. They subsisted on sales of paper, pencils, wallpaper, toothbrushes, and collections of church music that went through several editions. The Scott sold out its 5,000 copies in little over a year, then a second printing of 3,000, and a third went to press some months later, half of both reprintings presold to subscribers. During the 1840s, the Merriams paid Noah Webster some $3,000 for a fourteen-year copyright renewal to his *Dictionary,* which they brought out in a one-volume enlargement that discarded many of Webster's linguistic and lexicographical reforms. Their version proved to be so successful that they were later able to pay $250,000 to the Webster family for the copyright of a new official revision, and for the *Blue-Backed Speller,* as well, thus obtaining exclusive rights to two of the most successful books ever published in the United States.

Disturbed by the popularity of unauthorized hymnbooks being used by camp-meeting worshipers, the Methodist Protestant Church, one of the two new divisions of the denomination, gave its blessing to a collection by John Harrod that was enjoying great popularity among Southern members. The Methodist Book Concern issued various editions of the Harrod volume in a number of pocket sizes, including a "Pearl" edition, so small that "every child that can read ought to be put into possession of one."

This publication marked the first instance in which a leading Protestant sect took official recognition of the American people's changing taste in hymnody. Prior to 1830, Methodists generally used the large hymnbook issued in London some fifty years earlier, and the series of words-only pocket hymnals was generally based on that. The revised 1821 American edition of this 1780 *Collection of Hymns* "principally from the collection of the late Reverend John Wesley" remained in use by Methodist Episcopalians until after the Civil War. The Methodist Episcopal Church, South, brought out its own official hymnbook in 1847, shortly after separating from the main church. The first Methodist hymnal using printed music was published in 1878.

A great variety of revival-meeting hymnbooks was published to meet the demands of both rural and city churches in the north. Typical was Methodist Bishop Hanby's *Church Harp,* first printed in 1841, with two additional editions sold out within eighteen months. Although it did not contain music, it was one of the earliest to feature feet-washing hymns, with a number of choruses beginning with the words "Hallelujah, hallelujah" to be sung after other hymns. This practice of adding hallelujah choruses, which had become popular during the late 1830s, was inspired by black Christian camp-meeting participants. Hanby's familiarity with blacks and their culture came in no small measure from his involvement in the abolitionist cause. After he moved his family from Pennsylvania to Ohio in 1836, his house was a station on the underground railway, through which slaves passed on their way to freedom in Canada. His son Benjamin was moved by the family's antislavery feelings to write one of the most popular of all pre–Civil War ballads, "Darling Nellie Gray," the account of a woman slave who was sold away from her family to spend her life in Georgia and who is reunited with her lover only after death.

Traditionally, Episcopalians resisted change. The American edition of the *Book of Common Prayer,* with its metrical psalms, was adopted by the six-year-old Protestant Episcopal Church of the United States in 1790. It served for the next thirty years, until the singing of hymns was finally accepted by the Church of England. Although there was considerable resistance, twenty-seven hymns were added to the American service book. In 1826, hymns by Watts, Wesley, and other eighteenth-century writers were published as *Hymns of the Protestant Episcopal Church of the United States,* intended to be bound together with the *Book of Common Prayer*. These 212 hymns included texts by the hymnals's compilers, William Augustus Muhlenberg and Henry U. Onderdonck, both ordained clergymen, and verses by Francis Scott Key and other Americans.

The schism in 1741 between "Old Side" and "New Side" English Presbyterians over the modernization of music in the church by acceptance of a new version of the Tate and Brady psalter and the use of Dr. Isaac Watts's new translation of the Book of David continued in the United States until 1802. That year, the church's General Assembly adopted Yale president Timothy Dwight's edition of Watts's *Psalms,* which added new versifications of psalms Watts had omitted and a number of Dwight's alterations of the translations. An additional ninety-five hymns by Watts's contemporaries were added to the 168 in his first official Presbyterian hymnal. A musical edition of this hymnal first appeared in 1892.

Almost from the beginning of the Baptist movement in America, in 1639, religious and political differences within the denomination contributed to the creation of regional associations. By 1800, there were forty-eight, thirty in the South. The creation of a strong central organization suffered from the progress of these associations, from the struggle for nineteenth-century men's minds as well as their souls by evangelical revivalism, and from the impact of localism stimulated by the slavery issue. Whereas other major Protestant faiths built up national governing entities, the Baptists appeared unable to do so. Today, several dozen bodies administer and guide various boards, conventions, associations, assemblies, and organizations. There is no single Baptist hymnal in use among all the many adherents to this major faith. In spite of this, Baptist hymnody and spiritual songs have long been a vital influence on both religious and popular American music, and their course is one of the most colorful in the history of America's music.

During the first part of the last century, two hymn collections gradually came into general use by American Baptists, replacing native compilations prepared for local churches. New Englanders favored *Psalms, Hymns and Spiritual Songs of Watts, from the most approved authors,* compiled in 1818 by James Winchell, pastor of Boston's First Baptist Church. In the Middle Atlantic states, major Baptist churches made use of *The Psalms and Hymns of Dr. Watts, arranged by Dr. [John] Rippon,* prepared in 1787, when Rippon was pastor of a London church. It was reprinted in America five years later. An American edition of Rippon's "new arrangements" replaced this work in 1820. None of these books contained any music, though Rippon did publish a tune book of 100 hymns in 1791 to be used with his own first text collection.

The Christian Harmonist, collected by Samuel Holyoke and printed for him by the New Hampshire songbook publisher Henry Ranlet, was the first American tune book intended for Baptists. In *Music and Musicians in Early America,* Irving Lowens points out that Holyoke used a large number of verses from *Divine Hymns or Spiritual Songs,* compiled in 1784 by the Baptist preacher Joshua Smith, of Brentwood, New Hampshire, which had gone through eleven editions before Holyoke's work appeared. In addition, according to Lowens,

"Holyoke here attempted to compose in the folk idiom, and it is quite possible that some of the tunes were notated directly from the oral tradition."

In 1805, Ranlet produced *Christian Harmony,* the work of a Newbury, Vermont, tavern keeper, barrel maker, and farmer, Jeremiah Ingalls, who was in love with music and never hesitated to drop all work to join in song. Ingalls used the ground floor of his home as a tavern and conducted a singing school there as well. One of his melodies in the *Harmony,* "Northfield," survives on a recording and in Protestant hymnals to the present. Ingalls is credited by many as being the first to collect "Old Baptist" folk hymns, but he must share that honor with Holyoke.

Samuel Dyer's *New Selections of Sacred Music,* also for use by Baptists, went through six editions after it first appeared in Baltimore in 1817. Dyer was an Englishman, son of a Baptist preacher. Unlike the generally self-taught American compilers, Dyer was trained, taught by Thomas Walker, a London musician who worked on Rippon's tune book. He arrived in the United States in 1811, worked as a teacher and church musician in New York and Philadelphia, and formed a leading oratorio society in the latter. After a visit to England in 1815, he settled in Baltimore, having returned with anthems, odes, and choruses by modern composers, most of which had not yet been heard in America, which he used in his own tune books. He traveled along the Atlantic seaboard to promote sales of his hymnal. He also organized singing schools and led public performances of religious music in an effort to improve church singing, since he was especially opposed to the new vogue for shape notation, which was sweeping the South. Sales of his hymnal encouraged him to issue a collection of church anthems, whose sixth edition was eventually published by Firth, Pond, for whom his son, Samuel, Jr., worked as editor. Copyright to the Dyer hymnals passed into Oliver Ditson's hands during the Civil War.

Shortly after James Winchell's *Sacred Harmony* (1818) was published, James Loring, of the major Boston book-manufacturing business, Manning & Loring, published and copyrighted a tune book for that compilation. Loring produced other hymn collections and religious music, including the *Old Colony Collection of Anthems,* prepared jointly with the Handel and Haydn Society of Boston.

Probably the only failure by Lowell Mason among the many incredibly successful religious and educational publications was his venture into Baptist hymnody. Neither his 1831 *Manual of Christian Psalmody,* compiled with David Green, nor his 1834 *Union Hymns,* done with Green and Rufus Babcock, assistant pastor to the First Baptist Church, was used by Protestants of all denominations, though both contained music appropriate chiefly to Baptist services. In 1841, New England Baptists adopted *The Psalmist,* compiled by Baron Stow and Samuel F. Smith, local pastors. Stow was valedictorian of the first graduating class of the Theological Seminary of Columbia University, established in 1820. His collaborator on *The Psalmist,* Samuel Francis Smith, was a Harvard-trained minister who served as pastor to congregations in Maine and Boston and taught modern languages at Colby College before he joined the American Baptist Missionary Union in 1855 as its editorial secretary.

During a class reunion prior to Smith's death in 1895, his classmate and old friend Oliver Wendell Holmes read an original poem:

> And there's a nice youngster of excellent pith,
> Fate tried to conceal him by naming him Smith;
> But he shouted a song for the brave and the free,
> Just read on his medal 'My Country, 'tis of thee!'

When Smith was twenty-three, in 1831, and a theological student, he became friendly with Lowell Mason, for whose first childrens' school music book, *Juvenile Lyre,* he wrote original verses and translated foreign songs and poetry. He found the original music for Great Britain's royal anthem, "God Save the King," although he was not aware of that, and wrote words to the tune in a single setting. "My Country, 'tis of thee" was first sung at Fourth of July ceremonies in 1831, and was published shortly after by the sheet-music publisher Charles Bradlee, of Boston. In later years, Dr. Smith observed: "If I had anticipated the future of it, I would have taken greater pains with it. Such as it is, I am glad to have contributed this mite to the cause of American Freedom."

Despite the acceptance by northern Baptists of *The Psalmist,* their southern co-religionists were cool to the hymnal because it omitted many of the good old Baptist songs that had long been shouted out at camp meetings, Sunday services, and other occasions. Differences between Baptist hymnbooks was a relatively minor factor in 1845, when the southern wing of the church broke away to form the Southern Baptist Convention. Slavery was a major economic reality. Baptists in the South wished to preserve what they considered the denominational character of their belief, and therefore objected to active missionary work among blacks the world over. Many words-only song compilations had been and still were printed in Kentucky, southern Ohio, the Carolinas, and Tennessee prior to the formation in 1847 of the Southern Baptist Publication Society, in Charleston, South Carolina. In 1850, the society issued *Baptist Psalmody,* compiled by Basil Manly and his twenty-five-year-old son, Basil, Jr., who was pastor of Richmond's First Baptist Church and later enjoyed a long and distinguished career as a Southern Baptist leader. In 1859, the younger Manly published his *Baptist Chorals; a Hymn and Tune Book,* intended to supply "tunes adapted expressly to some of the choicest hymns" for use by owners of both the northern *Psalmist* and his earlier *Baptist Psalmist,* the most popular Southern Baptist hymnal available before the Civil War. Yet many of his rural brethren continued to worship to words and music from shape-note tune books.

The Unitarians, followers of belief in a conception of God as a single person, rather than in the Trinitarianism of other Protestant faiths, became a separate entity after 1785, when Boston's prestigious King's Chapel embraced the new theology. The city quickly became a stronghold of Unitarianism, and Harvard College became its Vatican. The American Unitarian Association was founded at Harvard in 1825 to serve as a public-relations and proselytizing agency for the 125 Unitarian churches then existing, most of them in New England and made up of socially prominent members. Though many good Unitarian hymnals and religious songs flowed from the literary elite making up these flocks, the major compilation came out in 1846, when two Harvard divinity students, Samuel Johnson and Samuel Longfellow, brother of the poet, compiled and edited *A Book of Hymns for Public and Private Devotions,* reflecting the Unitarian concept. During the Civil War, Longfellow, then a prominent Unitarian cleric, once more collaborated with Johnson, to edit *Hymns of the Spirit,* containing hymn texts written by leading American literary figures, among them Harriet Beecher Stowe, John Greenleaf Whittier, and Theodore Parker, the great preacher of the 1850s, as well as some of the editors' own work. The most recent *Methodist Hymnal* contains more songs by Samuel Longfellow than any other writer with the exception of Fanny Crosby, who wrote more than 9,000 hymns during a long and colorful career that extended into the twentieth century.

Nineteenth-century Congregationalism sprang from the spirit of questioning invoked in New England by the Second Awakening there during the 1790s. Coupled with a growing aversion to Unitarianism, many broke away from the conservative arm of the Presbyterian church and formed their own structure and seminaries. The faith was sufficiently organized by 1820 for its General Congregational Association to appoint a committee of members to compile a proper hymnal. After several years of inactivity, one of the committee members, a Yale graduate and ordained minister, Asahel Nettleton, took matters into his own hands. Despite poor health, for some ten years he had been conducting revivals of a comparatively moderate nature in rural Massachusetts and western New York, learning there many of the hymns that especially appealed to unsophisticated northerners. Drawing upon these, he compiled the 600-hymn collection *Village Hymns,* most borrowed, but with some original pieces of his own. Fifty "missionary songs" were included, among them the text to Reginald Heber's "From Greenland's Icy Mountains," the most well-known religious song intended for use by young ministers trained to "Christianize the heathen." No tunes were included, although names of suitable melodies were printed above each text. This hymnal went through several editions, and then Nettleton issued *Zion's Harp,* containing all of the tunes called for in *Village Hymns.*

Nettleton had come out of retirement to support friends who were troubled by the excesses of Charles Grandison Finney and others in the western New York camp-meeting movement. The first major nineteenth-century revivalist, Finney was considered by Nettleton's friends to be the re-creation of those flamboyant exhorters who had sprung up in the wake of George Whitefield's first Great Awakening, during the early 1740s. Nettleton undertook an unsuccessful crusade against Finney, but got little support from intellectual young clerics produced by the new Congregationalist seminaries. They, too, had embarked on personal ministries, using church pulpits as a sounding board for political radicalism.

Among them was Henry Ward Beecher, who in 1855 produced the *Plymouth Collection of Hymns and Tunes,* a highly logical combination of Nettleton's two volumes with printed notations above the words. Beecher was by mid-century the leading Congregational minister in America. His pulpit in Brooklyn's Plymouth Church served as the forum from which he gained newspaper headlines for his moral crusades. He enjoyed national prestige until his credibility suffered after a church member accused him of sexual misconduct in the early 1870s, prompting a lurid scandal.

In 1855, at the height of his fame, Beecher directed his brother, Charles, a fine musician and Congregational minister, and John Zundel, the Plymouth Church organist, to compile a new hymnal to replace the one prepared for the church in 1851. Zundel had been born in Germany, where he became an accomplished musician and served as a bandmaster for the Russian czar's Imperial Horse Guards and organist in a number of important Protestant cathedrals before he moved to America at the age of thirty-two. From 1850 until his retirement in 1878, he was Plymouth's chief organist and composer of much music expressly for use there.

Beecher envisioned the new hymnal as the greatest and finest of its kind and spent much time collecting hymns and suitable texts. When the work was completed in 1855, it contained 1,374 hymns, a number of them gathered from Roman Catholic sources. No religious printing house would undertake so large a publication, so Beecher prevailed upon a church member, Alfred S. Barnes, the leading publisher in New York of elementary and advanced textbooks, who believed that a "good book" was one selling millions, to engage in this vast job. Barnes proceeded to demonstrate that he was also a master salesman, even of church music. Despite protest from traditionalists against the inclusion of Catholic religious music, Barnes made such a huge commercial success of the new collection that he added a line of hymnals to his catalogue, stimulating others to do the same. It was A. S. Barnes's imprint, however, that appeared on the majority of successful hymnals for many years.

During this period, Barnes's chief competitor was Anson D. F. Randolph, who had learned the religious-book business as a teen-ager during the 1830s in the center of its activity in New York City, near where the American Bible Society had its offices. Randolph opened his own business in 1851 on Broadway, several blocks north of the Firth, Pond building, home of a leading popular-music publisher, and began selling religious and theological works. His first collection of hymns was a noncopyrighted volume of sacred poetry set to music, written for him by an Anglican minister. The success of the *Plymouth Collection* moved Randolph to put out the equally successful *Church Melodies,* compiled by Thomas Hastings, who, like his mentor and colleague Lowell Mason, was an enemy of folk hymns, the shape-note business, and all other new musical "aberrations."

Hastings, an albino and extremely near-sighted, grew up on the New York frontier and taught himself music from early instruction books. In 1816, at the age of thirty-two, he compiled the *Utica Collection,* a pamphlet of only a few pages to be used by the local singing society he served as director. It went through many editions, continually being enlarged, and became known in time as *Musica Sacra.* In 1832, Charles Grandison Finney asked Hastings to come to New York City to direct a group of choirs that had volunteered to sing during the evangelist's meetings. Hastings whipped the groups into top-flight order. Before his death, in 1872, he put together fifty collections and wrote 600 hymns and 1,000 approved melodies. *Church Melodies* (1858), among his best-known works, also appeared in a Baptist edition. The book was compiled for publication by Randolph and prepared with his son, Thomas S. Hastings, who became president of Union Theological Seminary.

In the year *Church Melodies* was printed, the Congregational Seminary at Andover, Massachusetts, issued another hymnal of major importance, *The Sabbath Hymn Book,* by Edward Amansa Park and Austin Phelps, teachers there. It rivaled the *Plymouth Collection* in size, with 1,290 hymns, and it, too, added to the interest of commercial-book publishers in the potential of denominational hymnals, a business that made many of them men of great wealth.

The Shape-Note Business

Notwithstanding the haughty contempt of Lowell Mason, Thomas Hastings, and other proponents of "scientific" (high culture) music, fasola solmization and its special notation flourished. Those Geneva type cutters, British music publishers, and Boston preacher-reformers who had pioneered the effort to improve singing among the unlettered through easy-to-read methods would have found much to please them in the spread of musical capabilities among rural Americans of the early nineteenth century. The earliest manifestation of new teaching techniques appeared in the early summer of 1798 when federal copyright was secured for *The Easy Instructor,* whose title page proclaimed the 106-page book to be

a New Method of teaching *Sacred Harmony,* containing the Rudiments of Music on an improved Plan, wherein the Naming and Timing the notes, are familiarized to the weakest capacity.

Likewise, an Essay on Composition, with directions to enable any person with a tolerable voice, to take the air of any piece of Music at sight, and perform it by word, without singing it by note. Also, the Transposition of *Mi;* rendering all the keys of music as easy as the natural key, whereby the errors of Composition and the press may be known. Together with a choice collection of Psalm Tunes, and Anthems, from the most celebrated Authors in Europe, with a number composed in Europe and America, entirely new; suited to all the metres sung in the different Churches in the United States.

Published for the use of Singing Societies in general, but more particularly for those who have not the advantage of an instructor.

Commenting on the new work in late August 1798, the *Philadelphia Repository and Weekly Register* noted,

it chiefly claims attention on account of a new method laid down for facilitating the learner in acquiring the knowledge of the notes as designated by four singing syllables, which is done by diversifying the shape of the notes: as for example, the shape of *Fa* is a triangle, *Mi* a diamond, *La* an oblong square, and *Sol* the usual form. It is evident that their different characters, indicating at sight the names of the notes, will greatly aid the student of Sacred Harmony.

The name William Little appeared as author of the first edition, and that of William Smith as well on succeeding printings of this first shape-note tune book, issued first in New York City and then in Albany over the following two decades. Influenced by *The Easy Instructor,* more than three-dozen shape-note collections came out, chiefly in the South, where the technique took firmest hold and is still observed in remote areas.

Andrew Law was apparently the first to make use of this copyrighted ''patent'' notation. He employed it in his 1802 *Musical Primer,* but only after reversing the square and triangle shapes in order to make the system seem to be his own creation. This seems a shoddy subterfuge, since he was one of the first to agitate for and secure protection by copyright for musical works.

The Harrisburg, Pennsylvania, newspaper owner, printer, postmaster, bookstore owner, and politician John Wyeth brought out his shape-note *Repository of Sacred Music* in 1810. It provided the former New Englander with his first profitable piece of book publishing, no mean success for the apprentice who had once operated a large printing establishment in Santo Domingo after attaining journeyman status. Wyeth was run out of that country by blacks rebelling against white French masters and made his way to Philadelphia as a common deck hand. When he acquired sufficient means, he bought into the Harrisburg weekly *Oracle of Dauphin County.* His *Repository* included songs by William Billings and other New England tunesmiths, and its *Second Part,* coming out in 1813 for use at Methodist camp meetings, contained the first of those ''folk hymns'' that Irving Lowens describes as ''a secular folk tune which happens to be sung to a religious text.'' The first part of the *Repository* reportedly sold more than 120,000 copies in five editions, and the second more than 25,000. Because Wyeth had no musical training, many historians, Lowens among them, deduce that his musical adviser was the Reverend Elkanah Kelsay Dare, a young Methodist minister, musician, and hymn writer, thirteen of whose pieces appear in it. Wyeth continued as an active job printer for other hymn compilers, publishing religious music for many denominations, as well as two self-help music instruction books in German, and some plagiarizations of the Smith and Little books.

The earliest songbook printed from shape-note type to appear in the South was Ananias Davisson's 1815 *Kentucky Harmony,* which came off the Wartman family press in Harrisonburg, Virginia. It was the standard 5-by-8¾-inch size, and like Wyeth's book it contained many American tunes by earlier composers, including Morgan, Billings, and Holyoke, alongside contemporary music by singing teachers who worked on the southern frontier. Davisson was a Virginia Presbyterian preacher and singing teacher who claimed authorship of a number of the book's songs. Success as a publisher led him to issue the 1820 *Supplement to the Kentucky Harmony* for use by camp-meeting Methodists, sold through agents in St. Louis, Louisville, Nashville, Knoxville, as well as in his home state of Virginia. Large sales led Davisson to open a printing office in Harrisonburg, which brought out James P. Carrell's *Songs of Zion* in 1822 and an enlarged edition in 1831. Carrell was a clergymen who later abandoned the calling to speculate in land, farms, and slaves, which made him wealthy enough to leave substantial bequests for Methodist printing and missionary work.

Allen Carden's 200-page *Missouri Harmony,* influenced by both the Wyeth and Davisson books, was printed for its author in Cincinnati and made available in early 1820. Carden intended it for use by his pupils in a school "for teaching the theory and practice of Vocal Music." The book became the most popular work of its kind throughout the Mississippi Valley and the Deep South, going through eight editions prior to 1858. Abraham Lincoln sang from this shape-note compilation of psalm tunes, hymns, and anthems to his sweetheart, Ann Rutledge, in the New Salem, Illinois, tavern owned by her family. An abridged edition was printed for the singing teacher during a visit to Nashville while on a tour in 1824. A Nashville newspaper printing office did the work, possibly from plates Carden carried with him, and the occasion marks the start of music publishing in the community that has become known as "Music City, USA." At some point prior to 1832, Carden sold his copyrights to Cincinnati printers.

Shape-note music paid for the education that made Samuel Lytler Metcalf an internationally famous doctor and chemist. Having grown up in Kentucky, Metcalf started to teach music there, and in 1817, at the age of nineteen, he compiled *Kentucky Harmonist,* "a choice selection of sacred music from the most eminent and approved authors of that science for the use of Christian Churches of every denomination." Wise beyond his years, Metcalf prudently employed a Cincinnati printer to make the book, and then used the profits from four editions printed over nine years to pay for his formal training at Transylvania College, in Lexington, Kentucky. He served as professor of chemistry there in later life and was the author of books on historical and scientific subjects that won him a world-wide reputation and an invitation to join the faculty of the University of Edinburgh, which he turned down.

The publication and sale of new shape-note songbooks boomed during the fifteen years after 1821, principally in the South, where ten of the sixteen known volumes appeared. That archenemy of patent notation and its teaching methods Lowell Mason made an inadvertent foray into the field in 1832 when the Cincinnati publishers of *The Ohio Sacred Harp,* which bore his name and that of his brother Timothy as authors, printed its music in shape notation. Knowing the prejudices of their Midwestern and Southern markets, publisher Truman & Smith noted in a foreward "that the *Sacred Harp* is printed in patent notes (contrary to the wishes of the authors) under the belief that it will prove more acceptable to the majority of singers in the West and South."

The Masons remained true to belief in the do-re-mi seven-note solmization, stating in their preface that "the most correct method of solmization is to apply a distinct syllable to each note of the scale, viz: the syllable DO to one, RA (ray) to two, MI to three, FA to four, SOL to five, LA to six, and SI (see) to seven. Indeed, by pursuing the common method of only *four* syllables singers are almost always superficial. It is therefore recommended to all who wish to be thorough, to pursue the system of seven syllables, disregarding the different forms of the notes."

Arguments among music teachers over the propriety of both systems of notation continued hotly. The shape-note faction scored a major triumph, within two years of *The Ohio Sacred Harp*'s publication, with the appearance of the first of the two long-lived shape-note tune books, *The Southern Harmony*. It enjoyed phenomenal sales for more than a century and could be found in the basic literature of some mass-singing meetings in the South long after World War II. Its compiler and harmonist, William Walker, of immigrant Welsh descent, was born in 1809 in South Carolina. He had only an elementary education and no formal music training, but his spirited presence at Baptist camp meetings earned him the name "Singing Billy." Walker was eighteen when financial circumstances made necessary a family move to Spartanburg, where he found greater opportunity by giving music lessons and appearing before large audiences in this recently founded county seat. Walker's first contact with organized musical activities developed the lifelong conviction that he said, "to praise the Lord on string instruments, the psaltery and the harp, as well as with the human voice, was not only a requisite, but a grand concomitant of religious worship.

Walker married at twenty-five, and in the process acquired a sympathetic brother-in-law, Benjamin Franklin White, equally untrained and a singing teacher. White was the naive one, trustful and inclined to share his joy in music for the sheer love of giving, often taking no fees for his lessons. The two began to gather the traditional Southern Appalachian tunes sung by blacks and whites, setting them down in the four-note fasola technique. By 1834, they had arranged over 200 songs and decided, because there was no publisher with appropriate music type in Spartanburg, that Walker should go north to find someone who could duplicate their work in mass quantities.

Walker found a printer in New Haven, Connecticut, and returned home with copies of the 248-page *Southern Harmony and Musical Companion*. His name appeared as author and compiler, and twenty-five of the songs were attributed to him as sole writer. He never spoke to his brother-in-law collaborator again, and soon moved south to Georgia.

The Southern Harmony became the most successful patent-note songbook issued prior to the Civil War, with more than 600,000 copies of its five editions sold. The Philadelphia stereotype printer Edward W. Miller was Walker's partner as publisher of the final four editions. "The Napoleon of the Book Trade," J. B. Lippincott, of Philadelphia, a leading bookseller of Bibles, prayer books, and literature to major Southern dealers, was the distributor for the Walker books. Walker traveled widely to promote sales, autographing copies for admiring buyers, with the letters *A. S. H.* (Author of *Southern Harmony*) appended to his signature. It became his custom to assemble and train a small group of the best local talent and then leave the territorial sales agency in its hands, with the pupils of the singing school each operated becoming the principal source of sales. A contemporary wrote: "Thousands and thousands have blessed the name of William Walker who sent the *Southern Harmony* into almost every home in the southern land, breaking up the fallow ground and creating . . . a thirsting for sacred music in the masses such as the round-note system has nor ever will accomplish.''

Wartime economic troubles in the South put an effective end to sales of the Walker books. When peace came, he capitulated to seven-syllable notation. In 1854, he had written, ''I have taught the four syllable patent notes, [Lowell Mason's], Italian seven syllables, and the numerals also, and in twenty-five years' experience, have always found my patent note pupils to learn as fast, and as correct as any.'' Only after hours of prayer did Walker announce in 1866 that God had revealed that a twenty-five-year-old system of musical notation designed by Professor Jesse Aikin, of Philadelphia, was now most acceptable to Him. The professor's *Christian Minstrel,* first issued in 1846, employed a seven-shape pattern that added three created by Aikin to Little and Smith's original patent notes. *The Christian Minstrel* had gone through more than 150 editions with little impact in the South before Walker's new tune book employing its method appeared in 1866. Unable to secure permission from the patent owners of Aikin's notation, Walker created his own version of it. Though it never enjoyed the success of its predecessor, the new *Christian Harmony* added significantly to the 750,000 copies of Walker books that had been sold by the time of his death, in 1875, with uncounted unauthorized printings of the originals since.

Walker's early collaborator B. F. White never swerved from his dedication to the traditional four-note fasola notation, first affirmed in his own *Sacred Harp,* printed in Philadelphia in 1844. This and Walker's book were the two most widely used collections to come out of the Southern United States. Filled with disappointment over the behavior of his brother-in-law, White moved his family to Georgia, just north of the Alabama border. A self-taught musician and a fifer during the War of 1812, White eked out a living for his large family by giving singing lessons, never turning away a pupil on account of inability to pay. The most promising of his students was a teen-ager, Georgia-born Elisha James King, with whom White compiled English hymns and psalm tunes, music by New England singing masters, local folk tunes and songs, and new works by Southerners. When their 262-page *Sacred Harp* came off Philadelphia stereotype presses in 1841, young King was dead, but his name appeared on the title page. A preface by White pointed out that he had ''taught music for the last twenty years, and being necessarily thrown among churches of various denominations and all the time observing their wants in . . . church music [had] in this work endeavoured to supply that deficiency which heretofore existed by placing all of the church music . . . in one book.''

Shortly after his *Sacred Harp* was introduced, the Southern Musical Convention was organized, with White as president, to produce fasola activities centered upon the new book. The organization was patterned after musical conventions first organized in the North by Lowell Mason to provide social pleasure and musical education. Like them, the *Sacred Harp* festivals took place over several days, but essentially they were devoted to instruction in sight-reading and concerts of solo and group singing of shape notes. Committees regularly revised and added to the contents of new *Sacred Harp* editions, which long continued to appear for use by practitioners of this now-esoteric singing art.

In 1851, White became editor of Harris County's first weekly newspaper, *The Organ,* which he also used as a promotional medium for fasola singing by reprinting songs from his collection. White eventually became county court clerk and was elected town mayor after the Civil War, in which he had served as commander of local militia. When Walker's *Christian Harmony* and its imitators gave currency to the seven-shape notation "Singing Billy" had espoused, White was instrumental in protecting the old tradition with new editions of his *Sacred Harp* in which he maintained that "we have been especially vigilant in seeking musical terms more appropriate to the purpose than the four note-names used in this book. But candor compels us to acknowledge that our search has been unavailing. The [four-note] scheme has had the sanction of the musical world for more than four hundred years; and we scarcely think that we can do better than abide by the advice 'Ask for the old paths and walk there.' "

The supporters of the newest thing, the seven-shape system, eventually drove a wedge between urban and rural followers of the tradition, a break that White lived to see in the last years before his death in 1879.

The First Great Urban Evangelists

Other than Bishop Francis Asbury, "Crazy" Lorenzo Dow, and a few others, the vast number of rural evangelists, whose inspired preaching impelled thousands of Americans from the Deep South to the Canadian border to seek salvation in public conversion to a belief in God and Christ, are lost to popular history. Those few remembered are known because of their connection with revival-meeting songs and collections of hymn words.

A conflict within the minds of early-nineteenth-century Americans over the place of the church in the order of things almost inevitably created the Second Awakening, led by nationally known revival preachers, men who could manipulate vast audiences into religious fervor. They have ranged from the first major revivalist, Charles Grandison Finney, most active from 1825 to 1835, on to Dwight L. Moody, Billy Sunday, and Billy Graham, and right up to contemporary practitioners of the electronic ministry. They have much in common, including an unswerving reliance on the value of religious music rooted in the popular idiom and performed by musicians and singers of professional caliber.

By 1830, Finney had become the most successful upper New York State and New England evangelist, leading great numbers of sinners to Christ during years of dramatically staged revival meetings and successfully making frontier religious assemblages respectable. In the late autumn of 1830, he received a letter from Joshua Leavitt, the editor of a religious laymen's weekly, the *New York Evangelist,* suggesting the adoption of a new hymnal, whose "favorite tunes and hymns of the various denomination" would certainly "aid in revivals of religion.'' Leavitt, thirty-six, had recently assumed the editorship of the *Evangelist,* which was subsidized by a number of wealthy patrons, men who found much of value in Finney's message. An ordained Congregational minister and ardent supporter of abolition and of temperance, he had already compiled the successful *Seamen's Devotional Assistant,* which was distributed by the Seamen's Friend Society. He had chosen 629 texts to serve ''pious sailors.'' The book's success persuaded him to prepare a collection of the ''lighter and more songlike hymns with rippling rhythms and sometimes 'chorusses,' '' which were sung at revival meetings. He chose as a model Nettleton's 1823 *Village Hymns,* with its accompanying collection of sixty-four appropriate melodies. Although he had no particular musical skill, he solved the awkwardness created by Nettleton's separately printed words and music by printing a single book in which the two appeared side by side. This *Christian Lyre* first appeared in weekly supplements to the *Evangelist* and then as a finished book in April 1831, printed and published by Jonathan Leavitt, at the time New York's most important publisher of religious and theological works.

Recognizing that people attending revival meetings showed ''a desire to use hymns and music of a different character from those ordinarily used in churches,'' Leavitt had dipped into the great treasury of popular music for his tunes. He used ''Home, Sweet Home,'' ''Auld Lang Syne,'' Charles Dibdin's ''Lowly Nancy,'' and simplified versions of the most likable melodies of Billings, Daniel Read, and other New Englanders. People approved, and the *Christian Lyre* had gone through twenty-six editions by 1846.

Not being intended for ''scientific musicians,'' the *Christian Lyre* immediately roused the ire of Lowell Mason and Thomas Hastings, who found its music ''insipid, frivolous, vulgar and profane'' but did borrow its ''pocket hymnal'' size for their own collection of *Spiritual Songs for Social Worship.* The Mason-Hastings book was clearly a response to Leavitt, who, they grumbled, ''in these enlightened days of reform'' asked worshipers to sing ''the current love songs, the vulgar melodies of the street, of the midnight reveller, of the circus and the ballroom, the very strains which of all others, we are told, are the best adapted to call forth pure and holy emotions, in special seasons of revival.'' The Mason-Hastings collection went through its last printing in 1839; Leavitt's, just before the Civil War, twenty years later.

Charles Grandison Finney, who was the first to use the *Christian Lyre* in his services, was born in 1792, spent his boyhood in central New York State and his adolescence in the remote and rugged Lake Ontario country. After a few years of precollege studies, he chose not to go to Yale, but got an education teaching school in New Jersey, from where he returned home to read for and be admitted to the local bar. At the age of twenty-nine, already a successful lawyer and religious skeptic, he went through a shattering conversion. Jesus Christ appeared before him in his office, giving ''the spiritual retainer to please His cause'' that Finney frequently cited during the many years of ministry that followed.

After starting on the streets of his small town, Finney extended his work to the bustling communities along the new Erie Canal, winning national attention through newspaper accounts of his incredible successes. With no formal religious training and only the license to preach granted by a rural Presbytery, the six-foot two-inche blond and blue-eyed preacher used an innate sense of theater and an orator's voice to pronounce "instant and eternal damnation" upon his listeners unless they repented. Among his improvements on the rural meetings was the "anxious seat," to which people could come and, individually, be made the subject of prayers. There Finney could engage in combat for the soul of the seat's occupant. He also created "protracted meetings"—several days of preaching, praying, and congregational singing. In urban versions of these frontier meetings, tailored to the demands of sophisticated city people, time was taken out only to sleep and eat.

Despite all the efforts of conservative clergy to curb his theatrics and restore Christian decorum to worship and dignity to the pulpit, Finney went unrestrained. The number of converts rising from the benches grew, and he increased the geographic range of his work. After refueling his soul with rest, he began a year-long crusade in New York City. He was supported by a number of wealthy local merchants, who were determined to attract the city's poor and new immigrants to the blessings and social discipline of an organized capitalist-oriented Presbyterianism. The *New York Evangelist* was established and financed to assist that cause.

The character of Finney's revivalism underwent a change in the summer of 1830, after he took a short vacation from his New York pulpit in response to an invitation from Rochester, New York, laymen. It proved to be, as William G. McLoughlin, Jr., writes in *Modern Revivalism:*

> the first city-wide campaign that deserves to be compared to the urban revivals of the post–Civil War era. In conducting it Finney made full use of the theories and practices of modern evangelism which he bequeathed to all professional evangelists for the succeeding century and a quarter. . . . Revivalism was becoming with Finney not only a trade but a respectable trade. It had to do so if it was to acquire and maintain the support of persons influential enough to carry through the revolution within the churches.

After an equally successful revival campaign in Boston, Finney returned to New York in response to a call from Lewis Tappan, one of the city's wealthy merchants who had supported his first visit. "This city must be converted or the nation is lost," Tappan had written. The merchant took over the Chatham Theatre, renting the space for $2,000 a year, and then spent $3,000 in renovating it. The Second Free Presbyterian Church was then housed there. It was "free" because there was no charge for the pews, which held between 2,500 and 3,000 people. Finney was paid $1,500 annually for his services and provided with a nearby house.

Aiming his evangelistic sights at the "prominent people"—the lawyers, politicians, merchants, and intelligentsia—Finney secured the services of a proper scientific musician, nearly blind Thomas Hastings, to direct the music. Hastings's presence made it evident that the character of revival music was being changed to accommodate the tastes of new communicants. The massed interdenominational choir of singers from twelve cooperating metropolitan-area churches sang only songs approved by Mason and Hastings, and they made proud their director and all exponents of scientific music training.

Gone with the hymns based on popular music that Leavitt had compiled was the rip-roaring brand of western revivalism that had brought Finney national prominence. The once spectacularly spellbinding evangelist was now a prudent and sedate cleric who relegated high-pressure preaching to the few months of summertime and several trips to Great Britain, during which he gave English-men occasional samples of American Bible thumping, the first they had wit-nessed since Lorenzo Dow's forays there in the early 1800s.

Finney resigned from both the Second Free Presbyterian Church and the mother faith in 1836, to become pastor of the new Congregational Broadway Temple, which had been built for him. Ill health and his growing ambivalence in the cause of abolition brought about his departure from New York, to be-come professor of theology at the new Oberlin College. There, he eventually became president, serving from 1851 to 1866.

During the decade of the 1830s, American population grew from 13 million to slightly over 17 million, nearly double that of 1820. The center of popula-tion, which had been eighteen miles southwest of Baltimore at the start of the century, had moved west to sixteen miles south of Clarksburg, Virginia. The seminaries and theological training schools being built by organized American Protestantism were unable to keep up with the demand for trained ministers to meet the requirements of the westward expansion. As a result of this failure, and the success of itinerant evangelists, educational standards were lowered, and many partly educated pastors were licensed to shepherd new communities. This, according to McLaughlin, "broke down the distinction between social classes, put the laity on an equal plane with the clergy, encouraged equality of the sexes, and pursued in a wild and fantastic way all manner of social re-forms."

The fire-and-brimstone pulpit techniques and unorthodox social conduct of these newly recognized frontier preachers, while acceptable to their flocks, brought down the wrath of conservative eastern superiors, and led sometimes to remov-als from the ministry after trials for heresy. Deviations from orthodoxy took many courses. Augustus Littlejohn was expelled when he turned his back on monogamy to share the blessings of "complex marriage" with the sisters of his congregations. The "irreverent prayer" ("God smite the Devil! God smite the whited sepulchre! Jesus Christ come down here and attend to these hard-ened cases!") with which Luther Myrick opened his meetings, accompanied by groaning, jumping, leaping, and stamping, led to his expulsion. Jedediah Burchard and his evangelist wife, it was charged in an unsuccessful attempt to curb his practices, made any church they entered "become a theater." Mrs. Burchard brought her spouse's dramatic style to bear on audiences of mothers and children, who otherwise were denied the blessings of evangelistic Presby-terianism.

On the other hand, Baptist revivalists did much to change the direction their faith was to travel. Because it had long sought to appeal to the poor and less well-educated for its converts, the Baptist church learned early the advantages of dramatic preaching, liberally larded with folksy gospel music. Generally, their songs were a far cry from John Calvin's basic precepts. Two of the best-known Baptist evangelists of the time, Elder Jabez Swan and Jacob Knapp, applied Finney's methods to their ministries. Though less dramatic than Finney at his peak, both paid as much attention to stage presence, costume, and delivery as did any actor on the New York stage. New Englanders and graduates of Hamilton Seminary, they fought dancing, gambling, the consumption of alcohol, and the influence of other denominations, and each gave up a pastorate in mid-career to take up itinerant revivalism.

Out of regard for his mostly poor and rural audiences, Swan, it was said, "never preached in a new suit of clothes until he had worn it through a rain storm." After thirteen years as a minister in New England and New York State, he began a full-time traveling career in 1841, holding three-month-long meetings until he was in his seventies. He often preached fifteen times a week and wrote his own hymns, often stopping in mid-harangue to sing one. He urged converts to sing his songs as they marched to the river for baptism by immersion and on their return to the meeting place.

After seven years of the traveling ministry, Jacob Knapp's fame in 1841 rivaled that of Finney, and he was making $2,000 a year. Much of that came from the pathetic pleas for free-will offerings during worship, as he cited an ill wife or pointed to the shabby clothing imposed on him by vows of poverty. When it was revealed that Knapp owned over $15,000 worth of real estate, funded by his followers, an investigation resulted in dismissal, the first such recorded, but certainly not the last to involve private gain by men of the cloth.

The Lunch-Hour Revival Movement

Traveling evangelists representing virtually all the Protestant creeds coursed across the nation during the 1840s and 1850s. Some of them were engaged in the work full time; others pursued the career only when temporary unemployment so indicated. More and more, temporal issues were becoming the abiding concern of middle- and upper-class Americans, whose way of life was subject to their vagaries. The problem of slavery, for one, was ever constant, splitting the nation, the churches, and many families along religious, social, and financial lines. Unparalleled prosperity seemed indicated as the permanent future state of the country. The national wealth, the number of banking houses, the value of interstate commerce, all had doubled in little more than ten years. More than $800 million in gold and silver had been added to the nation's treasuries since that morning in 1848 when a workman turned over a spadeful of California river bottom and unearthed a few golden nuggets. The constant westward expansion speeded up real estate speculation and railroad construction, the latter funded chiefly by the private investment of more than one billion dollars.

The bill came due on a summer's morning in 1857, when an Ohio financial institution became the first of 4,933 businesses that failed by the end of the year. The national monetary system closed down temporarily, and an additional 8,000 business establishments shut their doors the following year. Out of this twelfth depression since 1790 came a new religious movement, the third to shake the country in little more than a hundred years, the "Prayer Meeting Revival." Another middle- and upper-class, white Protestant, nonsectarian phenomenon, it moved businessmen and their employees to take matters into their own hands and, no longer relying on the intercession of the clergy, spend the noon hour in personal supplication.

Those Americans who had looked with disdain on rude frontier camp meetings now looked for help in the open prayer meetings that had been adopted by conservative ministers as a tool for increasing church attendance and tithing in the early 1850s. Big-city churches opened their doors during the lunch hour to "union prayer meetings," and those who were "losing treasure on earth" came in the hope that they could "lay up treasure in heaven." Daily, across the nation, 500,000 men joined this nonsectarian awakening. Each working day there were a dozen such meetings in New York, half that in Washington, three in Boston, and many in all the important northern and western cities. The new penny-daily newspapers made capital of the movement, recording its progress on the front page. Word of these meetings was also spread by the fast-growing electric-telegraph industry, whose services were coming into greater demand each day to report market quotations and other business items. Businessmen who had turned to public prayer in order to regain God's grace and blessings kept their associates in other cities in touch with the success of midday revivals by courtesy of the telegraph company, which sent the news free of charge during lulls in operation.

Many of the meetings in New York City were organized by the year-old Young Men's Christian Association, the YMCA, a social and religious organization patterned after the similarly named London group. Both had originally been funded by the wealthy in order to provide a respectable meeting place for their young employees, where Christian capitalist values could be affirmed by social and religious training, with a heavy accent on physical activities. It was understood that the latter would do much to lessen tensions imposed on these healthy youngsters by lack of access to the company of women. An inexpensive collection of favorite popular church songs, the *Union Prayer Meeting Hymns,* was issued by the Sunday School Union early in 1858, intended specifically for the businessmen's revival movement. Of all the stirring hymns inspired by that phenomenon, the favorite was the Reverend George Duffield's "Stand Up, Stand Up for Jesus!," the text of a sermon preached by Duffield's associate, Dudley A. Tyng, to a vast noontime gathering of 5,000 Philadelphians. A few days later, Tyng was dead, victim of an unfortunate accident, and on the following Sunday Duffield preached a sermon in his memory, ending with the eight stanzas of the new hymn. The words first appeared in Sunday School publications and then were widely reprinted. They came to the attention of George J. Webb, an English associate of Lowell Mason, who set them to music, which was published in the 1858 edition of *The Psalmist*. The hymn sold over a half-million copies in the next ten years, at a time when books of literature had an average sale of 1,500 copies.

The American Sunday School Movement

By 1860, the layman-controlled American Sunday School movement was reaching far beyond the young people normally regarded today as its constituency. Initially formed late in the previous century by the British philanthropist Robert Raikes to provide one day of education for the poor children who worked the other six in mills and mines, Sunday Schools sponsored by industry were introduced to America some time later. The immigrant inventor Samuel Slater, who founded the spinning-mill textile business in Rhode Island, chanced to overhear a group of his seven-to-twelve-year-old employees planning to raid a nearby apple orchard. Slater proposed to them, "You boys come to my house and I will give you all the apples you can eat, and I will also keep a Sunday School."

Schools of that sort, attached to various Protestant churches, had been formed earlier by the Wesleys in Georgia in the late 1730s, and in other Southern colonies just after the Revolution. In response to urging by Dr. Benjamin Rush, the physician, who advocated use of the Bible as a schoolbook, Philadelphians established the first urban Sunday or First Day School in 1790. Many merchants supported the institutions, which were run either by the church or by industry. Emphasis was placed on memorizing Biblical texts, hymns, and the catechism, and little attention was paid to reading, writing, or arithmetic, all regarded as purely a parental obligation.

The chief textbook in these early Sunday Schools was the venerable *New England Primer,* some eight to ten million copies of which had been purchased in America since its British forerunner was first registered with the Stationers' Company in 1683. The *Primer* included the Westminster catechism, some rhymes, and some hideous illustrations.

There were few collections of songs or hymns written especially for the young other than Watts's *Divine and Moral Songs,* his last little book; Ann and James Taylor's 1804 *Hymns for Infant Minds;* and Rowland Hill's *Divine Hymns in Easy Language,* intended as an index to all of Watts's childrens' songs, among them such grim items as:

> But, oh, what a horrible sight,
> When children, with anger and rage,
> Like lions will quarrel and fight,
> Which none can their anger assuage.

One victim of such early songs for children wrote in later life that youngsters "were solemnly exhorted to trail our voices to grim and ponderous tunes, which a hymn of equally unattractive character dragged its slow length along."

The first official American Sunday School Union hymnbook was compiled in 1819 after testing in various schools. Candidates for inclusion were printed on small cards and slip sheets, which were distributed to children, whose reactions were presumably noted. The responses were evidently dictated by grownups, for once the book was distributed, it became obvious that the music was not suited to children.

Some reformers agitated for revision, arguing that "if music is really to take hold of the feelings of children, it must be simple, quick and lovely in its general movements."

When the American Sunday School Union organized a publishing arm in 1824, a wave of educational reform followed that affected the entire nation. The union's stated purpose, "to disseminate useful information, circulate moral and religious publications in every part of the land, and endeavour to plant a Sunday-school wherever there is a population," spelled out the scope of its founders' ambitions. The union was an ecumenical venture, governed and administered by laymen, who supervised its missionary work and operated its chief enterprise, printing and publishing. In its first six years, it organized 6,000 schools, with 60,000 teachers and 300,000 pupils; brought out six million copies of primers, spellers, testaments, and hymnbooks; and issued periodicals—all within an annual budget of $76,000.

The age of students admitted to a union Sunday School showed a wide range. The very young were taught to read and write. Young adolescents were provided with advanced practical education, and adults were admitted to study and discuss the Bible under the supervision of lay teachers. In many schools, the Bible Study Group was larger than the entire congregation attending Sunday worship.

The union's early music publications included manuals and hymnbooks, among them *A System of Instruction in Music;* Thomas Hastings's *Juvenile Psalmody,* compiled for the Western Sunday School Union, based in Utica, New York; and Elam Ives, Jr.'s *Manual of Instruction in American Sunday-School Psalmody.* The last, a large work, was the fruit of its author's experience in teaching 5,000 children who had been trained to sing by rote how to sing a hymn scientifically "in one hour." The *Two-cent Hymn Book* for "houses of refuge" was issued by the union in 1826, as were various collections of songs suitable for meetings of Sunday School teachers and supervisors. The series of *Union Hymn Books* was repeatedly revised, coming out in editions of 20,000 to 30,000 copies each. By 1846, some 250,000 had been distributed.

The Sunday School Union's initial success and the commercial potential of music for children quickly came to the attention of printers and publishers specializing in secular literature and music for the young. A great number of religious-song collections aimed at this market appeared from the late 1820s until after the Civil War. Sunday School songs and books attained sales equal to, and often in excess of, those intended for the popular-music—buying audience. Yet none of these entrepreneurs enjoyed the commercial success and financial rewards attained by Lowell Mason, sometimes called the "Father of Singing Among the Children." It was a title on which he doted, but he deserved others, based on his remarkable understanding of the business of music education for the middle and upper classes, from which he made great profits.

The system of music education he created and promoted played a leading role in shaping the character of music that later generations of middle- and upper-class Americans perceived as proper to their social station. His influence—and that of his disciples Thomas Hastings, William C. Woodbridge, and their followers—did much to instill in the "cultured generations" of the post–Civil War period the belief that the music Europeans took most seriously was by its very nature the best, even though it might be difficult to enjoy at first hearing. As a result, popular music as known today had to await a new breed of music publishers, most of them first-generation Americans who heard in the street music around them a new and vital form that offered opportunities to make money, once they persuaded the owners of pianos that this music was worthwhile and that it occasionally possessed the very American genius that was making the nation a power.

Lowell Mason and Popular Religious Music

The Masons came to America in 1653 and settled in Medfield, Massachusetts. Six generations later, Lowell Mason was born, in 1792. He was musically precocious and could learn to play any instrument without instruction. After becoming the pupil of a number of neighborhood singing masters, from whom he gained an understanding of the possibilities of income from teaching, he began, at sixteen, to train and direct church choirs, accompanying them on his cello.

At the age of twenty, he jumped at the opportunity to travel to Savannah, with a neighbor who had been contracted to build a church organ there. When the chore was completed, Mason stayed on, finding work as a bank clerk in Savannah. He joined the local Independent Presbyterian Church and directed its choir. He also organized a Sabbath School that became one of the largest in the state and famous for the quality of its singing.

Mason's initial exposure to scientific musical theory, the German music that shaped his thinking from then on, resulted from a meeting with Frederich Abel, a recent arrival in America. Two years younger, Abel was the grand-nephew of C. F. Abel, who had produced concerts in London with J. C. Bach. Abel had been trained by his father and other German musicians, whose course of instruction he passed along to Mason. These studies included assignments to write original music and to reharmonize pieces by Mozart, Handel, and Beethoven. That training enabled Mason to complete a 320-page collection of psalm tunes, completely reharmonized by him, using approved church music as well as that by modern composers, chiefly German. Abel wrote a personal recommendation and sent Mason, book in hand, to George E. Blake, the Philadelphia publisher who had already issued some of the young German's piano music. Even though Mason was willing to forgo royalties, a misjudgment he never made again, Blake was not interested, nor was George Willig or any of the New York and Boston music publishers to whom Mason also went.

Mason's manuscript eventually came to the attention of Boston's Handel and Haydn Society, whose officials had been searching for exactly such a work. They asked the best-trained musician resident in the United States, Dr. George K. Jackson, to pass on its merits. Jackson recommended its publication after some revision and the inclusion of a few of his own hymns. *The Boston Handel and Haydn Society Collection of Church Music,* copyrighted by the society, appeared in 1822, printed by Richardson & Lord, of Boston. Little mention was made of Mason; the dedication paid tribute to Jackson's "great care and attention in revising and correcting" the book. A second edition, containing "additions and improvements," issued shortly after Jackson's death, dropped any reference to him. Mason later explained the absence of his own name in the early editions by saying he did not then wish to be known as a musical man.

As sales increased and new editions appeared, Jackson's ten original hymns were dropped, and eventually Mason's credit was changed from a single mention in fine print to large type on the title page as sole editor. Sharing in royalties from all eighteen editions, Mason netted an estimated $10,000 to $30,000 from sales of more than 50,000 copies.

His first taste of recognition as a writer of popular religious songs came in the mid-1820s after publication, as sheet music, of his setting for Bishop Heber's "From Greenland's Icy Mountains." A Savannah lady had discovered the words in a magazine and brought them to the handsome young bank clerk and choir director for an appropriate musical setting. The hymn first appeared in the 1827 edition of the Handel and Haydn Society's *Collection,* from which it was extracted for separate printing.

Mason gave Boston the first notice of his intention to train children in the art of singing during a visit to that city in 1826, when he was asked to speak at several local churches. "If music is not taught in childhood," he said, "much progress cannot be expected afterwards." It was a daring suggestion at the time.

Impressed not only by the public attention the *Collection* had received, but also by Mason's notions regarding education, a group of Boston businessmen arranged through three local churches for him to serve as their joint music director at an annual wage of $2,000, guaranteed for two years. Mason learned almost at once that it was not possible to serve three clergymen and three congregations. Only by supplementing his income with a salary from Boston's American Bank, where he was a teller, was he able to confine his musical duties to one, Dr. Lyman Beecher's Bowdoin Street Church, whose choir he directed for the next fourteen years, and made the group middle-class America's measure of quality. He also organized the first children's singing school in the United States, gradually increasing the size of its chorus from an initial half-dozen to 500 to 600 voices. For them, he wrote *Juvenile Psalmist* in 1832, a thirty-two-page work containing hymns and a question-and-answer introduction to music, and *Juvenile Lyre,* with Elam Ives, Jr., who had already written the Sunday School Union's first *Manual of Instruction.* Most of the translations of foreign songs used in the *Lyre* were by Samuel F. Smith, later author of

"My Country, 'tis of Thee." The *Lyre* also contained Mason's own setting, though not the one presently used, of "Mary Had a Little Lamb," a new piece written by *Godey's Lady's Book* editor Sarah Josepha Hale.

Shortly after he had returned to Boston in 1827, Mason was elected head of the Handel and Haydn Society, and served in that important position for the next four years, during which time he first exerted a tremendous influence on the city's musical future. Most of his ideas rested on a recently acquired familiarity with the Pestalozzian system of "psychologizing education," aiming for social reform through education of the individual young person, particularly applied to training children in music. He had been introduced to Pestalozzian precepts by William C. Woodbridge, a clergyman-educator who had spent time in Europe studying modern methods of education, chiefly elementary musical training. Mason borrowed German teaching books and new music written for the young that Woodbridge had brought back. He made free use of Woodbridge, Samuel Smith, and others to translate the German texts. Mason's new methods were first applied in late 1831 to the 100 pupils being trained on weekday afternoons at the Bowdoin Street Church. Within a year, the results were demonstrated in public by a series of free concerts that brought great acclaim and moved a group of Boston's music-loving merchants and literary figures to support formation of the Boston Academy of Music. With Mason at its head, the academy was dedicated to obtaining "for our country the advantages derived from vocal music in Switzerland and Germany."

During its first year, the academy trained 1,500 juvenile and adult students how to sight-read music, to sing, and how "to understand music and enjoy its performance," chiefly by attending concerts of ordinary church music in "the best style of performance." It was a plan of study that prevailed until 1847, when the academy closed its doors.

The first official textbook, compiled by Mason in 1834, the *Manual of the Boston Academy of Music,* had a significant effect on the countless number of Americans who were seeking to earn a living by teaching. It immediately became the essential tool of their trade. Its advocacy of a concentrated study of music, rather than the haphazard and casual part-time classes conducted by itinerant singing-school masters was to create a new and socially acceptable career for those trained in Mason's precepts. The *Manual* went through eight editions of several printings each prior to the Civil War. American music by Billings, Law, and others was included among the *Manual*'s contemporary German music, but Mason himself rearranged and harmonized these pieces in order to make them, too, properly "scientific." A narrow-minded isolationist American copyright law blessed the wholesale piracy of European music, and Mason ran as roughshod through the copyrights of his foreign idols as he did those of his fellow countrymen. Though few were aware of it, the *Manual*'s instructional text was lifted from a German book lent by Woodbridge.

Before he left the academy in 1838 for richer fields, having been placed in charge of all music education in the Boston school system, Mason issued a number of publications under the school's imprint that added substantially to the institution's financial well-being. One of these books was the *Boston Acad-*

emy's Collection of Church Music, which opened the doors of Protestant choir lofts to the music of Haydn, Mozart, Beethoven, Pergolesi, Cherubini, Romberg, Winter, Weber, Nageli, Kubler, and others. It was yet another step in Mason's determined crusade to reshape and improve hymnody by saving it from the evils of fasola solmization, which persisted among Southerners and the lower classes. By reminding educators and choir leaders that there were valid reasons for introducing alterations into books of psalmody, Mason added to his income with regular new editions.

The impact of Leavitt's *Christian Lyre* annoyed Mason, so he joined with Thomas Hastings, fresh from his work with Charles Grandison Finney in the great revivalist's New York crusade, to produce *Spiritual Songs for Social Worship.* The book's many editions, as well as those of other hymnals put together by Mason-influenced compilers, created an antidote to the "vulgarization" of church music.

During a prolific lifetime, Mason issued an extraordinarily successful catalogue of hymnbooks, and his sales and promotion techniques were little different from those developed by his fellow captains of American industry, one of whom he indeed was.

The most successful of Mason's works was his *Carmina Sacra* (1841), which sold over half a million copies in ten years, and in a revised edition became a cornerstone of the music-publishing business of Mason & Mason, established in the early 1850s by two of his sons. Eventually, all of Mason's copyrights were held by this company, including *The Hallelujah* (1854), to which was prefixed *The Singing School,* a manual for classes in vocal music; *Musical Notation in a Nutshell,* which sold more than 150,000 copies in its first four years; *The Psaltry* (1845), *Cantica Laudis* (1850), and *The New Odeon* (1855), each of which sold more than 50,000 copies within a few years; and *Mason's Mammoth Exercises* (1856), priced at $7.50 and containing sixty musical diagrams, each twenty-four-by-forty inches when opened, large enough to be read from the back of a schoolroom. In all, Mason compiled, edited, and collaborated on more than 80 collections, writing 1,126 original tunes and 497 reharmonizations or arrangements. His best-known hymns include "From Greenland's Icy Mountains," "Nearer, My God, to Thee," "Joy to the World," "Blest Be the Tie That Binds," "My Faith Looks Up to Thee," and "When I Survey that Wondrous Cross." After the death of one of his sons in 1869, the Mason brothers' catalogue was purchased by Oliver Ditson, of Boston, and so brought to that company most of Mason's best-selling works as well as those of his best-known associates.

An important secondary source of income came to Mason from the proceeds and spin-offs provided by the teachers' training classes, musical conventions, teachers' institutes, and normal institutes of music organized by the Boston educator and supervised or guided by him until his death, at the age of eighty, in 1872. In these Mason assumed a firm hand and permitted no heresy, which led one of his earliest disciples to defect and to write about "the arrogance of those who could endure nothing but the glorification of their idol," meaning Mason. Mason and his aides used high-pressure promotion and selling methods to push books and teaching aids. He organized his first summer teachers' class, twelve students, in 1832, after publication of the *Manual*. In 1839, 265 men and women attended the session. The first American Musical Convention was held in Boston in 1850, attended by 1,500 graduates of Mason's summer sessions, all of the participants ardent messengers of the music educator's gospel. From this, the movement spread over the country and thus directed the course of American public- and secondary-school education along the lines determined by Mason, and built up at the same time a prosperous market for his printed materials.

The first Normal Institute of Music was held in the summer of 1852 in New York City, with Mason and George F. Root as directors. The four-week session cost attendees ten dollars in addition to a four- to six-dollar charge for board, and offered day-long lessons in harmony, voice culture, composition, singing, and other subjects by a staff of specialists. Concerts of vocal and piano music were presented in the evenings.

The growth in the number of Americans who were taught to read and sing scientific music by the graduates of these Mason projects created an immense market for the popular religious songs that were being written on the principles inculcated by the Boston educator and his followers. The chief contributor to this popular and appealing hymnody was Mason himself; others were Hastings, George Webb, Henry K. Oliver, William B. Bradbury, George Root, and I. B. Woodbury, all of them regular participants in Mason's teaching sessions.

Bradbury and Woodbury became major pre–Civil War religious-song publishers and hymnists and helped to shape that income-producing aspect of the music business. The first church organ Bradbury ever saw was in the basement of Boston's Bowdoin Street Church. He had gone there in 1830, at fourteen, to study with Lowell Mason, having learned to play all the instruments available to him in his York, Maine, birthplace, where his father was a singing master and choir leader. As soon as he mastered the pipe organ, he was hired by Mason to play for the church choir, at a salary of twenty-five dollars annually. The instrument he played was so ancient that he had to press keys down to make the sound and then raise them to quiet it. Although he was soon hired away by another church, at a 400 percent increase in pay, Bradbury remained Mason's pupil at the Academy of Music.

Mason gladly recommended his now twenty-year-old pupil when authorities in Machias, Maine, asked for a teacher who could conduct three large singing schools as well as train a number of private pupils. After eighteen months in that rural community, where James Lyon, compiler of the 1760 *Urania*, had spent the last twenty-three years of his life, Bradbury returned to Boston to marry and then embark on a peripatetic teaching career in Canada. After responding to a call from the First Baptist Church of Brooklyn, he moved on to become organist at the Broadway Tabernacle, where his superb mastery of the church's newly installed pipe organ soon converted church members who had been angry over the introduction of the instrument. New fame came from the growing reputation he gained as director of a childrens' singing class. The Sunday School movement was in the first stage of expansion, and superintendents and officials of local youth groups flocked to see and hear the results of Bradbury's work. He assisted in the formation of children's choirs in other churches, instructing more than 600 in one. Out of this activity came his juvenile musical festivals, usually held in the vast tabernacle, where 1,000 children, seated on a gradually rising platform, sang the semiclassical pieces ordained by Mason. It was these demonstrations that persuaded New York authorities to add a music program to the public-school curriculum.

Bradbury brought out the first of his fifty-nine collections of popular religious songs in 1841, *The Young Choir,* for the use of his own pupils, which was adopted by progressive Sunday Schools around the nation. Many of his books, appearing on an average of two a year, were intended for the youth market, among them *The School Singer* (1843), *Young Melodies* (1845), *Musical Gems for School and Home* (1845), *Sabbath-School Melodies* (1850), *The Oriola* and *Golden Showers* (both 1862). Woodbury's most famous children's religious song, "Jesus Loves Me, This I Know," appeared in the last, its words coming from an 1860 novel, *Say and Seal,* by Anna and Susan Warner. In it a little boy was comforted by his Sunday School teacher, who sang to him this song, now familiar throughout the world.

More than two million copies of Bradbury's songbooks, Sunday School compilations, and hymnbooks for adults were sold. The most popular of the last was the 1858 *Jubilee,* which sold more than 250,000 copies. His hymns still in general use include "He Leadeth Me, Oh Blessed Thought," "Sweet Hour of Prayer," "I Think When I Read That Sweet Story of Old," "Holy Bible, Book Divine," "Saviour, Like a Shepherd Lead Us," and "There Is No Name So Sweet on Earth." Their long popularity runs counter to the opinions of many contemporaries who thought his talent trifling. But a later writer, Jacob Henry Hall, in *Biography of Gospel and Hymn Writers,* thought him "an excellent composer. His melodies have an easy, natural flow, and harmonies are among the best that American writers have produced." Credit for much of Bradbury's success must be shared with Thomas Hastings, who assisted in correcting his manuscripts before publication.

Bradbury was one of the first Americans to study in Europe. Between 1847 and 1849, he studied in Germany, at the institute founded by Mendelssohn for advanced training in piano, organ, voice, and harmony. After his return to America, he concentrated on writing, compiling, and publishing books, and personal involvement in the musical-convention movement. In 1854,, he formed a partnership with his brother, E. G. Bradbury, and the New York piano inventor F. G. Light, to make and sell keyboard instruments. They eventually introduced the Bradbury piano, one of the most widely known of the time.

Bradbury's steady need for new hymn texts brought him into contact with young poets, many of whom dominated the world of popular gospel songs through the remainder of the century. One was the blind poet Fanny Crosby, who had already written popular and sacred materials with George F. Root. She came to Bradbury's offices in lower New York in 1864 and became one of a group of verse writers and tunesmiths who supplied the publisher with the bulk of the hymns that filled his Sunday School songbooks. With Mary Ann Kidder, poetry editor of the *New York Leger,* and Josephine Pollard, temperance balladeer and hymn writer, Crosby wrote most of the words to which Bradbury set the tunes in his popular compilations for adult churchgoers.

Even as success was crowning his every effort, William B. Bradbury was slowly dying of the consumption that took his life in 1868, at the age of fifty-one. The Bradbury piano business was taken over by one of the factory foremen and eventually became the property of the Knabe Piano Company. Bradbury's catalogue of religious music, second only to that owned by Lowell Mason and his sons, was signed over by his wife and daughter to Sylvester Main, a former singing teacher and prominent church soloist. Main reorganized the business as Biglow & Main, in partnership with the merchant and church layman Lucius Horatio Biglow. In the postwar era they vied for sales with the John Church Company, of Cincinnati, the other major publisher in the idiom. The sales potential of this market is best attested to by the fact that publishers paid the trustees of Dwight L. Moody and his musical director, Ira D. Sankey, royalties in excess of $300,000 over a ten-year period from the sales of their hymnbook.

Isaac Baker Woodbury, born in 1819 in a Boston suburb, was apprenticed to a blacksmith, whom he left at thirteen to study music and the violin. He went to London and Paris for further study in 1838, and on his return taught and toured as ballad soloist for the popular Bay State Glee Club. Oliver Ditson published Woodbury's popular songs at this time, many of them musical settings of popular poetry: "The Rainy Day" and "Stars of the Summer Night," both by Longfellow, and "Be Kind to the Loved Ones at Home," "The Sailor Boy's Last Dream," and "Strike the Harp Gently."

With the Boston public-school music teacher Benjamin Franklin Baker, who became principal of the Boston Music School in 1851, Woodbury compiled *The Boston Educational Society's Collection* (1842) and *The Choral* (1845). These were the first in a long list of educational and religious songbooks that included *The Anthem Dulcimer,* which sold 125,000 copies in two years, and the Southern Baptist Publication Society's early *The Casket,* issued shortly after the denomination's split over the issue of slavery.

Poor health forced Woodbury to curtail his activities, so he returned to Europe to regain his strength. He, like fellow Americans Mason, Root, and Bradbury, was struck by the devotion and religious effect with which German worshipers sang "correctly" in their churches. One result of such visits was that many prosperous American churches gave up soloists and returned to full congregational singing, assisted by the introduction of the Germans' small black boards, on which movable numbers of hymns to be sung were presented to churchgoers.

After his return to New York in the early 1850s, Woodbury became a featured teacher-speaker and singing leader at musical conventions. His output of tune books and compilations became so great that a contemporary noted that his music was sung by more worshipers than that of any other American.

Woodbury's regular reviews of new printed music and books and his articles in the *Musical Review and Gazette* made him influential in promoting the trade and expanding its horizons.

In his last years of productivity, he became associated with Sylvester Main and his sixteen-year-old son Hubert, both of whom edited Woodbury's publications. Young Main revealed a knowledge of old church music far beyond that of anyone else of his years, an asset that continued to grow and proved to be a mainstay of Biglow & Main, where he worked until his death.

While on his way south on a business trip in the autumn of 1858, Woodbury was taken ill, and he died within three days. Thus his work on the new *Hymn Book of the Methodist Protestant Church* was ended; it was published under another editor the following year by the denomination's Book Concern. His hymns continued to enjoy great popularity throughout the Civil War, but by the turn of the century his tunes had disappeared from hymnals, and today they are in little use.

During the last year of Woodbury's life, an important publisher added religious songs for young people to his stock. Horace Waters, a founding member of the Board of Music Trade and rated in 1855 by the *New York Musical Review* as one of the city's three major music men, had come to New York in the late 1840s and gone into the piano business, adding music printing a few years later. Soon after 1855, he went into bankruptcy, but recouped his money in 1859 with the publication of *The Sabbath School Bell,* the most popular of its kind yet issued; it sold over one million copies in the next ten years. Waters listed himself as author-editor of the book, as he did with a dozen similar volumes appearing under his imprint before he abandoned the music business to pursue temperance and political activities.

Stephen Foster found Waters a disagreeable person who, in the early 1860s, treated him shabbily. Taking advantage of the songwriter's deplorable condition and hoping to cash in on his past success, Waters took forty-seven Foster songs, paying five to ten dollars for all rights. Twenty of these songs were printed in Waters's Sunday School songbooks. Waters's standards for these were higher than those of publishers who had no compunction about adapting old minstrel-song melodies to religious texts. For example, one made "Hear the Gentle Voice of Jesus" out of Foster's "Massa's in de Cold, Cold Ground."

It was precisely such usage of popular music that prompted the American Sunday School Union to institute a reform of juvenile hymnody, a movement that gained considerable impetus after the war. It was spurred by the success of a union publication, *Sunday School Anniversaries,* a significant milestone in the organization's drive for music expressive of gladness, which it perceived as being more conducive to the development of children's minds. New collections followed, with hymns and melodies written by outstanding authors and composers, and supervised by a merchandising and education genius, George Starr Scoffield, who ran the union's New York office and was responsible for all printed output.

Scoffield was sixteen when he went to work for the union in 1826. He worked his way up to salesman and then depository agent in the Philadelphia branch before he was placed in charge in New York in 1854. His vision was responsible for one of the union's proudest achievements, the *Ten Dollar Sunday School and Family Library,* made up of 100 books of from 72 to 250 pages per volume. In less than twenty years after its first appearance, one million sets of this remarkable work were distributed. Following the success of *Union Prayer Meeting Hymns,* compiled by a YMCA committee for use in the great prayer revival movement, Scoffield resumed printing of *Anniversary Hymns,* which had been started in 1825 and abandoned in the early 1830s. This series of new hymns for use on special occasions throughout the church year proved to be highly profitable. Out of this and the union's other postwar work with juvenile hymnody came one of the two elements (the evangelistic prayer meeting was the other) that would spark the gospel-song business, from whose roots the present-day Christian gospel-music movement sprang.

CHAPTER 6

The Music of
Black Americans 1800–1860

The first national legislation resulting from the combined efforts of dedicated white abolitionists and black activists ended the slave trade in 1808. By then, owing, ironically, to the ingenuity of a young tutor whose Yale College instructors had been in the van of the northern antislavery movement, the character of slavery in the South and the economy it sustained had changed dramatically. Eli Whitney went to South Carolina in 1792, and learned that the chief problem affecting the local economy was the difficulty of separating the seed by hand from Sea Island cotton. Having worked his way through college by using his skilled hands, he devised in ten days a working model of the cotton gin, which speeded up the seed-picking process and thus opened cotton production to major development. His 1794 patent was supposed to protect his invention, but the first model of his cotton gin was stolen and then reproduced in quantity, effectively stripping him of the tremendous royalties he could have earned.

Three years prior to Whitney's cotton gin, only thirty-eight bales of cotton were exported to England, where the raw material was needed by the textile industry. By 1805, this had grown to 146,000 bales, rising to three and a half million in 1860. The economic revolution in the cotton trade set off by Whitney's ingenuity sealed the fate of black freedom. The business of slavery expanded, despite the federal law that ended the trade.

The one million blacks living in the United States in 1800, nearly 200,000 of whom were free, increased to four and a half million by the outbreak of the Civil War, with only 13 percent of them freedmen, principally in the North. The decline in the manumission of blacks was due to the growing need for cheap labor in the cotton fields and the accompanying encouragement of child breeding to supply manpower. There were, however, large communities of free black people below the Mason-Dixon line, in Washington, Baltimore, Charleston, Mobile, and New Orleans, where black men supported their families much as did middle- and lower-class whites, working in the professions and as small businessmen, common laborers in factories, and daily workers.

The majority of Americans in the North, either remote from contact with blacks or too concerned with working up the economic ladder, avoided all involvement in the slavery issue until the war made continued inaction impossible. Many of them had found a palliative to qualms of conscience in the world of popular entertainment, with its burlesqued caricatures of the "darky" living in an unreal plantation world.

In the Southern and frontier states, fear of violence from slaves caused authorities to enact legislation that effectively stiffled any action to help the slaves. The first national effort to thwart total abolition began with the plan to send free Afro-Americans to Liberia, in western Africa, under the auspices of the American Society for Colonizing the Free People of Colour of the United States, organized by white Protestant clergymen in 1817 with the eager support of prominent Southern politicians and opinion makers. This project solidified the work of black leaders who thought of America as their home and the place where they hoped to make their future. By 1830, black abolitionists had issued the first Negro newspaper, *Freedom's Journal;* flocked to the first Negro convention, in Philadelphia; and supported Richard Allen, leader of the African Methodist Episcopal Church, in a course of action that led to formation of the American Antislavery Society in 1833. No free Americans were more disappointed in the inadequacy of Northern laws that sought to put an end to slavery in the confines of each separate state than a group of resolute whites who called themselves abolitionists. Their voice was the *Liberator,* edited by William Lloyd Garrison, a mild-mannered activist who once publicly burned a copy of the Constitution because it did not speak out against slavery.

With whites and blacks, Garrison had taken part in the formation of the Antislavery Society. He remained a director of the movement for twenty years, until a split developed between his radical white followers and the adherents of Frederick Douglass, a former slave who wished to work within the judicial and political system to achieve emancipation and equal opportunity. This schism involved practically all the 200,000 members of antislavery organizations.

Waves of whites began to swell the American population: 1.5 million during the 1840s, and 2.6 million in the following decade. In those areas where they chose to separate themselves from white social organizations, blacks did grow in number, but not in political strength. By the time of the Civil War, the AME Church had grown to more than 275 congregations, with 70,000 members, its own college—Wilberforce, in Ohio—and a magazine. This growth was in spite of the fact that small Charleston and New Orleans AME churches were discouraged by local authorities, and other Southern communities fought against even the introduction of the denomination. Only the Methodists and Baptists converted Southern Afro-Americans, though they insisted on segregating them in church. Yet nearly one sixth of the South's four million slaves were Christianized before the war.

Black Masons, Odd Fellows, and other fraternal groups in the North were never able to affiliate with the organizations' international white leaders, but their social activities flourished among growing affluent groups engaged in almost every trade and profession available to whites. Only a small number of those who had achieved wealth and real estate holdings through the exercise of shrewd business judgment and financial ability found the doors to real economic equality and social opportunity open to them.

Unions and labor guilds barred all blacks, and slave catchers often had the assistance of Northern whites in kidnapping escaped blacks for resale to plantation owners. Free blacks in many Northern cities were denied the ballot, a place on juries, and other civil rights to which they were qualified by both birth and condition of life.

Popular Music and Black Americans

Nowhere did the prewar black American poor live in such poverty as in large cities, where they were confined to racial and social ghettos in which their misery was occasionally equaled by that of immigrant white Irish and other Europeans: Little Africa in Cincinnati, Nigger Hill in Boston, Five Points in New York. To those and other sinkholes, curiosity-seeking whites went to watch black musicians, dancers, and entertainers. For more than a hundred years, the streets there had been offering unusual and compelling dances, music, and language, upon which whites drew for the blackface minstrel show that overwhelmed all other forms of pre–Civil War musical theater.

Minstrelsy and the Ethiopian song fostered the Northern white perception of the plantation as a pastoral idyll lived under a benevolent master and the loving fondness of his family. Instead, slave blacks lived under a lifetime sentence of forced labor. As new machinery was introduced to increase production, some blacks did begin to move up the ladder of technology in small ironworks, hemp mills, ropewalks, and other industries that sought to compete with Northern monopolies. On the plantations, clever blacks who had learned how to repair farm implements passed their skills on to the young. Many of these were among the slaves who came north by the underground railroad.

"Slaves were generally expected to sing as well as work," Douglass remembered from personal experience. "A silent slave is not liked by masters or overseers. 'Make a noise, make a noise' and 'bear a hand' are the words usually addressed to the slaves when there is silence among them. This may account for the almost constant singing heard in the southern states." White visitors generally regarded that singing as a mark of the carefree, happy life blacks were supposedly enjoying. Others remarked on the efficiency that up-tempo cheerful songs created. Only a few perceived that it was a means of permitting overseers to know where the field hands were.

Foreign travelers were poetic in recounting the glories of black singing. The Swedish novelist Fredericka Bremer, who traveled the length and breadth of America in the 1850s, went belowdecks of a Mississippi riverboat to hear the stokers sing. One of them, she wrote, "began an improvised song in stanzas, and at the close of each, the negroes down below joined in vigorous chorus. It was a fantastic and grand sight to see these energetic black athletes lit up by the wildly flashing flames of the fiery throats, while they, amid their equally fantastic song, keeping the time most exquisitely, hurled one piece of fire wood after another into the yawning fiery gulf.''

In the North, most urban blacks, like whites, became familiar with each new kind of music and new songs that made their way into the gathering places of the poor. Unless they were household servants, few blacks had access to modern musical instruments. When they did learn to play them, it began with that process of eavesdropping that had permitted slaves to become familiar with the white man's music since the summer of 1619.

By the time of the War of 1812, almost every middle- and upper-class white household in major cities had a least one instrument: a harpsichord or pianoforte, violin, clarinet, flute, guitar. Exposed to a persistent musical atmosphere, Philadelphia's blacks, like those in other large cities, soon took up this form of personal satisfaction. The programs of the Philadelphia Library Company of Coloured Persons, formed in 1833, included lectures, debates, and concerts. An 1841 publication, *Sketches of the Higher Classes of Coloured Society in Philadelphia, by a Southerner,* spoke of the ''universal love of European and white American music'' found among free blacks, a love ''cultivated to some extent—vocal and instrumental—by all.'' The women entertained on the piano, guitar, and other instruments ''with singing and conversation.''

During the 1820s and early 1830s, Philadelphia's music publishers—Willig, Blake, Klemm, and Bacon—published, along with white European-influenced dance music for the piano, flute, and guitar, military-band quicksteps and marches composed by James Hemmenway, a black who worked as a barber and hairdresser but also directed a military band and dance musicians who performed for both white and black functions in Philadelphia and its environs. When the city's Musical Fund Society moved out of Washington Hall, where Benjamin Carr had conducted concerts until his death, Hemmenway's Band was a regular feature there until the middle 1830s. The black musician had been a member of the all-black marching band led by Matt Black in the years after the War of 1812, along with Francis (Frank) Johnson, who became the best-known bandleader and keyed-bugle player in the United States.

Possibly of mixed blood, Johnson was born in 1792, and his musical education came first through eavesdropping, but later he was formally trained by musicians of both races who recognized his potential. Johnson initially played the violin, and by the time he was twenty-five he was famous as the fiddler who was leader of the black group that played for all the Quaker City's balls. In 1821, he formed the Coloured Black Band, at first with only himself on bugle, a fifer, and bass and side-drum players. In the half century during which a Johnson band played for dancers, marchers, and concertgoers, the size of the group grew to more than twenty-five instrumentalists, augmented with strings. For many years the basic cadre included the Appo brothers, who occasionally played in the Walnut Street Theatre orchestra, and A. J. R. Connor, whose songs and instrumental pieces were published in Philadelphia.

When Johnson's band was hired in the early 1820s to play for Philadelphia's State Fencibles, a white militia company and social group, many of the amateur soldiers resigned in protest. However, the verve and excitement of Johnson's music brought a change of attitude, and other white militia companies began to use similar black marching bands. During Lafayette's visit to the city in 1825, Johnson's military band and dance orchestra entertained at many of the public functions in his honor. The music Johnson wrote for these occasions, as well as other selections, were published for him and sold in the city's music stores.

Once Johnson's reputation became known nationally, publishers in other cities and in Europe issued music by this talented American, of whom the *Detroit Free Press* wrote in 1839, that "It may be said without fear of contradiction, that as a composer or musician, he stands without rival in the States."

His acceptance as a musician and composer had come slowly, however. In 1832, for example, when he accompanied the Fencibles to a national convention in New York, white musicians refused to perform until his band was removed from the line of march. It took years before white players recognized his ability, even though he was regarded as second only to Richard Willis, teacher of music at West Point and leader of its brass band, as the best American performer on the patented Halliday keyed Kent bugle.

Each summer Johnson took his musicians to Saratoga Springs, in New York State, where the upper class went to take the waters and escape the cities' heat. The Johnson band was a regular summer attraction there. From that base, he took his musicians on tours of the adjacent territory, playing in Buffalo, Detroit, and Toronto, before fashionable, wealthy, and appreciative audiences.

In the early summer of 1837, Johnson bade a temporary farewell to Philadelphia, and his fans and patrons gave their favorite bandleader a grand benefit ball, the proceeds of which were to pay passage to Europe for him and a few of his men. Later that year, he performed a series of morning concerts in a Regent Street concert room, playing the works of celebrated composers and also "Crows in the Cornfield," "Butter and Cheese," and his own keyed-bugle variations on "Yankee Doodle" and "Hail Columbia." He also appeared before the recently crowned ruler, Victoria. As a reward, Her Majesty presented the black virtuoso with a silver bugle, and he played his own "Victoria Gallopade" in her honor.

After some time on the Continent, Johnson returned to the United States and, following a tour of northern cities, to Philadelphia in late 1838. While abroad, he had purchased a large collection of music, some of it written in the "peculiarly celebrated" style of Strauss. He had also attended the highly profitable promenade concerts, introduced in Paris five years earlier. A large orchestra played concert music and popular dance tunes for audiences who occasionally listened while they engaged in chatting, drinking, eating, and sometimes sleeping. The theater pit or orchestra section was boarded over to make a large dancefloor, and a platform was erected on the stage for the musicians.

Johnson offered a season of similar concerts in the Great Saloon of the Philadelphia Museum, then the largest room in the United States. Three times weekly, during January and February 1838, between 2,000 and 3,000 people paid twenty-five cents to attend programs made up of the music of Balfe, Bellini, Johann Strauss, Auber, Meyerbeer, Boieldieu, and other contemporary European composers, as well as compositions and arrangements of popular contemporary songs by Johnson.

Johnson's Promenade Concerts were presented regularly in Philadelphia during the Christmas holiday season until his death, in 1844. Four months before, on December 23, 1843, Johnson had conducted what Eileen Southern, in "Frank Johnson and His Promenade Concerts," called "Philadelphia's first integrated concert—undoubtedly the first in the United States." In it, "leading white musical artists of Philadelphia joined forces with Frank Johnson's band to sing a 'Grand Concert of Vocal and Instrumental Music.'" Johnson also had earlier directed the 150-member Colored Choral Society of Philadelphia and his 50-piece orchestra in an oratorio in both a white Protestant and an African Presbyterian church.

Frank Johnson's band continued under the direction of A. J. R. Connor until after the Civil War. The professional men played alongside those who made bricks, cut hair, repaired shoes, or mended or pressed clothes by day, but together they entertained the City of Brotherly love by night with some of the best music heard in the United States.

None of these talented musicians ever achieved Johnson's prestige and popularity, nor did many others of equal ability. However, William Appo, Peter O'Fake, Henry R. Williams, and Connor, all from the Johnson group, attained some success, as did the banjo and guitar virtuosos Justin Holland and Horace Weston.

Hailed by fellow black Baltimoreans in his youth as "the most learned musician of the race," William Appo, with his brother Joseph, was a mainstay of the Johnson groups in which they performed and of Philadelphia theater orchestras. William taught music in both cities and in New York, where he eventually made his home.

The black flutist and guitar player Peter O'Fake played with the Johnson band throughout the 1850s under Connor's leadership. Earlier, before leaving his native Newark, New Jersey, where he had played church and popular music, he had been hired on at least one occasion to play in Louis Antoine Jullien's vast orchestra. O'Fake's black band played for social dancing in the New York metropolitan area for many years, and he was also active as a choir leader in the black Episcopalian church.

Born in 1813, to a middle-class black Boston family, musician and composer Henry R. Williams studied there in the days before Lowell Mason's theories of music education for the young had displaced the singing master. After playing for Johnson, he returned to Boston to teach and work in local bands and orchestras, and he was one of the city's black musicians in the band and orchestra of 2,000 instrumentalists assembled by Patrick Gilmore in 1872 for the Boston World Peace Jubilee. His music was published by Oliver Ditson, and he wrote arrangements for Gilmore's orchestras.

Horace Weston was born in 1825, the son of a middle-class black Connecticut teacher of music and dancing. Though he became a nationally known banjoist, Weston did not appear on the stage during the days of minstrelsy. When blacks were permitted to appear after the Civil War, he was among the earliest to be hired by Callendar's Georgia Minstrels, the first black troupe, with which he toured Europe.

Justin Holland (1819–1886), whose guitar instruction books were regarded as definitive texts, was born in Virginia but educated in Boston. He was already a fine guitarist by the time he went to Oberlin College at the age of twenty-two, and he became a professional player after his graduation. He settled in Cleveland, the city in which S. Brainard and his sons had built a family business into one of the country's largest music-publishing houses. For it, Holland provided many arrangements for guitar of leading popular songs, as well as solo music and piano and flute duets.

Among the best-remembered black marching bands were Sam Dixon's Brass Band, in Newburgh, New York, known in the late 1820s for their uniforms of yellow pants and red coats; the Hazzard Band of Philadelphia, second only to Johnson's aggregation during the late 1830s and early 1840s; Virginia's Richmond Blues Brass Band; and Robert's Band, the Scioto Valley Brass Band, and the Union Valley Brass Band, all active in Ohio during the 1850s. Half a century later, the *American Art Journal* wrote that "forty years ago nearly every regimental band in New York was composed of black musicians."

In the South, where a professional black musician had to be outstanding indeed, representing as he did a contradiction of the accepted folk myth that blacks were of a lower mental order, there were highly talented slave performers who compelled the admiration of both races. The fife-and-drum groups who played for eighteenth-century militia units were made up of black and white musicians and eventually evolved into larger musical groups when more complicated instruments became available. Small groups used violins, flutes, clarinets, banjos, tambourines, drums, triangles, mandolins made of gourds, and a horse's jaw bone, the teeth of which were scraped with a hollow stick. Former slaves recalled making music with tin cans, jew's-harps, or anything that would produce sound.

Solomon Northrup, a free black man of Saratoga Springs, New York, was lured to Washington, D.C., in 1841, by two white men and then sold into slavery in Louisiana. He was an accomplished musician, whose talent made him more valuable. He was especially busy during holidays, as he recalled in an autobiography published in 1853, after he had been rescued and returned north: "I was considered the Ole Bull of Bayou Bouef. My master often received letters, sometimes from a distance of ten miles, requesting him to send me to play at a ball or festival of the whites. He received his compensation, and usually I returned with many picayunes jingling in my pocket—the extra contributions of those to whose delight I had ministered." Such fiddlers as Northrup were considered a usual plantation luxury and provided their owners with additional profit beyond the income from their work in the fields or household.

A blind infant boy named Tom, purchased with his mother in 1849 by Colonel Bethune, a Georgia planter, provided his master with an asset that made the family fortune. At an early age he showed an extraordinary musical talent.

He was able to mimic any human or animal sound he heard, and, after being given access to the Bethune piano at the age of seven, amazed his owner by an ability to play any piece of music, no matter how difficult. This convinced his owner to give him special attention. The child's first public concert was given in Savannah in 1858, and from then until his death, in 1909, Blind Tom Bethune was exhibited throughout the United States and Europe by the family whose name he had been given. This amazing prodigy had a reported repertory of 7,000 pieces, some of his own composition. A major portion of each concert included improvisations on popular music of the day, in response to audience requests.

The "Black Swan," Elizabeth Taylor Greenfield, the first black concert singer to win fame both in the land of her birth and on the Continent, had a more traditional talent. Born in Mississippi in 1809 and taken to Philadelphia when still an infant, she was adopted by a white Quaker family named Greenfield. Like Tom's, her musical gifts made themselves known early, and she was given vocal lessons and permitted to sing for family and friends. She made her professional debut in 1851 and toured the northern United States during the next several years, being required to play to white-only audiences. Her programs were made up of the usual European art songs, pieces by Handel, Donizetti, Bishop, and Bellini, accompanied by piano, harp, or guitar.

A promoter took her to England in 1853, but he abandoned her before a single public performance. Harriet Beecher Stowe, in London basking in the first flush of adulation for *Uncle Tom's Cabin,* came to her assistance, introducing her to leading British patrons of things musical and cultural. They immediately leased Stafford House for a concert by the black American singer. Six of England's best-known vocal artists preceded the Black Swan, singing the most refined current parlor music. When her turn came, her voice, Mrs. Stowe wrote, "with its keen, searching fire, its penetrating vibrant quality, its 'timbre' . . . cut its way like a Damascus blade to the heart. It was the more touching from occasional rusticities and artistic defects, which showed that she had received no culture from art." She sang "Old Folks at Home," giving one verse in a soprano voice and the next in tenor. A guest "tried her voice by skips, striking notes [on the piano] here and there at random, without connection, from D in alt to first space in bass clef; she followed with unerring precision, striking the sound nearly at the same instant his fingers touched the key."

There was no such splendor when Elizabeth Greenfield returned to the United States. The spectacle of a black woman singing virtually the same repertoire as that with which the angelic Jenny Lind had captured the nation's adoration appeared to have no attraction. The Black Swan retired from public appearances to become a voice teacher in Philadelphia. When Hampton Institute emulated the example of the Fisk Jubilee Singers to raise funds for constructing new campus buildings, one of her pupils was among the student singing group, carrying on a heritage of talent from the world of slavery into the bright new world of freedom.

The Emergence of the Black Spiritual

While purportedly authentic "Negro" popular music was finding an international market for its printed copies and a universal audience for its white interpreters, a truly valuable black contribution to music was burgeoning in the South. Unperceived by most whites, among whom it was coming to glorious life, this peculiarly Southern black musical form awaited the war, to be brought to world attention.

The African Methodist Episcopal Church, most of whose members were in the North, still sang from an official hymnal, first issued in 1801 and revised in 1820. In it, Bishop Richard Allen, compiler of the work, had essentially clung to the hymns and liturgy that Methodism's founding father, John Wesley, had prepared for the American branch. So, too, had the members of the African Methodist Episcopal Zion Church. Together, the two had 75,000 adherents by the time of the Civil War, 5,000 of them in the AMEZ. Frederick Douglass chose to be a preacher in the latter church, but both branches remained active in support of the abolitionist movement, even after Douglass's break with militant white antislavery groups.

Almost from their first appearance in the South, AME preachers had found themselves viewed with suspicion by many whites, who saw them as potential leaders of slave insurrections. Even white missionaries found their position dangerous in rural regions. The Methodists had been the first to spread their gospel in the South, beginning after the Revolution. When white Baptists opened slave missions in South Carolina in 1808, there were fewer than 5,000 slave adherents to their belief in that state. The formation of the American Home Missionary Society in 1826 by representatives of the Presbyterian, Congregational, and some minor Reformed churches increased the work of black and white missionaries. In addition to baptizing, teaching, and preaching, they were asked to superintend the distribution of Northern charity to those most in need. When the largest Protestant denomination, the Methodist Episcopal Church, split over slave traffic and ownership, there were nearly 150,000 Southern members, a number that could have been far greater. In spite of Bishop Francis Asbury's policy of conciliation between the denominations, urban white Southern Methodists resisted all attempts to make their property members of any religious sect. Only a few more than 50,000 blacks were added to the Methodists' Southern branch in the first fifteen years after the split.

Slaves and free blacks who were permitted to attend worship sat in segregated sections, or listened from outside the building. Nevertheless, most chose their master's faith. On some plantations, black exhorters and ministers were allowed to hold Sunday worship, but black revolts brought about more repression of existing black congregation members. After Denmark Vesey's insurrection, which involved 9,000 slaves, was crushed in 1822, Charleston's AME church was razed, and the adjoining black-only graveyard alone remained to mark its former presence. Nat Turner's deep involvement with the Christian movement was cited as the reason for his leadership role in the 1831 revolt. He was known as the "Prophet" to his followers. After a reign of terror in which sixty whites and uncounted blacks died, Turner was executed, and not only did the slave code become more severe, but free persons of color suffered from new restrictive legislation, a repression that was a major factor in creation of the Antislavery Society.

The excellent and compelling singing for which Methodists were renowned undoubtedly contributed to their great success in the work of conversion. In spite of the segregation of black worshipers, the failure of white clergy to rouse religious fervor, and the discouraging of exclamations, responses, noises, or outcries of any kind, every effort was made to teach blacks the traditionally moderate hymns and psalms.

A Savannah minister who found blacks "extravagantly fond of music" was determined to "turn their taste to good account in their instruction." An advantage in teaching them good psalms and hymns, he proclaimed, "is that they are thereby induced to lay aside the extravagant and nonsensical chants and catches and hallelujah songs of their own composing; and when they sing, which is very often about their business or of an evening in their houses, they will have something profitable to sing."

Plantation owners who encouraged the conversion of their slaves used it to confirm their superior place in the "rightful order of things," thus enforcing respect and obedience in their chattel. God had become their ally in the trade in human beings, and they welcomed the missionaries' presence but insisted on sermons that would result in "good" servants who would eschew the worldly pleasures of secular song and the outlawed dance. As a result, the black spiritual, like the black man's traditional music and dance, was forced to go underground, to be done in privacy.

Southerners who professed ardent Christianity chaffed under charges by Northern abolitionists that the institution of slavery was outside the pale of that belief, and that owners of slaves supported missionary work only to assuage their consciences. Southern Methodists spent $1.8 million on that cause in the twenty years after 1844, in support of missions with a total flock of 10,000.

In order to discourage the fervor of black members, as well as whites who might be moved by it, the Southern Church of England dictated that only the *Book of Common Prayer*'s order of service be used, that only hymns and psalms be sung, with nothing added in the way of "extemporary address, exhortation or prayer." In 1845, Georgia passed laws providing that "no person of color, whether free or slave, shall be allowed to preach, to exhort, or join in any religious exercise with persons of color, either free or slave, there being more than seven persons of color present."

That direct and simple form of frontier Methodism, which was closer to John Wesley's open-air preaching than any other Protestant dogma, began to draw its membership from among common and generally illiterate people, attracting poor whites and black slaves to a greater degree than any other denomination. This was most evident in the camp meetings that became virtually an exclusive Methodist institution within a few years after the Gaspar River phenomenon of 1800. The whites who attended were usually too poor to own slaves or have an interest in the economy based on the institution of slavery, and so the meetings were generally nonsegregated at first. But after a few years, the blacks themselves separated from the white services to hear their own preachers and sing their own versions of revival songs. Laws forbidding separate meetings were soon forgotten, and the Methodist Episcopal Church, South, ordered separate black meetings to be presided over by black preachers. Separate meeting places were provided, and housing, cooking, and eating were segregated. Only in the all-camp meetings, conducted at the start and end of each day, did all participants come together, though they were seated in white and black sections, to sing the same hymns and occasionally listen to black preachers. Out of this separation came the first black religious church songs, based on improvised variations on Protestant hymnody, particularly the white camp-meeting songs.

Many blacks had already loosened the formal patterns of Watts and Wesleyan hymnody to embrace the catchy and magical Biblical images that appealed to their sense of ritual drama and song in religion. "Pull Old Satan Down," "Walk on, Jesus," "Shout Glory, Hallelujah to the Lamb," they sang. Words were married to rhythmic tunes; phrases were strung together in the age-old African call-and-response patterns and repeated again and again, eventually creating a private code that masked the hope of freedom on some distant day.

The singer and songwriter Henry Russell, not always the most authoritative of observers, but a reliable diarist, attended a Negro service in the 1830s and wrote:

> I often wondered whether it was possible that negroes could originate melody. I was desirous of testing them and I made up my mind to visit some negro meetings. . . . On entering the chapel at Vicksberg . . . one peculiarity . . . struck me very forcibly. When the minister gave out his version of the Psalms, the choir commenced singing so rapidly that the original tune absolutely ceased to exist—in fact, the fine old psalm tune thoroughly transformed into a kind of negro melody; and so sudden was the transformation by accelerating the time, that for a moment, I fancied, that not only did the choir but the little congregation intended to get up in a dance as part of the service.

The spectacle of blacks at worship became an attraction to which visitors were taken. In 1850, Fredericka Bremer was went by train from Charleston to a wood eighteen miles away. Thousands of worshipers were there, two thirds of them black and singing "as easily as we white folks talk." The blend of two races produced "a magnificent choir," dominated by "the black portion . . . as . . . their voices are naturally beautiful and pure." After midnight, she saw in the camp new converts still full of religious exultation and heard songs that were "extraordinarily wild and inaccountable," among them that "fragmentary bit of yodel, half sung, half yelled," which is now known as the "holler." The disjointed affirmations and prayers of the camp meetings' early days were becoming fervent, beautiful hymns.

Not until the war was ended did Northern and Southern whites alike learn the glories of true black spirituals, which had been seen only as a cultural oddity.

PART TWO

1861 to 1909

CHAPTER 7

"The Singin'est War" 1861–1865

Thirty-six hours after the first mortar shell had burst high over Fort Sumter, South Carolina, just before dawn of April 12, 1861, federal troops quartered there raised the white flag of surrender, and the bloodiest war in American history began. When it came to an end, just three days short of four years, 600,000 men were dead and a quarter million more were wounded or maimed.

In 1887, Brainard, of Chicago, published the 640-page collection *Our War Songs, North and South,* containing 438 songs well loved by the boys in blue and the boys in gray, whose annual reunions rang to their music. These old war songs were still sung after a quarter century.

More than 10,000 songs were published during the conflict, by a music business in which Northern entrepreneurs enjoyed the blessings of unrestricted materials—paper, ink, metal for type and plates—and access to maximum distribution. None of this was true in the South, where the major battles were fought and cities in which music publishers had established themselves were often under occupation. Control of the music business remained in the hands of the Board of Music Trade, as it did until the end of the century. The major piano manufactories were in the North; the making of printing presses and type founding were Northern monopolies; and 95 percent of the country's paper mills were located above the Mason-Dixon line. Just as the South's book-publishing business could not function successfully without access to supplies from the North, the fledgling Dixie music trade also learned to make do or do without.

Song Publishing in the Confederacy

After the war started, song publishers did continue to operate in Nashville, Macon, Mobile, and New Orleans, firms in the latter two cities having been part of the Northern sales and distribution networks. Others sprang up as federal troops tightened the noose around the faltering secessionist cause. Before the war ended, nearly 1,000 pieces of popular music were copyrighted in accordance with a new copyright law of the Confederate States of America. In a diplomatic move intended to sustain the support of Great Britain, the leading customer for its cotton crop, the South enacted legislation extending reciprocal protection to the British. Although authors and book publishers were well pleased with this move, the British government nonetheless consistently worked to mollify the United States, to whose storehouses it looked for wheat when crops failed.

Appropriately, the South's first song, George Robinson's "Palmetto State Song," written to salute those Carolinians who signed an agreement to withdraw from the union, was published by its oldest music house, that of the Seigling family of Charleston, but the plates for it had to be made by a Baltimore lithographic establishment. The major wartime Southern music publisher, Armand Blackmar, in business with his brother Henry Clay Blackmar, issued about half of the songs brought out during the hostilities. When the war started, these former Yankee music teachers had prospered. They, like most Southerners, thought that the South should fight, but also sing its own songs and dance to its own music. After federal troops commanded by General Benjamin Butler occupied New Orleans, Henry moved to Augusta, behind Confederate lines, to run the branch store that did most of the printing and distribution. Relying on an accent that confirmed his Yankee background, Armand continued to operate the New Orleans store until it was raided by Butler's men and all the merchandise was confiscated. He remained in Louisiana until peace came, but the songs he wrote were published under a pseudonym and issued by his brother. After the war, all their music was recopyrighted under United States law, and the Blackmars became well-known music merchants.

Philip Werlein, the other important prewar New Orleans publisher, was also put out of business by Butler's men. Only because he removed the store's stock of pianos and hid them under junk in his engraver's warehouse was he able to reopen his store in 1865. Under family operation, Werlein's was a landmark on Canal Street until after World War II.

Shortly after he arrived in Augusta, Henry Blackmar had advertised his readiness to fill all orders for currently popular and standard printed music "at Northern prices." In time, he developed a distribution chain in Atlanta, Columbia, Goldsboro, Macon, Mobile, Montgomery, Raleigh, Richmond, and Savannah. It was inevitable that John Hill Hewitt, manager of Augusta's Concert Hall, would turn up at the local Blackmar store. As the son of a music publisher and the brother of another, Hewitt had never been able to resist the business. Always ready to talk shop, he struck up a friendship with Blackmar, who was delighted to know a famous songwriter, and for a time Hewitt boarded with the store owner and his wife. He was under contract elsewhere while writing the music that won him the accolade "Bard of the Stars and Bars," so he did not place any songs with Blackmar until 1864, when he took over the Augusta store because Blackmar was in prison for having beaten his wife. Hewitt bought all of the Blackmar & Bros.' stock and good will. The retail value of the stock was in excess of $150,000 in inflated Confederate money, nearly four times the original cost. Approximately 15,000 pieces of popular music and about 3,700 standard publications were involved.

The staggering inflation that did much to bring about the defeat of the Confederacy hit the music business early. Items that had sold for thirty-five cents in 1861 soon cost three dollars. The size of sheet music shrank, and the paper was often so thin it made reading difficult and could not stand upright on a music rack. Moreover, the ink was usually only water infused with dye or lampblack.

The Confederacy's third major publishing house was headed by Hermann L. Schreiner, who was born in Germany in 1832 and came to the United States with his father, Johann, in 1849. The Schreiners settled in Macon, Georgia, to engage in the music trade. In 1861, they bought out W. D. Zogbaum, of Savannah, and later opened a third store under the John L. Schreiner & Sons banner in Augusta. Hermann gave up teaching music to devote all his time to the family business. While he was in New Orleans on a buying trip in 1862, the city was occupied by Butler's men, who were ordered to shut down the publishers of the seditious sheet music that was inspiring Southern patriotism. After returning to Georgia, Hermann sat down with his father to discuss what to do if federal troops invaded the state. He proposed that they concentrate on printing music, now that New Orleans had been cut off. With a pistol in his pocket, Hermann went north to Cincinnati to purchase a supply of old-fashioned music type and was able to buy a considerable amount from the local agent of a New York type founder. When wartime scarcities of metal made it impossible to produce engraved music plates, the Schreiners were thus in a position to print most of the new Confederate music.

The war's effect on music publishing was starkly shown in a Schreiner announcement of October 1863 calling attention to the 200 percent increase in the cost of paper and printers' wages. The retail price of all Schreiner publications was increased; dealers were given a fifty percent discount, with an additional ten percent on all orders for 100 copies of a song. In addition, all price marks on music were omitted, permitting local dealers to put their own in the center of the star symbol that the Board of Music Trade had made standard.

At the same time, the Schreiners informed the trade that the "celebrated poet and composer" John Hill Hewitt had entered into an exclusive arrangement with them, and was now in charge of the Augusta branch. Under the arrangement, they published some of Hewitt's most popular songs, including "Rock Me to Sleep, Mother" and "Somebody's Darling." Words to the latter were given by their author, Maria Ravenal de la Coste, of Savannah, to Hermann Schreiner, who dispatched them to Hewitt to be set to music. The songwriter's repetition of phrases and the addition of an appealing couplet made the song such a success that the Schreiners were hard put to keep up with demand, even though they had recently cornered the market in paper for sheet music. When a Georgia cotton mill burned down, they had salvaged 150 bales of damaged cotton and had it made into paper, giving them a two-year supply.

The Schreiners ended the Hewitt contract sometime in 1864, after discovering that he had been writing successful songs under a pseudonym and publishing them for sale through the Blackmars' Augusta store.

Colonel Blanton Duncan, a music engraver who became director of engraving and printing for the treasury of the Confederacy, went to the assistance of Southern music houses that could not deal with the Schreiner printing facilities because of federal troop activity. Using the government's lithographic facilities and printing presses, he moonlighted to produce vocal and instrumental music. His military connections made it possible for him to get his hands on the latest European music, brought through the blockade, which he reprinted for sale on a wholesale basis, cash on delivery.

With its type foundry and fifteen bookbinding plants, Richmond became the center of Southern book publishing, but comparatively little music was printed there during the war. Two Mobile music houses issued a total of twenty-seven items in that period, and fifty songs were printed in Tennessee, most of them by Nashville houses. That city's directory in 1855 carried the name of its most active publisher, John McClure. When the city was occupied by federal troops, he moved to Memphis, returning in 1868 and continuing to operate a music store there until 1882. Charles D. Benson, who brought out one of the South's best-known comic songs, "Here's Your Mule," opened a store in Nashville in 1858. In all, he published a dozen patriotic pieces, a collection of piano music, some marches, quicksteps, and dance music. "Here's Your Mule," written by Charles Stein, of Nashville, which was probably a Benson pseudonym, was sold by permission of the occupying forces. Its ubiquity made it the equivalent of World War II's "Kilroy Was Here." Unknown to the federal officers, its inspiration was the dashing Confederate cavalry raider John Morgan, and Benson printed a pro-Confederacy final verse that was sold only to known loyalists. He remained in the music business until 1882, although he added a line of men's furnishings in order to remain solvent in the era when Northerners effectively destroyed all Southern popular-music publishing.

Fewer than fifty Confederate music publishers issued the almost 1,000 copyrighted pieces of Confederate music known. Only a handful of them remained in the business once the war ended, especially after the Board of Music Trade strengthened its control over the business.

Not until country music became an important factor in the music business following World War II did Nashville, Atlanta, New Orleans, Memphis Shoals, and Macon music houses achieve international stature.

Song Publishing in the North

The inflation that is an inevitable concomitant of war, in addition to shortages of manpower following the drafting of thousands of men, forced costs up for the Northern music business. Paper rose 300 percent in price, and music publishers who had brought out sheet music on heavier paper with expensive engraved lithographic art during the first years of fighting were forced to reduce the quality of both paper and ink. Except for obvious best-selling items, covers appeared without illustration.

The sale of sheet music was also affected by a scarcity of small coins. The government began using postage and other stamps as currency, pasted on official Treasury paper, which also caused some consumer confusion, though shoppers and merchants became accustomed to it, and it remained in use until 1876. An act of Congress in March 1863 ended the ten-cent transcontinental rate that had done so much to introduce printed books, music, songsters, and paperbacks to western markets. A uniform letter rate of three cents per half ounce, regardless of distance, was installed. Creation of the Railway Mail Service, with special postal cars, and the inauguration of a domestic money-order service in 1864 eventually proved to be of significant benefit to large music houses with comprehensive catalogues of popular, art, and educational music.

In early 1859, Congress had shifted responsibility for maintaining the copyright deposits of publications of every nature from the Department of State to that of Interior. On February 18, 1861, just two weeks after the Confederate States of America was established in Montgomery, Alabama, the right of appeal to the Supreme Court in any suit involving copyright was extended to include authors and inventors.

One month before the war ended, Congress again added new provisions to the copyright law, requiring that a copy of every published work, including musical compositions, should be sent to the Library of Congress, free of postage and other expenses; a receipt would be returned by the librarian. If responsible copyright owners failed to do so within a year after publication, all rights to exclusive ownership were forfeited.

The new provisions, as well as the prosperity based on wartime inflation, may account for the increase of music copyrights filed in Washington. Donald W. Krummel, in the *International Musical Research Yearbook,* estimates that the decade of the 1860s saw a surge from the 5,000 titles registered annually during the 1850s to an average of 8,000, most of these after the conclusion of the Civil War.

Two major music printing and distribution syndicates dominated the wartime music business. Oliver Ditson, of Boston, headed one, which included Firth, Pond, until their separation in 1863; Lee and Walker, of Philadelphia, successors to the city's oldest and most successful firm, Willig; Lyon & Healy, two Ditson protégés who had been financed by him, in Chicago; and John C. Church, another of Ditson's bright young men, in Cincinnati. The second network usually included William Hall & Son, of New York; W. C. Peters, in Cincinnati; S. Brainard's Sons, in Cleveland; Henry Tolman, in Boston; D. P. Faulds, in Louisville; Henry Hempsted, a Milwaukee music dealer; and Root & Cady, in Chicago. The last-named firm had opened its doors in 1858 and, with exclusive contracts for the services of two of the most successful Northern songwriters, George Frederick Root and Henry Clay Work, produced an incomparable string of hit songs during the war.

Chauncey M. Cady and George Root's younger brother, Ebenezer Towner Root, were in their late twenties when they met in 1851. Cady was studying at

New York's Union Theological Seminary, and Root clerked in William Hall's fashionable music store at 239 Broadway and sang in public concerts and churches whenever the opportunity offered. The Roots were born on a farm near Shef-field, Massachusetts, George in 1820 and Ebenezer two years later, and re-ceived their elementary education in North Redding, a village not far from Boston. At thirteen George could play a tune on any musical instrument that came his way, and his dream was to play second flute in a Boston theater orchestra. Not as musically talented, Ebenezer went to South America with his father, the boy for his health and the parent to find work.

At eighteen, after promising his mother that she would never want for any-thing once he got a job, a pledge Root made good throughout her life, George went to Boston to learn music. He had found work as caretaker and fire tender in a music studio in return for the use of a piano and three dollars in hard cash weekly. The studio was housed in a remodeled theater also leased by Lowell Mason's Academy of Music and was thus the scene of church services and the American stronghold of the system of music training with which Mason turned around the course of "good" music in America.

Trained on the old fasola scale, young root was converted to Mason's do-re-mi notation, and his progress on the piano was so rapid that he got a job playing hymn accompaniments during Wednesday-night meetings in the Con-gregational church. After voice studies with George James Webb, Mason's chief assistant, and advanced lessons on his favorite instrument, the flute, Root was considered capable of teaching beginning students. He was hired at a sal-ary of eighty dollars a year by each of the five Boston primary schools where Mason was experimenting with music education.

Boston in the late 1830s was the scene of activity in popular music that would change music's character. Root was among the crowds that went to see the Swiss yodeling Rainer Family; heard John Braham, for more than twenty years the greatest English tenor; cheered John Philip Knight every time he sang "Rocked in the Cradle of the Deep"; purchases sheet music in Parker & Dit-son's music store; and were ardent fans of the great Henry Russell, whose music filled Root with delight. He was so taken with the Briton's songs, which helped him get out of his "elementary" writing state, Root wrote in his auto-biography, that he was soon able to play and sing them exactly the way the popular favorite did. Though Russell looked so pitiful singing "The Maniac," "The Gambler's Wife," and "The Old Sexton," feeling every word while performing, Root learned that, when the singing star retired to his dressing room, he "was said to have been much amused at the grief of his weeping constituents, showing that he had not really the heart in his song he appeared to have."

After a year, Root craved something of a higher order and moved on to the songs of Franz Schubert. It had been a rewarding time, however, for the music remained with him forever, teaching "the absurdity of saying that simple music keeps the tastes and musical culture of the people down."

Root participated as a specialist-instructor in the fifth annual Teachers' Class of Mason's Boston Academy of Music in 1841. The sessions brought together leading music teachers, singing masters, and choir directors for several days. Mason expounded on his methods of music education and philosophy of church music in the mornings, and Webb devoted the afternoons to secular music, training participants in part songs, glees, and madrigal singing. The evenings were get-togethers, open to all. There had been no voice training in the early meetings; now Root gathered together a small group for a half hour of instruction. This feature was thereafter an integral part of what became known as "music conventions."

With health restored, Ebenezer Root returned from South America in the early 1840s. His fine soprano voice had become smooth tenor, and Towner Root, as he wished to be called, determined to make music his profession. In 1846, he followed his brother to New York, to which the now prominent music educator had moved two years earlier.

George Root had not been able to resist the bright prospect presented to him by the Reverend Jacob Abbott, whose *Rollo* series of small paperbacks and other virtuous and simple books instructed thousands of nineteenth-century children on what to do to get to heaven and to avoid perdition's eternal flames. Abbott had opened a school for young ladies and wanted Root to become its music teacher. Within six weeks of his arrival in New York with a new bride, all of Root's time was taken up with teaching. Abbott's School for Young Ladies, the Rutgers Street Church Female Institute, and Miss Haines School for Young Ladies took so much of his attention that he had to turn his private lessons over to others. Root's version of the new methods of teaching the elementary principles of music were so much better and more attractive than anything seen before in sophisticated Gotham that he had no competition and was constantly in demand. His sisters came to the city to get an education at the schools where he taught; brother William found a place in a local business office; and Towner arrived to assist in teaching. Once reassembled, the Roots family became a New York rival of the singing Hutchinsons, but, as Root wrote, performed "music of a higher grade." Since no textbook available satisfied his special needs for "proper music," in 1847 he assembled *The Young Ladies' Choir* and published it in partnership with George Reed, of Boston. Reed was an old friend who had already brought out some popular songs written by the brothers; he remained involved with the Roots after Root & Cady was formed.

During Jenny Lind's record-breaking season of appearances in New York, George Root had an opportunity to attend every performance by speculating on the sale of tickets to her concerts. Then, at Jacob Abbott's suggestion, he went abroad for a year, staying most of the time in Paris. There he took voice lessons, met Louis Moreau Gottschalk and, through him, Hector Berlioz, who was then baffling conservative musicians with a radical new view of the art. Root refused, on religious grounds, to go to the theater or the opera.

On resuming his work at the New York Institution for the Blind upon his return, Root came into close contact with one of the school's most remarkable faculty members, Frances Jane (Fanny) Crosby, who taught history and English. Exactly his own age, she was a published writer, known nationally as

America's "Blind Poetess." Chancing upon Root one afternoon while he was at the piano picking out a melody, she suggested that the song be published. When Root noted that he had no lyrics, she immediately improvised the words she heard in the music, prompting a suggestion that the two collaborate. During the next summer, when both taught at Mason's Normal Academy of Music, they had a real opportunity to work together,

Root's understanding of the value to be found in "people's music" was one outcome of those weeks. He determined that he, like Foster, would write something "that all the people would sing."

The earliest Crosby-Root song was "Fare Thee Well, Kitty Dear," imitating Foster's "Ethiopian songs" be describing "the grief of a colored man on the death of his beloved." It was their usual procedure for Root to hum enough of the tune to give Crosby an idea of the meter and rhythmic swing he wanted. Crosby would supply words at once or provide them later, having retained the music in her head once she heard it. Towner Root took his brother's first hit, "The Hazel Dell," to his employer, William Hall, who bought it at once and signed its composer to an exclusive three-year contract for rights to all his "people's songs."

Not wishing to jeopardize the sales of his "more proper" music and teaching books, Root took the name G. Frederick Wurzel, the German word for root. As was the practice, Crosby received only a few dollars for all rights to her words, and the royalties, which eventually amounted to $3,000 from the sale of more than 125,000 copies, went to Root. This did not trouble Crosby, and they continued to work together, producing the first children's operetta or "cantata," The Flower Queen, in late 1852.

The modest talents of female students in academies, seminaries, and high schools were sufficient to earn those teachers who produced The Flower Queen and its successors sometimes astonishing profits. The $2,000 reaped from only two performances in St. Louis, from which Root earned only sixty cents, was not unusual. The children's cantatas were printed, merchandised, and distributed in the same way as popular sheet music.

During The Flower Queen's writing, Crosby usually showed Root several versions of what he wanted to be sung, and then he thought out the music, often doing so in the omnibuses and streetcars that carried him from one singing class to the next. Lowell Mason's two older sons had recently entered the bookselling and publishing business in New York and were eager to market copies of the cantata and any other music books Root cared to turn over to them. Among those publications was The Haymakers, of 1857, a paean to the joys of labor on the American farm that enjoyed its greatest popularity prior to the Civil War; it once filled Chicago's 2,300-seat Metropolitan Hall three times, at fifty cents a seat.

During the initial rush of creativity immediately after his return from Europe, Root conceived of a three-month summer session to train teachers not only in voice, as was now done at Mason's classes and conventions, but in the art of teaching harmony and general musical culture. He had some difficulty in persuading Mason to head the enterprise, and indeed succeeded only after he promised to do all the necessary advertising and reminded him that the sessions would increase the market for Mason's books and educational aids. The Mason brothers used their weekly magazine *The Musical Review and Choral Advocate* as the principal medium for selling the idea to the "right people" and reaped the profit from its use of Mason's teaching books, which they also published.

The first Normal Institute of Music was held in Dodworth's Hall on Broadway during the summer months of 1852. Mason headed the staff of instructors, and George Root, William B. Bradbury, Thomas Hastings, and others provided private lessons. Fees for each session were twenty-five dollars for the course, fifty dollars if private lessons were added. There were several hundred participants. For a number of years these institutes were the only ones of their kind in the United States, but in time the movement spread and became an important merchandising vehicle for printed music.

Root did not neglect his popular music, for he created a number of successful songs with Fanny Crosby: "They Have Sold Me Down the River," "Oh, How Glad to Be Home," "Proud World, Goodbye," "The Honeysuckle Glen," and "Rosalie, the Prairie Flower." The last was one of a group of six Root songs sold to Nathan Richardson, after his contract with Hall expired. A dedicated foe of such "trash," the music publisher, who was a wealthy musical amateur, was forced to resort to this people's music in order to show a profit from his elegant Boston music store. Root earned nearly $3,000 in royalties from "Rosalie" alone.

Another of his prewar hits with Crosby, "There's Music in the Air," a favorite with vocal quartets until well into the present century, was one of those written for the Masons' *Musical Review* on a regular weekly basis. When Chauncey Cady, the magazine's editor, sent a copyboy to pick up Root's newest piece, the composer rummaged through his desk and found a song he had written with Crosby and then thrown aside. Its success proved to him once more that it was hard to know when you would touch the people's heart.

Soon after Ditson's purchase of the Higgins brothers' *Chicago Musical Review*, Cady resigned from its editorship. He had been elected musical director of the local Musical Union, but his work as director of music for the First Congregational Church and the new Illinois State Normal University did not pay him enough, so he planned to open a music store in Chicago. Responding to the rosy picture Cady painted of the future in Chicago for a talented musician, Towner Root moved west to join his friend. He had long suffered as "Mr. Root's brother," and, having learned the music business from one of the country's most important man, he was ready for new fields to conquer. In late 1858, he and Cady opened their music store with "one of the largest and most attractive assortments of Musical Merchandise to be found west of New York."

George Root had given his brother enough money to buy a small interest in the new partnership and agreed to make their store his official headquarters whenever he was in the vicinity. In its first year of operation, Root & Cady became an important rival to Chicago's leading publishers, the Higgins brothers; it had a musical instrument and accessories department; the local agency for Steinway pianos and Hall's guitars, banjos, and flutes; rights to the northwestern market for Novello's inexpensive reprints of religious music; published the Mason brothers' catalogues; and had reciprocal agreements with Hall & Son as the Midwestern outlet for that publisher's printed music. The stock of military-band instruments was considered the largest and best west of New York. Business became so good that the floor above the store was rented for a piano and melodeon salesroom, and a 100-page, closely printed catalogue was issued.

At his brother's suggestion, George Root put in more capital and joined the firm as partner in charge of publications. In December 1860, he moved from a small room he had used as an office during his visits to a desk in back of the store. The war that broke out within a few months, putting an end to all music conventions and institutes, enabled him to devote full time to the music business. An ardent abolitionist, he perceived in the firing on Fort Sumter a God-given opportunity to rid the national soul of the canker of slavery that was destroying it, and a time when, he wrote, "anything that happened could be voiced in a song." Ready to write what he thought "would express the emotions of the soldiers or the people," he created the first of more than forty wartime patriotic songs. Inspired by Lincoln's call on April 15, 1861, for 75,000 volunteers to sign up for three months' service, he wrote "The First Gun Is Fired!" It was presented by the city's best-known male singers, Frank and Jules Lumbard, who also introduced many of his new pieces in the next four years, at a rally of patriotic Chicagoans. Broadside promotion copies of the words and music were handed out to the audience of 10,000. Within two days, the sheet music went on sale, and the broadside was made available at fifty cents a dozen for mailing to friends and loved ones. Root & Cady stocked their warehouse with new imported and domestic brass instruments to meet the demands of the military bands that were springing into being.

As the number of seceding states grew, Americans dedicated to preserving the union turned to patriotic music. In May, a committee of concerned citizens announced a contest for a new national anthem, posting $5,000 as a prize for its writer. Twelve hundred lyrics were submitted, 300 of them with music, before the competition closed in mid-June. Thirteen judges poured over the entries, only to announce that they had found none worthy of the award.

No longer hiding behind "Wurzel," George Root wrote the first popular hit as Root shortly before the year's end. He had been moved, as had most of the nation, by a set of verses written by the New England journalist Henry S. Washburn. "The Vacant Chair" had been inspired by the place waiting for a young lieutenant, killed in battle, that faced a grieving family at their Thanksgiving dinner. Thousands of Americans on both sides wept when they heard Washburn's words.

The ready facility with which Root now began to turn out appealing melodies that made him one of the North's most successful songwriters came, he said, from those "fourteen years of extemporizing melodies on the blackboard, before classes that could be kept in order only by prompt and rapid movements."

The music for his most important Civil War song, "The Battle Cry of Freedom," which reportedly sold between 500,000 and 700,000 copies in all forms, came to him as he was relaxing on a couch in Towner's home. Lincoln had recently issued a call for 300,000 volunteers to serve for three years. The words "Yes, we'll rally round the flag, boys, we'll rally once again, / Shouting the battle cry of freedom" came to his mind, with the stirring music, and the next morning he wrote down both. The song was already in production when the Lumbards came into Root & Cady's looking for something to use during a vast citizens' war rally to be held on July 23. They sang "The Battle Cry of Freedom," accompanied by a specially rehearsed orchestra and chorus that day, and at the fourth verse thousands joined in, singing the easy-to-remember phrases, so evocative of the call-and-response patterns of the popular hymns that had so long stirred camp-meeting worshipers and lunch-hour revival celebrants. Orders for the song poured in from dealers around the country, at least once for 20,000 from a single store, and kept fourteen printing presses busy.

Louis Moreau Gottschalk, who did not think much of most American popular music, told an Englishman, who had voiced that same judgment, about a melody being sung by regiment after regiment marching down New York's Broadway. "It has," he said, "animation, its harmonies are distinguished, it has tune, rhythm . . . a kind of epic coloration . . . which a battle song should have." He played this "obscure flower discovered on the heap of dirt that the poetasters and the musicasters have raised at the foot of their country's altar since the war began" throughout the wartime concert tour he made of America. In 1865, having paid $500 for Gottschalk's transcription of "The Battle Cry of Freedom," Root & Cady published an elaborate edition. Those who predicted they would never get their money back were stilled when the firm received more than 300 orders before publication.

The Hutchinsons added "The Battle Cry of Freedom" to their repertoire, and many entertainers who visited camps and hospitals to entertain the troops found it, along with "Home, Sweet Home," "The Star-Spangled Banner," "Listen to the Mocking Bird," and "Kingdom Coming," to be among the soldiers' favorites. The last song had been published by Root & Cady in early 1862, four months before George Root's hit. This bit of "Ethiopian business" came from the pen of Henry Clay Work. In the words of one contemporary tune-book compiler, it "set the whole world laughing, but there was about it a vein of political wisdom as well as of poetic justice that commended it to strong men." Its success was due to Cady's flair for promotion and the firm's effective advertising, for which he was chiefly responsible. For a week before the song was available for sale, street posters and newspaper pages carried the phrase "Kingdom Coming" in bold letters without any further explanation. The phrase became part of everyday lingo and won ever greater currency after Foster's old song promoters, the Christy Minstrels, introduced "Kingdom Coming" in a theatrical production of the same name. By early May, as the *Chicago Tribune,* boosting local products, reported, "the Negro melodists, theater orchestras and rural concert givers are producing it in every part of the country. The composer has worked himself into a popularity which must have astonished him."

Henry Clay Work, a solemn-looking, quiet, poorly dressed man, ten years

younger than George Root, had walked into the music educator's office with
the song in manuscript one day in the spring of 1861. It was, Root recalled
later, "elegant . . . full of bright, good sense and comical situations in the
'darkey' dialect . . . the melody decidedly good and taking, and the whole
exactly suited to the times." When Work told Root he was a printer, Root
said: " 'Well if this is a specimen of what you can do, I think you may give
up the printing business.' He liked that idea very much and an arrangement
with us was soon made." Root & Cady had found another prolific and successful hit maker.

"Kingdom Coming" soon sold at the rate of 3,500 copies a month. Its black-
English words did not trouble the sensibilities of those enlightened Northerners
who saw the struggle between the states as a crusade for emancipation. Southern black slaves became aware of the song almost as soon as did their would-
be liberators, chanting

> De massa run? ha, ha!
> De darkey stay? ho, ho!
> It mus' be now de Kingdom is comin'
> In de year ob Jubilo

They sang its verses to mock their owners, many of whom believed the words
and music to be a spontaneous expression of the black man's jubilation at the
thought of freedom.

The fervently religious, occasionally fanatical dedication to his own beliefs
had come to Henry Clay Work from his Bible-reading Connecticut Yankee
abolitionist father, whose chief purpose in life appeared to be securing freedom
for Christian black Americans. Henry was born in Middletown, Connecticut,
in 1833, and grew up on a farm in Illinois, to which his father had moved the
family in order to operate a station on the underground railroad. More than
4,000 escaping blacks were helped on their way to Canada by the family before
Alanson Work, after five years, was sent to prison. Pardoned in 1846 on condition that he leave the state, Work went to Canada, where Henry was later
apprenticed to a printer. Once he discovered a melodeon in the attic space
provided by his master, Henry developed his talent for music on that instrument, the only training he ever received. In 1853, he sold rights in his first
song to Ned Christy. A few years later, he went to Chicago to work as a
printer.

Inspired by those who had signed up in response to Lincoln's first call for
volunteers, Work wrote "Brave Boys Are They," which became a commercial
success for Hiram Higgins, the publisher who had already brought out Work's
"Lost on the Lady Elgin," a song that commemorated the tragic sinking of a
passenger steamboat on Lake Michigan in 1860.

With both Root and Work producing a growing list of songs, Cady correctly
boasted that Root & Cady was becoming the "country's leading purveyor of
patriotic songs." Root was not only prolific but also writing with the amazing
speed of his classroom days. His songs touched on all developments in the
war—both on the military scene and at home among those whose husbands,

lovers, and children were in battle or in prison camps. Although never important songs on the order of ''The Vacant Chair'' and ''The Battle Cry of Freedom,'' even his minor successes held a compelling mirror to the times.

His 1864 ''Just before the Battle, Mother,'' sold 100,000 copies in its first
year, synthesizing as it did the heartache felt at home and the new recruit's
dread of imminent combat. The Christy Minstrels took it on a trip to England
that year, where it also became a hit. The British could not believe that an
American wrote it and claimed that it had been inspired by the Crimean War
and written by one of their own. As the years passed, Root's original words
were lost, but the melody became a children's street song in England.

The miserable plight of federal soldiers in Southern prisons moved Root to
write the last of his great Civil War songs: ''Tramp, Tramp, Tramp, the Boys
are Marching.'' One tenth of all soldiers captured by either side—220,000
Confederate soldiers and 270,000 Union troops—died behind stockade walls,
those in the South often from the miserable circumstances created by the blockade. Like many of Root's later popular songs, ''Tramp, Tramp, Tramp'' was
written for Root & Cady's monthly magazine, *The Song Messenger of the
Northwest,* each issue of which carried the words and music of a new publication. A special New Year's extra had been scheduled for 1864, and Root,
interested in something else, had put off writing a new piece. After he turned
in the new song, within two hours of being pushed, his brother Towner commented,'' I must confess I don't think much of it, but it may do.'' It became
Root & Cady's second-greatest sheet-music seller.

Cady and the Roots saw *The Song Messenger* as another of the ''munitions
of war'' with which they were supporting the nation's just cause, as well as a
sound device to promote their products. The paper was sent wherever the United
States mails would take it. In order to get it to artists in small cities and towns,
Root & Cady addressed it to ''the principal Singer,'' relying on the local postmaster to make certain that it got to the most famous vocalist. It was direct-
mail promotion, and they were apparently the first in the music trade to use it.

Business became so brisk for the firm that in late 1863 two steam power
presses and a cylinder press, capable of 1,200 impressions an hour, were installed to print stereotyped music and a six-roller Adams press for music books,
to supplement outside production. Paper consumption had reached nearly a ton
weekly.

The considerable detail involved in handling the entire production of sheet
music and other materials was proving to be too great a burden for George
Root so Henry Work was named editor of *The Song Messenger* in early 1863.
The previous autumn, Root & Cady had entered the educational music-book
business, with George in charge of all text, teaching, and collections publications. The third book issued under his direction was his own *Silver Lute,* which,
with an enlarged edition in 1866, sold more than 200,000 copies. The Chicago
Board of Education was the first to adopt the *Silver Lute* as its official music
textbook. In three months, Cady reported to the music-trade press, more than
31,000 copies had been sold, and ''the demand for the book is so large that
the binders are unable to keep up with it.'' By the end of the year it was selling

1,000 copies a day. It was evident to the music trade by then that Root & Cady was now the Midwestern equal of Oliver Ditson and the most prosperous Board of Music Trade members, having sold 258,000 pieces of sheet music and 100,000 music books in the past twelve months.

Work had become a major contributor to that success. Unlike Root, he was a slow writer, taking several weeks to complete a song, having gone over it until the result was "like a piece of fine mosaic, especially in the fitting of words to music." He produced more than thirty songs for Root & Cady before 1866, when he left Chicago to settle in the East. Among them were patriotic war songs, ballads inspired by the conflict, and straightforward popular ballads, in which the firm also specialized. Among these were: "Grafted into the Army," about the $300 paid to be exempted from service; "Babylon Is Fallen," the sequel to "Kingdom Coming," which became well know but did not rival the commercial success of the first; "Corporal Schnapps," about the German volunteers who rushed to join Lincoln's army; and a temperance song written some years before Root & Cady published it.

As did all the Roots and Cadys, Henry Clay Work fought for the cause of temperance, and his "Come Home, Father," published in 1864, eventually became the official song of the National Prohibition Party. Vividly portraying the horrors of demon rum and its effect on a child, the ballad was interpolated into the play *Ten Nights in a Barroom*, which ran for most of the nineteenth century and well into the twentieth. Audiences went home red-eyed after they heard little Mary sing her sad plea:

> Father, dear father, come home with me now.
> The clock in the steeple strikes one. . . .
> You promis'd, dear father, that you would come home
> As soon as your day's work was done. . . .

Root & Cady offered a free copy of the song to anyone who could hear it without crying.

The song by which Work was best remembered and most hated in the South was "Marching Through Georgia," published in early 1865. General William Tecumseh Sherman, whose memory is sometimes evoked by his remark "War is hell," split the Confederacy in half after he left Atlanta in November 1864 and began a march to the sea. After six weeks with no news, President Lincoln received a telegram from Sherman: "I beg to present you as a Christmas gift, the city of Savannah, with one hundred and fifty guns, and plenty of ammunition, also about 25,000 bales of cotton." The song continued as a terrible reminder of that scorched-earth march when it remained in the mainstream of popular music; it served as the music for a woman-suffrage song, a square dance tune, and a college song. Sherman hated it.

Made a reasonably wealthy man by the proceeds of his contract with Root & Cady, Work took advantage of peace to make a pleasure trip to Europe. But in the depression that followed, he lost all his capital, invested in a New Jersey fruit farm, and went back to setting type. He wrote a few songs each year and published them through Root & Cady until the Chicago fire of 1871 in which the plates of his successful songs were destroyed. No longer bound by contract, he submitted music to other leading publishers, among them the Brainards, William Pond, John Church, Willis Woodward, as well as to Root & Sons and C. M. Cady, successors to the original firm. "Grandfather's Clock," published by Cady in 1876, proved to be a bonanza. It became so great a standard favorite that its rendition was mandatory in elementary-school festivities. Cady sold 800,000 copies of the sheet music in the first flush of its fame, netting the author substantial royalties. Work had written the song some years before, but he set it aside because it displeased him. Only after he ran into Cady, who asked for new material, did he retrieve it from a desk drawer.

With the success of "Grandfather's Clock," publishers were anxious to bring out his work despite the depression of 1877. His difficulty, he wrote, was in deciding to whom he should give a new piece. In 1882, he moved to Bath, New York, where his neighbors bragged that the writer of "Marching Through Georgia" lived among them. He wrote a group of minstrel songs for money. Woodward, a new publisher, paid outright in order to obtain the full copyright. One last great song remained, "The Silver Horn," put out some time later by Church, but it was neglected in the face of changing taste.

Both Root's and Work's songs did much to make the three partners in Root & Cady wealthy men. During the 1860s, when only 250,000 of the nation's 40 million citizens paid any income tax, which was based on annual earnings of more than $800, Cady and the two Roots averaged more than $10,000 annually from the music business. The national success of their popular music, including "Come Home, Father" and "Tramp, Tramp, Tramp," whose sales veteran music men predicted would "reach 200,000 thus beating anything known in the history of the trade," made them the peers of the eastern publishers. In recognition, they were voted into the Board of Music Trade in 1864. Chauncey Cady was elected secretary and treasurer of the board in 1866 and president in 1869.

Almost self-sufficient, doing all the necessary plate punching, engraving, lithography, stereotyping, printing, and binding on their premises, Root & Cady established profitable national and international business connections, equal to those of Oliver Ditson. Their 1865 sales were $260,000, out of the total of the city's $1,079,000 worth of musical merchandise, and they increased by 10 percent the following year, when Root & Cady sold 334,758 copies of sheet music and music books.

Some Civil War Songs and Their Writers

"The war was a fruitful theme for young poetic aspirants," the editor of Brainard's *Our War Songs–North and South* wrote in 1887. ". . . not infrequently they were set to music by those gifted with the power of song. Though they were often mere doggerel, they were eagerly read. . . . If the lines contained a happy hit or two, if they were calculated to arouse sentiment, if they had a good jingle, the verses usually were welcomed and sometimes even enjoyed a temporary popularity."

The people who wrote the best and the worst of the 10,000 songs reproduced on paper during the bloody war were as disparate as the American nation had become through waves of migration. "The poet forsook his higher strains to devote himself to the patriotic work of arousing the spirit of war and carnage, to lamentation over disaster, or the exultant paeans of victorious achievement. The great body of the people caught up the inspiriting melody, and the whole land resounded with the indomitable spirit of patriotic impulse and national pride."

As the war began, Firth, Pond was enjoying one of its greatest successes, "Viva l'America," the sort of music being written to instill a new spirit of nationalism as the ominous shadow of secession grew longer. The "God Bless America" of its day was written by Harrison Millard, then thirty, who was one of the most famous songwriters and voice teachers and a nationally known concert singer. He was one of those precociously gifted children who came under Lowell Mason's influence, choirboy at eight in his native city of Boston and member of the Handel and Haydn Society chorus two years later. When his voice changed to tenor, he successfully substituted for the society's principal male singer in a production of Handel's oratorio *Samson*. His song-writing career began about the same time, when Ditson published his first song. In 1851, he went to Italy to study voice and returned by way of London, where he appeared in concert and stage presentations. Through these years, Millard, who moved his music studio to New York in 1856, produced an almost ceaseless flow of songs, which continued until his death, in 1895, long after his kind of simple melody and accompaniment no longer appealed to sheet-music buyers. He had Root's gift for compelling melodies on occasion, but never his near-genius.

John Dwight Sullivan perceived " a gift for melody which well suits the average style of current Italian melody" in an 1855 *Journal of Music* review of Millard's "La Demanda." "Viva l'America" was his biggest hit, made so by the writer's consistent public performances of it at daily patriotic rallies. Infused with the love of country his song inspired in others, he volunteered for service in a New York regiment. In May 1861, his "Viva l'America" provided the climax of an afternoon of music and cannon fire for President Lincoln and 300 leading public figures at the Washington Navy Yard, where Millard was then stationed. Still a private, though he was soon to be commissioned, he conducted a glee club and vocal chorus, and Harvey Dodworth directed his famous band in a performance of the song.

As a first lieutenant in the infantry, Millard was twice mentioned in dispatches for bravery, but after four years of action he was so severely wounded that he was discharged. In recognition of his services, he was given position in the Boston Custom House, where he worked until retirement. During this time, he wrote most of his 350 popular songs, and nearly 400 adaptations of Italian, German, and French music, church anthems and hymns, and a four-act opera.

The wildfire rapidity with which Dan Emmett's walk-around song "Dixie" spread through the South, following its introduction in a New Orleans theater, made it inevitable that one day it would become the Confederacy's national anthem. Before then, other songs enjoyed that honor temporarily, at least one of which has survived to the present. James Ryder Randall was in his twenties and teaching English literature at a Louisiana college when he learned in 1861, that a friend had been killed in crossfire between federal troops marching through Baltimore and local residents. An ardent Southerner, Randall wrote a long poem, which appeared in a New Orleans newspaper and was widely reprinted throughout the South. Jennie Cary, received a clipping of the verses in Baltimore and sang them with her sister to Maryland troops. The melody the young ladies chose was "Lauriger Horatius," a Yale College song taken from the German "O Tannenbaum." In order to fit the words to the music, Cary added the phrase "My Maryland" to every second line in Randall's poem, and this gave it that extra quality which made it beloved on both sides of the struggle.

"Maryland, My Maryland" was heralded throughout the Southern states as their own "Marseillaise," but it never achieved the popularity of "Dixie" or "The Bonnie Blue Flag," written in 1861 to salute the South's original flag, a blue banner with a single star, which later was displaced by the Stars and Bars. Its writer, Harry Macarthy, was born in England, came to America in 1850 at the age of fifteen, and found work on the stage. Ten years later, he and his wife were popular favorites on the Southern theatrical circuits, appearing in shows that featured Macarthy's impressions, accompanied by comic songs, of the Irish, Germans, and blacks, at whose foibles back-country Anglo-Saxon audiences delighted to laugh.

Conflicting stories were told of the "Bonnie Blue Flag" 's origin, one having it that Macarthy was inspired when he watched an early 1861 secession convention to which a delegate came carrying a blue silk flag with a single star. The truth was probably that the "Arkansas Comedian," as Macarthy was known, wrote the song as a closing number for his "Personation Concerts" in order to cash in on the rising tide of patriotism. The music he used was an old Irish tune, "The Irish Jaunting Cart." The song made its first great impact at the New Orleans Academy of Music in the fall of 1861, on nightly audiences of soldiers on their way to the front in Virginia. They took the song with them, and its success promoted additional bookings for Macarthy, who toured the Deep South, then made his home in Richmond. He died in Oakland, California, in 1880 after an otherwise singularly unremarkable career.

The melody for one of Elvis Presley's hit songs of the late 1950s was appropriated from a song published during the war and popular with the troops, "Aura Lea." The music was by George R. Poulton, his only success, written for words by William Emerson Fosdick. Fosdick was a grandson of the pioneering frontier theatrical manager Samuel Drake, and his mother was an actress. After studying for the law, he wrote a historical novel, and on the strength of its reception by the Midwestern press he went to New York in 1852 to pursue a full-time writing career. His expectations were dashed when a blaze at the Harper publishing house destroyed the only copy of the work with which Fosdick expected to become famous. Home again in Cincinnati, he became known as a "true wit." He died in early 1862, a few years after "Aura Lea" had been set to music for the local publishing company owned by John Church.

After the war, veterans who were assigned to West Point brought the tune with them, and it became the traditional song "Army Blue." Producers of Presley's films believed it was time to show the world the he could sing something other than country and black rhythm-and-blues music. The song was revised slightly and, with new lyrics, for which Presley received partial credit, published as "Love Me Tender."

The music for Julia Ward Howe's "Battle Hymn of the Republic" was similarly borrowed. In fact, her song was the second successful appropriation of the camp-meeting hymn "Say Brothers, Will You Meet Us up in Canaan's Happy Shore?," allegedly written during the Millerite millennium of 1843. Credit for the tune's composition has also been given to South Carolina musician William Steffe, whose name became associated with the song when it was published in a Sunday School music book some years before abolitionist John Brown was hanged. Words memorializing Brown soon circulated, set to several different tunes.

In the spring of 1861, members of the 2nd Massachusetts Light Infantry began using the camp-meeting melody to poke fun at their sergeant, a Scottish-born John Brown, with the first line of the chorus, "Glory, glory hallelujah," sung three times. James E. Greenleaf, organist of Charlestown's Harvard Church, adapted the song for the Massachusetts regiment's band, and Patrick Gilmore added it to the repertory of his own elite bandsmen. Bay State volunteers on their way to the front beyond Washington marched along New York City streets to the strains and words of "John Brown's Body." By August, the song had spread as far west as Chicago, where Root & Cady added it to a new collection of popular songs. Greenleaf compiled five of the least offensive verses, added one of his own, and sold them to C. S. Hall, a Charlestown, Massachusetts, printer, who brought out a 6-by-9-inch penny ballad sheet. Encouraged by the response, Hall issued an edition with words and music. As public demand grew, other printers and publishers jumped on the wagon, four copyrights being granted in Boston alone in a single week in July 1861. The last, for "The Popular Refrain of Glory, Hallelujah," was issued to Oliver Ditson, but because Steffe was a native of Southern Carolina he was denied a share of the copyright "by virture of his citizenship in a foreign power" and lost all profits he may otherwise have received.

A leading Boston abolitionist and social leader, who accompanied her physician husband on a trip to Washington in December 1861, Julia Ward Howe visited the front-line troops. After experiencing a surprise attack, quickly routed, she returned to Washington along a highway clogged with singing men and heard "John Brown's Body" and its many verses. Later, she recalled that she had often wished that she, too, could write some words that might be sung to it.

This daughter of a New York banker and wife of a handsome Boston doctor attached to a hospital for the deaf, Samuel Gridley Howe, was a Unitarian preacher, a worker for the liberation of women, and the first female to be elected to the American Academy of Arts and Sciences. The Biblical imagery she employed in some verses that December night at Washington's Willard

Hotel became an immortal song. Back in Boston a few days later, she took the five stanzas she had written to the editor of *Atlantic Monthly*. Promptly titling it "Battle Hymn of the Republic," he paid her five dollars and printed the words in the magazine's February 1862 issue. They were immediately reprinted widely, appearing in a New York publication even before the *Atlantic* was on sale there. Newspapers carried them, and army hymnals printed the ennobling verses, which brought tears to the eyes of those who heard them. Prisoners of the Confederates sang them in defiance of their keepers.

Having copyrighted "Glory, Hallelujah" the previous year, Oliver Ditson locked his hold on the piece by publishing a new edition of "The Battle Hymn of the Republic, Adapted to the favorite melody of Glory, Hallelujah, written by Mrs. Dr. S. G. Howe for the Atlantic Monthly."

An earlier attempt by Mrs. Howe to write something that would move the people had met with little success. Entering a competition that offered a $5,000 prize for a new national anthem, she had suffered the same fate as had all other contestants, whose submissions were labeled by the judges as "bushels of rubbish . . . an enormous bulk of commonplace, watery versifications." Mrs. Howe's contribution was set to an old German melody.

Northern losses during the Peninsula Campaign of the first half of 1862, aimed at cutting off Richmond, finally brought Lincoln to the reluctant conclusion that the war could be won only with massive infusions of manpower. Losses during the Seven Days' Battles in the last week of June alone had been more than 15,800 on the federal side and more than 20,000 for the Confederates. On July 2, 1862, the President called for 300,000 more volunteers, a move that met with mixed response. Sensing the opportunity to boost morale with a song, George Root composed "The Battle Cry of Freedom."

A New York economist, financier, and ardent abolitionist, James S. Gibbons, had set his feelings down in a four-stanza poem, with the repeated chorus "We are coming, we are coming, our nation to restore; / We are coming, Father Abra'am, with three hundred thousand more." As Americans had been doing for more than a hundred years whenever they expressed in poetry their sentiments about a national crisis, Gibbons sent his work to a newspaper. It appeared, unsigned, in the *New York Evening Post,* of July 16, 1862. Because William Cullen Bryant, the *Post*'s editor, was a popular poet, many assumed that he had written the piece. It was reprinted widely and credited to Bryant. Publicly, he denied authorship, pointing to Gibbons. Within several months, twenty musical settings had been published, among them ones by Stephen Foster, George Poulton, and Patrick Gilmore.

Immediately after he had read the verses, Oliver Ditson sent them to a house composer and music editor, Luther Orlando Emerson, with the instruction, "Set these words to music instanter." The child of a Maine farm family whose progeny served to make up its own choir and orchestra, Emerson had been born in 1820. He abandoned a medical education for studies with one of the day's most famous music teachers, Isaac B. Woodbury. In 1847, he went to work as church organist in Salem, Massachusetts, for $100 a year, and ten years later went to work for Ditson as editor and compiler of collections of religious music. His first, the *Golden Wreath,* sold 40,000 copies within a year and was followed by a long series of similar works, all under the Ditson imprint. His *Harp of Judah* sold nearly 50,000 copies in the first three months of 1863 alone. Before his death, in 1915, he was responsible for seventy-two collections of music, instruction books and teaching manuals, numerous popular songs and works of art music, and had found time to conduct more than 300 music conventions. The nineteenth-century music historian W. S. B. Mathews wrote, in *A Hundred Years of Music in America,* that he was the best melodist of his kind, who "if he had received proper technical training when young would undoubtedly have distinguished himself as a composer of anthems and services, his sense of the dramatic significance of music being unusually acute." That gift served Emerson well in writing the music for the James S. Gibbons stanzas, the Ditson copyright that proved to be the best-selling of all versions.

After Lincoln ordered conscription in July 1863, efforts to raise an army of volunteers having failed, bloody riots took place in New York and other cities. About 1,000 people were killed, hundreds of shops looted, and fifty buildings burned in three days. Among the horrors was the looting and destruction of the home of the author of "We Are Coming, Father Abra'am." After escaping with his family without physical harm, Gibbons described the damages as an appropriate contribution to the war against slavery.

The exuberant words inspired by Lincoln's call for manpower gave the New York minstrel stage material for a comedy song on which the signature of William A. Pond appeared as the "Treasurer of the United States." By late 1863, steadily growing inflation had reduced the value of the first treasury notes issued without gold or any other metal to back them. Known as "greenbacks," from the green ink with which they were printed, some $450 million of the paper currency was issued before the war ended and was thus largely responsible for the doubling of the cost of living in the same period. Every night the country's leading minstrel man, Dan Bryant, brought audiences in the Mechanics' Hall theater to their feet with his rendition of "How Are You Greenbacks!," a variation on Gibbons's poem: "We're coming, Father Abra'm, one hundred thousand more, / Five hundred presses printing us from morn till night is o'er." The sheet music brought out by Pond & Son had a lithographed cover on which Bryant's visage appeared on a spurious ten-dollar bill with General Pond's autograph at the bottom.

The writer of "Tenting on the Old Camp Ground," Walter Kittredge, was a young New Hampshire neighbor of the successful singing Hutchinsons. More star-struck than other youngsters who lived nearby, Kittredge went to Judson Hutchinson for encouragement. Something in the youth, only three years younger than he was, struck a responsive chord in Judson, and he taught Walter to sing and play the melodeon and violin. Once Kittredge was eighteen and free to leave the family farm, he bought a horse and wagon to travel around rural New England singing and playing his own music. Hutchinson had been a good teacher, for as Kittredge recalled in his old age, "In my best days I thought I wasn't singing at my best unless I could make my audience first cry and then laugh on the very next song. That's the secret of popular singing. Make your audience understand by pronouncing plainly, and, if you feel the song yourself, you can carry them with you.''

For a time, he was employed by the Hutchinsons to fill in for family members who did not want to travel, but poor health and his wife and child persuaded him to return home. He never lost his love of music and began to write songs of every nature. A collection of these, *The Union Song Book,* was printed for him in 1862; it included some that the Hutchinsons had added to their extensive repertory.

Unable to put together $300 to buy a substitute, Kittredge was drafted and called up for service in late 1863. The night before he was to leave, he thought of what he was leaving behind and of what was to come, ''wishing for the war to cease . . . to see the dawn of peace.'' Putting his thoughts into words, he composed a melody for them on his violin. It took the army only a single look at his physical condition and past health for him to be rejected. A Boston publisher to whom he then offered the song for fifteen dollars turned it down, because he was looking for the sort of music George Root was writing, things like ''Rally Round the Flag,'' which the Hutchinsons had helped make a success.

The next spring Kittredge asked Asa Hutchinson to show ''Tenting on the Old Camp Ground'' and some other original music to his publisher, Ditson, which the singer did, for half of any royalties that might follow. This was certainly fair, for otherwise the song might never had had the national exposure that the Hutchinsons gave it. As a result, it became one of Ditson's most profitable copyrights, outselling most of the popular music he had yet printed, surpassing even ''We Are Coming, Father Abra'am.'' For many years ''Tenting on the Old Camp Ground'' was one of the most loved pieces of Civil War music sung at annual encampments of the Grand Old Army of the Republic and of the veterans of the Armies of the Confederacy.

The most popular song of the entire Civil War era, ''Weeping Sad and Lonely,'' sold one million copies after its publication in 1863 by Charles Carroll Sawyer and Charles W. Thompson, who did business out of the latter's home in Brooklyn, New York. Sawyer, author of the words, was twelve when, in 1845, his famous shipbuilder father moved the family from Mystic, Connecticut, to New York City. Though he began to compose verses and then popular music in his adolescence, it was not until the war that Sawyer won recognition for his song words.

''During the year 1861–2 many songs were published,'' he wrote at the head of the printed music in a later edition, ''but they were all filled with the love of a soldier for those whom he had left at home, and thinking it would cheer and comfort our brave boys, I composed and published the song 'Weeping Sad and Lonely', which seemed to reach into the hearts of both armies.'' It was soon almost impossible to supply the demand.

Little is known about Sawyer's publishing partner, Thompson, other than that he was a musician capable of arranging the original music Sawyer wrote for later publications. Distribution of their songs was handled by Ditson, in association with the Hall and Pond firms and Lee and Walker, of Philadelphia, but the copyright for "Weeping Sad and Lonely" remained in the original publishers' hands until after its first period of registration.

Its success amazed music critics of the time, one of whom wrote later:

> There is nothing in this sentimental song that enables one to read the riddle of its remarkable popularity during the Civil War. It had no poetic merit; its rhythm is commonplace, and the tune to which it is sung was of the flimsiest musical structure, without even a trick of melody to commend it. The thing was heard in every camp every day many times over—so much so that commanders banned it, hoping to save their men from its pacifist sentiments. Men chanted it on the march, and women sang it to piano accompaniment in all houses. A song which so strongly appealed to two great armies and to an entire people is worthy of a place in all collections of war poetry, even though criticism is baffled in an attempt to discover a reason for its popularity.

Its composer, Henry Tucker, was born in 1826 and died in 1882 after spending forty years as a professional songwriter. Little more is known about him than what appears on printed sheet music issued by several New York publishing houses. He continued to mine that vein of ballads appealing to both North and South, writing music and words for popular songs that depicted situations that transcended the color of military uniforms. None of them, not even "Weeping Sad and Lonely," matched the universal popularity and sales of "Sweet Genevieve," which he wrote in 1868 with George Foster, the friend and collaborator of Stephen Foster. Foster continued to insist until his death in 1928 that Genevieve was his wife, who died soon after they married and that the lyric was wrung from a grief-sticken heart. There is little evidence to support this fancy, but it is fact that he sold the words to Henry Tucker for a five-dollar bill, and thus left possession of a multimillion-copy American song in the hands of his song-writing partner.

"One remarkable feature of the period of the war songs" W. S. B. Mathews wrote, "was the extraordinary manner in which every note that caught popular favor was disseminated throughout the . . . country . . . no doubt due to the labors of the printing press and the unremitting and feverish interest . . . in the fortunes of war, and in every condition and sentiment that was connected with or grew out of it."

More to the point, the business of publishing and distributing popular songs on a national basis had come of age, galvanized by the war effort. Only the industry-controlled promotional process remained to be created.

CHAPTER 8

The Music of
God's Americans 1865–1909

The Singing Evangelists

The combination of true patriotism, concern for those who died and those who might come home, as well as the piety engendered by the great lunch-hour revival movement of 1857–1858, impelled the business world to engage in many acts of "Christian charity" during the Civil War. One of these was support of the Christian Commission, established at the urging of the YMCA to assist military chaplains and to perform charitable and spiritual works. Headed by a Philadelphia banker who raised over three million dollars from his associates for the purpose, the commission established libraries and provided reading materials to soldiers and sailors. In a single year, it distributed Bibles, testaments, tracts, and other "good reading material" in quantities as high as six million copies of a single inspirational exhortation and more than a million "knapsack" paperback hymnals.

Among the volunteer commission field workers was Dwight L. Moody, who left his church and YMCA work to erect prayer tents and nurse the wounded behind the lines. Moody had been born in Massachusetts in 1837, to a drunkard father and a soon widowed mother, who raised her family of ten on the kindness of neighbors and the produce from a two-acre farm. He never went beyond the local one-room school and was little affected by his family's Unitarian precepts. At seventeen he went to Boston to make his way in the commercial world and was converted to his employer's church. But the man's acts of Christian charity did not extend to the wages he paid, so Moody left for Chicago, where he found work in a boot-and-shoe store for thirty dollars a week. Within five years he had banked $7,000, made in part from loans at interest as high as seventeen percent a day, and was being paid $5,000 annually for work that included collecting past-due accounts from people damaged by the depression of 1857. Impressed by the businesslike way in which the YMCA functioned, Moody joined the organization and then founded his own Sunday School for the children of a slum district. The support of prosperous businessmen who were struck with his piety, determination to be the best, and hard work helped to make it "the largest this side of New York," as he wrote home.

During lunch-hour prayer meetings, Moody had brought passers-by in by demanding from them, "Are you for Jesus?" Such blunt, aggressive straight-forwordness in the religious work for which he left the shoe business in 1860 continued to bring financial support from the business world for his duties with the Christian Commission, his nondenominational fundamentalist church for the slum poor, founded in 1864, and the Chicago YMCA, whose president he was from 1866 to 1869. The church had grown into a vast congregation of the poor and downtrodden, people he had aroused with street-corner exhortations that won him the title "Crazy" Moody for his Christian fanaticism. He had never been ordained, and the gospel he preached was his own, made simple for those who were awed by the regular denominations. Businessmen were moved by him because he looked like a businessman, dressed like a business-man, and ran meetings like a businessman. Men of all social classes and eco-nomic states fell to their knees when his clear, melodious voice persuaded them to love Jesus and want to be saved.

Moody made several trips connected with his YMCA and Sunday School work to Britain, where he was invited to conduct a series of meetings in 1872. He had already engaged in the mass saving of city people's souls throughout the Midwest and in Philadelphia and Brooklyn, but he always considered the work to be only a part of his service to God. The Chicago fire of 1871 had not only destroyed the city's music business, but also Moody's home, church, Sun-day School, and the city's YMCA building. It was a challenge he accepted, so he raised money to rebuild them all.

In readying his foreign mission, Moody decided to take a hymn singer, for he had seen the power of stirring music at the urbanized camp meetings his services had become in the United States and also among the sick and wounded. His first choice was Philip Phillips, "the Singing Pilgrim," whose collection *Hallowed Songs,* containing many American hymns and a few English tunes, Moody intended to use, since most of the songs used in British churches and chapels could not be adapted to evangelistic services. A self-taught singer, Phillips owned a piano-and-organ store in Cincinnati, where he was also a partner in a religious-music publishing company, Philip Phillips & Co., one of the earliest to be devoted to the field. The first work issued by the company was a volume containing Phillips's own *Early Blossoms* and *Musical Leaves.* It was probably the best selling of many such books printed in the West, having sold nearly 750,000 copies.

When Pike's Opera House burned down in Cincinnati, taking W. C. Peters's entire stock and music plates, Phillips went to New York, to reopen his music house. There, he issued a number of other successful and popular compilations, one of which, the *American Sacred Songster,* printed in England, sold more than a million copies. Phillips had already made two tours of the British Isles, at a very "liberal compensation," part of the 4,000 song services he held in the course of his singing ministry. The Singing Pilgrim, a name taken from the title of one of his collections, declined Moody's proposal.

So, too, did Philip P. Bliss, once a promoter of printed songs for Root & Cady, who lead musical services at Moody's Chicago tabernacle and was now a singing evangelist. The gospel hymns Bliss was writing were to change not only the name by which these bright songs were called but also their musical character. Moody's final choice was Ira David Sankey, a fine singer whose talents were known only in the Midwest. Moody had met the thirty-year-old war veteran in 1870, when he was a delegate to a regional YMCA convention. After witnessing Sankey's ability to lead a congregation in song, he had persuaded him to come to work in the Chicago tabernacle.

Promising to pay Sankey $100 a month, the evangelist sailed, with his musical director, for England, arriving at Liverpool in June 1873. There was no one to meet them, two of the sponsors having died. Several months were to pass before the British public accepted the lay preacher and his hymn singer, whose role in worship was entirely unacceptable to the Anglicans and out of place in Calvinist and Methodist churches. It was Moody's meetings for middle-class merchants, common laborers and mechanics, and the poor that brought Sankey's hymn songs the almost fanatical devotion they enjoyed for years. He had been using Phillips's *Hallowed Songs* collection, but some hymns of his own composition brought about many requests for their publication. He wrote to Philip Phillips & Co. in New York, offering to send a dozen or more of the songs he had been singing—"The Ninety and Nine," "Jesus of Nazareth Passeth By," "Yet There Is Room," and others—if they could be published in the back of Phillips's collection. The offer was rejected, twice. Consequently, Moody agreed to subsidize manufacture of plates for a sixteen-page pamphlet, to be printed by Marshall, Morgan & Scott, cheap-book publishers. Sankey's *Sacred Songs and Solos* went on sale at six pence a copy, and as Sankey added new songs to his repertoire, revised editions were issued. Finally a words-only paperback was put on sale for a penny, two cents in American money, for the benefit of the poor, and *Hallowed Songs* was entirely discarded.

Once again businessmen came to Moody's aid, a group of them raising £2,000 to subsidize free mailing of an interdenominational London weekly, *The Christian,* to every one of the United Kingdom's 40,000 Protestant ministers. After an advertisement for Sankey's pocket hymnal appeared in the magazine, the collection became known to a wider circulation than was possible at the meetings alone, and it became a sensational seller. Copyright was taken out in Marshall, Morgan & Scott's name, and initial royalties were paid to Moody and Sankey. When sales grew, a committee of religious laymen was formed to supervise the payments, which finally amounted to £7,000 or $35,000. This money was turned over to Moody for completion of the rebuilding of his Chicago church.

The true origin of the word *gospel* to describe such songs is clouded. An English clergyman used the expression "singing the gospel" to describe Sankey's soul-stirring performances, and Philip P. Bliss named a compilation of his own songs, used by him on a singing revival tour, *Gospel Songs*. To whomever the credit belongs, such songs did confirm Moody's faith that most people liked singing.

> It helps to build up an audience—even if you do preach a dry sermon. If you have singing that reaches the heart, it will fill the church every time. There is more said in the Bible about praise than prayer, and music and song have not only accompanied all Scripture revivals, but are essential in deepening spiritual life. Singing does at least as much as preaching to impress the word of God upon people's minds. Ever since God first called me, the importance of praise expressed in song has grown upon me.

The crusade for English souls concluded with five months of triumph in London, where buildings seating 8,000 and 9,000 were erected especially for the pair. All classes attended, though Queen Victoria did not.

Moody's return home in August 1875 coincided with the growth of a national malaise. Corruption involving millions of dollars was exposed at the highest levels of government, reaching even into President U.S. Grant's Cabinet. Scandals in the operation of major city governments and wide-open profiteering by industrial "barons" led most to the belief that Christian principles were lacking entirely in the conduct of the nation's business and government.

Many business leaders, who saw Moody's conduct of his work for God as the vindication of American business, organized committees of laymen and clergy in leading cities to raise funds and set the stage for the evangelist's meetings. These were held several times each day except Sunday and extended over several months. In Philadelphia, the dry-goods merchant John A. Wanamaker headed the project; in New York J. Pierpont Morgan and Cornelius Vanderbilt; in Chicago, Cyrus McCormick and George Armour. A former Philadelphia railroad depot was converted into a building that would house 11,000. In New York, P. T. Barnum's Hippodrome was divided into two halls, seating 6,500 and 4,000. A new tabernacle that could later be converted into a "first class wholesale business house" was constructed in Chicago. Platforms capable of supporting immense choirs, carefully trained by Sankey, as well as dignitaries were installed in all of them, and in those in other large American cities.

Preparing for the great new crusade, Sankey put together a new collection of hymns, composed largely of those he had used abroad, with some by Philip Bliss. After discussion with the New York religious-music book publishers Biglow & Main, the title *Gospel Hymns and Sacred Songs* was adopted. Out of loyalty to George Root, Bliss had signed an exclusive contract with his old friend's new employer, John Church, of Cleveland, who would now handle all western printing and distribution of the completed work.

Copies of the new hymnal were on sale at all meetings and went in large number, prompting skeptics to say that Moody and Sankey were using the revivals to sell the publication. Although the royalty on a single copy was very small, proceeds from the first and the five succeeding volumes, in which James MacGranahan, George Coles Stebbins, and others collaborated, amounted to $357,338.64 in the first ten years. To avoid doubt as to his probity, Moody insisted that the money go to a committee of laymen, who would handle their distribution to "religious and educational institutions." Those proved to be chiefly the YMCA; after 1900, all royalties were paid directly to the trustees of the schools for men and women—Northfield and Mount Herman—Moody had established near his birthplace in Massachusetts. By then, 50 million Sankey hymnals had been sold.

These collections of simple but popular songs, in which harmony changed only once in a bar, sold in tremendous quantities, not only to those who attended revival meetings, but to all Americans. They were, for many, the true "hit" songs of the era. The multitudes who went to hear Sankey sing them and then were caught in Moody's "gospel net" usually applauded after they heard renditions of "Sweet Bye and Bye," "Where Is My Wandering Boy Tonight?," "Go Tell It To Jesus," and "Hold the Fort." In the middle of Moody's New York revival in March 1876, *The Nation* reported that Sankey's hymns "while written to religious words, are made attractive by many secular contrivances . . . a circus quickstep, a negro sentimental ballad, a college chorus, and a hymn all in one . . . ." The music of God's Americans had indeed undergone great changes in the past century, and at the time of that meeting audiences in another part of Brooklyn were succumbing to the charms of "Go Down, Moses" and "Roll, Jordan, Roll," as sung by the Fisk Jubilee singers.

When Dwight L. Moody retired from active ministry in 1892, the Bible Institute he founded in Chicago for training lay preachers was dubbed the "West Point of Christian Service." He died in 1899. Ira D. Sankey was still alive, and had just returned from a trip to the Holy Land, where he sang in the Tower of David, who had also "made a joyful noise unto the Lord." The 1903 edition of his *Gospel Hymns* contained 739 hymns, a far cry from the small pamphlet that had appeared in London thirty years before, and when the copyright expired to his *Sacred Songs* the next year, it was re-registered in his name only. He died in Brooklyn in 1908, the New York borough where extra trolley-car tracks had been laid to accommodate the crowds that came to hear him sing the gospel and Moody to preach it.

Following the death in 1867 of his employer, William B. Bradbury, young Hubert Platt Main, offered his father, Sylvester, the opportunity to purchase the company for which he worked as editor and manager of production. It was apparently successful because it was the exclusive publisher of Bradbury's music and teaching manuals and because of its talented staff of hymn and song writers. With his friend, fellow businessman, and layman church leader Lucius Horatio Biglow, the senior Main bought and reorganized the Bradbury interests into Biglow & Main, which became the most important publisher of sacred and gospel music books in the post–Civil War period. Eighteen million of the otherwise unknown number of music books sold in 1886 bore the Biglow & Main imprint. That success was due in great measure to Hubert Main, who was in complete charge of all publications, from the supervision of hymn writers, through the editing and proofreading, to merchandising of the final products.

Hubert Main had started in the music business in 1858, by helping I. B.

Woodbury edit one of his compilations. Next, he was the bookkeeper for a New York piano company, until Philip Phillips called him to Cincinnati for a similar position in his piano company, but actually he was hired to help the singer write down his music in preparation for printing and sale. Then he became editor of "the Singing Pilgrim's" early books. Fanny Crosby was already employed by Bradbury, the crown jewel among a group of women who wrote words to the religious music submitted for publication. The two were old friends, Fanny having known his father.

Blinded in childhood through the neglect of a household servant, Frances Jane Crosby was an extraordinary person, who believed that blind people could accomplish almost everything those with sight could. Her earliest musical training came in Ridgefield, Connecticut, during the 1830s from an itinerant singing teacher and from the music in Lowell Mason's *Handel and Haydn Collection,* which was lined out to her Presbyterian congregation. A few years later, in 1835, she was accepted by the New York Institution for the Blind, a four-year-old school that taught Louis Braille's system of raised letters and numerals, but Fanny's remarkably retentive memory allowed her to recite entire texts after one hearing. Among the joys now opened to her was poetry, which she first imitated and then began to write in her own way.

During the twenty years she spent at the institution, she progressed from pupil to professor, teaching children grammar, rhetoric, and ancient history, as well as the poetry that had brought her national fame as "America's Blind Poetess." George Root came to instruct music pupils, and after she chanced upon him at the piano they became collaborators, turning out a number of successful songs.

Her first acquaintance with cheerful modern religious songs came during revivals conducted at a Methodist tabernacle in 1850, where she also went through a soul-searing religious experience while singing one of Dr. Watts's great "old consecration hymns." She had learned to play the guitar and piano, and her musical training was expanded by Alexander Van Alstine, the blind teacher of music she married in 1858. Some time in 1864, after she had helped William Bradbury finish a church song, she began to earn her own living as a writer for the songwriter-teacher's publishing company, creating lyrics for both popular and sacred songs. She worked with Bradbury as she had with Root, either completing new songs with words written to order or creating them for him to write the music. Rarely did her name appear above the songs in published compilations. Bradbury also gave her other people's verses to correct or improve.

Philip Phillips worked with her on the book that gave him his nickname "the Singing Pilgrim," and, though she wrote most of the verses for it, she received no credit. Like Root and Bradbury, he did pay a few dollars for each. She always sat with an open book in her hand, held closely over her eyes, waiting for inspiration to come. It usually did quickly, occasionally bringing not only the words but often the music, too, which she sang to her publisher in a clear sweet soprano. In the forty-seven years Biglow & Main employed her, Crosby wrote 5,959 hymns, in addition to thousands she wrote or composed with others for other publishers, getting about three dollars for each. When she wrote a hymnal with her husband, Main rejected it, because he did not believe that people would buy a music book written by only two people. It may have been that which caused her to write under so many pseudonyms that her friends lost count at 204.

In 1867, William Howard Doane, with whom she collaborated on her best-known songs, came into her life. A wealthy corporation president who enjoyed a second, secret, career as a composer, he first considered music seriously after a heart attack at the age of thirty and began to compile hymnals. He was a talented writer but had little skill at turning a suitable couplet; Crosby proved to be the answer. Their collaboration began with the arrival of a letter from Crosby, who had never met him, that contained a poem he found fit exactly the music he was then working on. In the following years, he wrote more than a thousand songs with her, among them "Pass Me Not," O Gentle Saviour," "Safe in the Arms of Jesus," and "Rescue the Perishing," all finding a place in the hearts of churchgoers all over America.

Robert Lowry, with whom Crosby wrote many successful hymns, the best known of which was "All the Way My Saviour Leads Me," was a brilliant Baptist preacher who gave up the pulpit to serve as music editor for Bradbury and then for Biglow & Main, where he assisted in writing and compiling music for Sunday Schools. He was good at writing hymns that depended on brass-band martial music, and his "Shall We Gather at the River?" sounds best when sung by a spirited chorus accompanied by only a tambourine. His "I Need Thee Every Hour" was written to some verse given him by its author, Annie Hawks, a member of his Brooklyn flock.

Once all arrangements were completed for the publication of Sankey's *Gospel Hymns,* Fanny Crosby was drawn into the work. Not only were her older hymns scattered throughout the six volumes, but also she wrote new ones with Sankey, whose voice was beginning to lose its magnificent quality, and with George C. Stebbins and John Robson Sweney. Stebbins was associated with Moody for over twenty-five years as song leader and soloist and wrote "Though Your Sins Be as Scarlet" and "I've Got a Friend, Such a Friend" with Crosby. Sweney had commanded the band of the 3rd Delaware Regiment during the Civil War, and afterward became professor of music at Pennsylvania Military Academy, where he taught during his collaborations with Crosby, among them her well-known "Tell Me the Story of Jesus." For most of this time he was also song leader at the Sunday School where John Wanamaker was director.

In the nineteenth-century's final two decades, hymns like those written by the Queen of Gospel Song, as she was known internationally, were as popular and widely known as the best-selling sheet songs issued by the secular trade. Crosby's "Saved by Grace," J. M. Black's "When the Roll Is Called Up Yonder," and "The Ninety and Nine" were heard just as often as the most popular of Tin Pan Alley's hits that sold in enormous quantities during the Gay '90s.

Fanny Crosby was ninety-five when she died, still contemplating verses for a proposed hymnal and concerned as always about the poor masses among whom she had lived for so much of her active life. She remains in those of her songs that are occasionally recorded by new stars of the Christian gospel-song movement and in those hymns in the popular idiom that they themselves write, such as ''Put Your Hand in the Hand'' and ''One Day at a Time.''

Of all Fanny Crosby's collaborators, the one who most successfully crossed the line between popular and sacred song in the pre–Tin Pan Alley age was Adam Geibel, who, like her, was blinded as a child because of improper treatment. He was born in Germany in 1855 and brought while still a baby to Philadelphia, where he was trained in music and eventually became a prominent organist and conductor. His greatest success was in purely popular music, but he set some of Crosby's poems to music. During the 1880s, he wrote popular songs in New York, and in 1896 wrote the music for one of the era's most popular ''coon songs,'' ''Kentucky Babe,'' which became a favorite with barbershop singers. He formed Adam Geibel Music Co. to produce his Sunday School music, for which he wrote the melody to ''Stand Up for Jesus.'' His business was later purchased by the Hall, Mack Company, of Philadelphia, religious-music publishers. During the years Geibel was writing popular music, he was also organist at the Stetson Mission in Philadelphia, a time when his ''Sleep, Sleep, Sleep'' was written. The song served for many years as theme music for the Fred Waring orchestra, one of the most famous groups of the Prohibition Era.

Geibel was not the only writer of successful popular music to win some measure of prominence in the world of revivalist songs. Will Lamartine Thompson, who sold 265,000 copies of a song he wrote in ten minutes, ''Gathering Shells from the Sea Shore''—capitalizing on that success by noting it on all sheet music issued by him from East Liverpool, Ohio—made the transition from sacred to secular and back again with great ease. The son of an Irish immigrant banker who was also a patron of music, Thompson began serious study of the art in Boston at the Conservatory of Music and continued it in Leipzig. His first four popular songs, including the sibilant tongue twister that he had dashed off as an exercise, were rejected by S. Brainard's Sons, of Cleveland, even at twenty-five dollars for each. Thompson therefore opened his own music house in the town he grew up in and began to promote music by mail. He put ''Gathering Shells'' into the hands of the Carncross and Dixey Minstrel Company, which kept performing it until printing presses ran overtime to meet the demand for sheet-music copies.

Other Thompson songs were also successful in the next few years: ''Drifting with the Tide,'' ''My Home in Old Ohio,'' and ''The Old Tramp,'' whose line ''I'm only a poor wanderer, I've got no place to call home'' was popular in the year when a nationwide railroad strike paralyzed the nation. Thompson was intrigued by the great success of gospel songbooks, and so began to issue collections of such music, one of which included his ''Softly and Tenderly, Jesus Is Calling,'' in 1880. Thompson once called on Dwight Moody, who was seriously ill. The evangelist called the hymnist into the room and said, ''Will, I would rather have written 'Softly and Tenderly Jesus Is Calling' than anything

I have been able to do in my whole life.'' In 1892, Thompson transferred his considerable mail-order business in gospel music to Chicago, where a retail business was also carried on. After his death in 1909, the business became essentially jobbing and retailing, and was purchased by the Hope Publishing Company in 1916.

One of the most successful popular songs ever written by gospel songwriters was the result of a collaboration by mail, out of which the author got only three dollars and the composer got great royalties and international fame. Hart P. Danks, writer of the music, was trained as a child and became a choirboy. By the time the Danks family moved to Chicago in 1850, Hart's voice had changed to bass, though he was still not an adult. He pursued his musical training by study with W. B. Bradbury, when the country's finest voice teacher held a musical convention in that city. During the sessions, Hart presented a hymn he had written to his instructor, who was then in the process of compiling his *Jubilee,* which sold 200,000 copies. Bradbury took the song and included it in his book, an act that determined the youth to be a composer, rather than the builder his father wished him to be.

After marriage, Danks moved to New York, where he built a reputation as a highly competent writer of melodies the public liked, with such hits as ''Let the Angels In,'' ''Roses Underneath the Snow,'' and ''Don't Be Angry with Me, Darling,'' which sold in great quantity. His greatest success came in 1872, with ''Silver Threads Among the Gold,'' which sold 300,000 copies in the United States alone in the next ten years, and many more around the world, especially in Great Britain.

Danks had found his collaborator through the pages of a farm magazine, one of many periodicals to which Eben E. Rexford was selling stories and poems in order to pay his way through a Wisconsin college. Struck by the verses, Danks wrote to the author and sent three dollars for words to set to music. Rexford was delighted with the windfall and promptly dashed off nine additional poems, having already sold some verses to George F. Root, who had set them to music and printed them in sheet form and in music books. Danks kept the verses and sent the young writer eighteen dollars, with no explanation. Rexford never knew whether he ever received money for the words that made him famous and his collaborator one of the most successful songwriters in the rest of the nineteenth century.

As a result of its constant performance by the minstrel-show singer Richard Jose, ''Silver Threads Among the Gold'' had sold more than two million copies by 1900, and an additional one million in 1907, when it was revived, and concentrated song plugging by its publishers led to far greater and immediate sales. Ironically, the ''darling'' of the song, Danks's wife, left him the year the song was published. He died, an angry and lonely man, in a shabby Philadelphia lodging house. Near his body lay a piece of paper on which he had written, ''It is hard to die alone—since I kissed you, mine alone—you have never grown older.'' Rexford became a highly successful magazine editor, specializing in floriculture, and some of his verses for such publications were set to music; one of them, "Only a Pansy Blossom," became a hit. He was also a well-known hymnist, whose verses were used in Sankey's hymnals and compilations of sacred music.

The impact of the revival movement's gospel hymns was slow to be felt by denominations that had approved hymnals whose regular use was mandatory: Episcopal, Presbyterian, Methodist, and Congregational. Their hymnals were always published by an official book-manufacturing arm of the church, and they did not use printed music until late in the century, and, indeed, the *Episcopalian Hymnal* not until 1918. Tunes were named, and tune-book supplements were available, but they were not widely used until uniform congregational singing became universal in these churches. The *Methodist Protestant Hymnal* did not contain music until 1882, and a musical edition of the *Protestant Hymnal* was issued ten years later. Contemporary hymns, including those for gospel revivals by Sankey, Bliss, Crosby, Doane, Bradbury, and others, came slowly to the approved hymnals, the emphasis being on new translations and musical settings for old Latin hymns and those by Victorian English composers and a small group by Americans.

The success of Henry Ward Beecher's personally selected *Plymouth Collection,* which A. S. Barnes published as a favor to his minister, persuaded this prominent bookman to open a religious-music department. In 1862, he issued the first of a best-selling series of more than fifteen hymn collections by Charles S. Robinson, *Songs of the Church,* which continued to bring great profits to the Barnes firm over thirty years. A Presbyterian clergyman, Robinson had disagreed with his own music committee in the selection of appropriate hymns and argued against their dedication to "good music," the sort of " 'high art' that kills the spirit of the gospel in a preacher's heart more quickly than anything else in the world." At a time when the *Presbyterian Hymnal* had sales of more than 200,000 copies after its publication in 1866, Robinson's books— *Songs for the Sanctuary* (1865), *Psalms and Hymns* (1875), and many others— sold in quantities that kept publisher Barnes even more pleased. One reason for this success was Joseph Holbrook, who served as Robinson's music editor and selected popular melodies of the sort most formalists looked upon with disdain—Gottschalk's "Last Hope," for example.

The southern wing of the Presbyterian church, where musical tastes always tended more toward the secular, chose Robinson's 1875 collection as its official hymnal almost immediately after publication, and three years later chose one by a close associate of the clergyman-hymnodist.

The Baptists, whose religious songs had been a major influence on revivalist hymnody, prepared an official edition of the Robinson *Psalms and Hymns,* and they brought out their own *Hymnal* in 1883. Businessman William H. Doane, a hymn writer, too, was a music editor for this publication, and his musical orientation is reflected in the selection of seventeen hymns by Fanny Crosby and more of his own and those by Lowell Mason than of the most prominent and prolific contemporary English hymnists. Doane had pointed out in *Pure Gold* (1871), on which he collaborated with Robert Lowry and Crosby, that the "quiet revolution" resulting from the Sunday School movement had created congregations of a new sort who wanted songs of a "soul-stirring, strong and buoyant kind." Doane was correct in his understanding of what many classes of Baptists sought. The last nineteenth-century official collection to be issued by the American Baptist Publication Society, *Sursum Corda* (1898), whose Latin title alone affronted many, shifted its focus from sacred gospel songs to hymns heavily influenced by the new English writers. It was not accepted by most congregations. One factor in the consideration of its editorial committee may have been that the hold such copyright owners as Biglow & Maine had acquired over the most popular gospel songs permitted them to extract payments for permission to use out of all proportion to budgetary allocations. Another factor was certainly the determination of leading Baptist clergymen to elevate the music taste of their flocks.

The situation was different in the South, where worship under the open skies had exploded into the camp-meeting movement, and Sankey's gospel songs were heard during meetings held by itinerant evangelists. Southern Protestants had, like a fewer number in the north, learned that costly buildings, with stained-glass windows, massive pipe organs, and choirs, did not alone lead to grace, and many of the middle and poorer classes had abandoned them to the rich. For them, Sankey's *Gospel Hymns and Sacred Songs* took the place of ponderous volumes containing more than a thousand hymns, half of which were either unsingable or mere stuffing to warrant their cost.

With Moody as an example of what determination could attain, evangelists had adopted his modern business methods and gone on the road to sell the new kind of old-time religion. They became more effective when they began to use soloists, song leaders, and trained choirs, innovations they owed to the Chicago spellbinder, though few of them had ever been truly associated with him.

"The Moody of the South," Samuel Porter Jones, found that, even more than most Americans, those living in the remains of the old Confederacy were confused by what urban society was making of their country. War had decimated their ranks, ruined their lands, and made second-class citizens of them. He offered them the mercy of the Almighty. When he told the faithful to gain salvation by giving up gambling, drinking, swearing, and licentiousness and to return to regular Sunday church attendance, they rose to applaud and then went down on their knees to pray or walked to the mourner's bench to profess their faith. He packed a tent in Nashville that held 5,000 three times daily for a month and made 10,000 converts. This new "adjutant-general to the Lord Jesus Christ" was invited to bring his ministry of fervent Old Testament fundamentalism, show-business theatrics, and a message for the hopeful to every city with a population over 10,000. By the time he grew tired of it, in the late 1890s, he had exhorted all over America, though rarely in northeastern cities. Unlike Moody, who had asked for financial guarantees against all promotion and advertising, rent and other expenses, Jones lived on what was collected. When this failed to provide what was necessary, he gave the facts clearly and asked all to dig deeper for the tabernacle, the Bible never having mentioned "tabernickels."

Jones's grandfather and all his uncles had been Methodist preachers, but his father was a businessman and lawyer, who took up the cross only after the War Between the States. After graduation from an Alabama high school in 1867, at the age of twenty, Sam read for the law and was admitted to the Georgia bar. Drinking ruined him, and five years later he was stoking coal in a factory twelve hours a day. His grandfather converted him to temperance and the Methodist Episcopal Church, South. The former was a cause he worked for all his life, and the latter licensed him as a circuit preacher, first for small churches, and then, as word of his success spread throughout the South, for a series of Methodist meetings in larger cities, leading to the triumph in Nashville in 1885.

Fun, Jones said, "was the next best thing to religion," and, stripping down to his shirt sleeves, he expounded on the simple truths of the gospel, larding his sermons to born-again country faithful with slowly drawled anecdotes and homespun humor, which his dignified colleagues of the cloth deemed out of place. He found his Ira Sankey sometime in 1885, a twenty-five-year-old country singing teacher and Methodist choirmaster named Edwin Othello Excell, who had studied music formally at normal music schools conducted by George Root and his son Frederick. His basic education had been cut short in his teens, and he had worked as a plasterer and bricklayer for twelve years before determining on music as a lifetime career. In 1883, Excell moved to Chicago to open a publishing business and produce his own gospel songbooks. When he met Jones, he was as ready to go on the road demonstrating and selling his own printed materials as the evangelist was for a professional song leader. For the next twenty years, it was a Jones and Excell meeting to which crowds of Americans went, Excell leading the choir, which might be as large as 400 in his own "God Calling Yet" or "Let Him In," and the evangelist holding out his right hand while waiting for the sinners to come down the aisle, shake it, and get his "God bless you."

Sam Jones made more than $750,000 with his tongue. Excell built up a reputation as the country's best congregational song leader—Sankey having lost his voice—and became a major force in the publication of gospel music. By 1914, E. O. Excell Co. had sold about 10 million books and was selling nearly half a million annually. At the time of his death, in 1921, (while he was assisting in a revival meeting,) Excell's company was the largest hymnbook publisher in America, with annual sales of one million, but it had become essentially a wholesaler.

The 2,000 to 3,000 songs Excell wrote and published appeared first in his *Triumphant Song* series. The first of five volumes came out in the late 1880s and the last in 1896. His countless songs for Sunday Schools, written in association with Methodist Bishop John H. Vincent during the late 1880s, were published in such compilations as *Excell's Sunday Songs* and *Day School Songs* during the next decade. The "Amazing Grace" sung today was first published in his *Coronation Hymns* in 1910.

Bishop Vincent was minister to Chicago's Trinity Methodist Church during the Civil War and found the Sunday School there dull, dreary, and backward in imparting lessons. His work to improve the knowledge of subjects taught in

Sunday Schools was augmented in 1874 with the organization of the Sunday School Assembly at Lake Chautauqua, in western New York State. For two weeks, a group of forty men and women, who had paid six dollars for the course, were instructed in study of the Bible and its concordance and in Holy Land geography, the better to teach their charges. The school grew, and the unchaperoned young people were kept out of harm's way by an enlarged course, prayer, and hymn singing. Excell served as music editor for Vincent when the cleric instituted education by mail with International Sunday School Lessons, in conjunction with publication of literature, religious studies, and histories in three-by-five-inch paperbacks issued by the Chautauqua Press. For more than half a century, during which time tented Chautauqua also went on the road, the lake site served the growing American middle class as a camp-meeting, where they learned to worship culture in an atmosphere that grew, though slowly, ever less governed by the strict precepts laid down by Vincent and his associates. Secular music first entered the carefully controlled precincts in 1880, and, after Carl Maria von Weber's "Invitation to the Dance" had broken the ice, the programs were enlarged to include European art music, Sousa marches, and later even such popular songs of the day as "The Little Brown Church in the Vale" or "Ta-ra-ra-boom-de-ay."

Sam Jones was a regular attraction under Chautauqua tents and at the lake until the last years of his life, when he spoke chiefly on the evils of Old Demon Rum. He made certain that his audience learned and then sang at the top of their voices the temperance ballads that were intended, as were Sankey's, to bring people to a vision of the right. J. H. Herbert's comic plantation song "De Brewer's Big Hosses Cain't Run Over Me" was a favorite of Jones. Its composer had left a promising medical career to go on the road with a popular temperance lecturer, for whom he wrote and led audiences in rousing songs intended to bring thousands to sing the sobriety pledge. It was a natural progression for Herbert and others like him to write gospel hymns; he became prolific and internationally celebrated for his song books for the YMCA, religious music, and instructional manuals.

It was the concentration on unrelenting jeremiads against alcohol that persuaded a number of college-educated ordained clergymen that the path to a modern progressive gospel lay in a new evangelism. The most prominent of these was Benjamin Fay Mills, a Congregationalist who reduced the system and procedures of his citywide campaign to a booklet. It began with advance publicity and went through each step of a revival meeting, a blueprint to which members of each working committee were obliged to adhere strictly. Born in New Jersey in 1857, Mills became an evangelist in 1887 but did not formalize his plan for a new ministry until 1891. Choirs of between 100 to 150 were required at each meeting in each cooperating church, of which there might be anywhere from two dozen to eighty, and a choir of 600 voices was needed for the large meeting hall where a final two weeks of evangelism concluded seven weeks of intense activity. Mills's music director made arrangements with Biglow & Main to provide Sankey hymnals free of charge to the choirs in return for a stand in every church or meeting place where the hymnals could be sold by company representatives, for not less than thirty cents, by then a standard merchandising practice in the religious-book-publishing business. The dimensions of this marketplace were tremendous, Mills alone speaking to five million persons in his twelve years as a revivalist.

Support of the Reverend Mills's ministry fell off sharply as he increased his attacks on big business, charged major companies with cruelty to strikers, reproached church trustees for ownership of disease-infested tenements and the Presbyterian and Methodist churches for practices that rivaled those of gutter politicians. In 1899, abandoned by the city churches that once had fought one another for his services, Mills retired to become a Unitarian pastor in California.

Dwight Moody suffered a massive and fatal heart attack that year, and Reuben A. Torrey, the director of the Moody Bible Institute and pastor of the Moody Tabernacle, jumped in to fill the master evangelist's commitments. Two years later, Torrey began the career that made him and his music director, Charles A. Alexander, the Moody and Sankey of the twentieth century. Son of a New York banker, educated at Yale College and Seminary, Torrey had become the first paid music superintendent for Moody, at $5,000 a year, in 1889. A call to conduct meetings in Australia took the evangelist and Torrey overseas in 1901, and before their return, four years later, the two had spread the revivalist gospel in the Far East, India, and the British Isles. Success abroad made Torrey much in demand in the United States, and he devoted the next six years to revival meetings in most major American cities. As Moody's successor in fact, if not in spirit, Torrey appeared to industrialists and merchants as a shadow likeness of the businessman evangelist who had restored their public image as true Christians.

In *Modern Revivalism,* William G. McLoughlin, Jr., correctly points out that "Torrey would never have been a successful revivalist had it not been for his singing partner, Charles McCallom Alexander. Though only eleven years younger than Torrey, Alexander's methods of evangelism were as different from his as the mid-Victorian era was from the Jazz Age." A Tennessean, born in 1867, Alexander had left a small college in that state to travel with a Quaker evangelist, and then left him to get professional training at the Moody Bible Institute. After working with Moody at the 1893 Chicago World's Fair, he joined Milan B. Williams, a fundamentalist on the order of Sam Jones, and it was from this association that Torrey called Alexander in 1901.

Alexander was the earliest to abandon the pipe organ, and the melodeon, which Sankey had used so often, for the concert piano. In the half-hour song-service prelude to Torrey's appearance, Alexander sometimes pitted the crowd against a large choir in a competition to see who could sing louder, or the men against the women, the balconies against the main floor. As it had been said of Sankey, more people came to hear and see Alexander than Torrey, who did not think of himself as an advocate of the old-time style of revival.

Alexander conceived of himself much as does a contemporary singing star and had a personal publicity man and a comfortable style of life, which became possible after he married the daughter of the wealthy British chocolate maker

Cadbury. It did not take him long to become aware of the profits that lay in publishing his own songsters and hymnals, which were used exclusively by the choirs he trained and directed and sold to faithful audiences. Three volumes of *Alexander's Songs* had been published in England by Marshall Bros. Perhaps because his music may have been appropriated by British publishers, Alexander was unscrupulous in pirating music for his American gospel songbooks, a portion of whose profits he gave to the Moody Bible Institute Colportage Association, retaining the lion's share for himself. The Association, a wing of Moody's business operation, had been formed to distribute and publish Christian literature, the name adapted from *colporteur,* one who stocks religious books and tracts. Around 1900, Moody's Bible Institute began to sell songbooks, among them Alexander's *Revival Hymns,* edited with David Brink Towner, a hymnist and head of the institute's music department, who had written successful popular music before pursuing a career as a hymn writer and music educator. As head of the music program at the institute, Towner was responsible for the training of the period's best choristers and song leaders, including Charles Alexander. The Colportage Library also issued a number of hymn collections in a pocket-sized small edition, the music business having learned that the public would still pay thirty cents or more for a few gospel songs they liked rather than larger sums for larger official denominational hymnals. The book series included others by Towner, among them one with E. O. Excell, *Famous Gospel Hymns.* The institute cut all hymnbook production in 1920, but in the first half of the twentieth century it sold more than one million copies.

With the New York market controlled by Biglow & Main, who shared the majority of religious-music book sales with John Church, Chicago and the Midwest had become centers for such publishing ventures. There were the institute, with its limited output and Excell's staggering one, Hope Publishing Co., Will L. Thomas & Co., Tullar-Meredith, and the Bilhorn Folding Organ Co., which also issued religious music.

Hope Publishing, in Chicago, acquired Biglow & Main in 1920, and the E. O. Excell catalogue in 1931. The firm had been founded in 1892 by a ninety-pound hunchback Methodist revivalist, Henry Date, who compiled his gospel-song repertoire expecting to get a publisher for it. Finding none, he issued a sixty-four-page sampler to promote the 224-page *Pentecostal Hymns,* for whose printing he borrowed money. While continuing his evangelistic work in the Midwest, he paid a Chicago publisher twenty-five cents each to fill orders that came in as a result of his promotional piece. As business increased he employed a boyhood friend from England, George H. Shorney, to manage it, and Elisha Albright Hoffman, an evangelical minister, and J. H. Tenney to serve as music editors for future publications, the contents of which Date usually selected personally. The firm was incorporated in 1902, and its catalogue grew steadily, concentrating on music for Sunday Schools, most of it written and compiled by Charles Hutchinson Gabriel, an Iowa farm boy who learned music on a reed organ and who eventually became director of music for one of San Francisco's largest Episcopalian churches. Gabriel had come to Chicago in 1895. As a member of Hope's staff, he wrote thirty-five gospel songbooks, eighteen Sunday School and children's songbooks, nineteen collections of anthems, twenty-three cantatas, and innumerable compilations of music for men's and women's voices. His song "When All My Labors and Trials Are O'er," published by Excell in 1900, was inspired by "Old Glory Face," the superintendent of a rescue mission in St. Louis. By 1914, it had been translated into at least seventeen languages and had appeared in print millions of times.

Tullar-Meredith was a study in contrasts in the backgrounds that brought it to evangelism and its music. Grant Colfax Tullar grew up in near poverty and was sent to a woolen mill when he was ten, but he found work as a shoe-store errand boy in his early teens. He had only one year of formal education, just after he was converted at a Methodist camp meeting in 1888 at the age of nineteen. He then spent the years 1891 to 1900 as song leader for an evangelist. Isaac H. Meredith was born to a financially comfortable middle-class family that provided music lessons before he was ten and was proud of his progress when he became organist of the local YMCA, where he continued to play until he took up evangelistic work in 1890. Three years later, the Tullar-Meredith Company was formed, to handle their gospel songs, the latter's having already been published by Excell and Bilhorn. Tullar's best-known hymn, "Face to Face with Christ, My Saviour," which can still be found in the Baptist hymnal, was published by them in 1899, when the firm had moved its headquarters to New York City. This successful Sunday-School and church-music publishing house was sold following Tullar's death in 1950.

Profits from the sale of a portable folding reed organ weighing less than seventy pounds went into religious work and the gospel-song publishing house owned by the Bilhorn Folding Organ Company of Chicago. The instrument was invented by Peter Philip Bilhorn when he needed such an instrument in his evangelistic work. Bilhorn was a popular singer in German beer gardens and music halls before he found Christ during a revival and was converted. He left his full-time job of managing the family's carriage factory to his brother and began to study music seriously with Frederick Root and opera tenor Jean de Reszke. He then traveled with a number of itinerant revivalists. After becoming well known for his song-leading work, he was called to direct the choir of 4,000 voices at an international Christian Endeavour convention in London, after which he served as the modern revivalist Billy Sunday's chorister until 1908. This former popular singer wrote more than 2,000 gospel hymns and a number of volumes of sacred music, almost all of which were published by the Bilhorn brothers' company. The first song he ever wrote, "I Will Sing the Wondrous Story," is his best known. It was written in 1886 to verses by the man who had converted him and was first published in Sankey's *Sacred Songs and Solos*. It became one of the most popular numbers in the collection.

The family's organ business continued long after the vogue for evangelist hymns had declined, and the Bilhorn portable organ was a familiar sight during World War II, when chaplains in all branches of the armed forces used it in their services.

After increasingly angry quarrels over the conduct of his business affairs, Charles Alexander left the evangelist with whom he had been associated for seven years to join John Wilbur Chapman, whom Moody had once called "the greatest evangelist in the country." Trained at a Midwestern college and seminary, Chapman was converted personally by Moody in 1878, when he was a teen-ager, and was licensed to preach at the age of twenty-two, in 1881. He served in various pastorates, each one of them more prestigious, until he arrived at New York's exclusive Fourth Avenue Presbyterian Church by way of John Wanamaker's Philadelphia Bethany. Chapman had taken out several years during this rise to eminence to work with Moody and on his own as a revivalist, and was appointed a vice-president of the Bible Institute in 1896. This progress was observed by church authorities, and in 1901 he was named secretary of the presbyterian General Assembly's committee on evangelization. He gave up his New York church two years later to devote full attention to the problems facing revivalism in urban centers and his role in it. Out of this work came his "Simultaneous Evangelistic Campaign," which called for teams to work in churches, halls, theaters, and other buildings at the same time. He and the man he knew to be the best of his kind, Charles Alexander, conducted the main meeting in a large centrally located place. The method utilized as many as twenty-seven teams of evangelists and song leaders at a time, conducting 990 simultaneous meetings to a total attendance of more than 700,000. Special sessions were held for actors, shop girls, business leaders, their employees, habitual drunkards, and those "Magadalenes of the Avenues," prostitutes. Chapman believed that "spiritual dignity and grace" were fundamental to revivalism, and his almost timid platform manner and sentimental sermons were in keeping with that judgment. Those who wanted the excitement of down-home revivalism got their money's worth in Alexander's performances, as always bordering on a vaudevillian's techniques, a reward for staying to observe the main order of business. Chapman's businesslike conduct of revivalism won support from the commercial world, but when this tapered off, he, with Alexander and his English wife as added attractions, spent most of his time on tours around the world.

Another team of revivalists had come to the fore, one that drew more on the professional actor's stagecraft, the dynamic changes that had come to popular music and its associated technology, and the average American's concern about his place in a world where big business and big labor appeared to be locked in mortal combat and he was somewhere in the middle. Billy Sunday and Homer Rodeheaver came to center stage, and their mission was to spread the gospel of American Christianity and the value of that individualism that had made the country what it used to be.

A "rube of rubes," William Ashley Sunday called himself. He had been born in an Iowa log cabin and never graduated from high school, because he wanted to join a nearby town's baseball team. He got to the big leagues and starred in the outfield for the Chicago Whitestockings, in the days before they wore "sox," for several hundred dollars a month, training in the winters by stoking coal in railroad engines. Like so many before him, he was converted by a small-time itinerant evangelist and gave up all worldly pleasures except baseball, but he soon left that, too, to become an eighty-three-dollar-a-month

Chicago YMCA worker. He picked up most of his theology in Bible class there.

When Chapman made his initial foray into evangelism in 1894, Sunday was his advance man, getting things in order for the meetings, and substituting when the great man's train was late. Sunday's first sermons were lifted from Moody, but gradually he refined them to plain, practical preaching, with something of both Jones and Moody in him. Newspapermen began to compare his pulpit appearances to popular entertainment, and well worth the love offerings Sunday called for to support his work. He picked up tricks from other workers in the field, wearing shirt sleeves, breaking furniture in his anger at sin, jumping to the pulpit to wave the American flag, speaking 300 words a minute in short, terse sentences full of language from the sports field that his listeners easily understood. He grew in the esteem of his fellow Americans until they ranked him in 1914 as eighth in the list of their favorite great men.

When Billy Sunday hit New York in 1917, the war in Europe was turning men's minds from concern for themselves to the job of saving the world for democracy. Still, he drew an audience of one and a half million over ten weeks. It was the last great hurrah for the almost 2,000 evangelists who had staged nearly 35,000 revival meetings in the previous five years.

"Rody," Homer Alvin Rodeheaver, a trombone-playing choir leader and soloist, gospel-song composer and publisher, spent twenty years with Billy Sunday, from 1910 until 1930, when people were asking for repeal of the Prohibition Amendment to the Constitution, which Sunday had done so much to achieve. Much like Alexander in the way he conducted the hour-long warm-ups before Sunday's appearances, Rodeheaver was more up-to-date in the songs he wrote and published. Trombone in hand, with which he sweetly played the melody line of gospel songs, he directed choirs of as many as 2,000 voices, accompanied by two pianos, in music heavily influenced by popular music, for an average of more than 500 meetings annually.

Rodeheaver had left an Ohio farm at seventeen to go to Ohio Wesleyan University, where he became a cheerleader for the sports teams. During the war with Spain, he had served as trombonist in a Tennessee regimental band, and then had joined several evangelists prior to becoming music leader for Billy Sunday. Almost immediately on assuming that post, Rodeheaver formed a publishing company in association with one of Sunday's pianists, to maintain control over songs they both were writing as well as others whose copyrights they had purchased outright. Business was soon so brisk that Rodeheaver brought his brothers in to operate financial and production affairs and the mailing and promoting of Homer A. Rodeheaver Co.'s music and hymn books. With the acquisition of Praise Music Publishing, of Philadelphia, the enterprise became a major force in religious music, displacing Biglow & Main, whose management was chiefly concerned with maintaining ownership of profitable old copyrights. A number of outstanding hymnists were signed to exclusive contracts, among them George Rennard and Charles Gabriel, who gave the firm two of the twentieth-century's best-selling gospel hymns, "The Old Rugged Cross," by the former, and the latter's "Brighten the Corner Where You Are." Rennard's classic was voted by army chaplains during World War II the most popular Protestant hymn of all time and the favorite gospel song as well. "Brighten the Corner," with its syncopated rhythms, was a particular favorite of Sunday's audiences, and was used by Rodeheaver to get the spirit moving. In his autobiography, he wrote: "When the tabernacle was filled we would have one section on one side sing the first phrase of the chorus, then, jumping across the tabernacle, the section on the opposite side sing the second phrase, the chorus choir would sing the third phrase, and then we would pick out the ten back rows of the tabernacle, often nearly a short city block away, to sing the last 'Brighten the Corner.' " It was an antiphonal device he used with many evangelistic hymns, but none had this song's universal popularity.

The Hall, Mack Company, of Philadelphia, founded in 1895, had sold gospel songs and books by the hundreds of thousands when Rodeheaver bought the business in 1937. With it came the firm's manager, C. Austin Miles, a pharmacist turned gospel songwriter, whose 1912 "I Come to the Garden Alone" ranked second in the military clergymen's poll of all-time favorite Protestant hymns. Its waltzlike melody and sentimentally pietistic sensuality, when sung by Rodeheaver and a woman member of Sunday's staff, made it the most popular of the dramatic duets.

As a privately owned and operated enterprise, Rodeheaver's music firm was not obliged to make its financial status public. However, the veteran religious-song leader told *Life* in September 1945 that he had already realized gross sales in excess of seven million dollars, and ten years later the music-business trade press reported his annual sales to be more than a million copies of music and books. This is far below the 18 million copies Biglow & Main had sold in 1886, when production costs and retail prices were lower, a clear indication of the way in which Americans' interest in gospel hymnody had decreased in spite of Rodeheaver's continuing efforts to turn that tide. In the course of promoting his products, he was the first gospel singer to go into the recording studio, which he did for many of the major firms before he formed his own label, Rainbow Records, the earliest of its kind. He was also the first to promote gospel songs and religious hymns on the radio, using that medium to merchandise low-priced folios of selected copyrighted music in his catalogue.

The songs for which Rodeheaver, Alexander, and other song leaders became famous were not, as Billy Sunday's musical director wrote in his memoirs, "intended for a Sunday morning service, nor for a devotional meeting—[their] purpose was to bridge the gap between the popular song of the day and the great hymns and gospel songs, and to give men a simple, lilting melody which they could learn the first time they heard it, and which they could whistle and sing wherever they might be." That was the identical principal that made Tin Pan Alley ruler of the popular-music world during this period in the development of American music.

The Shape-Note Business

The roots of the modern South's religious-music publishing business, which was started prior to World War I by James D. Vaughan, Virgil Oliver Stamps, and J. R. Baxter, run back to a self-taught Pennsylvania Mennonite music teacher whose family went into Virginia's Shenandoah Valley just after the American Revolution. Joseph Funk was in his thirties when he came across music books, usually printed in the North, that used easy-to-learn-by patented notation, with four symbols denoting the entire musical scale. Despite their great cultural heritage, Funk's German neighbors were, in their own pastor's words, "backward in the practice of the vocal art," particularly in church, and he determined to remedy that. In 1816, he took the manuscript of his compilation, *Choral-Musick,* written in German, to a job printer equipped with "buckwheat" notation, who had recently printed Ananias Davisson's *Kentucky Harmony* in that patented type. Sixteen years later, Funk had become a leading music teacher in the valley, and for his English-speaking pupils he published *Genuine Church Music* in that language. Like the first work, it contained an elementary guide to music and a number of tunes to which favorite church hymns were sung. It went through nineteen editions in the next forty years, a total of 80,000 copies. In 1851, the work's name was changed to *Harmonia Sacra,* more in keeping with the style of Lowell Mason and his Northern elitists, but it became known to less sophisticated Southerners as "Hominy Soaker," something Funk deplored. All books following the early editions were manufactured and shipped from a log print shop in the Funk family's hometown, known after the Civil War as "Singer's Glen."

When he returned from the war, Aldine S. Kieffer, Funk's grandson, devoted his entire time to management of the family publishing business. Born on a Missouri farm in 1840, where his father taught him music before his death when the boy was seven, Aldine had gone with his mother to Virginia. Grandfather Funk continued his music education, and taught him the printing business when he was tall enough to stand and set type. The firm of Joseph Funk & Sons continued to expand as he grew up, and when Aldine was sixteen, he began to teach in singing schools under his grandfather's direction, using the new *Harmonia Sacra.*

Joseph Funk died, at the age of eighty-five, while Aldine was in a prisoner-of-war camp, where he had had opportunity to exchange music books and gospel-song collections with men in both gray and blue. One of the latter was a boyhood friend and fellow singing-school pupil, Ephraim Ruebush, who later became his partner in the Ruebush Kieffer Company, the first important patent-note music-publishing company in the South.

"Singing Billy" Walker, a nationally known singer and four-syllable book compiler, whose *Southern Harmony* had already sold thousands of copies, learned from God in a dream sometime after the war that the seven-shape system was one He now preferred, so he began to publish his books in the new fasola type. The Funks had been using a similar patent-note type font since the first publication of the Hominy Soaker. Kieffer went to work with his uncles to restore the printing office that had been abandoned after Funk's death. The first publication to come off the press was a small book for Sunday Schools and revival meetings, the *Christian Harp,* which sold 168,000 copies in the next ten years.

Other elements than the new typography were affecting the Southern religious-music trade. Among them were: the urban evangelistic revival meetings in the

North; the increased production and distribution of inexpensive melodeons, including Bilhorn's folding organ; the new kind of gospel music, highly influenced by contemporary popular music written by Sankey, Doane, Bliss, and others; and the South's black spirituals, which the North was only beginning to recognize as a real form of musical art.

To educate the masses in seven-shape sight-reading and -singing, Kieffer opened the first of his Normal Music Schools and, in order to advertise his books, began publication of *Musical Millions,* the trade's first important promotion and publicity paper. To it and Aldine Kieffer, who was "the defender of popular notation and mass singing" to his friends and "the Don Quixote of Buckwheat Notes" to the critics, is due more credit than to any single person or means of communication for the success of the Southern music business and musical education. Edited by Kieffer, its pages printed not only his verse and judgments of music's progress but also the same material that was used in leading trade papers and publishers' house organs printed in the North, the progress of teachers who used Ruebush-Kieffer publications in their work, and accounts of the extraordinarily large sales of new publications. One result of the paper's proseletyzing activity was Biglow & Main's decision to print its successful Sankey hymnals in shape-note editions, followed by a rush of Southern Methodist, Baptist, and Presbyterian publishing offices to do the same with their hymnals. Kieffer was also responsible for contact with composers, authors and publishers in connection with use of their copyrighted music. The most popular of his songbooks, issued by Ruebush-Kieffer, which was organized in 1872 and moved to nearby Dayton six years later, was the 1877 *Temple Star,* which sold more than 500,000 copies.

When Kieffer looked around for someone to head the Virginia Normal School, the first of its kind in the South to hold annual sessions, it was suggested that he employ B. C. Unseld as principal. A West Virginian of German stock, Unseld had taught himself music on a cardboard piano keyboard and then a melodeon when he rose from clerking in a country store to supervision of the books of a railroad line. He was twenty-two when he took six months out to study music formally with Eben Tourgee, and, when his teacher established the New England Conservatory of Music, Unseld was put in charge of business affairs there.

After Kieffer offered him the post, starting with the summer 1884 session, Unseld also agreed to go to Nashville to teach the Fisk Jubilee Singers the "chaste music" that would be expected of them on European tours in addition to the spirituals they were singing with great success throughout the United States. Although he had been trained in "scientific" music by his Northern teachers, Unseld came in time to appreciate that the South, having been disastrously defeated, was looking for a cultural and intellectual life of its own. Putting away his prejudices, he offered not only the usual conventional fare of education in genteel music, but also training in the rural musical language of patent notation. Until his death, in 1923, Unseld spent part of the year at Normal Music Schools in North Carolina, Tennessee, and Missouri, the rest in the North.

As it had in the North, music education in the South soon embraced music of other than a religious nature. Graduates of the Normal Music Schools proudly displayed the accomplishments of their pupils during singing conventions, where shape-music lovers assembled. New musical literature printed and sung in the buckwheat-note tradition began to grow: comic songs, patriotic songs, love songs—all the elements of Northern secular vocal music. Nearly two dozen periodicals, supplementing the *Musical Millions'* promotional work on behalf of fasola singing, were launched prior to 1900, aimed at readers in the Deep South and as far west as Texas.

To serve this new market better, Kieffer sent Anthony Johnson Showalter, the son of a distinguished singing teacher and a graduate of the Virginia Normal Music School, to Dalton, Georgia, next to Dayton the second-greatest Southern center of rural singing and music. Born in Virginia in 1858, Showalter had studied with Unseld and later with Horatio Palmer and the Roots, father and son. One of his earliest books, *Harmony and Composition,* published in 1882, was the first music-teaching book written by a Southern author. Within a year, Showalter who was not only a musician but also a sound and practical businessman, opened his own firm, the A. J. Showalter Company, the most important of the second-generation Southern patent-note publishers, which sold three million songbooks in fifty years. The most successful of sixty books the firm published, in round or shape notes, was Showalter's *Class, Choir and Congregation,* which contained secular songs and sold 400,000 copies.

"A. J." was known as one of the best singing-convention song leaders, in 1904 being paid $500 for leading an all-day singing by an enormous group of shape-noters at the Atlanta Southeastern Fair. Many of them were graduates of his own musical institutes, held throughout the South and Southwest, in connection with which he edited, for a quarter of a century, *The Music Teacher,* the Showalter Company house organ and promotional publication.

The giants of the South's religious-music-publishing third generation—Vaughan, Stamps, and Baxter—were graduates of the normal institutes and also conducted schools to teach both kinds of notation and singing. Until regular notation triumphed over the past, all continued to promote shape-note singing and composition, publishing the majority of hymnbooks and Sacred Harp collections. Few of the country-music singers and songwriters whose music, blended with the black man's rhythm and blues, became rock 'n' roll were outside the influence of buckwheat-note music, the gospel song, and fa-so-la singing. This last and the Afro-American musical tradition were the major factors in the music of white Protestant Southerners.

CHAPTER 9

Black Music in America
1860–1909

The Spirituals

The surrender of Fort Sumter had inflicted a never-closing wound to the soul of many Americans in May 1861, among them General Benjamin Butler, a Massachusetts politician who had supported Jefferson Davis for the vice presidency of the United States on the Democratic ticket. Now, having wangled a commission, he was chafing to punish the rebels. Once word spread that this white general in command of Fort Monroe welcomed refugee black slaves, boatloads of men, women, and children poured into the military installation at the entrance to Chesapeake Bay and were immediately put to work as servants and laborers. Southern plantation owners protested this appropriation of their property, which led Butler to remind them that slaves were "contrabands of war," and he refused to return them. Delighted with the phrase, Americans took it up and used it to label all slaves. Fort Monroe's facilities grew too small to accommodate the runaways, who spilled over into the countryside around Hampton, Virginia. As conditions daily became more desperate for the black people, the Congregational, abolitionist-inclined American Missionary Association sent its representatives to set up some means for their relief. Among those who came to help was Lewis C. Lockwood, a former YMCA secretary, who arrived in September 1861 and immediately fell victim to the charm and majesty of a particular "prime deliverance melody" sung by the contrabands, whose repeated chorus—"Go down to Egypt—tell Pharaoh, / Thus saith my servant, Moses / Let my people go!"—rang, he said "like a warning note in the ear of despotism."

In December, three verses of the twenty Lockwood had taken down and sent to friends, with the music as he heard it, appeared in the *New York Tribune*. This was, according to Dena J. Epstein, in *Sinful Songs and Spirituals,* the first appearance in print of the text of a Negro spiritual. Within two weeks, Horace Waters, the New York music publisher–prohibitionist and foe of slavery, is-

sued "The Song of the Contrabands—'O let my People go' " in a printed
edition selling for twenty-five cents, with Oliver Ditson as co-publisher. Lockwood was credited with both words and music, the latter rewritten and then
arranged in slapdash fashion by Thomas Baker, once a member of Jullien's
famous orchestra, now musical director for Laura Keene who had been performing similar editorial functions for Waters since 1853. In April 1862, the
song was featured in *Harp of Freedom,* a thirty-two-page abolitionist songbook
sold by Waters for five cents "in order to awaken a deep interest in behalf of
the 'contrabands' whom God, in his providence, has cast upon the Free North,
to clothe and educate." "Go Down, Moses" was the only true song of black
Southern slaves in the paperback—the others were antislavery verses written to
popular melodies—and it was the first of its kind to find mass distribution in
printed sheet-music form. Waters's publications failed, however, to reveal to
Americans the real glory of black America's spirituals.

Nor did two more of these religious folk songs, published at her own expense in November 1862 by Lucy McKim, a young professional musician of
Philadelphia who was more capable than Lockwood of writing down these wild
and sad words and music. She was nineteen years old when she accompanied
her father, James, a well-known leader of the abolitionist movement, on a tour
of inspection of conditions among the contrabands crowded into Port Royal,
South Carolina, after Union forces had taken that harbor in November 1861.
The number of blacks there grew even more quickly than at Fort Monroe, since
they were not only runaways in search of freedom but also those abandoned by
white masters fleeing from ruthless Yankee soldiers. Several volunteer groups
sent teachers and missionaries to Port Royal, which had been selected by the
government as the site for an experiment to ascertain how capable blacks were
of learning and working in a state of freedom. The Port Royal Relief Committee of Philadelphia was particularly active in the project and had sent the McKims.

Finding it "difficult to express" in "mere musical notes and signs" the
entire character of the black songs she heard in Port Royal, Lucy McKim
nevertheless sent to the leading music magazine of the day, John Dwight's
Journal of Music, copies of two songs she had published, "Poor Rosy, Poor
Gal!" and the "triumphal anthem 'Roll, Jordon, Roll.' " She had heard the
latter for the first time on the July 4, 1862, when thousands of blacks marched
behind the Stars and Stripes in procession, "cheering them for the first time as
the 'flag of *our* country.' " The songs were published as No. 1 and No. 2 of
Songs of the Freedmen of Port Royal "collected and arranged by Miss Lucy
McKim," part of a group of eight spirituals whose publication was never completed. Probably at the instigation of his employee John Dwight, Oliver Ditson
undertook publication of "Roll, Jordon, Roll," using plates Lucy McKim had
paid a Philadelphia engraver to cut, but without any evident success.

Many accounts of the black folk music that people from the North were
hearing for the first time appeared in abolitionist periodicals and newspapers
and in major literary magazines and journals. None of them lighted the spark
of public demand that sometimes resulted in printed publication, not even those
by Thomas Wentworth Higginson. He was a militant Unitarian preacher, who

was tried for attempting to break into a Boston jail to free a fugitive slave; became a fervent supporter of John Brown in the dark and bloody days in Kansas and at Harpers Ferry; and was named commander of the first regiment of Civil War soldiers recruited from former slaves, the First South Carolina Volunteers. Using his experiences with his soldiers, which he recounted in a diary, he wrote an article for *The Atlantic Monthly*, "Negro Spirituals," in June 1867, and then a full-length book, *Army Life in a Black Regiment*. In both he detailed the songs, though not the music, he had heard in South Carolina. He wrote in the *Atlantic* that there was "no parallel instance of an oppressed race thus sustained by the religious sentiment alone."

Charles Scribner, the New York book publisher who had initially expressed interest, finally rejected the manuscript of the first collection of black America's spirituals, *Slave Songs of the United States*. Its compilation had been a labor of love for William Francis Allen, Charles Pickard Ware, and Lucy McKim Garrison, who had married Wendell P. Garrison, son of the abolition movement's leader, who was literary editor of *The Nation*. Allen and Ware were cousins, Harvard graduates, with some modest musical abilities, but certainly not on the order of Mrs. Garrison's. Ten years younger than Allen, Ware had joined his sister in Georgia's sea islands immediately after graduation in 1862. Almost at once he began to collect songs by the free slaves whose work he supervised on corn and cotton plantations. In three years he was ready, he wrote to Allen, to contemplate their publication. A trained philologist, Allen, who had first gone to the South in 1863 as a volunteer teacher of contrabands, was greatly interested in the slaves' songs, sinful as well as spiritual, and had discussed a similar project with Wendell Garrison. Lucy Garrison proved to be the catalyst in bringing the work to printed reality. With Garrison, she was chiefly responsible for correspondence with other collectors of slave songs, among them musicians, army officers, newspapermen, and missionaries, whose contributions to the completed book were invaluable.

Published by A. Simpson & Co., of lower Manhattan, a recently formed literary enterprise, *Slave Songs of the United States*, was first offered for sale in a four-page prospectus. Containing the words and music of 136 slave songs, the book came off press in September 1867 and received mixed reviews. Ditson turned down an offer to bring out a second edition using the original plates, but one did appear in 1871, after which the book disappeared from general circulation, emerging in 1929 in a reprint edition that recognized it as a major contribution to research in American music.

In spite of these and other efforts to bring the Negro spiritual to the attention of more white Americans, the music was virtually unknown outside the South. It needed some polished entertainer whose "acceptable" renditions in places of mass public entertainment would make popular this music with words that even its admirers admitted were in a barbarous, Africanized sort of English. That performer proved to be a group of nine black college students—only one of whom had not been a slave—trained in the genteel music of the day by their school's treasurer, a young white man from Cadiz, New York, George L. White. They were enrolled at Fisk University, in Nashville, Tennessee, which was founded by the American Missionary Association in 1866. Around the time of publication of *Slave Songs,* with which White was probably not familiar, he had been placed in charge of music education and training at Fisk. Though his own education ended in high school at the age of fourteen, he had taught in Ohio schools and trained black choruses in Sunday Schools. Beginning with the approved music they learned to sing from notes, White moved his pupils up, at the insistence of a young pianist and singing student, to the music of leaders of the normal institute movement, and finally to *Esther,* a popular little operetta for Sunday School classes written by William Bradbury. When the Hutchinson Family played in Nashville in 1870, White saw a new dimension in the public performance of popular music, and his charges soon learned something about stage presence.

The Fisk group sang before white and black audiences, never mixed, around Nashville, but in 1871, when the young college, whose finances had never been good, required new funds, White took the young singers and their black accompanist on the road in search of paying audiences. Early programs featured white popular music, such as "Home, Sweet Home" and Foster's "Old Folks at Home," both done in the proper parlor-music style. But the inclusion of a slave hymn, remembered from the singers' own past, brought audiences to their feet. Though it proved to be successful and profitable in the collection plates, singing "slave songs" as public entertainment troubled some of the singers. When they resigned from the group, they were replaced by other Fisk students.

Many who came to listen were puzzled by the group's appearance, since they had been exposed only to burnt-cork performers in minstrel shows. To establish their entertainment as different, White, who was beginning to demonstrate an inborn sense of showmanship unusual for a college teacher, changed the group's name to "The Jubilee Singers." It was under that name that they appeared in New York City in the winter of 1871 and gave a successful concert at Henry Ward Beecher's Plymouth Church. The press, which had been exposed to abuse from Beecher's pulpit, took to calling them "Beecher's Nigger Minstrels," and rooming-house owners, whose quarters had been reserved in advance and who believed them to be a company of burnt-cork entertainers, immediately turned the students away when it was apparent they were not white.

The Jubilee Singers' big breakthrough came as a result of Patrick Gilmore's grand notion that a mighty International Peace Festival, held in Boston, was an appropriate way to celebrate. The bandleader and cornet star, who was also a songwriter and music publisher on occasion, had presented the first of his great Boston festivals just after the war, directing an orchestra of 1,000 and a chorus of 10,000 before an audience of 50,000 in a newly constructed coliseum. The musicians and choristers were so spread out on the stage that Gilmore could not provide a proper downbeat. Consequently, a table near his podium held buttons, which he pressed to fire a starting cannon that cued his performers.

When financial arrangements for the Boston 1872 festival broke down, Oliver Ditson came to the rescue with $50,000 to ensure presentation of the eighteen-day gathering. Letters from President Grant to the heads of European governments brought the most famous military bands to Boston; Johann Strauss came to conduct his "Blue Danube," and soloists from around the world performed. Using a six-foot baton, Gilmore rehearsed an orchestra of 2,000 and a chorus of 20,000 in a newly built auditorium that could hold 100,000. The choruses, including the Jubilee Singers, performed "The Battle Hymn of the Republic" at the first performance, with a black group from Boston singing the verses. The number of the assembled musicians may have confused the orchestra, which began to play on too high a pitch, and failure loomed until the Fisk singers took over the verses. When the song ended, men threw their hats into the air and the auditorium rang with cries of "The Jubilees! The Jubilees! The Jubilees forever!" The Fisk singers had arrived as star performers, accepted by white audiences, even though they were black and devoted a large portion of their programs to black spirituals and songs.

White brought in Thomas Freylinghaysen Seward to help him with an official *Jubilee Songs as Sung by the Jubilee Singers,* which Biglow & Main was to publish, to replace similar unauthorized collections that had been sold in connection with concerts by the Fisk group. More than a hundred slave songs and spirituals transcribed and arranged by Seward, among them "Swing Low, Sweet Chariot," "Turn Back Pharaoh's Army," "Steal Away, Jesus," and "Go Down, Moses," appeared in the final work, which had many reprintings. Seward, who had studied with Lowell Mason, George Root, and Thomas Hastings and had taught at Teachers College (later, part of Columbia University), became vocal coach and musical director for the Jubilees on their European tours, which raised more than $175,000 for Fisk in six years. People who had known black music only through the white minstrels who used the traditional tambourine and bones, with fiddles, banjos, and blackface make-up, were amazed by these black singer-performers. There was much of Stephen Foster's influence on the arrangements Seward made for them. The new renditions made it easier for white audiences to cope with Africanized English in songs that success made increasingly Euro-American.

Other black colleges in the South, principally Hampton Institute, formed similar singing groups and sent them, too, out on the road to bring back money to overcome insufficient benefaction from Northern whites. In the early 1900s, these groups were often quartets of singers. The Victor Talking Machine Company recorded one from Fisk, and the first number selected for them to sing was "Old Black Joe." The Negro spiritual was now also an important element of a concert singer's repertory, and music publishers brought out many volumes of the music, arranged by whites and, as their competence became known, by black graduates of segregated Southern colleges. In the absence of recognized composers, spirituals fell into the public domain, though many, in newly arranged versions with new verses that made the original lines proper English, were copyrighted in the names of contemporary musicians.

Minstrels and the Millionaires of Minstrelsy

Colonel Higginson had speculated about whether some of the slave songs were really the product of "some leading mind" after he witnessed what appeared to be the actual composition of several. However, it was generally assumed that the spirituals, like all folk music, were the result of a process that grew by accretion, unconsciously. Such was the belief of many whites who went to see a post–Civil War innovation, the colored minstrel show, featuring black performers who often had to dab burnt cork on their faces in order to comply with the general image of a true minstrel man. There had been some black minstrel troupes, performing much the same material as white ones, prior to the end of the war; one of them entertained Higginson's soldiers in Charleston in 1863. By 1870, as Robert C. Toll found in his research for *Blacking Up,* some twenty had appeared, all but one of them above the Mason-Dixon line. Most played on the sympathies of the North, for they billed themselves as "former slaves who had lived in bondage" and were making their way in the world by performing "Plantation Melodies . . . the true songs of the Sunny South." The most successful was the Brooker and Clayton Georgia Minstrels. Charles Hicks, the black manager and part owner, went into business for himself, and, with a few recruits from the group he was leaving, made up a company—the Georgia Slave Troupe Minstrels—of five musicians, two end men, and an interlocutor. It was reportedly these performers who first used the riddle "Why does a chicken cross the road?" The company grew, and Hicks took his men abroad, returning in 1872 when he sold his interest to a white tavern owner, Charles Callender. This, the most famous company of delineators of "genuine darky life in the South, introducing peculiar music and characteristics of plantation life," came into the control of another white man, Colonel Jack Haverly, in 1878. One of America's great showmen, Haverly already owned several all-white minstrel companies, some touring theatrical companies, a number of theaters in New York, Chicago, and San Francisco, and interests in mines and mills. The empire Haverly was building eventually rivaled that of P. T. Barnum and proved to be an incubator for musical and dancing talents. Haverly changed the character of his all-white minstrel performances. His United Mastodon Minstrels performed expensive extravaganzas set in locations around the world, which were inspired by the stage "spectacles" that were attracting sell-out houses. His Colored Minstrels, meanwhile, provided a home for Negro talent in Southern settings: the cornfield, canebrake, barnyard, and on the levee and flatboat.

Both the surge of national interest in such popular white gospel songs as the Moody and Sankey hymns and the popularity of the Fisk Jubilee Singers, with their spirituals and slave songs, were responsible for the inclusion of religious songs in the minstrel show for the first time during the mid-1870s. Their use was greater in the black programs, where vocal groups of varying size sang jubilee and plantation music. Almost every white troupe had its own imitations of the Jubilees or the Hampton Singers, groups named the Georgian Students or the Hamtown Students, who parodied the true songs or sang new religious material provided by professional songwriters, many of whom also appeared with the company as performers. The most successful was Will S. Hays, whose full-time occupation was "river editor" for the *Louisville Courier-Journal,* but who wrote the minstrel favorites "Angels, Meet Me at the Cross Roads" (1875), "Early in de Mornin' " (1877), "Meet Me by de River Side" (1877), and

"Keep in de Middle ob de Road" (1878). Hays also supplied the minstrels with popular, comic, and novelty songs, among them "Old Uncle Ben, the Colored Refugee" (1869), "Who's A-Gwine to Take Care of Me?" (1876), "Roll Out, Heave Dat Cotton" (1877), "Hannah, Is You Dar?" (1880), and his most famous tear-jerker, which lived to become an early country-music favorite, "Little Old Log Cabin in the Lane" (1875). Charles A. White, a major late-nineteenth-century music publisher and a partner in White, Smith & Co., was another favorite with minstrel singers. His "I'se Gwine Back to Dixie" (1874) and "The Old Home Ain't What It Used to Be" (1874) were written for minstrel companies, the latter dedicated to Charles Hicks.

The (George) Primrose and (Billy) West Company, formed by two song-and-dance men who left Haverly to form their own troupe in 1877, made its owners the first millionaires of minstrelsy with shows that gradually deleted all blackface performers. They were the first to send integrated companies on the road, although the two races never appeared on stage at the same time except in the finale.

Marking the success of Primrose and West, most white companies reduced the "darky humor" of their programs except for banjo numbers and scenes set on plantations. Of the major stars, only Lew Dockstader, a song-and-dance minstrel, played in blackface throughout a long career that began during the Civil War and ended with his death in 1924. He was regarded as the last of the great kings of minstrelsy. Dockstader trained many white performers in the theater arts, among them Al Jolson, whose performances in blackface, with wooly wig and white gloves, continued through a career in the theater, motion pictures, and radio. Dockstader's nearest rival for the crown he won was Al G. Fields, who died in 1921. Fields began as a circus musician and clown, and traveled with a road company of *Pilgrim's Progress*, with Haverly, and on a wagon show before he organized Fields Minstrels, whose forty-one years of touring back and forth across America set the longest record known by any company of blackface performers; it continued until 1928, seven years after its founder's death.

No black men other than Charles Hicks and Billy Kersands had a record of longevity even approaching that of Dockstader and Fields, nor did any black minstrel troupe. As the popularity of white minstrelsy declined with the advent of other, more sophisticated, forms of popular entertainment—vaudeville, the player piano, the phonograph, and motion pictures—so did that of colored minstrels, whose appearances were more and more relegated to rural and back country places. There were slightly more than fifty new colored minstrel companies in the 1870s, and about thirty-five in the following decade. By 1895, when the end came for black minstrelsy in the North, the three important black minstrel companies still working—McCabe, Young and Gray's Pavilion Minstrels, Richard and Pringle's Georgia Minstrels, and the Hicks and Sawyer Consolidated Minstrels—were all owned and managed by whites.

Billy Kersands, who started with the original Georgia Minstrels, remained active when black minstrel shows went south, playing in vaudeville and still dancing the Virginia Essence he had performed before European royalty and

American mobocracy. Danced to "Old Folks at Home" played in 6/8 time, the Essence was Dan Bryant's old shuffling dance in which Kersands appeared not to move his feet at all. Kersands' comedy was based in part on a large wide mouth, in which he could place two billiard balls and still sing songs he sometimes wrote himself, and the dancing and singing that made a show without him like a circus without elephants. Hicks, on the other hand, gave up performing early to make use of his ability to put together talented companies and run them with the discipline of a drillmaster. Even after whites monopolized the business, Hicks was still in demand as an advance man and publicity agent, for he was regarded as one of the best at getting audiences to "belly up" to the box office and buy tickets.

The First Great Black Songwriters

As the vogue for both black and white minstrelsy appeared to be ending, the experience black men had gained from it served to get many of them into the second phase of their contribution to the theatrical stage. Black songwriters benefited, too, when their talents were recognized by white music publishers and by white and black theatrical producers. The songs of James Bland, Bob Cole, J. Rosamund and James Weldon Johnson, Bert Williams, Alex Rogers, Gussie Davis, and Ernest Hogan, among others were as popular as those by white composers and authors during the "coon song" and ragtime-music days of the late nineteenth and early twentieth centuries. There had been professional black songwriters before them, however, entertainers who wrote many of the songs they sang onstage. The most famous were Sam Lucas, who had danced and sung alongside Kersands in the original Georgia companies, and the banjo king Sam Devere, who could make his instrument, "sing, talk, and cry."

Born to poor but free parents in Ohio in 1850, Lucas was nineteen when he first donned an end man's burnt cork, and he was recognized as the grand old man of the Negro theater when he died in 1916. He began to write his own songs while working with Callender's Jubilee Minstrels. "De Day I was Sot Free," "Shivering and Shaking Out in the Cold," and the popular spirituals "I'se Gwine in de Valley" and "Put on My Long White Robe" were among them, but the crowd's favorite as long as he sang was his "Carve Dat Possum." Not content to be a minstrel man, Lucas aspired to the legitimate stage and leaped at the opportunity to be the first black man to play Uncle Tom in the play based on Harriet Beecher Stowe's novel. With the diamond-studded jewelry he always carried, instead of trusting his money to banks, he went south with a white Little Eva who was so fat that she brought jeers rather than tears from the audience. The result was a disaster, and Lucas had to pawn some of his jewelry to get back north to work at barbering, a job he continued to do between engagements. He was featured in the all-black productions that combined minstrelsy with the white man's musical and paved the way for black musical comedy. He also played in England for several years before appearing on Broadway in A Trip to Coontown in 1899, the first Negro musical to run for three seasons. Lucas then played in the next Cole-Johnson musicals, leaving finally to become a vaudeville monologist. When moviemakers turned to *Uncle Tom's Cabin* for one of their early three-reel productions during World War I, Lucas was again hired to play the leading role, but, after catching pneumonia while shooting the frozen-river scene, he died.

"Good old Sam" Devere was one of the greatest banjo players. His notes came off the strings of his instrument it was said, like a "veritable Niagara of titillating music." At least two of his songsters were published during the 1870s, *Sam Devere's Burnt Cork Songster* and *Sam Devere's Combination Songster,* and in 1882 Charles D. Blake & Co., of Boston, issued *Sam Devere's Album of Original Songs,* which was also published in England by Arthur Chappell & Co. It contained six songs: "Butterfly Dude," "Annie Who Plays the Banjo," "That Sweet Scented Handsome Young Man," "Riding on the Elevated Railroad," "Our Hired Girl," and "Dar's a Lock on de Chicken Coop Door."

James A. Bland, a black songwriter whom many of his contemporaries considered to be the equal of Stephen Foster and John Philip Sousa, was a member of Haverly's European Minstrels, of which Kersands and Sam Lucas also were part. His father, an examiner in the Patent Bureau and later an attorney, was a member of the black civil service aristocracy formed in Washington, D.C., in the years following the Civil War. Bland studied at Howard University but spent more of his time entertaining friends with song than at his books. He organized a government clerks' glee club, whose members he had known while serving as a page in the House of Representatives, and wrote his first popular songs for this group. He may also have performed with minor black minstrel companies, but the first of which he is known to have been a member was Callender's Original Georgia Troupe, for he had been inspired to practice the art after seeing George Primrose in action. He moved to Boston in 1875 to manage and star in performances by a local minstrel company, and he began to sell his songs to the Boston publishing house owned by John F. Perry, who had recently left White, Smith & Perry, which he had helped form in 1867. Bland's greatest song, which many incorrectly believe Stephen Foster composed, "Carry Me Back to Old Virginny," was written to be sung by the Original Black Diamonds, with which Bland performed beginning in 1876. Perry did not copyright the song until three years later.

In the next several years, many of the 700 or more songs Bland wrote were published, not only by Perry but by White, Smith, the New York firm owned by S. T. Gordon, and other firms. His work included comic and sentimental songs for the minstrel stage and proper parlor ballads in which no trace of Africanized English appears. In 1879, the other songs by which he continued to be known were published: "Oh! Dem Golden Slippers," "In the Morning by the Bright Light," and "In the Evening by the Moonlight." When his "De Golden Wedding" came out in 1880, Perry printed on the back cover of the sheet music that "Oh! Dem Golden Slippers" had already sold more than 100,000 copies. Ironically, only thirty-eight songs by James Bland were ever deposited for copyright in the Library of Congress. The majority of them became the property of other entertainers.

Oblivious to his loss, Bland starred in Haverly's Carnival of Genuine Colored Minstrels, playing banjo, singing, cavorting as an end man, and being treated as the darling of some of America's most famous people. Black minstrelsy was in its heyday. Haverly took his minstrels to England, all sixty-five of them, male and female. Sixteen end men wielded their bones and tambourines, as quartets sang the songs of jubilee and spirituals, the bass and tenor soloists warbled sentimental ditties, Billy Kersands filled his large mouth with chinaware, and James Bland introduced "Oh! Dem Golden Slippers."

Bland liked the English and their island so much that he returned in 1884 with an even larger group of minstrels, and then decided to remain when his fellow artists returned to the United States. Abandoning all minstrel make-up and trappings, he enjoyed the acclaim that had been his in America and earned as much as $10,000 a year in addition to royalties from sales of his music during his twenty years away. Then it all came to an end, and he was back home, working at a desk in a Washington office, the one-time idol of two continents now a clerk. The newspapers did not even record his death in Philadelphia on May 5, 1911. Some sixty-six years after it had been written, "Carry Me Back to Old Virginny" was adopted as its official song by the Old Dominion, the state of Virginia, whose legislators were unaware that a black man had written it.

During the time Bland was in Europe, a number of changes had taken place in black entertainment, including the inevitable collapse of minstrelsy in major northern cities and the very shape and character of popular-music publishing. The songs of the "Ethiopian business" at which Stephen Foster excelled, the "plantation songs" of Will Hays, C. A. White, and others, the "darky music" of the minstrel shows, all now fell under the label "coon songs."

Persuaded to do so by Sam Lucas, Sam T. Jack, theatrical producer and founding father of "girlie" burlesque, presented in 1891 *The Creole Show*, a blend of burlesque with healthy dollops of the minstrel show. Sixteen beautiful black women and a number of leading black performers, including Lucas, a black female interlocutor, but with men in the traditional end positions, played to packed houses, and then continued in new editions for the next half-dozen years. More than forty black actors and actresses who went on to greater fame passed through the casts of such interpolations as a burlesque *Pinafore*, "Tropical Revelries," "Washday on the Levee," and other mixtures of vaudeville, minstrelsy, drama, and slapstick. In 1895, a black publicist, John W. Isham, who had worked for Jack, introduced *The Octoroons*, a mélange of Harrigan and Hart, burlesque, minstrel show, and variety, with an all-black cast, and followed it the next year with *Oriental America*, the first all-black musical to play on Broadway. It had much less burlesque and even fewer elements of the minstrel show; instead, it offered operatic arias sung by the best-trained black voices white New Yorkers had yet heard.

A vogue for coon songs dominated the new Tin Pan Alley following the success of M. Witmark, the most prominent of the new breed of music houses, with "All Coons Look Alike to Me." Its writer, the black entertainer Ernest Hogan, who was a veteran minstrel quartet singer and end man, became a national figure as a result of the song's popularity. Music-business apocrypha has it that Hogan heard the song, with a different melody, in a Midwestern honky-tonk as "All Pimps Look Alike to Me," voiced by a prostitute whose lover had died; further, that after Hogan wrote a new melody and changed the noun to "Coons," Isidore Witmark rewrote the melody for the verse and added some new words to the second chorus. The song became one of the ragtime era's greatest hits, selling well in the United States and abroad.

This was not the first use of the now generally distasteful word in popular music. It dated back to 1834, when George Washington Dixon sang "Old Zip Coon" on the New York stage, and during the early 1880s sheet-music copies sold well of "The Coonville Guards," "The Coon Dinner," and "New Coon in Town." Any song in black dialect was labeled a "coon song," as was any involving black persons. Irving Berlin's "Alexander's Ragtime Band," with "it's de bestest band what am, my honey lamb," clearly falls within the genre's scope, although by that time the description was being abandoned by many in Tin Pan Alley. Such songs gradually became known as "novelty songs." The Depression classic associated with Fats Waller, "Your Feet's Too Big," which was featured in the Broadway success *Ain't Misbehavin'*, was the work of a successful songwriter of the coon-song era, and except for its slightly more modern melody might well have been a hit in the 1900s. Many of the novelty rhythm-and-blues songs of the late 1940s and the 1950s had exactly the same flavor.

The "ragtime" arrangement of Hogan's hit was the first of its kind to be published and did much to make the song famous internationally. It was the work of a white Chicago musician, Max Hoffman, who was paid five dollars for it and an additional five dollars for a ragtime orchestration. Though Witmark & Co. usually paid only a dollar fifty for such work, evidently they realized what Hoffman had done for them and the song. So did competing music men, who sent much of their new material to Hoffman for arranging, in time making it necessary for him to hire only highly talented musicians for the theater orchestras he directed, so that he could farm out extra work to them. However, it was the inherent musical qualities of Hogan's tune, which Hoffman brought to the fore, that made "All Coons Look Alike to Me" popular with ragtime pianists. In 1900, when an international ragtime pianist championship was held in New York, those who reached the semifinal level were required to perform it in original variations.

An outstanding blackface comedian, Hogan was ranked by many critics higher than the great Bert Williams, though, as James Weldon Johnson wrote, "he lacked Williams' subtlety and finish." On the heels of his success as a songwriter, Hogan joined Sissieretta Jones's ensemble of black variety artists, dancers, comedians, and musicians. This touring group continued for almost twenty years, chiefly in the South, and was one of the early bridges between the old blackface minstrel show and the new musical comedy written and performed by blacks. Dubbed the "Black Patti," Madame Jones, who had been born in Rhode Island in 1868 and studied music at the Boston Conservatory, made her first impact on New York critics in 1892. She had already been acclaimed for her singing in small American cities and during a long tour of Central America. On her return to New York, she was chosen to be one of the leading attractions at the Grand Negro Jubilee, held in Madison Square Garden in April 1892. She then toured Europe and major American cities. After a scheme for her to sing *Aïda* and *L'Africaine* at the Metropolitan Opera House fell through, her managers assembled a production by the Black Patti Troubadours, in which the soprano's talent was confined to operatic and standard selections. As plans for new productions grew more ambitious, Ernest Hogan was one of the talented black musicians and performers called to join the company as writer and performer.

Hogan left the Black Patti troupe in 1898 to join a production at the Casino Roof Garden, on Broadway, of *Clorindy, or The Origin of the Cakewalk,* words by Paul Lawrence Dunbar and music by Will Marion Cook, the first black operetta in the new syncopated style. Dunbar, then twenty-seven, had already written some of the verse and fiction that would make him famous. Cook, the son of Oberlin College graduates (his father was a lawyer), was born in Washington in 1865, sent to Oberlin to study music at the age of thirteen, and given advanced training in Germany, where the great Joachim taught him the violin. After his return to America in 1895, he studied for a time with Anton Dvořák at the New England Conservatory of Music, and then went to New York City, where he was regarded as the best trained of all black musicians working there. It was inevitable that he would try his hand at the new syncopated black-influenced music that was sweeping the land. *Clorindy* opened with "Darktown Is Out Tonight," sung by Hogan and the entire company of twenty-six black performers, the first of four Dunbar-Cook songs that brought audiences up to the roof garden, after the all-white show downstairs concluded, throughout the summer of 1898. The others were "Jump Back, Honey," "Hottest Coon in Dixie," and "Who Dat Say Chicken in This Crowd?" In later years, Cook recalled that when he was working on the last song at the family piano, his mother came in from the kitchen to shout, "Oh, Will! I've sent you all over the world to study and become a great musician, and you return such a nigger!"

At the end of the summer, Hogan left to go to Australia, and *Clorindy* was incorporated into *A Senegambian Carnival,* starring the team of Bert Williams and George Walker, for which Dunbar and Cook provided the music. A brief road tour followed before the cast of sixty was told that the management had decided to close because of poor attendance. However, Dunbar and Cook were now recognized as the nearest rivals to the popular black song-writing-and-comedy team of Bob Cole and Billy Johnson. One of the most versatile men in the history of black theater, Cole was in his late twenties, an excellent singer, dancer, and comedian, best known for his tramp act. He played several musical instruments and was capable of writing the book, music, and songs for a musical, directing it, and coping with all the problems of managing the entire production. After going to New York from Georgia, where he had attended Atlanta University, he managed and appeared with a side-street black stock company and then began to write for the stage. The white managers of Sissieretta Jones hired him to write for her earliest Troubadour productions. After he fell out with the management over money and was replaced by Hogan, Cole determined to produce an all-black full-length musical comedy of his own.

His partner, Billy Johnson, was from South Carolina and had appeared with several minstrel companies during the 1880s and written songs for them. Johnson had also been a member of the *Creole Show* and *Octoroons* casts before he joined Cole to stage and write music for Black Patti's earliest shows. Their production of the full-length *Trip to Coontown* had stormy sailing during its out-of-town performances, but, with financing from an affluent stage-struck black South Carolina youth, it opened in early 1898, with Cole and Johnson starring as the tramp and a flimflam artist. Sam Lucas was brought in sometime later in a major supporting role. The production ran for three years, during which, unlike the past, when they had to sell all rights to white producers for a flat amount, Cole and Johnson were able to pay themselves a portion of the receipts as royalties. It was an argument over the division of this money during a time when Cole was seriously ill that led to a complete break between the two. Johnson went on the road with *A Trip to Coontown,* and later, after moving to Chicago, he played in local black musicals. He died after a fall in 1916.

Clorindy's success, and that, the following summer, of another Cook musical, *Jes Like White Folks,* the Cole-Johnson hit, and the general acceptance of black entertainers in the best vaudeville houses indicated that brighter days were truly in store. The Marshall Hotel, on West 53rd Street, had become the gathering place for black theater, literary, and music figures. Bert Williams and his partner George Walker could be found there regularly, as could Ernest Hogan, back from Australia and starring in vaudeville. Later, he had the leading part, the "unbleached American," in *Rufus Rastus* (1906), with songs by Tom Lemonier, Joe Jordan, and Hogan. It was predicted that this success would be followed by an even greater one with *The Oyster Man,* a play with music by Will Vodery, but during rehearsals in 1907 Hogan died of exhaustion. In the encomiums that followed, he was acknowledged to have been the greatest performer ever seen in the American black theater. There may be some merit to the belief that Hogan's death was hastened by despair over the scorn shown him by members of his own race because of "All Coons Look Alike to Me." When pressed, Hogan had always argued that the song had come along at a time when music needed a new direction, and, as a result of its success, the way was made easier for blacks to find a place in the world from which they had long been barred. Ironically, the song's great success also led white lynch mobs that roamed New York City streets during a race riot in 1900 to look for Hogan, Bob Cole, and Billy Johnson as potential victims.

The Marshall was also the spawning ground for the first important black popular orchestra, the Memphis Students, formed by Joe Jordan, the songwriter and musician whose hit songs included "Oh, Say Wouldn't It Be a Dream," "Sweetie Dear," "Lovie Joe," sung by Fanny Brice in Ziegfeld's *Follies of 1910,* "The Raggedy Rag," and "That Teasin' Rag," written in 1909 for Ada Walker, wife of the stage star. The last song served as the chief melodic strain for "The Original Dixie Land One Step," made famous by the Original Dixieland Jass Band in 1917. Jordan's complaint about that plagiarism made the Victor Talking Machine Company remove the band's record from the market and change the label to credit Jordan with the "Introduction" of "That Teasin'

Rag.'' His name appeared on only the first printing of the sheet music. Though born in Cincinnati, Jordan learned piano rag in St. Louis and then worked as a musician in Chicago before he arrived in New York in 1904, at the age of twenty-two. He published his own music for a time, but most of it was never brought out, at least under his own name. He did, however, become much in demand as a theater-orchestra leader and arranger in both New York and Chicago, and also worked for Florenz Ziegfeld. During the Great Depression, he was the conductor of the Negro Orchestra Unit of the New York Federal Theatre Project which produced Orson Welles's all-black *Macbeth*. After World War II, he joined the faculty of the Modern Institute for Music, in Tacoma, Washington. The Memphis Students, which Jordan had organized in 1905, were neither students nor all from Memphis, but the name appealed to international vaudeville, variety, and music-hall audiences. Including seventeen men and women who not only played the usual instruments, but also sang and danced, the group was booked by leading vaudeville houses almost at once.

Among other important songwriters who could be found at the Marshall in the early 1900s were the stuttering comedian Irving Jones, writer of "I'm Living Easy," "You Missed Your Man," "La Pa-ma-la," and "St. Patrick's Day Is Bad for Coons"; the minstrel man, actor, and music publisher Shepherd Edmonds, writer of "I'm Gonna Live Anyhow Until I Die," "You Can Fool All the People All the Time," and "That Will Bring You Back" before he retired from the music business to become the first Negro private detective in America; and Chris Smith, the baker who taught himself to play guitar and piano while waiting for the bread to rise, and joined a medicine show with his partner Elmer Bowman, traveling for the next several decades. His songs, many of which were recorded during the early 1900s by the Edison's National Phonograph Company, include "Never Let the Same Bee Sting You Twice," "Good Morning Carrie," "He's a Cousin of Mine," "Down in Honky Tonk Town," "Come After Breakfast, Bring Your Lunch and Leave Before Supper Time," and his greatest hit, "Ballin' the Jack," written in 1912 when whites picked up a dance blacks had been doing for years. It became a hit after being sung in the *Ziegfeld Follies of 1913*. (The producer's name became part of the title in 1911.) Many of Smith's songs were written with R. C. McPherson, who sometimes used the pseudonym Cecil Mack and who formed the first black popular-music publishing company, Gotham-Attucks Music, in New York, around 1906. In addition to the songs written with Chris Smith, McPherson's hits included "You're in the Right Church but the Wrong Pew," "Please Go Way and Let Me Sleep," "(That's Why They Call Me) Shine," "Teasing," "Charleston," "Runnin' Wild," and "Old Fashioned Love." With Harry Burleigh, Will Marion Cook, the Johnson brothers (J. Rosamund and James Weldon), and Will Tyers, McPherson was one of the black founding members of the American Society of Composers, Authors and Publishers, in 1914.

Gussie L. Davis, next to Bland the most successful black songwriter in the last decades of the nineteenth century, had gone to live in New York City during the 1890s, and later moved into a house in its suburban section of

Whitestone. Much like Bland, he did not concentrate on any one style, but wrote all the descriptive songs, maudlin ballads, sentimental Irish ditties, and plantation and coon songs publishers wanted. Born and educated in Cincinnati, he wrote his first successful song in 1881, at the age of eighteen. Unable to find a publisher, he paid twenty dollars to a local printer, who brought it out as sheet music. Recognizing his lack of musical training, Davis applied to a local school of music, but was rejected on account of his color. He went to work there as a porter at fifteen dollars a month and the promise of private lessons. During this period he wrote and sold some songs to the John Church Company. After three years, he was hired by a local printing office to write twelve new songs, among which was his first great hit, "The Light House by the Sea" (1886). A wealthy white Cincinnatian, George Propheter, Jr., who had aspirations to be a songwriter, signed a contract for Davis's exclusive services and opened a Cincinnati music-publishing company, with later, a branch office in New York. The arrangement continued until Propheter's death, and in its course Davis wrote some 300 songs, a few of them to words by his publisher. Among the songs that "had an immense sale," according to sheet-music-cover advertising, were "Baby's Laughing in Her Sleep," "Irene, Goodnight," "The Light House by the Sea," "The Hermit," and "Don't Move Mother's Picture." Most of Davis's songs during this time were waltzes, which were featured by white minstrel singers around the United States, none of whom knew the writer's color. Davis had learned, as he once told a newspaper interviewer, that women had become the "supporters of the music dealers." Because men were able to whistle the tunes they heard and liked, and women could not, the female sex bought the greatest amount of sheet music, he said. And because society frowned on the use of "unrefined" songs, women bought and played waltz songs and descriptive ballads.

His "Fatal Wedding" (1893), whose lyrics were credited to a popular singer who sang the song constantly; "Picture 84" (1894); "Down in Poverty Row" (1895), to words by the Briton Arthur Trevelyan, who had shared the popular 1901 "My Samoan Beauty" with another black writer, Will Accoe; and "In the Baggage Coach Ahead" (1896), all sold in great quantities, the last reported to have gone over the million-copy mark. Imogene Comer, a white "female baritone" and singer of descriptive songs, and black Billy Johnson, who sang it every night in Black Patti's show, plugged it to its success. Bonnie Thornton, a tiny white soubrette, had performed the same function, single-handed, for "Poverty Row."

Gussie L. Davis had become one of the most successful songwriters on Tin Pan Alley, a fact confirmed in 1895 by the *New York World*. In a promotion intended to raise circulation, the newspaper held a competition, with an award of $500 and a gold medal for the writer of the song voted best by its readers. Davis was selected, with James Thornton, Charles Graham, Felix McGlennon, Charles K. Harris, Harry Dann, Percy Gaunt, Raymond Moore, Joe Flynn, and Charles B. Ward, as competitors and won a second prize of $500 in gold for his "Send Back the Picture and the Ring." After a serious illness, from which he recovered in the summer of 1899, Davis began to prepare for a road tour with the black actor Tom McIntosh in a production centered on the farce comedy "A Hot Old Time in Dixie." Stricken again, he died in October 1899.

Gussie Davis's place as America's top professional black songwriter was taken within a few years by the new song-writing team of Bob Cole and the Johnson brothers. James Weldon Johnson was twenty-eight and J. Rosamund two years younger when they first began to work with Cole in the summer of 1899. The sons of a middle-class Jacksonville, Florida, family, both had received advanced education, James at Atlanta University and Rosamund, who, taught by his mother, played the piano at the age of four, at the New England Conservatory of Music. After touring for one year in *Oriental America* as a principal singer, Rosamund returned to Florida, where James was teaching in a local high school and studying for the law. At Rosamund's prompting, they wrote some songs to be used by his music pupils and a comic opera, *Toloso,* which satirized the new American imperialism that had brought on the Spanish-American War. With the manuscript of their musical and a letter from a local music-store owner to the Witmark brothers in New York, they went north and auditioned the work for the music publishers. A round of Broadway producers followed, with not much success, but a chance meeting with Cole resulted in a love song, "Louisiana Lize," whose exclusive singing rights were sold for fifty dollars to May Irwin, the leading white comic star, and given to the Joseph S. Stern Company for publication.

The brothers spent the following winter in Florida getting ready for another assault on Tin Pan Alley, during which they wrote "Lift Every Voice and Sing," which is now the official song of the National Association for the Advancement of Colored People. It was published by Stern. Cole was waiting for them in New York in the summer of 1900, and the three entered into a partnership that lasted until Cole's death, each member receiving an equal share of profits from more than 200 songs and any plays in which they were featured. In addition to some new songs for May Irwin, they wrote "Run, Brudder Possum, Run" for the Rogers brothers' new musical, *In Central Park,* starring the pair of former vaudeville performers who had become serious rivals to the Broadway stars Weber and Fields.

It was the success of the possum song that brought about a connection with producers Klaw and Erlanger, one of the most powerful factors in the theatrical business. With the Marshall Hotel, where the Johnsons and Cole lived, as their headquarters, they wrote and sold a number of songs to major musical productions featuring white casts, and then were called by Klaw and Erlanger, whose stage director had been looking for the writers of "Run, Brudder Possum, Run." Their first major assignment followed, writing three songs for an extravagantly spectacular pantomime, *The Sleeping Beauty and the Beast.* Another fortunate break was the acceptance of their song "The Maiden with the Dreamy Eyes" by Florenz Ziegfeld for his production of *The Little Duchess,* starring his wife, the beauteous Anna Held. In working on that song, James had reasoned that, rather than write songs for the black musical theater or whites who sang coon songs, they should write the kind of songs for which a large market existed, ones young men took along when courting, to be played by their girls, giving both sexes an opportunity to vent their sentiments decorously.

This judgment proved to have considerable merit, for fifteen of their songs were accepted by producers of major Broadway musicals. With the manuscripts in hand, the three went to talk business with their publishers, Joseph W. Stern and Edward B. Marks. The result was the first contract given by a New York publisher to black songwriters. It was for three years of exclusivity, a cash guarantee to be paid monthly, and repayment only out of semiannual royalties. James then returned to Florida to head a new high school; Rosamund and Cole were signed to work in vaudeville as a singing-and-dancing team at salaries that began at $300 a week. By June, fortune appeared to be beaming on all three. Indebtedness to Stern and Marks had been repaid out of sheet-music sales, and there was a $1,500 check with their June 1902 statement. Cole and Johnson had moved up to the top vaudeville houses and were playing two shows a day; their new song "Under the Bamboo Tree" had been taken for Marie Cahill's new production. With it and "The Maiden with the Dreamy Eyes" both selling well, James gave up teaching. The trio turned an entire floor of the Marshall into the home and headquarters of one of the year's most successful theater-music teams. Royalty checks doubled and then doubled again from the sales of their hits "Mandy, Won't You Let Me Be Your Beau," "Nobody's Looking but the Owl and the Moon," "Tell Me, Dusky Maiden," "The Old Flag Never Touched the Ground," "My Castle on the Nile," and "Oh, Didn't He Ramble," written by Cole and Rosamund under the pseudonym Will Handy.

They wrote the music for two new Klaw and Erlanger productions, one of which, *Humpty Dumpty,* opened the magnificent New Amsterdam Theatre, on 42nd Street off Broadway, and ran for 123 performances. Cole and Rosamund continued to work as headliners on the national Orpheum vaudeville circuit and on a tour of Europe, at salaries that were now over $3,000 a week. New popular song hits by them continued to roll off Stern and Marks's presses: "Lazy Moon," "Congo Love Long," "My Dusky Princess," "Gimme de Leavin's," "The Countess of Alagazam," "Hottentot Love Song," and "Fishing," with which Marie Cahill stopped the show every night.

Despite their success, Cole was restive. He thought they should capitalize on the fame their appearances were bringing and establish a theatrical production company of their own to do their own musicals. After a farewell engagement at New York's Palace Theatre, they retired from vaudeville to star in *The Shoo-Fly Regiment,* an all-black musical for which Cole wrote the book, Rosamund the music, and James the lyrics. Shortly after the show opened in 1906, James assumed the first of several government posts he filled during his life, that of consul at Puerto Cabello, Venezuela. A more European operettalike work followed in 1908, *The Red Moon,* with book and lyrics by Cole. The production ran for two years, and, when it closed, its stars and creators announced that they were retiring from the musical theater to resume their careers in vaudeville. Cole began to suffer from nervous problems, but Rosamund wrote two more musicals, *Mr. Lode of Koal,* with Bert Williams, Alex Rogers, and J. A.

Shipp, and *Hello Paris,* with L. Leubrie Hill, a black songwriter who became one of the most important World War I black show-business entrepreneurs.

Bob Cole died in 1911. Rosamund Johnson continued his theatrical activities at home and abroad. For a time, he was musical director for the Hammerstein Opera House in London. In 1914, he was named director of the Music School for Colored People, and during the 1930s he played in a number of all-black productions on Broadway, among them the original *Porgy and Bess.* He died in November 1954, at eighty. After leaving the diplomatic service, James Weldon Johnson served as NAACP national secretary for fourteen years, wrote many books of literature and about the black experience, and was hailed as an outstanding black poet. He returned to teaching during the 1930s, at Fisk University and at New York University, where was a visiting professor when he died in 1938.

Though they were the equal of the best white writers for the musical theater for almost a decade, Bob Cole and J. Rosamund Johnson had not been able to support the large companies of performers and complicated scenery *The Shoo-Fly Regiment* and *The Red Moon* called for. When they left Broadway to play in the popular-priced theaters in the South, the almost all-black audiences were uneasy with the writers' attempts to break away from the stereotypes and racial conventions imposed by white theater owners. Many came expecting to see a Bert Williams and George Walker, but neither Cole nor Rosamund was one, nor, indeed, an Ernest Hogan, and dwindling box-office receipts confirmed that fact.

Williams and Walker were both born outside the Deep South—Williams in 1874 in the Bahamas, and Walker the year before in Lawrence, Kansas. At the age of two, Williams was taken to Riverside, California, where he graduated from high school and then went to San Francisco and joined a minstrel company. Made up of a Mexican trombone player who doubled as caravan driver, and five white and four black minstrels, the troupe played in lumber and mining camps along the coast. Williams and Walker met around 1893, when the latter joined the minstrels as an end man. He was already an extraordinary dancer, and soon taught Williams many steps, finally working up the act in which they played with medicine shows and on vaudeville circuits, reaching New York in late 1895. The coon song was already all the rage, and many white singers had again taken to smearing black make-up on their faces before they sang the latest new songs.

Billed as "Williams and Walker, The REAL Coons," the pair opened at Koster and Bial's Music Hall on the present site of Macy's department store in New York and played for a record run of forty weeks. Wearing blackface to cover his light complexion, Williams was the stuttering, self-effacing clown; the dapper and dancing Walker fed him the straight lines. In a short time, Bert Williams proved himself to be the equal of the best white or black writers of successful ragtime songs. One of the songs the pair sang was his "Dora Dean, the Hottest Thing You Ever Seen," toasting a beauty in *The Creole Show's* glamorous line of black female dancers.

Its success led to two rather unusual occurrences in the popular-music business. A postal regulation forced the publisher to call back the original edition and change ''hottest'' to ''sweetest'' so the song could be sent by mail. A suit for plagiarism by another black entertainer brought a decision by the California court hearing it that raised the issue of morality in copyrighted music. Williams was declared the original author of the song, but the court held his copyright to be questionable because the song's lyrics were indecent, particularly the use of ''hottest'' in the edition deposited for registration.

Assisted by two lovely young black women, with Williams shuffling along behind him, Walker, dressed like a black dandy, introduced white New Yorkers and then all America to the cakewalk. The traditional African circle dance, to which slaves added movements mimicking the grand-march parade of their minuet-dancing masters and mistresses, part of which was later absorbed into the minstrel show's walk-around, became the ''chalk-line walk'' during the mid-nineteenth century. It was danced by blacks with pails of water on their heads, the prize going to the couple who lost the least water. In time, the prize became a lavish cake. The once-rude dance had been transformed into a thing of exuberant elegance when George Walker danced it with two charmers to the ragged-time music of 1896. White high society was quick to respond to the colored billboards showing Williams and Walker and their assistants prancing in the cakewalk, and the lower classes joined them almost at once in taking up the dance. Cakewalk competitions were held in public places ranging from aristocratic ballrooms to Coney Island beer parlors. Even the presumably staid Britons succumbed to the cakewalk's lures after Williams and Walker, billed as the Tobasco Senegambians, introduced the dance during their first visit to that country, in 1897.

The success of Cole's *Trip to Coontown* persuaded white theatrical managers that there were profits in the new all-black shows he, Ernest Hogan, Will Marion Cook, Jesse Shipp, Alex Rogers, and others were pioneering. That understood, it was child's play to perceive the commercial potential of Bert Williams's talent. He had already mastered the stagecraft that was to make him one of the greatest comedians of any color in any age. In an article in the *American Magazine* of December 1917, Williams revealed the genesis of his slow delivery:

> When I was a lad I thought I had a voice, but I learned differently in later years. I did not take care of it and now I have to talk all of my numbers. . . . I study very carefully the acoustics of each theater I appear in. There is always one particular spot on the stage from which the voice carries better more clearly and easy than from any other. I make it my business to find that spot before the first performance, and once I find it I stick to it like a postage stamp. People have sometimes observed that I practice unusual economy of motion. . . . It is to spare my voice and not my legs that I stand still while delivering a song.

Williams and Walker appeared on the stage in several all-black productions that failed, before the successful *Sons of Ham* (1900), with a book by them and Jesse Shipp, music by Will Marion Cook, and lyrics by Alex Rogers. A black writer from Nashville, Rogers wrote some 2,000 songs, the best known for Williams and Walker, "Bon Bon Buddy, the Chocolate Drop," "I'm a Jonah Man," "I May Be Crazy, but I'm No Fool," "Adam Sinned Because He Had No Mammy," "Elder Eatmore's Sermon on Casting Stones," a comic monologue, and the song Williams had to sing before he was allowed to leave the stage, "Nobody," for which the actor wrote the words. As was true of all the Williams and Walker musicals produced in the next seven years, the *Sons of Ham* departed from New York after a short but respectable run to play for at least a year on the road.

In Dahomey, the first of three musical satirizations of various aspects of the modern Negro's life, this one dealing with the "Back to Africa" movement, actually opened *on* Broadway in 1903, the first black musical to do so, at the New York Theatre, between 44th and 45th Streets. The score was by Cook and Rogers, with Paul Lawrence Dunbar providing some of the lyrics. Cole and Johnson's popular "My Castle on the Nile" was interpolated, as were some other popular hit songs of the day. Cook's classically trained talent was an important ingredient in the show's success, particularly in the finale, his "On Emancipation Day," with its grand march and cakewalk. The production played fifty-three times and then went to London for an unexpected run of 251 performances, followed by a tour of the leading provincial cities before it returned to New York. From there it went on a cross-country tour that visited Williams's home state of California.

The same artistic team functioned in the creation of the final two Williams and Walker shows, *Abyssinia* (1907) and *Bandana Land* (1909). Williams introduced his famous pantomime poker game in the latter and sang its hit song "Late Hours." During the road tour of *Bandana Land,* Walker appeared to be losing control of himself and was subject to spells of deep despond. His wife, Ada Overton Walker, stepped in and, dressed in male attire, sang his songs when he was confined to one of several hospitals. He was returned to one on Long Island, where he died in 1911. George Walker's continuing fight for better conditions for black professional actors and musicians and the physical energy he expended in that struggle have been cited as the chief factors contributing to his death. Another may have been the despair felt by this uneducated man who, like Bob Cole, saw his work denigrated by many cultured blacks as blind imitations of white patterns that the other race could do better.

During Walker's long illness, Williams appeared in *Mr. Load of Koal,* with music by J. Rosamund Johnson, books and lyrics by Shipp and Alex Rogers, with some interpolated songs, including "That's a Plenty," written by Williams and Henry Creamer. A new face in New York, Creamer, from Virginia, was another of the talented young black songwriters Williams encouraged by using their music in his stage appearances. With Turner Layton, Creamer wrote "Dear Old Southland," " 'Way Down Yonder in New Orleans," and "If I could Be With You One Hour Tonight" during the 1920s. After the musical's run of sixty-two performances on Broadway, Williams played in major vaudeville houses catering to white patrons and then joined *Ziegfeld's Follies* of 1910, in which the talented comedienne Fanny Brice also made her Broadway debut. As the only black in the cast, Williams immediately became the victim of racial prejudice, and some fellow players threatened Ziegfeld with a boycott. The producer was adamant, compromising only by putting Williams in comedy sketches and dances exclusively with male players. Within a few years, when critics had hailed Williams as one of the most finished actors on the American stage, Ziegfeld presented him with all the leading performers, male and female, in every one of the *Follies* after 1911. Williams remained loyal to the man who had been first to integrate the musical theater and turned down offers to appear in vaudeville for twice the income he was making with Ziegfeld. Cole and the Johnsons had learned earlier of the producer's attitude toward black talent. Asked to go to Ziegfeld's apartment for a conference on *The Little Duchess,* they were barred from entering by an officious doorman. Learning of this, Ziegfeld informed the building's owners that, if his black guests were not sent upstairs at once, he and his wife, Anna Held, would vacate the building, with proper coverage of the event in the newspapers.

In 1901, Williams recorded the first of nearly eighty songs, initially for the Victor Talking Machine Company, and two years later for the Columbia Phonograph Company, with whom he remained until his death. Although not the first black man to make phonograph records, Williams was the first black artist to have a sustained career in the recording business. (George W. Johnson, a former slave who was discovered while panhandling along Washington streets, recorded cylinders of the first song written by a black American to be recorded, the black minstrel banjoist Sam Devere's 1888 "The Whistling Coon," and two other songs, "The Laughing Song" and "The Whistling Song," for Edison in 1898.) Williams always recorded the songs that he sang onstage, and Columbia's record catalogues continually mentioned that Williams was a *Follies* star. Williams's 1914 success, "The Darktown Poker Club," a hit both on the stage and as a recording, was written with Will Vodery, a young Philadelphian who had received formal music training and, in 1904, had left the University of Pennsylvania to write music for the stage presentations starring the man whose protégé he had become. Vodery wrote part of the music for *Abyssinia,* and arranged the music for *Bandana Land,* serving as musical director for the show in the United States and on the subsequent tour of Europe. Ziegfeld first learned of Vodery's abilities through his songs that were interpolated into *Follies* scores and engaged him to write special material and do arrangements for ensuing extravaganzas glorifying the American white girl, which he did until the 1920s. After service as leader of a black regiment's military band during World War I, Vodery studied at the Paris Conservatory and then wrote the music for Williams's last, and unsuccessful, stage show, *The Pink Slip,* retitled *Under the Bamboo Tree,* during whose first performance Williams collapsed and died. Vodery was also staff arranger for Stern and Marks. As one of the black music world's most respected figures, he was a great influence on Duke Ellington during that young Washingtonian's early days in New York City. When the talking pictures' success with musical presentation increased the demand for composers and arrangers, Vodery spent three years in Hollywood. Generally little known to the white world, Vodery remained a major contributor to the world of black musical theater until his death in 1951.

Bert Williams's early abandonment of that world in 1910 for the *Follies* was one of many signals that the first, brilliant and vibrant, period of its growth was coming to an end. Black bohemia was moving uptown to Harlem, where all-black audiences remained its principal patron until the Prohibition period. In the decade that began with *A Trip to Coontown,* however, when all the black musical comedies and extravaganzas that had been produced were related to the stereotype created by the Ethiopian business, and men like Hogan, Williams, Walker, and even, on some occasions, Cole and Johnson were obliged to wear the low-comic's burnt cork, gross-lipped mouth, and wooly wig, their dances and music were nonetheless unfettered by past conventions.

Cakewalks and Coon Songs

The dashing Louis Moreau Gottschalk's contribution to the course of a new kind of vernacular American music, growing out of the fusion of African rhythms and European harmonies with which the young composer and pianist had grown up in New Orleans, gave the first inkling of such a development to Europeans in the late 1840s and to his fellow Americans just before the Civil War. Many of his black-influenced piano pieces, including "La Bamboula—Danse des Nègres," in which a kind of cakewalk rhythm may be discerned, and "Le Bananier," a precursor of classic ragtime, were issued by the Escudier Brothers, of Paris, publishers of Berlioz and Verdi. Shortly after Gottschalk's return to the United States in 1853, a leading New York music publisher, General William Hall, contracted with him for all American rights to his music and published most of his New Orleans pieces among the sixty works he printed before Gottschalk's sudden and permanent departure in 1865.

During his transcontinental tours in the war years, Gottschalk, billed as "the greatest pianist now before the public," played piano pieces whose sources lay in African rhythms, the Spanish habanera, Negro street songs, and Latin-American music, in a repertory that thrilled many who played the piano. Because of the growth of transcontinental mail service, anyone could order, for quick delivery from New York, printed copies of Gottschalk's music for as little as twenty-five cents a copy plus postage.

Other significant contributions to the growth of ragged music were less exotic but equally important. Yet it was European-influenced classical art music that created the major difference between Tin Pan Alley ragtime, the blues, and jazz, which were in a similar incubation stage. The "classic" ragtime of Scott Joplin was, unlike them, composed music, written to be performed exactly as its creator intended.

In the post–Civil War years, black music involving embellished and syncopated melody lines, played against the "slow drag" of parade music, was developed in Midwestern saloons, wine rooms, and brothels. Its creators were side-street and back-alley musicians who played their "jig" or "rag" interpretations of familiar songs, schottisches, quadrilles, and marches on pianos and with small bands. Many of them were trained musicians from middle-class families, who found such Negro-influenced music as Gottschalk's and that being used in minstrel shows more inspiring than the repertory imposed on them by teachers trained in the correct parlor music of the day. Others, self-taught, learned by jigging on any piano available.

Chicago, where more railroads began and terminated than anywhere else, became a gathering place in 1893 for these musicians from all around the United States. They had been drawn by opportunities for work created by the city's great Columbian Exposition, not only on the fairground, but also in the vast red-light district, which had grown larger for the occasion. Ragtime musicians from Missouri, Kansas, Tennessee, and southern Illinois took advantage of the special penny-a-mile excursion fares and created a convocation of their peers without parallel. In the months during which 12 million Americans gaped at the wonders of the nation and those to come, a tremendous interchange of thinking about jig music took place in cutting contests featuring showpiece instrumental music and the exchange of ideas and techniques. Among those most influenced were white musicians, some of them members of the many bands and small orchestras spotted around the exposition, who heard that raggy syncopation in the fair's amusement area and in the red-light district. A few were members of John Philip Sousa's great band, particularly his spectacular instrumental star Arthur Pryor, master of the trombone smear. In later years, a vast number of Americans got to know ragtime through the novelties Pryor wrote after 1896 and recorded with members of the Sousa band: "A Coon Band Contest," "Mr. Black Man," "Razzazza Mazzazza," and "Southern Blossoms."

Syncopated popular music had began to change the character of American songs before the Chicago exposition, but afterward it was being described as the "coon song." Professional entertainers and songwriters had heard it in sporting houses and drinking establishments. Theodore Metz, a bandmaster for a white minstrel company, first heard his "A Hot Time in the Old Town" in an all-colored whorehouse. Henry Sayer, press agent for a Broadway show, found "Ta-ra-ra-boom-de-ay" in Babe Connor's place in St. Louis, rewrote its "unspeakable" words, and saw his finished piece become world famous after a British actress did some daring leg kicks as she sang it. It became a million-copy seller for its publisher. Sportswriter Charles Trevathan, gave "The Bully Song," as done by one of Madame Connor's ladies, to white May Irwin and made her the ranking "coon-shouter" of the day. A now-unknown white minstrel man heard "Who Stole the Lock on the Henhouse Door" at a gilded house of ill repute and made it part of the blackface gentry's repertory. The alcoholic vaudeville performer and songwriter Jim Thornton did not find his song in a brothel, but heard it played by black musicians for Little Egypt in the *Streets of Cairo* sideshow on the Columbian Exposition midway. Sol Bloom, later chairman of the Foreign Affairs Committee of the House of Representatives, but then managing the dancer, published Thornton's "She Lives on the Streets of Cairo." Ernest Hogan found there the jig-time dance melody he used for "The Pas Ma La" and his hit "All Coons Look Alike to Me."

It was a black piano player, so light-complexioned that he had passed for white all his life, who provided Tin Pan Alley with the first true rag song that became a national hit. The kind of music Benjamin Robertson Harney, of Mid-dleboro, Kentucky, played was still called "jig piano" when he opened in February 1896 at Keith's vaudeville theater in New York and delighted audi-ences with his "genuinely clever plantation Negro imitations and excellent piano playing." The act included three people. Harney's white wife opened with a coon song and then returned in blackface for the finale to reprise the song in proper English. Harney played some piano music and then sang his own "Mis-ter Johnson, Turn Me Loose" and "You Been a Good Old Wagon but You Done Broke Down," after each of which Strap Hill, a black ragtime singer and player from Memphis, repeated the song from his perch in the balcony. Harney imitated him so skillfully that the show had to stop each time for an encore.

Harney was twenty-five years old but had behind him several years of saloon back-room entertainment. That was followed by tours throughout the Midwest and Chicago during the exposition, after which he joined a white minstrel com-pany, where he became famous for "Ben Harney's Celebrated Stick Dance," which remained part of his vaudeville act until the end. Calls for sheet-music copies of his songs sent New York publishers on a mad race, with Frank Hard-ing winning when he bought "Mister Johnson" in time to put it on sale in April. The Witmark brothers bought it from Harding later that year, after Isi-dore Witmark had visited Kentucky to authenticate Harney's claim to the songs and brought both out in new editions. May Irwin had already demonstrated her incomparable ability to make a song a hit by singing it regularly, along with "The Bully Song," and arrangements were made by the Witmarks for her to become chief booster of the two Harney songs. The Witmark staff arrangers had not yet mastered the art of simplifying syncopated playing, so the original editions contained only a few interludes of real ragtime accompaniment, ar-ranged by the Chicago theater-orchestra leader Max Hoffman.

Harney's success in New York was followed by a tour on the Keith Mid-western circuit as a top-billed performer, ending in Chicago sometime in early 1897. Because of May Irwin's plugging and his own sensational public appear-ances, "Mister Johnson" had become a hit and "You Been a Good Old Wagon" was not far behind, compelling such nearly instant imitation that within the year more than 600 "Negro songs" were issued by major houses. Harney's new kind of popular music was generally advertised as coon song, and only after the tide of instrumental rag music overwhelmed Tin Pan Alley later in 1897 did publishers begin to apply "rag" to any syncopated song or instru-mental selection in march tempo. Contributing to the success of such songs from the start was the fact that they were ideal accompaniment for the cakewalk dancing made famous by those Kolored Kings of Komedy, Williams and Walker.

The editorial problem involved in putting rag notation down on paper was quickly solved by the major music publishers' staff arrangers, most of whom were trained white musicians. In 1897, S. Brainard's Sons' Chicago branch published the first instrumental selection that can be termed true ragtime, "The Mississippi Rag," written by William H. Krell, the white leader of a band to whose music Chicagoans were dancing the cakewalk, the ragtime two-step, and occasional polkas and waltzes. Ironically, the first rag written by a black musician did not appear until December 1897, when Tom Turpin's "Harlem Rag" was published by a St. Louis music dealer, who soon sold it to Joseph Stern in New York.

Becoming aware of raggy music's growing popularity, a Chicago music publisher, and owner of music sections in some leading Chicago department stores, Sol Bloom, saw a need for a self-instruction ragtime teaching book. He turned to Theodore Northrup, a white musician, and had him put down on paper Ben Harney's raggy versions of some favorite parlor music, including the venerable "Old Hundred" and "Annie Laurie," to which Northrup added some elementary ragtime training exercises. It was issued in September 1897 as *Ben Harney's Rag Time Instructor*. Many of Northrup's examples of what Harney did on the keyboard were puzzling, but the book sold so well that the Witmarks acquired the copyright from Bloom, a former employee, and used their extensive merchandising facilities to make it available throughout America.

Harney went on from triumph to triumph in vaudeville, eventually making three tours around a world whose inhabitants called for more and more of the music he had introduced. After appearing for many years as the "real inventor of ragtime," Harney ended all professional activity because of a heart attack in the early 1920s. The Harneys lived the rest of their lives in near poverty, supported by money from the Actors' Fund. His last great hit had come out in 1899, "The Cake-Walk in the Sky," advertised by the Witmarks as "a ragtime nightmare." Frank Witmark was the first music man to capitalize on the phenomenon of ragtime words. He added a "jig" version of the lyrics used by Harney in his vaudeville act to the sheet music—for example, making "And they all bowed down to the king of the coons / Who taught them the cake walk in the sky," "Agan thegay agaul bogowd dogon to thege kinging agove cagoons / Whogo tagot there cagake wagauke gin thege skigi"—which soon had everybody ragging any and every song's words.

The success of ragtime songs and the leading music publishers' determination to capitalize on the craze, which began to sweep America after 1896, required white and black professional songwriters to add a new category to their output. Paul Dresser, the Indiana songwriter and former blackface minstrel, who was already a top writer, although his "On the Banks of the Wabash" and "My Gal Sal" were still in the future, joined the coon-song parade in 1896 with "I's Your Nigger If You Wants Me, Liza Jane." Eighteen-year-old Georgie Cohan cut his songwriting teeth on jig song with "I'll Have to Telegraph My Baby," "Who Says a Coon Can't Love," "The Warmest Baby in the Bunch," "When My Lize Rolls the Whites of Her Eyes," and a dozen others for the Witmarks, hoping to make the fortune from sheet music that would enable him to leave the stage. Blind gospel songwriter Adam Geibel wrote many coon songs for White, Smith, in Boston, including his "Kentucky Babe," a favorite, with or without darky dialect, of singing quartets of both sexes. Irving Jones became one of the most successful black writers of raggy songs, beginning with "When a Coon Is in the Presidential Chair" and "You Ain't Landlord Any More," both of which the stuttering comedian sang in vaudeville. Bert Williams dashed off "Mammy's Little Piccaninny Boy," and George Walker wrote "The Hottest Coon in Dixie." Pausing among the waltz songs that had made him famous, Gussie Davis sold Stern and Marks "Get on Your Sneak Shoes, Children." While hundreds of popular songs in black dialect were being offered to the public, the Witmarks boasted "the best high-class coon song," Barney Fagan's "My Gal Is a High Born Lady," which the white minstrel show and vaudeville clog dancer sold them for $100.

The white composers who appear to have best captured the cakewalk's exuberance and ragtime essence in instrumental compositions generally were trained musicians. Frederick Allen Mills had left his post as head of the violin department at the University of Michigan in the early 1890s to go to New York, where he became a free-lance musician. His first important song was "Rufus on Parade" (1895), written under the pseudonym "Kerry Mills," which he always used. In 1897, came both words and music for "At a Georgia Camp Meeting," which he hoped would demonstrate that respectable rag songs could be written reflecting the true Negro spirit by using realistic subjects. No publisher was interested in such blasphemy, so Mills published the song himself. John Philip Sousa, who had already demonstrated that he sometimes had an ear for dance music, but wrote marches that sold equally well for use in social dancing, was given Mills's new piece by Arthur Pryor and helped make it the national anthem of the cakewalkers. Mills followed with other two-step marches— "Whistling Rufus," "Happy Days in Dixie," "Impecunious Johnson"—then in 1904 wrote the music and published, with words by Andrew Sterling, "Meet Me in St. Louis, Louis." His next important hit, "Red Wing," written in 1907, is generally believed to be an authentic nineteenth-century folk song but was published as an "Indian Intermezzo." The profits Mills realized from his cakewalk hits enabled him to become a major publisher of popular songs. Among the successful hits he brought out were the 1897 "Asleep in the Deep," the scores for George M. Cohan's Broadway shows (written by the brash young theater genius between 1900 and 1910, after he left the Witmarks and before he began a short-lived publishing venture of his own), which brought out "Forty-five Minutes from Broadway," "Give My Regards to Broadway," "Mary's a Grand Old Name," and "You're a Grand Old Rag" (later, Flag), the early Gus Edwards songs, and such other hits as "Waltz Me Around Again, Willie," "He Walked Right In, Turned Around, and Walked Right Out Again," and "The Longest Way 'Round Is the Shortest Way Home." The size of Mills's catalogue and its popularity qualified him for a place among the eighty-seven-member Music Publishers Association in 1906, when he was one of the syndicate of five major music houses that effectively ended cut-rate sheet-music sales in major department stores. The transposing piano Mills maintained in his New York offices attracted many of the one-finger songwriters of the 1900s, among them Irving Berlin.

Two instrumental rags rivaled the success of Mills's "At a Georgia Camp Meeting" in 1897, one of them, "Eli Green's Cake Walk," by a young woman who demonstrated sheet music in a Troy, New York, department store. Sadie Koninsky went to New York with the manuscript and a letter to Joseph Stern from her employer. With lyrics written to order by a successful Tin Pan Alley balladeer, the piece was a hit in both instrumental and vocal versions. Koninsky went back to Troy and opened her own publishing company, but never had another hit. "Smoky Mokes," an equally popular hit in 1897, was written by Abe Holzman, like Mills and most other white writers of successful ragtime instrumentals the product of formal music education. Trained at the New York Conservatory of Music, Holzman went to work for Leo Feist as a staff arranger, then became head of the firm's band and orchestra music department. Feist named Holzman's composition "Smoky Mokes" and promoted it and other ragtime pieces he published through the Feist Band and Orchestra Club, whose mail-order customers paid a dollar a year in return for twelve new instrumentals guaranteed to become hits, and found that it was true that "You Can't Go Wrong With a Feist Song." Holzman's syncopated pieces were published not only for solo piano, but also for mandolins, guitars, zithers, and banjos, single and in combination as well as for orchestra in ten, fourteen, and full group parts and for military bands. The major publishers dealing in ragtime instrumental music—Mills, Remick, Stern, and the Witmarks—all did the same, and in order to extract all possible profit from each work also issued it as popular songs with "humorous darky texts."

Holzman's chief competitor as a successful ragtime composer was Max Hoffman, who had come to the United States at the age of two and while still a teen-ager was playing violin in Chicago theaters. He was only twenty when he was promoted to the post of leader, but was already writing arrangements for vaudeville performers and local music publishers. It was Hoffman's transcription of Ben Harney's performance of "Mr. Johnson Turn Me Loose" for Witmark (because the pianist could not write music) that created new opportunities for him. His success opened another career, taking down and generally improving melodies dictated to him by other musically illiterate songwriters. The Witmarks were the first to use Hoffman arrangements to promote their hit rag songs with a series of "rag time medleys," long instrumental pieces for solo instruments, as well as orchestras and bands, that contained melodies of a half-dozen or more of the publishers' best-selling coon songs. In 1901, Hoffman began to write the music for the annual Rogers brothers' musical comedies, which were published by the stars' own music company. He next worked for Ziegfeld, writing songs for Anna Held productions and the first *Follies,* in 1907. Later, he was staff composer and musical director for Klaw and Erlanger productions.

The writer of the year 1900's best-selling syncopated cakewalk instrumental, J. Bodewalt Lampe, was a Dane who had left Europe at an early age, studied music and the violin, then organized bands and orchestras in the Chicago area. He also worked as a free-lance arranger for local music publishers and in 1900 wrote "Creole Belles" and published it himself. Jerome Remick bought it later that year and hired him to work in the firm's band and orchestra department, where Lampe remained for nearly twenty years. During the 1920s, he was in charge of music for the famed Trianon Ballroom in Chicago. The success of "Creole Belles" came around the time the cakewalk fad was coming to an end, but this last of the great marching two-step instrumentals found a place in early New Orleans jazz literature and may be heard in costume motion pictures of that period as a reminder of times past.

Despite the decline in publication of Tin Pan Alley's ragtime instrumental music and songs, beginning around 1900, the number of amateur piano players was increasing steadily. The production of pianos and player pianos reached its all-time high in 1899, when more than 365,000 were manufactured, and it continued to average 300,000 annually until just after World War I. Publishers kept the word *rag* alive, however, by using it more than ever in the titles of new songs and demanding its use in the lyrics of up-tempo, syncopated popular songs, in order to continue attracting customers who liked its sound. Many were learning to rag the keyboard from the one-dollar Axel Christensen *Instruction Book for Rag-time Piano Playing,* which made it possible to master the technique in "ten easy lessons." Beginning in 1903, in a Chicago office where he taught pupils at fifty cents a lesson, Christensen eventually built fifty studios in every part of the nation and also had a mail-order business that provided self-instruction to several hundred thousand people during the next three decades. His magazine *Rag Time Review,* which began publication in 1914, was equal parts fan publication, trade paper, educational journal, and sounding board for those who regarded ragtime as "the one true American music."

The introduction and successful merchandising of music mechanically reproduced by the player piano and phonograph machine and recordings supplemented Tin Pan Alley's boosting of ragtime music and coon and rag songs. Annually, thousands of Americans were learning to "play" the Pianola and the Victrola.

In the coin-operated music machines' first years, there were few that did not offer the "Maple Leaf Rag," "Smoky Mokes," the songs of the Johnson brothers and Bob Cole, Harry von Tilzer, F. A. Mills, Victor Herbert, George M. Cohan, and other music being promoted by Tin Pan Alley.

That was also true of the disks and cylinders manufactured by the young phonograph industry, which found ragtime songs and piano music especially compatible to its relatively primitive technology. The sounds of large instrumental groups, most women's voices, the true violin, and the piano in particular could not be captured satisfactorily on acoustic recordings until just before World War I. Some of the sixty-four members of Sousa's band, but never with their leader participating, began to record ragtime music for the phonograph industry in August 1897, cutting "Levee Revels, an Afro-American Can-hop" and Arthur Pryor's "new Negro oddity—Orange Blossoms" for Emile Berliner, in Washington, D.C. Earlier that year the recording industry's first studio band, the Metropolitan Orchestra, which later joined Victor, had made Theodore Metz's "Coon Town Capers" and Kerry Mills's "At a Georgia Camp Meeting." All of the ragtime music recorded by instrumental groups before the war was exactly that and had no vocal choruses. The following April, Sousa's band recorded the Mills cakewalk, which had already entered Sousa's concert repertory and was recorded by the band at least seven additional times before 1912, a period during which the group made forty-five cakewalk, two-step march, coon- and rag-song instrumental recordings for Berliner and the Victor Talking Machine Company. "Creole Belles," "Whistling Rufus," Metz's "Hot Time in the Old Town Tonight," and Pryor's "The Passing of Ragtime" were the most demanded numbers, and the most frequently recorded.

Apparently earlier than Sousa's musicians first recorded, the "King of the Banjo," Sylvester "Vess" Ossman, had already cut "Eli Green's Cake Walk" for Berliner, and certainly on October 9—accompanied by Fred Gaisberg, the teen-age recording pioneer on piano—recorded one of Max Hoffman's ragtime medleys, featuring a number of the Witmarks' coon songs. The banjo was ideally suited to the demands of early acoustic technology, and, as the most skilled performer on that instrument willing to enter the recording studios, Ossman became a well-known recording personality, appearing on Columbia, Edison, and Victor labels for nearly two decades.

Coon songs were a programing staple for the recording companies almost from the earliest days. They were all sung by whites. A group known as the "Standard Quartette," all "gentlemen of color," George W. Johnson, and Bert Williams were the leading pioneer black recording artists. All of the other leading coon-song and black-dialect vocalists before World War I were white, the best known being Charles Asbury, David C. Bangs, Arthur Collins, Billy Golden, Silas Leachman, Bob Roberts, Len Spencer, Billy Williams, and the "First Lady of Phonograph Records," Ada Jones.

This racial discrimination, if indeed it was industry policy, did not extend to black songwriters. The *Edison Phonograph Monthly,* distributed to jobbers and dealers beginning in March 1903, contained suggestions for local promotion to increase record and phonograph sales. A list of the next month's releases was printed regularly, with comments and information about the writers, publishers, content, and sometimes the lyrics of new recordings. All of the black songwriters discussed here were regularly mentioned, with references to past successes or current activities in vaudeville and the musical theater.

Classic Ragtime, Its First Rise and Fall

The makers of piano rolls had been recording the best selling of all instrumental ragtime compositions, "Maple Leaf Rag," for several years before the United States Marine Band made the first phonograph recording of Scott Joplin's classic, in October 1906. Vess Ossman recorded it, accompanied by a band conducted by Charles A. Prince, music director for Columbia in New York, the following March. Sheet-music sales had already gone over the million mark, a success that astounded residents of Tin Pan Alley. They rationalized this seeming miracle by claiming that, whereas few buyers could play Joplin's rag, there were "lots who like to play *at* it." The retail value of a million seller at fifty cents a copy was $250,000, but by not being in New York, the Missouri publisher probably got only a fraction of that. The writer received a penny a copy, $10,000 spread out over four years, with additional sums during the next decade.

Prior to the late 1890s, a few songs selling thousands of copies over a period of several years had been brought out by publishers in hinterland communities, but, with Tin Pan Alley's domination of music-publishing channels of merchandising and promotion, such a miracle was no longer regarded as possible. In fact, whenever a song from inner America indicated any potential for real success, it was immediately purchased outright by a major house. The publisher of "Maple Leaf Rag," John Stark, a piano dealer in Sedalia, Missouri, had occasionally issued music written by members of his family or local musicians, principally to stimulate the sales of his instruments and to build good will. When he did venture into rag-music publication, he usually paid twenty-five dollars in advance for all rights and an additional twenty-five dollars when the song sold 1,000 copies. His production facilities were simple—a hand press in his music store, operated by a member of the family.

There were several versions of Stark's acquisition of "Maple Leaf Rag." The most reasonable is that, after having been turned down by other publishers, Joplin brought it to him as a matter of course. By some whimsy of fate, Stark happened to be the man who perceived the rag's unique qualities.

Born in the Arkansas part of Texarkana, three years after the Civil War, Scott Joplin became familiar in childhood with the classical European musical tradition. His mother played the banjo, on which Scott became proficient by the age of seven. His father had been a household slave musician, playing the prevalent European-influenced parlor and dance music for his wealthy Texan owners. He kept his violin after freedom and brought it out at night to play for his wife and small family. Scott's uncanny memory for any music he heard, his genuine talent, and the gift of perfect pitch won him music lessons from educated members of the town's black community. After his father abandoned the family, his mother became a day worker in local white homes and was able to squirrel away enough money to buy a battered old square piano, the instrument destiny had intended for Scott. Once he had mastered the instrument, through the teaching of a part-black barber, musician, and music teacher who also opened wide his knowledge of classical European music, Joplin began the career of itinerant Midwestern musician that finally brought him to Sedalia and John Stark.

Following Emancipation, the increasing availability of inexpensive upright pianos led to the replacing of the banjo as the black musician's favored instrument by the keyboard, which was better equipped to cope with emerging raggy-time syncopation. Joplin soon became known as one of the best musicians in eastern Texas, both as a member of small black orchestras that played for dancing and as a genuine "professor" of the piano. At the age of sixteen, he formed a small vocal group of young black friends, which worked with him for four years. In 1888, he went in search of greater opportunities and the company of peers. After several years of wandering, he settled in St. Louis, to which many of the Midwest's best black pianists had gravitated and which he used as a base for travels through eastern Missouri and into the Ohio Valley, reaching Chicago for the 1893 exposition. Two years later, he formed a chorus, which included two of his brothers. They traveled as far east as Syracuse, New York, performing the type of material Gussie Davis used in his vaudeville act.

Two such waltz songs written by Joplin were published in that city by local piano and music dealers.

Joplin was living in Sedalia in 1897, enrolled in the music school of the local white-endowed College for Negroes, and playing in brothels, saloons, and, on the cornet, in an all-black twelve-member concert band that also performed the newest rag songs and cakewalk music. Recognizing his special musical qualities, a small group of young black pianists gravitated to him, among them several disciples of his own kind of ragtime pianism: Scott Hayden, all of whose rags were written with Joplin, Arthur Marshall, whose early rags were published by Stark, and white Brun Campbell, known as the "Ragtime Kid" before he was sixteen. In December 1897, the first rag by a black composer, "Harlem Rag," was published, rousing in Joplin the determination to get his own rag (a word he did not favor) music into print. Tom Turpin, writer of "Harlem Rag," which was inspired by a brief trip to New York, had been Joplin's great friend during his stay in St. Louis. Five years younger than Joplin, and the son of a café and saloon owner in whose establishments he played, Turpin was mentor to a number of young black pianists, among them Louis Chauvin and Joe Jordan, who was later a successful musical director and songwriter.

Joplin had already sold "Original Rags" to a Kansas City publisher, who did not bring it out for two years, and only then at the suggestion of a white musician, Charles N. Daniels, his music editor and song plugger. The work was published as "arranged" by Daniels and "picked" by Joplin. When Joplin walked into Stark's store in the summer of 1899, he had with him several manuscripts, some of them written with Hayden and Marshall, one of them "Maple Leaf Rag." Its title honored the Maple Leaf Club, a black men's social and gambling hangout, which Joplin made his headquarters whenever he was in Sedalia. Several years of reworking and rearranging the piece had produced a work for which Stark immediately paid fifty dollars. The contract that both signed called for a penny royalty on each copy sold, ten free copies to the composer, and a discounted price of five cents each for all copies he wanted to buy, none to be sold for less than twenty-five cents. The manuscript was sent off to St. Louis for printing. Of the first edition, only 400 copies were sold in the following year.

The popularity of cakewalk-march and two-step dance music notwithstanding, the sheet-music-buying public was slow to discover "Maple Leaf Rag." Word of mouth, increasing performances by professional entertainers who had learned to cope with Joplin's unorthodox music, and Stark's use of promotional puffery that labeled his composer the "King of Ragtime Writers" and his music "classic ragtime" had their effect, and in late 1900 orders from eastern chain stores for large quantities of the sheet music began to arrive. To be nearer the national market, Stark moved to St. Louis and traded 10,000 copies of his hit for the small printing office. He added other rags to his catalogue, by Joplin and by black musicians he was teaching, and began to dream of making New York his base of operations. On a trip to St. Louis in 1903, the veteran songwriter and New York newspaperman Monroe Rosenfeld went to the Stark offices, by then in handsome larger quarters, where he interviewed Joplin and dashed off a story about his "quaint creation." Rosenfeld also had a good word for a new Joplin work, "The Entertainer," which, with another composition, "Solace," was featured in the 1974 film *The Sting* and helped to win a post-humous Pulitzer Prize for the black musician.

This revival of interest in Joplin's music was stimulated by a recording: "Scott Joplin: The Red Back Book," a product of the composer, musician, and educator Gunther Schuller's dedication to American vernacular music. For the recording, Schuller edited and restored the original arrangements of seven of Joplin's piano pieces, published by Stark in *Standard High Class Rags* (c. 1906). Having observed the success of New York publishers with inexpensive arrangements of successful songs and instrumental music for an eleven-piece combination of instruments, to be played by vaudeville pit bands, on park bandstands, or for dancing and as salon music, Stark followed suit. Better known as the *Red Back Book* because of its brilliant cover, the collection of arrangements served musicians for many years. Eleven of the fifteen rags included were by Joplin, with the obvious choices of "Maple Leaf Rag" and "The Entertainer." Stark called attention to this publication, as he did all items in his catalogue, by flowery mailings to jobbers and retailers.

Relations between Stark and Joplin began to vary from friendly to antagonistic, depending on how quickly the publisher would accede to the composer's insistence on publication of ever more inventive music, intricate by commercial standards and ambitious by artistic ones. In spite of Stark's five-year contract for his exclusive services, of nearly fifty instrumental pieces—rags, waltzes, and marches—written by Joplin between 1899 and his death in 1917, Stark published fewer than two dozen. The rest were brought out by Joplin and by other publishers, in Boston, St. Louis, Chicago, and New York. He had been studying with a German musician, who used as a text *A Manual of Simple, Double, Triple and Quadruple Counterpoint,* and spoke to his friends Turpin, Marshall, and Hayden of plans to write music that would wait twenty-five years before people recognized its qualities. Preoccupied with plans to open a New York branch, Stark had adamantly refused to publish *A Guest of Honor,* a ragtime opera Joplin had written and taken on an abortive tour in 1903. Still, his most successful writer continued to bring him music that the publisher recognized as too subtle and difficult for the average amateur pianist to essay. Speedier tempos and execution characterized the ragtime instrumentals that Tin Pan Alley then preferred; yet Joplin insisted that his music must be played slowly, each note as it was written. Other publishers were eager to bring out Joplin works, hoping that lightning would strike again, but the public rarely perceived the worth of their "wierd and intoxicating effects," as Joplin himself described them. To help, he prepared *School of Ragtime—Six Exercises for Piano,* published at his own expense in 1908.

Shortly after Stark opened the Stark Music Printing and Publishing Co., in New York—adding nearly 200 publications to the several hundred issued in St. Louis before 1910, when the operation there was closed—Joplin followed him east. The proceeds from the sale of two coon songs to a St. Louis music house financed the trip. The black musicians and entertainers who gathered at the Marshall Hotel in Manhattan were skeptical when they learned that Joplin was planning to jump from ragtime to grand opera, and that he expected to have the score completed shortly. To them, ragtime was not classical music, as Joplin thought.

Joplin had remarried and was operating a boardinghouse with his new wife, Lottie. He supplemented his royalties and money from new music by teaching and working in vaudeville but spent his free time on his opera, *Treemonisha*. Sales of classic ragtime had fallen off. Quick to perceive a new market, the publishing business concentrated on music that was more dance- and less piano-oriented: ragtime songs and simplified arrangements of the flashy music of vaudeville pianists who "ragged the classics." Cakewalk and two-step dancers who had pranced to the slow march-time of rag rhythms were now devotees of the turkey trot, grizzly bear, and bunny hug. The favorite music of the sleek ballroom team of Vernon and Irene Castle, who popularized many of these fast new dances, was Irving Berlin's song (originally done in a coon dialect) "Alexander's Ragtime Band," which was neither true nor classic rag, possessing only a ragtime touch of Foster's "Old Folks at Home." After having luck with a number of rag songs—"Yiddle on Your Fiddle, Play Some Ragtime," "Ragtime Violin," and "Oh, That Beautiful Rag"—Berlin had given a rag-song touch to a piece he had not been able to sell and revised the lyrics of "Alexander and His Clarinet," producing the song that sold a million and a half copies of sheet music in the next few years and made him a partner in a leading music-publishing company.

Turning his back on the popular-music business, which indeed then had little interest in him, Joplin was determined to get *Treemonisha* produced. Unable to find a publisher, he had paid for printing its 230-page vocal-piano score, with its twenty-seven songs, in 1911. Despite a favorable review of it in *The American Musician* of June 24, 1911, which stated that he had "created an entirely new phase of musical art and had provided a thoroughly American opera, dealing with an American subject, yet free from all extraneous influence," no one came forth to fund even a run-through of the opera. That occurred in 1915, with Joplin at the piano, in a rented theater in Harlem to an invited audience, not one of whom evinced any public encouragement. The reason may have been that *Treemonisha* was so much a product of the culture of its time. As Gunther Schuller wrote, it was "the result of a three-way cross-breeding of elements—mid-nineteenth-century European opera, Afro-American dance forms, and turn-of-the-century American popular idioms." This "curious alchemical mixture of musical styles and conceptions" bewildered even the most musical of people who attended that reading.

The syphilis he had contracted during his days of wandering had been lurking for many years, but now struck with dreaded full force. Joplin's mind began to wander, and no page of the Symphony No. 1, to which he devoted much time, was ever found. His piano playing became erratic, as the piano-music rolls he made in 1916 indicate, even after they were doctored by staff arrangers. After a few months, he was committed to a New York City mental hospital. On April 1, 1917, he was dead.

Less than a year later, the first American composer of vernacular music to win a Pulitzer Prize, George Gershwin, wrote "The Real American Folk Song (Is a Rag)," to words by his brother, Ira.

When John Stark was told of Scott Joplin's death, his printed comment was "a homeless itinerant, he left his mark on American music." Soon after, the house that "Maple Leaf Rag" built drew upon its stock of unpublished Joplin rags and brought out "Reflections Rag—Syncopated Musings," which proved to be one of his best. Though the St. Louis red-light district where rag had flourished was shut down, putting many rag writers out of work, Stark continued to print music by them, much of it what Joplin would have approved, but the number issued dropped steadily. Soon almost all income was derived exclusively from Joplin's masterpiece.

John Stillwell Stark died a little more than ten years after the man whose name he had made known internationally, and a few months after Mrs. Lottie Joplin renewed the initial copyright of "Maple Leaf Rag" and assigned it to Stark & Company, the original publisher.

CHAPTER 10

The American Musical Theater 1865–1909

Popular Music on the Post-Civil War Stage

Charles II of England, whose appreciation of the unveiled female form was a contributing factor to the creation of London's licensed royal theaters, would have been a delighted spectator at Niblo's Garden, on Broadway, the night of September 12, 1866. Alarmed at what was to be performed there, New York's clergy had been threatening hellfire and damnation for weeks to all who went to see the dozens of beautiful coryphées imported from Milan, Berlin, Paris, and London in the "as little as the law allows" promised by the management.

The "grand magical spectacular drama" they saw, *The Black Crook,* was the profitable resolution of potential disaster that began with the burning to the ground of the Academy of Music, chartered by the New York legislature to present grand opera and other entertainment with a "facility for education." Two of the producers had originally leased the Academy of Music, as the only proper venue, for the first American appearance of a Parisian classical ballet troupe. Their theater suddenly gone, the pair made an agreement with William Wheatley, manager of Niblo's, to join them in presenting the ballet company in his house. Wheatley had his own ideas and went to work to create a vehicle in which the dancers could be shown to greater financial advantage, one of the spectacular extravaganzas with which the British actress Laura Keene had made large sums of money during the Civil War. The first woman to become a theatrical manager in America, Keene had made her first great success as the producer and star of *Our American Cousin,* in whose title role she was featured the night President Lincoln was assassinated.

When the Civil War began, Keene's theater was the only house in New York City with the sinking stage, trap doors, and heavy stage machinery that permitted rapid shifting of the elaborate scenery utilized in lavish musical burlesques featuring singing, dancing, pantomime, and grand tableaux. This was a new form of American theater that had grown out of British pantomime, and to it Keene added the attraction of women actresses and dancers dressed in the barest minimum of clothing in several long-running "grand spectacle burlesques" that quickly became known as "leg drama."

Wheatley found a suitable vehicle for his proposed grand spectacle in *The Black Crook,* a four-year-old manuscript the one-time carpenter and navy veteran Charles M. Barras had been trying to peddle, and he agreed to pay Barras seventy-five dollars a week in royalties. Such an agreement was necessary because of the revised Copyright Act of 1856, which secured performing rights in copyrighted dramatic compositions to their owner. Barras saw his original "magical and spectacular drama in four acts" disappear as emphasis was placed on the dancers and their made-in-Paris costumes, so he threatened to withdraw his script. Time was too short to replace it. Wheatley raised the weekly fee to $1,000.

Most of the early songs, dances, and instrumental music for the production were written by Thomas Baker, an English-born violinist who had been Laura Keene's musical director and house composer. One of the musicians brought to America by the great Jullien in 1853, Baker remained, finding work in the theater and as editor for music publishers, to one of whom, William A. Pond, he sold his part of the *Black Crook* music.

The Black Crook ran for sixteen months, 475 performances—a new record: Keene's leg drama *The Seven Sisters,* for which Baker also wrote the music, had run half that time. It grossed over one million dollars, making more than $600,000 for its producers. More important, from the historical point of view, was that the success demonstrated to theatrical producers that full-length spectaculars using music, song, and dancing, particularly when the last was done by seminude women, were profitable. A number of productions of *The Black Crook* were mounted around the country, for all of which Barras licensed local performing rights. Baker's music, not similarly protected, was used freely, as was any new music written to suit the demands of local dancing and singing talents and any popular songs interpolated by various musical directors. New material of all types was constantly added, to replace material that threatened to pall or to suit new performing talent. As a result, music publishers in many parts of the country offered sheet music of selections from the production, demand for which was created by live performances. William Pond and his syndicate of co-publishers from coast to coast had the largest selection, sixteen, including Baker's music and that of Giuseppe Operti, conductor for the New York revival in 1871.

Barras was also making money from the sales of a novel based on his playscript, *The Black Crook, a Most Wonderful History,* but his ownership of the stage piece came to an end after the issue of morality entered a court action seeking an injunction against an unlicensed rival production in San Francisco. The court ruled for the defendant, and Barras said that "the piece under dispute was not even subject to copyright since it cannot be denied that this spectacle of 'The Black Crook' merely panders to the pernicious curiosity of very questionable exhibitions of the female person." Barras was not alive, having died in an accident in 1873, to receive royalties from later revivals of the production in New York City, which continued until the early 1890s.

The hit in most early *Black Crook* productions, "You Naughty, Naughty Men," was brought from England by the soubrette who sang it nightly in New York. This polite version of the racy and suggestive songs "waiter girls" were singing in the concert saloons of lower Manhattan was immediately published in America by H. E. Dodworth, leader of the Niblo Garden pit orchestra, who normally would have been asked to write or supply all supporting music, a principal function of a house music director in both dramatic and musical theaters.

Even as Broadway musical productions were providing the means of promotion for New York music publishers, whose songs were in demand as a result, the city's music rooms and concert saloons were performing a similar function for songwriters, who supplied the entertainers with a steady stream of new material. Little of this was published by the large houses unless a great demand became evident. Instead, one looked for the words in the sheet-music-size *Comic and Sentimental Singer's Journals' Containing All the Popular Songs of the Day,* which sold for two cents and were printed and distributed nationally by such job printers as Henry de Marsan, of New York. Established before the Civil War, Marsan's house, he boasted, was "the oldest Publishing-Establishment of the kind, and the first that introduced in the United States the publishing of the penny sheet songs and ballads." A stock of 2,300 different songs was always available, as were such pocket songsters as *The Black Crook,* which had only one of the musical burlesque's songs but many other currently popular songs, and other paperbacks bearing the names of entertainers and minstrel singers who featured some of their contents.

Musical stage entertainment changed considerably during and after the Civil War. Except for one or two of the major companies, most minstrel troupes were out on the road, because of a decline in New York City's enthusiasm for them. Regular seasons of opera in the rebuilt Academy of Music brought in audiences who had once attended performances of drama but had switched their loyalties; lovers of "genteel comedy" and comic opera looked to Laura Keene and *The Black Crook* and its followers. For the common man, there were the concert saloons and music rooms, which had sprung up to fill the void left by the minstrels' departure. That move had been speeded by passage of the Concert Hall Act of 1862, which put the low-priced minstrel show out of business in New York City by denying a license to sell alcoholic beverages (their major source of income) to any place of business where a curtain separated the audience from the entertainers. In addition, the beautiful waiter girls who had dispensed alcoholic and personal refreshment to patrons could no longer do so. Boy waiters replaced them. Dressed in street clothes, the girls mingled with customers once city police began to do little to enforce the legislation. The performers were separated from the patrons by large fans rising from the floor in some concert saloons. In 1870, more than 600 music halls flourished in Manhattan below Houston Street and in the Bowery district.

The most famous and popular was the "music hall of the masses," the American Concert Hall, or "444," its address on Broadway, a former minstrel theater. Hundreds were turned away nightly, unable to gain admission to see the entertainment or to visit a saloon attached to the hall. The soon-to-be highest-paid variety entertainer in America, Tony Pastor made it his home base. Born Antonio Pastore in New York in 1837, he had started singing for money at the age of six, worked as a blackface minstrel infant prodigy in P. T. Barnum's Museum four years later, and toured as the "clown prince of song" with circuses throughout the 1850s. It was during this time that he first sold pocket songsters with words to his songs, a source of income that continued throughout his career as an entertainer.

When the Civil War restricted travel, Pastor returned to New York and made his first appearance at 444 in April 1861, in a typical program of varied entertainment. A few nights later, after having learned its little-used words from some sheet music, he sang "The Star-Spangled Banner" to a crowd already infused with patriotism by the South's secession, and roused all to join in on each chorus. The city became his overnight. Every victory, setback, and political crisis was fair game for the songs he sang, ones he wrote himself, drawing on events of the day and generally set to well-known melodies, and ones borrowed from other performers or purchased for a few dollars from songwriters, who eventually submitted as many as a hundred new works a week for his inspection.

When the war ground to an end, Pastor opened his Opera House on the Bowery, an area workingmen and immigrants regarded as theirs and where the well-dressed and cosmopolitan rarely ventured. For the following ten years, the "No More Seats" signs went up early every night when the new "aristocrat of the Bowery" offered three-hour-long programs of varied popular entertainment, at an average of thirty cents a person. Every performance included sentimental songs, humorous ballads, and topical ditties. And there were always Tony Pastor Song Books available for a few coins. Few entertainers who became famous during the next decade failed to bring in their new act at Pastor's. Every few weeks a new burlesque of some popular stage work was offered. Drawing on the tremendous success of *The Black Crook*, Pastor instituted a corps de ballet of his own, ten "first class young ladies." He put them to work with his company of resident comic actors, who performed in the afterpiece burlesques. The result was *The White Crook*, a parody of Wheatley's hit, in which the men dressed in pink tights and the dancers wore jockeys' clothing. The legitimate musical theater, located north of Houston Street to just above Union Square, provided material aplenty for more of these spoofs, not only at Pastor's, but also in other music rooms and by minstrel companies.

When *The Black Crook* ended its run in early 1868, Wheatley was ready with another pretext for public display of the female body, *The White Fawn*, which had a cancan danced in pink tights to music by the house orchestra leader, Edward Mollenhauer. One of three German brothers who became well-known musicians and composers, Edward had fled military service and joined Jullien's orchestra for its tour of the United States, where he remained and found work in the theater. Like Baker, he sold his score to Pond, who was acquiring most of the scores and interpolated songs offered in New York's musical burlesque spectacles.

Many dancers in *The Black Crook* and *The White Fawn* were blondes, born so or made so with the aid of chemicals, and, with the comely legs and yellow hair of Lydia Thompson and Her British Blondes in several other musical burlesques in New York and on tour, it seemed that blondes and bodies were going to stay on the city's stage.

Even the long-running series of *Humpty Dumpty* comic spectaculars had their Corps of Coryphées, who appeared in tights and ravishing clothing and also much less. Written by their star, the first great American stage clown, George L. Fox, the *Humpty Dumpty* shows used Mother Goose characters but put them into contemporary situations involving many aspects of American and international social and political life. Fox built up such a large following of children that he became the first to offer Wednesday matinees of musical theater for them. By the early 1870s, moreover, fourteen of New York's sixteen theaters offered leg shows to audiences of generally respectable persons.

The continuing success of such theatrical productions as *Uncle Tom's Cabin* and *Ten Nights in a Barroom,* both with songs interpolated, had already proved that people would come to the theater to see a single attraction, instead of the potpourri of entertainment that had previously prevailed. By the end of the Civil War, it was generally believed by theatrical managers that the play could be more important than the players. This led to establishment of the "combination" system for touring companies. Headed by an actor-manager "star," the groups of actors were accompanied by scenery from the New York production and the nucleus of an orchestra, which would be augmented by local musicians. As in New York theaters, each traveling group had its own musical director, responsible for all music used on stage. With scripted plays, this meant music before and after the performance, between the acts, and for the singing and dancing numbers. Some music was usually by the director, but most selections were instrumental arrangements of operatic arias, social dances, and popular songs.

Other than the minstrel men, Joseph K. Emmett was the first stage star to write his own songs, for a series of comedies in which he played the German immigrant Fritz Van Vonderblinkinstoffen, to whom yodeling on his "mouth harmonicon" was natural. An American, Emmett had served a minstrel apprenticeship and worked as a low-Dutch comic song-and-dance entertainer in concert saloons before he starred in his first play, *Fritz, or Our Cousin German.* Thomas Baker had written some dialect songs for him, but Emmett trusted his own more and began to slip them into the action. His famous "Lullaby—Go to Sleep My Baby, My Baby, My Baby," which remained popular until the end of the century, began as a guitar song called for in the original script. As the play continued in New York for a long run, changes were made and new business added, and "Lullaby" eventually became the climax of the evening in a "grand parlor social scene." Emmett later played Fritz in sequels, writing new songs for all of them and making national hits out of "Sweet Violets,

Sweeter Than All the Roses," "The Cuckoo Song," "The Mountain Song," and "Come Back Baby." They were made famous not only by Emmett, but also by the German comedians who imitated him, but they did not appear for sale as sheet music chiefly because the international star did not wish the counterfeit Emmetts to have the music as he sang it. There was also his awareness of the experience of J. W. Lingard, one of the first famous female impersonators, a Briton who introduced his song "Captain Jinks of the Horse Marines" to America. Emmett had worked with him in the first years of the song's popularity and had seen how American publishers took advantage of the copyright laws to capitalize on public demand for Lingard's song. As a non-American, Lingard could not secure copyright. Twelve of the twenty members of the Board of Music Trade violated their own self-imposed "courtesy of the trade" agreement and simultaneously brought out Lingard's fellow Englishman George Leybourne's "Champagne Charlie," in 1867, when it was being sung in concert saloons and by street singers and heard from all the thousands of street hand organs. The same was true of Lingard's "Walking Down Broadway," "The Grecian Bend," and "On the Beach at Long Branch," all of which were sung every night by Tony Pastor. Leybourne, though he was not in the United States, had his "The Man on the Flying Trapeze" and "Up in a Balloon," popular in the late 1860s, issued by many American firms, together with parodies of "Champagne Charlie Is My Name"—"Bourbon Bob," "Rein-wein Sharlie," and others. American publishers even used the same lithographed picture of Leybourne, dressed as a British swell, on the sheet-music covers of their bootleg editions. Emmett finally agreed, in 1878, to John Church's offer to publish his songs in their "only correct and authorized" printings, with a royalty on all sales.

The stock market panic of 1873 affected the economy for more than a decade, causing New York producers to look for new and less expensive kinds of musical theater. George Fox, Emmett, *The Black Crook,* and a few other attractions were unscarred and continued to play to packed houses. The white traveling minstrel business, having purged itself of excesses of vulgarity in order to attract sober mid-American audiences, dealt with the economy by its own kind of combination system, consolidating into a dozen or so large companies that only occasionally played the major eastern seaboard communities. New York remained the almost exclusive domain of the San Francisco Minstrels, Dan Bryant's old company, and its ribald burlesques of stage plays, and musical extravaganzas.

Stage musicals suffered. A production of the first American musical with a score by a single team of writers, *Evangeline,* which ran throughout the 1880s and early 1890s, played only two weeks in New York, in the summer of 1874. So, too, a year later, did *Around the World in Eighty Days,* the first of the Kiralfy brothers' miracles of lavish scenic spectacle, ballet, procession, and music, which matched *Evangeline*'s success in the next decade. However, a former synagogue now housing the Theatre Comique was threatening to put Tony Pastor's Opera House out of business, owing particularly to its headliners Harrigan and Hart, a comedy team. Pastor introduced Ladies Invitation Night, when women accompanied by a ticket-buying male were admitted free of charge. He also raffled off sewing machines at Saturday matinees and gave flowers and candy to wives, who now began to fill his house, but to no avail. Nor did raffled hams, turkeys, or hat and dress patterns help. Pastor began to cast about for a new kind of variety for a house uptown to restore his fortunes.

His nemesis, the Theatre Comique, with Harrigan and Hart, was being packed every night with a new kind of stage entertainment. The bill was traditional: a comic sketch, a ballad singer, the feature—Harrigan and Hart and their players—and the afterpiece. The difference was the feature, a song and a playlet based on it. These were written by Harrigan, to music by David Braham, the English musician who had migrated to America at the age of sixteen and worked with Jullien. He met Harrigan at Pastor's during the summer of 1872, when Harrigan and Hart in a blackface act were part of Pastor's first group of traveling variety performers.

Edward "Ned" Harrigan, born in New York in 1844 to first-generation Irish-American parents, had grown up with a great variety of people, on whom he later based his songs, his nine full-length Mulligan plays, some two dozen other stage works, and eighty or so playlets, many with songs and incidental music. Looking back on his work in 1889, he said, "It began with the New York 'bhoy', the Irish American and our African brother. As these grew in popularity I added the other prominent types which go to make up life in the metropolis and in every other large city of the Union and Canada . . . the Irishman, Englishman, German, low German, Chinese, Italian, Russian and Southern darky." The sympathy and understanding of them with which he wrote put his work many levels above the minstrels' caricatures and brought the upper classes to the Comique's box seats and the lower orders to its galleries to see life in the city's tenements, in its Irish and Negro volunteer militia, among the squatters along the New York Central's right of way, and the pretentious social climbing Irish newly rich.

After six years of wandering, which took him finally to San Francisco and a concert saloon, Harrigan returned to New York in 1870. Needing a partner for his variety turn, he found Tony Cannon, soon replaced by Hart, who sang like a nightingale and was pretty enough to be a rival of the great Lingard. Then came Tony Pastor and after that the engagement at the Comique. When Harrigan determined to write both songs and plays, he turned to David Braham, who was a patient teacher, in time his father-in-law, and who helped him work out the system that produced more than 180 published songs. Once the script was completed, Harrigan turned the song words over to Braham, who was a fast worker, able to deliver the entire score for a full-length play in less than a month, with many songs being completed in five or ten minutes. The tunes he composed on his violin generally had a snap at the end.

All of the Harrigan-Braham songs were published by William Pond, beginning with "The Mulligan Guard," written in 1873 for a playlet that became a full evening's stage piece in 1883. Harrigan had taken his song to Pond hoping the publisher would bring it out with a handsomely engraved cover showing Harrigan and Hart in costume, which would serve as valuable advertising for them. Pond rejected it, but after he heard the team sing it and read their favorable notices, he bought it outright for fifty dollars, signed the songwriters to an exclusive contract, and published "The Mulligan Guard"—with a portrait of the comedians in guard uniform on the cover—in song, guitar, and quickstep editions, for forty cents each. In the collection of Harrigan and Braham songs issued by Pond in two volumes between 1883 and 1892 were their best-known songs: "The Babies on Our Block" (1879), "Whist! The Boogie Man" (1880), "Paddy Duffy's Cart" (1881), "I Never Drink Behind the Bar" (1882), "The Widow Nolan's Goat" (1882), "My Dad's Dinner Pail" (1883), "Maggie Murphy's Home" (1890), and dozens of others. In the larger cities, they had become latter-day folk songs. Even small children knew them, from illustrated cartoon-and-text books issued by the paperback trade.

The surge of immigration from northwestern Europe during the Civil War stimulated the growth of the foreign-language theatrical tradition. In this new wave of immigrants were many educated people who were familiar with the waltz music of Josef Lanner and the Strauss family and the sophisticated comic operas of Jacques Offenbach, conductor at the Théâtre Français in Paris. The son of a German Jewish cantor, Offenbach had gone to Paris to study cello at the age of fifteen, in 1833, and after working his way up to the conductor's stand took over management of a small theater, where no more than four speaking parts were permitted in any single operetta. He then began to write the first of more than 106 one-act and full-length works. An extraordinarily facile composer, he turned out at least four new ones each year, to the delight of all Europe, where they also were sung in English and German translations. His *Grande Duchesse de Gérolstein* proved to be his most popular in the United States after its performance at New York's French Theatre in 1867, a short time after its world premiere. Oliver Ditson included it in his popular *Beauties of the Opera* series. Hundreds of songs, in English translation, as well as instrumental and dance music, including the cancans, from Offenbach operettas were issued as sheet music by major publishers, and productions by "parlor opera" professional and amateur groups proliferated around the country, many adapted to American tastes and to suit the capabilities of local singers and musicians. Blackface minstrels mocked them with rowdy burlesques.

The popularity of Offenbach's music grew ever greater after such charming European performers as Mademoiselle Aimée from Paris and the English Emily Soldene offered brazen displays of the cancans gymnastic high-kicking in his *Geneviève de Brabant, Belle Hélène,* and *Blue Beard.* Comic opera became an important element in the American musical theater, even though it was disdained by self-appointed spokesmen for the cultured class.

Having always believed that there was a lot of money in him if "only someone could dig it out," Edward Everett Rice, found that it was opéra-buffe, comic opera, that would do so. His songs and music graced *Evangeline,* called "the jolliest entertainment of the age." It was born after he and his friend J. Cheever Goodwin saw Lydia Thompson and her blondes perform in Boston around 1871. Rice, who played the piano but could not write music, suggested that the pair compose a burlesque extravaganza to which one might take the whole family without feeling shame. Goodwin had already rewritten librettos for some of Offenbach's operettas to make them suitable for viewing by Bostonians, and the libretto he provided for Rice's music was strained of any obscenity in language or stage action. The work was loosely based on Longfellow's epic poem, but Evangeline was played by a man and her lover, Gabriel, by a curvaceous woman in male attire of varying kinds. It took place in the Wild West, darkest Africa, a balloon, and on a remote tropical island, with its own spouting whale, who fancied the heroine, and had a happy ending. One of the production's most popular features was the dance performed by Evangeline and a papier-mâché heifer occupied by two men, in the front end of which the great stage comedian Henry F. Dixey made his debut.

Rice dictated the music, for twenty-seven songs, to an arranger and also made suggestions about the songs' musical settings. *Evangeline* was shown at Niblo's Garden in the summer of 1874 and then sent back to Boston for more work. With changes in the libretto and some new songs, it was revived for the first of many times two years later, in Boston, where it grossed more than $40,000 for an eight-week run. It made its triumphant return to the New York stage in the summer of 1877. *Evangeline* became known as the "cradle of stars," because many headliners made their first appearance behind the footlights in one of its revivals. Sometime in 1875, Louis F. Goullaud, of Boston, published the first complete piano-vocal score of this "musical comedy," as Rice and Goodwin called it, binding thirty-one of *Evangeline*'s songs and instrumental music in cloth to sell for three dollars. Many of the selections were also issued separately. The new Manhattan publishing company of T. B. Harms, founded by brothers Tom and Alex, who soon challenged William A. Pond's monopoly of Broadway musical scores, became Goullaud's New York distributor in 1878.

The first comic opera written by an American resident, Julius Eichberg's *The Doctor of Alcantara,* was issued in a piano-vocal score by Oliver Ditson in 1862. Eichberg was born in Germany in 1824, studied music at the Brussels Conservatory, was director of an opera troupe in Geneva, where he became acquainted with Robert Schumann, and came to the United States in 1857. Two years later, he was appointed director of music at the Boston Museum, one of the city's oldest playhouses, for whose resident company he wrote the three-act opera, with a libretto by Benjamin Edward Woolfe. It proved to be a very successful work, and was regularly performed by professional companies around the country and by church choirs and other amateur groups, prompting publication by Ditson in 1879 of a revised edition. None of Eichberg's other comic operas was as successful. In 1867, Eichberg founded the Boston Conservatory of Music, and was director of music education for the city's public schools during the 1870s. Until his death, he was a leading music educator and well known as a composer.

Having observed that his profits from *Evangeline* increased as each new element of leg drama crept into its revivals, Rice dropped his notions about propriety and, in 1879, turned again to Longfellow, for his *Hiawatha*. The new musical comedy never approached the success of *Evangeline,* nor did any of those he wrote and produced up to the early 1900s except for *Adonis* (1884), which ran 603 times on Broadway. His excellent judgment of new musical talent for the theater was affirmed at least twice in the last years of his career. *Clorindy, or The Origin of the Cakewalk,* the "first Negro operetta in the new syncopated style," was produced by Rice for a trial run in 1898, during his "Summer Nights" at the Casino Roof Garden. Six years later, he gave Jerome Kern his first theater assignment: to write additional songs for a production of *Mr. Wix of Wickham,* part of whose original music Rice had written.

One reason for the failure of *Hiawatha,* which had pleasant but inadequate music, was the presence of the English team of W. S. Gilbert and Arthur Sullivan in America and the tumultuous success of their *H.M.S. Pinafore* and *The Pirates of Penzance.* These demonstrated that American audiences were open to music that was both popular and musicianly, particularly when it was sung by singers who could act. This was equally true of Offenbach's operettas, but they were regarded as exotic and foreign, and such success as they enjoyed usually depended on the ability of translators, singers, and musical directors, who had never seen the original productions presented under the composer's supervision. Offenbach himself complained about this when he visited the United States during its centennial celebration in 1876.

Americans were scarcely aware of Gilbert and Sullivan when their one-act comic opera *Trial by Jury* was performed for a few weeks in late 1875, shortly after its London premiere. Three years later, however, the nation discovered *H.M.S. Pinafore,* and a new national mania was born. During the year in which England began slowly to take this wickedly modern Jack Tar operetta to its heart, hundreds of amateur and professional productions were mounted in the United States, among them those by juvenile opera companies, blackface minstrel troupes, and church choirs raising funds for charity. Pirated editions of *Pinafore*'s catchy songs appeared by the dozens, and orchestral music for live productions was written by each theater's musical director from a piano score. Currently popular songs were interpolated, characters and plot were generally garbled (a seven-foot female impersonator played Little Buttercup, and the orphan hero was impersonated by a young woman in one production), and Sullivan's orchestral coloration, so essential to *Pinafore*'s charm, was nonexistent.

Theater and opera companies began to call for more Gilbert and Sullivan, and the same musical pirating was repeated with *Trial by Jury* and *The Sorcerer,* their earlier works. In Philadelphia, young John Philip Sousa, music director of the Original Philadelphia Choir Opera Company, which was booked into a Broadway theater, was called on to write overnight a complete orchestral accompaniment for the latter. He worked from a collection of its songs. Success helped sales of American editions of Sullivan's earlier parlor ballads "Onward, Christian Soldiers," written in 1871 for a children's hymnal, and "The Lost Chord." For years, Sullivan, a one-time Chapel Royal chorister, had been selling his ballads to London publishers for £5 each, until Chappell & Co. offered to pay a royalty on sales of printed copies.

Pinafore was originally produced in London by the Comic Opera Company, a syndicate of investors headed by the holder of a monopoly to sprinkle water on the city's dusty streets, publishers George Metzler and Frank Chappell, and the impresario Richard D'Oyly Carte. A royalty of about thirty dollars was paid for each performance of *The Sorcerer,* but after a falling-out, the water monopolist and the publishers were ousted, and Gilbert and Sullivan became partners with D'Oyly Carte, sharing in all profits after expenses, and about twenty-two dollars for each performance of *Pinafore.*

The growing royalty-free use of *Pinafore* in America annoyed both Gilbert and Sullivan, particularly after medical problems prevented Sullivan from accepting a two-week engagement paying $5,000 to conduct in Philadelphia. D'Oyly Carte was dispatched to arrange for a production with English performers under the direction of the author and composer. John Ford, who managed theaters in New York, Philadelphia, Baltimore, and Washington, agreed to pay $4,000 a week for their services and to present not only *Pinafore* but also a new two-act piece Sullivan was at work on, at his usual slow pace. Yankee music-publisher pirates were to be foiled by keeping all musical arrangements and the original manuscript under lock and key between the performances of a New York company and three touring units. In order to secure English copyright, which was granted only after a first performance within the country, a run-through production of *The Pirates of Penzance,* with only piano accompaniment, was performed in a remote provincial watering place.

The New Year's Eve 1880 performance in New York City was a triumph. The *American Register* said of *Pinafore* that it had started "the regeneration of the modern stage in our native land." Undeterred by D'Oyly Carte's security methods, American publishers attempted to bribe members of the theaters' pit orchestras for the parts, sent musical stenographers night after night to take shorthand notes of the lyrics and the libretto, and finally got enough to print spurious piano-vocal scores. However, the genuine article, published by William A. Pond prevailed, so the first of many generations of Americans soon became true Savoyards (a name given those who devotedly attended each new Gilbert and Sullivan production at the Savoy Theatre in London), able to mouth every single word and note along with the performers onstage.

In 1875, Tony Pastor advertised his new home on Broadway, across from Niblo's and a few doors above the Theatre Comique where Harrigan and Hart reigned, as "the acknowledged Vaudeville Theatre of the Metropolis . . . cherished by the Ladies, Children and the Cultured Mass of amusement-seekers." Managers in San Antonio and Louisville were also labeling their places of entertainment vaudeville theatres, but Pastor made the name stick and used it for the rest of his career. On his stage, German, Italian, Irish, and other dialect comedians of both sexes sang and danced to a growing supply of novelty songs. The chaste and respectable material Pastor offered for a twenty-five-cent piece now included "protean acts," good-looking young women dancing and singing sentimental songs and changing their costumes with great speed to appear in attire suitable to the words they sang. Every one of Pastor's three-hour-long performances came to an end with the traditional afterpiece, which then was a burlesque of the most recent stage musical presentation, using costumes and scenery that accurately represented the originals. The beauteous corps de ballet was ending its brief career in variety's gaslight, to find a harbor in girlie burlesque, for Pastor now looked for genuine talent as well as good looks. Though it was not his intention, or that of other managers, the new variety-vaudeville theater became a nesting ground for talented performers.

That was also true of the new minstrel companies. Faced with serious competition from touring combination theatrical groups and traveling variety shows that were bringing the newest material from Manhattan to the heartland, the minstrel companies began to reexamine and overhaul their offerings. The most attractive qualities of the extravaganza-spectacle and comic opera—in short, of every new musical advance—were now being offered to audiences who became more exacting in their tastes with every passing year. J. H. Haverly's United Mastadon Minstrels were no longer traditional blackface singers, dancers, and comedians, but, instead, professional entertainers capable of offering elegant and eye-filling spectacle and singing equal to the operatic or concert stage, suitable for family viewing. In the process of consolidation that reduced the number of traveling minstrel shows from sixty to twelve by 1880, individual talents who had been sufficient to carry a company became part of large groups of their true equals. Many of the major male minstrel stars on the late-nineteenth-century stage learned their skills as members of Haverly's troupe or the Primrose and West company, the first to reintroduce "white minstrelsy" to America. With a larger orchestra and a truly disciplined singing cadre, Primrose and West left blackface humor and songs to music publishers, vaudeville, phonograph records, and cylinders, and provided Americans with many of their hit songs during the 1880s.

New and ambitious music publishers were beginning to challenge the hold on printed-music sales by members of the Board of Music Trade, known as the Music Publishers Association during the 1880s, most of whom were monopolizing the wholesale business, and had only a minor retail trade. Because of this control of distribution, middlemen jobbers were not attracted to the business.

Tom Harms, who eventually loosened Pond's hold on theater music, and Willis Woodward, owner of *Woodward's Monthly Magazine,* were among the earliest to see the obvious advantages of giving the minstrel star or vaudeville performer who featured their songs a share in the profits from sheet-music sales, or, if they wrote their own material, a larger royalty. Frank Howard, of Primrose and West, realized more than $200,000 in royalties from songs he wrote or on which his name appeared after he had bought them for a few dollars. Harms paid Howard thirteen cents a copy for his "Only a Pansy Blossom" in 1883, a ballad the singer had obtained for a five-dollar piece from a fellow entertainer. Such a large royalty was unusual from the new popular-music publishers, but songs that the minstrels and vaudeville artists featured on their tours and offered for sale in theater lobbies made money, and the few cents paid in royalties were welcome. The going rate in such cases was from five to eight cents. Banks Winter, composer of one of the best-selling songs of the 1880s, "White Wings," had little trouble selling it to Woodward for a high royalty once he became a member of the Primrose and West minstrel troupe and sang his song regularly. Before that, it had been turned down by every publisher in New York. With more capital to invest than Harms had, Woodward published most of the hits featured in minstrel shows and was able to lure songwriters away from Harms. Paul Dresser, a blackface minstrel end man and brother of the novelist Theodore Dreiser, became one of early Tin Pan Alley's greatest songwriters. Starting as a teen-age entertainer with a traveling medicine show, Dresser finally joined Primrose and West as an end man. For years, he continued to publish the *Paul Dresser Song Book,* a paperback songster containing words to the songs he sang along with all others used in every performance. Harms published Dresser's first major success, "The Letter That Never Came," in 1886, but when Woodward offered him greater royalties, Dresser joined the magazine publisher as an exclusive writer, though he left a few years later to become a partner in his own music house.

Woodward's reluctance to pay minstrel performers who were not songwriters for boosting his songs brought about new competition that eventually put him out of business. The fifteen-year-old boy soprano Julius Witmark was signed by Primrose and West in 1885 and immediately accepted Woodward's offer of a share in the new song "Always Take Mother's Advice," provided he sang it regularly on a forthcoming national tour. Witmark's continued performances of the song were central to its success, but when he went to Woodward to collect his royalties, all he received was a twenty-dollar gold piece and a pat on the shoulder. In revenge, Julius and his brothers opened M. Witmark & Sons in 1885, using their father's name because they were all under legal age. Long after the boy soprano had become the boy tenor, he continued to promote his brothers' songs and other family-owned copyrighted songs. He later became an executive in the company, which owned one of the greatest pre-1900 collections of published popular music.

Within a few years, the company had its own offices on Broadway, south of Union Square, and had become a stopping-off place for professional songwriters, looking for ten and twenty dollars in return for their newest composition, and singers from Tony Pastor's, the minstrel companies, and variety houses, looking for new material. As a result of their success with new popular songs, M. Witmark & Sons had as many as a thousand manuscripts submitted in a single month, so many that it adopted a hit-or-miss policy in taking any for publication.

Their only true competition, other than Woodward, was T. B. Harms, in business since 1898 and specializing in the theater music and songs William Pond had long monopolized; and Spaulding & Gray, formed in 1888 by a clerk in Ditson's New York store and a professional boxer turned comedian and songwriter. Frank Harding, who once issued successful popular songs from his job-printing office on the Bowery had now, like Ditson, become a wholesale-retailer of music he owned.

Even the most imaginative and energetic of these new music men, however, waited for orders to come in as a result of the plugging of their songs by stage and variety performers before they engaged in any real boosting themselves. Too small to own more than a single piano, not yet prosperous enough to employ staff songwriters and song demonstrators, too far removed from the intrigue of the Music Publishers Association and awareness of proposed international copyright, they were poised on the edge of a veritable music-business miracle, which would demonstrate the potential in the purely popular song trade.

Frank Harding, another of the pre-1890 publishers who concentrated on minstrel-show and variety-hall songs, did not pay performers to sing his music. Instead, he charged them to print 2-by-4-inch pictures of them on the covers of sheet music to be to distributed with their "compliments." Back covers of Harding publications were festooned with paid advertising for butchers, plumbers, coal dealers, photographers, and other tradesmen. Harding's job-printing office on the Bowery had been turned over to him by his former minstrel-man father in 1879. Located in the midst of a cluster of variety theaters, the building had a room that was always available for a poker game to the songwriters who were performers or who wrote material for them. Those who lost their money at cards could always get five or ten dollars from Harding for their newest effort or the promise of one. "There was no use in giving them more than ten dollars at a time," Harding told Edward Marks in the mid-1930s, three decades after this veteran music man had sold all his copyrights to Marks, an early giant of Tin Pan Alley. "A man could get damned drunk on ten dollars. I used to buy beautiful songs . . . six for twenty-five dollars."

In order to promote his music, each day Harding placed small stacks of recently printed songs on a counter in his office. Performers who had paid to get their pictures on the covers cleared the counter by noontime. Having purchased the privilege, they were eager to distribute the songs to fellow artists, theater managers, bookers, musicians, and others. This realistic approach to the vanity of actors and singers brought about the great success of Harding's "Drill, Ye Tarriers, Drill," "Where Did You Get That Hat?" and "December and May," the last with words by E. B. Marks. A ladies' notions salesman and would-be songwriter, Marks learned the business from Harding and was one of the first traveling drummers to take a sideline of sheet music on trips outside New York. Between regular business calls, he visited local music stores and piano dealers.

The first great female singer to come out of the variety houses was Lillian Russell, whose name was coined by Tony Pastor, according to his account of their relationship. Helen Louise "Nellie" Leonard had already sung minor roles in revivals of *Evangeline* and *Pinafore* when Pastor heard her sing some concert ballads. He immediately put the svelte blonde under contract, for seventy-five dollars a week. She made her vaudeville debut in his 14th Street theater, part of the Tammany Society's modern building in the heart of New York's new entertainment area around Union Square. In a few weeks, the "transmigrated nightingale [who] looked like Venus after her bath," as the *New York Mirror* reported, was starring in a Pastor burlesque of Gilbert and Sullivan's newest comic opera, *Patience*. Though never the abiding American favorite that its predecessor would be, *Patience* was such a profitable venture for the Comedy Opera Company partners that D'Oyly Carte took home $100,000 from the "definitive" production in the winter of 1881. He had exported his own

British brand of bunkum to stimulate interest in *Patience,* "an Aesthetic Opera" that dealt with a dairymaid who was forced to choose between a poet of the outdoors and a languid, white-lily-bearing poet who bore a striking resemblance to Oscar Wilde. D'Oyly Carte sent Wilde himself on a lecture tour of the United States. In a short time, his velvet knee breeches, flaming-red silk handkerchief, and extravagantly brazen comments on any American subject built up a vast audience for the new comic opera, whose London run was making more money than the British prime minister's salary. In an excess of amiability, after *Patience* had played for six months, D'Oyly Carte sold American rights to his friend Edward Rice, who revived the work, with Lillian Russell as the dairymaid. American comic opera had found a crown princess, and she was being paid $250 a week. In 1898, the figure had grown to $2,500 a week, and expenses for a tour of Germany.

During the years in which Russell starred at the Casino Theatre in musical stage works written by Gilbert and Sullivan, Gustave Kerker, Offenbach, Audran, Millöcker, Julian Edwards, Reginald De Koven, and John Stromberg, among others, she acquired and got rid of innumerable lovers and three husbands, all of the latter connected with the theater. Her second, Edward Solomon, was an English composer, an intimate of Arthur Sullivan and D'Oyly Carte, and the writer of several successful comic operas created for her. Solomon's *Billee Taylor,* in which Russell appeared in the 1885 revival, included one of the major hit songs of the time, "All on Account of Eliza." In their several years of marriage, which came to an abrupt halt when Solomon was arrested for bigamy while on a trip home to England, Broadway's "Royal Queen of Operatic Songs" enlivened her appearances on stage by wearing the snug-fitting clothing of young boys or sailors and also the expensive and stunning gowns and spectacular hats that became her trademark. As age added pounds and she tipped the scales at 165, she refused to wear tights, a decision approved by a court after her producers took the matter there.

In 1899, Lillian Russell was thirty-eight and ruler of all she surveyed when she agreed to appear with the German-dialect comedians Joe Weber and Lew Fields in one of their combined vaudeville–stage musical–travesty presentations. She received $1,250 a week and expenses, guaranteed for a season of thirty-five weeks, with all the gowns and hats to be paid for by the producers. Music for the Weber and Fields two-part productions, which bridged the gap between vaudeville-burlesque and classic American musical comedy, was written by John "Honey" Stromberg, who was working for the Witmarks as an arranger in 1895 when his first song, "My Girl's a Corker," began to sell large quantities of sheet music. He accepted an offer from the two comedians to be in charge of all their music, to be published by a company they had organized. Within a short time, however, it became evident that none of those involved had any ability to operate a publishing house in the competitive atmosphere of Tin Pan Alley, so it was sold to the Witmarks, for $10,000. Among the string of Stromberg hits were "I Sigh for a Change," "My Blushin' Rosie," "Kiss Me Honey Do," and other coon songs he wrote for Russell to sing in the vaudeville portion of Weber and Fields' presentations. One of the latter, "Come Down, Ma Evenin' Star," was written, to Robert B. Smith's lyrics, for *Twirly-Whirly* (1902), a production Stromberg never saw. He had promised Russell a great new song, and the manuscript was discovered among his possessions after his death by suicide, brought about by poor health and disastrous investments in New York real estate. It and Stromberg's "When Chloe Sings," neither sung in dialect, became a regular feature of Russell's vaudeville appearances in the years before her final retirement at the end of four decades, during which she was the unchallenged queen of the American musical stage.

Lillian Russell was already a high-priced artist when D'Oyly Carte brought *The Mikado* to New York in 1885. Gilbert and Sullivan and the Comedy Theatre company were again having problems with American publishers and piracy. William A. Pond, their authorized publisher in the United States, was able to obtain an injunction against an unauthorized production that would have preceded the official New York premiere. This new legal verification of Gilbert and Sullivan's monopoly of the American comic-opera stage, which otherwise was the exclusive domain of European composers, was successfully challenged in the same year by Willard Spenser, a young and wealthy musical amateur from Philadelphia.

Though looked down on by the New York press, the City of Brotherly Love had been an important factor in American music of all kinds for many years. It was the home of a major comic-opera company, one of America's greatest songwriters, Septimus Winner, and William Fry, composer of America's first grand opera, *Leonora*. John Philip Sousa had but recently left his post as conductor for the city's comic-opera company, for which he had written several works, to lead the United States Marine Band in Washington. The city also boasted two major American music publishers, one of whom, Lee and Walker, had published a waltz by Spenser in 1867, when he was still a teen-ager. Fifteen years later, however, Spenser had great difficulty in rousing any professional interest in a new comic opera with Japanese characters, *The Little Tycoon*. He had already shown the manuscript to D'Oyly Carte's American representative, without success. The manager of a Philadelphia theater finally agreed to present the piece, in early 1885, and within a few months it proved to be amazingly popular, at least with local audiences. New York critics did not like *The Little Tycoon* when it had a brief run there that spring. They pointed out its similarities to *The Mikado,* which was currently enjoying success in London and due in New York shortly. Spenser could only respond that he had copyrighted the piece in October 1882 and that the producer of *The Mikado* may have had access to his composition some years before Gilbert wrote the libretto for his Japanese comic opera. More than 2,000 performances of *The Little Tycoon* by the original Philadelphia company followed before Spenser took back all rights and began to publish and license it himself. For many years, two of its songs, "Heel and Toe We Always Go" and "Love Comes Like a Summer Night," remained among America's favorite parlor music. *The Little Tycoon* neared its 10,000th professional performance in 1940, six years after its writer's death, and there had been more than 6,000 performances by amateur opera groups. Spencer's *The Princess Bonnie* (1894) and *Miss Bob White* (1901) had each had nearly 3,000 performances by then, in spite of the New York critics' continuing antipathy.

Spenser's success was even more unusual in light of the 1887 failure in Philadelphia and some other cities of Reginald De Koven's first comic opera, *The Begum,* with a libretto by the Chicago newspaperman and music critic Harry B. Smith, who eventually wrote the books and some 6,000 lyrics for more than 300 musicals. The son of an Anglican clergyman, De Koven was born in Connecticut and went to England with his family when he was fourteen. After completing his education at Oxford, he went into business in 1879, but found time to study music, orchestration, and composition in Europe, where for a time he was a pupil of both Franz von Suppe and Leo Delibes. He returned to America thoroughly Anglicized, with an accent and sporting a silk hat, sable-lined coat, and gold-headed cane. His habit of looking at musical scores through a lorgnette infuriated the Tin Pan Alley songwriters who came into contact with him, who called him Reggie. A wealthy Chicago heiress, however, found him entrancing and married him. He had moved to Chicago and started to work with Harry B. Smith. Their first effort failed, as did their *Don Quixote* two years later.

Robin Hood, completed in 1890, might have suffered a similar fate had it not been for a song interpolated at the last moment that became a popular hit. The work was offered to the Bostonians, the nation's most popular light-opera company, which had misgivings about yet another flawed Smith–De Koven opera but finally did present it, in costumes borrowed from other productions, after a total expenditure of $109.50. The role of Allan-A-Dale was played as a breeches part by a contralto, Jessie Bartlett Davies, who complained after the first performance that the score did not give her a show-stopping aria and threatened to leave. De Koven went to the theater's piano to play and sing a song he had written to words by a British poet, Clement Scott, which, with his setting of Eugene Field's "Little Boy Blue," had been published by the Boston Music Company. Recognizing the appeal of "O Promise Me," the actress urged that it become part of the score and soon was singing it night after night to standing ovations. Despite the popularity it was gaining, as well as the orders for sheet-music copies that began to pour in from music stores, Gustave Schirmer, Jr., owner of the Boston Music Company, did nothing to promote the song. The son of the New York piano manufacturer and major American publisher of European concert music, young Schirmer had been brought up to rely on traditional music-business practices and would not consider engaging in modern merchandising and popular song-boosting tactics. He concentrated, instead, on the growing sales of piano music and art songs by Ethelbert Nevin. After Schirmer returned to New York to operate G. Schirmer, he brought out a vocal score and selections from *Robin Hood* in 1891. Despite Schirmer's neglect, in time "O Promise Me" became one of the company's best-selling copyrighted pieces and a favorite with ballad singers and vaudeville performers.

Notwithstanding the song's increasing success, as well as that of two other selections from *Robin Hood,* "Brown October Ale" and "The Armorer's Song,"

De Koven continued to work toward his dream of writing music that would be heard in the Metropolitan Opera House. He wrote eleven more works for the Broadway musical theater with Harry Smith, who had also begun to work with other composers and songwriters, including John Stromberg, with whom he wrote Weber and Fields shows. De Koven's music was often called cold and uninspiring, even imitative. A rumor said that he had stolen the melody for "O Promise Me." De Koven told a newspaperman that all composers imitated one another and that the last thing America needed was the new kind of American music that popular songs were providing. Two Smith–De Koven musicals were produced by Ziegfeld, and starred his future common-law wife, the ninety-eight-pound French entertainer whose perfect hourglass figure and such songs as "Won't You Come and Play Wiz Me" made Anna Held's name a household word. *Papa's Wife* (1899) was highlighted by the presence of the first sixteen beautiful Ziegfeld show girls parading to De Koven's music, but the hit of the show was "I Wish I Really Weren't, but I Am," a popular song interpolated into the score, because its publisher was ready to part with hard cash. In Ziegfeld's 1901 *Little Duchess*, the producer eliminated both the script and much of the score to make way for popular music written by Tin Pan Alley songwriters. An effervescently buoyant Anna Held stopped the show each night with the Johnson brothers and Bob Cole's "Maiden with the Dreamy Eyes," the latest in a string of hit songs the three black songwriters had placed in a dozen musical productions.

When Blanche Ring tired of De Koven's music for *The Jersey Lily* (1903), she turned to former minstrel man Billy Jerome and Hungarian immigrant musician Jean Schwartz's "Bedelia" to get the ovations to which she had grown accustomed.

Reginald De Koven turned his back on Broadway in 1913. He formed the Philharmonic Orchestra of Washington, D.C., and remained its conductor for three seasons. He also wrote piano sonatas, ballet music, and two operas, *Canterbury Tales* (1917), which the Metropolitan Opera produced, and *Rip Van Winkle*, written the year before his death, in 1920. When *Robin Hood* was revived in 1945, it lasted only two weeks on Broadway, having become the type of musical theater that palled.

Robin Hood's success notwithstanding (the Bostonians gave a 1,200th performance in early 1891), the future for a thoroughly American musical theater appeared far from bright as the "Gay '90s" began. De Koven's scores had reeked of the British and European art music he admired, and Gilbert and Sullivan's hand lay heavily on those who sought to imitate their success and set their plots in the exotic Orient. The most popular of 1891's productions by a native-born writing team, *Wang*, with a libretto by J. Cheever Cowdin, of *Evangeline* fame, and a score by a German-trained American who was also a part-time painter, Woolson Morse, was set in Siam and had very little American about it but its advertising slogan: "*Wang* Goes With a BANG!" Yet revivals of a limited repertory of European comic operas and operettas and new works by their writers could be counted on to attract audiences, as witness the 200 performances of the German Karl Millöcker's *Poor Jonathan,* starring Lillian Russell, after its October 1890 opening. The hit of the newest Harrigan and Braham score was "Maggie Murphy's Home," another of the European-influenced waltz songs to which even such new music publishers as the Witmarks looked for the largest sheet-music sales.

The major hit of the road tour of Charles Hoyt's comedy with music *A Trip to Chinatown* was still another in the "tempo di valse" tradition, "The Bowery," words by Hoyt to music by Percy Gaunt. A Briton who had grown up during the time robust music-hall songs were replacing broadside ballads as the Englishman's darling songs, Gaunt went to the United States and learned about the American theater and its music by working for David Braham on the Harrigan and Hart shows. Many things had not changed in a hundred years, and, as had been true when James Hewitt and Alexander Reinagle provided music and directed the orchestra for the earliest American musical productions, Broadway producers still employed a single individual to serve as musical director and to provide music for the dancing and songs that were loosely incorporated into the action. Such simple cues as "Let's gather around the piano," "I love a good quartet song," or "Sing me a song" introduced a waltz song or parlor ballad.

Economic vagaries affected the New York Philharmonic Orchestra, which was reduced from one hundred in the late 1860s to less than sixty thirty years later. This made available a cadre of highly professional musicians for the major theaters' orchestras. Musicians employed for three dollars a performance formed the standard concert-saloon combination of piano, one or two violins, viola, flute, clarinet, cornet, trombone, double bass, and drums, with a battery of noise-making gadgets. Occasionally, a theater would advertise the presence of a thirty-piece orchestra, created by considerable doubling of the usual instrumentation.

Suddenly, like an Indian summer, in one last great burst of vitality the popular waltz song delivered its commercial masterpiece, the best selling of its kind, "After the Ball." It was the work of a self-taught banjo player from Wisconsin, Charles K. Harris, who could not write music and, like many songwriters of the period, dictated to a professional musician, who put it down on paper for a few dollars. Harris had some familiarity with the music business, having sold some songs to the Witmarks, so he was aware that continued boosting by a leading stage personality was important. The traveling original company of *A Trip to Chinatown,* on the road before its official New York premiere, was playing in Milwaukee, and Harris sought out the company's leading baritone, J. Aldrich Libby. Though Gaunt was responsible for all the show's music, a starring player was in the position to interpolate songs of his own selection, and Libby did this for Harris after an orchestration in the desired key was provided, at the writer's expense, a cigar in lieu of the five dollars Harris did not have. A five-minute standing ovation followed Libby's rendition of the song's three long verses and six encores of its chorus. After the promise to Libby of $500 and a share of sales income, the song became part of every performance of *A Trip to Chinatown.* Julius Witmark, who was also in the cast, offered Harris $10,000 for all rights to the song, for which orders were beginning to pour in as the production moved nearer to New York. While thinking over the offer, Harris got an order from Oliver Ditson for 75,000 copies, which was worth $14,250. Sales grew still larger after Sousa added "After the Ball" to the programs of his large band during an engagement at the Chicago World's Fair. Harris decided to publish the song himself and soon was clearing $25,000 a month as sales of "After the Ball" went over the five-million mark. Those young music publishers who had believed that there was money in popular music were now certain of the fact.

The difference in attitudes between Ditson and the Witmarks revealed, in hindsight, the direction in which success lay for the new music publishers. Established and conservative, Ditson had become a wholesale-retailer and would not venture capital on a risky property. Young and bold, the Witmarks were eager to gamble on a song of whose success they felt sure. It was this willingness to back judgment with money and the investment of their own and their employees' ability to boost a song to popularity that heralded the maturity of Tin Pan Alley's new music business. The number of new music-publishing ventures, operating on the shoestring that had become the American way, began to multiply.

Despite the panic of 1893 and ensuing financial difficulties, and due in no small measure to the success of Gaunt's "The Bowery" and "Reuben and Cynthia"—two of the five songs Harms brought out in vocal score—and of "After the Ball," A Trip to Chinatown had run for 650 performances by 1893, returned for another hundred a year later, and was revived by Ziegfeld in 1912 as A Winsome Widow, starring the Dolly Sisters, and with Mae West in the cast. None of the old songs remained, for music had changed, and the hit of the show was a ragtime number, "By My Baby Bumble Bee." The old-fashioned waltz song had had its day.

Some producers of the new lyric theater continued to trust their luck to European imports and native-grown comic opera, none of which cost more than $10,000 to mount. Musical scores were always written to preselected librettos in less than three months by European-born composers who had worked their way up from a place in the orchestra pit to the conductor's desk. Typical were Gustave Kerker, director of music for the Casino Theatre, and the Viennese Ludwig Englander, who started in America at a theater on the Bowery. Already an accomplished cellist by the age of seven, when his family moved to Louisville, Kentucky, Kerker was leading the local playhouse orchestra when Edward Rice heard his first operetta and recommended Kerker to the management of the new Casino Theatre. Lillian Russell reigned for many years over this modern temple to music, which was also the home of the renowned Casino Girls, who sang in chorus, danced politely, and marched in military drills. Kerker conducted almost all of the 571 New York performances of the English operetta Erminee, music by the Viennese-born Londoner Edward Jakobowski, which included the celebrated "heart" song, "Dear Mother, in Dreams I See Her." Although sheet-music publishers, magazines, and newspapers used its music with impunity, Robert Aronson, producer at the Casino, was reluctant to chance legal action after the affirmation of Gilbert and Sullivan's rights to

The Mikado. In return for permission to present an "authorized" production and use Jakobowski's orchestrations, Aronson paid $120,000 in royalties to the English copyright holders for a total of 1,256 performances by three companies, in New York, Philadelphia, and Boston.

Most American composers for the musical theater were not paid any money other than their salaries as musical director, but from time to time Kerker freely interpolated his own songs and music into revivals of old favorites. His *Castles in the Air* (1890) did have 100 performances, but generally the Casino owners continued an unadventurous policy of light lyric opera, little of it either daring or modern.

Other than Harms, most of the publishers around West 28th Street in New York were not yet interested. Following the passage of a revised copyright law in 1891, which provided reciprocal international protection, Harms had effected a relationship, allowing simultaneous publication, with the London publishing firm of Francis, Day & Hunter, established by three English variety artists who now controlled a majority of England's popular music. The majority of music men, however, regarded the musical theater merely as an exploitative medium. Using such celebrities as J. Aldrich Libby, whose lithographed face was appearing with greater frequency on sheet-music covers, publishers were spending from $25,000 to $75,000 annually for boosting their songs. Asked by a *New York Herald* reporter in late 1893 whether he was comfortable pushing such big-money hits as "After the Ball" and "Two Little Girls in Blue," Libby replied, "Of course to the trained ear of a professional these songs are somewhat disappointing. But the recompense comes in the wider audience that a singer has for his simpler themes." Though the songs, he said, might be "tawdry from a classical standpoint, still [they] contain a homely sentiment that is beneficial in its moral influence." They were also becoming more beneficial to the publishers' income.

Through his connection with Francis, Day & Hunter, Harms got control of the music in an imported British production in 1894 that affected the character of American musical theater for more than a decade; it was *A Gaiety Girl*. He had already brought out the vocal score and six individual songs from another important innovation, Ludwig Englander's *The Passing Show,* with libretto and words by Sydney Rosenfeld, a Virginian active in the theater since 1874 as author, producer, and director. Aware of a recent new direction being taken by vaudeville in France—a comic revue with a series of variety acts tied together by a script that commented on recent events, while the undraped female body was used for scenic effects—Rosenfeld created his "topical extravaganza . . . reviewing the past events of the year," chiefly theatrical. Unadorned bodies appeared in a series of Living Pictures, a ballet was performed whose French title implied the salaciousness for which Paris was noted, and a line of "six colored youths" in a plantation dance catered to the growing taste for coon-song music. The Casino's management found this form of sophisticated vaudeville a solution to recent box-office problems and embarked on a summertime policy of similar "reviews" with music chiefly by its principal musical director, Gustave Kerker.

During one of her trips back home in the 1870s, after she and her British Blondes had captivated Americans, Lydia Thompson had popularized the form of full-length burlesque, in which they had appeared in the United States. The Gaiety Theatre in London became the new form's English stronghold, with a brilliant company of singers, comedians, and chorus girls. Constantly seeking to keep up with the newest developments in America, the Gaiety management presented a series of comic operas blended with the farce comedies that had become all the rage in America in the early 1890s. Their 1893 offering, *A Gaiety Girl,* was imported to New York the following year, and, although a leading critic found it an "undefinable musical and dramatic mélange," musical-theater lovers were enchanted with its sentimental ballads and comic songs, burlesque and civilized melodrama, the new dancing, in which swirling skirts covered what once had been exposed by tights, and, particularly, the Gaiety Girl ensemble of fashionably dressed and trim chorus girls. True American musical theater had received a setback from which it did not fully recover for a decade. American producers were affected by the new British imports, and some tried, rarely succeeding, to match the sparkling qualities of the genuine article. Its popularity soon exceeded that of Gilbert and Sullivan, compounded by a series of musical comedies from England with scores by the Britons Sydney Jones, Lionel Monckton, and Ivan Caryll. Kerker's 1898 *Belle of New York* was so influenced by the Gaiety musicals that it ran for more than a year in London after having failed to rouse any great enthusiasm in the city that inspired it. Such family trade as did come to the Broadway theater was in search of burlesque to which one could bring the children, and continuous vaudeville was already beginning to syphon off many of this audience. More to the point, the creation of a theatrical syndicate was producing a new effect on dramatists, composers, actors, and producers.

By the mid-1890s, some 200,000 miles of railroad track linked New York City to an America in which some 5,000 theaters in 3,500 cities provided one form or another of professional entertainment. "Direct from Broadway" companies and musical attractions made it possible for any local showman with the funds and a theater capable of holding a large audience to obtain larger profits than ever achieved from the resident stock companies that had been a major ingredient of show business for nearly a century. The competition for New York productions and performers became more high-pressured each August as theater owners from around the country came in search of their next season's attractions. Only one out of twenty theatrical productions left New York with a penny of profit; they expected to reap a large return from one or two years on the road before a final, farewell, appearance on Broadway. To subsidize expensive transportation costs, runs in large centers were punctuated by performances in smaller nearby communities.

Out of the inevitable confusion, circuit managers and theatrical booking agents emerged—middlemen who brought order out of chaos and supplied a steady supply of attractions throughout the year. In 1896, six major booking agents formed a theatrical trust, which became known as "the Syndicate." It was headed by Marc Klaw and Abe (Abraham Lincoln) Erlanger, who already controlled most, if not all, theaters in the Southern United States. Beginning with sixteen first-class houses and smaller places between, the Syndicate, within a decade, controlled more than 700 important playhouses. Relieved of all responsibility for arranging their annual programs, theater owners eagerly affiliated with the Syndicate, and placed implicit trust in the judgment of the producer members. Theaters were, therefore, forced to accept what was sent, regardless of quality. The Syndicate could call for revision and remove or replace songs. The nation's taste soon became that of the Syndicate and of theatrical producers who cast their lot with it.

The Syndicate's destruction did not occur until 1916. The Shubert brothers, refugees from czarist oppression, had joined Klaw and Erlanger in an aborted vaudeville trust expected to break B. F. Keith's hold on variety entertainment. When that failed, the brothers, with backing from wealthy financiers and political figures, bested Klaw and Erlanger and shaped the course of post–World War I musical theater. Until then, however, it was the Syndicate's world. Klaw and Erlanger, for example, sold exclusive rights to the music from their productions to publishers and purchased long options on the works of every European musical-comedy writer.

Until the Shuberts acquired a ten-year lease for the Casino Theatre in 1902, every musical theater in New York except Weber and Fields' Music Hall, was operated by the Syndicate. Yet, no matter how long its stay on Broadway, a play was adjudged successful on the basis of out-of-town revenues. Some musicals played as many as five years away from New York. Sousa's *El Capitan* was on the road for four consecutive years after its initial run in a Syndicate house, which added to the reputation of the March King.

Even before his resignation from the Marine Corps, in 1892, John Philip Sousa's marches, to which people danced the popular two-step, were hailed as the best of their kind. This son of an immigrant trombone player in the Marine Band had been apprenticed to that group at the age of fourteen and received his entire musical education there. When Jacques Offenbach visited the Philadelphia Centennial Exposition in 1876, Sousa played first violin in his great orchestra of a hundred musicians. This was after he had played in the Ford Theatre pit orchestra in Washington and traveled with a nude-girl Living Picture troupe throughout the Midwest. Though his ambition, after serving as musical director for the famous Philadelphia Amateur Opera Company, was to write the sort of comic operettas that were making Gilbert and Sullivan rich and famous, he also wrote minstrel songs and variety shows. His first published operetta was performed during his second year as the Marine Corps bandmaster, but it was the marches that he composed especially for that group that made him known internationally. Most of the early pieces were sold, with full-band score and a piano reduction, for thirty-five dollars, or less. His early publisher, Harry Coleman, purchased two musical-instrument factories with profits from the sale of Sousa's marches.

Though never a good businessman, Sousa did become a millionaire, part of that fortune coming from a contract with the John Church Co., of Cincinnati, guaranteeing him royalties that eventually rose to 15 percent of retail price from sales to military bands around the world and for dancing the two-step. In a single quarter, July–September 1894, Church paid him royalties of $6,588.59 for two marches, "Liberty Bell" and "Manhattan Beach." David Blakely, a businessman who managed Patrick Gilmore, persuaded Sousa to form a civilian concert band, promising him an annual salary of four times his Marine Corps pay of around $1,800 and a share of all profits from concert tours. Under terms of their agreement, Blakely owned all the copyrights for music Sousa wrote for the band. After Blakely's death, in 1897, a protracted court action followed, ending with an order that Sousa surrender to the estate the entire band library, as well as income from compositions written between 1892 and 1897. During the prolonged litigation, the bandmaster became extremely reluctant to add any large sums to his income, and when, in late 1897, the New Haven Theatre, where his new operetta, *The Bride-Elect,* had its first performance, offered him $100,000 for all future performance rights, he refused the Syndicate theater's proposal. He also rejected an offer of $10,000 for newspaper-publication rights to a march based on one of the operetta's songs.

None of Sousa's later stage works duplicated the great success of *El Capitan* (1898), certainly his most performed operetta. Moreover, as a heavy schedule of concerts both in the United States and abroad absorbed most of his time, his theatrical activities dwindled. His last stage work, the variety extravaganza *Everything* (1918), used some of his own incidental music and songs by several Tin Pan Alley writers, among them Irving Berlin. Sousa was rarely enthusiastic about popular music, and only after cylinder recordings of such popular ragtime hits as "Smoky Mokes" and "At a Georgia Cake Walk," made by members of his band under Arthur Pryor's direction, attracted crowds of the new music's devotees to his concerts were those and other syncopated selections included on his programs. A consummate egoist, Sousa believed that once he played even a street melody, it became respectable. Millions around the globe evidently agreed throughout the three decades during which he ruled the popular concert-band world.

The Irish-born musician and conductor Victor Herbert was an unusual figure in the American musical theater, where most composers had long been content to give all rights to their music for little more than their salaries as musical director. His European experience had made him aware that music publishers could be aggressive administrators of dramatic-performance rights and could become very wealthy men. When the Bostonians, in search of new material, asked Herbert to write a work for them, he insisted on proper compensation: no less than a five percent royalty to him and his collaborator, no interpolation of popular songs by others, and control of the final libretto. The opera company agreed, and in *Prince Ananias* (1894) they acquired a work that became one of the most popular in their repertoire for the next several years.

Born in Dublin in 1859, Herbert got his musical training in Germany and then worked as a cellist in European concert and theater orchestras. He had no thought other than to marry the principal singer of the Stuttgart Opera Company and continue his career as a concert artist and composer. Then his fiancée accepted an offer to join the Metropolitan Opera Company in New York, with the understanding that Herbert would be a member of its orchestra. The Herberts arrived in 1886. He soon won the admiration of opera and theater musicians and composers for his genial disposition, genuine talent as a conductor, virtuosic cello playing, and skill as a composer of both light and concert music.

His *Prince Ananias* was followed by three more of the thirty-five stage musicals he wrote in thirty years. Among these early works was *The Goldbug* (1896), in which Bert Williams and George Walker, the black comedians who had taken New York by storm, made their first, but short-lived, appearance in a Broadway musical. In 1898, Herbert was appointed conductor of the Pittsburgh Symphony Orchestra, and it became clear that with the burden of new duties he needed an aggressive music publisher to deal with theatrical producers and promote his music for the stage. A friend brought the jovial Irishman and the Witmarks together, and an agreement was concluded that remained in effect until after World War I. During that period, almost all of Herbert's popular lyric works were published in piano-vocal score by the Witmarks. His concert and grand-opera music was handled by G. Schirmer.

Despite his arrangement with the Witmarks, whose silent partner the trade believed he had become, Herbert's business sense prevailed on two occasions, and new operettas were published by others. In 1906, Joe Weber, having broken his long partnership with Lew Fields, was starring in a new comic opera, which had a burlesque afterpiece by Herbert that lampooned Wagner's *Lohengrin*. Weber insisted that the music he had commissioned from Herbert be brought out by Charles K. Harris, the publisher to whom he had sold publication rights of all his productions. Herbert assented and was pleased by the fine printing job done on the vocal score and the royalty checks sent him for the music of *Dream City and The Magic Knight*. A few years later, when producers who had purchased rights for a road tour of the production intended to drop Herbert's original music and use a new score, copyright owners Harris and Herbert sued and were successful: the original music was retained. After the original producer sold *The Rose of Algeria* (1908) to Lew Fields, because he found the music too sophisticated for his audiences, Harris again got all publication rights. When George M. Cohan and his business partner, Sam Harris, auctioned off the assets and copyrights owned by Cohan and Harris Music—a company formed to compete with the large music houses—Charles K. Harris purchased the rights they had acquired to one of Herbert's lesser efforts, *Little Nemo* (1908), an operetta based on the popular newspaper cartoon figure of that name.

The prevailing musical-theater practice of interpolating purely popular songs to attract less sophisticated ticket buyers infuriated Herbert, and he insisted on a clause in his contracts forbidding it. Generally, most prominent composers and their publishers were satisfied by a $1,000 penalty for every new song inserted into a score. However, Lew Fields, the producer, and Herbert's lawyer evidently omitted the interpolation clause in the contract for *It Happened in Nordland* (1904), whose star, Marie Cahill, was notorious for boosting new popular songs on the legitimate stage. She continued to plug a song published by Detroit businessman Jerome Remick, "The Best I Get Is Much Obliged to

You,'' with increasing frequency, but Herbert was powerless to do anything. He was further embarrassed because it was said that he was incapable of writing his own music. The music director became ill, so Herbert took over the conductor's baton for a time. When Cahill began to plug the song, which was enjoying great sales, he handed the orchestra over to its first violinist until she finished it. Fields supported Herbert, and Cahill withdrew from the cast. Blanche Ring, an equally aggressive song booster, took her place. From that point on, Herbert's attorney carefully scrutinized contracts to avoid repetition of this incident, which received a great deal of gossip and newspaper space.

The Witmarks proved to be exactly the sort of go-getting publishers Herbert was looking for, and by the middle of 1899 he was writing to thank them for the most recent royalty check and complimenting their "excellent showing in the way of sales." He had personally supervised, as he did all his life, the work of the Witmark employee who prepared a vocal score, orchestral selections, and dance arrangements of songs from *The Fortune Teller* (1898). Due to its exploitation as a popular song by the Witmarks, "Gypsy Love Song" went on to sell two million copies of sheet music. By plugging them in vaudeville, on phonograph records and piano rolls, and in restaurants and theaters, the Witmarks made hits out of many songs from Herbert comic operas: "Toyland" and "I Can't Do That Sum" from *Babes in Toyland* (1903); "Kiss Me Again" from *Mlle. Modiste* (1905), taken from Herbert's trunk for Fritzi Sheff to sing in a display of popular stage-song styles and then expanded, and also "The Mascot of the Troop" and "I Want What I Want When I Want It"; six Tin Pan Alley–influenced songs from *The Red Mill* (1906), "Everyday Is Ladies' Day with Me," "Good-a-Bye, John," "In Old New York," "Isle of Our Dreams," "Moonbeams," and "Because You're You"; and, in 1910, "I'm Falling in Love with Someone" and "Ah, Sweet Mystery of Life" from his master musical-theater work, *Naughty Marietta,* whose orchestrations of near-symphonic quality were a response to the challenge of voices recruited from the Metropolitan and other major opera companies. "Ah, Sweet Mystery of Life" was originally an instrumental entr'acte piece to which words were added at the suggestion of a member of the cast. Though it was not a major success in a season when thirty-four musicals were offered, *Naughty Marietta* outlived all the others.

Both Herbert and Sousa were active in the battle for copyright revision that led to the revised act of 1909. Following its passage, both signed with the National Phonograph Company, Edison's organization, but only Herbert actually participated in recording cylinders and disks; Sousa left that to his assistants.

Because all of Broadway's spectacle and music theaters were controlled by the Syndicate, virtually all of the Witmarks' pre-1910 musical comedies and operettas—those by Herbert, Julian Edwards, Gustav Luders, Karl Hoschna, A. Baldwin Sloane, Richard Carle, Manuel Klein, and others—played in Klaw and Erlanger houses. The Witmarks maintained excellent relations with Klaw and Erlanger and became the first new serious competition for Tom Harms as leading publisher of musical-theater songs and scores in the late 1890s. With reciprocal international copyright protection affirmed by federal law in 1891, Chappell and Boosey, both London publishers of popular songs and musical stage works, opened branches in New York to deal with theatrical producers. Boosey, for one, ended its relationship with William A. Pond & Co., stripping that veteran firm of many hits from the British stage and music halls. Francis, Day & Hunter, of London, on the other hand, used Harms as its American sub-publisher. Tired of the stresses of music publishing and promotion, Harms increasingly relied on one of his arrangers and pluggers, Max Dreyfus, to whom he sold a majority interest early in the new century. For years, Harms prospered, owing to the success of the Gaiety's musical comedies in America.

In 1900, the musical comedy *Florodora* arrived in the United States. Set on a tropical island of that name, it brought to Broadway a line of six 130-pound singing and dancing "typewriter girl" chorines, who duetted nightly with an equal number of handsome young men in the show's hit song, "Tell Me Pretty Maiden (are there any more at home like you?)" *Florodora* ran for 505 performances, followed by many more on the road and in regular revivals. It made $10,000 a week in the first year on Broadway. Its packed house always included wealthy men who had already seen it a dozen times but slipped in nightly just before the major song. Another British import that year, *The Messenger Boy,* with music by Ivan Caryll and Lionel Monckton, also enjoyed more than 100 performances.

The Syndicate monopoly received its first serious blow in the musical theater when Sam Shubert brought *A Chinese Honeymoon* from London, where it had had an unheard-of run of 1,000 performances. It played in the Casino Theatre, which he had leased for a year with a borrowed $20,000. To be safe, he added some American popular songs published by Shapiro, Bernstein & Co., a partnership of Maurice Shapiro and Louis Bernstein. The firm was soon regarded in the trade as the Shuberts' "official music house." Incessant boosting by Shapiro and Bernstein of their song "Mister Dooley," by William Jerome and Jean Schwartz, saluting the hero of America's favorite Irish-dialect sketches, written by Peter Finley Dunne, helped the new Shubert production run 375 times in New York, followed by a number of touring companies. Schwartz was a young and recent Hungarian immigrant who had fallen in love with syncopated popular music. Taking advantage of the piano lessons given him by a sister who had studied with Franz Liszt, he became the first sheet-music demonstrator in a department store and later joined the Shapiro, Bernstein staff. Like other successful music houses seeking to promote songs thought to have a strong potential for success, Shapiro, Bernstein paid stage performers and provided many gratuitous services in order to have these songs interpolated into operettas and stage musicals. This form of boosting made hits out of his songs "Rip Van Winkle Was a Lucky Man," "Bedelia," and "Chinatown, My Chinatown," among others. With Jerome, a former minstrel man and vaudevillian, Schwartz wrote complete scores for many long-running theatrical presentations. Their first, *Piff!!! Paff!!! Pouf!!!* ran for almost a year at the Casino in 1904, and *The Ham Tree* (1905) was a starring vehicle for the blackface team of McIntyre and Heath for more than five years. In the Jazz Age, Schwartz no longer turned out hit songs or hit scores, but he continued to provide workmanlike music for Shubert revues.

The "second Victor Herbert," as he was considered in 1904, Gustav Luders was another of the period's major European-born operetta composers. A native of Germany, where he had studied the violin, piano, and composition and served in the kaiser's band, he had come to America in 1888. He found work in Milwaukee theaters and the Schlitz beer garden there. Charles K. Harris met him and encouraged him to move to Chicago, where music publishers were looking for trained people to put down on paper promising songs offered for publication by musically illiterate amateurs. Luders took down "My Gal Is a High Born Lady" from minstrelman Barney Fagan, and his name was on all the copies of that successful Witmark song. In addition to working for the Witmark branch office, Luders was in charge of music for a Chicago theater owner, who commissioned him and a local newspaperman, Frank Pixley, to create a new operetta, which he proposed eventually to take to New York. Pixley had already written a successful play and the Americanized libretto for *Florodora,* and their collaboration was a triumph on the road. *The Prince of Pilsen* followed. It had more than 5,000 performances, playing simultaneously in New York and Chicago. Its songs "The Message of the Violet" and "The Heidelberg Stein Song" were great hits, and its constantly repeated query "Vass you effer in Zinzinnati?" became a national catch phrase. Hit songs continued to appear in Luders's eight succeeding musicals, two of them written with American humorist George Ade, which filled houses everywhere on the road, where *The Prince of Pilsen* was still playing. Yet times had moved too fast for Luders. After his last musical was savaged by New York critics, he was found dead in his hotel room, from a broken heart, his publisher Isidore Witmark always maintained.

Karl Hoschna, another Witmark employee who became an outstanding composer for the lyric stage, got his first job there after he had written a letter offering to give up his well-paying place in Victor Herbert's orchestra for a lowly copyist's wages. He was only twenty years old, but fear of what an oboe's reed might be doing to his head made it impossible for him to continue playing the instrument. Born in a province of Austro-Hungaria, Hoschna had studied at the Vienna Conservatory, served as a bandmaster in the Austrian Army, and joined Herbert in 1896. At Witmark, he became Isidore's trusted assistant and so learned the business from a man who had become a respected figure on Broadway. Isidore Witmark was an expert at doctoring a scene, placing a song so that it would have the greatest effect on an audience, and recognizing genuine talent. He encouraged Hoschna, who first wrote only songs. His first complete score, *The Belle of the West,* never got to Broadway, but did well on tour and produced a minor hit, "My Little Lassoo." Hoschna's ability first showed in his fourth effort, *Three Twins,* written to order for the governor of California, whose wife had written the successful play on which it was based. Hoschna was paid $100 for the completed score, and his friend Otto Hauerbach, an advertising copywriter who later changed his name to Harbach, got the same for the lyrics. A Danish-American born in Utah, Hauerbach was an English teacher working toward a doctorate at Columbia University and making a living through writing jobs. He had already written an operetta with Hoschna that was never produced. Three Hauerbach-Hoschna songs did much to keep *Three Twins* going for 255 performances, making it 1908's biggest musical hit: "The Little Girl Up There," "The Yama Yama Man," which made a star out of Bessie McCoy and won her Richard Harding Davis as a husband, and "Cuddle Up a Little Closer, Lovey Mine." The last had been written earlier for a vaudeville performer who failed to pay the $100 promised. It was sung in *Three Twins* as a pretty love song, and won a vast record and sheet-music public when done as a ragtime song in black dialect.

Isidore Witmark sold the work of this brilliant new writing team to the producers of three operettas in 1910. Two foundered almost at once, but the third, *Madame Sherry,* for which Hauerbach wrote both lyrics and book, ran for 231 performances, longer than another masterpiece produced that season, *Naughty Marietta.* Dancing in many styles had become standard on stage, and Hoschna provided *Madame Sherry*'s chorines with outstanding music in his "polka français" to Hauerbach's "Every Little Movement Has a Meaning All Its Own," which was repeated throughout the evening. It became one of the following year's best-selling songs after the Theatrical Syndicate took the production to almost every city in the nation. Despite their success, writer and composer found it impossible to keep out interpolated songs. However, the production benefited from "Put Your Arms Around Me, Honey," which young Albert von Tilzer, its writer and publisher, persuaded one of the featured players to boost.

Hoschna's last complete score, his tenth, written for *The Girl of My Dreams,* which had been touring for more than a year before it opened in New York in 1911, provided at least two hits but failed to stay on Broadway for more than a month. Hoschna was dead by the end of the year, but the two hit songs, "Doctor Tinkle Tinker" and "Every Girlie Loves Me but the Girl of My Dreams," were heard everywhere. The following year, Hauerbach collaborated with another Middle European, Rudolf Friml, on one of the few early twentieth century's great operettas, *The Firefly.*

Having built up a respectable fortune from his ragtime hits, which had made him one of Tin Pan Alley's most important publishers, F. A. Mills saw great opportunities on Broadway. Although all the important stage composers were connected with the Witmarks, that independent-minded vaudevillian George M. Cohan, determined to conquer the musical theater, refused to do business with them. He was still rankled over past dealings with the Witmarks when he was fifteen, in 1893, and had sold a song for ten dollars and royalties. When it appeared in print, editing had given it a professional quality, but the comic vaudeville routine he and his family had been successfully singing on tour was now a sentimental ballad of the kind he parodied. His parents had taken him on stage at the age of four months, so he was the product of a medium now becoming a major component of the entertainment business. He had been given some elementary music lessons by a pit-band violinist, but he never used more than four or five notes, always in a major key, in the songs he wrote from the age of ten until shortly before World War II. He sold "I Guess I'll Have to Telegraph My Baby" to one of the Witmarks' lesser competitors, and laughed when it edged out some top Witmark tunes. He also began to write parodies and patter songs to order for other vaudeville performers, using his facility with words and his few notes. When the ragtime and coon-song craze proved successful, he became one of the most prolific writers in that idiom.

Inspired chiefly by Ned Harrigan's human comedies, peopled with familiar types and with ballads and topical songs that gave voice to what audiences felt, Cohan, in 1901, elaborated on a sketch the Four Cohans had been using in vaudeville and created *The Governor's Son,* a play with more than a dozen of the brash, toe-tapping songs that became standard Cohan fare. It ran in a small downtown New York theater before Cohan took it on the road for a long and successful run. He followed the same formula again, with similar success, two years later, and was ready to test Broadway audiences with a self-starring vehicle in 1904. F. A. Mills was now his publisher, and the cough-drop salesman who was also managing a professional prize fighter, Sam Harris, entered his life at this point. In time, he became co-producer of all Cohan shows and by 1911 was the owner, with Cohan, of seven theaters, two in Chicago and five in New York. When the 26-year-old Cohan went to see Abe Erlanger with one act of a play he had dashed off at top speed—as he always did, with both words and music—the theater-owner agreed to participate in financing *Little Johnny Jones,* a play with music. Coming at a time when contrived European-influenced operettas and British musical comedies ruled the theater, the down-to-earth, truly vernacular dialogue and the show-stopping songs of this production found a responding streak in the audience, one Cohan carved out for his own. "Give My Regards to Broadway" and "I'm a Yankee Doodle Dandy," from *Little Johnny Jones,* gave Mills smash hits on the order of his own "At a Georgia Camp Meeting."

When Erlanger asked Cohan whether he could write a play without a flag, the response was that he could write one without anything but a pencil, and he did: *Forty-five Minutes from Broadway,* his first work without a role for any of his family. Written within a few weeks, this ordinary show about ordinary people recouped the $10,000 spent to mount it within a few days and kept adding money to Cohan's account for years from road tours and revivals. So, too, did three of its songs, "Mary's a Grand Old Name," "Forty-five Minutes from Broadway," and "So Long, Mary."

Cohan's next production, *George Washington, Jr.* (1906), was inspired by a Civil War veteran who had held a folded American flag in his hands during a funeral the actor attended. As he talked to Cohan about the past and his experiences in the war, he stroked the flag, calling it a "grand old rag," and before Cohan returned to his apartment the melody and much of the lyric was composed. The challenge then was to write a patriotic play suitable to the sentiments the song roused. It was exactly that way of working that brought him negative criticism. *Life* once disparagingly described his work as "mainly consisting of several bars of well-known patriotic or sentimental songs strung together with connecting links of lively and more or less original musical trash. The words fitted to these curious contraptions are of the kind of unmetrical stuff that children compose and call poetry.'' Typically, Cohan responded, in part, in a paid advertisement, ''I write my own songs because I write better songs than anyone else I know of. I publish these songs because they bring greater royalties than any other class of music sold in this country. . . .'' Americans evidently agreed with him, and they showed it on the road for *George Washington, Jr.* They bought more than one million copies of ''You're a Grand Old Flag,'' in which Cohan had replaced the word *rag* after protests from veterans and patriotic groups. Congress gave him a medal for it and for his World War I hit ''Over There,'' the first such honor ever awarded to an American songwriter. The 1908 *Fifty Miles from Boston* produced Cohan's last great musical-theater song, ''Harrigan,'' a heartfelt tribute to the man who had inspired him to write for the legitimate stage, Edward ''Ned'' Harrigan.

At a testimonial dinner given by all elements of the Broadway theater for Cohan, the actor-songwriter and producer of six hits running on Broadway and concurrently on tour in 1910, his friend Marc Klaw pointed out that Cohan represented

the spirit and energy of the twentieth century—a concentrated essence, four-cylinder power—a protest against and apology for the elimination of the palmy days of the drama. Who would want to go back to the *Uncle Tom's Cabin* days when the scene in the last act with gates ajar and the red fire burning was a fine representation of hell with a label ''Heaven'' on it, when you can get Georgie Cohan, with banners flying, drums playing and fifes blowing to the merry tune of ''The Grand Old Flag'' or ''Yankee Doodle Dandy?'' . . . This youngster struck a universal chord in his songs and plays, and that is why we know and love him.

Only George M. Cohan could, at this dinner, get the Shuberts and Marc Klaw together. The battle between the Syndicate and the upstart immigrants had grown hotter after the success of the latter's *Chinese Honeymoon.* The tide of fortune generally went with Klaw and Erlanger, but there were occasional victories for the three brothers. Their *Fantana* (1905) sprang from Sam Shubert's suggestion to Harry Smith for a musical extravaganza. When the script was completed, Shubert called in young Chicagoan Raymond Hubbell, who had already provided the brothers' second successful musical, *The Runaways.* It had filled the Casino Theatre in New York for 167 performances, following a full year in Chicago, and was now beginning what became a five-year run on tour. Barely twenty-one when he wrote it, Hubbell had worked for Charles Harris as a staff arranger and music editor, and then moved to New York on the basis of *The Runaways'* success. The Shuberts spent $75,000 on *Fantana* before it began a 298-performance stay in New York, and ensured its success by inserting the Witmarks' newest popular-song candidate for boosting, ''Tammany,'' another of the ''Indian novelties'' popular in the early twentieth century. Never a distinguished composer, Hubbell was a profit maker and consequently a favorite with the brothers, who produced many of the thirty musical comedies and revues he wrote before 1930.

In July 1905, the Shuberts acquired considerable financial backing from a group of Cincinnati financiers and politicians and broke the contract with Klaw and Erlanger, under which they had been granted access to Syndicate theaters in return for twenty-five percent of the profits from all productions playing in them. It was the first time in theatrical history that show business had gone to big business for funds, and an economic war between the two theater-owning factions followed. Two years after Sam Shubert's death, in 1905, his brothers had put together a circuit of fifty-nine theaters, in the largest American cities— not a great number in contrast to the Syndicate's several hundred, but one to which they could send out productions for a forty-week season. A temporary truce took place that year with the formation by Klaw and Erlanger in partnership with the Shuberts of a combined advanced vaudeville "world theater trust," which was to control theaters not only in America but also in England, France, Germany, and Austria. When this illegal combination in restraint of trade on an international level collapsed of its own weight, the battle between an established monopoly and one in process of maturation resumed.

The bankers' panic of 1907 was due to currency difficulties that had troubled the American economy since the inflationary excess of Civil War financing. It had many repercussions, not the least of which was a need for entertainment cheaper than the legitimate theater. An increasing number of theaters around the country, particularly the popular-priced houses, therefore, began to convert to vaudeville. There had already been a decline in the number of companies traveling on the road, and it continued at a greater rate over the next decade.

Klaw and Erlanger, however, had a major asset: performance rights for a new operetta, *The Merry Widow,* that was a great success all over Europe. Colonel Henry W. Savage, a producer associated with the Syndicate, had seen Franz Lehar's hit in Vienna—where its lovely music was performed nightly by the composer's concert band—and had bought the rights to an English-language version published by Chappell. The failure of any New York producer during the past seven years successfully to revive any of those once-popular Viennese operettas, as well as the increasing Americanization of those by the current generation of European-born Americans, seemed to be a clear indication that theater audiences had lost their taste for the medium. Yet Savage had been heartened by the great success a few months earlier of the London production and so embarked on a major promotion campaign. Almost immediately after its opening, a few days before the failure of a New York bank heralded the panic of 1907, *The Merry Widow* was a national phenomenon. Its songs—"I Love You So," "I'm Happy at Maxim's," and "Vilia"—were heard everywhere and appeared not only in editions issued by Chappell's New York branch, but also in pirated copies based on the original Austro-Hungarian publication, whose copyright status was questionable. Within a year, there had been more than 5,000 performances in the United States. Cylinders, phonograph records, and piano rolls of the songs sold in great quantities. The waltz danced by the Merry Widow and her blue-blooded lover was changing the character of stage dancing, from that by regimented masses a more personal kind, and it created a revolution in popular dance styles that had been dominated by the jerky movements of the military two-step and the raggy cakewalk promenade.

Savage's success sent other producers and American representatives of European publishers scrambling off to Europe in search of equally profitable Viennese-waltz operas. Only two by Oscar Straus and Leo Fall's *The Dollar Princess* (1909) approached the popularity of Lehar's triumphant musical piece. Not related to the Strauss family (he used only one *s* in his name), Oscar Straus was a native of Vienna, where Lehar now occupied the place of honor long reserved by that city for the two Johann Strausses. Leader of the orchestra and composer at the most fashionable cabaret, where his burlesques, parodies, and light operas were first performed, Straus became the object of spirited bidding by American producers following the great popularity of *A Waltz Dream* (1908) and *The Chocolate Soldier* (1909), the latter based on George Bernard Shaw's sardonic *Arms and the Man*. In it, *The Merry Widow* waltz found a new rival, "My Hero," which became a show-stopping hit on Broadway and the road for many years.

The flimsy romantic plots of these waltz operas provided a welcome relief from the stresses of the third great financial crisis in a generation, and so, too, did the glamorized leg-and-vaudeville spectacles that Straus preferred to label "revue" and that Florenz Ziegfeld, Jr., introduced to New York in 1907. The latter had gotten his start in the entertainment world during the Chicago World's Fair of 1893, for which his father, a Chicago music educator, served as director of music. Displaying the world's strongest man in flesh-colored shorts, young Ziegfeld cleared $5,000 a week at a Chicago food-and-entertainment theater. He followed that financial triumph with a series of vehicles tailored to the special talents of his new wife, Anna Held, suggesting racy European wickedness even in the songs he selected for her to sing, "Won't You Come and Play Wiz Me?" and "I Can't Make My Eyes Behave." When Held appeared at Koster and Bial's in 1898, Ziegfeld had one of her backdrop curtains painted to duplicate the professional copy of a Witmark song, "I Wants Dem Presents Back." Each note of the melody line was a large cutout through which the head of a young black boy poked out on cue as Held sang. The Witmarks had no great expectations for this coon song's success, but Held made it a rage almost overnight.

Ziegfeld's formula remained constant: a New York run and then on the road until summer, when the couple went to Paris for rest and to create their next sexy farce. The public was titillated by the sight of the splendid Held legs on theatrical posters and in publicity pictures, and by newspaper accounts of the milk-filled tub in which she bathed and sometimes met the press. Having learned that occasional glimpses of various portions of the Held anatomy created a viable box-office commodity, Ziegfeld compounded the effect in 1906 by glorifying the girls who served as chorines in his productions. House records were broken when an increasing number of the handsome young ladies he selected displayed legs, arms, and shoulders with stage magic that sometimes made them appear nude, paraded in superb costumes that did not neglect to feature surprising décolletage, and in general transported the wickedness of the Folies-Bergère to Broadway.

Aware of Ziegfeld's generally difficult financial position and knowing the exact amount of ticket-sale revenue, because he was generating it in their theaters, Klaw and Erlanger offered to finance a New York version of Paris's Folies and to pay him $200 a week to produce it on the roof of their New York Theatre. Ziegfeld spend $13,000 for the *Follies of 1907,* a large production budget for the time, with weekly costs of $4,000, half going to the featured star of the show. There were fifty bosomy Anna Held Girls (though she did not appear in the production), who danced, marched, drummed, and bathed onstage in a large pool. The wickedly naughty Salome dance, with which Mary Garden was scandalizing audiences at the Metropolitan Opera House, was parodied, as were Theodore Roosevelt, John D. Rockefeller, and other political and financial figures in the true revue's obligatory sketches. *Variety* correctly reviewed the *Follies* as "vaudeville entertainment," because of its succession of variety turns, skits, dancing, and songs. Following a run out of New York, where it made $120,000, the *Follies* returned to Broadway. To get people to come back, Ziegfeld regularly changed leading performers, skits, and interpolated new popular songs. Nora Bayes boosted "Budweiser's a Friend of Mine" and the Jean Schwartz–William Jerome "Handle Me with Care" for half the run, and vaudeville's Gibson Bathing Girls played for a week. Marc Klaw was ready to try the same thing the following summer, once again in a rooftop theater, with no air conditioning and only a canopy to keep off rain. The appeal of stars singing popular songs, glorified girls, and the revue format packed theaters for more than two decades. The *Ziegfeld Follies* are remembered today, however, mostly for their songs and those who played and sang them— Fanny Brice, Bert Williams, Eddie Cantor, Van and Schenck, Paul Whiteman, Ruth Etting, and Helen Morgan.

The musical-theater business over which Ziegfeld, George M. Cohan, Victor Herbert, Klaw and Erlanger, and the Shubert Brothers ruled in 1910 had seen many changes in a decade. Among the 408 Broadway and traveling groups announced in 1900, there had been eighteen musical-comedy and comic-opera companies. Fifteen original musical productions by composers residing or born in America were presented, and those comprised about one fourth of all offerings in New York in the 1899–1900 season. Despite Herbert's triumph with *Naughty Marietta* and the long-running *Florodora, Fantana,* and Luder's *Prince of Pilsen,* almost all musical shows made their profits on the road, where the Theatrical Syndicate dictated what would be shown. There, sold-out houses were the rule when *The Merry Widow, The Chocolate Soldier,* and *The Dollar Princess* were put on. The black musical theater had come and then had moved uptown to New York's Harlem. The old-formula comic operettas appeared to have had their day, though occasionally one would surface and soon disappear for the road, where people were less sophisticated. For the first time, the American public had a reasonably permanent souvenir of some of the music and songs from presentations it had taken to its heart, by means of player-piano music rolls and phonograph recordings and cylinders.

And there was vaudeville.

Vaudeville and Popular Music

Joseph K. Emmet, in his "Fritz" shows, Ned Harrigan and David Braham, with their string of Harrigan and Hart plays with music, Tony Pastor, and all their imitators had been proving for many years that the common man's "common music" could pack theaters. It was a lesson that the originators of "clean" vaudeville learned quickly. Sometime around 1887, a few theater owners in New York and other large cities followed Tony Pastor's example and adopted a "family policy." The most popular places of wide-open mass entertainment, however, continued to be the men-only theaters, dime museums, and concert saloons, where amiable feminine companionship was never absent and blunt earthy songs could always be heard. Pastor's chief competition for the New York family trade—the glorified concert saloon operated by the women's haberdashers Koster and Bial, which was packed nightly by couples and families who came to eat, drink, and watch a high-class variety program that usually also featured imported artists—had originally been a free-and-easy hangout for prostitutes. In its small Cork Room, just off the Concert Hall, where only champagne was sold and each cork was nailed to the walls or ceiling, men came to mingle with the cancan chorus and the stars, found there after each performance. The room also became a regular stop for music publishers.

Koster and Bial's and a few similar places around the nation had excellent orchestras. Pastor's Music Hall had one of admitted poor quality, and, around the country, places where variety entertainment was provided usually had only a pianist. Occasionally a drummer was added to create special sound effects. When singers and dancers needed, and demanded it, an orchestra of piano, clarinet, cornet, trombone, string bass, drums, and sometimes other instruments, directed by a violinist, became a feature of many large halls.

Two New Englanders, Benjamin Franklin Keith and Edward Franklin Albee, were the first showmen outside New York City to adopt a policy of continuous family variety entertainment. In July 1885, having accumulated sufficient capital from a pirated *Mikado,* which was so successful that a road company was sent out, Keith and Albee offered continuous vaudeville from 10:00 A.M. to 11:00 P.M.; admission was ten cents, with a chair available for five cents more, prices soon raised to twenty cents for both. Mrs. Keith was on hand to make certain that any performer who indulged in such profanity on stage as "slob" or "son of a gun" was immediately discharged. Keith and Albee expanded their holdings with theaters in Providence, Philadelphia, and, finally, New York in 1893, where they bought the Union Square Theatre, in the middle of what long had been Pastor's exclusive domain.

The center of New York's entertainment business had already moved uptown once more, to an area north of Madison Square Garden and above 34th Street.

Gilbert and Sullivan were among the first to open up this district when their comic operas played in a theater at Herald Square. The new Madison Square Garden occupied an entire block and was larger than any European amphitheater. Across the street from the Metropolitan Opera House at 39th Street and Broadway was the new Casino Theatre, home of light opera and the famous "Casino girls," symbolized by Lillian Russell and predecessors of Ziegfeld's glamorous girls. Koster and Bial were persuaded by the impresario Oscar Hammerstein to lease space in his new Manhattan Opera House on 34th Street and Broadway for a music hall, and there their higher-class vaudeville at advanced prices continued to attract the city's families, for a few more years. As ever, the music publishers followed the move uptown, to 28th Street near Sixth Avenue, soon to be known as "Tin Pan Alley."

Political tension and a failing economy once again dealt the theater and the music business a serious blow. The collapse of a vast London financial house and the issuance of silver coinage, which had been reduced by half its value in less than twenty years, brought on the worst depression yet in American history. Lasting from 1893 to 1896, it put theatrical and variety entertainment out of the reach of the average American. The majority looked for cheaper amusements, and vaudeville provided it for them in an increasing number of theaters. Ironically, seeking to compete with vaudeville, Koster and Bial offered a program of fourteen short Edison motion pictures, the first presence in a modern theater of the medium that would destroy the business in the next three decades.

Modern vaudeville began in January 1893 when F. F. Proctor, owner of a church converted to a theater, inaugurated continuous vaudeville in New York. The city was flooded with advertising suggesting "After Breakfast Go to Proctor's, After Proctor's Go to Bed." Beginning each day except Sunday with a "milkman's matinee" and closing with a "supper show," Proctor built up a family trade for inexpensive vaudeville. To cut costs as times grew worse, he presented top-billed entertainers only at the evening show and cut the music to a piano only. Other managers did the same. Tony Pastor resisted continuous vaudeville for nearly three years, maintained his price of one dollar for reserved seats (no longer available at his competitors' houses), got rid of the acting company and all afterpieces and musical burlesques, and began to feature single "singing women." Others followed suit. Hammerstein announced that he would pay $3,000 a week for the popular French singer Yvonne Gilbert. Ziegfeld built his spectacular productions around Anna Held. Among the imported singing stars were Vesta Tilley, Marie and Alice Lloyd, and Cissie Loftus, but there was a crop of American singers who gave them excellent competition in the struggle for vaudeville audiences' favor: Lottie Gilson, who introduced the "singer in the gallery," a young boy who sang with her; Maggie Cline, who made "Throw 'Em, Down, McCluskey" a best seller for Frank Harding; Bonnie Thornton, the wife of songwriter Jim Thornton and the best booster of "She May Have Seen Better Days," "My Sweetheart's the Man in the Moon," and "When You Were Sweet 16"; Maude Nugent and her "Sweet Rosie O'Grady"; the female baritone Helene Mora, who popularized "Comrades," "Kathleen," and "Those Wedding Bells Shall Not Ring Out"; the Bowery Girl, Annie

Hart, of "Who Threw the Overalls in Mrs. Murphy's Chowder" fame; Emma Carus; May and Flo, the Irwin Sisters; and a hundred other coon shouters, soubrettes, comediennes, song-and-dance ladies, Irish singers, female baritones, Bowery Brunhildes, and singers bound inextricably to songs they made famous, all of them now, alas, forgotten.

The new music publishers were backstage regulars at the vaudeville houses. The Witmarks; Ed Marks and Joe Stern; Tom Harms; Leo Feist; Charles K. Harris; F. A. Mills, publisher of ragtime and cakewalk hits; Pat Howley and Fred Haviland; Spaulding and Kordner, for whom young George Cohan was Americanizing the English popular songs they had acquired. They made fifty or sixty visits a week to pass around copies of their newest songs, buy champagne or beer, give out cigars, recommend tailors—in short, do everything they could to boost their newest publications. The objects of their attention were, in addition to the women singers, comedy pianists, sweet singers, Negro delineators, baritones, tenors, bassi profundi, whistlers, balladeers, song-and-dancemen, countertenors, female impersonators, duos, and quartets.

As the importance of the variety artists in making songs into hits became obvious to them, the cost of boosting began to rise above the price of such good-will entertainment as a drink, a cigar, a dinner, a friendship. Musical-theater performers had already learned that publishers would pay large sums and a share of royalties to promote music, and now it was the vaudeville performers' turn. The songwriter L. Wolfe Gilbert, a self-proclaimed "dean of Tin Pan Alley," insisted that it was a Chicago music publisher, Will Rossiter, who instituted the practice of giving theatrical trunks and rings, paying for gowns and hotel bills, buying advertisements in theatrical papers, and all the other forms of paying for play that became known as "payola." If Rossiter *was* the father of payola, it came late in the 1890s, after national vaudeville circuits had been created, and years after most music publishers were emulating the "royalty ballad" payments created by London music publisher Boosey.

By 1899, Americans of all classes were getting a lot of entertainment for their money in the sixty-seven vaudeville theaters. The four Keith houses alone entertained more than five million people a year and employed 3,500 actors; the annual payroll was half a million dollars. Vaudeville artists may have offended the taste of sophisticated Americans, but they rarely offended their sense of decency. Male attire was forbidden to female performers, blunt language could bring instant dismissal, and a high plane of respectability and moral cleanliness was demanded in each performer's contract. Women and children were not the majority of audiences, but they regarded the first-class houses as the only place of public entertainment in which they considered themselves safe.

The absence in the theater pit of any musical instrument other than a piano surprised most stage performers when they first played in vaudeville. The rise of ragtime songs and music, however, had made it more acceptable. Two pianists worked five hours each a day, except on Sundays, when blue laws were in operation, and they appeared to know every piece of popular music ever written. Monday mornings were hectic in vaudeville houses, for they were rehearsal periods, during which each act's musical selections were established as pianist and performers fixed the final routines. Because selections were not yet used more than once on a program, every singing performer, and, if they had one, personal accompanist attempted to get as early a place on the rehearsal schedule as possible, in order to lay claim to specific songs they had been paid to boost. Stage doormen were bribed to swear who had arrived first, the backstage crew was overtipped, pianists were paid off—all to establish proprietary rights to songs. In large cities, publishers' local representatives smoothed the way for stars, took them to dinner, paid for wine and bribes, and made certain that the local press would be out in force and write good reviews.

Women singers, in particular, had added supporting players and stage props to their acts: a singer in the gallery, a talented whistler in the balcony, a bald-headed man near the stage to whom they could direct a love song, a group of ''picks''—talented black (and later white) child dancers and singers to feature in the act's finale—expensive lamps to be plugged into an electrical outlet near the accompanist's piano, lavish furs, stunning clothing ''directly from Paree,'' stage sets and jewelry, most of it paid for by publishers, particularly when the performer was a national personality who ''headlined'' the show.

During the 1890s, most performers secured engagements through the services of individual agents, ''bookers,'' who received 10 percent in return and worked for the artist in negotiations with vaudeville managers. Having observed the success of the Theatrical Syndicate and hoping similarly to centralize all booking and control salaries, a group of vaudeville managers representing the majority of the variety houses organized the Vaudeville Managers Association in 1900. Under the association's aegis, a satellite organization, later the United Booking Office, guaranteed a longer work year to performers who cooperated with the VMA, soon dominated by Keith and Albee. Despite an aborted strike by a protesting group of performers, the White Rats (Star spelled backward), VMA's power grew, and profits increased for its affiliated member theaters. Performers, however, continued to suffer economic abuse. A blacklist of variety artists who spoke out against UBO's excesses was established. As a result, performers grew more reluctant to fight the system, which was exacting as much as a twenty percent commission from them.

Among the independent bookers who had been barred because of UBO's near monopoly was William Morris, a semiliterate Austrian immigrant in his late twenties. His best clients were often non-VMA theater owners looking for variety artists, and he supplied them with talent despite continued efforts to put him out of business. Morris, a highly talented showman himself, became the most successful independent booker in New York, and under his guidance prosperous competition with the monopoly developed. In one instance, his suggestion that an orchestra take the place of the pianist resulted in a regularly packed vaudeville house directly next to the Keith-Albee flagship theater in Boston. The result was the return of large groups of musicians to the orchestra pit of every major vaudeville theater in America. This meant that singing performers had to furnish their own musical arrangements, though this was soon underwritten for major stars by music publishers.

When economic depression began to affect legitimate-theater ticket sales in late 1906, Klaw and Erlanger joined the Shubert brothers in the United States Amusement Company, created to build and operate a national circuit of all-star vaudeville theaters. With millions evidently at his disposal, Abe Erlanger hired William Morris to be principal booker, with a million-dollar five-year contract. Despite word from VMA that any artist who went with Morris would be black-listed for life by the UBO, Morris was able to sign seventy-five headline acts, for a million dollars.

Many stage and vaudeville performers had noted the advances being made by organized skilled workers and their craft unions and began to work for similar gains. Among the first such undertakings was one by black artists. With Bert Williams, George Walker, Bob Cole, and Rosamund Johnson as leaders, an all-Negro actors group was formed, its membership coming from the 270 black principal performers and more than 1,000 other professional black artists. An action resulted in a 33⅓ percent increase for vaudeville musicians, who were receiving only two dollars a performance. The White Rats organization was revived and, as the Associated Artists of America, eventually received a charter from the American Federation of Labor. In 1911, with secret backing from Albee, a countergroup, the National Vaudeville Artists, was formed, in which membership as well as resignation from the White Rats was required before a UBO booking was possible. This spirit of opposition to managerial practices helped. Morris was still able to buy talent, though he had to pay more; talent costs for a Morris presentation neared $10,000 a week, whereas Albee spent less than half that. In the first of his twenty-five tours of the United States, the Scottish singer Harry Lauder proved to be a major attraction in Klaw and Erlanger's "advanced vaudeville" theaters. A former mill boy and coal miner, Lauder was England's highest-paid performer when Morris signed him in 1907 for $3,500 a week and got packed houses in return. The British pho-nograph industry had already recognized Lauder's appeal in 1902, and after Thomas Edison heard him, the kilted ballad singer recorded a dozen of his highland songs for Edison. Another attraction with whom Morris drew audi-ences away from the Albee houses was Annette Kellerman, whose diving, swimming, and posing in flesh-colored one-piece bathing suits were evidence of how far family vaudeville had swerved from Mrs. Keith's censorship. Heavy competition and changing public morality, owning to the melting-pot American national character were indeed making "indigo" musical and theatrical mate-rial palatable to both management and mass audiences.

Then almost overnight Albee's competition disappeared. After secret nego-tiations, in return for $250,000 in cash and the assumption of $1.5 million in talent contracts signed for Klaw and Erlanger theaters by William Morris, the masters of the United States Amusement Company agreed to stay out of the vaudeville business for ten years. In a letter signed by Albee, the members of the Associated Artists of America were assured that there was no blacklist and they were urged to forget all old scores. Morris, however, as unrelenting as ever in his hatred of Albee, rejected an offer of $50,000 a year to become chief booker for UBO. Instead, he opened a new management company, with Harry Lauder as his main attraction.

With Klaw and Erlanger and the Shuberts disposed of, Albee went back to gobbling up any competition. He expressed only disdain for the new kind of show business evolving from penny arcades, small-time variety houses, and moving-picture nickelodeons. But less affluent white urban Americans and their immigrant neighbors were making the business profitable, as they pressed millions of five-cent pieces into the palms of small-time entrepreneurs.

Long before several hundred of the 5,000 nickelodeons in the United States in 1907 were opened in New York City, music publishers had been playing a role in the development of the American motion-picture industry. Anyone could go into business. A seventy-five-dollar Edison Kinetoscope could be rented for a few dollars, films of from 100 to 1,400 feet in length, costing ten cents a foot, could be leased, vacant stores were readily available, and illustrated song slides were free for the asking from music publishers seeking to get the widest possible audience for their music. Initially, a pianist provided all the music during the half-hour performance, but, as in vaudeville, competition forced the addition of drums or a violin, until finally a five-piece orchestra was usually ensconsed just below the screen. For variety and to lessen rumored eyestrain, live entertainment was added, more than one illustrated song was programed, and the length of each show and its price were increased. Often the performers were hired to clear the house of people who wanted to stay for another show, but very quickly movie-theater owners learned that a first-class "pic-vaude" combination made money, so by 1907 two million people, one third of them children, were going to the movies every day. Within two years, movie-only theaters were closing their doors because of competition from 2,000 small combination houses around the country. The business had become so vast that the Motion Picture Patents Company was formed, a trust that leased 5,000 movie projectors and rented about 2,000 reels a week. Both the vaudeville-only and the pic-vaude houses were taking a large bite out of the $850 million spent on personal entertainment in 1909, most of it going to the variety impresarios. In 1906, Keith had merged with F. F. Proctor and thus got control of six theaters in New York with a capitalization of eight million. Four years later, Keith's chain in that city had a total capacity of nearly 10,000 seats for each performance. An estimated million New Yorkers were going to large and small vaudeville houses each week and spending nearly a half-million dollars for admission.

Vaudeville had already created its own millionaire barons, the four owners of important circuits around the nation: Keith, now so wealthy he was leaving most management decisions to Albee; S. Z. Poli, a sculptor brought to New York to work in a waxworks who became the leading New England variety-house owner (his estate was valued at $30 million); the Californian Martin Beck, former German waiter, builder of the Palace Theatre on Broadway, who introduced fifteen-piece orchestras in 1909 and handed out printed programs; and Percy G. Williams, who began with a medicine show after the Civil War, built one of New York's first boardwalks, and sold his theaters to Albee in 1912 for around six million dollars, after having been a thorn in UBO's side for many years. The nickelodeons, too, had produced their first millionaire: Marcus Loew, a furrier who began with coin-slot phonographs and such "peek movies" as "In My Harem" and "Her Beauty Spot." He moved to ownership of an interstate nickelodeon circuit and began to present vaudeville in the group of quality theaters he was assembling. By the 1920s, he had built 125 deluxe vaudeville theaters; the crown jewel was his State Theatre, on Broadway and 45th Street, in New York City. The year before Loew died, at the age of fifty-seven, in 1927, Will Rogers called him the "Henry Ford of show business." When the Palace, two blocks north, began to charge three dollars for admission, Loew's State was bringing high-quality variety to the people for fifty cents a seat.

Vaudeville had not yet created any millionaires in the ranks of performers. In the years before World War I, singers of popular music began to climb to the head of each bill and became the industry's best earners. Harry Lauder was indisputably the highest-paid man in variety, earning at least $4,000 a week. In the same salary range were Lillian Russell; the comedy team of Weber and Fields, reunited for a brief time; Eva Tanguay, "the 'I Don't Care' Girl," a headliner wherever she appeared; Bert Williams, who had recently joined Ziegfeld in the first *Follies* and became the biggest of the big-timers; and the glamorous Gertrude Hoffman, wife of Max Hoffman, the music editor and composer of the Rogers brothers' shows. Touring with an orchestra of thirty musicians and a line of Hoffman Girls, who were the best dancers on any stage, she did imitations of a dozen single women headliners, among them, May Irwin, singer of "The Bully Song," "Mr. Johnson, Turn Me Loose," "When You Ain't Got No Money, Well You Needn't Come 'Round," and "I Couldn't Stand to See My Baby Lose." President Woodrow Wilson offered Irwin the post of secretary of laughter in his Cabinet after she gave up coon shouting for the legitimate stage. She left that for vaudeville, to tour in a one-act play, *Mrs. Peckham's Carouse,* which George Ade sold to her for $200. When she got bored, despite one of variety's highest weekly salaries, her sister Flo carried on in the role of an alcoholic housewife who never once moved from her chair. Another success was Vesta Victoria, a darling of London, whose brilliant singing portrayals of various character types combined satire with great sensitivity. She was the girl who "waited at the church," complained with sulky innuendo that daddy wouldn't buy her a bow-wow, made "Poor John," who took her to see his mother before he asked for her hand in marriage, a song that became so popular that the great Yvette Guilbert got permission to sing it on her first appearance in the United States in order to prove that even a French cabaret singer knew America's favorite music.

Because of long-held nationalistic antipathy to the British on the part of average Americans, it took doing, but by the late 1890s American vaudeville audiences were cheering English music-hall performers. The great success of songs from London had smoothed the way for Felix McGlennon's "Comrades," "Actions Speak Louder Than Words," "Mr. Captain, Stop the Ship," and, especially, "And Her Golden Hair Was Hanging Down Her Back," which Monroe Rosenfeld, an American newspaperman and songwriter, "produced," or, more properly, merely copyrighted because of the quirk in American law; "Tell Me, Pretty Maiden," and indeed the entire score of Leslie Stuart's *Florodora;* Harry Dacre's "Playmates," "On a Bicycle Built for Two," "Sweet

Katie O'Connor," and "Elsie From Chelsea"; and many other British music-hall songs.

One of the best and best-paid British performers in America was Albert Chevalier, a singing Cockney comedian in costermonger's "pearly" garb, whose songs, many of which he wrote—"In the Old Kent Road," " 'E Can't Get a Roise Out of Me," and "My Old Dutch," a tribute to his wife—brought tears and laughter. Vesta Tilley made Felix McGlennon's "Daughters" an international hit before she came to New York City after many years on the London stage and in its music halls. Dressed in elegantly immaculate men's formal evening dress, or as a Bow Street Bobbie, one of Her Majesty's sailors, or smoking a cigar, Tilley was one of the best male impersonators in singing "Burlington Bertie," "There's a Girl Wanted There," and "Following in Father's Footsteps." Alice Lloyd, sister of the great Marie Lloyd, who could never capture audiences in America as she had done in England because of her bluntly indigo material, was one of the first performers to copyright a bit of stage business: the use of a mirror to reflect a spotlight onto bald heads in the audience as she sang "Won't You Come and Splash Me" or "Be Good, Be Good, My Father Said."

American vaudeville artists relied for their music on Tin Pan Alley's products, not only because music publishers paid them to do so but also because audiences responded best to the syncopation and raggy rhythms of the new songs. Among those who were being paid $1,500 a week or more was Blanche Ring, whose vaudeville act was made up almost entirely of the songs she had made hits: "Bedelia," which sold three and a half million copies after she interpolated it into one of Reginald De Koven's failures, *The Jersey Lily* (1903); "I've Got Rings on My Fingers"; "Yip-I-Addy-I-Ay," introduced by her in *The Merry Widow Burlesque* (1908); "In the Good Old Summer Time," first rejected by music publishers because "seasonal" songs had a limited life; "The Belle of Avenue A," introduced in *Tommy Rot* (1902); and one of the earliest airplane songs, "Come Josephine in My Flying Machine." Another well-paid performer, and one of the best "hoofers" in vaudeville, was Eddie Leonard, writer of "Ida Sweet as Apple Cider," which saved his job with the Primrose and West minstrels when he introduced it in 1902; "Roll Dem Roly Boly Eyes," which he shared with Blanche Ring; "Mandy Won't You Let Me Be Your Beau," and "Dreamy Eyes." Leonard was featured, in blackface, in the racially integrated *The Southerners* (1904), which had music by Will Marion Cook, and was a popularizer of Johnson and Cole's "Li'l Gal," from *The Shoo-Fly Regiment* (1907), and black songwriter Shep Edmonds's "I'm Gonna Live Anyhow Till I Die." Jim McIntyre and George Heath, starting in 1874 and becoming the greatest and best paid of the blackface comedy teams, were the first white men to dance the buck and wing on stage. They were important popularizers of coon songs, particularly "Alexander, Don't You Love Your Baby Any More?," which Andrew Sterling and Harry von Tilzer wrote for them, in turn inspiring Irving Berlin's "Alexander and His Clarinet." Emma Carus, another vaudeville headliner, born in Germany but a great American coon shouter, introduced Berlin's revision of "Alexander," the great 1912 success "Alexander's Ragtime Band."

The queen of singing women stars for many years was Nora Bayes, born Dora Goldberg, who appeared for a time with the second of her five husbands, Jack Norworth, her collaborator on "Shine on Harvest Moon." They introduced it in Ziegfeld's *Follies of 1908,* to such nightly applause that Ziegfeld brought it down from the New York Theatre Roof for his production later that year of *Miss Innocence,* starring Anna Held, Bayes, and Lillian Lorraine. When a plump, ungainly, but talented young blackface singer stopped the show each night with "Moving Day in Jungle Town," a coon song inspired by Theodore Roosevelt's recent hunting trip in Africa, Bayes ordered that the singer be fired. Because she was a star of the first magnitude, Ziegfeld consented, and so, Sophie Tucker was out of her first Broadway show. When Ziegfeld asked her to wear tights, Bayes left, in order to preserve her image as a lady of style and taste.

Nora Bayes first became known to the public in 1902, as the "Wurtzburger girl," after she introduced Harry von Tilzer's "Down Where the Wurzburger Flows" in a vaudeville theater in Brooklyn and continued to boost it steadily for the songwriter-publisher. It was the first of many songs she made popular: "Come Along My Mandy," an English music-hall coon song; an Americanized version of the British "Has Anybody Here Seen Kelly?"; "Mister Moon Man"; "Apple Blossom Time in Normandy"; "Over There," which she featured soon after George M. Cohan introduced it in a show for troops (it sold 400,000 copies of sheet music during 1917 alone, some two million by the end of 1918); and "The Japanese Sandman" in 1920, when jazz-inflected popular music was beginning to appear, with which Bayes was never truly comfortable. But loyal fans continued to come to see the "best popular singer" until her death, in 1928. By then, almost all the great song stylists of the early big time were gone, those possessors of clear enunciation, clear voices, and dramatic ability, all later considered old-fashioned. But Sophie Tucker was thriving, "the last of the red hot mamas," as she was known until her death, in the television age that dealt the final death blow to vaudeville.

CHAPTER 11

Popular Music in the Age of Gigantism 1866–1909

The growth of industry that made the United States a major international giant by the end of the century had started before the War of 1812, when European powers, particularly France and Great Britain, put great economic pressure on America's foreign commerce. The construction of factories brought about by the cutting off of European products increased gradually and doubled by 1859; it was then speeded up by the War Between the States. The production of munitions, food, and textiles for both the military and civilians, as well as the transportation needed to distribute them, increased in proportion. Manufacturing had almost tripled since 1820, and the output doubled again by the end of the century. Workers in factories grew from 400,000 to five million in the same period.

Commercial meat-packing, for example, a $30-million business in 1830, was the country's second largest in 1900, with an annual gross in excess of $800 million, the result of the growth of cities, where 10 million people lived in 1900. Immigration rose from about 5,000 a year in 1800 to more than a million a year after the depressed economy and epidemics in Italy, and racial restrictions, pograms, and massacres in Russia filled westbound steamships in the 1890s and early 1900s. This influx had been preceded by the arrival of 1.3 million Germans in the years 1840 to 1860 alone and more than a million Irish in the 1850s. These new Americans all played a role in shaping the nation's culture. Germans and western Europeans brought art music and the resources for music education. Eastern and southern Europeans found little opportunity for creative expression except in the growing business of popular entertainment. From them came not only stage performers of every caliber but also those who roamed city streets grinding out the newest popular song on a hand organ.

Track mileage linking centers of industry expanded sevenfold, to 200,000 miles in 1900. The value of manufactured products increased from $1.8 billion to more than $13 billion. Nine tenths of all wealth was in the hands of one tenth of the population, however, including those of 3,800 millionaires. Among these captains of finance were many who regarded themselves as trustees for their poorer brethren and distributed gifts to cultural, educational, and musical institutions. Henry Lee Higginson, of Boston, wanting the good music of German masters he had enjoyed during his student days in Vienna to be available to at least the better class of Americans, endowed the Boston Symphony Orchestra in 1881, with the promise that he would maintain it until the project was self-sustaining.

Andrew Carnegie, who thought that "the concentration of business . . . in the hands of the few . . . [was] not only beneficial but essential to the progress of the race," was one of the first businessmen to utilize the new industrial art of public relations, the development of favorable opinion toward such concentration. He established many philanthropies, and new capitalists followed his example, expecting to earn their own share of the public's regard. One of Carnegie's gifts was his Hall of Music in New York, which opened in 1891. It proved to be, among other things, the newest of the concert halls where American piano makers could demonstrate their most expensive products when they were played on by European virtuosos imported at great expense and high fees. Wealthy Americans learned, for example, through advertising in the pages of quality magazines, that Polish pianist Ignace Paderewski used only the Steinway, the "instrument of the immortals," and could purchase one for their family parlor, with the hope that some of his prowess was built into it.

Just prior to the Civil War, the piano business entered its golden age, which came to an end just before the Great Depression of the 1930s. This was the time when popular music was beginning to spread widely and rapidly, a process that usually began out of doors, especially for such best sellers as "The Battle Cry of Freedom," "Tenting on the Old Camp Ground," "The Battle Hymn of the Republic," and other rousing songs that built up enthusiasm on the home front for the bloody conflict. Professional singers and well-rehearsed choirs and instrumental groups introduced and sang them regularly. As they had during the lunchtime revivals, listeners joined enthusiastically in the refrains, singing from words distributed by employees of music publishers or local music retailers. Publishers cherished the long verses that developed these songs, during which the crowds were usually silent, for in order to learn them and their music people had to buy the published product.

Other kinds of popular music—love songs, ballads, and comedy pieces—generally were played in public in a theater or a concert saloon. There, singers were accompanied by a pianist, who pounded out the repeated pattern of "ump-pah" chords in four-four time, to which most songs were then set.

In 1866, $15 million was spent on pianos, meaning 25,000 new instruments in American homes. Most of these were American products, and served not only as a music maker but also as a symbol of a family's station, culturally and financially. Surrounded by loving family and friends, that daughter due next for marriage demonstrated the value of the lessons she had undertaken as she provided accompaniment to family concerts of approved music. And when she was wed, her new provider found it as necessary to acquire a family piano as a kitchen range.

With the growing importance of the piano as a household fixture, music publishers, particularly the leading members of the Board of Music Trade, found an extremely lucrative market. Oliver Ditson alone carried about 33,000 pieces for the piano, and within ten years some 200,000 works for the instrument were published in the United States. A considerable number of them were for voice and piano, and were simple and tasteful.

The author Wilson Flagg interviewed a professional singer who stated that there were four kinds of parlor songs in that post–Civil War period. The best featured rhythm, "not formal or very apparent" and demanded a trained vocalist. Then there were songs "by ordinary composers, which are [not] intrinsically melodious [but] full of musical platitudes and plagiarisms." Among these were the current hit songs, popular today and gone like the mayfly tomorrow. Then came the "singsong airs in which the rhythm, or the swing of the movement, is not sufficiently varied to conceal its uniformity," the old favorite British songs of the early 1840s. The last kind were tunes that "soon pall upon a sensitive ear," in a minor mode, like the old folk music of Scotland and Ireland.

The business of great hits in sheet music, particularly in the West, where Root & Cady had led the way, collapsed almost at once with peace in 1865, and then music books, both religious and secular, became most profitable. George F. Root's 1868 *Triumph,* for singing schools and with an introduction for congregational singing, sold some 90,000 copies in its first year and brought a $30,000 profit to the publisher. The business of publishing music for God's postwar Americans became one of the most profitable, the Moody-Sankey hymnbooks alone keeping such companies as John Church, in Cincinnati, and Biglow & Main, in New York, out of Ditson's acquisitive hands for many years.

It was a relatively small group of composers who wrote those simple and natural melodies, set to the most elemental harmonies. They were, W. S. B. Mathews wrote, "brightened up with a few stock passages, arpeggios, and the like, simple and easy to be executed by players of small attainment, but modelled upon [work of] first-class writers." He bitterly condemned these works, which represented, to him, the average musical consciousness of mid-century America. He was referring to those darlings of the music trade—Addison F. Wyman, Charles Grobe, James Bellak, Thomas P. Ryder, Charles D. Blake, and others—whose printed music, truly suited to the market of eager young women, sold consistently in great quantities. All of these writers made money, several receiving large amounts. Mathews conceded, however, that even these "parasites upon poetic music have their uses. While they occasionally take up space which might be better occupied, they do, nevertheless, afford delight to many whose interest in music is so slight that nothing less easily assimilated would stand a chance of being received. Of these works it might be said [they represent] the effort of composers to adapt themselves to the newer and more democratic and untrained public.''

Wyman's ''Silvery Waves,'' was held back by the Brainards two years, before publication, because they believed it was not commercial. Fourteen years after its New Hampshire-born composer died, the piece had sold nearly one million copies, and his other popular pieces—''Woodland Echoes,'' ''Music Among the Pines,'' ''Wedding Bells March,'' ''Evening Parade March,'' and similar trifles—were not far behind.

James Bellak appeared to be in a contest for productivity with Charles Grobe. When the Board of Music Trade issued its one and only *Complete Catalogue of Sheet Music and Musical Works* in 1870, Bellak was just a few hundred works behind Grobe. Little is known about him, but, like his rival, Robert Offergeld has written, his music was ''not musical at all but industrial, like Grand Rapids rococo furniture,'' and it enjoyed similar vast sales.

Charles D. Blake, starting later, outproduced both Grobe and Bellak. Born in Walpole, Massachusetts, in 1847, he began to study music at age seven and produced the first of more than 3,000 works three years later. In time he studied with John Knowles Paine, years before that conservative German-trained Yankee was named the first professor of music at Harvard—probably the first in the nation. Blake had little difficulty getting his music into print, and he was such a successful writer that White, Smith & Co., a new Boston firm, signed him to an exclusive contract. After it came to an end eighteen years later, Blake established his own company. Many of his piano pieces sold enormously, chiefly because he had a nose for what was commercial, a quality that served him as the publisher of ''Rock-a-bye Baby in the Tree Top,'' certainly the most famous lullaby in history. The music had been improvised by fifteen-year-old Effie Crockett when she was caring for a crying infant; the words came from the old *Mother Goose Book,* first printed in the mid-eighteenth century. When her music teacher heard the song, she took it and the young lady to Blake. He immediately offered to publish it, provided that she supply three additional verses to go with the traditional lyric. Fearful that her father would object, she used her grandmother's name, Canning, on the printed copies.

Eleven years older than Blake, Thomas Phylander Ryder was born in Massachusetts but did not begin to study piano until he was fourteen. His progress was rapid, and before he was twenty he was playing the organ in Boston churches, eventually at the Tremont Street Baptist Church. His pieces were mostly for the piano, and after his ''Chanson des Alpes'' was published by White, Smith in 1880, he became one of the handful of best-selling writers in that idiom. Hundreds of copies of his music adorned the nation's music racks.

In spite of their financial success, Mathews found all these works ''more or less open to criticism upon the ground of their obvious aim at pleasing mainly the uncultivated taste.'' However, he added, anyone who could write 1,200 pieces successively and ''please the public in all of them, is in a better position to judge the variety of qualities entering into the successful performance of such a task.''

Those music publishers who monopolized the ''uncultivated'' market had no complaints about the quality of their product, for which piano teachers were the most aggressive salesmen. They received a 50 percent discount from most of the leading houses—Ditson, Hall, Peters, Church, Brainard, and White, Smith—which controlled the jobbers' market, and collected an average of eight to ten dollars for sheet music in addition to every twenty dollars paid them for twenty lessons. In the spring of 1884, a new publication for piano teachers, *The Etude*, published in Lynchburg, Virginia, by Theodore Presser, questioned the morality of the piano teacher–music publisher relationship. One fourth of every dollar spent for music education, he wrote, went for sheet music, on which the publishers realized a profit of 500 to 600 percent, even after the discount they gave the teachers. Although production costs has fallen because of the advanced printing process in general use, and therefore an eight-page piece of music could be produced for less than two and a half cents a copy, sheet-music prices remained the same as during the Civil War. In addition, the importation of European music was also controlled by a few publishers, who routinely doubled the original price, attributing the increase to a 25 percent import tax. A 20 percent tariff on all imported printed matter using lithography had been imposed in 1842 in order to put an end to the importation of indecent and obscene prints. It was raised to 25 percent during the Civil War and re-mained there, with minor variations, until 1890, when 10 percent was added. Four years later, music was completely exempted. Throughout this period, however, two copies of any piece of music could be ordered at one time for educational purposes, free of all duty.

Presser pointed out that music received through the mail was not subject to the duty and that teachers who ordered from Germany, for example, were al-lowed a 40 percent discount, so a selection that cost an American teacher $3.34 could be purchased by him in Germany for $1.50. American music published abroad could also be ordered at greatly reduced prices. The Music Teachers National Association, in which Presser was a leading figure, tried to effect a change in the situation without much success. At its annual meeting in 1885, the group came out in favor of reciprocal international copyright, which would inevitably lead to reduced prices. Here, too, they were unsuccessful.

Due in no small part to their relations with music publishers, many piano teachers earned more than an accredited professor of music and were regarded as solid citizens by their communities—no longer the lowly ''fiddlers'' of the past. In 1887, according to a report issued by their association, they had a half-million pupils, almost all of whom learned from printed music sold them by their teachers. Having tasted the profits from supplying printed music for the piano, of which 800,000 had been manufactured in the preceding thirty years, some music publishers ventured into manufacture of the instrument. This had been a standard adjunct of the trade for such pre–Civil War publishers as Wil-liam Hall; Firth, Pond; W. B. Bradbury, and Lowell Mason's sons. Of these, only the last survived, as the Mason & Hamlin Company. John Church did enjoy great financial success during the last decade of the century with his Everett instrument, but hardly on the scale of the nation's three best-known firms: Knabe, Chickering, and Steinway. Baltimore's William Knabe & Co., formed in 1837, opened luxurious quarters in New York City in 1864 and entered into energetic competition with the Steinway company on East 14th Street. The Steinwegs had left their home in the Hartz Mountains of Germany in 1850 and opened in New York as Steinway & Sons three years later. Their earliest instruments had a full iron frame in a square piano box and an arrangements of strings in two layers, bass over treble, to produce a fine tone. By 1860, this prize-winning technology was applied to grand pianos, which were proclaimed, in the first general advertisement to use testimonials by famous pianists, as "most novel, ingenious, and important." Steinway built a larger factory during the war, between 52nd and 53rd Streets. By 1880, seven of every ten American pianos sold in Europe were made by Steinway, a rate almost equaled in the United States.

Steinway had overtaken its leading American rival, Chickering, who had been making pianos since 1843, a dozen years after its founder, cabinetmaker Jonas Chickering, opened his Boston shop. When the Steinways reached America, Chickering was manufacturing 15 percent of all pianos sold in the country. Two years later, in 1853, 500 workers turned out 2,000 instruments annually in a new Boston factory, the largest of its kind until Steinway's new factory, which was bigger than any other building in the United States except the Capitol. The rivalry between the two firms continued even after Jonas Chickering died. In 1867, after each had spent about $80,000 on a press and advertising campaign in Paris in connection with the great exposition there, Steinway won the first gold medal and Chickering a lower award. Acclaimed by such eminent European musicians as Rossini, Berlioz, Liszt, and Anton Rubinstein, the American piano and its Steinway and Chickering manufacturing families had become world renowned.

Music Publishing in the Midwest

As Towner Root and Chauncey M. Cady had anticipated, the presence of George Root in their new building near Chicago's Crosby Opera House attracted not only successful songwriters and composers but also the Midwest's young aspirants to fame and fortune. Among these was James Ramsay Murray, a Scottish-born musician taught by Root during prewar musical institutes in New England. Apprenticed to a Massachusetts rubber manufacturer, he won his employer's patronage, which enabled him to pursue a musical career. In 1863, while serving as an army musician, Murray submitted a song written with his cousin, a Union officer, and it became one of Root & Cady's best-selling items. "Daisy Deane" enjoyed a long life; in time it was arranged by Salvation Army musicians to be one of the organization's "war cry" songs, to rouse public support.

When Murray was mustered out of the service, Root offered him a position as assistant in the publishing department, eventually promoting him to be editor of *The Song Messenger* in 1870. The firm's annual business then exceeded a half-million dollars, one third of all income of Chicago's music business. In 1881, after the John Church Company purchased the entire Root & Cady book catalogue, Murray headed the book-publishing department. In that capacity, he wrote music for Sunday Schools, popular gospel songs, and a number of collections of church music. His *Pure Diamonds* for Sunday Schools sold more than 500,000 copies. His best-known song was the version of "Away in a Manger"—incorrectly attributed to Martin Luther for many years—that was published as "Luther's Manger Song" in *Dainty Songs for Lads and Lasses,* issued by Church in 1887.

The celebrated nineteenth-century singing evangelist and gospel songwriter Philip Paul Bliss first came to George Root's attention during the war, when he submitted an original melody for publication and asked only for a serviceable flute in return. Always on the lookout for bright men, Root felt that he had found one. He took the melody and revised it a bit, then sent the instrument off in the mail. A few months later, Bliss wrote again, outlining his history and asking for a position. He had been born in a log cabin in western Pennsylvania in 1838 and learned to love music from his hymn-singing parents. He had begun working on farms and in lumber camps at the age of eleven and joined the Baptist Church at twelve. Two years earlier, he had heard the sound of piano music through the open windows of a house. Astounded, he ventured inside, only to be thrown out after asking the young lady to "play some more!" While studying with local musicians, he attended one of W. B. Bradbury's music conventions, on the strength of which he found employment as a teacher.

Root sent for him in 1864, which began an association that lasted for four years, during which time Bliss served as a song booster, promoting the firm's copyrights throughout the surrounding territory, holding conventions, and giving concerts of the company's music, at which his magnificent voice was accompanied by his wife at the piano. Bliss was guaranteed an annual sum; when the proceeds of these public appearances failed to match it, Root & Cady made up the difference.

Root & Cady published a number of Bliss's popular songs before a meeting with Dwight L. Moody changed the young musician's future. He began to sing regularly at prayer meetings conducted by that businessman-turned-clergyman, who knew the power of an appealing soloist in revival work. Bliss's golden hair and beard and his Apollo-like physique compelled the full attention of worshipers to his fine booming voice, and won him the post of director of music at Chicago's First Congregational Church.

In 1870, he sent a new hymn, "Hold the Fort," to Root, and it became quickly known to Christians around the world. An example of its appeal is that the melody serves today for Ghana's national anthem. That hymn song and others—"Pull for the Shore," "Let the Lower Lights Be Burning," "Dare to Be a Daniel," and those he wrote with Fanny Crosby, Robert Lowry, Ira Sankey, and Moody himself—introduced the style that awakened people and led them to Christ. With catchy words and simple music, influenced by the minstrel-theater march and walk-around, these songs were sung and whistled long after the prayer meeting had ended. Had there been a Tin Pan Alley at the time, its music men certainly would have fought to publish this new kind of gospel song. They sold in editions of many thousands through the years. None was better than Bliss at their creation. His first collection, *The Charm,* brought out by Root & Cady in 1870, called them "Sunday School music," but that was soon changed to what they are known as today, "gospel songs."

Moody persuaded Bliss to take up the career of singing evangelist, and his activities were not unlike those he had performed for Root & Cady on the road. Printed sheet music and books of his and others' songs were on sale at each service, and he was available for hire by professional revivalists. After Root & Cady suspended business in 1871, Bliss began to publish his collections through Biglow & Main, of New York, and he earned significant royalties from the success of *The Tree* (1872), *Sunshine for Sunday School* (1873), *Gospel Songs for Gospel Meetings* (1874), and printed copies of individual songs.

In early 1874, Bliss joined a Civil War officer, Major Daniel Webster Whittle, in a religious ministry. A former jeweler, a poet, and now a lay preacher, Whittle spoke and Bliss sang at revival meetings throughout the Midwest and Deep South. Shortly after Christmas of 1875, Bliss and his wife left their children with friends and went by railroad to join a gospel meeting planned for Moody's Chicago Tabernacle. Just as the train was crossing a ravine in Ohio, the bridge gave way, plunging the engine and cars into the river below. Flames burst out, and Bliss, who had been hurled through a window, went back into the flaming wreckage to find his wife, saying, "If I cannot have her, I will perish with her." Their bodies were not found.

As Root & Cady's representative on the Board of Music Trade, Chauncey Cady had ample opportunity to watch the "Nestor of the Music Business" at work. Oliver Ditson was quick to purchase any music-publishing business in trouble or offered for sale, and Cady soon launched his own plan to do the same in the Midwest. His first acquisition was a minor one: the catalogue of Florenz Ziegfeld, Sr., founder and director of the Chicago Academy of Music. Trained as a pianist at the Leipzig Conservatory of Music under Ignaz Moscheles, Felicien David, and others, Ziegfeld was still a young man when he refused an offer to head a Russian conservatory and emigrated to Chicago. Although he was one of that city's most important musical figures, he was overshadowed by his son, the great glorifier of the American girl. During the 1893 Chicago World's Fair, the senior Ziegfeld opened a music hall, in the hope of raising funds for the academy. For it, he sent his son off to Europe to bring back the best concert artists available. The talent proved to be second-rate, and the project prospered only after young Ziegfeld brought in the world's strongest man, Sandow, whose exhibitions of muscular agility rivaled the pelvic gyrations of "Little Egypt," the nautch-dancing queen of the fair's popular-entertainment area.

It was Cady's purchase of Henry Tolman's catalogues that stamped the firm as a major force, not only in the Midwest but also nationally. It added thirty-five years of copyrights and engraved plates to the many thousands already owned, and contributed an important part of the 1.2 million copies of printed music of all kinds sold by Root & Cady in 1868. The company's catalogue issued the following year was nearly 500 pages long, listing 8,498 titles and 104 music books, all acquired within a decade, a feat that made even the eastern giants jealous. Horatio Richmond Palmer's collection of music for singing classes, *The Music Queen,* proved to be a fine seller. Cady had taken over Palmer's catalogue in early 1868, after the music teacher–composer's duties required all of his time. Born in New York State in 1835, Palmer was a member of his father's church choir at nine, and while still in his teens was director of the choir and organist, already recognized as a brilliant teacher. Succeeding volumes in Palmer's "Song" series, *The Song King, The Song Monarch,* and *The Song Herald,* each sold upward of 200,000 copies, the first two for Root & Cady initially and then for John Church. In later years, Palmer headed the large New York Church Choral Union, dedicated to the improvement of religious song, and was also in charge of the music department for the Chautauqua assemblies. The gospel hymn for which he is best remembered, "Yield Not to Temptation," was written in 1868 for Root & Cady.

Even the shrewdest eastern publishers, Ditson and his senior partner, John C. Haynes, had failed to perceive the potential market in Chicago and the Midwest. When one of the Ditson clerks, Patrick J. Healy, decided to open a music store there in 1863, his employer told him that he would be lucky indeed if the store was doing $100,000 a year after a decade. Actually, a year after opening for business, Healy and his partner, George Washburn Lyon, were making that and more.

Lyon was born in Massachusetts in 1833, went to work for Charles Keith's Boston music store while still a boy, and then was hired by Ditson. A student of the violin and the harp, he later concentrated his interest on the manufacture of the latter instrument. The firm was nationally known after the early 1870s for the instruments he produced. Younger by seven years, Healy was born in County Cork, Ireland, and came to America while still a boy. He started working for Ditson at the age of ten, after having been an errand boy for George Reed and Henry Tolman. Ditson became fond of him and encouraged him to go to night school, where he learned reading, writing, and bookkeeping. This led to his becoming a company accountant and, later, confidential clerk to Ditson. In 1863, Ditson offered to set Healy up in business as a Midwest associate in Chicago, St. Louis, or San Francisco. After consulting his friend Lyon, Healy chose Chicago, prompting his mentor's skepticism.

Lyon & Healy first shared a store with a local piano dealer, whose business they absorbed in 1871. By that time they had an annual profit of about $500,000. The Ditson Company maintained its financial interest in the firm until 1890, when the Chicago operation was organized as a separate corporation, though it still functioned as a primary Midwest agency. Lyon then withdrew from the partnership, selling his interests for $250,000. Under the original name, the firm operated the country's largest music store, with Ditson's copyrighted music as its chief stock, and was listed on all covers as secondary publisher. In 1895, a Lyon & Healy executive, J. F. Bowers, was elected president of the Board of Music Trade's successor, the Music Publishers Association, a position to which he was perennially reelected. He also served as president of the Talking Machine Jobbers National Association, and the National Piano Dealers Association, an indication of the company's eminent position within the music business.

In 1868, Lyon & Healy began its own music magazine, *The Musical Independent,* with William Smith Babcock Mathews as editor. One of the late nineteenth century's foremost music critics and piano teachers, Mathews was born in Vermont in 1837. A precocious youngster, he profited from Lowell Mason's music-education programs, and at fifteen was deemed sufficiently qualified to earn his living as a music teacher in a New England academy. His formal education had stopped at the district-school level, but he eventually taught himself Greek, Latin, French, and German, as well as classical literature and metaphysics. When the Civil War broke out, he was teaching music in a Georgia seminary, from which he immediately resigned. He was forced to stay behind Confederate lines, however, and consoled himself with the only two books he had been able to retain, the Beethoven piano sonatas, and Bach's "Well-Tempered Clavier." When peace came, he went to Chicago and an Episcopalian organ loft. He edited the Lyon & Healy magazine until fire put an end to that aspect of the company's activities.

Though he never wrote music, Mathews was a prominent music educator, critic for Chicago's *Tribune* and *News,* lecturer, and associate editor of Theodore Presser's magazine, *The Etude.* He was, as a contemporary wrote, "one of the most widely read writers upon musical subjects writing in the English language, and his work is distinguished for its perspicacity, intelligence, and, like his piano-forte conceptions, for polished 'phrasing.' "

In the first issue of *The Musical Independent,* Mathews wrote that one of the publication's chief concerns was "new and attractive music . . . the chief element of which is, that it is melodious and practicable." No one in Chicago bore better witness to that element than the local writer and sole publisher of what proved to be the most lasting popular ballad of the late 1860s, "When You and I Were Young, Maggie." He was James Austin Butterfield, who arrived in the city in 1867, having already published the song in Indianapolis. He intended to pursue a career in serious music while living off the proceeds of his sheet-music sale. In short order, he was appointed director of the choir for which Mathews played. He also taught voice culture and harmony. Born in the hunting country of Hertfordshire in 1837, he was given a tiny violin made by his father soon after he learned to walk. At the age of four he could sight-read music, and at six he played the violin alongside his father in the village orchestra. When his parents refused to permit his admission to the Westminster Abbey choir, he was apprenticed to a tradesman. He made his way to America at nineteen.

When the Civil War started, he was in Tampa, Florida, heading a music academy. He moved north to Indianapolis, where he taught voice and violin, and also write the first of 150 popular songs. "When You and I Were Young, Maggie" was written in 1866 and first advertised in Indiana's earliest music magazine, a house organ and promotion medium for J. M. Butterfield, the small independent company he had formed. The song's appealing lyric and undemanding octave-and-two-note range won the interest of sheet-music buyers; it sold more than a quarter-million copies within a few years, even though sheet sales had collapsed in the Midwest. American minstrel companies took the song to England, where it found a happy home in the mainstream of sentimental Victorian ballads.

Butterfield had found the words in *Maple Leaves,* a book of original poetry by Canadian George Washington Johnson, published in 1864. The Maggie of that poem had actually lived, been married to Johnson, her schoolteacher, and died that same year. In Chicago, Butterfield devoted himself to composition and music education for the rest of his life. One of his comic operas, the five-act *Balshazzar,* had 1,000 public performances during his lifetime. As one of a handful of small independent music publishers, Butterfield presented no serious competition to Root & Cady, who would, however, have been delighted to own his copyrights.

Times were good and getting better in Chicago in 1870, when fire destroyed the Lyon & Healy store, temporarily ending the partners' music business. A little more than a year later, on the night of October 9, 1871, George Root learned that a great fire downtown was spreading and that the Root & Cady building was gone. The $125,000 loss for the firm's partners was a small part of the $196-million disaster, which leveled 17,500 structures on 2,125 acres of metropolitan Chicago. The city's music trade was almost wiped out, and its publishing activities went into a serious decline, which continued for almost ten years, until S. Brainard's Sons moved from Cleveland and became the major Midwest music enterprise.

After the fire, many musicians and teachers who promoted printed music sales left town for greener pastures or went into other lines of work. The original Root & Cady company was dissolved, and two new bodies were created. George Root assigned all the real estate holdings he had amassed to the new partnership of Towner Root, Chauncey Cady, and William Lewis, who had been manager of the firm's musical-instrument division. It was to assume all liabilities, open a general music-merchandising store, and print music books. The new firm of George D. Root & Sons (sons Frederic and Charles and his brother William) was to conduct a general business in printed music and books. However, Root & Cady's insurance companies defaulted on their obligations, and in order to salvage any credit all sheet-music plates were sold to Brainard's and all music books to John Church, for a total of $150,000. With this money Chauncey Cady felt he could establish the new company, so contracts were signed for new pianos, band instruments, and other associated wares, which went on sale in a new building.

For the first time, however, Cady's sound business judgment appeared to have deserted him. A public disclosure in February 1873 indicated that he had erred, overestimating the value of assets and future potential, and that the company had actually been forced into bankruptcy several month before. Towner Root and William Lewis then formed a new company, after George Root purchased the entire bankrupt stock of merchandise at a bargain rate, thus forcing Cady out of the business. In 1875, the new Root & Lewis merged with George

Root & Sons to form Root & Sons Music Company, whose principal stock was owned by the John Church Company, a tangled web of business dealings worthy of Byzantium.

Cady was in New York City by that time, where he capitalized on a chance meeting with Henry Work by obtaining the manuscript for "Grandfather's Clock," which brought him considerable profits. When he died in 1888, he had been reduced to running the Southern agency for his old friend W. W. Kimball. Towner Root died six years later, still active in E. T. Root & Sons, general music dealers, formed in 1880, after he had withdrawn from Root & Sons Music Co.

During these business mergers and sales, George Root remained active as a composer and songwriter, author, and leader of musical conventions. He was at his desk daily until his death, the same year as Towner's. John Church, for whom he worked as editor of publications and of the firm's house organ, published all his music. Regularly honored with degrees from leading educational establishments, Root was eulogized some years before his death as the creator of popular songs "within the comprehension of the masses," songs that had "an elevating influence and [were] admirably adapted for raising the standard of music, which has been the one great object of his life."

Copyright and the Music Business

As one of its first acts of international diplomacy, the Confederate States of America had signed a reciprocal copyright protocol with Great Britain. However, in the postwar years, native anti-intellectualism as well as political distrust of the North contributed in large measure to making the South a hotbed of political opposition to any similar action by the United States Congress. A curious alliance of disparate personalities and interests continually thwarted international copyright legislation, until at last President Benjamin Harrison signed a new act in 1891.

For more than half a century, the absence of proper laws enabled book and music publishers to create a profitable trade in noncopyrighted printed materials, to the financial detriment of writers, composers, and authors in the United States and Great Britain. In the case of American vernacular music, it served as a restraint on the publication and promotion of music that appealed to the lower classes, to whom inexpensive popular entertainment was becoming increasingly available. Soon after the Civil War ended, the battle for protection resumed, and petitions for new laws affecting foreign works began to descend on Congress. The battle lines were established, and remained firm until almost the end of the fight. On one side was labor—the printers, typesetters, lithographers, and others involved in the manufacture and sale of books, who feared loss of income from any change in the federal laws. With them were Democratic politicians and the people of rural areas in the South and West, whose sentiments were constantly stirred up by editors of country newspapers. By 1890, some 12,000 independent country weeklies were serving small communities of less than 10,000 inhabitants and farm country with as few as 300 persons. At least half of these papers used "patent insides and outsides" supplied by about two dozen companies, the largest being the American Press Association of New York. Patent stereotype plates were sold to the newspaper owners for twenty-five cents a column. They contained not only advertising, but also serialized British novels, which were free of copyright under the current law. Because any change in this delicate balance would seriously affect the income of newspaper editors, whose subscription rates had fallen to an average of $1.50 a year by the 1880s, readers were subjected to propaganda against change from the only source of information available to them. Their national representatives were well aware of resulting local attitudes and remained in the forefront of the opposing forces.

The most important of the latter were the cheap-book publishers and reprinters, who, like music publishers, reaped their largest returns from editions of non-copyrighted properties. Each of the several groups fighting revision of the law was a potent adversary, and many of them, like the American Press Association, supported powerful Washington lobbyists.

By the 1880s, writing had become more than the gentleman's pastime it was regarded a half century earlier, and major publishers in the centers of American literary activity—New York, Philadelphia, and Boston—began to join efforts to obtain a new law. So, too, did the conservative "best" people of the northeast, who were chiefly Republicans. Although the Music Teachers National Association was a strong proponent of revision, only two figures connected with American music were active to any visible degree in the final period of the fight: Oliver Ditson, in the last year of his life, and Reginald De Koven, music critic for the *Chicago Daily News,* one of that city's favorite composers for the theater. His social position as the husband of a leading Chicago heiress undoubtedly played a part in his appointment as secretary of the Chicago branch of the American Copyright League in February 1890; other members were meat packer George A. Armour and merchant Marshall Field, as well as some local authors.

Having studied music in England and France, De Koven was certainly aware that composers and authors of musical-theater works there had been in the forefront of the long struggle to obtain payment for the use of their works, particularly in Spain, Italy, and France. The Spanish General Association of Writers and Authors, formed in 1874, became the Society of Authors, Composers and Proprietors of Dramatic Works six years later. Because of the organization's strength and membership, which included composers of the popular zarzuelas (operetta or vaudeville with alternating music or song and dialogue), every theatrical producer had first to obtain and pay for permission from the society before mounting a musical production. In Italy, Giuseppe Verdi and Arigo Boito were leaders in the formation, in 1882, of a society of composers and publishers, Societa Italiana Autori e Editori. The group's principal concern was a revision of their young nation's 1865 copyright law, which had established registration and deposit of works. In a short time, it was successful in getting passage of new legislation, which gave composers the right to take legal action in order to control public performances of their music. This society was modeled on France's Société des Auteurs, Compositeurs et Editeurs, founded in 1851 and based on the principle of protection of public performances of stage works first enacted by Louis XVI and strengthened two years later with a ban on unauthorized performances. Through the following years, the collection of performance fees proved to be very difficult. So a court action was brought in 1847 by two composers against a Paris café for unauthorized performances of their music. Local and higher courts found for the plaintiffs, which led to SACEM's formation. In thirty years, collections rose from a few thousand francs to several million as continued court action affirmed the validity of performance licensing. SACEM established collection agencies in a number of European countries without similar protective organizations, among them Belgium, where a law protecting musical and other intellectual property was finally enacted in 1885.

Following SACEM's example, composers and authors in other countries formed their own national groups, and in 1886 representatives of fourteen nations met in Berne, Switzerland, out of which came the Berne Convention, which protected authors' rights. It was signed by all the participating countries, including Great Britain, France, and Germany, within two years. The original convention stipulated that a writer complying with the copyright law of his country enjoyed full protection against pirated editions and unauthorized translations in all signatory nations. Interestingly—for it soon affected music around the world—mechanical reproduction of music was not included in the first Berne Convention, in which it was regarded as not constituting any deprivation of authors' rights. The United States did not join the Berne Convention nations, as could have been expected after decades of opposition to international copyright.

Action for international copyright resumed when Charles Dickens arrived in 1867, on his second American lecture-and-reading tour, and once again importuned the natives for a law to protect foreign authors. He was followed almost immediately by Anthony Trollope, whose mother had acquired her dislike of Americans in the early 1830s, when she operated a Cincinnati variety store, an antipathy her son shared. He had been passed over for promotion in the British Post Office, though he had invented the pillar mailbox, and had little love for the authorities. Yet he accepted his government's official suggestion and undertook while in America to add his voice to the cause of reciprocal copyright.

A number of proposed bills to that effect were introduced in Congress and quickly buried, due to the efforts of labor and the cheap-book reprinters and despite the presence of renowned foreign lobbyists. Among the suggestions offered was one by New York publisher William A. Appleton, who revived the 1859 proposal of a "manufacturing proviso," which would grant international copyright on the basis of domestic manufacture of foreign works, using only made-in-America materials. Despite its attraction for labor, the proposal, which also called for banning all foreign publications and protection only for those that had been assigned by their original writer to an American publisher, also failed of passage. Many publishers were against the manufacturing clause, fearing it would prove to be too expensive in the face of domestic costs far higher than those in Europe and Canada, where many of them were manufacturing. Most American publishers were still making far greater profits from material copyrighted abroad than were the foreign owners.

The "courtesy of the trade" policy put into place by book publishers prior to the Civil War remained in effect until nearly the end of the century. It was announced by a published initial claim which was supported by an agreement to make some payments to the European writer. Only established authors enjoyed this privilege. Publisher members of the Board of Music Trade, who were rarely known to pay foreign composers, also maintained a courtesy policy, and generally refused to jump one another's claims to successful works. Nonmembers were never so courteous, and created a major industry problem through their sometimes brazen duplication of choice music.

Both book and music trades suffered from rampant Canadian piracy. A series of Canadian copyright laws favoring local manufacture culminated in an 1889 act, which required publication within Canada no more than a month after protection elsewhere. If not complied with, the new law made any copyrighted American book or piece of music free to local publishers, who then shipped their product back into the United States.

The Congress had not opposed most of those changes intended to patch the stingy original act of 1790. In 1860, supervision of the registration and deposit function was entrusted to the Library of Congress and its librarian, and postage-free delivery of all books, musical compositions, maps, and pamphlets was enacted, followed, in 1865, by enactment of a penalty of twenty-five dollars for each failure to make a proper deposit. A recording fee of fifty cents for each transaction was instituted in 1870, as was a penalty of one dollar for every sheet of printed material found that had been manufactured without the copyright owner's written permission, half of the collected sum to go "to the use of the United States." The policing and collection function for this was left to the copyright owner, who had to apply to civil courts for redress.

The final, successful, drive for international copyright began in the mid-1880s. Authors had permeated the halls of Congress, and one of them, the governor of New York State, Theodore Roosevelt, was a powerful figure in Republican circles. The American Copyright Club, which William Cullen Bryant and several hundred other poets and writers had formed in 1843, twelve years before publishers began a similar group, was now the American Copyright League. As the foremost group fighting for new copyright laws, this association was a key factor in the final triumph, having formed many supporting groups around the country after proselytizing by touring writers. The league supported a number of bills, even though its members were often divided over the manufacturing clause, which proponents of international copyright recognized as essential in order to gain the support of organized labor, without which most such legislation had generally foundered. In their concern to have the sort of united front that operated in other nations, authors persuaded their publishers to form a similar lobbying group. This led to the new American Publishers' Copyright League in late 1887. A join Copyright Conference in 1889 included the Typographers Union, which insisted on the manufacturing clause as a condition for its cooperation. Other unions involved in the printing trade were brought into line the following year when Samuel Gompers, president of the American Federation of Labor, proclaimed his support of international copyright. So, too, did the Music Teachers National Association.

Throughout the 49th, 50th, and 51st Congress bills affecting international copyright were regularly pushed aside by more pressing legislation. Finally, after the clock was stopped at midnight on March, 3, 1891, the combination of conference recommendations, resolutions, and amendments to the proffered Platt-Simonds Act was passed by both houses, the first major revision of the United States Copyright Act of 1790. President Harrison signed the bill that night.

Its provisions became effective the following June 1. Among them, the music business noted that copyright protection was extended to twenty-eight years for both resident and nonresident authors if reciprocal copyright existed between the two nations involved; books, chromos, and lithographs had to be manufactured in the United States to obtain copyright; foreign copyrighted books and plates could not be imported for sale; two copies only of foreign books could be imported, subject to duty. In addition, the secretary of the Treasury was required to issue to all collectors of customs and all postmasters regular weekly lists of new copyright entries. Book and music publishers who had long been the victims of cheap counterfeit foreign editions of their property now had allies in their fight against piracy.

Changing Technology and Distribution

As *The Etude* correctly pointed out in 1884, sheet-music prices established during the Civil War still prevailed despite the improved lithographic-duplicating process, which lowered costs of reproduction greatly. Early in the 1880s, most music publishers also profited by abandoning the remaining vestiges of stunning colored lithographed covers, which had been the glory of pre-war publications, in favor of poorly printed photoengravings and halftone reproductions of photographs. The saving did prove to be a boon to theatrical performers and minstrel-show, variety-hall, and concert-saloon vocalists, whose visages adorned the covers of songs they had written or were performing or boosting. Many houses dropped all illustrative art and used only passe-partouts to hold crude drawings that had some bearing on the contents or the performers.

The quality of halftone engravings increased dramatically once the publishers of some 1,000 daily newspapers learned that the monotonous uniformity of typeset columns of words alone could be profitably broken up by illustration. In spite of protests from church groups, a hundred of these papers were brought out in regular Sunday editions during the 1880s, for which the price was raised to five cents. They contained a variety of photo-illustrated contents. In 1888, the Sunday *New York World,* whose daily circulation exceeded 300,000 copies, at one penny each, printed the words and music for Monroe Rosenfeld's "With All Her Faults I Love Her Still" as a circulation-boosting stunt. It proved so successful that the *World* regularly reprinted sentimental ballads, many written by Rosenfeld, who was then a company employee. Other Sunday papers picked up the scheme, and music publishers initially were pleased to grant permission for the reproduction of songs in their entirety by this new group of free boosters. But when sales of fifty-cent sheet music suffered as a result, the publishers began to refuse. The papers then exerted pressure by dangling pages of free publicity to musical-theater producers, who, in turn, promised not to give publication rights in their new productions directly unless the music publishers assented. The matter was resolved when publishers and songwriters presented a united front. A compromise was effected: only those songs not expected to attain any meaningful sales appeared in Sunday papers. These "Sunday supplements" were printed on cheap paper and usually had cartoons on their covers, drawn by newspaper staff artists. At the insistence of an important composer, quality colored art decorated the supplements, which often appeared in Sunday newspapers from coast to coast.

Sheet-music cover art took on new quality, as well as color, in the early 1890s. The success of popular comic weeklies—*Judge, Puck,* and *Life*—stimulated interest in a return to colored lithographed illustration. *Puck* regularly printed a double-page colored center spread, which was quickly adopted by other publications. This use of color in popular art led to its use by the aggressive new music houses—Witmark, F. A. Mills, Leo Feist—who brought out sheet music with colored illustrated covers created by talented artists and influenced by new movements in art. Each cover also featured the usual halftone inset of the star committed to boosting the song.

Another important means of mass distribution of popular music, one the publishers supported for many years in the interests of publicity, was the product of that "other music business." It dated back to the "one side only" broadsides of the Tudor period, which eventually became the words-only songsters. The Civil War had stimulated distribution of pocket songsters, which were issued by job-lot printers. Typical of them was Henry De Marsan, of Chatham Street, New York. Having operated a successful wholesale and retail stationery business throughout the 1850s, De Marsan now opened a "song depot," to handle penny song slipsheets and ballads. He built up a catalogue of 2,300 songs, always on hand. During the war, he had adorned his song-words publications with colored illustrations. Sometime in 1868, he began the *Weekly Comic and Sentimental Singers Journal,* an eight-page, 8-by-10 1/2-inch black-and-white biweekly collection of fifty songs of the day "sung in concert-rooms, theatres, and opera-houses in the United States and Great Britain." Selling for two cents a copy, it was distributed by agents throughout the northeast, as far west as Buffalo, and as far south as the Baltimore-Washington area. Unlike the traditional songster, De Marsan's *Journal* always contained a single page of music, generally a noncopyrighted foreign work or one he purchased from a member of the songwriting fraternity. Pond, Ditson, the British firm of Boosey and Co., and other leading publishers were delighted with this added exposure of their wares. In return, De Marsan published the names and addresses of publishers of the sheet music for the song words he reprinted.

Others who brought out collections of song words included the toy-book publisher William Wrigley; members of the Tousey family, one of whom, Frank, was among the founders of the first American humor magazine, *Judge,* in 1881; Pauline Lieber, who acquired the De Marsan catalogues in the 1880s; Robert De Witt & Co.; and Henry J. Wehman. These dime-book publishers and job printers resorted to this line of cheap-book production only after cheap pirated English fiction and public-domain American novels threatened to destroy the entire book business of the United States. Beadle & Co., which had started on the profits from prewar dime books of popular songs, produced more than four million copies of ten-cent novels during the hostilities. Their success attracted other publishers, and by 1870 their dime and half-dime novels were selling in great quantities, too. The invasion was based on well-known English and American fiction, rather than the potboiler original novels Beadle had commissioned. Within two years, more than a dozen publishers were engaged in the new business, among them the Canadian John W. Lovell, who published as many as seven million books a year. He operated out of a printing plant just across the border, near Rouse's Point, New York. Paying no more attention to music copyright than he had to those for literature, he established a "popular" line of song-word and music books, providing yet another source of concern for the Board of Music Trade and its members.

Mr. Edison's Wonderful Talking Machine

The first believable mechanical enhancement of a human voice was most probably the work of a primitive shaman who successfully amplified or distorted his own or that of an acolyte in order to persuade the disbelieving of the potency of the mystical forces he controlled or whose earthly agent he was.

Only after Alexander Graham Bell and Thomas Edison separately stumbled on new findings was the world provided with the serendipitous creation of a technology that would change both the form of mass-duplicated music and the mechanics of its production.

In 1877, Edison, only thirty, was already being hailed as America's most important inventive genius. He was profiting from the patented carbon transmitter that delivered speech "loudly," with which he proposed to improve the telephone Bell had introduced a year earlier, probably just in time to beat Edison to its construction. Edison had in common with his major American rival for world acclaim an interest in aiding those who were hard-of-hearing; he himself was showing signs of deafness, from a blow to his head in childhood. And deafness in his family had initially led Bell to experiment with a "speaking telegraph," to assist deaf-mutes in learning to speak. Out of this came the accidental creation of the telephone.

In new experiments with Bell's telephone, Edison stumbled on the principle of the phonograph, after an embossing needle he was using to capture vibrations on paraffin paper accidentally pricked his finger. "There is no doubt," he wrote in a notebook that day, July 18, 1877, "that I shall be able to store up and reproduce accurately at any future time the human voice perfectly." He began to work on a machine for that purpose.

Edison's press agent made a premature disclosure of this new project, hailing it as a "talking machine." Edison then disclosed the device to the editor and staff of *Scientific American* in early December. A cylinder prepared in advance asked about the editor's health and how he liked the new phonograph, said that it was itself feeling well, and then bade all good night. The prototype of this recording and reproducing machine had been built to Edison's specifications, at a cost of eighteen dollars, in about thirty hours. While examining it for final approval, Edison spoke into his phonograph: "Mary had a little lamb." After a second diaphragm-and-needle unit was adjusted, the words were repeated, and Edison confessed later that he had never been so surprised in all his life.

The press gave wide attention to the "New Jersey Columbus," and helped to build the craze for the phonograph. People began to pour into Menlo Park, New Jersey, the home of Edison's laboratories, many coming on special excursion trains organized by the Pennsylvania Railroad. Several hundred tin-foil phonographs were manufactured, for distribution by a syndicate of investors, including Bell's father-in-law, which paid Edison $10,000 to perfect his invention and $50,000 for production costs, plus a 20 percent royalty on all sales. A few months later, the investors formed the Edison Speaking Phonograph Company of Connecticut. Edison's public-relations people had mounted a major campaign, including a demonstration of the machine at the White House, and in press interviews Edison always predicted a rosy future for the project. The United States was divided into territories in which exhibition rights to the phonograph were individually leased, a song promoting the device was published by G. Schirmer, and large brass demonstration machines, selling for eighty dollars, went into production. Public interest was great, and some exhibitors made as much as $1,800 in a single week from demonstrations of prerecorded cylinders and on-the-spot recordings of instrumentalists and members of the audience. In the July 1878 issue of *The North American Review,* Edison expounded on the possible use of his phonograph, most of them obvious in hindsight: dictation, the preservation of literature through recorded readings by a first-class elocutionist, recorded performances by great singers, to help the blind, in education, as a speaking toy. In another interview, he made this interesting suggestion: "It may be used as a musical composer. When singing some favorite airs backward it hits some lovely airs, and I believe a musician could get one popular melody every day by experimenting in that way."

By the autumn of 1878, the novelty was beginning to wear off, tin-foil recordings were proving too fragile for untrained users, royalties from the public showings were declining, and Edison himself had been struck by the suggestion that he was capable of inventing artificial light for home use. He accepted a contract from the newly formed Edison Electric Light Company for his exclusive services for a period of years, to perfect and then supervise the installation of indoor lighting with an incandescent lamp. By 1880, the phonograph was another half-remembered phenomenon to most Americans, though not to the owners of some 2,000 machines that had been sold during the initial exploitation.

At the height of public reaction to his invention, Edison had told one newspaperman that it was his child and he expected it to be "a big feller and support me in my old age." Now, with another child gestating and bright prospects looming for a far greater financial future, he said that it really had been "a mere toy, which has no commercial value."

Seeking to remind the world of the great contributions to man's learning the House of Bonaparte had made, Emperor Louis Napoleon III had created an annual award in the name of the Italian physicist Alessandro Volta, a protégé of his Corsican grandfather. In 1880, 50,000 francs ($20,000) were awarded as the year's Volta Prize to Alexander Graham Bell for his telephone. Though the world was honoring him for his genius, Bell had not yet received a single penny from his creation, so he used the prize money to establish a much-needed laboratory in Washington, D.C. An English-born cousin, Chichester A. Bell, and an American accoustic engineer, Charles Sumner Tainter, joined him, and among the projects on which they embarked was improvement of Edison's phonograph.

Several major results of their work were patented after four years of effort: cylinders made of wax-coated cardboard to replace Edison's fragile tin foil; an improved diaphragm with a fluctuating stylus guided by the recorded grooves; and a clockwork and then electric battery-powered motor instead of the original unsteady hand-cranked device. Private proposals were made to Edison by intermediaries, who sought collaboration on all future experiments, a pooling of patents, and joint selling of a new machine based on the Bell research. But the incandescent lamp had been perfected, leaving Edison free for other projects. He directed his assistants to resume work on his now ten-year-old invention, one he had seemingly discarded. His publicity staff was turned loose to create a public image of him as the man who had never forgotten the phonograph.

Early in 1887, Bell and his associates sponsored the first public demonstration of the new "graphophone," its name a reversal of the Edison machine's to avoid charges of piracy. In June, the American Graphophone Company was formed, and a manufacturing plant was opened in Bridgeport, Connecticut, financed by a group of investors located chiefly in the nation's capital. Among them were some who had been principals in merchandising the Remington typewriter as a standard piece of office furniture; they saw the dictating phonograph, a use Edison had espoused, as an ideal adjunct. The Isaac Pitman shorthand system, which had appeared in 1837, was proving to be difficult to master, and the Gregg system was a year away. The vast amount of reporting being done in Washington, where the business of all three branches of government was taken down by hand and then transcribed for reprinting, made the city an ideal initial market in which to prove the worth of either the Bell or the Edison machine, and American Graphophone investors intended to profit from one of them.

These plans quickly became known to the Edison people, and work in Menlo Park concentrated on the dictating and voice-transcribing aspect of the phonograph. Despite its early entry in the field, the Graphophone had not yet made any real progress and needed additional financing. This was provided by a northern financier, Jess H. Lippincott, who had recently acquired a million dollars from the sale of his family's glass-tumbler business. He spent a fifth of the sum to purchase an exclusive contract for the American promotion and sales rights to the Bell dictating machine.

The rush to reestablish primacy in the business-machine market made rough financial going for Edison, as costs for research and development mounted. To rekindle public interest, the press was persuaded to report on the "frenzy of toil" going on in New Jersey, and much emphasis was placed on music when famous musicians were brought in to test and approve the new models. Although he had no musical training and was growing deafer, Edison made his tastes will known. Beethoven was a favorite, but Wagner unwelcome. Vocal artists were accompanied by solo instruments only, orchestral backing in Edison's judgment serving only to boom "the cannon around a singing mouse." Italian artists, who often caused the stylus to jump off the cylinder, were recorded personally by Edison, and with great caution. The press was finally permitted to see a perfected Edison phonograph at 5:00 A.M. on June 16, 1888, in ample time for the morning editions. A machine was dispatched to Colonel George E. Gouraud, Edison's London representative, with whom, it was announced, all future correspondence would be exchanged on experimental blank wax-phonograms. Using his considerable European social contacts, Gouraud made good use of the blanks. Disraeli, Gladstone, Florence Nightingale, Lord Tennyson, Sir Arthur Sullivan, all spoke messages to the great inventor into the horn of his Improved Phonograph at London's Edison House. Sullivan said he was "terrified at the thought that so much hideous music may be put on record forever."

Lippincott was still convinced that the machine's future lay in supplying dictating equipment to the government and business. To corner the supply of a machine whose financial prospects he considered as promising as those for the typewriter, Lippincott created the earliest recording-business trust by using the balance of his million dollars to acquire control of Edison Speaking Phonograph Company stock. His new North American Phonograph Company was open for business in July 1888. It served as sole agent for Edison's dictating phonograph and also had a contract with Graphophone to take at least 5,000 machines annually. The Edison Phonograph Works would construct new business machines and would retain the right to manufacture and distribute any musical recordings.

Like the American Bell Telephone Company, on which he modeled his operation, Lippincott began to lease rights to thirty-three subcompanies in various states and territories around the nation. The most important of these was the Columbia Phonograph Company, formed by some of Graphophone's original investors to operate as sole franchise holder and distributor of both the Edison and the Bell machines in Delaware, Maryland, and the District of Columbia. A fee of forty dollars a year was charged for rental of each machine, and all profits were shared with North American.

In 1890, beset by both financial and physical problems, Lippincott fell to the ravages of infantile paralysis, and his major creditor, Thomas Edison, got control of North American.

An estimated 1,700 dictating machines were in use by July 1891, but only about 100 of them were Graphophones. Active resistance to the use of the machines by organizations of stenographers and other office workers, because of the noise and acrid odors emanating from the batteries that powered them, dissuaded many potential customers. Many machines had been returned because of the difficulty of operating them. Columbia had already begun to sell its machines outright for about $150 in order to unload stock, and others were about to do the same.

The money initially received from Lippincott had gone into building a large factory in West Orange, New Jersey, where hundreds of workers built the phonographs, and another in a nearby town for production of wooden cabinets to house them. The first use of these facilities in connection with recorded music was the daily output of 500 talking dolls, which began in 1889. The twenty-two-inch ceramic head and clothed metal bodies housed one of twelve nursery-rhyme cylinders. More important was the production, beginning in May 1889, of music cylinders for use in coin-slot phonographs. Some of these, only a few thousand of which were in use by 1891, were already supporting companies that had not been able to rent their supply of dictating phonographs.

Louis Glass and W. S. Arnold, owners of North American's San Fancisco operation, had, earlier, obtained a patent for a coin-actuated attachment for multiple-tube phonographs through which a number of listeners could hear music selections. They had then sold their patent, "for blood money," to the Automatic Phonograph Company, which leased equipment for sixty dollars a year. There were others, as well, engaged in improving nickel-in-the-slot devices.

Because the Edison Company was not yet producing music cylinders for sale, many franchise holders and coin-machine operators employed local talent to record their own. The art had not yet advanced from the point at which every recording was a true original performance, which could be duplicated in quantity only by using a number of phonographs for each "round" or take. Singers still rarely recorded in front of fewer than three machines; instrumental groups were usually surrounded by ten. By attaching as many as ten additional machines by tubes to the ten master machines it was possible to produce about 2,000 cylinders, though of varying quality from the original.

In May 1889, the Edison Phonograph Works began to supply local companies with masters and then quantities of cylinders. The selections included instrumental, solo, and quartet vocals and parlor-orchestra and military-band selections. Early the following year, however, the shipments were stopped, the company protesting that, around the country, some companies were making their own blank cylinders, infringing on Edison's patents.

North American issued its first printed catalogue for the coin-machine trade in mid-1890 and brought out subsequent lists for several years. Columbia did advertise recordings for home use late in its first year of operation, but most of its products went into the coin machines. Initial brochures advertised records of "orchestras, of brass bands of eight pieces, cornet solos, flute, piccolo, violin, organ, piano, banjo, and other musical records . . . which give subscribers at home at all times a high class of music. We have whistling solos by artistic whistlers, which are very popular." They were indeed, and those made by a government clerk, John Yorke Atlee, became a staple of the Columbia catalogue. His recordings brought in more nickels than all others except those by eight members of the United States Marine Band, which sold originally for $2.00 a cylinder. About 100 selections were recorded for Columbia before 1892 by this band, including new pieces by Sousa for which the group had won national fame, current popular music—"Little Annie Rooney," "Down Went McGinty"—and military / concert-band standards—"The Anvil Chorus" with a real anvil, and Strauss waltzes. With studios in Washington, Philadelphia, and New York, Columbia was able to select its repertory from the newest and most popular music of any type being played in these entertainment centers.

Coin-machine operators, who were placing one third of all available phonographs in locations where people congregated in great numbers, were the best customers for recorded music. Their cylinders could be heard in hotels, saloons, train stations, ferry waiting rooms, even church fairs. Customer cheating by use of slugs, wads of paper, or ice, the regular daily change of selections, and maintenance problems were the chief topics of discussion at the second annual convention of phonograph companies in June 1891. Louis Glass, father of the jukebox, reported on activity in San Francisco, where in a six-month period five of his machines had brought in over $3,000, the most popular operating as many as ten hours daily. It was the consensus of the conventioneers that their future lay in music and the coin-operated phonograph. Nearly a thousand were in regular use, and it was anticipated that the number would continue to grow.

The Board of Music Trade

With the war over, many knowledgeable persons in the music trade expected a marked decline in sheet-music sales. Those of Root's "Tramp, Tramp, Tramp," Work's "Marching Through Georgia," the pirated northern versions of Hewitt's "All Quiet along the Potomac," and, particularly, Sawyer's "When This Cruel War Is Over" had been commercial near-miracles. Now, songs would never again sell copies by the thousands and also appear as ballad slipsheets and in paperback songsters. Representatives of an industry that had been fattening on the copyright-free music of Europe had reason to believe that the rapidity with which popular music had swept both North and South was, like the paper on which it was printed, ephemeral, the product of a vanishing time, when music was written in the temporary cause of national unity. The *Tribune*'s correspondent in Niagara Falls, where the Board of Music Trade held its meeting in July 1865, reported the observation (probably fed him by a board member) that "in Europe sheet music is for the rich and aristocratic, and on the average costs twice as much as in this country." This was an argument against international copyright cited for decades by book publishers, whose commercial interests in this matter coincided perfectly with those of the music-trade monopolies.

In the postwar period, major publishers strove to stimulate public realization of the dignity and importance of musical culture. Factors contributing to that expected happy event were the influence of the prewar teachers' institutes fathered by Lowell Mason, the growing number of educational music periodicals, the concert-going tradition stemming from the 1850s' tours by European stars, the rising appetite for European light opera, the influx of Middle Europeans with a strong musical tradition, and the coming of age of the American pianoforte-manufacturing industry.

It was a commonly held belief among many musically trained people that the most popular vernacular music was unusually borrowed from older and better-trained composers. William Mason, for example, was fond of telling about the time when he was listening to a group of black roustabouts who were singing what sounded to him like the "Anvil Chorus," up to a point when they veered away from all resemblance to it. True to his father's training, he tried to correct their error, only to learn that what they really were essaying was Root's "Tramp, Tramp, Tramp."

In fact, a new kind of educated songwriter was emerging from the very elements that such men as William Mason expected to increase the national constituency for advanced art music. Hart Pease Danks, W. B. Bradbury, Robert Lowry, Philip Bliss, Fanny Crosby, James A. Butterfield, whose "When You and I Were Young, Maggie" had already matched the immense sales figures of the wartime hits, J. P. Webster, and Ira Sankey were all typical of the new breed. They touched an instinctive commonality of millions of people. Their songs, generally first published in music books, then, when popularity dictated, as sheet music, were soon selling in quantities rivaling those of the most successful Civil War songs.

The established music publishers apparently failed to perceive the proportions of this new market. They left its exploitation to independent new small firms, principally Biglow & Main, of New York. They did, however, show some interest in popular quartet and waltz songs; music of the "plantation," the new name for black-dialect music, and pieces sung by popular entertainers. But these Board of Music Trade publishers tended to concentrate on vocal and instrumental parlor music, which was most in demand by the middle and upper classes. Their salesmen had for long been musicians who eked out a living by teaching the piano and singing to the children of those Americans. By the late 1870s, the two giants, Ditson and Brainard's, and one or two others shared in one out of every four dollars spent on music education in the home.

Great strides were made after the Civil War in public-school music education. As a result, the level of amateur piano performance rose from that of the simple pieces commonplace in the 1840s to a familiarity with works that piano virtuosos introduced. Beginning with the appearance of Sigismund Thalberg in 1855, Americans were made aware of what the piano was capable, not only through touch, but by a new conception of melodic delivery. In the 1872–73 season, the Steinways paid Anton Rubinstein $40,000 for a national tour, to promote their instruments. The forty-three-year-old pianist and conductor of the Russian Imperial Court Orchestra proceeded to set a new standard of pianistic excellence.

The growth of advanced music schools and conservatories contributed to the rise in excellence of teaching and led to formation of the Music Teachers National Association in 1876. With Theodore Presser as the driving force, this group of men and women grew from an initial several dozen to almost 1,000 by 1890. It was the only organization connected in any way with music that lobbied consistently and aggressively for a reciprocal international copyright law. Many of its members wanted something that would protect American composers in Europe, where they themselves had studied and composed music.

Presser was one of them, having studied at the Leipzig Conservatory after advanced education at the New England Conservatory of Music in the early 1870s. A native of Pittsburgh, he had clerked for a local music store before beginning his professional career as a teacher in the Ohio-Virginia region. In 1883, he started *The Etude,* a monthly publication for teachers and students of the pianoforte. Eight to twelve pages in each issue were given to études, exercises, and teaching pieces. Initially, he had hoped to attract at least 5,000 subscribers, needed to support the magazine, but it soon became the voice of the music teachers' association and helped to fund the publication of modestly priced music-teaching pieces by the publishing company Presser founded in 1886 in Philadelphia.

During its eleventh meeting, in 1887, the association announced that half a million young Americans were studying the piano, in one out of every 125 households. In 1900, the first year such census figures were available, 92,000 Americans were employed full time as music teachers and musicians, more than twice the 43,249 in Great Britain, long considered a far more cultured nation.

A number of major differences between music teachers and music publishers became public soon after the formation, in 1855, of the Board of Music Trade, whose avowed purpose was to adopt and sustain a fixed uniform price for all music published. William Hall's intention to reduce prices for noncopyrighted foreign music had sparked the board's birth and industrywide resistance to this move to charge the same for American and European music, a policy book publishers had abandoned. In 1857, a group of music teachers established the first formal organization to fight the board's monopoly. Only the financial panic of 1857 and the Civil War stifled this movement.

When it appeared in 1864 that the war might be coming to an end, the board formalized its dealer-discount policy and added many regular and small retailers to the music teachers as recipients of the 50 percent discount. The move clearly was intended to make more products available in the territories where music teachers had been enjoying their own monopoly of sales by virtue of the traditional markdown.

During the following years, some board members challenged the rule of the few houses that controlled the organization: Ditson, Hall, Lee and Walker, Root & Cady. A stiff fine or expulsion was the price. Many new, nonmember, firms had become active by 1869, F. W. Helmick in Cincinnati, Benjamin W. Hitchcock in New York, White, Smith & Perry in Boston, among them. The major British house, Boosey & Co., opened an office in New York during the late 1860s. In addition, there were many publishers of ballad slipsheets, songsters, and song-word periodicals.

The music publishers also tried to make things easier for music retailers, in their competition with music teachers' sales, by issuing monthly periodicals dedicated to the advancement of the art of music. There were Brainard's *Musical World* (1863), Root & Cady's *Song Messenger of the Northwest* (1864), and Dwight's *Journal of Music,* which Ditson took over from its founder in 1858. All served as catalogues of their publishers' merchandise and as means of self-instruction. J. L. Peters advertised that, for a three-dollar annual subscription, each of the 20,000 recipients of its *Musical Monthly* received more printed music than could be had by spending fifty dollars for sheet music at retail. S. Brainard's Sons promised two dollars' worth of music in each number of *Musical World,* which sold for fifteen cents an issue, $1.50 for a year, and offered five premium collections of music for an additional ten cents. Music teachers and retail dealers who could not afford to stock large varieties of printed music were the victims of the usual trade policy of immediately filling all individual mail orders upon receipt of the full retail price, which was listed on the back cover of all printed music. To make selection easier, the music was given a number, which was its grade of difficulty: 1. easiest; 2. easy; 3. moderately easy; 4. medium; 5. difficult; 6. very difficult; 7. greatest difficulty.

At its 1869 meeting in Niagara Falls, with Chauncey M. Cady presiding, Julius Lee, of Lee and Walker, as vice president, and William Hall's son Thomas as secretary and treasurer, the Board of Music Trade approved the publication of a *Complete Catalogue of Sheet Music and Musical Works* published by its members. Dena J. Epstein has written, in an introduction to a reprint: "Presumably, the volume was to have been offered for sale, but an extensive search of music journals for the years 1869–1872 failed to uncover a single announcement or review of the *Catalogue,* any indication of its purpose, or the slightest hint of the identities of the compilers." Because it contained the copyrighted music of only twenty of the nearly 100 firms known to have been engaged in printing both the words and the music of selections that can be designated as "popular," the *Catalogue,* does not reflect the extent of the published music of the period 1825–1870. There were by 1869, as White, Smith & Perry, a Boston music firm, pointed out in the first edition of its house organ, *The Folio* "many new people in the music publishing field," of which the company was one, and it was not yet a member of the Board of Music Trade. Consequently, its songs, including its hits "Little Footsteps" and "Shoo Fly, Don't Bother Me," did not appear in the *Catalogue.* However, as was the trade practice, a successful song brought almost immediate imitation by the publication of new pieces with the same or similar titles, in the expectation that customers would buy what was available. Hall brought out "Little Footsteps That Are Lost," and Louis Tripp, of Louisville, Kentucky, "Shoo Purp, Don't Bodder Me," both of which are listed in the *Catalogue.* "Shoo Fly" had been popular with black soldiers during the war and was published by White, Smith as written by Billy Reeves and Frank Campbell but arranged by one of the day's most famous minstrel-show singers, Rollin Howard. The twentieth-century's practice of "cutting in" a star performer as author of a popular song, honed to sharper edge than ever during Stephen Foster's lifetime, was prevalent by the 1870s.

The first successful songwriter to become a major music publisher, Charles A. White, was born in 1832 on a farm in rural Massachusetts. At twelve he built a violin out of a cigar box and taught himself to play so well that a British teacher of physical training, in which dancing was an important element, hired him to play during lessons. For many years after that, White was a teacher of dancing. He entered the music business just before the Civil War, when he opened a Boston music store in partnership with W. Frank Smith, who had clerked for Oliver Ditson. White wrote some popular songs, which Ditson published, but when his own firm was nearly bankrupt after two years, he realized it was because they were selling music they did not own. Raising $900 from the sale of a pleasure sailing boat, White opened a publishing company in partnership with Smith and John F. Perry, another music dealer, in 1867. Almost from the start, it was successful. "Shoo Fly" sold nearly 200,000 copies in sheet music and a gallop arrangement, and "Little Feet" did almost as well. An experience with his first published effort had taught White how to protect himself from one form of piracy. Ditson had published it as well as another, with virtually the same melody and the same title, and had refused to hear White's complaint. So, early in his publishing career, his "Moonlight on the Lake" sold 500,000 copies after he countered any effort by rival houses to mislead the public with similar titles by writing "When 'tis Moonlight on the Lake" and "When 'tis Starlight," waltz songs that did almost as well as the original.

Regarding himself as a businessman first, but songwriting as a profession out of which he intended to make money, too, White wrote more than 1,500 copyrighted pieces before his death. The melody and verse for his first hit, "Put Me in My Little Bed," were written in less than fifteen minutes, and the song was an immediate success. His ability to write attractive melodies and simple lyrics was the firm's chief asset for years. In 1870, "Come, Birdie, Come" did almost as well as his first song. He did not, as he once said, "strike fire every time, because it was almost impossible to hit on a popular idea every time," but he had surely learned the art of satisfying large numbers of people with his music. "When 'tis Moonlight on the Lake" was the first of his quartet songs to be performed in four-part harmony, with considerable use of an echo effect, which was very popular at that time.

During the 1870s, when Boston was one of the major centers of the minstrel-show business, White wrote and published songs for use by local and national companies. His "The Old Home Ain't What It Used to Be," "I'se Gwine Back to Dixie," and "The Little Old Log Cabin in the Dell" (written after Will S. Hays's hit of almost the same title) were all successful, but not as much as those brought to the firm by a young black minstrel performer named James A. Bland. They were all published by White, Smith & Perry, but when Perry left to go into business the next year, Bland went with him, and many of his greatest songs bore Perry's imprint.

Charles White's most successful song, "Marguerite," sold more than a million copies in the twenty years after its creation in 1882, principally because it was interpolated into the record-breaking melodrama *The Old Homestead*. The song was written almost to order, when Smith said that a new love song would be appropriate as the firm's next publication. "I went home and picked up my old violin," White recalled in an 1890 interview. "The idea had come to me of a young woman leaving the country and her rustic lover to go to the city. The rustic lover realizes that she would soon forget him and he is sorrowful and despairing. That was the idea I wanted to get out. It isn't necessary for me to put my feet into ice water and my head in a bag in order to write a song. As soon as my fingers grasped the neck of the violin the tune came to me." Because he was a songwriter, White was different from most music publishers of the time. He took his newest child backstage to the old Boston Theatre, where Denman Thompson was starring in *The Old Homestead*. After hearing White perform the new piece, Thompson ordered that it become part of the production, where it remained until well into the next century.

As a businessman, White considered American popular music inferior to the foreign compositions the public appeared to prefer. Therefore, he was against passage of the international copyright law.

White, Smith had been admitted to membership on the Board of Music Trade in 1883, but resigned from it in 1890, convinced that the board needed to become a combination of the largest retail dealers and major music publishers in order to offset the inroads of new music houses. White, Smith was by then one of the most important music publishers in the country, with nine branch offices and a new five-story headquarters building in Boston. Music of all types came off the firm's presses, printed for publishers of all sizes both in the United States and abroad, as well as for private individuals. In addition, the firm operated a Canadian printing plant for French-language music and another solely for Spanish publications. It was one of the few firms not sponsored or founded by Oliver Ditson to remain a major twentieth-century music publisher. Most of the major pre–Civil War firms had been absorbed by Ditson, including Mason Brothers, Lee and Walker, William Hall, and J. L. Peters. Ditson also held a half-interest in the John Church Company, of Cincinnati.

The rock on which the house of J. L. Peters, music publisher of New York, had rested for a decade was Will Shakespeare Hays, born in 1837 in Louisville, Kentucky, where he continued to live until his death in 1892. He was by profession a newspaperman, for most of his life the writer of a column in the *Courier-Journal* devoted to the Ohio River, its commerce, lore, and rivermen. He was also a talented and successful postwar white songwriter in the Stephen Foster tradition, and produced at least 500 songs, which sold many millions of copies in total, as well as additional quantities of collections, folios, songbooks, music for the violin and the piano, and at least one large instrumental work. He had only slight knowledge of theory and harmony. In his youth, he had learned to play several instruments, but he always played new pieces on a piano for some trained musician to put down on paper.

He was twenty-five when he sent his first successful song, "Evangeline," to

Silas Brainard, in Cleveland, and though he got no money for it, he continued to turn out others, most of which were published by D. P. Faulds, of Louisville, in whose music store he clerked. His "Drummer Boy of Shiloh" was published on both sides of the battlefront. "My Sunny Southern Home," first printed in Louisville, became so popular in the Confederacy that Union General Butler vowed to put its author into prison should he ever chance upon him. After the war, John Peters became the first publisher to encourage Hays, by paying for his songs; he gave him twenty-five dollars each for several, among them the successful "Write Me a Letter from Home," which sold more than 350,000 copies, and "We Parted by the Riverside," which sold 300,000.

In August 1867, Peters signed Hays to an exclusive contract, which gave the composer a two-and-a-half-cent royalty on all printed copies of his music sold. This was extended three years later, and when the Oliver Ditson Company purchased Peters in 1877, Hays became a Ditson writer. He was then regarded as the most successful American songwriter, "having sold more copies and more songs than any five men," according to his hometown newspaper, the *Courier-Journal.* His total sale at the time was more than three and a half million copies. "Nora O'Neal" (1866) had already sold 250,000 copies; "Mollie Darling" (1871), 150,000; "Shamus O'Brien," 200,000.

Hays had written black-dialect verse for his newspaper column, and, with the growing national popularity of minstrel shows suitable for a family audience, he used it again. His plantation songs became extraordinarily well known. "Early in de Mornin'," "Roll Out, Heave dat Cotton," "Angels Meet Me at the Cross Roads," "Keep in de Middle ob de Road," "Oh, Sam!," "Susan Jane," and "Little Old Log Cabin in the Lane" became part of the repertory of most itinerant white minstrel companies and served as a model for young black songwriters entering the business by way of black minstrelsy. In 1923, when the hillbilly-music industry was born, with a recording session by Fiddlin' John Carson, in Atlanta, Georgia, Hays's "Little Old Log Cabin in the Lane," slightly altered by time and usage, and then regarded as a piece of authentic fold music, was chosen as the A, or preferred, side on the *OkeH* release that resulted.

During the four years he was a member of the Board of Music Trade (1873–1876), John Peters, who had served as president in the last two, saw the trade settle down to prosperity for the few and difficulties for the many. According to Lyon & Healy's *Musical Independent,* one publisher, certainly Oliver Ditson, had made a fortune, and two had become rich, one of them probably Silas Brainard, who had recently died. Only about 1,200 selections in the board's 1870 *Catalogue* had warranted a retail order for 25 copies, and fewer than 100 an order for as many as 200. One new song in a thousand ever sold more than a thousand copies, and the run-of-the-mill songwriter was fortunate to average sales of 500 copies.

As the United States celebrated its centennial in 1876, twenty-eight publishers were regarded as major firms, slightly fewer than half of them board members. William Hall, the independent rebel who had precipitated the creation of the board, was dead, as was his old War of 1812 comrade John Firth. Root &

Cady was no longer a functioning music publisher; its surviving partners were laboring for others in the business or nibbling at the trade's edges. Horace Waters had quit the publishing game to devote his time to piano sales and the cause of temperance. He left his business in the hands of one of his former clerks, Charles Tremaine, once a member of a singing family.

In 1859, Oliver Ditson had moved into the Midwest market by sending his twenty-year-old clerk John Church to Cincinnati to take over the David Truax catalogue, purchased outright the previous year. Beginning with a half-interest junior partnership, Church had prospered, and he bought out Ditson in 1870. Changing the firm's name to John Church & Co., he proceeded to build an extensive business in general musical merchandise and publications. His position was recognized in 1872 by election to the presidency of the Board of Music Trade, to succeed Chauncey Cady, whose own company had collapsed. Church provided half of the $150,000 with which Cady attempted to restore his firm, and thereby came into possession of publications that were to make him an even more important music man throughout the remainder of the century. Among these were Horatio Richmond Palmer's *Song King* and *Song Queen* series, which sold more than 200,000 copies, and his popular religious song "Yield Not to Temptation."

George F. Root joined the Church firm as editor and held musical institutes under company sponsorship, which served to promote instructional manuals and texts. Church's monthly magazine, *The Musical Visitor,* which Root edited, became the official journal of the Chautauqua Musical Reading Club. This company-operated mail-order business offered a four-year course of home music study based on Church book and music publications, sold to members at a discount. In association with Biglow & Main, Church co-published Moody and Sankey's *Gospel Hymn* series, which sold millions of copies around the world. The company did not neglect secular music. It brought out many songs associated with stars of the white minstrel theater in the 1870s and 1880s. Among them was Gus Williams, star and songwriter of the popular German-dialect *Fritz* musical stage plays, whose songs enjoyed vast sales.

In the east, Ditson's two sons were beginning to make their own marks. The older, Charles, who had learned the business as a clerk, was admitted to partnership in 1867 and put in charge of the New York branch, then named for him, which eventually absorbed the Mason brothers, Firth, Son & Co., William Hall & Son, and J. L. Peters. The firm, a major adjunct to the large wholesale and retail Ditson trade, was also chief retailer to music teachers and dealers in the central states. With the acquisition of the major Lee and Walker catalogue in 1875, James W. Ditson, the younger son, moved to Philadelphia to head a firm bearing his name. As the largest retail house in that area, it handled the parent firm's wholesale trade throughout the South. James's tragic death in 1881 reduced the branch to a subsidiary operation, run by employees.

Second in rank to Oliver Ditson, John C. Haynes ran the Boston company and enabled his mentor to engage in a number of commercial ventures, which included presidency of the National Bank of Boston and trusteeship of the Boston Safe Deposit Company and the Franklin Bank, which Ditson had originated and managed. When Oliver Ditson died in 1888, Haynes assumed full charge of the giant enterprise, but he did not neglect his own considerable commercial holdings, which included real estate in Boston and the Midwest. Although not a trained musician like Ditson, Haynes had introduced many musical innovations: the first American publication of Mendelssohn's *Songs Without Words,* already the most important collection of solo piano music in Europe; Beethoven's complete piano sonatas, a daring venture at the time; and Nathan Richardson's *New Method for the Piano,* which made more than one million dollars in a decade. He had demonstrated his considerable managerial abilities in the early 1860s, when Ditson decided to add musical-instrument manufacture and put him in charge. The John C. Haynes & Co. division became, in time, one of the best-equipped instrument factories in America and made a half-million dollars annually. Having served as secretary-treasurer during the Civil War, Haynes became an important presence on the Board of Music Trade in the mid-1870s, being named vice-president and, in 1877, acting president.

By then, S. Brainard's Sons, of Cleveland, was reckoned to be second only to Ditson as a music publisher, wholesaler and retailer. Following the death of their father, in 1871, Charles and Henry shared in the purchase, for $150,000, of the Root & Cady plates. With this popular-music catalogue, they left educational and religious publishing to Church. They then began to diversify, dealing in all major makes of musical instruments and opening an electrotypy factory and a bindery that were fully equipped to print music on order for amateur songwriters. For twenty-two dollars, one could obtain 100 copies of a four-page song, with illustrated title page, and copyright registration. The Brainards were founding members of the Board of Music Trade, but not until 1880 was one of them, Henry, made an officer. The main Brainard office had been moved to Chicago, where Charles was in charge. A creditable musician, he had worked as a salesman in the Cleveland store before being made a partner in 1865 and given control of *Musical World,* which served as a chief advertising medium and public-relations tool. Through this house organ, Charles announced, in August 1879, the presence in Chicago of a major music house, with more than 20,000 pieces of music and 100,000 music plates.

The growth and size of the music-publishing trade was posing a major problem of overproduction and of overstocking by retailers. William Pond pointed out to *The American Art Journal* in August 1879 that because there was so much competition, and despite a disposition not to publish so much, many houses feared the displeasure of composers and songwriters and consequently brought out music they knew would not recoup production costs. He ascribed the concentration of business in a few large houses to the fact that some firms were so badly underfinanced they could not endure the strain of competition. There had already been several proposals to reorganize the Board of Music Trade as a result, one of them a suggestion to form a subordinate Dealers Protective Association. This may have been Pond's suggestion, for the trade press hinted that he was usually fined for his conduct at board meetings. The proposal was rejected, and annual meetings evidently degenerated into such splits over policy that they were recessed. The group was regarded as defunct in late 1879.

A rebel element appears to have prevailed in 1880, when Pond was elected president and new rules of conduct were approved at a meeting involving every large music publishing house in the country, with White, Smith, of Boston, as a new member. Overproduction, price fixing, and overstocking continued to take their toll. Major music pirates had emerged in the United States to disrupt the trade, offering copyrighted music owned by Board of Music Trade members at one sixth its retail price. The piano-manufacturing industry produced about 45,000 instruments in 1880, valued at around $12.5 million, and demand was growing for inexpensive printed music. The courtesy-of-the-trade policy instituted at the formation of the board remained a tentative gentlemen's understanding, although the American book trade, from which the music men had borrowed it, now recognized individual ownership of a European work provided some payment was made to the author. Five separately owned versions of the popular noncopyrighted "La Manola" were listed in the board's 1870 *Catalogue,* as well as three waltz arrangements of it and two hornpipes. Ten years later, the most popular version was "The Manola Waltz," arranged by an American and published by Edward Schuberth, of New York, who was not affiliated with the board. Another nonmember, the Philadelphia music publisher W. F. Shaw, issued Schuberth's version in one of his own cut-rate music folios. Though Schuberth understood that going after Shaw was a difficult task, one with little prospect of victory, he undertook to test an issue the major houses preferred to avoid for fear of rocking the boat. Shaw's defense was that an arrangement of an uncopyrighted work could not itself be protected. Schuberth prevailed, but Board of Music Trade publishers condemned Shaw, not for his piracy, but for failure to comprehend "what it means to occupy the position a respectable music publisher, understanding the nature of his business and willing to respect the rights of his colleagues and the musical profession."

The cheap library explosion, beginning in the mid-1870s, which nearly wrecked the American book business had a simultaneous counterpart in the music trade. Much of it was centered in Canada. In the early twentieth century, representatives of the Music Publishers Association complained to Congress that low-priced, pirated reprints of their most popular music were still being advertised and sold in the United States, despite pending copyright law changes. On at least two occasions—in 1882, by a group of member and nonmember publishers, and three years later—a committee circularized dealers and the trade and paid for advertisements calling attention to Canadian reprints being openly sold at "extraordinary and tempting" prices. A reward of forty dollars was promised for any information leading to the conviction of any persons engaged in the business. Retail dealers in the states who carried these publications, as well as persons who purchased them, were warned that they were violating the Copyright Act. Despite this and other campaigns, the practice remained rampant until a new copyright regulation involved the active intervention of postal authorities.

Retail dealers were having their own problems. Independent sheet-music jobbing had not yet been introduced, and they had to travel to the offices of the few leading wholesale-retail music publishers, where they were often misled by song titles deliberately similar to those of hits, or to order their stock by mail. There were no sheet-music traveling salesmen to stimulate interest in new publications or keep the retailers aware of what was afoot in the business. The publishers had learned from the difficulties created for piano manufacturers by their itinerant drummers. Few had any loyalty to the parent organization; they promised greatly reduced wholesale prices in order to make sales and build up commissions. Though volume did increase, profits fell, and manufacturers soon reduced the number of their traveling salesmen and relied on mail orders or regular visits to their plants by piano dealers. There was also a new regulation that required orders for at least $300 worth of printed music in order to qualify for a 50 percent discount. Shelves were piled with overstock as a result, making easily available Canadian reprints especially intriguing. Music teachers, with their guaranteed markets, were another problem, as was the fact that the publishers were making a 1,400 percent profit from the retail mail-order business they stimulated by listing items for sale on the back of every piece of printed music.

Small wonder that, although they were sold at double their European cost, cheap German, French, and English reprints of the classics were creating a million-dollar annual market. As the retail music market had extended westward, European publishers had terminated the exclusive sales agencies assigned to a few East Coast publishers.

Small wonder, too, that such men as W. F. Shaw, B. W. Hitchcock and his fifteen-cent *Monthly Musical Gem* magazine, and Richard Saalfield and his five-cent-music publishing company were regularly pilloried at Board of Music Trade meetings. Saalfield offered dealers a new kind of retail sheet-music business, one based on increased volume and profits owing to his drastically reduced wholesale prices. With his catalogue of 600 items, and new ones added daily, he hoped to recruit music stores and instrument dealers ready to throw up sheet music altogether because sales were too small and dead stock piled up, absorbing profits. His sales pitch seemed irresistible: "If you take hold of our five-cent music you will sell at least ten copies . . . and you will make 150 per cent profit." A person who "buys one piece at 30 or 40 cents" will "take ten or twenty different pieces at 5 cents. . . . If you keep a sample copy of each piece on your counter . . . persons will pick up on an average ten pieces that they otherwise would never have taken."

Saalfield's main office was in New York City. His brother operated a branch in Chicago, where the reduced-price market continued to flourish long after the office in the east was closed. Two similar firms were organized in Chicago, National Music Company and Chicago Music Company, which placed their publications in cheap-music stores and on sidewalk stands, where reprints of the same European music the eastern companies sold at eight times the cost were mixed with new popular songs written for them. Often their editions could not be distinguished from the hits they capitalized on. J. P. Webster's "In the Sweet By and By" was issued as "Piano Variations" on it, with the title in large type and no mention of the arranger, George Schlieffarth, the most prolific Chicago composer of five-cent music. Ditson and Lyon & Healy brought suit for infringement, and were in turn sued by Webster's widow for having failed to share their profits from "over a million copies sold in five-cent form." Songwriters got little money from this business. Schlieffarth once testified that he had written more than 1,500 copyrighted compositions, many of them for National and Chicago, for which he received only $5,000 in royalties. His hit "Who Will Buy My Roses Wild?," which sold at least 100,000 copies, netted him eighty-three dollars.

Saalfield was never able to build up a national distribution system or a large enough volume of sales and went bankrupt within a year. There were other publishers engaged in the cheap-music business, however, who were less ambitious than Saalfield and appear to have prospered.

Brainard's was not prospering and, in mid-1883, sold a part interest in the business to a local music dealer, W. F. Albright. The following year, another outsider, E. L. Graves, replaced the retiring Henry Brainard, and Charles Brainard returned to the Cleveland office. Business started to improve under Albright and Graves, who initiated new methods of operation. In 1884, the company reported its worth as approaching half a million dollars, from 31,720 active titles and 50,000 copyrights. Around the same time, *The American Art Journal* estimated, from the questionably accurate measure of music-plate ownership as reported by the publishers, that William Pond followed Ditson and Brainard's in worth, with about 11,000 publications; below Pond were S. T. Gordon & Son, New York, 8,300; John Church & Co., 6,000; White, Smith & Co., 5,600. Four years later, when industry gossip said that Charles Brainard, in poor health, was anxious to give up the music business, John Haynes offered $80,000 on behalf of the Ditson Company, but he withdrew after being asked to add another $20,000. It is an indication of changing times in the music business that ten years earlier Ditson had paid J. L. Peters $125,000 for a catalogue that ranked below that of Brainard's. In a sweeping reorganization in 1889, S. Brainard's Sons was incorporated as an Illinois music publisher and dealer, with a capital stock of $250,000. Charles Brainard remained a partner with Albright, but a new man entered, H. F. Chandler, once a salesman for the company and now associated with a Chicago music-plate manufacturing and printing business. The Cleveland facilities were shut down, and all stocks of printed music and books were moved to Chicago. Three firms there took over all printing work and effected a 25 percent reduction from previous production costs.

From the perspective of a century, it is evident that most major houses were wallowing in a slough of inertia. Dedicated to maximizing profits from their copyrights at the expense of the public retail business, they had created many of the evils besetting the trade. Retailers proclaimed that there no longer was any money in sheet music, since it was difficult to maintain a complete stock without accumulating an increasing amount of dead material. The once-regulated fixed discount policy was out of control, by either an association of music publishers or the trade itself, further reducing profits and tending to drive marginal operations out of business.

A few new and specialized publishers had entered the business during the

1880s, particularly in New York City, the center of the variety entertainment Tony Pastor pioneered and the home of musical stage works that could recoup production expenses and make substantial profits, though only on the road. The earliest of the new publishers specializing in popular music to achieve any success with songs that leading publishers rejected, missed, or completely ignored was Willis Woodward, a magazine publisher and printer, who issued his first popular song in 1883. The following year, he had one of the decade's biggest hits, "White Wings," purchased for twenty dollars by the man Woodward credited on the sheet-music cover with its authorship, Banks Winter, a minstrel-show tenor, who received an eight-cent royalty on every copy sold. It had become standard practice for the newer publishers to pay performers who boosted their songs either a small sum regularly or a royalty ranging from six or eight cents to as much as fourteen cents a copy. This practice, the twentieth century's payola, had come by way of England. It began on January 3, 1866, when the publisher John Boosey presented contralto Charlotte Sainton-Dolby at his first "Ballad Concert." The songs she introduced were not serious music; instead, they were what soon became known as "royalty" ballads, because a royalty was paid to Madame Sainton-Dolby. After that, every other important singer contracted by Boosey and rival ballad publishers was paid. Newspaper advertisements announcing such performances were paid for by the publishers and appeared whenever royalty singers concertized. Although the public was never aware of it, almost every important vocalist was part of the game. Antoinette Sterling introduced Sullivan's "The Lost Chord" and sang it at every Boosey concert for the next twenty years, collecting a sheet-music royalty throughout that time. Singers became so associated in the public's mind with their royalty songs that contracts for concerts required them to sing their hits. Because the system remained secret, a half century later questions were still being raised about its morality.

The 1890s ragged-time songs, musical-comedy successes, and co-publication with major London music houses lay in the near future for individuals who, with a few exceptions, knew little about words and music and cared less, but perceived that money could be made in popular music and intended to get their share of it. With little or no experience, they were ready to promote and merchandise music after the new fashion being used by big business. Knowingly or intuitively, they applied precepts of salesmanship being expounded by John Henry Patterson, the genius of the American Cash Register Company, who looked for salesmen who could be trained, rather than those born to the profession, and emphasized that familiarity with the product must be inculcated in the customer in order to maximize sales.

The Pianola and the Victrola

A pianista, invented in France and generally regarded as the earliest mechanical piano employing the vacuum principle, was shown at the 1876 exposition in Philadelphia. It got no great response from Americans, who were spending their money for the true instrument in ever greater numbers. By 1880, piano mechanic John McTammany of Worcester, Massachusetts, whose tombstone epitaph hails him as "Inventor of the Player Piano," had developed the first of his mechanical-toy "Organettes," on which any child "old enough to use hands intelligently" could produce "any desired melody or harmony, sacred or secular, from the most plaintive dirge to the most lively dance music," by cranking a perforated paper roll and pumping the small bellows, which provided the air to activate organ reeds. McTammany had taken out the first of fifteen patents dealing with his device in 1866. He eventually sold all of them to the Mechanical Organette Company. The head of this enterprise was William B. Tremaine, of the New York music-publishing and piano-business family, who merchandised McTammany's now improved toy as a superior musical instrument for use by adults. Some year later, Tremaine purchased the Aeolian Organ Company and in 1888 bought the patents and plant of a Boston automatic-music-roll manufacturing company. His twenty-two-year-old son, Henry, left his job as salesman for a paper company to join his father, and succeeded him in 1890 as head of this assortment of companies.

In the words of a contemporary, young William Tremaine "without any experience in the business," had had "the great advantage of nothing to forget" and was able to apply modern corporate strategies. He moved the troubled Mechanical Organette Company uptown into expensive and impressive offices, from which he engaged in a series of acquisitions and reorganizations that were financed by men of wealth charmed by his forceful and aggressive personality. He next established a new Aeolian Organ and Music Company, one of a number throughout the northeast dealing in automatic organs and pianos and the manufacture of perforated music rolls. In 1895, Edwin Scott Votey, a partner in the Detroit organ-building company that supplied Aeolian its instruments, perfected a pedal-operated machine that, when attached to a piano, enabled one to play the instrument mechanically, using music rolls. By nature a craftsman, rather than an entrepreneur, Votey turned exploitation rights for his machine over to Tremaine, who introduced the "Aeriola," a self-playing piano late in the year. The empire-in-embryo grew again in 1899 when Tremaine was elected president of a reorganized Aeolian Company. He owned many patents acquired by merger and pooling and engaged in the manufacture of pianos, player-piano attachments, and perforated rolls. In three years, upright and grand Aeolian pianos to which Voety's "Pianola" attachments were affixed were the majority of about 75,000 player pianos sold, for which more than a million music rolls were bought annually.

The first commercially successful coin-operated player piano was introduced in 1898 by the Wurlitzer Company, of Cincinnati, Ohio. It used a cylinder containing ten selections of currently popular music, any one of which could by played and repeated for a nickel a time. A coin-operated piano using paper rolls was introduced by Wurlitzer in 1902 and, with continuing improvements, remained a successful item until the Depression of the 1930s, when coin-operated phonographs supplanted all other machines that reproduced music mechanically. By that time, at least sixty-five separate companies had been involved in the coin-operated player-piano business.

Wurlitzer also made the PianOrchestra, manufactured in many different sizes and quickly duplicated by others under many names. These machines used paper rolls that duplicated mechanically almost all the instruments of a full symphony orchestra. Coin-operated machines had a common price of a nickel a play, and the type of music offered was keyed to the location, ranging from classical and salon music in hotels and expensive restaurants to the latest popular songs in beer gardens, dancing pavilions, ice-cream parlors, arcades, lobbies of nickelodeon theaters, and amusement resorts. George Gershwin was a child when he first heard popular music, played by a coin-operated piano in a neighborhood store. Much the same was true for most urban Americans during the years preceding World War I.

A four-page color advertisement placed by Aeolian in *Cosmopolitan* in 1902 stunned the piano world and player-piano dealers. Exactly 8,131 different selections were already on Aeolian rolls, it said, and an additional 250 were to be added every month. The music included classic pieces by Scarlatti, Bach, Haydn, Rubinstein, Schubert, Chopin, Beethoven, Mendelssohn, Moskowski, Liszt, Wagner, Verdi, Mascagni, Suppé, and Gounod, and popular music— Strauss waltzes, Sousa marches, parlor songs, ragtime hits, and selections from Broadway musicals.

Despite many innovative features, the Pianola, like all other mechanical piano attachments, depended on its primary programing material, a perforated paper roll. The earliest were laid out mathematically, and the original, or master, was duplicated from it by workmen. It was left to the operator, who supplied the necessary pneumatic power by pumping foot pedals, to create musical expression. Beginning in 1891, a wavy line running the full length of the roll was introduced. When a lever controlling tempo was moved, a pointer following this line, and various tempos and sound effects were produced mechanically, for players who generally were without any musical training.

In the beginning, player-piano attachments affected only sixty-five notes of the eighty-eight-note instrument. Moreover, until the war, rolls did not contain the words of popular songs; in order to sing along, one had to buy the sheet music. The Vocalstyle Music Company, of Cincinnati, was the first to stencil words on paper rolls, around 1909, but these were principally for art music. Sing A Word player rolls of popular music with lyrics running along the right side became standard in 1916. Publishers charged four cents for the right to print these, and eight cents for "high-priced" songs, plus two cents for each roll manufactured, as required by the 1909 Copyright Act. In 1919, the Music Publishers Protective Association raised the rates for words to six and twelve cents.

German technology introduced in America after 1904 made it possible to record an actual performance. Master rolls were made on a electrically powered pneumatic piano to whose keys and pedal electric keys were attached, these in turn indicating with a pencil on the master roll exactly how long pedal and keys were depressed—longer for soft notes, shorter for loud ones. Mechanical control of perforations that provided more realistic shadings of expression came soon after, providing for the first time a reasonably close mechanical approximation of the original artist's performance. It became the fashion to invite friends to home concerts by Paderewski, Debussy, Grieg, or Victor Herbert.

In 1903, Henry Tremaine's mechanical-piano empire was the largest in the world, with capital of $10 million and factories in the United States and Germany. It controlled eleven American, German, Austrian, and English manufacturing and operating companies, and manufactured the Aeriola, Aeolian Orchestrelle, Pianola, Metrostyle Pianola, Pianola Piano, and the Aeolian Pipe Organ, as well as the Weber, Steck, Wheelock, and Stuyvesant pianos, the Vocalian and Votey organs, the British Orchestrelle, and the pianos of the Choralion Company of Germany and Austria.

Player-piano industry sales grew from one out of every eight of the 364,545 pianos manufactured in 1909 to a peak, in 1921, of 208,541 of the 341,652 made and sold that year.

Not until after the depression of 1893–1895 had been weathered did the early player piano and Edison's wonderful talking machine move out of the coin arcade and into the family parlor. Only a relatively small portion of Edison's business-machine production was making its way into government and commercial offices, much of the rest being equipped for coin-slot operation. Because of their cost and mechanical unreliability, many rented phonographs for use in the home carried with the lease the regular services of a competent repairman-mechanic. While Edison stubbornly maintained his determination to promote his invention as a business machine, the Columbia Phonograph Company, largest and most successful of the franchise holders, concentrated on vernacular music for its program material and moved aggressively into the coin-operated automatic-phonograph market. Its slot machines could be rented for $125 a year or bought outright for $250. The rental for Columbia's new headquarters in Washington was paid by profits from a company-operated Phonograph Parlor in the same building. Washingtonians cued up there by the dozens to drop their nickels into one of the hundred or so machines. Columbia Phonograph Parlors were established in other major cities, and one on the boardwalk in Atlantic City was particularly successful. By the end of the decade, Columbia had expanded across the nation and was located in London, Berlin, and Paris. Elegant showrooms were opened, where the company's musical performers made regular personal appearances. Nearly 3,500 persons jammed into the New York display hall on one occasion in 1898 to see and hear music performed by yodelers, xylophonists, vocalists, and former street musician George W. Johnson.

The depression years were troubled ones for Edison, who was plagued by a series of lawsuits disputing his control of patents basic to talking-machine development and manufacture. In addition, he was forced to recognize that the popularity of coin machines and their two-minute cylinders of popular music had turned the industry away from supplying the business world. So he set his assistants to work on a cylinder player to be used in the home. He was also spurred to the effort by Columbia's introduction of a spring-driven American Graphophone, which sold for seventy-five dollars. To frustrate continuing litigation, he placed his North American Phonograph Company in bankruptcy, effectively shutting off the supply of all Edison phonographs and blank cylinders. Many of his smaller franchise holders went out of business as a result. Columbia, with its own cheap new machine and company-owned blank-cylinder factory, set up by a technician hired away from Edison, thus gained even greater domination of the market. Competition was decimated further by the first of a series of price cuts, a 40 percent reduction from the early 1890s' standard of one dollar to two dollars per cylinder.

While Columbia was consolidating its position, a resident of Washington was at work experimenting with many of Columbia's singers and musicians on the flat disks, or "plates," he had perfected. Born in Germany, Emile Berliner was nineteen when he came to the United States in 1870 to work in a Washington dry-goods store. Of a scientific turn of mind, he had experimented with improvements for Bell's telephone in his boardinghouse-room laboratory. There, he created a transmitter that the Bell Telephone Company purchased from him for a large sum along with his services as consultant. After several years in Germany, where he opened a telephone-instrument manufacturing company, he returned to Washington and went to work engraving sound vibrations on metal by chemical action and a hand-cranked machine on which to reproduce them. In 1888, he demonstrated these at a meeting of scientists and proclaimed that his methods made possible "as many copies as desired" of a single master recording. Only a German novelty maker showed any interest. Operating under a license from Berliner, he manufactured five-inch Celluloid or rubber discs, which, with small hand-driven reproducing machines, he put into expensive toys.

However beautiful and round the tone of Berliner's Improved Gramophone and more natural his flat plates, their virtues were little known outside Washington in 1895. Some friends had made a small investment in the United States Gramophone Company, which controlled all the patents, then leased them to the Berliner Gramophone Company, formed by Philadelphia financiers. In a position to manufacture and promote his inventions on a modest scale, Berliner moved to Philadelphia, where Columbia saw no great challenge in an operation that revolved around a record store, probably the first of its kind. A limited number of twelve-dollar Seven-Inch Hand Gramophones and plates of music and recitation were sold. The instrument resembled those used in the German toys. Its major weakness, when compared with Columbia and Edison machines, was the uncertainty of turntable speed produced by manual operation.

The Wizard of Menlo Park had returned to the phonograph wars, having formed the National Phonograph Company out of the remains of North American. From its factory came a new Edison hand-wound spring-driven Home Phonograph, which sold originally for forty dollars, but was driven down to thirty dollars within a year by Columbia's competition. The Edison laboratories had also developed a new method to mass-produce records, using a pantograph to make five masters at a time and duplicating them at least five times before they wore out. The record business was finally getting off the ground, just as the economy improved and consumers were attracted by cheaper players, an increasing and varied repertory, and Columbia's price-cutting tactics that reduced popular cylinders to fifty cents each, five dollars for a dozen. For the rest of the decade, Columbia remained the leader of some ten companies, which produced a half-million cylinders and records in 1897, and 2.8 million two years later.

The first to issue a numerical catalogue, in 1895, borrowing from Edison's early system for identification of recordings, Columbia was the earliest company to sign a performing group to an exclusive contract: the Marine Corps Band, which was stationed in close proximity to its recording studio. When two men from New York came to Washington to record the band on masters to be auctioned off, Columbia obtained an injunction, thus getting legal sanction for its franchise in the District of Columbia and its agreement with the band.

By 1898, some recording artists had become well-known public personalities. They sang or played the same material for any company that paid them the usual two dollars for each master made. Only a small group of performers had mastered the very exacting voice control that was needed for recording. They had to sing with distinctness and strength and show expression without too much variation of tone. The work asked for gymnastic ability, as well. "For notes that are soft and low you must thrust your head into the receiver," a Columbia executive explained, "and must draw it out again as rapidly or slowly as you increase the volume of sound. In a piece that has sudden changes the singer's head keeps bobbing back and forth all the time . . . a soprano . . . must put her head as far as it will go into the horn when she's on her very low notes, and when she soars to the heights she must draw quickly back and sing straight to the ceiling."

Columbia sought to curb its artists' gypsylike habits and keep them out of rival studios by signing them to a year's contract for their exclusive services. The best known were Vess Ossman, the banjoist; Steve Porter, Len Spencer, and Billy Golden, vocalists; Minnie Emmett, soprano; and members of the new Columbia house orchestra.

The mechanical genius of a young Camden, New Jersey, machine-shop owner and builder of models for inventors, Eldridge Reeve Johnson, put Berliner's flat disk into serious competition by turning the inefficient hand-wound record player into what became the world-famed Victrola, which gave its name to any talking machine using flat records. It had become obvious that, in order to compete with Columbia and Edison cylinder players, the Berliner Gramophone needed motor power like theirs, rather than hand power, to turn records at constant speed. Several devices were tried unsuccessfully before Johnson came into the Philadelphia office with an improved hand-wound motor and soon after, in the summer of 1896, received an initial order for 200 of them. The Berliner board of directors then signed an agreement with a New York promoter, Frank Seaman, giving him exclusive United States sales rights to the Gramophone. An expensive advertising campaign was mounted by Seaman, and by Christmas he was unable to fill all the orders for a twenty-five-dollar improved model, even though Johnson was stepping up production to 1,500 motors a week. The machinist had also developed a new sound box, resulting in improved quality.

All new seven-inch recordings were made of Celluloid, rather than vulcanized rubber. Their louder sound was an advantage over cylinders. It resulted from Johnson's experiments with a thick wax blank master, which was electroplated after recording and used for stamping copies. Owing to the complicated state of affairs involving earlier patents, Johnson registered only part of his new process, which he supervised personally and in great secrecy in a new Camden factory, where all Gramophone component parts were also manufactured.

On the staff was one of the truly giant figures of early recording-industry history, Fred Gaisberg. In his early twenties, Gaisberg had left Columbia, where he had worked with the major talent, to join Berliner, and then got his new company to duplicate its best-selling cylinder hits on Gramophone masters. Half of the 500,000 cylinders and disks produced in 1897 were sold by Seaman, and the following year his total sales of all records (715,000 of the total of 1.5 million cylinders and disks manufactured) and players went over the million-dollar mark.

Columbia resorted to a vitriolic advertising campaign, seeking to remove Berliner as a serious competitor. It compared the quality of Berliner's records to "the braying of a wild ass" or "escaping steam," in which it was joined editorially by the major talking-machine trade paper. Legal action followed.

Frank Seaman responded to American Graphophone's suit, brought to enjoin him from selling the Berliner talking machine, by reorganizing his company into the National Gramophone Corporation, which began to merchandise a slightly modified imitation of the Improved Gramophone. He had long been discontented with his share of profits, which had fallen off by a third in 1899 as a result of the anti-Gramophone war. He assented to a decree affirming Columbia's ownership of certain patents basic to Johnson's operations, and began a joint manufacture of the Zonophone with Columbia and American Graphophone, leaving the Berliner management to build a new sales organization. A month later, Seaman got an injunction of his own, which restrained Berliner from selling its own products in the United States.

When the order was filed, Emile Berliner was on his way to Europe to inspect the progress of his growing international operations. A Canadian subsidiary had been the first of these, formed in 1897, with his son Herbert in charge. William Barry Owen, who had been trained as a lawyer and learned the business from Seaman at National Gramophone, was then dispatched abroad to sell Berliner's European rights for a million dollars. A year followed before the English Gramophone Company was formed with Owen as managing director. Parts were shipped from Camden for assembly in England, and Gaisberg was sent to London to take charge of recording activities. In late 1898, some hydraulic presses, manufactured in America, were set up under a tent in Hannover, Germany, pending the erection around them of the world's first record factory, owned by Berliner's brother Joseph. During the building, production continued, from masters Gaisberg made in London of an entire gamut of popular music. Again demand outpaced production, stimulated by Owen's extravagant use of Seaman's promotion and advertising techniques.

Edison had been a presence in Europe since Colonel Gouraud's first demonstrations of the talking machine. Columbia, too, had already opened branches in Paris and Berlin, and was about to in London. In Paris, the young Pathé brothers were building their cylinder–talking-machine business into a major enterprise, with a catalogue of 1,500 selections. France and a few other European countries were at the coin-slot-machine stage, waiting until the public indicated a readiness to take the phonograph into the home.

Between Gaisberg's industry in the recording studio and Owen's go-getting enthusiasm for the business, Europe was being made aware that the Gramophone plate was no longer a toy and that Berliner's Gramophone was superior to cylinder players. German and French Gramophone companies were opened in 1899. In several other countries, local agencies were established and at least a hundred selections were taken down on zinc masters, then rushed off to Hannover for pressing. By 1900, a European catalogue of 5,000 separate selections was available, and with it ample stocks of Berliner Gramophones made in Eldridge Johnson's Camden plant.

Operating from a new fully integrated pressing and manufacturing operation in Canada, where he had moved to avoid further litigation, Berliner looked to Europe for his profits during 1900, while Johnson brought lawsuits through which he hoped to terminate an injunction that had stopped him from operating in the United States. With Berliner's departure, he had found himself the possessor of considerable Berliner merchandise for which he had not been paid and could not deliver, owing to the court's ruling. He also had on his hands new wax masters of recent Berliner releases that he had been making secretly and knew to be superior to the originals. Staking $5,000 on the venture, he opened Consolidated Talking Machine Company in the autumn of 1900 and began to merchandise Improved Gramophones, selling for from three to twenty-five dollars, and new Improved Gramophone records. Public response was immediate, bringing Columbia and Seaman back to court. They charged that Consolidated was a front for Berliner, and asked that Johnson be enjoined from any use of the word *Gramophone* and its manufacture. The injunction was denied, although Johnson was forbidden to employ the disputed name. While awaiting appeal, which he believed would be denied, Johnson left the word *Gramophone* to Berliner and came up with one of his own: *Victor*.

After a tug of war and horse trading between the Berliner interests and Johnson, the Victor Talking Machine Company was incorporated in October 1901, capitalized at two million dollars, with 60 percent of the stock issued to Johnson and the balance to Berliner. It appeared that the record business would be divided between Johnson's Victor disks and the Edison and Columbia cylinders. A young workman, Joe Jones, who had worked for Berliner in 1896, upset this balance of power when the United States Patent Office issued him, after more than four years, a patent on the basic principle of Johnson's secret wax-master process. Its own perfector had failed to do the same for fear of making it available to rival companies. Columbia acquired this Jones patent through American Graphophone in 1902 for $25,000 and began to issue its own disk recordings. Another lawsuit followed. It was resolved in 1903 by an agreement that Victor and Columbia would pool their disk patents and operate under a cross-licensing arrangement. Until expiration of basic patents the companies owned and monopolized, it was impossible for any new record company to enter the business without infringing or paying high license fees.

The three giants had varied products: Edison, cylinders only; Victor, disks only; Columbia, both. Production of recorded music multiplied ten times in a decade, from 2,750,000 to 27,500,000 in 1909, with a cylinder-to-disk production ratio of two to one at the start, and one to nine in 1914, several years after Columbia adopted a disks-only policy. The number of cylinder and record players grew in proportion from an estimated near million produced by 1904. Victor alone produced 250,000 talking machines in the next five years.

Distribution systems were in place by 1904, with mail-order and an expanding commercial outlet chain for the sale of players, cylinders, and disks well established. Victor had more than 10,000 dealers and a million-dollar-plus annual profit. Edison used an exclusive jobber system. Columbia had its initial American Graphophone franchise holders as a base, to which a variety of leading business establishments were added. Recordings or machines could be purchased in locations ranging from small "mom-and-pop" stores, bicycle shops, variety stores, and the catalogues of major mail-order houses, to the largest music specialty houses and fancy metropolitan department stores. By controlling manufacture and distribution and offering a discount of about 45 percent on all production, Victor and Columbia fixed prices and kept such major department stores as Macy's from selling at the customer discounts that made that firm the largest in the world.

Columbia and Edison began to mass-produce molded cylinders simultaneously but independently. These offered two minutes of popular music for thirty-five cents, less on a hard wax surface that was eventually advertised as being "indestructible."

While rivalry between Columbia and Victor grew hotter, despite their rapprochement, Thomas Edison continued to cater to a mid-American market of rural and small-town people. Many of them saw him as one of their own, a man who might now walk with kings of finance and princes of power but was still their kind. He had lighted the world, made pictures move and machines talk, and they placed their faith in him and his products. Acting as his own director of artists and repertoire, despite growing deafness, Edison chose the music he recorded and the performers who sang it or spoke it. He specialized in ragtime, coon songs, Sousa, Herbert, sentimental ballads, and monologues. When his dealers complained that competitors were cornering the high-class trade with operatic disks, he began a two-minute Grand Opera series. His faithful audience scorned it, and more sophisticated buyers preferred it on longer Victor records.

When their supply of blank cylinders was closed off by the introduction of a new molding process, Edison franchise holders gave up any recording activities and expanded their coin-slot-machine operations. Because Edison and American Graphophone phonographs were sturdier and more reliable than the Victor machines, they became standard equipment in penny arcades and record parlors. Soon, a new branch of the industry came into existence: "Penny

Vaudevilles,'' in which one could hear the newest cylinders for the smallest American coin. The first of these, with nearly 100 ear-tube-equipped Edison Penny Coin-Slot Machines, was opened on Union Square in New York. It was operated by a corporation capitalized at $500,000, which eventually built up a chain of thirteen around the country. On a single holiday, an estimated 200,000 persons crowded into these fourteen vaudevilles and spent at least ten cents each. Any city of more than 10,000 inhabitants could support such a business, and it spread rapidly, yielding substantial profits. The automatic-phonography industry did not use disks until 1908, when the first automatic coin machines went on sale, but by that time the nickel-in-the-slot Peerless Player Piano was beginning to displace recorded music with that of the paper music roll. Within a year or two, an end came for the coin-slot automatic-phonograph industry, though it returned in the early 1930s, when desperate economic times brought back this poor man's concert hall.

In 1909, seeing that the cylinder was also losing popularity, Edison shut down all European recording and manufacturing operations and turned to his principal market, the small-town household. The common people stayed with him until the end, in 1929, when Thomas A. Edison, Inc. ended manufacture of all phonographs, cylinders, and disks. Only radio sets and dictating machines remained, the last of Edison's wonderful talking-machine miracles.

During the period when cylinders were in the final decade of their supremacy, Eldridge Johnson and his men, among them Calvin Child, who was in charge of Victor's new Manhattan recording studios, slowly forged ahead of Columbia and a few independents to become the largest talking-machine business in the world. Much of this progress resulted from contributions made by British Gramophone, which included ''little Nipper,'' the dog listening to ''his master's voice,'' which appeared on all Victor records beginning in 1902. Artist Francis Barraud had painted a dog peering into the horn of an Edison cylinder phonograph in 1893 and offered it for sale to a company representative, who declined it. It stayed in Barraud's studio until 1899, when he decided to make some changes and borrowed a Gramophone horn to use as a model. William Barry Owen purchased the reworked picture for £100 and had lithographed prints made of it, which were distributed to all branches and foreign agencies, and to America, where Johnson was taken by it. British Gramophone itself did not use the art until 1909, and copyrighted it as an official trademark the next year.

Fred Gaisberg's duties as man in charge of artists and repertory for British Gramophone, which was now operating under the Victor company's patent-sharing with Columbia, sent him around the world in quest of talent. In Russia, where people of all classes had quickly fallen in love with the talking machine, a local pressing plant was constructed to meet the demand. The leading St. Petersburg Gramophone shop was operated by an enterprising and imaginative merchant, who suggested that a new line be introduced: recordings of the stars of the Imperial Opera. The response was great and immediate to the resultant high-priced editions bearing red labels, as a symbol of quality and luxury. This suggested to Gaisberg and Owen that British Gramophone record a luminary at

La Scala, Milan's opera house. It was a mission of destiny for Gramophone and Victor. Arrangements were nearly canceled when the home office cabled that the ten-pound fee was exorbitant and forbid the project. But Gaisberg, figuring that a sale of 2,000 for each of the sides would pay the fee, recorded Enrico Caruso's rich, strong voice, the answer to a recording man's dream. The ten records made a net profit of £15,000, and also ended reluctance by major performers to sing into the acoustic recording horn. Gramophone's first Red Label catalogue was issued in September 1902, and included recordings by most of the leading stars of Europe's Golden Age of Opera. The price of ten-inch Red Label records was raised to one pound in early 1903, after a contract was negotiated with the legendary Italian tenor Francesco Tamagno, which guaranteed the first royalty payment to a recording artist—four shillings or 20 percent of the retail price on every record sold.

Emile Berliner had first suggested the royalty-payment system. His speech in Philadelphia to the Franklin Institute on May 16, 1888, out of which came the first entrepreneurial investment in the Gramophone, included this prediction: "Prominent singers, speakers or performers may derive an income from royalties on the sale of their phonoautograms and valuable plates may be printed and registered in order to protect against unauthorized publication."

On the twenty-fifth anniversary of that occasion, Berliner returned to the Franklin Institute and, pointing to his own remarkable contributions, from which Eldridge Johnson had produced the modern Gramophone, reminded his audience that

> the machine which hitherto had confined itself to popular musical tastes, to low comedy, simple songs, cornet and clarinet solos and to military music, rapidly improved to such a degree that it began to appeal to grand opera stars, to the great masters of the piano, to the wizards of the violin, to symphony orchestras, to virtuosi of every kind of musical instrument and to celebrated actors and elecutionists. The gramophone repertoire expanded to comprise the whole gamut of audible phenomena and voice reproductions in particular became so startingly perfect that big hotels were able to have their orchestras accompany the great singers of the day as they appeared by proxy out of the horn of the talking machine.

There is certain truth in Berliner's hyperbole, but as Gaisberg wrote in *The Music Goes Round:*

> Stringed instruments we recorded by a subterfuge. We substituted the Stroh violin for violins and violas, for a 'cello we used a bassoon, and for the doublebass a tuba. The Stroh violin was invented by the late Augustus Stroh. Its four strings were stretched over a diaphragm-resonator to which was attached a horn. . . . In some ways acoustic recording flattered the voice. . . . The inadequacy of the accompaniments to the lovely vocal records made in the Acoustic Age was their greatest weakness. There was no pretense of using the composer's score; we had to arrange it for wind instruments entirely. The articulated tuba tone was altogether too insistent. Though marked advances were made in the technique of manufacture which reduced the surface noise on the disc, nevertheless the artist and the selection had invariably to be selected with care so as to cover up all instrumental deficien-

cies. Only full, even voices of sustained power could be utilized, and all nuances, such as pianissimo effects, were omitted.

Influenced no little by the Gramophone Company's success, both Columbia and Victor opened their New York studios to stars of the Metropolitan Opera Company and other vocal luminaries for new lines of celebrity recordings to be sold for premium prices. With access to the British company's catalogues through an exchange agreement, Victor had a considerable advantage. Its first announcement of Red Label, or "Red Seal," records included several from Caruso's 1902 session. Recording fees began jumping, due in no small measure to the competition for the singers. Marcella Sembrich recieved $3,000 for three songs from Columbia, which got the same number of selections from Edouard de Reszke for a third of that amount, a task that took only a half hour of the basso's time. With superior financial resources, which Johnson was ready to commit to the improvement of his products, and lavish advertising, intended to create an image of his talking machine as "the greatest musical instrument in the world," Victor won the battle and had the concert celebrity field to itself for many years.

Intentionally or not, Victor advertising had much in common with that of the Aeolian Company for its Pianola, which was being established as the "Royal Road to Music in the Home." Both organizations delighted in multipage advertisements, in color, run in major general-interest magazines. Victor used a double-page display to herald its exclusive association with "the greatest tenor of modern times," Enrico Caruso. In early 1904, a contract was signed with him that was to pay him $4,000 for the first ten sides, $10,000 for the next ten, and forty cents a disk, plus an advance on royalties of $10,000, for the next ten. His income from this source during his lifetime has been reckoned at from two to five million dollars.

Similar advertising displays greeted the first appearance of Eldridge Johnson's new and improved "piano-finished" cabinet Victrola in September 1906. Completely self-enclosed, with an internal horn, space in which to store Victor records, and a lid that hid the reproducing apparatus, it sold for $200. By the end of 1906, Victor had an earned surplus of six million dollars.

All advertising hoopla notwithstanding, the original $200 Victrola was never responsible for more than 20 percent of Victor phonograph sales until after 1910. During the few remaining years that the cylinder enjoyed two thirds of all sales of prerecorded music, the Red Seal line generally accounted for less than one fifth of all Victor production and about three percent of total disk sales. In 1912, the Red Seal catalogue contained 600 recordings; many of these were duplications, and only a fraction of the total repertory. Not until after World War I, did Red Seal production increase to one fourth of all Victor disks manufactured. This lasted for only a few years before sinking again below 20 percent, where it remained. It did, however, provide income out of all proportion, due to the higher prices for the celebrity line, starting at a dollar fifty. Double-faced popular records were standard after 1908 but Red Seals were pressed on one side only until 1923. Twelve-inch solo disks by Caruso cost three dollars; when he sang with other Victor stars, the prices went up—six dollars for the quartet from *Rigoletto* and seven dollars for the sextette from *Lucia*. With unusual candor, Victor had stated in 1905 trade-paper advertising that its popular artists sold more than three fourths of all disks manufactured in Camden, but that grand opera was good for the company's public image and attracted the higher classes. This remained its responsibility until technology made it possible to record the orchestra with some semblance of reality, and the function was then assigned to conductor-performers.

Despite all its high-blown dedication to culture, Victor looked for its profits to the masses of Americans who began to buy Victrolas in great quantities after an enclosed-horn table-model phonograph was introduced by Columbia and then improved and duplicated at even lower prices by the Camden factories. After 1912, this poor-man's Victrola made up about half of all talking machines bearing the little Nipper trademark.

The Victrola's mass audience was learning to "play" not only the phonograph but the piano as well, without hands. What Daniel J. Boorstin has called "mass production of the moment," produced first by the camera, was being extended to the musical experience. The market for popular music was apparently limitless. Music publishers and leading performers promoted it. It was inexpensive to record. Columbia, Victor, and Edison had taken care not to extend the royalty-payment system to operatic stars by making either full-time or piecework employees of musicians, accompanists, instrumentalists, singing groups, and vocalists who recorded popular music. Each label had several bands, one or two accompanists, and a few well-known singers on staff, and paid two dollars a song to all others. Because of the volume of production, with as many as fifteen to twenty sides made in a day, the money was good, better than many could earn in vaudeville. Without needing the magnetism necessary to make a live audience warm up to them, record singers—one out of every ten a woman—found singing into a horn financially rewarding.

In the next decade, total record sales climbed over $100 million, not to be exceeded until after World War II, despite the advent of electrical recording in the age of the microphone.

The Pursuit of Copyright Revision

American music publishers were never a visible lobbying presence at any copyright hearing in Washington during the 1880s. Then, in early 1888, a time when its founder was suffering from a severe mental illness that rendered him incapable of making business judgments, the Oliver Ditson Company joined the American Publishers Copyright League, possibly because the firm owned more than 3,000 music books. After its July 1890 meeting, when agitation for international copyright appeared to be winning the battle, however, the Board of Music Trade announced that it had taken no action regarding copyright.

British music publishers, on the other hand, had reason to be concerned about new legislation affecting copyright, for several of their own country's acts had already affected their livelihoods. That of 1843 had stripped Thomas

Boosey of the foreign copyrights in his catalogue, including the four most valuable properties in the British music trade, *La Traviata, La Sonnambula, Rigoletto,* and *Il Trovatore.* The same act added musical composition to the 1833 law that fixed a penalty of forty shillings for each unlicensed public performance of a dramatic work. Legislation in 1882 and 1888 required publishers to affix a notice reserving public performance rights on every newly printed piece of music, which had generally been done only on musical-theater works. Publishers who used royalty concerts to promote the popularity of their parlor ballads and the music did not comply. In order to stimulate public performances and thus sales, printed notices allowing the songs to be sung without license were common.

The prospects of reciprocal international copyright with the Americans, after fifty years of work, was pleasing, but a manufacturing proviso in the proposed legislation raised vigorous outcries and requests for the British government to make formal protest. The proposed law would compel all music sold in the United States to be printed from type or engravings made in the country, on paper of local manufacture, by American nationals. Certain clauses of the Berne Convention affecting foreign copyrights were another matter of great concern. The new law would add to them a significant problem for a music trade already suffering from promiscuous discounting, which was making sheet-music retailing unprofitable.

American music men, however, looked forward to the bill's passage, since it would leave to them all publication of European music and would keep prices of foreign music at the same level as copyrighted American works.

With long experience in the American music business, Novello, Ewer & Co., of London, asked its U.S. Counsel Lauriston L. Scaife, for an opinion as to whether the manufacturing clause would really affect music, since it was not specifically mentioned. *The Congressional Record* for the final day before the bill's passage, March 3, 1891, reported that music had indeed deliberately been excluded, together with dramatic compositions, photographs, and other works of ''fine art.'' This compromise had occurred after pressure from labor, authors, dramatists, and the Music Teachers National Association. Otherwise, they claimed, such works created or published in Europe because their duplication or publication in the United States might be too expensive would strip their creators and composers of copyright.

On Scaife's advice, Novello tested the new law by depositing for copyright in Washington a work composed in England and printed wholly from British type on British paper. In a carefully staged public incident, Librarian of Congress Ainsworth Rand Spofford accepted it, having already ruled that musical compositions were exempt from the manufacturing provision. This decision extended only to the music; it did not include librettos, song lyrics, or any words accompanying music. Almost immediately, the French writers' and composers' society, SACEM, opened an office in New York, and European publishers began to enter an average of 200 works monthly for copyright. Theodore Presser, who had been a major proponent of a new copyright law and was publishing educational music by American composers at considerably reduced prices, sent his manuscripts to Germany for printing and on their return deposited them for American copyright. Other American music men, chiefly the small group that determined policy for the Board of Music Trade, protested that, with cheaper labor and production costs in Europe, their foreign competitors, increasingly active in America, had a decidedly unfair advantage.

The pragmatic Witmarks, most successful of the new music men, sent Isidore off to London to effect reciprocal working arrangements with members of the British Music Publishers Association, whose songs now enjoyed American copyright and could share in profits. He signed contracts with Charles Sheard, an important popular-music house, and Reynolds & Co., which specialized in costermonger songs, which became American hits after the British music-hall stars' invasion of vaudeville. An American was employed to be a permanent Witmark representative in Europe. Boosey & Co. opened a new New York branch and withdrew its "cheap"-music agency from the Pond Company. Francis, Day & Hunter, special victims of the old law, when their hits "Annie Rooney," "Comrades," and others had been pirated widely by Americans, entered into a co-publication deal with Harms.

In June 1892, members of the British Music Publishers Association agreed to give financial support to an action in America against the Ditson Company, and its few remaining, but unspecified, supporters on the Board of Music Trade, for having violated the United States copyright law by bringing out four copyrighted Novello works. During the delay that followed, Brainard's Sons resigned from the board, in early 1894, followed shortly by the John Church Company. This left John Haynes and Charles Ditson, William Pond's heirs, and a Washington music publisher–piano dealer to face the defeat handed down by a circuit court in June. After losing on appeal the next spring, Ditson declined to take the matter to the Supreme Court.

American music publishing came of age, insofar as the legislative process involving copyright was concerned, on June 11, 1895, when the new Music Publishers Association of the United Stated was voted into being. Seventeen members, with the Witmarks among ten charter members who had never participated in Board of Music Trade affairs, agreed to work toward an "elevation of the tone and character" of their business; correct abuses and ameliorate "evils which may affect the trade"; establish an industry credit bureau; and support any "action toward a revision and improvement of the administration of the present copyright system, with the view of making it an adjunct of greater value to the publishing interests in this country than it is now."

William M. Treloar, a Kansas City music publisher who also served in the House of Representatives, was soon persuaded that copyright revision was good for both his constituents and the music business, and offered a bill to revise the 1891 act. Initial copyright would last forty years, with a twenty-year renewal under the new proposal. Provisions for seizure and destruction of pirated music and music books were made more stringent. Music was added to a revised manufacturing clause.

Of the twenty-nine association members who supported this bill, only five, spearheaded by Boston's White, Smith and the Arthur P. Schmidt Company, opposed the revised manufacturing clause. The German-born Schmidt had opened a Boston retail music store in 1876, which specialized in imported contemporary concert music. He then developed an interest in young Americans who had made their first reputations in his native country and could not find an American publisher for their works. He was the first to bring out a printed full orchestral score by an American composer, J. K. Paine's First Symphony, and his best-selling music in 1895 included piano pieces by Edward MacDowell, many of whose compositions had already been published in Germany. The complicated concert music Schmidt wished to issue could be engraved in Germany at half its American cost, and a change in the manufacturing clause could have a serious effect on his business. It would also leave MacDowell's early pieces to the mercy of American reprinters.

Several copyright acts were approved in 1897, two of which dealt with part of Treloar's proposal. A Copyright Department was formed, to be financed by the government; the law against book and music piracy was strengthened, particularly to impede imports from abroad bearing a spurious American copyright notice, and penalties were increased. Quickly, Canadian and European printers began to ship work without such a notice.

The January 3, 1897, act added the words *and musical* to statutes adopted in 1856 that required permission from the copyright owner of a dramatic composition in order to give a public performance. It was the birth of a privilege whose financial returns to authors created vast changes in American music and publishing throughout the next century. The change had been offered on behalf of Arthur Tams, to protect such musical productions as operas, farces, comedies, extravaganzas, and other forms of music theater popular in the 1890s. While stage manager of the Casino Theatre, Tams had started a collection of musical and vocal scores of stage productions and prompt books containing handwritten directions and warnings about presentation. These rarely passed out of the possession of a theater's musical director or stage manager. Beginning in 1885, in a small basement room, he had built up the most important stage-music library in the country. He began to rent orchestral and vocal scores, instrumental and vocal parts, managers' guides, and other material necessary for either professional or amateur productions. Next he added cantatas, childrens' operettas, masses, and similar musical works, and rented copies to a market of 20,000 church choirs, 3,000 vocal societies, and countless music clubs and societies, involving more than a half-million persons. This business was perfectly legal, because Tams purchased the copies of protected works he rented out. When special orchestral instrumental parts could not be obtained from the publishers, he had them prepared himself. Many composers supported his operation, because his purchase and the subsequent promotion of their music added print royalties.

The Music Publishers Association operated on the principle that the 1897 performing-right provision still applied only to dramatic compositions. (Until 1909, only three actions involving public performance of copyrighted musical work without permission were brought, all dealing with commercial theater use.) Many of the new publishing houses started building their own rental li-

braries or orchestral and vocal scores; the first operated by the Witmarks opened
a year after the law went into effect. Though it annoyed them, Tams's library
was regarded as properly operating within the law. When works other than
those for the theater were added, however, warnings went to his customers,
citing the law for which he was responsible. A printed circular sent out by G.
Schirmer, Novello, Schmidt, the three Ditson companies, Boston Music, Boosey,
and Edward Schuberth pointed out that the use of rented copies deprived their
authors of royalty compensation. Tams countered with a lawsuit, charging the
publishers with conspiring to prevent him from carrying on his rental business.
The defendants won. Tams and his customers then went to Congress for a new
law, and achieved the introduction of a bill providing for rental of music for
performances given for charitable purposes. The bill had to wait for more pressing
business to be taken care of. The publishers, meanwhile, were not concerned
about payment of a fee for the performance of their purely popular music,
because that would interfere with their promotional activities. Moreover, piracy
by and shipment of music from Canada to mail-order customers and music
retailers in the United States were well in hand under new regulations. After
the 1891 reciprocal copyright law, publication of music from theatrical productions had proved to be another addition to their profits, and they negotiated
with producers and theater managers for publication rights to music they owned
by virtue of employing composers to write it. In order to assure the collection
of additional income from performance rights in England, where American operettas and musical comedies were beginning to enjoy popularity, publishers
had to arrange "copyright performance" there and also deposit publications
simultaneously in the United States and England. The special one-time performance required casting, rehearsal, and an invited audience, to each member of
whom the admission price of a guinea was advanced, then retrieved at the end
of the evening.

British music publishers noted the successes of their American and French
colleagues in achieving legal protection and began to move, too.

The late-eighteenth-century custom of printing on sheet music a price double
that expected was still in force in England and led to confusion among the
sheet-music buyers who had become important customers of British music pirates. The streets of London and every large provincial city were filled with
sheet-music peddlers hawking counterfeited sheet music at half the trade price.
Passage of a bill in 1902 failed to curb these sales and, relying on a law that
permitted seizure of property known to be counterfeited, members of the British Music Publishers Association emulated their American cousins and employed retired soldiers and policemen to raid the premises of shops known to
be selling it, strip sidewalk hawkers of their sheet-music supplies, and break
into printing offices. As many as 300,000 copies were flushed out in a single
week, but piracy still flourished.

In April 1905, the nineteen members of the British Music Publishers Association announced they would no longer spend money to acquire news songs,
pay to advertise royalty concerts where their old songs were featured, or enter
into any new contracts that involved royalty payments to vocal artists. The

British music-printing trade was forced to close temporarily as association members devoted their time to prosecution of pirates and lobbying for stricter legislation. Chappell alone spent £10,000 in support of a new bill promising prison terms of twelve months or more at hard labor. The bill became an act in 1906, and its sponsor, T. P. O'Connor, a member of Parliament and publisher of London's major entertainment-business weekly, was guest of honor at a banquet in London during the spring and one later in New York. The American reception and dinner was held under auspices of the Music Publishers Association.

At the thirteenth annual meeting of the Music Publishers Association, on June 11, 1907, one topic of discussion was the growing tendency on the part of some members "to slaughter" their copyrights by selling the music in bulk at drastic discounts to such price-cutting outlets as the five-and-ten-cent stores and the major department stores. There was also a report on the organization's fight for copyright revision, particularly in regard to perforated music-roll and cylinder-disk manufacturers, who used copyrights freely on the same royalty-free basis as had music publishers themselves for more than a century.

The Witmarks were conspicuously absent from this meeting. Isidore Witmark had suggested strongly to James F. Bowers, twelve-term association president, that he not run again for the presidency because of a conflict of interest that was threatening to upset the progress of a favorable new copyright law. Bowers was reelected. He was general manager of Lyon & Healy, which was Midwest representative of the Aeolian Company. This collusion had been brought to the attention of Congress and President Theodore Roosevelt as a result of its exposure during the first of three copyright hearings in June 1906. Cries of "monopoly" had followed, and opponents had threatened him with passage of an amended and consolidated copyright law.

The initial consolidated and revised copyright bill offered for consideration by the Senate and House Patent Committees on June 6, 1906 had come out of conferences called by Librarian of Congress Herbert Putnam. In his words, those invited to assist in framing the proposed legislation included "writers of books, writers of plays, composers of music, architects, painters, and sculptors, photographers and photoengravers, the publishers of books, newspapers, periodicals, music, and prints, and the manufacturers, printers, typographers, and lithographers . . . the creators of works which are to be protected and the publishers through whom the property in these becomes effective and remunerative." The Music Publishers Association was represented by eight members. R. L. Thomae, of the Victor Talking Machine Company, was the only employee of any recording company present, but he was there as a music publisher. He was in charge of Victor's music copyright department, which had spent $35,000 to buy compositions to be recorded by its artists. Other figures from the musical world were the delegates from the Manuscript Society, an association of lesser composers of serious music.

Among the terms affecting music in the proposed bill was an increase in the duration of copyright to the life of the author plus fifty years; making a misdemeanor of any unauthorized performance of a dramatic or musical composition for profit; and the addition to the specific rights of copyright owners in the original Copyright Act of the following: "To make, sell, distribute, or let for hire any device, contrivance, or appliance especially adapted in any manner whatsoever to reproduce to the ear the whole or any material part of any work published and copyrighted after this act shall have gone into effect, or by any means of any such device or appliance publicly to reproduce to the ear the whole or any material part of such work."

Proceedings the first day dealing with music began merrily with testimony from John Philip Sousa, who confessed that he wrote better music when he was better paid, and from Victor Herbert on behalf of "brother composers whose names figure in the advertisements of these companies who make perforated rolls and talking machines, and who have never received a cent."

The first jarring note was struck when C. Howlett Davis, an inventor, appearing in opposition to the bill, referred to a "complete monopolisitc octopus, in which the Aeolian Company forms the head and brains, and the Music Publishers' Association the body, the independent publishers the writing arms, and the composers the suckers and baiters." He referred to a scheme engineered by Bowers and Aeolian executives to resolve the issue of whether or not the mechanical reproduction of music by a perforated music roll was an infringement of the copyright laws. Agreeing to pay all costs for a legal action that would be taken up to the Supreme Court, Aeolian had entered into secret contracts with many members of the Music Publishers Association. The arrangement would give Tremaine's piano combine exclusive rights to draw upon the catalogues of participating music firms for a period of thirty-five years, with a royalty of 10 percent on each roll sold once the issue of infringement and property rights was resolved in the copyright owners' favor.

An action had been brought by White, Smith against the Apollo Company, maker of player pianos and piano rolls, charging illegal use of two copyrighted pieces, "Little Cotton Dolly" and "The Kentucky Babe Schottische," coon songs written by Adam Geibel, the blind songwriter and sometime collaborator with Fanny Crosby. The lower courts found for the defendant, and the case was sent to the Supreme Court. Should the decision be confirmation of the lower courts', the new property right dealing with "devices reproducing to the ear any musical work," introduced by Walter Bacon, of White, Smith, on behalf of the Music Publishers Association, would affirm the right of the publishers to enter into the Aeolian contracts.

In the atmosphere of the times, when Theodore Roosevelt had won reelection because of his trust-busting activities and general antimonopoly legislation, Davis's disclosure of the conspiracy provided a stunning advantage to the manufacturers. They took up the monopoly cry and charged that it would cost them and the public millions. Because Aeolian rolls could be played only on Aeolian Pianola attachments, excessive wholesale prices would be fixed, and all independent player-piano companies would be forced out of business. Although such composers as Sousa and Herbert might gain under the proposed law, they argued, most songwriters would not, being compelled by conditions in the marketplace to go to the publishers, who would impose their own terms.

The record and cylinder companies complained that they had been locked out of the preliminary drafting sessions, that Thomas, the Victor representative, was there as a music publisher rather than a manufacturer.

Nathan Burkan, attorney for the Witmarks, who, with other association members, had signed with Aeolian, and counsel for the association painted the arrangement as a logical action on the part of clients who were not seeking to participate in any monopoly. Litigation costs being high, Aeolian's offer was a veritable act of charity. The exclusivity clause was not different from Victor's with Caruso or one of their own with Herbert or Sousa.

It was not until after the second round of hearings that the music publishers realized what tremendous assistance the independent player-piano manufacturers and record companies had been given by Davis's testimony. Bowers had proved to be an ineffectual witness when it became obvious that he had personally recruited for Aeolian the signatory publishers. There was a considerable effort on Burkan's part as well as that of the few publishers represented to minimize the possible danger in the Aeolian contracts. A recent adverse appeals court decision was cited as terminating the arrangement, as were unusual recent contracts with composers who reserved to themselves the right to permit mechanical reproduction of their music, hence taking that right out of the publishers' hands. It had been admitted that about fifty-six publishers had signed with Aeolian, but Burkan cautioned lest all publishers should be punished for "the alleged wrongs of a few."

The manufacturers argued that the proposed bill was unconstitutional, that perforated music rolls and recordings were not "writings" and thus were outside the scope of the present law; and that phonograph recordings helped, rather than harmed, popular songs. Countless letters from music publishers to Columbia, Edison, and Victor were introduced, all pleading for a recording to be made of a particular new song, sheet music and orchestrations of which were often attached.

Two new elements were introduced, both of which would seriously affect the future of music publishing, and neither of which brought any great reaction from the publishers present: public performance for profit, and compulsory licensing with a two-cent royalty fee. Arthur Tams's church-choir and singing-club customers had been effective lobbyists. Legislation proposed by the American Bar Association, after consultation with leading music publishers, none of whom had objected, included a "for-profit" exemption in the public-performance section. Compulsory licensing was a suggestion from the Victor representative, and the two-cent-royalty proposal was from a witness appearing on behalf of the Wurlitzer Company. He had computed the average royalty on all sheet music published at one and a half cents a copy, but favored the slightly larger sum as the most that could be collected without having the manufacturers pass it along to the public.

The record companies pointed to growth of the sheet-music business since 1900—from $2,272,385 at manufacturers' value to $4,147,784 four years later— and projected that for 1906 at $6 million, a 163 percent increase in six years, a period when sales of phonograph disks and cylinders steadily increased as well.

Some European developments next proved to be embarrassing for the American music business. T. P. O'Connor proved to be less helpful than they had hoped. His 1906 bill offered to Parliament originally contained language lumping record makers with sheet-music pirates. Talking-machine men persuaded him to change the language so that the law did not cover perforated music rolls, records, or cylinders. Then Aeolian's arrangements with the publishers proved to have an international counterpart when it was revealed that the player-piano combine's German division had made similar agreements with publishers there. Once the law was changed to cover mechanical reproduction, Aeolian controlled most German music, and competitors could make perforated rolls only by paying for permission.

The second round of copyright hearings effectively split the popular-music houses away from the Music Publishers Association. The old music publishers, with their large holdings of better-class music, were on the other side. Their interests were best served by a new copyright law that affirmed their rights to make the Aeolian deal and by a new section beneficial to music whose copyrights had expired or would soon expire. it read: "that additions to copyrighted works and alterations, revisions, abridgements, dramatizations, translations, compilations, arrangements or other versions of of works, whether copyrighted or in the public domain, shall be regarded as new works, subject to copyright under provisions of this act."

The popular-music publishers, who needed the law in order to collect for the use of their music on music rolls and records, were in a quandry: how to disassociate themselves from Bowers and Aeolian, with whom many had signed, and still maintain solidarity in their fight for revision. Nathan Burkan assumed an even more important role in their councils, winning for himself a place of trust among them. He had recently been victor in a protracted case involving a highly successful and profitable piracy, getting a jail sentence for the offender, which brought him more publisher clients.

Following Bowers's reelection as association president, the Witmarks, Leo Feist, G. Schirmer, Boosey, Carl Fischer, Fred Haviland, and a few other music houses resigned from the Music Publishers Association and subsequently formed the New York Music Publishers Association. Isidore Witmark and Nathan Burkan went to the Capitol to find out how bills got passed through the Congress. They learned quickly that a national constituency for copyright revision had to be built and money spent. The phonograph interests had already formed the American Musical Copyright League, and Witmark set about building a counterpart. He worked from a list of between 5,000 and 6,000 people whose songs had been rejected by the Witmark Company. Saying to each that, like other music publishers, he had been forced to turn down such attractive songs as theirs because of the inroads the record and piano-roll companies were making in costs, he urged them, their relations, and friends to write to their congressmen and senators and plead the songwriters' cause.

Victor Herbert continued to be the most active and effective composer spokesman in Washington. He continued that role as president of the new Authors and Composers League of America. Witmark's amateur songwriters joined en masse, paying one dollar for a membership card, and continued their letter-writing campaign.

The new session of Congress required introduction of new bills, and in January 1907 several were filed, among them Senator Alfred B. Kittredge's pro-music revision and Representative Frank D. Currier's, which favored the manufacturers' interests.

The final hearings began on March 27, 1908, a month after the Supreme Court had ruled for the defendant in White, Smith versus Apollo, making it imperative that copyright protection be extended to cover mechanically recorded music. Antitrust sections were added to the bill, one making mandatory the termination of any copyrights upon proof of their involvement in violation of national or state laws concerning trusts or monopolies.

Early in the proceedings an attempt was made by a typographers' union leader to insert the word *music* in the manufacturing clause. This was quickly supported by the player-piano interests, who hoped to focus the publishers' activities on this, rather than on the basic issue of extending copyright to cover mechanical production of music. After being convinced by the other side that the proposed addition would harm, rather than help, American printers, the union representative told the committee that labor opposed the change, so the issue was dropped. When the hearings concluded, the stalemate between music interests and the record and paper-roll manufacturers appeared as strong as ever and their positions more rigid. Yet a majority of committee members were convinced that new legislation was essential.

Herbert and Sousa had held publicly, and most publishers privately, that the proposed two-cent royalty was inadequate, that the fee should be based on the reputation of the composer and the cultural worth and artistic quality of his music. Now, with the present session of Congress nearing an end, and with the prospect that the entire campaign would have to be fought again, Herbert capitulated and accepted the flat two-cent rate. Manufacturers were brought into line with an assurance that, once a piece of music was recorded, it would be available to anyone else seeking to duplicate it mechanically, and at the same two-cent rate.

Five minutes before his term expired, Theodore Roosevelt signed the 1909 act "to amend and consolidate the acts respecting copyright."

A provision that had elicited little interest or activity on the part of songwriters and music publishers—the exclusive right "to perform the copyrighted work publicly for profit if it be a musical composition and for the purpose of public performance for profit"—was to play a major part in the future of American music of all kinds. The time lay not too far ahead when income from that source would provide the major portion of financial returns from copyrighted music.

Tin Pan Alley

The final phase in the move of the late nineteenth century by New York's popular-music business away from the Union Square theater and variety-house district to Tin Pan Alley began in late 1893, when M. Witmark & Sons located at 49–51 West 28th Street, in Manhattan. Within a few years, the shabby thoroughfare received the name by which it became world-famous in a newspaper article written by the press agent, journalist, womanizer, inveterate gambler, and songwriter Monroe H. Rosenfeld. Music-business apocrypha has it that he was visiting the Harry Von Tilzer Music Company offices when he first heard the firm's piano, fixed to produce the tinkling syncopation of a new kind of popular music by interweaving paper strips between its strings, and it inspired his immortal description of 28th Street's sounds.

The activities of music men concentrated in this district during the next two decades, before the business again moved uptown with show business, apparently did not figure in the 1899 Department of Commerce report, which listed music sales by eighty-seven music publishers worth $2.25 million at manufacturers' cost. Nor did sales by important representatives of European houses: Chappell; Boosey; Francis, Day & Hunter, and H. W. Gray, new owner of Novello's interests in America; the German Breitkopf & Härtel; and Ricordi, of Milan.

Testifying during the December 1908 copyright hearings, the Witmark attorney, Nathan Burkan, who also represented the New York Music Publishers Association, sought to remove his clients from any potential penalties to be imposed by Congress on the eighty-seven American publishers involved in the Aeolian paper music-roll monopoly, the owners of exactly 381,589 compositions. Burkan spoke on behalf of the 117 publishers that he claimed, owned the majority (503,597) of currently copyrighted pieces of American music. The statistic was heavily loaded in his favor by the inclusion of the catalogues of the foreign houses. Yet there were important omissions of new popular-music houses from Burkan's list—Joseph Stern, Jerome Remick, Leo Feist, F. A. Mills, for example, and the remaining 112 companies, including the John Church business, with 35,000 compositions; the T. B. Harms catalogue of 25,000 copyrights, owned by Max Dreyfus and songwriter Jerome Kern following Harms's death in 1906; and the Witmarks, with 15,000. Many now-famous, but then smaller, Tin Pan Alley names *were* cited by Burkan: the Sam Fox Publishing Co., Von Tilzer, Maurice Shapiro, the Joe Morris Company, Gotham-Attucks Music Co. (the first black-owned publisher), P. J. Howley & Co., and Gus Edwards Music Publishing Co.

Though he promised to do so, Burkan never supplied the list of eighty-seven offending music houses, at the top of which was the oldest and most important nineteenth-century American publisher, the Oliver Ditson Company, of Boston. This venerable firm, whose founder was now dead, had become the prototype of a wholesale-retailer operation, with little or no interest in the new vernacular music until music stores ordered copies of "hit" songs. Two thousand music dealers around the country had found it easier to send orders to a wholesale house with Ditson's stock, rather than to the small new publishers, when they needed a few copies of a new song. The Boston firm carried, as its advertising boasted, "seven miles of printed music and music books, with over 100,000 copyrights of its own." Although Ditson did advertise in leading art and parlor-music magazines and papers, it had no salesmen to visit retail dealers, nor did it engage in promotion of its own music. It relied instead on regular mailings of booklets and thematic lists to some 30,000 musical people in the United States and Canada.

Appearing on behalf of the Edison phonograph interests during the Washington hearings, the company's house counsel, F. L. Dyer, pointed to the demand of American people for noncopyrighted foreign music, in which the leading members of the old Board of Music Trade had specialized for much of the nineteenth century. There had been, he said, no attempt on the part of piano-roll, cylinder, and record manufacturers "to advance one cause against the other." The amount of foreign music they recorded represented 70 percent of all selections placed on sale. "The people themselves, having the opportunity of taking either, demand 70 percent of the foreign music and only 30 percent of the American music," dramatic testimony to the antiquated sales and merchandising policies of the established music business. The new music publishers had already made a considerable change in the way American popular music was being published and promoted. Thus, the ratio was soon reversed.

The Witmark brothers' first five years on West 28th Street marked a time when, Isidore Witmark wrote a half-century later, "the taste of the nation swung . . . away from the servitude to three-quarters time and the polite, moral, four-four of the sentimental ballad. Already the negroid rhythms of the minstrel show had been insinuating a new tempo into the national consciousness . . . such shows contained both the fast and slow rhythms that were to come forth one day in the guise, respectively, of 'ragtime' and 'blues.' "

The novel methods for promoting their products went back to Great Britain's "royalty concerts" and Willis Woodward's first experience of paying singers to use his songs. Sometime in 1884, this former magazine publisher, then a "yellow music" merchant, as popular music was then known, visited a New York theater where one of his songs was regularly rendered by the company tenor. On asking, Woodward learned that it had cost the performer sixteen dollars for the orchestration and a lead sheet. He offered to provide the same material for "White Wings," which was then just beginning its climb to success, saving the singer the money. News spread, and Woodward found many others ready to get the same bargain. This forced rival houses to match his offer. Some years later, the Witmarks introduced the "advance," or "professional," copy, provided to all talent without charge. It was followed by the grant of "exclusive" rights to sing a new piece and "push" it by frequent performances, for which the singer got anywhere from ten to fifty dollars a week. The arrangement was sweetened by paying for advertising to promote the artist.

During the 1880s, hit songs enjoyed popularity for as long as eighteen months, and those writers productive and important enough to be paid royalties got as much as eight or nine cents a copy on sales of regular editions. Few, however, were paid for sales of instrumental versions. Most popular yellow music was sold at a 40 to 60 percent discount, and averaged fifty cents at retail. Prices dropped by a fifth when the panic of 1893 struck, seriously affecting such new music houses as Stern, Feist, Remick, Howley, Haviland, and, in Chicago, Will Rossiter Music, owned by an English draftsman who introduced many promotional devices that made his and other Tin Pan Alley products known around the world.

After hearing the celebrated Irish tenor and songwriter William Scanlon sing in a Chicago theater, Rossiter had tried his own hand at writing a popular song in the early 1890s. When his initial effort, on which he used the pseudonym W. R. Williams, was rejected by all the Chicago music houses, he brought it out himself and promoted it by singing it in public wherever and whenever he could. Touring minstrels picked it up and made "Sweet Nellie Bawn" the first of many hits published by Rossiter, among which were songs by many future song-writing greats: Jimmie Monaco, Egbert Van Alstyne, Al Piantidosi, Gus Kahn. He did turn down Charles K. Harris's "After the Ball" in 1892, but helped the young banjoist-songwriter find a printer and introduced him to the importance of copyright registration. During the 1893 Columbian Exposition in Chicago, fairgoers packed a section offering free programs of popular music in such great number that the competing performances by the Chicago Symphony Orchestra, under Theodore Thomas, were forced to close. Rossiter took advantage of this display of public taste by immediately printing and selling throughout the Exposition grounds vast numbers of words-only songsters containing the day's favorite songs.

Rossiter, Chicago's most important music man throughout the following twenty years, was second by only two days in bringing out the earliest printed ragtime number, Warren Beebe's "Ragtime March," in 1897. This became a publication of his Band and Orchestra Club, which distributed twelve monthly arrangements of the firm's best-selling songs for a dollar, another Rossiter innovation. His flair for attention-getting promotion was best typified by the large folders he distributed to band and orchestra leaders to hold their musicians' music. The Rossiter name was spread across the back of these in three-inch letters and served as a point of focus for audiences. The words-only booklets continued to come out, and to them was added a line of inexpensive material for stage and vaudeville performers, who called him "Uncle Will." Rossiter preferred to buy his songs outright for as little as possible, but after paying $7,000 for all rights to "Meet Me Tonight in Dreamland," in 1909, he spent $10,000 to promote the sentimental ballad. It sold more than two million copies. He followed this with his own "I'd Love to Live in Loveland with a Girl Like You," another multimillion-copy seller.

Such giant sales were still far in the future for his New York counterparts in 1893, but their belief that there was money in popular music was spreading. In Cincinnati, a syndicate of local investors, among them a pork packer and a distiller, put more than a million dollars in the John Church Company, reorganized after the founder's death, to help it operate as a music publisher and wholesale and retail musical-instrument dealer, capitalized at five million dollars. An early order of business was the negotiation of a contract with John Philip Sousa, promising him a fifteen percent royalty on all and any printed music sales.

Necktie salesman Joe Stern, who played melody with one hand and faked with the other, and corset salesman Ed Marks, composer of verses for all family occasions, started with far less capital. They opened in a rented office on 14th Street with a dollar's worth of used office furniture and only $100 in the bank. Marks had already enjoyed some small success with songs published by

Frank Harding, whose new publications he had carried on the road and sold on a commission basis to small variety shops and music stores. There was little financial return to songwriters who didn't publish their own material, Marks had learned. In 1894, he and Stern put their talents together and wrote the lachrymose waltz song "The Little Lost Child." The work was arranged for them in piano-copy form by George "Rosey" Rosenberg, a free-lance musician who did such chores for a dollar or less. The success of that song and their "Mother Was a Lady, or If Jack Were Only Here" made possible a move uptown to two rooms with a piano. Though a number of important vaudeville and music-hall singers had taken up their maiden effort, the song's most important boosting came from the first set of illustrated song slides used to promote a popular song. Having seen the single stereopticon slide that was used as the backdrop in Denham Elliott's perennial tear-jerker *The Old Homestead* when a male quartet sang Robert Lowry's "Where Is My Wandering Boy To-night?" Marks got the idea of using a set of slides to illustrate an entire song. George H. Thomas, house electrician at the theater where the Elliott company was playing, used a patrolman from a Brooklyn police station to pose for the still shots depicting the tragic story of an abandoned little girl who is rescued from death from exposure by a kind New York City cop. The song was three years old, which caused Marks some difficulty in persuading a tenor in the Primrose & West company to use the ten slides. But it stopped the show. Use of the gimmick spread like wildfire, and a new subsidiary branch of the music business came into existence. Songs were written expressly for use with slides, generally of the tear-inducing kind, and often requiring as many as fifty separate poses. The song-slide manufacturers remained in business even after the advent of talking pictures, since organists used "follow the bouncing ball" to lead audiences through the day's top hits.

Their first two hits and the song-slide phenomenon enabled Stern and Marks to give all their time to the music business. Taking Woodward's practice of paying for orchestrations one step further, they began to issue stock arrangements of each new song. These were distributed free of charge to orchestra leaders. Other publishers soon did the same. As demand for orchestrations grew out of proportion to production costs, publishers stamped on all professional copies: "Send 10 Cents for Orchestra Store." From this, they began to realize a small profit.

With at least one multimillion-copy seller, "The Little Lost Child," to their credit, Stern and Marks attracted the leading professional writers and as the century came to an end the Jos. W. Stern & Co. imprint graced the covers of these major hits: "Whisper Your Mother's Name," "You're Not the Only Pebble on the Beach," "Elsie from Chelsea," "I Don't Care If You Never Come Back," "Take Your Clothes and Go," "I Don't Like No Cheap Man," "Sweet Rosie O'Grady," "Down in Poverty Row," "Take Back Your Gold," and "You Can't Keep a Good Man Down."

One of their early, and not very successful, publications was "Those Lost Happy Days," written by a corset-company advertising manager, Leo Feist, a friend who had helped them with advertising, cover layouts, and distribution.

Feist did his own song boosting, sending copies of the song to dry-goods stores around the country, autographing covers for sheet-music-department salesgirls, and even, he once recalled, giving them theater tickets he had purchased and then punched "to make them seem like complimentaries." His relationship with Stern and Marks came to an angry end when he asked for a partnership and was turned down. Bitterness prevailed for many years, until Feist admitted to Marks that his demands may have been unreasonable. It is not known whether Marks apologized for the troubles he created for Feist. However, the break led to a new career. Feist rented a small room with an upright piano and began full-time work with music after he had trained his assistants at the corset company and then resigned. Monroe Rosenfeld gave Feist his first song hit in 1894, "And Her Golden Hair Was Hanging Down Her Back," which the newspaperman had lifted from an English hit by Felix McGlennon. The American copyright did not protect the song, and only after Feist became aware of the true author did McGlennon's name also appear on the sheet music. Success brought larger quarters, but for several years Feist had difficulty in the music trade, where word of his estrangement from Stern and Marks had spread, Printers were fearful of offending the now-important publishers by working for Feist, and jobbers were reluctant to handle his catalogue. He had given up song writing and hired Abe Holzman to be company pianist and arranger. When the ragtime craze spread, Feist ordered a cakewalk instrumental, which Holzman called "Echoes of the South" because "echoes of anything sells." Conditioned by his experience in the dry-goods business, Feist looked for a more compelling title, and came up with "Smoky Mokes." He then created the myth that Holzman was a European conservatory-trained musician who had succumbed to ragtime. The instrumental sold in amazing numbers and provided financial resources to fund the future Tin Pan Alley giant, who created the first company slogan in the trade: "You Can't Go Wrong with Any Feist Song."

Patrick J. Howley, a young Scottish hunchback, whose partnership in music publishing with Fred Haviland and Paul Dresser ended in bankruptcy, met his future associates in the mid-1880s at Willis Woodward's office. Haviland was just out of his teens and well on his way to being in full charge of purchases of sheet music published in New York for all the Ditson branches. He had earlier worked for a Brooklyn stationer and music publisher. Howley was a man-of-all-work for Woodward, responsible, among other things, for dealing with songwriters, one of whom was the former seminarian and minstrel man, now actor, Paul Dresser, who had already won fame with "The Letter That Never Came," published by Harms, and a number of Woodward publications. An ambitious man, Howley demonstrated to Dresser exactly how Woodward was defrauding him of royalties and suggested that the two join in their own publishing company. Haviland had already become involved with Howley in a secret understanding to handle publication for him of a waltz he had bought outright from a Charles Ditson customer. After dedicating it to the star of a Broadway play, Haviland got permission to sell the sheet music during the play's year-long run. Boys went through the aisles at all intermissions selling the music. Pooling two hundred dollars, the three joined in ownership of the

George T. Worthy Company, music publishers, operating out of a small office near Broadway. Dresser was on the road most of the time, touring in New York successes; his partners kept their jobs and handled the new business after hours.

For almost two years, the company floundered. Haviland's involvement was discovered by his employers, and he was discharged from his eighteen dollar-a-week position. He was forced to earn a living by doing odd jobs while running the new F. B. Haviland Company. In 1895, the three struck pay dirt with Dresser's "Just Tell Them That You Saw Me," the product of an afternoon's tinkling at the company piano. An enterprising button firm made a button with the song title on it, and soon comedians, newspaper editors, tailers, and bankers were using the name, which had become a catchword for the fashionable young men of New York.

Four additional Dresser hits came out that year, followed in 1896 by seven more. The business was now housed in elegant new quarters, typical of the other successful houses, and had on staff pianists and arrangers. Now retitled Howley, Haviland & Co., the firm was besieged by professional writers eager to have a share in its remarkable streak of luck. "I wouldn't take no royalty," he announced. "All I want is money when I needs it and I wants it." Because his songs were usually successful, he could have made much more, from royalties.

One of Howley, Haviland's chief asset was an inside plugger, charged with demonstrating new songs to visiting performers. Max Dreyfus was a slight young man who had grown up with European art music in cultured environs. Within a few years, he left to join Harms as arranger and house pianist. His importance there grew as his employer became more and more a slave to the bottle; Tom Harms died in 1906. With financial backing from relatives and several London music publishers, Dreyfus acquired control of the Harms Company. Additional money was, evidently, supplied by Jerome Kern, not yet twenty. He had come across the Hudson from Newark to get into the music business; his first job was in the billing department of Stern's jobbing plant, the General Music Supply Company, established around 1900 to fight the five major music jobbers, who controlled the business. It had become their practice to fill large orders for hit songs by including copies of songs for which there was little or no demand. Kern was pleased when his talent appeared to be recognized by Stern's publication, in 1902, of his first piece, an instrumental work, "At the Casino." The following year he offered to put some mooney he had recently inherited into the business, but he was turned down. Soon after, he left his seven-dollar-a-week job as a Stern song plugger in the John Wanamaker Department Store and went to work for Dreyfus at Harms, as a plugger and staff writer, at a five-dollar increase in salary. Though the Witmarks had a virtual monopoly of Broadway musical scores, Dreyfus was able to arrange the interpolation of some Kern songs into hit productions and then sent the young writer to London, for seasoning and experience. Sometime just before 1905, after Kern was back to New York, Harms moved to roomy, well-furnished offices on West 45th Street, with Kern as a partner. His financial interest eventually became 25 percent of a business that flourished as Dreyfus revealed an uncanny genius for discovering promising young talent. Among the giants of the American musical theater he sponsored were Rudolf Friml, George Gershwin, Vincent Youmans, and Richard Rogers.

Another new employee at Howley, Haviland during Max Dreyfus's tenure there was Theodore Dreiser, still years away from his successful novels. He had left his advertising-agency job in the Midwest to become a free-lance writer in New York. His fond brother, Paul Dresser, created on-the-job training by having the music house subsidize a new magazine, *Every Month,* beginning in 1895, with Dreiser as editor. Each issue contained four pieces of music published by the company, articles about the theater and songwriters, and expressions of the editor's philosophy. It was aimed at the women's market, and lasted two years, having lost $50,000 for its sponsors.

The sum appeared trivial in light of the firm's astounding success. It published "I Can't Tell Why I Love You, but I Do, Do, Do," by teen-age Gus Edwards; "The Sidewalks of New York," by Charlie Lawlor and Jim Blake, an actor and a hat salesman; Dresser's "The Blue and the Gray," "On the Banks of the Wabash," "Just Tell Them That You Saw Me," and many others. George Evans, the Honey Boy, brought to the office "In the Good Old Summer Time," which was introduced by Blanche Ring. The song was an overnight sensation. Clifton Crawford gave it "Nancy." Then, in rapid succession, it published "Just Because She Made Them Goo Goo Eyes," "Ain't That a Shame," "Bill Bailey Won't You Please Come Home," "Keep the Golden Gates Wide Open," "Goodbye, Dolly Gray," "Mandy Lee," and "In the Baggage Coach Ahead."

Dresser continued, however, to be the company's nonpareil hit writer. Between 1897 and 1901, he had twenty-seven consecutive successes. He had tried his hand at coon songs with some profit, but it was the sentimental, tear-inducing ballads of a fading generation with which this three hundred-pound, six-foot monument to generosity and the high life was most comfortable, music to which the pump organ installed in his hotel apartment, on which he wrote his melodies, was ideally suited.

As income from sheet-music sales declined seriously, Dresser began to view his partners with suspicion and became active in the firm's general operations for the first time whenever his vaudeville engagements took him to New York. The failing business and exasperation with Dresser's complaints drove Haviland to sell his share in the company for $8,000, a fraction of its previous worth. In 1904, he opened F. B. Haviland Publishing Company. He then hired away from his former associates, for twenty-five dollars a week, hit-songwriter Theodore Morse, making him the highest-paid house pianist and staff writer in the business. Morse had written the million-copy-seller "Dear Old Girl," which had helped keep Howley, Haviland & Co. temporarily out of bankruptcy. He had also served as Dresser's personal musical amanuensis. Within a year of working with Haviland, he was a full partner, and had written "Blue Bell," "Down in Jungletown," "Arrah Wanna," "Keep on the Sunny Side," and "I've Taken Quite a Fancy to You," all substantial successes.

Equally incompetent to run their business, Dresser and Howley watched it go into inevitable bankruptcy. The heartbroken songwriter opened his own firm on 28th Street, resting his hopes for a return to fame and fortune on a new song, "My Gal Sal," inspired by a prostitute he had known in his youth and never forgotten. He had earned and spent a half-million dollars, but was now forced to live with a sister, at whose home he died in January 1906. Within a year, "My Gal Sal" sold more than a million copies. It and "On the Banks of the Wabash," made the official state song of Indiana, survived Dresser.

The last of the great houses formed late in the century, Shapiro, Bernstein, was still controlled by family members in 1985. Louis Bernstein and Maurice Shapiro went into business together late in the century, confident they could break the Witmarks' evident monopoly on the services of musical-theater performers for boosting songs. They began effecting business arrangements in mass lots with stage performers. Money seemed to be no object, as Tin Pan Alley learned when it became public that they had given a diamond ring worth $500 to the great hit maker Lottie Gilson for a year's worth of song-boosting services. To attract her and other stage performers, Shapiro and Bernstein looked for writers of songs that lent themselves to dramatization and stage action.

They found exactly that in Harry Von Tilzer, a Midwesterner in his late twenties who had been singing in circus and burlesque shows since the age of fourteen. Born Harry Gumm, he used his mother's family name with the aristocratic prefix on stage. He went to New York, and for the next six years wrote special songs for Tony Pastor and other variety artists, getting as much as two dollars each for about 3,000 pieces. In 1898, he and his collaborator, Andrew Sterling, used the back of an order to pay three weeks overdue rent to put "My Old New Hampshire Home" down on paper. When none of the major houses showed any interest, they sold it to a job printer who occasionally published music, W. C. Nunn, for fifteen dollars. Nunn also brought out another Von Tilzer–Sterling piece, "I'd Leave My Happy Home for You." Shapiro and Bernstein bought both and began to boost them after paying Von Tilzer a flat $4,000 royalty in advance and giving him a job in their office as song plugger and writer. The two songs together eventually sold three million copies.

Realizing that it would be cheaper to make Von Tilzer a partner rather than pay him royalties, Shapiro and Bernstein had their best-selling songwriter's name painted on the office door and sent him west to run their Chicago branch. There, he began to work with Arthur Lamb, an English lyricist whose "Asleep in the Deep" had become the national anthem for every vaudeville basso and baritone. Bernstein loved their "Spider and the Fly," "Mansion of Aching Hearts," and "Jennie Lee," but turned down "A Bird in a Gilded Cage," because "it's about a whore." It was not published until Lamb made her the married woman whose "beauty was bought for an old man's gold."

With five hit songs under his belt, Von Tilzer realized that their profits were greater than his share of the company's. He left to form his own company, in whose offices on 28th Street Monroe Rosenfeld gave a new name to the music business. Soon after Von Tilzer's defection, Maurice Shapiro left the firm, to spend several years in Europe. On his return around 1904, he had a short business association with Jerome M. Remick, in Shapiro, Remick Music Publishing Co.

A wealthy young man from Detroit, who found access to the stage a royal road to the beds of actresses, Jerome Remick had purchased the local publishing firm of Whitney, Warren, whose offices were a regular way station for touring vaudevillians. His earliest musical success came from ragtime songs, the first of which was "Ma Ragtime Baby," written by a local black bandleader, Fred Stone, whose musicians played for all the best society in southern Michigan. So great was Stone's influence in Detroit that he organized the first all-black musicians' union there, to which whites had to apply for membership in order to work in the city. Remick's first million-copy seller was the result of his purchase in 1901 of "Hiawatha—A Summer Idyl," the first of many "Indian" intermezzos. Others were "Navajo," "Tammany," "Red Wing," "Indianola," "Silver Heels," and "Anona." The last was supposedly written by Mabel McKinley, the former President's niece, who sang it in vaudeville and got an injunction whenever another performer tried to sing it on the same stage. "Hiawatha" 's writer and first publisher was Charles N. Daniels, a white Kansas City musician, who joined Remick in Detroit as staff arranger and writer. He later became a major West Coast music publisher and motion-picture songwriter, under the name Neil Moret.

In 1904, Remick went east to conquer Tin Pan Alley, and the Broadway chorus lines, and had that brief partnership with Maurice Shapiro, who left after a time and once again joined Louis Bernstein. Never loath to spend money when it would produce a profit Shapiro, Bernstein got the exclusive right to all Shubert brothers' musicals, which later included all the Winter Garden songs made by Al Jolson. The Witmark hold on theater music was effectively broken.

Jerome Remick, too, continued to enjoy success. Appropriating Rossiter's music-folder attention-getters, he began to hand them out along Broadway, where audiences got to know the name strung out in three-inch-high letters across the folders. One of Remick's chief business talents was an ability to select knowledgeable, devoted men to work for him. The head of his professional department, Mose Gumble, was with the organization until his death, in 1947, years after it had been sold to Warner Brothers and Remick was back in Detroit as president of the leading local dairy company. Hired away from Shapiro, Bernstein in 1904, where his fifteen-dollar-a-week salary as a song demonstrater was among the industry's highest, Gumble made early million-copy hits out of "In the Shade of the Old Apple Tree," "Shine on Harvest Moon," "Put On Your Old Grey Bonnet," and "By the Light of the Silvery Moon." Remick himself bought the last. Having heard that sheet-music jobbers were looking for its owner, Remick found him. It was Gus Edwards, who had been using the song in his children's act for the past two years. Remick proposed $7,000 for the copyright, but, well aware of how valuable the song had become, Edwards held out and got $20,000. There were people in the business who laughed at Remick in the early days, but his determination to be a success was responsible for his quick rise to a place among Tin Pan Alley's leading merchandising and promotion innovators. His reputation as an industry loner grew in 1906 after he signed exclusive contracts with a number of major department stores around the country to operate their sheet-music departments, thus closing them to his rivals. It was a move that disrupted the business for a number of years.

In the economic hard times following the panic of 1893 to 1895, the cost of advertising to launch a new song was fixed at around $1,300: $250 to publish 10,000 professional copies; $50 to print the star's picture on the cover of regular copies; advertising in the trade papers $500; an initial payment of $500 to the performer guaranteeing to feature the song regularly. But only one out of every 200 songs published made a substantial profit, and fewer than one half got back the initial $1,300 spent on them. In 1975, American record manufacturers, who had taken over the process from print publishers, asserted that 77 percent of all record releases did not get back the initial production and exploitation costs.

Beginning in the late 1890s, the music business found itself confronted with the first (and far from the last) national debate regarding its best-selling product, in this case the ragtime song. There has been earlier fulminations against certain kinds of popular music, chiefly patriotic songs. British ballads were burned during the Revolution, as was "Dixie" in the time of an even bloodier conflict. Septimus Wimmer was jailed for having written a "McClellan for President" song in 1864, the Hutchinsons managed too offend almost every part of the American establishment with their music, and "Weeping, Sad and Lonely, or When This Cruel War Is Over" was barred from the front lines during the Civil War because of its effect on the troops. Congressional intervention resulted in the deletion of some Confederate songs from later editions of Brainard's *Our War Songs, North and South.*

However, not until open war was declared on the ragtime song by the press, pulpit, and women organized to be of service to some worthy cause was there such a national manifestation of opposition to "inferior music." It was not aimed at classical ragtime. Joplin's "Maple Leaf Rag" had just been published and probably had not yet sold its first few thousand copies. The best of society was dancing to "Smoky Mokes," "At a Georgia Camp Meeting," and Arthur Pryor's "Coon Band Contest." There can be little doubt that a considerable amount of racism was involved in this operation, which, then as later with rhythm and blues and rock 'n' roll, was coated with a patina of concern for public morality. Edward A. Berlin, in *Ragtime,* discusses many elements of this war, among them "attempts at repression" and "suggestions of moral, intellectual and physical danger." However, he lists no earlier published expression of these fears than that in the *Musical Courier* of September 13, 1899, which sounded what appears to be the earliest battle cry:

> A wave of vulgar, filthy and suggestive music has inundated the land. Nothing but ragtime prevails, and the cake-walk with its obscene posturings, its lewd gestures.
> . . . Our children, our young men and women, are continually exposed to the contiguity, to the monotonous attrition of this vulgarizing music. It is artistically and morally depressing, and should be suppressed by press and pulpit.

It is thought that this was really another blast against people who would not advertise in his publication by the magazine's owner, Marc A. Blumenberg.

An avowed enemy of popular music, which was "repugnant" to him, he had long been a vitriolic enemy of Victor Herbert's musical comedies and light music, about which his magazine wrote, "there is not a single original strain in anything he has done," "everything written by Herbert is copied." This led to a suit for libel, won by the composer. Long before this, Herbert and his publisher, Witmark, had refused to advertise in the *Musical Courier* and been subjected to attacks in the magazine. In 1898, the editor of *Musical America* editorialized on "Organized Blackmail," without naming Blumenberg and his publication. He cited examples of a "certain notorious musical paper" that was blackmailing artists, music-trade organizations, and publishers. As the most successful publisher of ragtime songs, M. Witmark & Sons was ripe for this.

Whatever Blumenberg's real motives, his dolorous tirade roused the proponents of "good music" to action. At its national meeting in 1901, the American Federation of Musicians sought to ban ragtime, asking members to boycott the music, and "do all in their power to counteract the pernicious influence exerted by 'Mr. Johnson,' 'My Coal-Black Lady' [both Witmark publications] and others of the negro school. . . . The musicians know what is good, and if the people don't, we will have to teach them."

Such attacks posed a new problem for the music business, which recurred from time to time, always equating vernacular music with the debauchery of children and a general debasement of musical taste, and making it responsible for the declining sales of concert and art music as well as a general decline in public morality.

By then, the ragtime-coon song finally seemed to lose much of its attraction for the Witmarks and a handful of other houses, which began to specialize in "production music," that written for musical comedies or four-act plays. The scenery, general trappings, and larger orchestra of a Broadway presentation added an additional ingredient to a song's potential for success, as did its repetition during weeks of evening and matinee performances. It was, moreover, from such a repertory that most orchestras in large hotels, plush restaurants, and vaudeville houses chose their nightly selections.

By 1906, the American theater was a $200-million enterprise, with major investments in theaters around the country, whose offerings were controlled by the Klaw and Erlanger syndicate, or those newcomers the Shubert brothers. With approximately 400 theaters, the former booked 700 theatrical companies annually, employing about 30,000 persons, on a payroll of $1.75 million. In total, more than 100,000 persons worked in this field, and more than five million dollars was spent on newspaper advertising and the transportation of touring companies. Few theatrical productions earned back from a Broadway run the $10,000 to $75,000 it had cost to mount them. It was from road tours that Victor Herbert, George M. Cohan, and other well-known composers of production music got their greatest royalties. In a single year, Cohan, who wrote book, music, and lyrics, earned about $32,000 from performances of *George Washington, Jr., Little Johnny Jones*, and *Forty-Five Minutes from Broadway*, all running concurrently across the nation. This was over and above his royalties as performer and producer. The composer of a full production score received a share of box-office receipts, ranging from the usual one and a half percent to the five and six Cohan and Herbert demanded and got. In most cases, the printing, promotion, and merchandising of production music was determined by the producer, who had already been given an advance of several thousand dollars against royalties in return for the grant of exclusive publication rights. This made possible the monopolization of production music by the Witmarks; F. A. Mills; Shapiro, Bernstein; Harms; and Haviland.

Publishers worked actively to have individual pieces promoted by the very effective "three-song prima donnas" of vaudeville and by interpolation into the scores of musical comedies and into the action of plays. Only a few composers were able to secure contracts barring interpolation, and even then leading ladies flagrantly violated the provision.

Professional managers, such as Mose Gumble, of the Remick firm, spent much time making sure that audiences, including those at the vaudeville houses, would take up catchy refrains or insist on encores. Plants, voices in the gallery, stooges, or water boys were paid to plug songs or encourage audience response. Many water boys, among them Al Jolson, were recruited from synagogue classes. Harry Von Tilzer was particularly adept at creating stunts to bring attention to his new songs. For "Down Where the Wurzburger Flows," nightly he assisted the young actress who introduced it in remembering supposedly forgotten lines. An apparently sleeping man was roused at every performance by the first notes of his "Please Go Way and Let Me Sleep" to join the onstage vocalist in her rendition. The Wurzburger breweries used his "Down Where the Wurzburger Flows" to promote sales by paying whistlers to introduce its melody in beer halls. The success of a popular song depended as much on the cleverness of the professional manager and his song pluggers as on its inherent appeal.

The Witmarks had learned early that sales, no matter how large, of purely vernacular songs could not support a venture looking for large profits. Taking the lead among Tin Pan Alley publishers, the firm began its own music magazine, opened a talent bureau for vaudeville performers and amateurs, and helped arrange concerts and performances by church and educational groups. When it bought out its first complete musical-comedy score, *The Isle of Champagne*, by Charles Byrne and William W. Furst, in 1892, it also produced arrangements of all its songs for social and popular dances and for various combinations of instruments. The general practice was immediately established that the songwriter would not be paid any royalties on their sales, which ostensibly were part of the exploitation and promotion process.

After Isidore Witmark acquired American rights to "better-grade" British and European music on one of his early trips abroad, the Witmark *Black and White Series* was instituted, with American music of the "higher class" added soon after. Because energetic promotion and aggressive advertising had long brought prosperity to wholesale-retailers, it became attractive to the new music-business jobbers. Music for the voice was added to the Witmark series, sacred as well as art and concert, all arranged for solo and various combinations of voices, offered in at least three keys. Stern, Feist, and a few others copied this by issuing their own folios of "higher-grade" compositions and educational and operatic works. Sales grew steadily, despite increasing competition for the lucrative trade. It was this market, whose wholesale prices were fixed by a general understanding among the firms involved, that continued to grow with increasing sales of production music.

The strictly popular-song side of the business was beginning to suffer by 1906 from a variety of problems. Performers asked for more money and more gratuities for song boosting. The proliferation of professional copies cut into the sale of regular copies of songs that failed to achieve the hit category. Wholesale prices for all popular music had been cut in half, from the twenty to thirty cents of the 1880s and early 1890s. The mounting number of potential hits stemming from the corresponding growth of new houses shortened the life of a successful song, from the eighteen months of the past to three to six months, and big sellers were crowded out by new candidates for public favor.

In May 1908, the *American Musician* carried a list, based on trade sources, of songs that were selling in large quantities, most earning their writers a five-cent royalty. The statistics were often at variance with those generally accepted, but they are evidence that sales claims of this and many other periods in music-business history cannot be accepted as accurate.

Over a million copies:
"After the ball," Charles K. Harris; published by writer ("A Trip to China-town" on other side)
"Bedelia" (1903), William Jerome and Jean Schwartz; Shapiro, Bernstein & Co. ("The Jersey Lily")
"In the Shade of the Old Apple Tree" (1905), Harry H. Williams, Egbert Van Alstyne; Shapiro, Jerome Remick Co.
"Love Me and the World is Mine" (1906), David Reed, Ernest R. Ball; M. Witmark & Sons
"Mr. Dooley" (1902), William Jerome, Jean Schwartz; Shapiro, Bernstein & Von Tilzer ("A Chinese Honeymoon")
"Under the Bamboo Tree" (1902), Bob Cole and Rosamund Johnson; Jos. W. Stern & Co. ("Sally in Our Alley")

800,000:
"Always" (1899), Charles Horwitz and Frederick V. Bowers; M. Witmark & Sons
"Because" (1898), Charles Horwitz and Frederick V. Bowers; M. Witmark & Sons
"All Coons Look Alike to Me" (1896), Ernest Hogan; M. Witmark & Sons
"By the Watermelon Vine, Lindy Lou" (1904), Thornton S. Allen; published by writer
"My Sweetheart's the Man in the Moon " (1892), James Thornton; Frank Harding

500,000:
"Hiawatha" (1901), Neil Moret (Charles N. Daniels); Jerome Remick / Whitney-Warner Publishing Co.
"I'm Afraid to Come Home in the Dark" (1907), Harry H. Williams and Egbert Van Alstyne; Jerome H. Remick & Co.

"I Wants Dem Presents Back" (1896), Paul West; M. Witmark & Sons (Featured by Anna Held in Ziegfeld productions)
"Golden Rod" (1907), Mabel McKinley; Leo Feist & Co.
"Sweetest Story Ever Told" (1892), R. M. Stultz (Featured on minstrel shows)
"Violets" (1900), Julian Fane and Ellen Wright; G. Ricordi & Co.

In their often desperate search for copy to fill the pages of bloating Sunday editions, many reporters fell back on the popular song when all else failed. Such stories were filled with accounts of the great sums to be made from a simple popular song. It was usually pointed out that young women bought most of the plaintive songs written, and warned hopeful amateurs never to use more than an octave and a note, more being "dangerous." The creation of these usual "quantums of balderdash and rot," as the *American Musician* characterized them in a story appearing in an early January 1907 issue of the Sunday *New York Sun,* was made to seem easy.

The situation for most songwriters was neither easy nor rosy. Only about twenty-five production writers and songwriters were then under contract to a music publisher and receiving the five-cent royalty for their compositions. The other few who were paid a royalty were special cases, star performers, or freelancers who made the rounds with new material and bargained for the best deal.

The "game" of writing songs, as Nat D. Mann, himself a composer and manager of the Witmarks' Chicago office, wrote in a remarkably candid article for *Music Trade Review* was not what it had been five or six years before, when a song that became popular could make a fortune for its writer. Nor did many composers who supplied publishers with most of their best-selling pieces know anything about theory or harmony, generally whistling or "faking" a melody for a staff musician or arranger to put down.

> The popular songwriter of today, as soon as he gets an idea, immediately goes to his publisher to have it arranged. . . . In forty-nine cases out of fifty the publisher generally has the entire melody rewritten by one of the arrangers and when it is played over for the "composer" or "author" they immediately suffer with an enlargement of the cranium, forgetting entirely that there is hardly a sequence of the notes as he originally conceived it, and that the entire melody has been rearranged, notes cut out, and other substituted. Nevertheless he gets all the royalties and credit for it, while the man who actually did the entire work gets from $1 to $2.50 for his labor. It generally depends upon the ability of the arranger as to what he will receive for arranging a pianoforte copy for publication.

Nor was there much profit in song writing, Mann added. "The author gets from 1 to 3 cents per copy; if he is unknown he sometimes gets 1 cent per copy. . . . The royalties are generally divided between the author and composer, so it is easy to figure 'the tremendous fortunes' the songwriters of today are making."

Such successful songwriters as Charles K. Harris, Harry Von Tilzer and his brother Albert, Gus Edwards, and Carrie Jacobs Bond did make fortunes out of their hits, by being their own publishers, and were possessed of sufficient business acumen to compete with the established firms. In the case of Mrs.

Bond, music publishing was forced upon her after the sudden death of her husband and a sidewalk fall that incapacitated her. In order to support herself and a young son, she opened a rooming house and wrote children's songs for Brainard's. The royalties were small or nonexistent, so she began to publish new pieces on her own, though with little success. Encouraged in 1903 by Jessie Bartlett Davies, star of the Boston Opera Company, Mrs. Bond issued some new songs intended for an adult market. Her printer's unpaid bill rose to $1,500 after she brought out *Seven Songs* in book form. Included were "Just A'wearyin' for You" and "I Love You Truly," two of her three hits, which, with "A Perfect Day" (1909), sold millions of copies. Going from store to store, at first she was able to sell only a few books each week, and suffered a serious breakdown. A Chicago druggist friend paid the printer in return for a 10 percent interest in Bond House, her publishing company. In time, demand began to build for separate copies of her songs.

After a slow recovery, Carrie Bond, in 1908, opened an office in Chicago in conjunction with her grown son. Within a year, nineteen employees were operating the booming business. Though never part of Tin Pan Alley's tradition of music, Carrie Jacobs Bond and her modestly artistic songs were in the true vernacular tradition—simple melodies with words easy to remember. A considerable degree of their "quality" appeal was due to the matte-finished linen paper on which the songs were printed, warranting the slightly higher price that millions of Americans equated with higher-class music.

Mrs. Bond's songs were promoted without charge chiefly by art- and concert-music soloists seeking to broaden their appeal to ticket buyers. The popular music firms meanwhile found the cost of song boosting rising ever higher, particularly with the popularity of the phonograph record and cylinder and the growth of music-machine parlors. As a result, recording artists and coin-machine owners were added to those being paid for exploitation. When competition among publishers to secure recordings kept growing, one of the best-known artists, Len Spencer, opened an office to represent a dozen firms exclusively, bringing advance copies of new songs to the attention of recording executives and his fellow performers and serving in general as a song plugger, assigned only to the record business.

Several music men had already been involved with that industry: Julius Witmark as an early recording artist on Berliner's experimental disks, and Joe Stern and Ed Marks as cylinder manufacturers. In 1897, Stern and Marks opened the Universal Phonograph Company, in a building near their 20th Street offices equipped with recording devices and a studio. Songs published by them were chiefly used by the same free-lance artists who worked for Columbia and Edison, but they also cut hit songs owned by others, to meet a public demand that was limited only by the industry's generally small output. Because the "round" system permitted manufacture of only seven cylinders at a time, the proliferating independent manufacturers had no problem disposing of their product. Universal's records sold for a dollar each, or a dozen for ten dollars, and their fame spread as far as England, from which orders came for the entire Universal output. What appeared to be a profitable side venture collapsed, however, once

Columbia developed a secret dubbing system that increased production by 500 percent. This was followed by an announcement from Edison's National Phonograph Company of a restriction on sales of blank cylinders, effectively destroying all competition by such small manufacturers as Stern and Marks and about two dozen other companies.

With restrictions on entering the music-roll or recording business, and prices of music falling, leading New York firms concentrated their energies to combat the surreptitious printer and establish a controlled distribution system.

That eternal enemy of their trade the printed sheet-music pirate had become more sophisticated and imaginative. On October 28, 1905, Garret J. Couchois was convicted in New York City of counterfeiting the Carl Fischer firm's trademark on pirated copies of its song "Hearts and Flowers." He was sentenced to thirty days in the city prison and fined $500, as stiff a punishment as allowed under the law. After the decision was unanimously affirmed by higher courts, Couchois pleaded guilty to having done the same with other publishers' trademarks and copyrights.

Couchois had created a gigantic scheme to pirate every successful piece of music on the market, and nearly succeeded in disrupting the entire popular-music business, particularly that dealing in the "higher type" of music. Using the name Jones, he took authentic copies of sheet music to a photoengraver, who made exact electroplate reproductions, which were then shipped to a printing plant he operated in a rural New Jersey factory.

In the case of Boosey & Co.'s best-selling "royalty" ballad "The Holy City," Couchois-Jones duplicated the signature of its composer, which was stamped on every authentic copy to ensure against counterfeiting, by making a similar stamp of his own. After buying ten copies of the song at Boosey's New York store and securing an invoice of his purchase, Couchois changed the figure from 10 to 10,000, and reduced the total price to an amount far below the customary one. With this as proof that his counterfeited copies were authentic, he sold them to jobbers. He did the same with other hit songs similarly manufactured and distributed. Agents in his employ around the United States used documents forged by him to sell counterfeited editions sent them from the New Jersey printing plant. Months passed, while Couchois flooded the country with his pirated sheet music at far below usual wholesale prices, which threatened to bring the business to its knees, before the scheme was discovered and the villain arrested.

Relying on the failure by Congress to fix criminal penalties for piracy, Couchois was tripped up only by counterfeiting the publishers' imprints on his printed copies, a violation of New York laws. Other sheet-music pirates were thereafter careful not to duplicate his error. Not until a criminal penalty for duplicating copyrighted music without permission was eventually mandated by federal law did sheet-music piracy as a major problem end.

The first, temporarily effective, move by leading Tin Pan Alley music houses to control distribution and fix the price of their sheet music on a uniform basis took place in 1907 with formation of American Music Stores. This was a little more than half a century after creation of the Board of Music Trade of the

United States for much the same purpose. Production music, prices of which were strictly controlled already, and in which the American Music Stores' founders specialized, had remained the most profitable music-business product. However, in those large stores where a single publisher had a contract giving him control over purchasing and display, sheet music from successful musical comedies published by others was not featured or available for purchase. Local theater managers complained, and future relations with producers were impaired. Individual popular songs, on the other hand, were approaching a different commercial crisis. The volume of their sales to jobbers was strong and increasing, but individual orders were usually only for the big hits. Legitimate retail dealers found baffling the practices of music-firm commission salesmen, particularly their insistence on selling to them at the usual wholesale price and then getting larger orders for the same items at a considerably reduced cost from competing five-and-ten-cent and department stores. Many of these had become such large outlets for the most important hits that publishers were forced to sell at special prices or lose their business entirely. By selling sheet music at retail for as little as six or eight cents, they created public demand in general.

The R. H. Macy store in New York was a particular vexation to the music firms. Having just won a protracted court case against the American (Book) Publishers' Association, the store's owners, who advertised that it would undersell all competition, now prepared to discount most of its stock. For years prior to the legal action, most of the book trade and the American Booksellers Association had strictly enforced their rules against discounting of any kind. They had blacklisted such violators as Macy's, forcing it to take losses on books in order to retain customers.

The current shaky status of the sheet-music business, aggravated by the Supreme Court's finding favorable to Macy's, was further upset by contracts signed by Jerome Remick with a number of leading department stores around the country that gave him control over their sheet-music operations and thus an opportunity to feature only his production music. These problems led to the formation in early 1907 of American Music Stores. With an initial capital of $25,000, provided by the Witmarks, Leo Feist, Kerry Mills, Charles K. Harris, and Fred Haviland, the new group prepared to establish a chain of its own stores and to operate sheet-music departments for others from coast to coast. These would carry each partner's entire catalogue of music and also purchase all the other publishers' material at regular wholesale prices.

They would strongly maintain the prevailing retail rate for all stock. Harris told a reporter for the *Music Trade Review* that when dealers warred on each other by cutting prices, the American Music Stores would attempt to restore "an amicable understanding. Ruinous competition is farthest from our intentions; but if competitors feel inclined to slash music in order to run us out they will be up against a hard game, for we will . . . meet them on their own ground . . . our object is to again place the retailing of music on a profitable and honorable basis, and eliminate absolutely the bushwackers and guerrillas, as well as the cut-throat methods that have characterized the trade for too many years."

The Supreme Court decision in August 1907, finding that the book publishers' combine had indeed acted in restraint of trade against Macy's, freed the giant department store to resume even more drastic underselling of many fixed-price items, including some affecting the music business: phonograph machines, musical instruments, including pianos, and printed music. The American Music Stores had by then made contracts with fifty major stores, including a few in New York, and set up its own branches in other cities. In addition, Maurice Shapiro, Max and Louis Dreyfus on behalf of Harms, the firm of Francis, Day & Hunter, and Fred Hager, a recording-company executive and songwriter, and his partner, J. Fred Helf, had created their own retail operation, the United States Music Stores, capitalized at $200,000.

Heavily involved in the Washington copyright hearings, Isidore Witmark found time to become the architect of a strategy to combat the massacre of prices for sheet music resulting from a price war between Macy's and Siegel, Cooper, spawned by the Supreme Court finding. He proposed that the partners in American Music Stores use their branch in a store on 14th Street in New York for a one-cent sale of sheet music, and keep it going for twenty weeks, if necessary, to bring Macy's and Siegel-Cooper, also on 14th Street, to their knees.

Starting with the Witmarks' biggest hit of the day, "Love Me and the World Is Mine," which sold for twenty-three cents wholesale, Witmark offered to throw in all his other best-sellers provided the others would join him. Hit songs published by others would be bought at the standard discount and added to the one-cent sale. Nothing would be sold C.O.D. or by mail, and only a single copy of each song could be purchased by a customer. As another gambit, Witmark suggested recruiting fifty to sixty people to go to both Macy's and Siegel-Cooper on the first day of the sale and "tantalize the music clerks and managers by showing them the penny ad and asking Macy's, who claimed to be cheaper than anybody else, to meet it." Some of these people would choose a dozen pieces of music and then put down twelve cents for them, demanding that the store stand behind its promise to beat all prices.

On October 11, 1907, advertisements appeared in all major New York papers for an "Unprecedented Sale of Copyrighted Music, published at from 50 to 60 cents a copy—no old or shopworn stocks: nothing but the biggest and latest HITS by the greatest songwriters . . . ON SALE TOMORROW AT 1¢ A COPY" at Rothenberg's. Police reserves were called, later on that Saturday, to quell crowds frustrated when it was announced that the entire sheet-music stock was exhausted. Macy's finally called the conspirators to effect a truce. One was made, and American Music Stores' penny-a-copy printed-music sale came to an end, after Macy's and its rival ended their massacre of sheet-music prices, which had bottomed out at one to three cents a copy.

It had been a costly victory. The *American Musician* reported three months later that this "coterie of publishers" had sustained a loss of $20,000, and that American Music Stores was in trouble. This was promptly denied by the partners, most of whom were then deeply involved in the copyright-revision process.

The sudden end to the price war was a boon, not only to Macy's and Siegel-

Cooper, but to all the partners in American Music Stores, who realized almost immediately that Witmark's strategy was going to cost more than any of them cared to pay. Moreover, it had little effect on the "cheap stores" and independent retailers, who continued to sell the leading hits for less than a dime. Within a few years, the growth of F. W. Woolworth's five-and-ten-cent stores, where nothing cost more than a dime, and that of his competitors established the ten-cent price as standard for almost all printed sheet music other than standard and production songs. Publishers locked out of the musical theater were the principal victims of this situation: Albert Von Tilzer; Ted Snyder, with whom young Irving Berlin soon entered into partnership; Gotham-Attucks, the black-owned firm; Joe Morris, in Philadelphia, and other songwriter-owned companies. Partners in American Music Stores and United States Music Stores, and also Jerome Remick, were able to control displays of production music in the sheet-music sections of stores with whom they had contracts or in the retail operations they ran, but they were forced to accept wholesale prices lower than the usual when orders for large quantities of their big hits came from cheap stores.

Isidore Witmark found himself excoriated as the "Judas of the music trade" by the smaller publishing houses after the copyright hearings for having prevented addition of the word *music* to the manufacturing clause. His action was of greatest benefit to those large firms that, like his own, had reciprocal arrangements with major European houses, and those like Schirmer and Carl Fischer who generally had their music printed in Germany.

Few among those who participated in the negotiations preceeding the new copyright law realized the full implications of the legislation. None of them could possibly envision the five-billion-dollar industry that came out of the compulsory-licensing and public-performance-for-profit provisions. Nor could they have predicted the dramatic changes in public taste, developing technology, government intervention, vicious infighting between publishers and songwriters, or the vast conglomeration of their business on an international scale that would touch the American popular song and its creators in the following decades.

Bibliography

General

America's Taste 1851–1959: The Cultural Events of a Century Reported by Contemporary Observers in the Pages of the New York Times. New York: Simon & Schuster, 1960.

Austin, William F. *Susanna, Jeanie and The Old Folks at Home: The Songs of Stephen Foster from His Time to Ours.* New York: Macmillan, 1975.

Barzun, Jacques. *Berlioz and His Century: An Introduction to the Age of Romanticism.* New York: Meridian Books, 1956.

Batterbery, Michael and Ariane. *On the Town in New York: A History of the Eating, Drinking and Entertainment from 1776 to the Present.* New York: Scribner, 1973.

Berger, Max. *The British Traveller in America 1836–1860.* New York: Columbia University Press, 1943.

Blom, Eric. *Music in England.* Baltimore: Penguin Books, 1942.

Bode, Carl. *The American Lyceum.* New York: Oxford University Press, 1950.

———. *Antebellum Culture.* Carbondale: Southern Illinois University Press, 1970.

Boorstin, Daniel J. *The Americans: The Democratic Experience.* New York: Random House, 1973.

———. *The Americans: The National Experience.* New York: Random House, 1965.

Branch, E. Douglas. *The Sentimental Years, 1836–1860.* New York: Appleton-Century, 1934.

Brooks, Van Wyck. *The Confident Years, 1885–1915. New York: Dutton, 1952.*

———. *The Flowering of New England.* New York: Dutton, 1936.

———. *New England: Indian Summer.* New York: Dutton, 1940.

———. *The Times of Melville and Whitman.* New York: Dutton, 1947.

———. *The World of Washington Irving.* New York: Dutton, 1944.

Carson, Gerald. *The Polite Americans: 300 Years of More or Less Good Behaviour.* New York: Macmillan, 1966.

Case, Victoria, and Robert Ormond Case. *We Called It Culture: The Story of Tent Chautauqua.* New York: Doubleday, 1948.

Chase, Gilbert. *America's Music: From the Pilgrims to the Present.* New York: McGraw-Hill, 1955.

Chevalier, Michel. *Society, Manners and Politics in the United States 1833–34*. Translated by John William Ward. Ithaca, NY: Cornell University Press, 1961.

Dannett, Sylvania, and Frank E. Rachel. *Down Memory Lane: Arthur Murray's Picture History of Social Dancing*. New York: Greenburg, 1954.

Davidson, Marshall B. *Life in America*. 2 vols. Boston: Houghton Mifflin, 1951.

Dictionary of American Biography. Multivolume. New York: Scribner.

Dictionary of National Biography. Edited by Leslie Stephen and Sidney Lee. 21 vols. with suppl. London: Oxford University Press.

Dulles, Foster Rhea. *A History of Recreation: America Learns to Play*. New York: Appleton-Century-Crofts, 1965.

Durant, Will and Ariel. *The Age of Napoleon*. New York: Simon & Schuster, 1975.

Ehrenberg, Lewis Allen. "Urban Night Life and the Decline of Victorianism: New York City's Restaurants and Cabarets 1890–1918." Diss. University of Michigan, 1974.

Elson, Louis. *The History of American Music*. New York: Macmillan, 1925.

Evans, Tom and Mary. *Guitars: From the Renaissance to Rock: Music, History, Construction and Players*. New York: Paddington Press, 1977.

Franks, A. H. *Social Dance: A Short History*. London: Routledge & Kegan Paul, 1963.

Furnas, J. C. *The Americans: A Social History of the United States*. New York: Putnam, 1969.

Garraty, John A. *The American Nation*. New York: Harper & Row, 1971.

Goldin, Milton. *The Music Merchants: The Colorful Chronicle of the Impresarios, Entrepreneurs and Patrons Who Popularized Serious Music in America*. New York: Macmillan, 1969.

Grimsted, David. *Notions of the Americans, 1820–1860*. New York: Braziller, 1970.

Grove's Dictionary of Music and Musicians. Edited by Waldo Selden Pratt. 6 vols. New York: Macmillan, 1928.

Grunfeld, Fred. *The Art and Times of the Guitar: An Illustrated History of Guitars and Guitarists*. New York: Collier Books, 1959.

Harris, Neil. *The Land of Contrasts, 1880–1901*. New York: Braziller, 1970.

Harrison, Harry F., as told to Karl Detzer. *The Story of Tent Chautauqua*. New York: Hastings House, 1958.

Hart, Philip. *Orpheus in the New World: The Symphony Orchestras as an American Cultural Institution*. New York: Norton, 1973.

Hershkowitz, Leo. *Tweed's New York: Another Look*. New York: An Anchor Book, Doubleday, 1978.

Hiller, Ralph, ed. *The Concerto*. Baltimore: Penguin Books, 1952.

———. *The Symphony*. Baltimore: Penguin Books, 1949.

Hitchcock, H. Wiley. *Music in the United States: An Historical Introduction*. Englewood Cliffs, NJ: Prentice-Hall, 1969.

Holbrook, Stewart H. *The Age of the Moguls*. Garden City, NY: Doubleday, 1953.

Howard, John Tasker. *Our American Music: Three Hundred Years of It*. New York: Crowell, 1954.

Jones, Howard Mumford. *The Age of Energy: 1865–1915: Varieties of American Experience*. New York: Viking, 1971.

———. *O Strange New World: American Culture: The Formative Years*. New York: Viking, 1964.

———. *The Pursuit of Happiness*. Cambridge, MA: Harvard University Press, 1953.

Kmen, Harry A. *Music in New Orleans 1791–1840: The Formative Years*. Baton Rouge: Louisiana State University Press, 1966.

Lang, Paul Henry. *Music in Western Civilization*. New York: Norton, 1941.

Lang, Paul Henry, ed. *One Hundred Years of Music in America*. New York: Grosset & Dunlap, 1960.

Loesser, Arthur. *Men, Women and Pianos: A Social History*. New York: Simon & Schuster, 1954.

McCarthy, Albert J. *The Dance Band Era: The Dancing Decades from Ragtime to Swing*. London: Spring Books, 1971.

McCue, George, ed. *Music in American Society, 1776–1976: From Puritan Hymn to Synthesizer*. New Brunswick: Transaction Books, 1977.

McDowell, Tremaine. *The Romantic Triumph 1830–1860*. New York: Macmillan, 1933.

Mackerness, E. D. *A Social History of English Music*. London: Routledge & Kegan Paul, 1964.

McNamara, Brooks. *Step Right Up: An Illustrated History of the American Medicine Show*. New York: Doubleday, 1976.

Marrocco, W. Thomas, and Harold Gleason. *Music in America: An Anthology from the Landing of the Pilgrims to the Close of the Civil War*. New York: Norton, 1964.

Marzio, Peter, ed. *A Nation of Nations: The People Who Came to America as Seen Through Objects, Prints and Photographs at the Smithsonian Institution*. New York: Harper & Row, 1976.

Mathews, W. S. B. *A Hundred Years of Music in America: An Account of Musical Effort in the United States During the Past Century*. New York. AMS Press, 1970. Reprint of 1889 ed.

Matthiessen, F. O. *American Renaissance*. New York: Oxford University Press, 1946.

Mellers, Wilfrid. *Music in a New Found Land: Themes and Developments in the History of American Music*. London: Barrie & Rocklif, 1964.

Miller, Perry. *The Life of the Mind in America: From the Revolution to the Civil War*. New York: Harcourt, Brace & World, 1965.

Minnegerode, Meade. *The Fabulous Forties*. Garden City, NY: Garden City Publishing, 1924.

Mueller, John H. *The American Symphony Orchestra*. Bloomington: Indiana University Press, 1951.

Mussulman, Joseph A. *Music in the Cultured Generation: A Social History of Music in America*. Evanston, IL: Northwestern University Press, 1971.

Nettl, Bruno. *Folk and Traditional Music of the Western World*. Englewood Cliffs, NJ: Prentice-Hall, 1959.

Nevell, Richard. *A Time to Dance: American Country Dancing from Hornpipes to Hot Hash*. New York: St. Martin's Press, 1978.

Nye, Russell Blaine. *The Cultural Life of the New Nation, 1776–1830*. New York: Harper Torchbooks, Harper & Row, 1963.

———. *Society and Culture in America, 1830–1860*. New York: Harper Torchbooks, Harper & Row, 1974.

———. *The Unembarrassed Muse: The Popular Arts in America*. New York: Dial, 1970.

Parrington, Vernon L. *Main Currents in American Thought*. 3 vols. New York: Harcourt, Brace, 1927–1930.

Probst, George E., ed. *The Happy Republic: A Reader in Tocqueville's America*. New York: Harper Torchbooks, Harper & Row, 1962.

Raynor, Henry. *Music and Society since 1815*. New York: Schocken Books, 1976.

Richardson, P. J. S. *The Social Dance of the Nineteenth Century*. London: Herbert Jenkins, 1960.

Riegel, Robert E. *Young America 1830–1840*. Norman: University of Oklahoma Press, 1949.

Rosenthal, Harold, ed. *The Mapleson Memoirs: The Career of an Operatic Impresario, 1858–1888*. New York: Appleton-Century, 1966.

Rourke, Constance. *American Humor: A Study of the National Character*. Garden City, NY: Doubleday, 1953.

———. *The Roots of American Culture*. New York: Harcourt, Brace, 1942.

Sachs, Curt. *A History of Musical Instruments*. New York: Norton, 1940.

Schlesinger, Arthur M. *Political and Social History of the United States 1829–1925*. New York: Macmillan, 1925.

Schlesinger, Arthur M., Jr. *The Age of Jackson*. Boston: Little, Brown, 1946.

Schwartz, Harry W. *Bands of America: A Nostalgic, Illustrated History of the Golden Age of Band Music*. New York: Doubleday, 1957.

Seldes, Gilbert. *The Stammering Century*. New York: John Day, 1928.

Smith, Harry Nash. *Popular Culture and Industrialism 1865–1890*. New York: New York University Press, 1967.

Spillane, Daniel. *History of the American Pianoforte*. New York: Spillane, 1890.

Spiller, Robert E., and Harold Blodgett. *The Roots of National Culture: American Literature to 1830*. New York: Macmillan, 1949.

Stone, James. "Mid-Nineteenth Century American Beliefs in the Social Value of Music." *Musical Quarterly,* January 1957.

Sullivan, Mark. *Our Times: America Finding Herself*. New York: Scribner, 1927.

———. *Our Times: The Turn of the Century*. New York: Scribner, 1927.

Susman, Warren. *Culture and Commitment*. New York: Braziller, 1970.

Swan, Howard. *Music in the Southwest 1825–1950*. New York: Da Capo Press, 1977.

Taylor, William A. R. *Cavalier and Yankee: The Old South and American National Character*. New York: Braziller, 1967.

Trachtenberg, Alan. *Democratic Vistas 1860–1880*. New York: Braziller, 1970.

Upton, George F. *Musical Memories: My Recollections of Celebrities of the Half-Century 1850–1900*. Chicago: McClurg, 1908.

Wann, Louis. *The Rise of Realism, 1860–1900*. New York: Macmillan, 1949.

Wetzel, Richard D. *Frontier Musicians on the Conoquenessing, Wabash and Ohio: A History of the Music and Musicians of George Rapp's Harmony Society, 1805–1906*. Athens: Ohio University Press, 1976.

Wood, Gordon S. *The Rising Glory, 1760–1820*. New York: Braziller, 1970.

Woodward, W. E. *The Way Our People Lived: An Intimate American History*. New York: Dutton, 1944.

Black Americans' Music

Allen, William F., Charles F. Ware, and Lucy McKim Garrison. *Slave Songs of the United States*. New York: Peter Smith, 1929.

Anderson, Jervis. *This Was Harlem: A Cultural Portrait, 1900–1950*. New York: Farrar, Straus & Giroux, 1982.

Aptheker, Herbert, ed. *A Documentary History of the Negro People in the United States*. New York: Citadel, 1951.

Bakewell, Dennis C., ed. *The Black Experience in the United States: A Bibliography Based on the Collections of the San Fernando Valley State College Library*. Northridge, CA: San Fernando Valley State College Foundation, 1970.

Bennett, Lerone, Jr. *Before the Mayflower: A History of the Negro in America, 1619–1964*. Baltimore: Penguin Books, 1966.

Bland, James. *The Album of Outstanding Songs*. New York: Edward B. Marks Music, 1947.

Botkin, B. A. *Lay My Burden Down: A Folk History of Slavery*. Chicago: University of Chicago Press, 1945.

———. *A Treasury of American Folklore*. New York: Crown, 1944.

Brawley, Benjamin: *A Social History of the American Negro*. New York: Collier Books, 1970.

Brown, Sterling A. *Negro Poetry and Drama and the Negro in American Fiction*. New York: Atheneum, 1969.

Butcher, Margaret Just. *The Negro in American Culture, Based on Materials Left by Alain Locke*. New York: Knopf, 1956.

Charters, Ann. *Nobody: The Life of Bert Williams*. New York: Macmillan, 1970.

Charters, Samuel R., and Leonard Kunstadt. *Jazz: A History of the New York Scene*. New York: Doubleday, 1962.

Courlander, Harold. *Negro Folk Music USA*. New York: Columbia University Press, 1963.

Cuney-Hare, Maude. *Negro Musicians and Their Music*. Washington, D.C.: Associated Publishers, 1936.

Dalby, David. *Black Through White: Patterns of Communication in Africa and the New World*. Bloomington: Indiana University African Studies Program, 1971.

Daly, John C. *A Song in His Heart: The Life and Times of James A. Bland*. Philadelphia: Winston, 1951.

Damon, S. Foster. "The Negro In Early American Songsters." *Papers of the Bibliographical Society of America,* Vol. 28, 1934.

———. *Series of Old American Songs*. Providence, RI: Brown University Library, 1936.

Daughtry, Willia Estelle. "Sissieretta Jones: A Study in the Negro's Contribution to 19th-Century Entertainment." Diss. Syracuse University, 1968.

Davidson, Basil. *The African Genius*. Boston: Little, Brown, 1969.

de Lerma, Dominique-René. *Bibliography of Black Music*. Vol. 1, *Reference Materials*. Vol. 2, *Afro-American Idioms*. Westport, CT: Greenwood Press, 1981.

———. *Black Music in Our Culture*. Kent, OH: Kent State University Press, 1970.

Dennison, Sam. *Scandalize My Name: Black Imagery in American Popular Music*. New York: Garland, 1982.

Dillard, J. L. *Black English: Its History and Usage in the United States*. New York: Random House, 1972.

Dixon, Christa. *Negro Spirituals from Bible to Folksong*. Philadelphia: Fortress Press, 1976.

Dowd, Jerome. *The Negro in American Life*. Chicago: Century, 1926.

Dundes, Alan. *Mother Wit from the Laughing Barrel*. Englewood Cliffs, NJ: Prentice-Hall, 1973.

Emery, Lynn. *Black Dance in the United States from 1619 to 1970*. Palo Alto, CA: National Press Books, 1972.

Epstein, Dena, J. "The Folk Banjo: A Documentary History." *Ethnomusicology* 19, September 1975.

———. *Sinful Songs and Spirituals: Black Folk Music to the Civil War*. Urbana: University of Illinois Press, 1977.

————. "Slave Music of the United States Before 1860." *Music Library Association Notes* 20, Spring / Summer, 1963.

Fisher, Mark Miles. *Slave Songs in the United States*. Ithaca, NY: Cornell University Press, 1953.

Fletcher, Tom. *The Tom Fletcher Story: 100 Years of the Negro in Show Business*. New York: Burge, 1954.

Floyd, Samuel A. "J. W. Postelwaite of St. Louis." *Black Perspective in Music,* Fall 1978.

Floyd, Samuel A. with Marcia J. Reisser. "Social Dance Music of Black Composers in the Nineteenth Century and the Emergence of Ragtime." *The Black Perspective in Music,* Summer 1980.

Franklin, John Hope. *From Slavery to Freedom: A History of Negro Americans*. New York: Knopf, 1967.

Gaines, Francis Pendleton. *The Southern Plantation: A Study in the Development and the Accuracy of a Tradition*. New York: Columbia University Press, 1924.

Genovese, Eugene D. *Roll, Jordan, Roll: The World the Slaves Made*. New York: Pantheon Books, 1974.

George, Carol V. R. *Segregated Sabbaths: Richard Allen and the Rise of the Independent Black Churches*. New York: Oxford University Press, 1973.

Goodrich, John, and Robert M. W. Dixon. *Blues & Gospel Records 1902–1942*. London: Storyville, 1969.

Grissom, Mary Ellen. *The Negro Sings a New Heaven*. New York: Dover, 1969. Reprint of 1930 ed.

Gutman, Herbert G. *The Black Family in Slavery and Freedom, 1750–1925*. New York: Pantheon Books, 1976.

Hamilton, Charles V. *The Black Preacher in America*. New York: Morrow, 1972.

Hatch, James, and Omanii Abdullah. *Black Playwrights 1823–1977*. New York: R. R. Bowker, 1977.

Hodge, Francis. "Charles Mathews Reports on America." *The Quarterly Journal of Speech,* December 1950.

Hughes, Langston, and Milton Meltzer. *Black Magic: A Pictorial History of Black Entertainers in America*. New York: Bonanza, 1967.

Jackson, Bruce, ed. *The Negro and His Folklore in Nineteenth-Century Periodicals*. Austin, TX: American Folklore Society, 1969.

Jackson, George Pullen. *Down-East Spirituals and Others: Three Hundred Songs Supplementary to Spiritual Folk-Songs of Early America*. New York: J. J. Augustin, 1942.

————. *White and Negro Spirituals: Their Life Span and Kinship*. New York: J. J. Augustin, 1943.

Johnson, James Weldon. *Along This Way: An Autobiography*. New York: Viking, 1933.

————. *Black Manhattan*. New York: Knopf, 1930.

Johnson, James Weldon, ed. *The Book of American Negro Spirituals*. New York: Viking, 1925.

Katz, Bernard, ed. *The Social Implications of Early Negro Music in the United States*. New York: Arno Press, 1969.

Levine, Lawrence W. *Black Culture and Black Consciousness: Afro-American Folk Thought from Slavery to Freedom*. New York: Oxford University Press, 1977.

Levy, Eugene. *James Weldon Johnson*. Chicago: University of Chicago Press, 1973.

Lomax, Alan. *Folk Songs of North America*. Garden City, NY: Doubleday, 1960.

————. *Mister Jelly Roll*. New York: Duell, Sloan and Pearce, 1950.

Lomax, John and Alan. *American Ballads and Folk Songs*. New York: Macmillan, 1934.

————. *Folk Song USA*. New York: Duell, Sloan and Pearce, 1947.

Lovell, John, Jr. *Black Song: The Forge and the Flame. The Story of How the Afro-American Spiritual Was Hammered Out*. New York: Macmillan, 1972.

Marks, Edward B. *They All Sang*. New York: Viking, 1935.

Marshall, Herbert, and Mildred Stock. *Ira Aldridge, the Negro Tragedian*. Carbondale: Southern Illinois University Press, 1958.

Mitchell, Loften. *Black Drama: The Story of the American Negro in the Theatre*. New York: Hawthorn Books, 1967.

Murdock, George Peter. *Africa: Its Peoples and Their Culture*. New York: McGraw-Hill, 1959.

Nathan Hans. *Dan Emmett and Negro Minstrelsy*. Norman: University of Oklahoma Press, 1962.

————. *Dan Emmett and the Rise of Black Minstrelsy*. Norman: University of Oklahoma Press, 1977.

Oliver, Paul. *Blues Fell This Morning*. London: Cassell, 1960.

————. *Savannah Syncopaters: African Retentions in the Blues*. London: Studio Books, 1970.

Ottley, Roi, and William J. Weatherby, eds. *The Negro in New York: An Informal Social History*. New York: New York Public Library, 1967.

Patterson, Cecil Lloyd. "A Different Drum: The Image of the Negro in the 19th Century Popular Song Books." Diss. University of Pennsylvania, 1961.

Rabateau, Albert J. *Slave Religion: The 'Invisible Solution' in the Antebellum South*. New York: Oxford University Press, 1978.

Ricks, George Robinson. *Some Aspects of the Religious Music of the American Negro*. New York: Arno Press, 1977.

Roach, Hildred. *Black American Music*. Boston: Crescendo Books, 1973.

Roberts, John Storm. *Black Music of Two Worlds*. New York: Morrow, 1972.

Sampson, Henry T. *Blacks in Blackface: A Source Book on Early Black Musical Shows*. Metuchen, NJ: Scarecrow Press, 1980.

Schafer, William J. *Brass Bands and New Orleans Jazz*. Baton Rouge: Louisiana State University Press, 1977.

Simpson, George Eaton. *Black Religion in the New World*. New York: Columbia University Press, 1978.

Southall, Georgia. *Black Tom: The Post-Civil War Enslavement of a Musical Genius*. Minneapolis: Challenge Productions, 1979.

Southern, Eileen. "Frank Johnson and His Promenade Concerts." *The Black Perspective in Music,* Fall 1977.

————. "Gussie Lord Davis, Tin Pan Alley Tunesmith, in Retrospect." *The Black Perspective in Music,* Fall 1978.

————. *The Music of Black Americans*. New York: Norton, 1971.

Southern, Eileen, ed. *Readings in Black American Music*. New York: Norton, 1971.

Stearns, Marshall and Jean. *Jazz Dance: The Story of American Vernacular Dance*. New York: Macmillan, 1968.

Tannenbaum: Frank. *Slave and Citizen: The Negro in America*. New York: Knopf, 1947.

Toll, Robert C. *Blacking Up*. New York: Oxford University Press, 1974.

Walker, Wyatt Tee. *Somebody's Calling My Name: Black Sacred Music and Social Change*. Valley Forge, PA: Judson Press, 1979.

Walser, Richard. "Negro Dialect in 18th-Century American Drama." *American Speech,* December 1955.

Winter, Marian Hannah. "Juba and American Minstrelsy." *Chronicles of American Dance.* New York: Henry Holt, 1948.

Wittke, Carl. *Tambo and Bones: A History of the American Minstrel Stage.* Durham, NC: Duke University Press, 1930.

Woodward, C. Vann. *The Strange Career of Jim Crow.* New York: Oxford University Press, 1974.

Yoder, Don. *Pennsylvania Spirituals.* Lancaster: Pennsylvania Folklife Society, c. 1961.

British Street and Parlour Ballads

Appleton, William W. *Madame Vestris and the London Stage.* New York: Columbia University Press, 1974.

Baily, Leslie. *The Gilbert and Sullivan Book.* London: Cassell, 1951.

————. *Gilbert and Sullivan and Their World.* London: Thames and Hudson, 1973.

Bettany, Clemence. *100 Years of the D'Oyly Carte Opera Company and Gilbert and Sullivan.* London: D'Oyly Carte Company, 1975.

Boosey, William. *Fifty Years of Music.* London: Ernest Benn, 1931.

Brahms, Caryl. *Gilbert and Sullivan: Chords and Dischords.* Boston: Little, Brown, 1975.

Bratton, J. S. *The Victorian Popular Ballad.* Totowa, NJ: Rowman & Littlefield, 1975.

Calder-Marshall, Arthur. *If You Have Tears, Prepare to Shed Them Now: The Ballads of George R. Sims.* London: Hutchinson, 1969.

Carse, Adam. *The Life of Jullien: Adventurer, Showman-Conductor, and Establisher of the Promenade Concerts in England, together with a History of Those Concerts up to 1895.* Cambridge: Heffer, 1951.

A Century and a Half in Soho: A Short History of the Firm of Novello, Publishers and Printers of Music 1811–1961. London: Novello, 1961.

The Chappell Story 1811–1961. London: Chappell, 1961.

Cheshire, D. F. *Music Hall in Britain.* Rutherford, NJ: Fairleigh Dickinson University Press, 1974.

Cooper, Martin. *Opera Comique.* London: Parrish, 1949.

Delgado, Alan. *Victorian Entertainment.* New York: American Heritage Press, 1971.

Disher, Maurice Wilson. *Victorian Song from Dive to Drawing Room.* London: Phoenix House, 1955.

Fitzsimmons, Raymund. *The Charles Dickens Show.* London: Geoffrey Bles, 1970.

Gammond, Peter, ed. *The Best Music Hall and Variety Songs.* London: Wolfe, 1972.

Hand, John. *Irish Street Ballads.* Liverpool: Denvir's Penny Irish Library, 1873.

Henderson, W. *Victorian Street Ballads: A Selection of Popular Ballads Sold in the Streets in the Nineteenth Century.* London: Country Life, 1938.

Hindley, Charles. *The Life and Times of James Catnach, Ballad Monger.* London: Reeves and Turner, 1878.

Honri, Peter. *Working the Halls.* London: Saxon House, 1973.

Humphries, Charles, and William C. Smith. *Music Publishing in the British Isles from the Beginning until the Middle of the Nineteenth Century.* London: Cassell, 1954.

Hyman, Alan. *The Gaiety Years.* London: Cassell, 1975.

Lee, Edward. *Music of the People: A Study of the Popular Song in Great Britain.* London: Barrie & Jenkins, 1970.

McQueen-Pope, W. J. *The Footlights Flickered.* London: Herbert Jenkins, 1959.

————. *The Melodies Linger On: The Story of Music Hall.* London: W. H. Allen, 1950.

————. *Pillars of Drury Lane.* London: Hutchinson, 1955.

————. *Theatre Royal, Drury Lane.* London: W. H. Allen, 1951.

Mander, Raymond, and Joe Mitchenson. *The Lost Theatres of London.* London: Vista Books, 1967.

————. *Revue: A Story in Pictures.* New York: Taplinger, 1971.

————. *The Theatres of London.* New York: Hill & Wang, 1975.

Nettel, Reginald. *Seven Centuries of Popular Song: A Social History of Urban Ditties.* London: Phoenix House, 1956.

————. *Sing a Song of England: A Social History of Traditional Song.* London: Phoenix House, 1944.

Neuburg, Victor. *The Penny Histories.* New York: Harcourt, Brace & World, 1964.

Pearsall, Ronald. *Edwardian Life and Leisure.* New York: St. Martin's Press, 1973.

————. *Edwardian Popular Music.* Rutherford, NJ: Fairleigh Dickinson University Press, 1975.

————. *Victorian Popular Music.* Detroit: Gale Research, 1973.

————. *Victorian Sheet Music Covers.* Detroit: Gale Research, 1972.

Priestley, J. B. *The Edwardians.* London: Sphere Books, 1970.

Raven, Jon, ed. *Victoria's Inferno: Songs of the Old Mills, Mines, Manufactories, Canals and Railways.* Manchester: Broadside Press, 1978.

Richardson, P. J. S. *The Social Dance of the Nineteenth Century in England.* London: Herbert Jenkins, 1960.

Rowell, George. *The Victorian Theatre.* Oxford: Clarendon Press, 1956.

Scholes, Percy A. *Mirror of Music 1844–1944: A Century of Musical Life in Britain as Reflected in the Pages of the* Musical Times. 2 vols. London: Novello and Oxford University Press, 1947.

Speaight, George, ed. *Bawdy Songs of the Early Music Hall.* London: David & Charles, 1973.

Spellman, Doreen and Sidney. *Victorian Music Covers.* London: Evelyn, Adams & Mackay, 1969.

Taylor, Deems, ed. *A Treasury of Gilbert and Sullivan.* New York: Simon & Schuster, 1941.

Traubner, Richard. *Operetta.* New York: Doubleday, 1983.

Turner, Michael. *A Casquet of Gems.* New York: Viking, 1969.

————. *Just a Song at Twilight.* London: Michael Joseph, 1975.

————. *The Parlour Song Book.* New York: Viking, 1973.

Unger-Hamilton, Clive, ed. *The Entertainers.* New York: St. Martin's Press, 1980.

The Universal Songster or Museum of Mirth. 3 vols. London: George Routledge, n.d.

Walsh, Colin. *There Goes That Song Again: One Hundred Years of Popular Song.* London: EMI Music Publishing, 1977.

White, R. B. *Life in Regency England.* New York: Putnam, 1964.

Wilson, A. E. *Edwardian Theatre.* New York: Macmillan, 1952.

Young, Kenneth. *Music's Great Days in the Spas and Watering Places.* London: Macmillan, 1968.

Church Music

Ahlstrom, Sydney E. *A Religious History of the American People.* New Haven, CT: Yale University Press, 1972.

Benson, Louis F. *The English Hymn, Its Development and Use in Worship.* New York: George Doran, 1915.

Blackwell, Lois S. *The Wings of the Dove: The Story of Gospel Music in America.* Norfolk, VA: Donning Press, 1978.

Brown, Theron, and Hezekiah Butterworth. *The Story of the Hymns and Tunes.* New York: American Tract Society, 1906.

Bruce, Dickson D., Jr. *And They All Sang Hallelujah: Plain-Folk, Camp-Meeting Religion, 1800–1845.* Knoxville: University of Tennessee Press, 1974.

Bucke, Emory Stevens, ed. *Companion to the Methodist Hymnal.* Nashville: Abingdon Press, 1970.

Curti, Merle. *The Growth of American Thought.* New York: Harper & Row, 1964.

Douglas, Charles W. *Church Music in History and Practice.* Revised by Leonard Ellinwood. New York: Scribner, 1962.

Duncan, The Reverend Canon. *Popular Hymns: Their Authors and Teachings.* London: Skeffington House, 1933.

Ellinwood, Leonard. *The History of Church Music.* New York: Morehouse-Gorham, 1953.

Elson, Ruth. *Guardian of Traditions: American Schoolbooks of the Nineteenth Century.* Lincoln: University of Nebraska Press, 1964.

Findlay, James F., Jr. *Dwight L. Moody: American Evangelist, 1837–1899.* Chicago: University of Chicago Press, 1969.

Foote, Henry Wilder. *Three Centuries of American Hymnody.* Cambridge, MA: Harvard University Press, 1940.

Frazier, E. Franklin. *The Negro Church in America.* New York: Schocken Books, 1964.

George, Carol. *Segregated Churches: Richard Allen and the Rise of the Independent Black Churches.* New York: Oxford University Press, 1973.

Green, Archie. "Hear These Beautiful Sacred Selections." *1970 Yearbook of the International Folk Music Council.* Edited by Alexander L. Ringer. Urbana: University of Illinois Press, 1970.

Hall, Jacob Henry. *Biography of Gospel Song and Hymn Writers.* Chicago: Fleming H. Revell, 1914.

Heilbut, Tony. *The Gospel Sound: Good News and Bad Times.* New York: Simon & Schuster, 1971.

Hopkins, Charles H. *The Rise of the Social Gospel In American Protestantism.* New Haven, CT: Yale University Press, 1940.

Jackson, George Pullen. *Another Sheaf of White Spirituals.* Gainesville: University of Florida Press, 1952.

———. *Down-East Spirituals and Others: Supplementary to Spiritual Folk-Songs.* New York: J. J. Augustin, 1937.

———. *Spiritual Folk-Songs of Early America: Two Hundred and Fifty Texts and Tunes, with An Introduction and Notes.* New York: J. J. Augustin, 1937.

———. *White and Negro Spirituals: Their Life Span and Kinship.* New York: J. J. Augustin, 1943.

———. *White Spirituals in the Southern Highlands.* Hatsboro, PA: Folklore Associates, 1964.

Johnson, Robert A. *The Frontier Camp Meeting: Religion's Harvest Time.* Dallas: Southern Methodist University Press, 1955.

Julian, John. *A Dictionary of Hymnology.* New York: Dover, 1957. Reprint.

Lorenz, Ellen Jane. *Glory Hallelujah: The Story of the Camp Meeting Spiritual.* Nashville: Abingdon Press, 1980.

McLoughlin, William G., Jr. *Modern Revivalism: From Charles Grandison Finney to Billy Sunday.* New York: Ronald Press, 1959.

Metcalf, Frank. *American Psalmody 1721–1820.* New York: C. F. Hartman, 1917.

––––––. "The Easy Instructor: A Bibliographical Study." *Musical Quarterly,* January 1937.

––––––. *Writers and Compilers of Sacred Music.* New York: Metcalf, 1925.

Morehead, James and Albert. *Best Loved Songs and Hymns, Popular, Patriotic and Folk Songs, Church Hymns and Gospel Songs, Spirituals and Carols.* Cleveland: World Publishing, 1865.

Ochse, Orpha. *The History of the Organ in the United States.* Bloomington: Indiana University Press, 1975.

Polack, W. G. *The Handbook to the Lutheran Hymnal.* St. Louis: Concordia Publishing House, 1942.

Reynolds, William Jensen. *Companion to the Baptist Hymnal.* Nashville: Broadman Press, 1976.

––––––. *A Joyful Sound: Christian Hymnody.* 2nd ed. New York: Holt, Rinehart & Winston, 1978.

Rice, Edwin W. *The Sunday School Movement.* Philadelphia: Union Press, 1917.

Rich, Arthur Lowndes. *Lowell Mason: The Father of Singing Among the Children.* Chapel Hill: University of North Carolina Press, 1946.

Rodeheaver, Homer A. *Twenty Years with Billy Sunday.* Chicago: Rodeheaver, 1936.

Rosenberg, Carroll S. *Religion and the Rise of the City: The New York City Mission Movement.* Ithaca, NY: Cornell University Press, 1971.

Routley, Erik. *The Music of Christian Hymnody: A Study of the Development of the Hymn since the Reformation, with Special Reference to English Protestantism.* London: Independent Press, 1958.

Ruffin, Bernard. *Fanny Crosby: The Queen of Gospel Song.* Philadelphia: United Church Press, 1976.

Sallee, James. *A History of Evangelistic Hymnody.* Grand Rapids, MI: Baker Book House, 1978.

Sizer, Sandra S. *Gospel Hymns and Social Religion: The Rhetoric of Nineteenth-Century Revivalism.* Philadelphia: Temple University Press, 1978.

Stevenson, Robert. *Protestant Church Music in America: A Short Survey of Men and Movements from 1584 to the Present.* New York: Norton, 1966.

Sweet, William Warren. *Religion in the Development of American Culture.* New York: Scribner, 1952.

––––––. *Revivalism in America: Its Origin, Growth and Decline.* New York: Scribner, 1944.

Tamke, Susan. *Make a Joyful Noise Unto the Lord: Hymns as a Reflection of Victorian Social Attitudes.* Athens, OH: Ohio University Press, 1978.

Walker, William. *A History of the Christian Church.* New York: Scribner, 1959.

Washington, Joseph R., Jr. *Black Religion: The Negro and Christianity in the United States.* Boston: Beacon Press, 1964.

Civil War Music

Bernard, Kenneth. *Lincoln and the Music of the Civil War.* Caldwell, ID: Caxton Printers, 1966.

John Brown and the Union Right or Wrong Songster. San Francisco: D. E. Appleton, 1862.

Crawford, Richard, ed. *The Civil War Songbook: Complete Original Music for 37 Songs.* New York: Dover, 1976.

Eliason, Robert E. *Keyed Bugles in the United States.* Washington, D.C.: Smithsonian Institution Press, 1972.

Emurian, Ernest K. *Stories of Civil War Songs.* Natick, MA: W. A. Wilde, 1960.

Fagan, W. L. ed. *Southern War Songs: Camp-fire, Patriotic and Sentimental.* New York: M. T. Richardson, 1890.

Glass, Paul. *The Spirit of the Sixties.* St. Louis: Educational Publishers, 1964.

Harwell, Richard B. *Confederate Music.* Chapel Hill: University of North Carolina Press, 1950.

————. *Songs of the Confederacy.* New York: Broadcast Music, 1951.

Heaps, Willard A., and W. Porter. *The Singing Sixties: The Spirit of the Civil War Days Drawn from the Music of the Times.* Norman: University of Oklahoma Press, 1960.

Hoogerwerf, Frank W. *Confederate Sheet-Music Imprints.* Brooklyn: Institute for Studies in American Music, 1984.

Luper, Albert, ed. "Civil War Music." *Civil War History* 4, No. 3, September 1958.

McDowell, Lucien L. *Songs of the Old Camp Ground.* Ann Arbor: Edwards Brothers, 1937.

Our National War Songs: A Complete Collection of the Grand Old War Songs, Battle Songs, National Hymns, Memorial Hymns, Decoration Day Songs, Quartettes, etc. Enlarged ed. Chicago: S. Brainard's Sons, 1892.

Our War Songs, North and South. Cleveland: S. Brainard's Sons, 1887.

Silber, Irwin. *Songs of the Civil War.* New York: Columbia University Press, 1960.

Songs of Dixie: A Collection of Campsongs, Home Songs, Marching Songs, Plantation Songs by Favorite Authors. Chicago: S. Brainard's Sons, 1890.

Southern War Songs: Camp Fire, Patriotic and Sentimental. New York: W. T. Richardson, 1890.

The Stars and Stripes Songster No. 2. New York: American News, 1864.

Wharton, H. M. *War Songs and Poems of the Southern Confederacy.* New York: Winston, 1904.

White, William Carter. *A History of Military Music in America.* New York: Exposition Press, 1944.

Wilson, Edmund. *Patriotic Gore: Studies in the Literature of the American Civil War.* New York: Oxford University Press, 1962.

Copyright

Barnes, James J. *Authors, Publishers and Politicians: The Quest for an Anglo-American Copyright Agreement 1815–1854.* Columbus: Ohio State University Press, 1975.

Birrell, Augustine. *Seven Lectures on the Law and History of Copyright in Books.* London: Cassell, 1899. Reprint: New York: Augustus M. Kelley, 1971.

Bishop, William Wallace. "The Struggle for International Copyright." Diss. Boston University, 1959.

Bowker, Robert Rogers. *Copyright, Its History and the Law: A Summary of the Principles and Practices of Copyright with Special Reference to the American Code of 1909 and the British Act of 1911.* Boston: Houghton Mifflin, 1912.

Charvat, William. *Literary Publishing in America 1790–1850.* Philadelphia: University of Pennsylvania Press, 1959.

Congressional Globe. 32nd Congress. Washington, D.C.: 1832.

Congressional Record: The Proceedings and Debate of Congress. Washington, D.C.: U.S. Government Printing Office, 1880–1891.

Copyright Enactments: Laws Passed in the United States since 1783 Relating to Copyright. Washington, D.C.: Library of Congress, 1978.

Finkelstein, Herman. "The Composer and the Public Interest." *Law and Contemporary Problems,* January 1954.

———. "Public Performance Rights in Music and Performance Rights Societies." 7 *Copyright Problems Analyzed.* New York: Commercial Clearing House, 1952.

Lehman-Haupt, Hellmut, Lawrence G. Wroth, and Rollo Silver. *The Book in America: A History of the Making and Selling of Books in the United States.* New York: R. R. Bowker, 1951.

Mott, Frank Luther. *Golden Multitudes: The Story of Best Sellers in the United States.* New York: Macmillan, 1947.

———. *A History of American Magazines 1850–1865.* Cambridge, MA: Harvard University Press, 1938.

———. *A History of American Magazines 1865–1885.* Cambridge, MA: Harvard University Press, 1938.

Nowell-Smith, Simon. *International Copyright Law and the Publisher in the Reign of Queen Victoria.* Oxford: Oxford University Press, 1968.

Peacock, Alan, and Ronald Weir. *The Composer in the Market Place.* London: Faber & Faber, 1975.

Peterson, Lyman Ray. *Copyright in Historical Perspective.* Nashville: Vanderbilt University Press, 1969.

Publisher's Weekly. 1889–1891 passim.

Putnam, George Haven. *The Question of Copyright: Comprising the Text of the Copyright Law of the United States, a Summary of the Copyright Laws at Present in Force in the Chief Countries of the World, Together with a Report on the Legislation Now Pending in Great Britain. A Sketch of the Contest in the United States, 1837–1891, in Behalf of International Copyright, and Certain Papers on the Development of the Conception of Literary Property, and the Results of the American Act of 1891.* New York: Putnam, 1904.

Ringer, Barbara. "Two Hundred Years of Copyright in America." Speech to Patent, Trademark, and Copyright Section of American Bar Association, August 10, 1976.

Scheinman, Walter. "Copyright Influence on British and American Drama." Thesis. Cornell University, 1947.

Sheehan, Donald. *This Was Publishing: A Chronical of the Book Trade in the Golden Age.* Bloomington: Indiana University Press, 1952.

Tebbel, John. *A History of Book Publishing in the United States.* Vol. 1, *The Creation of an Industry 1630–1865.* New York: R. R. Bowker, 1972. Vol. 2, *The Expansion of an Industry 1865–1919.* New York: R. R. Bowker, 1975.

Tryon, W. S. "Nationalism and International Copyright: Tennyson and Longfellow in America." *American Literature* 24, 1952.

U.S. Senate Reports Vol. 7. Washington, D.C.: U.S. Government Printing Office, 1886.

Waters, Edward N. *Victor Herbert: A Life in Music.* New York: Macmillan, 1955.

Witmark, Isidore, with Isidore Goldberg. *From Ragtime to Swingtime: The House of Witmark* New York: Lee Furman, 1939.

Jazz and Ragtime

Berlin, Edward. *Ragtime: A Musical and Cultural History.* Berkeley: University of California Press, 1980

Blesh, Rudi. *Shining Trumpets: A History of Jazz*. New York: Knopf, 1946.

Blesh, Rudi, ed. *Classic Piano Rags: Complete Music for 81 Rags*. New York: Dover, 1973.

Blesh, Rudi, with Harriett Janis. *They All Played Ragtime*. New York: Oak Publications, 1971.

Collier, James. *The Making of Jazz: A Comprehensive History*. Boston: Houghton Mifflin, 1978.

Foster, George Murphey. *The Autobiography of Pops Foster as Told to Tom Stoddard*. Berkeley: University of California Press, 1971.

Haskins, James. *Scott Joplin: The Man Who Made Ragtime*. New York: Doubleday, 1978.

Hasse, John Edward, ed. *Ragtime, Its History, Composers and Music*. New York: Schirmer, 1985.

Hasse, John Edward, with Frank J. Gillis. Liner notes for "Indiana Ragtime: A Documentary Album." Indianapolis: Indiana Historical Society, 1982.

Hentoff, Nat, and Albert J. McCarthy. *Jazz*. New York: Rinehart, 1959.

Gammond, Peter. *Scott Joplin and the Ragtime Era*. New York: St. Martin's Press, 1975.

Jasen, David A. *Recorded Ragtime 1897–1958*. New York: Archon Books, 1973.

Jasen, David A., ed. *Ragtime: 100 Authentic Rags*. New York: Big 3 Music, 1979.

Jasen, David A., with Trebor Jay Tichenor. *Rags and Ragtime: A Musical History*. New York: Seabury, 1979.

Lawrence, Vera Brodsky. *The Complete Works of Scott Joplin*. New York: New York Public Library, 1982.

Oliver, Paul. *Aspects of the Blues Tradition: A Fascinating Story of the Richest Vein of Black Folk Music in America*. New York: Oak Publications, 1969.

Schafer, William J., and Johannes Riedel. *The Art of Ragtime: Form and Meaning of an Original American Art Form*. Baton Rouge: Louisiana State University Press, 1973.

Schuller, Gunther. *Early Jazz*. New York: Oxford University Press, 1968.

Stearns, Marshall. *The Story of Jazz*. New York: Oxford University Press, 1956.

Tichenor, Trebor Jay, ed. *Ragtime Rarities*. New York: Dover, 1975

Waldo, Terry. *This Is Ragtime*. New York: Hawthorne Books, 1976.

Music Publishing

Applebaum, Stanley, ed. *Show Songs from "The Black Crook" to "The Red Mill." Original Sheet Music for 60 Songs from 50 Shows, 1866–1906*. New York: Dover, 1975.

Austin, William W. *Susanna, Jeanie and The Old Folks at Home: The Songs of Stephen Foster from His Time to Ours*. New York: Macmillan, 1975.

Barragan, Maude. *John Howard Payne, Skywalker*. Richmond, VA: Dietz Press, 1953.

Berhrend, Jeanne, ed. *Louis Moreau Gottschalk's Notes of a Pianist*. New York: Knopf, 1964.

Bierley, Paul S. *John Philip Sousa, American Phenomenon*. Englewood Cliffs, NJ: Prentice-Hall, 1973.

Bio-Bibliographical Index of Musicians in the United States since Colonial Times. New York: AMS Press, 1972. Reprint of 1956 ed.

Bordman, Gerald. *Jerome Kern, His Life and Music*. New York: Oxford University Press, 1980.

Boyd, Patricia. "Performers, Pedagogues, and Pertinent Methodological Literature of the Pianoforte in Mid-Nineteenth Century United States." Thesis. Ball State Teachers College, 1975.

Bradley, Van Allen. *Music for the Millions: The Kimball Piano and Organ Story.* Chicago: Regnery, 1957.

Brink, Carol. *Harps in the Wind: The Story of the Singing Hutchinsons.* New York: Macmillan, 1947.

Brooks, William. Liner notes for "The Flowering of Vocal Music in America." New World LP 231.

———."Progress and Protest in the Gilded Age: Songs from the Civil War to the Columbian Exposition." Liner notes for "The Hand That Holds the Bread." New World LP 267.

Browne, Ray E. "American Poets in Nineteenth Century 'Popular' Songbooks." *American Literature,* January 1959.

Burton, Jack. *The Blue Book of Broadway Musicals.* Watkins Glen, NY: Century House, 1952.

———.*The Blue Book of Tin Pan Alley: A Human Interest Anthology of American Popular Music.* Watkins Glen, NY: Century House, 1950.

Byrd, Joseph. Liner notes for "Popular Music in Jacksonian American." Musical Heritage Society album 834561.

Charles, Norman. "Social Values in American Popular Music." Thesis. University of Pennsylvania, 1958.

Charters, Ann. *Nobody: The Story of Bert Williams.* New York: Macmillan, 1970.

Charvat, William. *Literary Publishing in America 1790–1850.* Philadelphia: University of Pennsylvania Press, 1959.

Chorosch, Paul, and Robert Fremont, eds. *More Favorite Songs of the Nineties.* New York: Dover, 1975.

Claghorn, Charles Eugene. *Biographical Dictionary of American Music.* Nyack, NY: Parker Publishing, 1973.

———.*The Mocking Bird: The Life and Diary of Its Author, Sep. Winner.* Philadelphia: Magee Press, 1937.

Coad, Oral S. "The Plays of Samuel Woodworth." *The Sewannee Review,* April 1919.

Cohan, George M. *Twenty Years on Broadway and the Years It Took to Get There.* New York: Harper, 1925.

Cohen, Norm. Liner notes for "Minstrels and Tune Smiths: The Commercial Roots of Early Country Music 1902–1923." John Edwards Memorial Foundation LP 109.

Crawford, Richard A. *Andrew Law: American Psalmist.* Evanston IL: Northwestern University Press, 1968.

Davison, Sister Veronica. "American Musical Periodicals 1853–1899." Diss. University of Minnesota, 1973.

Debas, Allen G. Liner notes for "The Early Victor Herbert: From the Gay Nineties to the First World War." The Smithsonian Collection LP 30366.

Degen, Bruce N. "Oliver Shaw, His Music and Contributions to American Society." Diss. University of Rochester, 1971.

DeKoven, Anna. *A Musician and His Wife.* New York: Harper, 1926.

De Shin Bone Alley Screamer: All de Nigga Songs Ever Wur Writ. New York: Turner and Fisher, c. 1834.

Dichter, Harry, and Elliott Shapiro. *Handbook of Early American Sheet Music.* New York: R. R. Bowker, 1941.

Disher, Maurice Willson. *Victorian Song: From Dive to Drawing Room.* London: Phoenix House, 1955.

Dodworth, Allen. *Dancing and Its Relation to Education.* New York: Harper & Brothers, 1900.

Dreiser, Theodore. "Birth and Growth of a Popular Song." *Metropolitan Magazine,* November 1898.

————. "Whence the Song." *The Color of a Great City.* New York: Boni & Liveright, 1923.

Eliot, Coleman. *The Oliver Ditson Company: The Story of Its Development and Remarkable Success in the Field of American Music.* Promotional brochure. Boston: Ditson, n.d.

Epstein, Dena J. Introduction to *Complete Catalogue of Sheet Music and Musical Works, 1870.* Board of Music Trade of the United States of America. New York: Da Capo, 1973. Reprint of 1870 ed.

————. "The Haymakers and George F. Root." Liner notes for "The Haymakers." New World LP 234.

————. "Music Publishing in Chicago Before 1871." *Notes* 3, 1944.

————. *Music Publishing in Chicago Before 1871: The Firm of Root & Cady 1858–1871.* Detroit: Information Coordinators, 1969.

Evans, Charles. *American Bibliography.* 13 vols. New York: Peter Smith, 1941.

Ewen, David. *American Popular Songs: From the Revolutionary War to the Present.* New York: Random House, 1966.

————. *Great Men of Popular Music: The Stories of America's Trend-setting Songwriters, Their Lives, Their Times, Their Work from 1746 to 1965.* Englewood Cliffs, NJ: Prentice-Hall, 1970.

————. *The Life and Death of Tin Pan Alley.* New York: Funk & Wagnalls, 1964.

Ewing, George W. *The Well Tempered Lyre: Songs and Verses of the Temperance Movement.* Dallas: Southern Methodist University Press, 1977.

Filby, F. W., and Edward G. Howard. *Star Spangled Books: Books, Sheet Books, Newspapers, Manuscripts and Persons Associated with "The Star Spangled Banner."* Baltimore: Maryland Historical Society, 1972.

Fisher, William Arms. *One Hundred and Fifty Years of Music Publishing in the United States, 1783–1933: An Historical Sketch with Special Reference to the Pioneer Publisher Oliver Ditson Company.* Boston: Ditson, 1933.

Floyd, Samuel A., with Marcia J. Reisser. "Social Dance Music of Black Composers in the 19th Century and the Emergence of Ragtime." *The Black Perspective in Music* 8, No. 2, Summer 1980.

Foner, Philip S. *American Labor Songs of the Nineteenth Century.* Urbana: University of Illinois Press, 1975.

Foster, Damon S. *Series of Old American Songs.* Facsimiles. Providence, RI: Brown University Library, 1936.

Foster, Stephen Collins. *Songs, Compositions and Arrangements.* Indianapolis: Foster Hall Reproductions, 1933.

Freedland, Michael. *Irving Berlin.* New York: Stein & Day, 1974.

————. *Jolson.* New York: Stein & Day, 1972.

Fremont, Robert. *Favorite Songs of the Nineties.* New York: Dover, 1975.

Fuld, James J. *American Popular Music 1875–1950.* Philadelphia: Musical Americana, 1956.

————. *The Book of World Famous Music: Classical, Popular and Folk.* New York: Crown, 1966.

Fuld, James J., ed. *A Pictorial Bibliography of the First Editions of Stephen Foster.* Philadelphia: Musical Americana, 1957.

Geller, James H. *Famous Songs and Their Stories.* New York: Macauley, 1931.

Gellerman, Robert F. *The American Reed Organ: Its History, How It Works.* Vestal, NY: Vestal Press, 1973.

George Christy's Essence of Old Kentucky: New and Popular Songs, Interludes, Dialogues, Funny Speeches, Darkey Jokes, and Plantation Wit. New York: Dick & Fitzgerald, c. 1850.

Gerson, Robert A. *Music in Philadelphia.* Philadelphia: Theodore Presser, 1940.

Gilbert, Douglas. *Lost Chords: The Diverting Story of American Popular Songs.* New York: Cooper Square, 1970.

Goldberg, Isaac. *Tin Pan Alley: A Chronicle of American Popular Music.* New York: Atlantic Paperbooks, Frederick Ungar, 1970.

Goldin, Milton. *The Music Merchants: The Colorful Chronicle of the Impresarios, Entrepreneurs and Patrons Who Popularized Serious Music in America.* New York: Macmillan, 1969.

Graham, Philip. *Showboats: The History of an American Institution.* Austin: University of Texas Press, 1931.

Grau, Robert. *The Business Man in the Amusement World.* New York: Broadway Publishing, 1910.

———. *Forty Years Observation of Music and the Drama.* New York: Broadway Publishing, 1909.

Green, Stanley. "Hits from Early Musical Comedies." Liner notes for "I Wants to Be an Actor Lady." New World LP 221.

Hamm, Charles. Liner notes for "An Evening with Henry Russell." Nonesuch LP 71307.

———. *Yesterdays: Popular Song in America.* New York: Norton, 1979.

Harding, Rosamund E. M. *The Pianoforte: Its History Traced to the Great Exhibition of 1851.* Cambridge: Cambridge University Press, 1933.

Harris, Charles K. *After the Ball: An Autobiography.* New York: Frank-Maurice, 1926.

———. *How to Write a Popular Song.* New York: C. K. Harris, 1906.

Harris, Neil. *Hum Bug: The Art of P. T. Barnum.* Boston: Little, Brown, 1973.

Haviland, F. B. *How to Write a Popular Song.* New York: Haviland, 1910.

Hewitt, John Hill. *Shadows on the Wall, or Glimpses of the Past: A Retrospect of the Past Fifty Years.* AMA Press, 1971. Reprint of 1877 ed.

Hill, Richard S. "The Mysterious Chord of Henry Clay Work." *Musical Library Association Notes,* March, June 1953.

Hitchcock, H. Wiley. *American Music Before 1865 in Print and on Records.* Brooklyn: Institute for Studies in American Music, 1976.

Hoogerwerf, Frank W. *John Hill Hewitt: Sources and Bibliography.* Atlanta: Emory University General Libraries, 1981.

Hoover, Cynthia A. Liner notes for "19th Century American Ballroom Music." Nonesuch LP 71313.

———. *Music Machines—American Style.* Washington, D.C.: Smithsonian Institution Press, 1971.

Howard, John Tasker. "The Hewitt Family in American Music." *Musical Quarterly* 17, 1931.

———. *Our American Music: Three Hundred Years of It from 1620 to the Present.* New York: Crowell, 1946.

———. *Stephen Foster: America's Troubadour.* New York: Crowell, 1946.

Howard, Joseph Edgar. *Gay Nineties Troubador*. Miami: Joe Howard Music House, 1956.

Huggins, Coy Elliott. "John Hill Hewitt: Bard of the Confederacy." Diss. Florida State University, 1964.

Hunsberger, Donald. Liner notes for "Home Spun America: Marches, Waltzes, Polkas and Serenades: Music for the Social Orchestra; Songs of 19th Century Patriotism, Temperance & Abolition, & Popular, Sentimental Tunes of the Hutchinson Family Singers." Vox Box 5309.

Hutchinson, John Wallace. *Story of the Hutchinsons*. 2 vols. New York: Da Capo Press, 1977. Reprint of 1896 ed.

Jablonski, Edward. *The Encyclopedia of American Music: From Folk songs to Rock, Jazz to Symphony, Gospel Songs to Oratorios, and Tin Pan Alley to Opera*. New York: Doubleday, 1981.

Jackson, Richard. Liner notes for " 'Angels' Visits' and Other Gems of Victorian Music." New World LP 220.

The James Bland Album of Outstanding Songs. New York: E. B. Marks Music, 1946.

Johnson, H. Earle. *Musical Interludes in Boston 1795–1830*. New York: Columbia University Press 1943.

Johnson, James Weldon. *Along This Way: An Autobiography*. New York: Viking, 1933.

———. *Black Manhattan*. New York: Knopf, 1930.

Jones, F. O. *A Handbook of American Music and Musicians, Containing Biographies of American Musicians, and Histories of the Principal Institutions, Firms and Societies*. New York: F. O. Jones Canaseraga, 1886.

Jones, Howard Mumford. *The Harp That Once: A Chronicle of the Life of Thomas Moore*. New York: Henry Holt, 1937.

Jordan, Philip D. *Singin' Yankees: A Biography of the Hutchinson Family*. Minneapolis: University of Minnesota Press, 1946.

Jordan, Philip D., with Lillian Kessler. *Songs of Yesterday*. Garden City, NY: Doubleday, Doran, 1941.

Kahn, E. J., Jr. *The Merry Partners: The Age and Stage of Harrigan & Hart*. New York: Random House, 1955.

Kaufmann, Helen L. *From Jehovah to Jazz: Music in America from Psalmody to the Present Day*. New York: Dodd, Mead, 1937.

Keefer, Lubov. *Baltimore's Music: The Haven of the American Composer*. Baltimore: J. J. Furst, 1962.

Kinkle, Roger. *The Complete Encyclopedia of Popular Music and Jazz 1900–1950*. New Rochelle, NY: Arlington House, 1975.

Klamkin, Marian. *Old Sheet Music: A Pictorial History*. New York: Hawthorne Books, 1975.

Kobbe, Gustav. *Famous American Songs*. New York: Crowell, 1906.

Krohn, Ernst C. *Missouri Music*. New York: Da Capo Press, 1971.

———. *Music Publishing in the Middle Western States Before the Civil War*. Detroit: Information Coordinators, 1972.

Krummel, Donald W. "Counting Every Star, or Historical Statistics on Music Publishing in the United States." *Interamerican Musical Research Yearbook 1974*.

———. "Philadelphia Music Engraving and Publishing 1800–1820: A Study in Bibliography and Cultural History." Diss. University of Michigan, 1958.

Lang, Paul Henry, ed. *One Hundred Years of Music in America: A Centennial Publication on the Anniversary of G. Schirmer & Co.* New York: Grosset & Dunlap, 1960.

Lawrence, Vera Brodsky. "Micah Hawkins, the Pied Piper of Catherine Slip." *The New-York Historical Society Quarterly*, April 1978.

———. *The Piano Works of Louis Moreau Gottschalk*. New York: Arno Press, 1969.

Lehman, Carrol J. "Benjamin Carr: His Contribution to Early American Music." Diss. University of Iowa, 1975.

Levy, Lester, M. *Flashes of Merriment: A Century of Humorous Songs of America, 1805–1905*. Norman: University of Oklahoma Press, 1971.

———. *Give Me Yesterday: American Music in History, 1890–1920*. Norman: University of Oklahoma Press, 1975.

———. *Grace Notes in American History: Popular Sheet Music, 1820–1900*. Norman: University of Oklahoma Press, 1967.

———. *Picture the Songs: Lithographs of Sheet Music of Nineteenth-Century America*. Baltimore: The Johns Hopkins University Press, 1976.

Lichtenwanger, William. "The Music of 'The Star Spangled Banner.' " *The Quarterly Journal of the Library of Congress*, July 1977.

Loggins, Vernon: *Where the World Ends: The Life of Louis Moreau Gottschalk*. Baton Rouge: Lousiana State University Press, 1958.

Lowens, Irving. *A Bibliography of Songsters Printed in America Before 1821*. Worcester, MA: American Antiquarian Society, 1976.

———. *Music and Musicians in Early America: Aspects of the History of Music in Early America and the History of Early American Music*. New York: Norton, 1964.

McCabe, John. *George M. Cohan, the Man Who Owned Broadway*. Garden City, NY: Doubleday, 1973.

McClure, J. B., ed. *Edison and His Invention*. Chicago: 1895.

MacLaughlin, M. C. "The Social World of American Popular Songs." Thesis. Cornell University, 1968.

McNeil, W. K. "Syncopated Slander: The Coon Song 1890–1900." *Keystone Folklore Quarterly*, Summer 1972.

Mandel, Alan. Liner notes for "An Anthology of Piano Music 1780–1970." Desto LP 6445 / 47.

Marcuse, Maxwell. *Tin Pan Alley in Gaslight: A Saga of the Songs That Made the Gay 90's 'Gay'*: Watkins Glen, NY: Century House, 1959.

Marks, Edward B. *They All Sang: From Tony Pastor to Rudy Vallee*. New York: Viking, 1935.

Marrocco, W. Thomas, and Harold Gleason. *Music in America: An Anthology from the Landing of the Pilgrims to the Close of the Civil War*. New York: Norton, 1964.

Martin, Deac. C. T. *Book of Musical Americana*. Englewood Cliffs, NJ: Prentice-Hall, 1970.

Marzio, Peter C. *The Democratic Art: Chromolithography 1840–1900*. Boston: David Godine, 1979.

Mathews, W. S. B. *A Hundred Years of Music in America:* New York: AMS Press, 1970. Reprint of 1889 ed.

Mattfeld, Julius. *Variety Music Cavalcade 1620–1969*. Englewood Cliffs, NJ: Prentice-Hall, 1971.

Milligan, Harold Vincent. *Stephen Collins Foster*. New York: Schirmer, 1920.

Minstrel Songs Old and New: A Collection of World-wide, Famous Minstrel and Plantation Songs, including the Most Popular of the Celebrated Foster Melodies, Arranged with Pianoforte Accompaniment. Boston: Ditson, n.d.

Montgomery, Elizabeth Rider: *The Story Behind Popular Songs*. New York: Dodd, Mead, 1961.

Montague, Richard A. "Charles Edward Horn: His Life and Works." Diss. Florida State University, 1959.

Moody, Richard. *Ned Harrigan: From Corlear's Hook to Herald Square.* Chicago: Nelson-Hall, 1980.

Mooney, Hughson. "Popular Music Before Ragtime 1840–1890." *Popular Music and Society* 5, 1977.

———. "Popular Music Since the 1890s." *American Quarterly,* Fall 1954.

Morath, Max, ed. *Favorite Songs of the Nineties.* New York: Dover, 1973.

Morris: Joan. Liner notes for "Songs of the Great Ladies of the Musical Stage." Nonesuch LP 71330.

———. Liner notes for "A Treasury of Turn-of-the Century Popular Songs." Nonesuch LP 71304.

Newsom, Jon. "The American Brass Band Movement." Liner notes for "The Yankee Brass Band: Music from Mid-Nineteenth-Century America." New World LP 312.

———. Liner notes for "Songs by Stephen Foster." Vol. 2. Nonesuch LP 71333.

———. Liner notes for "Who Shall Rule This American Nation: Songs of the Civil War Era by Henry Clay Work." Nonesuch LP 71317.

Offergeld, Robert. *The Centennial Catalogue of the Published and Unpublished Works of Louis Moreau Gottschalk.* New York: Ziff-Davis, 1970.

———. "Gottschalk & Company: The Music of Democratic Sociability," with additions by Edward A. Berlin. Liner notes for "The Wind Demon and Other Mid-Nineteenth-Century Piano Music." New World LP 267.

Pearsall, Ronald. *Victorian Sheet Music Covers.* London: Evelyn, Adams and Mackay, 1969.

Perkins, Charles C., and John S. Dwight. *History of the Handel and Haydn Society.* New York: Da Capo Press, 1977. Reprint.

Raph, Theodore. *The Songs We Sang: A Treasury of American Popular Music.* New York: A. S. Barnes, 1964.

Redway, Virginia Larkin. "The Carrs, American Music Publishers." *Musical Quarterly,* January 1932.

Rich, Arthur Lowndes. *Lowell Mason: The Father of Singing Among the Children.* Chapel Hill: University of North Carolina Press, 1946.

Ringer, Barbara. "Two Hundred Years of Copyright in America." Speech to Patent, Trademark and Copyright Section of American Bar Association, August 10, 1976.

Roffman, Frederick S. Liner notes for "Naughty Marietta." Smithsonian Collection, complete recorded performance.

Root, George Frederick. *The Story of a Musical Life.* Cincinnati: Church, 1891.

Rossiter, Will. *How to Write a Song and Become Wealthy.* Chicago: Rossiter, 1898.

Ruffin, Bernard. *Fanny Crosby: The Queen of Gospel Song.* Philadelphia: United Church Press, 1976.

Salzman, Eric. Liner notes for "Moore's Irish Melodies." Nonesuch LP 79059.

Sampson, Henry T. *Blacks in Blackface: A Source Book on Early Black Musical Shows.* Metuchen, NJ: Scarecrow Press, 1980.

Sankey, Ira. *The Story of the Gospel Hymns.* Philadelphia: Sunday School Times, 1906.

Scanlon, Mary B. "Thomas Hastings." *Musical Quarterly,* April 1946.

Schonberg, Harold. *The Great Pianists.* New York: Simon & Schuster 1963.

Shapiro, Elliott. "Ragtime." *Music Library Association Notes,* June 1951.

Sheean, Vincent. *Oscar Hammerstein I.* New York: Simon & Schuster, 1957.

Sherman, Robert L. *Actors and Authors with Composers and Managers Who Helped Make Them Famous: A Chronological Record and Brief Biography of Theatrical Celebrities 1750–1950.* Chicago: Robert L. Sherman, 1951.

Smith, Gregg. *America's Bicentennial Songs, from the Sentimental Age, 1850–1900*. New York: Schirmer, 1975.

Smith, Harry B. *First Nights and First Editions*. Boston: Little, Brown, 1931.

Sonneck, Oscar. *Early Secular Music*. Washington, D.C.: Library of Congress, 1905. Enlarged and revised by William Treat Upton, Washington, D.C.: Library of Congress, 1945.

———. *The Star Spangled Banner*. New York: Da Capo Press, 1969. Reprint of 1914 ed.

The Sousa Band: A Discography. Washington, D.C.: Library of Congress, 1970.

Sousa, John Philip. *Through the Years With Sousa*. New York: Crowell, 1910.

Southern, Eileen. "Gussie Lord Davis (1863–1899), Tin Pan Alley Tunesmith: In Retrospect." *The Black Perspective in Music*, Fall 1978.

Spaeth, Sigmund. *A History of Popular Music in America*. New York: Random House, 1948.

———. *Read' em and Weep*. New York: Doubleday Page, 1926.

Spillane, Daniel. *History of the American Pianoforte*. New York: Spillane, 1890.

Steinway, Theodore. *People and Pianos*. New York: Steinway & Sons, 1961.

Stephens, John Anthony. "Henry Russell in America: Chutzpah and Huzzah." Diss. University of Illinois / Urbana, 1975.

Stone, James T. "The Merchant and the Muse: Commercial Influences Before the Civil War." *Business History Review*, March 1956.

Tatham, David. *The Lure of the Striped Pig: The Illustration of Popular Music in America 1820–1870*. Barre, MA: Imprint Society, 1973.

Tawa, Nicholas. *Sweet Songs for Gentle Americans: The Parlour Song in America 1790–1860*. Bowling Green, OH: Bowling Green State University Press, 1980.

———. "The Ways of Love in the Mid-19th-Century American Song." *Journal of Popular Culture*, Fall 1976.

Taylor, Deems, ed. *A Treasury of Gilbert and Sullivan*. New York: Simon & Schuster, 1941.

Taylor, Deems, ed., with John Tasker Howard. *A Treasury of Stephen Foster*. New York: Random House, 1946.

Thorson, Theodore Winton. "A History of Music Publishing in Chicago 1850–1960." Diss. Northwestern University, 1961.

United States Songster: Choice Collection of About One Hundred and Seventy of the Most Popular Songs. Cincinnati: J. A. James, 1937.

Upton, George P. *Musical Memories: My Recollections of Celebrities of the Half Century 1850–1900*. Chicago: McClurg, 1908.

Upton, William Treat. *Anthony Philip Heinrich*, New York: Columbia University Press, 1939.

Urkowitz, Steve, and Lawrence Bennett. "Early American Vocal Music 1720–1850." *Journal of Popular Culture* 12, No. 1, 1978.

Vinson, Lee, ed. *The Early American Songbook*. Englewood Cliffs, NJ: Prentice-Hall, 1974.

Wagner, John Waldorf. "James Hewitt: His Life and Works." Diss. Indiana University, 1969.

Waters, Edward. *Victor Herbert: A Life in Music*. New York: Macmillan, 1955.

Weinlein, William J. *A Checklist of American Music Publications*. Detroit: Information Coordinators, 1970.

Westin, Helen. *Introducing the Song Sheet: A Collector's Guide to Song Sheets*. Nashville: Nelson, 1976.

Whitcomb, Ian. *After the Ball*. London: Allen Lane / Penguin Books, 1972.

White, John L. *Git Along, Little Dogies: Songs and Songmakers of the American West.* Urbana: University of Illinois Press, 1975.

Wier, Albert E., ed. *The Book of a Thousand Songs: The World's Largest Collection of the Songs of the People, Containing More Than a Thousand Old and New Favorites.* New York: Mumil Publishing, 1918.

Wilk, Max. *Memory Lane: The Golden Age in American Popular Music 1890 to 1925.* New York: Ballantine, 1976.

Winder, William Craig. "The Life and Music Theater Works of John Hill Hewill." Diss. University of Illinois, 1972.

Witmark, Isidore, and Isidore Goldberg. *From Ragtime to Swingtime: The House of Witmark.* New York: Lee Furman, 1939.

Wolf, Edwin, II. *American Song Sheets, Slip Ballads and Poetical Broadsides 1850–1870.* Philadelphia: The Library Company of Philadelphia, 1963.

Wolfe, Richard J. *Early American Music Engraving and Printing: A History of Music Publishing in America from 1787 to 1825 with Commentary on Earlier and Later Practices.* Urbana: University of Illinois Press, 1980.

———. *Secular Music in America 1801–1825.* 3 vols. New York: New York Public Library, 1964.

Wollcott, Alec. *The Story of Irving Berlin.* New York: Putnam, 1925.

Work, Henry Clay: *Songs.* New York: Da Capo Press, 1974. Facsimile ed.

Zellers, Parker. *Tony Pastor, Dean of the Vaudeville Stage.* Ypsilanti, MI: Eastern Michigan University Press, 1971.

Periodicals

American Art Journal. New York, 1864–1905.

American Musical Journal. New York, 1834–1835.

The American Musician. 1884–1905.

The American Musician & Art Journal. 1905–.

The Billboard. New York, 1894–.

Boston Musical Times. 1860–1871.

Dwight's Journal of Music. Boston, 1852–1881.

The Etude. Philadelphia, 1875–.

Metronome. New York, 1871–.

The Music Trade Review. 1875–.

Musical Courier. New York, 1895–.

New York Musical Review & Choral Advocate. 1850–1872.

United States Musical Review. New York, 1867–1874.

Variety. New York, 1905–.

Pianolas, Victrolas and the Mechanical Music Business

Aldridge, Benjamin. *The Victor Talking Machine Company.* New York: RCA Victor, 1964.

Bauer, Roberto. *Historical Records 1898–1908/9.* London: Sidgwick & Jackson, 1947.

Bowers, David. *Put Another Nickel In.* New York: Bonanza Books, 1966.

Brooks, Tim. "Columbia Records in the 1890s: Founding the Record Industry." *Association for Recorded Sound Journal* 1, 1978.

———. "A Directory to Columbia Recording Artists in the 1890s." *Association for Recorded Sound Journal* 2/3, 1978.

The Edison Phonograph Monthly 1903–1909. Exact reproduction by Wendell Moore. Louisville: Pennant Litho, 1976–.

Fagan, Ted, and William R. Moran. *The Encyclopedic Discography of Victor Recordings 1900–1903.* Westport, CT: Greenwood Press, 1983.

Gaisberg, Fred. *The Music Goes Round.* New York: Macmillan, 1942.

Gellatt, Roland. *The Fabulous Phonograph 1877–1977.* New York: Macmillan, 1977.

Giovannoni, David. ''The Phonograph as a Mass Entertainment Medium: Its Development, Adaptation and Pervasiveness.'' Thesis. University of Wisconsin, 1980.

Johnson, E. R. Fenimore. *His Master's Voice Was Eldridge R. Johnson.* Milford, DE: State Media, 1974.

Koenigsberg, Allan. *Edison Cylinder Records 1889–1912, with an Illustrated History of the Phonograph.* New York: Stellar Productions, 1969.

Krivine, J. *Juke Box Saturday Night.* Secaucus, NJ: Chartwell Books, 1977.

Moogk, Edward B. *Roll Back the Years: History of Canadian Recorded Sound and Its Legacy: Genesis to 1930.* Ottawa: National Library of Canada, 1975.

Moore, Jerrold Northrup. *A Matter of Records: Gred Gaisberg and the Golden Era of the Gramophone.* New York: Taplinger, 1977.

Ord-Hume, Arthur W. J. D. *The Player-Piano: The History of the Mechanical Piano.* New York: A. S. Barnes, 1970.

The Phonograph and How to Use It: Being a Short History of Its Invention and Development, Containing Also Directions, Helpful Hints, and Plain Talk as to Its Care and Use, Etc. New York: National Phonograph Company, 1900.

Proceedings of the 1890 Convention of Local Phonograph Companies. Nashville: Country Music Foundation, 1975. Reprint.

Reed, Oliver, and Walter L. Welch. *From Tinfoil to Stereo: The Evolution of the Phonograph.* New York: Howard Sams / Bobbs-Merrill, 1959.

Roehl, Harvey. *Player Piano Treasury: The Scrapbook History of the Mechanical Piano in America.* Vestal, NY: Vestal Press, 1973.

Rust, Brian. *The American Record Label Book: From the Nineteenth Century through 1942.* New Rochelle, NY: Arlington House, 1979.

———. *The Complete Entertainment Discography from the Mid-1890s to 1942.* New Rochelle, NY: Arlington House, 1973.

———. *Jazz Records 1897–1942.* 4th ed. New Rochelle, NY: Arlington House, 1978.

Schicke, C. A. *A Revolution in Sound: A Biography of the Recording Industry.* Boston: Little, Brown, 1974.

Smart, James R., and Jon W. Newsom. *''A Wonderful Invention'': A Brief History of the Phonograph from Tinfoil to the LP.* Washington, D.C.: Library of Congress, 1977.

Show Business

Baines, Jimmy Dalton. ''Samuel S. Sanford and Negro Minstrelsy.'' Diss. Tulane University, 1976.

Bernheim, Alfred L. *The Business of the Theatre: An Economic History of the American Theatre 1750–1932.* New York: Benjamin Blom, 1964. Reprint of 1933 ed.

Blair, Walter. *Native American Humor 1800–1900.* New York: American Book, 1937.

Bordman, Gerald. *The American Musical Theatre.* New York: Oxford University Press, 1978.

———. *Jerome Kern, His Life and Music.* New York: Oxford University Press, 1980.

Brown, Col. T. Allston. *Fun in Black or Sketches of Minstrel Life*. New York: R. M. DeWitt, 1974.

Carse, Adam. *The Life of Julien: Adventurer, Showman-Conductor and Establisher of the Promenade Concerts in England, together with a History of Those Concerts up to 1895*. Cambridge: W. Heffer & Sons, 1951.

Churchill, Alan. *The Great White Way: A Re-Creation of Broadway's Golden Age of Theatrical Entertainment*. New York: Dutton, 1962.

Coad, Oral Sumner, and Edwin Mimms. *The American Stage*. New York: U.S. Publishers Association, 1929.

Csida, Joseph, and June Bundy Csida. *American Entertainment: A Unique History of Popular Show Business*. New York: Watson-Guptill, 1978.

Daughtrey, Willia Estelle. "Sissieretta Jones: A Study of the Negro's Contribution to Nineteenth Century Entertainment." Diss. Syracuse University, 1968.

Davidson, Frank. "The Rise, Development, Decline and Influence of the American Minstrel Show." Diss. New York University, 1952.

DiMeglio John E. *Vaudeville USA*. Bowling Green, OH: Bowling Green State University Press, 1973.

Dormon, James H., Jr. *Theater in the Ante Bellum South*. Chapel Hill: University of North Carolina Press, 1967.

Dunlap, William. *Diary. 3 vols*. New York: New-York Historical Society, 1930.

Enkvist, Nils Brik. *Caricatures of Americans on the English Stage Prior to 1870*. Port Washington, NY: Kennikat Press, 1968. Reprint of 1951 ed.

Freedley, George, and John A. Reeves. *A History of the Theatre*. New York: Crown, 1968.

Gilbert, Douglas. *American Vaudeville: Its Life and Times*. New York: Dover, 1963.

Green, Abel, and Joe Laurie, Jr. *Show Biz from Vaude to Video*. New York: Henry Holt, 1951.

Grimsted, David. *Melodrama Unveiled: American Theatre and Culture*. Chicago: University of Chicago Press, 1969.

Harris, Neil. *Hum Bug: The Art of P. T. Barnum*. Boston: Little, Brown, 1973.

Havens, Daniel. *The Columbian Muse of Comedy: The Development of a Native Tradition in Early American Social Comedy, 1787–1845*. Carbondale: Southern Illinois University Press, 1973.

Henderson, Mary C. *The City and the Theatre: The History of New York Playhouses—a 235-Year Journey from Bowling Green to Times Square*. New York: Clifton, 1973.

Hewitt, Bernard. *Theatre USA 1668–1957*. New York: McGraw-Hill, 1959.

Higham, Charles. *Ziegfeld*. Chicago: Regnery, 1972.

Hodge, Francis. "Charles Mathews Reports on America." *The Quarterly Journal of Speech*, December 1950.

———. *Yankee Theatre*. Austin: University of Texas Press, 1964.

Hornblow, Arthur. *A History of the Theatre in America*. 2 vols. New York: Benjamin Blom, 1965. Reprint of 1919 ed.

Hoyt, Harlowe R. *Town Hall Tonight: Intimate Memories of the Grassroots Days of the American Theatre*. Englewood Cliffs, NJ: Prentice-Hall, 1945.

Hughes, Langston, and Milton Meltzer. *Black Magic: A Pictorial History of Black Entertainment in America*. New York: Bonanza Books, 1967.

Lamb, Andrew. *Jerome Kern in Edwardian England*. Brooklyn: Institute for Studies in American Music, 1985.

Laurie, Joe, Jr. *Vaudeville, from the Honky-Tonks to the Palace*. New York: Henry Holt, 1953.

Leavitt, M. B. *Fifty Years in Theatrical Management 1859–1909*. New York: Broadway Publishing, 1913.

Lewis, Philip. *Trouping: How the Show Came to Town*. New York: Harper & Row, 1972.

Ludlow, Noah Miller. *Dramatic Life as I Found it: A Record of Personal Experience, with an Account of the Rise and Progress of the Drama in the West and South, with Anecdotes and Biographical Sketches of the Principal Actors and Actresses Who Have at Times Appeared upon the Stage in the Mississippi Valley*. New York: Benjamin Blom, 1966. Reprint of 1880 ed.

MacKinley, Sterling. *Origin and Development of Light Opera*. Philadelphia: David McKay, 1927.

McLean, Albert F., Jr. *American Vaudeville as Ritual*. Lexington: University of Kentucky Press, 1965.

Magriel, Paul, ed. *Chronicles of the American Dance*. New York: Henry Holt, 1948.

Marks, Edward B. *They All Had Glamor: From the Swedish Nightingale to the Naked Lady*. New York: Globe Publishing, 1944.

Marston, William Moulton, and John Henry Feller. *F. F. Proctor, Vaudeville Pioneer*. New York: Richard R. Smith, 1943.

Mitchell, Loften. *Black Drama: The Story of the American Negro in the Theater*. New York: Hawthorn Books, 1967.

Moody, Richard, *American Takes the Stage: Romanticism in American Drama and Theatre, 1750–1900*. Bloomington: Indiana University Press, 1955.

―――. *Dramas from the American Theatre, 1750–1900*. Bloomington: Indiana University Press, 1955.

Morrell, Parker. *Lillian Russell and the Age of Plush*. New York: Random House, 1940.

Nathan, Hans. *Dan Emmett and the Rise of Negro Minstrelsy*. Norman: University of Oklahoma Press, 1977.

―――. "Dixie." *Musical Quarterly*, January 1949.

Odell, George C. D. *Annals of the New York Stage*. 15 vols. New York: Columbia University Press, 1927–1949.

Paskman, Daily, and Sigmund Spaeth. *Gentlemen Be Seated*. New York: Doubleday, Doran, 1928.

Quinn, Arthur Hobson. *A History of the American Drama from the Civil War to the Present Day*. New York: Crofts, 1923.

Root, Deane Leslie. *American Popular Stage Music, 1860–1880*. Ann Arbor: UMI Research Press, 1981.

Sheean, Vincent. *Oscar Hammerstein I*. New York: Simon & Schuster, 1957.

Smith, Cecil. *Musical Comedy in America*. New York: Theatre Arts Books, 1950.

Smith, Solomon Franklin. *Theatrical Management in the West and South for Thirty Years*. New York: Benjamin Blom, 1968. Reprint of 1868 ed.

Sobel, Bernard. *Pictorial History of Vaudeville*. New York: Citadel Press 1961.

Stagg, Jerry. *The Brothers Shubert*. New York: Ballantine, 1969.

Stone, Henry Dickinson. *Personal Recollections of the Drama or Theatrical Reminiscences: Sketches of Prominent Actors and Actresses, Their Chief Characteristics, Original Anecdotes of Them, and Incidents Connected Therewith*. New York: Benjamin Blom, 1969. Reprint of 1873 ed.

Toll, Robert C. *Blacking up: The Minstrel Show in 19th Century America*. New York: Oxford University Press, 1974.

―――. *On with the Show!: The First Century of Show Business in America*. New York: Oxford University Press, 1976.

Traubner, Richard. *Operetta: A Theatrical History*. New York: Doubleday, 1983.

Vernon, Grenville. *Yankee Doodle-doos: A Collection of Songs of the Early American Stage*. New York: Payson & Clark, 1927.

Wallace, Irving. *The Fabulous Showman: The Life and Times of P. T. Barnum*. New York: Knopf, 1959.

Wemyss, Francis. *Chronology of the American Stage from 1752 to 1852*. New York: Benjamin Blom, 1968. Reprint of 1852 ed.

Werner, M. E. *Barnum*. New York: Harcourt, Brace, 1923.

Wittke, Carl. *Tambo and Bones: A History of the American Minstrel Stage*. Durham, NC: Duke University Press, 1930.

Zeidman, Irving. *The American Burlesque Show: A History*. New York: Hawthorn Books, 1967.

Index